Lecture Notes in Computer Scie

T0250730

Commenced Publication in 1973
Founding and Former Series Editors:
Gerhard Goos, Juris Hartmanis, and Jan van Leeuwen

James H. Anderson   Giuseppe Prencipe
Roger Wattenhofer (Eds.)

Principles of Distributed Systems

9th International Conference, OPODIS 2005
Pisa, Italy, December 12-14, 2005
Revised Selected Papers

 Springer

Volume Editors

James H. Anderson
University of North Carolina at Chapel Hill
Department of Computer Science
Chapel Hill, USA
E-mail: anderson@cs.unc.edu

Giuseppe Prencipe
Università di Pisa
Dipartimento di Informatica
Largo Bruno Pontecorvo 3, 56100 Pisa, Italy
E-mail: prencipe@di.unipi.it

Roger Wattenhofer
ETH Zurich
Computer Engineering and Networks Laboratory
8092 Zurich, Switzerland
E-mail: wattenhofer@tik.ee.ethz.ch

Library of Congress Control Number: 2006938989

CR Subject Classification (1998): C.2.4, D.1.3, D.2.7, D.2.12, D.4.7, C.3

LNCS Sublibrary: SL 1 – Theoretical Computer Science and General Issues

ISSN   0302-9743
ISBN-10   3-540-36321-1 Springer Berlin Heidelberg New York
ISBN-13   978-3-540-36321-7 Springer Berlin Heidelberg New York

Springer is a part of Springer Science+Business Media

springer.com

© Springer-Verlag Berlin Heidelberg 2006
Printed in Germany

Typesetting: Camera-ready by author, data conversion by Scientific Publishing Services, Chennai, India
Printed on acid-free paper   SPIN: 11795490   06/3142   5 4 3 2 1 0

Preface

The 9th International Conference on Principles of Distributed Systems (OPODIS 2005) was held during December 12–14, 2005 in Pisa, Italy. It continued a tradition of successful conferences with friendly and pleasant atmospheres. Previous OPODIS conferences were held in Chantilly (1997), Amiens (1998), Hanoi (1999), Paris (2000), Mexico (2001), Reims (2002), La Martinique (2003), and Grenoble (2004).

The OPODIS conference constitutes an open forum for the exchange of state-of-the-art knowledge on distributed computing and systems among researchers from around the world. Following the tradition of the previous events, the 2005 program was composed of high-quality contributed papers by experts of international caliber in this scientific area. Papers were sought soliciting original research contributions to the theory, specifications, design and implementation of distributed systems, including:

- communication and synchronization protocols
- distributed algorithms, multiprocessor algorithms
- distributed collaborative environments
- embedded systems
- fault-tolerance, reliability, availability
- grid and cluster computing
- location- and context-aware systems
- mobile computing and networks
- peer-to-peer systems, overlay networks
- performance analysis of distributed algorithms and systems
- real-time systems
- security issues in distributed computing and systems
- sensor networks
- specification verification and testing of distributed systems

This year, a particular focus was placed on real-time systems and wireless networks.

In response to the call for papers for OPODIS 2005, 109 papers in the above areas were submitted from 30 countries from around the world. Each paper was reviewed by at least three reviewers, and judged according to scientific and presentation quality, originality and relevance to the conference topics. The Program Committee selected 30 papers for presentation at the conference. In addition to the submitted technical papers, the program included two exciting invited talks, by David Peleg (Weizmann Institute of Science, Israel), and by Giorgio Buttazzo (Scuola Superiore S. Anna of Pisa). We are grateful that these two distinguished experts accepted our invitation to share with us their views on various aspects of the field.

It is impossible to organize a successful program without the help of many individuals. We would like to express our appreciation to the authors of the submitted papers, the Program Committee members and the external referees. We would also like to thank the OPODIS Steering Committee members, in particular the chairman Philippas Tsigas, who supervised and supported the continuation of this event. We owe special thanks to the Organizing Committee chair, Giuseppe Prencipe (Università di Pisa, Italy), the publicity chair, Thomas Moscibroda (ETH Zurich, Switzerland), and Andreas Wetzel (ETH Zurich, Switzerland) for his assistance with the electronic submission and reviewing system.

December 2005   James H. Anderson and Roger Wattenhofer

Organization

OPODIS 2005 was organized by the Dipartimento di Informatica, Università di Pisa, Italy.

Organizing Institutes

Organizing Committee

Vincenzo Gervasi	Università di Pisa, Italy
Thomas Moscibroda	ETH Zurich, Switzerland (Publicity)
Giuseppe Prencipe	Università di Pisa, Italy (Chair)
Andreas Wetzel	ETH Zurich, Switzerland (Submissions)

Steering Committee

Alain Bui	Université de Reims Champagne-Ardenne, France
Marc Bui	Université de Paris 8/EPHE, France
Hacène Fouchal	Université Antilles-Guyane, France
Roberto Gomez	CEM-ITESM, Mexico
Nicola Santoro	Carleton University, Canada
Philippas Tsigas	University of Chalmers, Sweden (Chair)

Program Committee

Tarek Abdelzaher	University of Virginia, USA
Luis Almeida	Universidade de Aveiro, Portugal
James Anderson	University of North Carolina at Chapel Hill, USA (Co-chair)
Anish Arora	Ohio State University, USA
Ted Baker	Florida State University, USA
Joffroy Beauquier	Université de Paris Sud, France

Referees

Sébastien Tixeuil
Nir Tzachar
Akira Uchiyama
Takaaki Umedu
Paolo Valente

Nicolas Vidot
Shengquan Wang
Bettina Weiss
Josef Widder
Reuven Yagel

Hirozumi Yamaguchi
Shen Zhenhui

Sponsoring Institution

Università di Pisa

Table of Contents

Session 3: Self-stabilizing Systems

Session 4: Peer-to-Peer Systems and Collaborative Environments

Session 5: Sensor Networks and Mobile Computing

Session 6: Security and Verification

Session 7: Real-Time Systems

Session 8: Peer-to-Peer Systems

Session 9: Sensor Networks and Mobile Computing

Distributed Algorithms for Systems of Autonomous Mobile Robots

David Peleg*

Department of Computer Science, The Weizmann Institute of Science, Rehovot, Israel
`david.peleg@weizmann.ac.il`

Over the last five decades, mobile robots have been the focus of extensive research and development activities, with numerous applications for industrial tasks, military operations, search and rescue missions and space exploration, as well as some home applications.

Systems consisting of a group of autonomously operating mobile robots (sometimes referred to as *robot swarms*) have attracted considerable interest throughout the past twenty years, due to their potential for providing flexible, low-cost solutions in hazardous situations (e.g., military operations, toxic environments or fire fighting). The idea is to deal with such applications using swarms consisting of many small and simple robots, with very limited capabilities (e.g., low energy sources, limited communication means and weak processors). The use of tiny, functionally simple and cheap robots may make it acceptable to lose some of the robots, so long as the team manages to achieve its collective goals.

The main research efforts invested so far in mobile robots focused on the main engineering aspects of providing physical functionalities. Nevertheless, it seems clear that the design of very large robots swarms makes it essential to reconsider also control and coordination issues. For instance, managing the movements of a robot swarm involves new and interesting algorithmic problems due to the need to coordinate the movements of the individual robots and avoid collisions and over-crowding. Coordination tasks studied so far in the literature include gathering a robot swarm to a single point, pattern formation, flocking (or following a leader), partitioning, spreading and searching.

Most existing experimental settings of robot swarms involve small swarms (of, say, up to a dozen robots), which allow centralized control. However, future robot swarms, consisting of tens of thousands of robots, can no longer be controlled centrally in an efficient manner, and it seems that certain tasks may need to be managed by distributed protocols. Indeed, there have been a number of recent studies on distributed coordination and control protocols for robot swarms. From the point of view of the community of distributed algorithms and systems, this presents an interesting new distributed model that differs in a number of key aspects from the traditional models, and raises some intriguing research problems.

The talk will review this exciting research area, present some of the main problems and issues raised by it, and discuss directions for future study.

---

* Supported by the Israel Science Foundation (grant No. 693/04).

J.H. Anderson, G. Prencipe, and R. Wattenhofer (Eds.): OPODIS 2005, LNCS 3974, p. 1, 2006.
© Springer-Verlag Berlin Heidelberg 2006

Real-Time Issues in Mobile Wireless Networks

Giorgio Buttazzo

Scuola Superiore Sant'Anna, Pisa

The use of cooperating mobile robots is requested in an increasing number of application domains, including civil protection, surveillance, environmental monitoring, under-water exploration, and space missions. In most of these applications, the robot units are required to acquire sensory information, localize themselves in the environment, plan trajectories, avoid obstacles, and cooperate with the other robots to reach a common goal.

To achieve such objectives, the development of a team of cooperating robots poses several interesting problems from a research point of view, such as the real-time execution of acquisition and control processes, the efficient management of computational resources, the software control of energy consumption, the real-time communication protocols on wireless networks, and the development of distributed agreement algorithms for reaching a consensus in collective decisions. Moreover, small mobile robots are often controlled by micro-controllers having low computational power and limited resources, hence satisfying timing constraints requires the use of efficient operating systems and algorithms that can guarantee a predictable behavior both in normal and overload conditions.

This talk will present some of the most challenging problems to be solved in order to support the development of mobile wireless networks of cooperating robots.

J.H. Anderson, G. Prencipe, and R. Wattenhofer (Eds.): OPODIS 2005, LNCS 3974, p. 2, 2006.
© Springer-Verlag Berlin Heidelberg 2006

A Lazy Concurrent List-Based Set Algorithm

Steve Heller[1], Maurice Herlihy[2], Victor Luchangco[1], Mark Moir[1],
William N. Scherer III[3], and Nir Shavit[1]

[1] Sun Microsystems Laboratories
[2] Brown University
[3] University of Rochester

Abstract. List-based implementations of sets are a fundamental building block of many concurrent algorithms. A skiplist based on the lock-free list-based set algorithm of Michael will be included in the Java™ Concurrency Package of *JDK 1.6.0*. However, Michael's lock-free algorithm has several drawbacks, most notably that it requires all list traversal operations, including membership tests, to perform cleanup operations of logically removed nodes, and that it uses the equivalent of an atomically markable reference, a pointer that can be atomically "marked," which is expensive in some languages and unavailable in others.

We present a novel "lazy" list-based implementation of a concurrent set object. It is based on an optimistic locking scheme for inserts and removes, eliminating the need to use the equivalent of an atomically markable reference. It also has a novel wait-free membership test operation (as opposed to Michael's lock-free one) that does not need to perform cleanup operations and is more efficient than that of all previous algorithms.

Empirical testing shows that the new lazy-list algorithm consistently outperforms all known algorithms, including Michael's lock-free algorithm, throughout the concurrency range. At high load, with 90% membership tests, the lazy algorithm is more than twice as fast as Michael's. This is encouraging given that typical search structure usage patterns include around 90% membership tests. By replacing the lock-free membership test of Michael's algorithm with our new wait-free one, we achieve an algorithm that slightly outperforms our new lazy-list (though it may not be as efficient in other contexts as it uses Java's RTTI mechanism to create pointers that can be atomically marked).

1 Introduction

Lists are a fundamental building block for concurrent data structures, both in their own right, and as the basis for many types of search and dictionary data types [12]. We consider three kinds of list operations: inserting a list entry, removing a list entry, and testing whether an entry is in the list.

This paper introduces the *lazy list*, a simple new concurrent *list-based set* algorithm with a number of novel concurrency-related properties. To explain the novel aspects of lazy lists, we start with an overview of different ways to synchronize lists. *Coarse-grained* locking, which uses a single lock to protect the entire

J.H. Anderson, G. Prencipe, and R. Wattenhofer (Eds.): OPODIS 2005, LNCS 3974, pp. 3–16, 2006.

list, has the advantage of simplicity, but provides no concurrency. With *lock coupling* (sometimes called "hand-over-hand" locking) [1], a thread acquires the lock for each successive entry before releasing the lock for its predecessor. Lock coupling provides more concurrency than coarse-grained locking, but threads may acquire many successive locks, which is undesirable because lock acquisition typically involves expensive atomic operations (such as compare-and-swap). Moreover, concurrent threads moving through the list may contend for locks even if they are searching for unrelated list entries. Valois [14] was the first to suggest a non-blocking implementation of a concurrent list-based set. Harris [3] and later Michael [10], presented highly efficient lock-free algorithms for list-based sets. Fomitchev and Ruppert [10] present more complex algorithms that provide an amortized cost guarantee for all operations that is provably linear in the length of the list. Michael's algorithm is the basis for a concurrent skip-list data structure in the Java™ Concurrency Package of JDK 1.6.0.

As in most previous list-based set algorithms, we represent a set as a sorted linked list. In our new lazy list algorithm, insertion and removal operations are *optimistic*: each operation searches the list without acquiring any locks or interfering with other threads. When an operation locates the entry it is seeking it locks that entry and its predecessor and checks for synchronization conflicts. If no conflict is detected, an entry is inserted or removed, and otherwise the locks are released and the operation is restarted.

This optimistic approach to insertion and removal has the advantage that insert and remove calls that access non-adjacent list entries never interfere. In the absence of synchronization conflicts, these operations acquire only a constant number of locks. Entries are removed from the list in a *lazy* manner: the entry is first marked as removed (the "logical" removal), and then it is physically unlinked from the list (the "physical" removal). The simplifying power of lazy techniques has been exploited by Harris [3] and Michael [10] for concurrent lists, and by Maier [9] in more general contexts. Nevertheless, the algorithms of Harris and Michael require the ability to perform an atomic compare-and-swap on two fields at once: a Boolean marked field and a reference field to the next entry in the list (the equivalent of an `AtomicMarkableReference` in the Java Programming Language). Since in many systems it is unacceptable to "steal a bit" from a reference, one must use alternative techniques. In modern object oriented languages, one can have two trivial (empty) subclasses of a node object and use a *run time type identification* (RTTI) mechanism [2] to determine which subclass the current instance belongs to, where each subclass represents a state of the bit. In languages without RTTI support, one can use an additional level of indirection, adding a pointer to a special dummy node to signify that the bit is set. This is the mechanism used to implement `AtomicMarkableReference` in the Java Concurrency Package, which unfortunately can introduce significant performance penalties.

Perhaps the most substantial advantage of the new algorithm is that membership test operations are *wait-free* [4]. The lock-freedom progress property of the membership test in Michael's algorithm guarantees that if some threads are executing method calls, and at least one thread continues taking steps, then at least one thread will complete its call, but makes no progress guarantee for any individual thread. Wait-freedom is a stronger progress property that guarantees that any thread that continues taking steps in executing a method call, will eventually complete the call.

The membership test of our algorithm acquires no locks, requires no synchronization, and never interferes with any concurrent operations. This last property is particularly important because it is reasonable to expect that in most real-world applications, membership tests are by far the most common operations. In Michael's lock-free list algorithm, and unlike in ours, if a thread traversing the list encounters an entry that has been logically but not physically removed, then the thread must stop to complete the physical removal. Physical removal requires calling a compare-and-swap operation, and if several concurrent threads attempt to remove the same entry, then only one will succeed, and the rest will be forced to abandon their traversals and start over. While the number of such removals is likely to be small, our empirical testing shows that when there is a high level of concurrent traversals, contention among threads competing to perform the removal causes a large number of traversals to be abandoned and restarted.

By contrast, in the new lazy list algorithm, only the remove operations are required to perform physical removals, while the insertion and (more importantly) membership query traversals are not delayed by physical removals. The wait-free nature of the membership operation means that ongoing changes to the list cannot delay even a single thread from deciding membership. We note that our wait-free membership test is of independent value: one can readily replace the membership test in Michael's algorithm with the lazy list's new membership test, allowing it to obtain improved performance by eliminating the need for physical removals.

To evaluate our new lazy list algorithm, we implemented it in the Java™ programming language and conducted a series of benchmarks comparing our new algorithm to known algorithms on a 16 node SunFire™ 6800 cache coherent bus-based multiprocessor machine. We found that when there is a high fraction of membership tests (as in search structures) the new lazy list algorithm and a new version of Michael's algorithm that uses our wait-free membership test, outperform all others by a factor of two or more. The good performance of our new version of Michael's lock-free list depended on the use of Java's RTTI mechanism. We also found that as the fraction of membership queries dropped, the relative performance advantage of the lazy list disappeared, and the new version of Michael's list with our wait-free membership test showed the best performance.

In summary, we conclude that adding the new wait-free membership test always offers a performance advantage and has no performance penalties. For applications with a high fraction of membership tests, one should definitely use the new algorithms, while the choice of which algorithm to use—the new lazy list, or Michael's lock-free list with our new wait-free membership test—seems to depend on the cost and availability of mechanisms for implementing the equivalent of `AtomicMarkableReference` in a given system and language.

Following our initial presentation of the algorithms in this paper, a complete formal treatment was provided by Vafeiadis et al in [13]. We therefore focus on providing an informal and easily accessible explanation of why our new algorithm works, and refer the interested reader to [13] for the detailed correctness proofs.

2   The New Algorithm

We present our concurrent linked-list implementation in the context of a list-based set object. For our purposes, a *Set* provides three methods:

- The add(x) method adds x to the set, returning *true* if and only if x was not already in the set.
- The remove(x) method removes x from the set, returning *true* if and only if x was in the set.
- The contains(x) method returns *true* if and only if the set contains x.

For each method, we say that a call is *successful* if it returns *true*, and *unsuccessful* otherwise.

Linearizability [6] is a standard correctness condition for concurrent data structures. The list-based set implementation that we present is a linearizable implementation of a set object. To prove this it is enough to identify, for each method call in each possible execution history, a *linearization point*, a single operation when the method call "takes effect". For example, the linearization point defines exactly when add(a) adds an entry, a point during the execution of the method immediately before which a is not in the set, and immediately after which a is in the set.

Lock-freedom is a progress property that guarantees that if some threads are executing method calls, and at least one thread continues taking steps, then at least one thread will complete its call. It guarantees that the system as a whole continues to make progress, but makes no progress guarantee for any individual thread. *Wait-freedom* is a stronger progress property that guarantees that any thread that continues taking steps in executing a method call, will eventually complete the call.

As noted earlier, following our initial presentation of the algorithms in this paper, a complete formal treatment was provided by Vafeiadis et al in [13]. We therefore focus here on giving an informal and easily readable explanation of why our new algorithm works.

We represent the set as a sorted list of entries. As shown in Figure 1, the Entry class has four fields. The key field is the set element. Our algorithm works for any ordered set of keys that has maximum and minimum values and is well-founded, that is, for any given key, there are only finitely many smaller keys. This is trivially satisfied by most real-world key types because the size of the key is fixed; for simplicity, we present our algorithm assuming that the keys are integers. We will use the well-foundedness assumption to technically capture the notion that the progress of a membership query in Michael's algorithm is lock-free while the new algorithm's membership query is wait-free.

```
private class Entry {
    int key;
    Entry next;
    boolean marked;
    lock lock;
}
```

Fig. 1. List entry: an entry keeps track of the set element itself (the key), the next entry in the list, a marked field to denote logical removal of the entry, and a `lock` field for synchronization

The list is maintained in `key` order, providing an efficient way to determine whether a given key is in the list. We sometimes abuse notation slightly and use the same symbol to refer to an entry and its associated key (entry a will have key a and so on.). The `next` field is a reference to the next entry in the list, the `marked` field indicates if its associated key is logically removed or still in the data structure, and the `lock` field is a lock used for synchronization.

We assume that the `add()`, `remove()`, and `contains()` methods are the *only* ones that modify entries, a property sometimes called *freedom from interference*. We require freedom from interference even for entries that have been removed from the list, since a thread may unlink an entry while it is being traversed by others. In a language such as Java, we can rely on the garbage collector to recycle unreachable entries. In a programming language without garbage collection, this property can be maintained by using methods like ROP [5] or SMR [11].

The list has two kinds of entries. In addition to *regular* entries that hold elements (keys) in the set, we use two *sentinel* entries, called `head` and `tail`, as the first and last list entries. The sentinel entries contain the minimum and maximum key values, respectively; we assume that these values are never added, removed or searched for. Ignoring the details of synchronization for the moment, the top part of Figure 2 shows a schematic description of how a key is added to the set. Each thread has two local variables used to traverse down the list: `curr` is the current entry and `pred` is its predecessor.

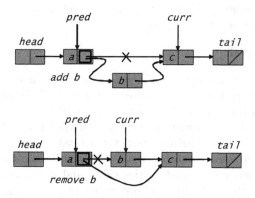

Fig. 2. Insertion and removal of list entries

To add a new key to the set, a thread sets the local variable `pred` to `head` and `curr` to `head`'s successor, and moves down the list, comparing `curr`'s key to the key being added. If they match, the key is already present in the set, so the thread returns *false*. If `pred` precedes `curr` in the list, `pred`'s key is lower than the inserted key, and `curr`'s key is higher, then the key is not present in the list. Therefore, the thread creates a new entry b to hold the key, sets b to point to `curr`, and then sets `pred` to point to b. The key is now a member of the set.

Removing a key is similar: we scan the list to find the relevant adjacent pair of entries. The target entry is removed from the list in two steps: first, its `marked` field is set to *true*, indicating that the entry has been *logically* removed from the list, and second, the predecessor entry's `next` field is redirected to point to the successor entry, *physically* removing the entry from the list. As discussed more precisely later, the removal "actually happens" when an entry is marked, and the physical removal is just a way to clean up.

2.1   The `remove()` Method

As shown in Figure 3, when the `remove()` method attempts to remove the entry with key k, it scans through the list without acquiring any locks, traversing both marked and unmarked entries. The `remove()` method uses two local variables: `curr` is the current entry and `pred` is its predecessor. When `curr` is set to the first entry with a key greater than or equal to k, the traversal stops, and the method locks `curr` and `pred`. Because there is a gap between the unsynchronized traversal and the lock acquisition, it is necessary to *validate* that the method has locked the correct entries. What can go wrong? There are three obvious problems: the `curr` entry could have been removed, the `pred` entry could have been removed, or another entry may have been inserted between `pred` and `curr`. Surprisingly, perhaps, these are the *only* things that can go wrong, and moreover, they can be detected very efficiently. It is enough to check that `curr` and `pred` are both unmarked, and that `pred`'s `next` pointer points to `curr` (see Figure 4). If these conditions hold, the entries are adjacent and present in the list. If the validation succeeds, the `remove()` method logically removes the entry, physically removes the entry, releases both locks and returns *true*. If the entry with key k is absent, the method unlocks the entries and returns *false*. If the validation fails, the thread restarts the method.

2.2   List Traversal

For an unsuccessful `remove()` call, the linearization point is the point at which it finds (reads the pointer to) a marked entry with the same key or the first unmarked entry with a larger key. For a successful `remove()` method call, the linearization point is the moment the entry is marked (line LR of Figure 3).

We pause momentarily to discuss list traversal. The list traversal in the `remove()` method in Figure 3 seems straightforward: simply follow the list pointers. The same approach is used in the `add()` and `contains()` methods. It is important to note that this traversal differs from those of other concurrent list-based set algorithms in the literature in two important ways:

- it requires no additional synchronization (such as acquiring locks [1] or cleaning up logically removed nodes [10]), and
- it traverses both logically and physically removed nodes.

This latter property, which allows us to achieve the former, is the key to our algorithm's good performance. Figure 7 shows how a concurrent physical removal of a node during thread A's traversal can cause it to traverse a physically removed part of the list. The traversal works correctly because we assume the freedom from interference property which implies that nodes, even if they are removed from the list, are not recycled (freed back to the available memory pool) as long as they are reachable. Thus, if a node is removed while it is being traversed, the

```
public boolean remove(int key) {
    while (true) {
        Entry pred = this.head;
        Entry curr = head.next;
        while (curr.key < key) {
            pred = curr; curr = curr.next;
        }
        pred.lock();
        try {
            curr.lock();
            try {
                if (validate(pred, curr)) {
                    if (curr.key != key) {       // present
                        return false;
                    } else {                     // absent
LR:                     curr.marked = true;      // logically remove
                        pred.next = curr.next;   // physically remove
                        return true;
                    }
                }
            } finally {                          // always unlock curr
                curr.unlock();
            }
        } finally {                              // always unlock pred
            pred.unlock();
        }
    }
}
```

Fig. 3. The lazy `remove()` method: removes entries in two steps, logical and physical

```
private boolean validate(Entry pred, Entry curr) {
    return  !pred.marked && !curr.marked && pred.next == curr;
}
```

Fig. 4. The lazy lists validation

traversing thread will continue to follow the list of pointers and eventually reach its target node. Our algorithm maintains the property that if an entry was in the list when a given thread started searching for it, it will remain reachable from this thread's `curr` pointer as long as it is not removed.

2.3   The add() Method

Like the `remove()` method, the `add()` method (Figure 5) scans the list without acquiring locks, until `curr` is set to the first entry with a key greater than or equal to the key to be inserted. The method locks both entries, validates them, and if an entry with the specified key is not already present in the list, inserts a new entry, unlocks the entries, and returns *true*. The remaining cases are just as in the `remove()` method. For an unsuccessful `add()` method call, the linearization point is the moment at which the entry is observed to be unmarked in the list. For a successful `add()` method call, it is the moment when `pred.next` is set. We note that one can make the `add()` method more efficient by locking only

```
public boolean add(int key) {
  while (true) {
    Entry pred = this.head;
    Entry curr = head.next;
    while (curr.key < key) {
      pred = curr; curr = curr.next;
    }
    pred.lock();
    try {
      curr.lock();
      try {
        if (validate(pred, curr)) {
          if (curr.key == key) { // present
            return false;
          } else {                // not present
            Entry entry = new Entry(key);
            entry.next = curr;
            pred.next = entry;
            return true;
          }
        }
      } finally { // always unlock
        curr.unlock();
      }
    } finally { // always unlock
      pred.unlock();
    }
  }
}
```

Fig. 5. The add() method

```
public boolean contains(int key) {
  Entry curr = this.head;
  while (curr.key < key)
    curr = curr.next;
  return curr.key == key && !curr.marked;
}
```

Fig. 6. The lazy list's wait-free `contains()` method

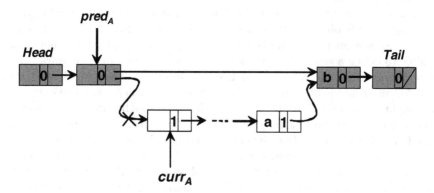

Fig. 7. Linearizing an unsuccessful `contains()` method calls is a bit tricky. Dark nodes are physically in the list and white nodes are physically removed. During a traversal of the list by thread A, the sublist starting at the node pointed to by `curr` (and schematically represented by "...") may be disconnected from the main list by a concurrent `remove()` method execution. Both nodes with items a and b can still be reached, and the determination if an item is in the list is based solely on the mark-bit.

the `pred` node, but for the sake of keeping our algorithm simple, we omit this optimization here.

2.4   The Wait-Free `contains()` Method

The key to the performance of our algorithm is the new wait-free `contains()` method. This method is of independent interest. For example, we show in Section 3 that it can readily replace the lock-free `contains()` method in the algorithm of Michael [10] to provide improved performance.

The `contains()` method scans the list, just like the `remove()` and `add()` methods, ignoring whether nodes are marked or not, until `curr` is set to the first entry with a key greater than or equal to the sought-after key. Instead of locking the entry, however, it simply returns *true* if and only if the `curr` entry is unmarked with the desired key. This is correct since the list is ordered and so, if a node is removed, it must be marked or not present in the list.

It is easy to see that this method is wait-free. First, notice that because the universe of keys is well-founded there are only a finite number of keys that are smaller than the one being searched for. According to the algorithm, entries with lower or equal keys to a given entry will never be added ahead of it (i.e. so that they are reachable from it) even if the entry points into the list but is logically and physically removed from the list. Thus, each time the traversal moves to a new node, the new node has a larger key than the previous one, and this can happen only finitely many times, which implies that traversal is wait-free. This contrasts with Michael's membership test [10] which is only lock-free [4], since it can be forced to restart its traversal from the beginning of the list infinitely often if the same item is re-inserted and removed, and it fails each time when attempting to clean it up.

A successful `contains()` method call is linearized when the marked field of a matching entry is observed to be false. Linearizing an unsuccessful `contains()` method call is a bit tricky, and is a good example showing that it is not always possible to define a single linearization point for each method that works for all method calls in all executions. In particular, simply choosing the linearization point for an unsuccessful `contains()` as the point at which a marked entry with the sought-after key or an entry greater than the sought-after key is found is incorrect. Consider the following scenario. Assume that entry a is marked and thread A is attempting to find the entry matching a's key. While A is traversing the list, curr_A and all entries between curr_A and a including a are removed logically and physically. Thread A would still proceed to the point where curr_A points to a. It would then detect that a is marked and therefore no longer in the list. Linearizing at this point is correct in this case. However, consider what happens if while thread A is traversing the removed section of the list leading to a, and before it reaches the removed a, another thread adds a new entry with a key a to the reachable part of the list. Linearizing the unsuccessful `contains()` method at the point at which it observed the marked entry a would be wrong, since it occurs *after* the insertion of the new entry with key a to the list.

We therefore linearize an unsuccessful `contains()` method call within its execution interval at the earlier of the following points: (1) the point where a removed matching entry is found and (2) the point immediately before a new matching entry is added to the list. As can be seen, this linearization point is determined by the ordering of events in the execution, and not predetermined as a specific point in the method execution.

3   Performance

We evaluated our new algorithm on a SunFire™ 6800 cache coherent bus-based multiprocessor machine with 16 1.2 GHz processors. The algorithms were implemented in Java 1.5.0. We varied the percentage of `contains()` method calls and the percentage of `add()` and `remove()` method calls. Each thread randomly selected both the type of call to make (respecting the given percentages) and the operand for it; operands are integers in the range 0..1023. We repeated this test suite both with and without an additional load of 16 threads performing computation in order to evaluate the sensitivity of our results to background load, but do not report the additional load tests here as there were no significant differences noted. In all our benchmarks, we measured *throughput*: the total number of calls completed over the course of 8 seconds, averaged across three runs. We tested six different list algorithms in all.

- *Coarse* – We use a single `java.util.concurrent.ReentrantLocks` lock to protect all access to the list.
- *Fine* – This is a *fine grained* hand-over-hand locking (lock-coupling) [8, 1] list-based implementation using a lock per list entry. Threads traverse down the list holding multiple locks at a time, releasing the earlier acquired entry's lock only after acquiring the next one in the list.
- *LockFree* – This is a *lock-free* list implemented according to Michael's algorithm [10], using the `AtomicMarkableReference` of JDK 1.5.0 to allow a markable next pointer per entry. As in our algorithm, the mark is used to denote that an entry is logically removed. Unlike in our algorithm, the `contains()` method is lock-free and not wait-free as calls do not traverse marked entries, instead, they clean them up before continuing traversal down the list.
- *LockFreeRTTI* – This is the lock-free list of Michael's algorithm [10] using the Java RTTI mechanism to distinguish marked entries. Such mechanisms are not available in all languages. Achieving the effect of marking a bit in the `next` pointer is done more efficiently than with `AtomicMarkableReference` by having two trivial (empty) subclasses of each entry object and using RTTI to determine at runtime which subclass the current instance is, where each subclass represents a state of the mark bit.
- *NewLockFreeRTTI* – This is *LockFreeRTTI* with Michael's lock-free `contains()` method directly replaced by the new wait-free `contains()` method of this paper, one that does not clean up marked entries and instead traverses them in a wait-free manner.
- *NewLazy* – This is the new lazy list algorithm of this paper, with its new wait-free `contains()` and an optimization of the `add()` method to use only a single lock.

The top of Figure 8 shows the results of running a benchmark with 90% `contains()` method calls, 9% `add()` method calls and 1% `remove()` method calls (left) and another benchmark with 50% `contains()` method calls, 45% `add()` method calls and 5% `remove()` method calls (right). The 90/9/1 ratio and the high fraction of `add()` method calls to `remove()` method calls are considered typical of search structures, a common application of linked-lists [7].

If we look at the graph of the 90% test on the lefthand side of Figure 8, we see that the two new algorithms, the lazy list and the new lock-free list with a wait-free `contains()` method, outperform all others by a factor of two or more, including both versions of Michael's lock-free list, the one implemented with `AtomicMarkableReference` and the one implemented with the RTTI mechanism. The reason for this is as follows: even though there is a very small fraction of `remove()` method calls, there are many concurrent `contains()` method traversals, and in both of the original versions of Michael's algorithm they all compete to clean up the same small set of logically removed entries. All traversals that

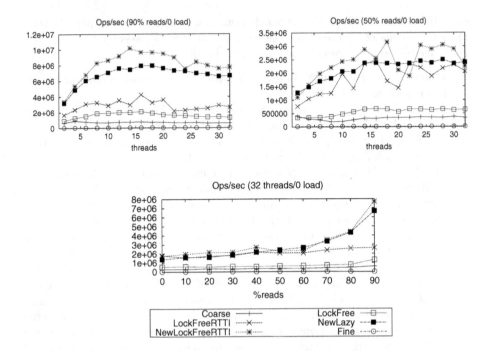

Fig. 8. The top two graphs show the change in throughput as concurrency increases to 32 threads with 60% and 90% of the operations being contains() method calls, and a 9/1 ratio of add() to remove() method calls. The bottom graph shows the change in throughput for the case of 32 threads as the fraction of contains() calls increases to 90%.

fail must restart, leading to a significant overhead. The new version of Michael's algorithm with RTTI and our wait-free contains() method performs slightly better than the lock-based lazy list. However, the reader is reminded that many languages do not have the equivalent of RTTI.

The graph of the 50% test on the righthand side of Figure 8 shows what happens when we drop the fraction of contains() method calls. As can be seen, the lock-free RTTI-based implementation of Michael's algorithm stays at about the same throughput level, yet the performance of the two new algorithms deteriorates because (1) the large number of additional add() method calls in the new version of Michael's algorithm incur cleanup contention (they fail attempts at cleaning up the same entries) and must restart their traversals, and (2) the add() method calls in the lazy list acquire more costly locks and fail validation at a much higher rate, forcing them to restart their traversals.

The bottom graph of Figure 8 shows the change in throughput for the case of 32 threads as the fraction of contains() method calls increases (maintaining the 9/1 ratio of add() and remove() method calls). As can be seen, from 50% and onward the two new algorithms outperform all others, and have more than twice their throughput at 90%. The choice of which algorithm to use, the new lazy list,

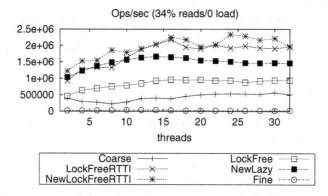

Fig. 9. The graph shows throughput as concurrency increases with a 34%, 33% and 33% ratio respectively of `contains()`, `add()`, and `remove()` method calls

or Michael's lock-free list with our new wait-free membership test, for typical search applications with a high fraction of memberships tests, seems to depend on the cost of implementing the equivalent of `AtomicMarkableReference` in a given system and language.

The graph in Figure 9 shows the change in throughput when running a benchmark with 34% `contains()` method calls, 33% `add()` method calls and 33% `remove()` method calls. Though this is not a typical search structure access pattern, we present it here to explore how the algorithms compare across a wider range of loads. As can be seen, the throughput of the lock-free RTTI based implementations drops slightly, and the performance of the lazy list drops more significantly. As before, this is due to the further increase in the number of costly lock acquisitions and of failed validations.

We conclude that even with higher `add()` and `remove()` method call rates than we expect in many applications, our results show how to improve on the performance of previous algorithms. Furthermore, without using any nonstandard language tricks, our new algorithms soundly beat previous ones.

4   Conclusions

We introduced the *lazy list*, a simple new concurrent list algorithm based on lazy marking and deletion of nodes. Perhaps the most substantial advantage of the new algorithm is a *wait-free* membership test operation, an operation that can readily replace membership tests in other list-based set algorithms such as Michael's lock-free lists [10].

Various optimizations to our algorithm are possible. As noted earlier, one can make the `add()` method more efficient by locking only the `pred` node. One can also add an optimization whereby threads "prevalidate" the state of an entry before acquiring the entry locks, thereby saving the cost of acquiring them upon failure.

Most importantly, we believe the algorithmic approach introduced in this paper, the combination of lazy lock-based list manipulation coupled with wait-free traversal, can lead to simpler and possibly more efficient algorithms for related data structures such as concurrent skip-lists and other search structures.

References

1. R. Bayer and M. Schkolnick. Concurrency of operations on b-trees. *Acta Informatica*, 9:1–21, 1977.
2. B. Eckel. *Thinking in Java (2nd Edition)*. Pearson Education, 2000.
3. T. Harris. A pragmatic implementation of non-blocking linked-lists. *Lecture Notes in Computer Science*, 2180:300–314, 2001.
4. M. Herlihy. Wait-free synchronization. *ACM Transactions on Programming Languages and Systems*, 13(1):124–149, January 1991.
5. M. Herlihy, V. Luchangco, and M. Moir. The repeat offender problem: A mechanism for supporting lock-free dynamic-sized data structures. In *Proceedings of the 16th International Symposium on DIStributed Computing*, volume 2508, pages 339–353. Springer-Verlag Heidelberg, January 2002. A improved version of this paper is in preparation for journal submission; please contact authors.
6. M. Herlihy and J. Wing. Linearizability: A correctness condition for concurrent objects. *ACM Transactions on Programming Languages and Systems*, 12(3):463–492, July 1990.
7. D. Lea. Personal communication.
8. D. Lea. *Concurrent Programming in Java(TM): Design Principles and Patterns*. Addison-Wesley, second edition edition, 1999.
9. Corinne Maier. *Hello Laziness: Why Hard Work Doesn't Pay*. Orion, London, 2005. ISBN: 0752871862.
10. M. Michael. High performance dynamic lock-free hash tables and list-based sets. In *Proceedings of the fourteenth annual ACM symposium on Parallel algorithms and architectures*, pages 73–82. ACM Press, 2002.
11. M. Michael. Safe memory reclamation for dynamic lock-free objects using atomic reads and writes. In *The 21st Annual ACM Symposium on Principles of Distributed Computing*, pages 21–30. ACM Press, 2002.
12. M. Moir and N. Shavit. *Chapter 47 – Concurrent Data Structures – Handbook of Data Structures and Applications*. Chapman and Hall/CRC, first edition edition, 2004.
13. V. Vafeiadis, M. Herlihy, T. Hoare, and M. Shapiro. Proving correctness of highly-concurrent linearisable objects. Technical report, Microsoft Research, Cambridge, UK, 2005.
14. J. Valois. Lock-free linked lists using compare-and-swap. In *ACM Symposium on Principles of Distributed Computing*, pages 214–222, 1995.

Efficiently Implementing a Large Number of LL/SC Objects

Prasad Jayanti and Srdjan Petrovic

Department of Computer Science, Dartmouth College, Hanover, New Hampshire
{prasad, spetrovic}@cs.dartmouth.edu

Abstract. Over the past decade, a pair of instructions called load-linked (LL) and store-conditional (SC) have emerged as the most suitable synchronization instructions for the design of lock-free algorithms. However, current architectures do not support these instructions; instead, they support either CAS (e.g., UltraSPARC, Itanium) or restricted versions of LL/SC (e.g., POWER4, MIPS, Alpha). Thus, there is a gap between what algorithm designers want (namely, LL/SC) and what multiprocessors actually support (namely, CAS or RLL/RSC). To bridge this gap, a flurry of algorithms that implement LL/SC from CAS have appeared in the literature. The two most recent algorithms are due to Doherty, Herlihy, Luchangco, and Moir (2004) and Michael (2004). To implement M LL/SC objects shared by N processes, Doherty et al.'s algorithm uses only $O(N + M)$ space, but is only non-blocking and not wait-free. Michael's algorithm, on the other hand, is wait-free, but uses $O(N^2 + M)$ space. The main drawback of his algorithm is the time complexity of the SC operation: although the *expected amortized* running time of SC is only $O(1)$, the *worst-case* running time of SC is $O(N^2)$. The algorithm in this paper overcomes this drawback. Specifically, we design a wait-free algorithm that achieves a space complexity of $O(N^2 + M)$, while still maintaining the $O(1)$ worst-case running time for LL and SC operations.

1 Introduction

In shared-memory multiprocessors, multiple processes running concurrently on different processors cooperate with each other via shared data structures (e.g., queues, stacks, counters, heaps, trees). Atomicity of these shared data structures has traditionally been ensured through the use of locks. To perform an operation, a process obtains the lock, updates the data structure, and then releases the lock. Locking, however, has several drawbacks, including deadlocks, priority inversion, convoying, and lack of fault-tolerance to process crashes.

Wait-free implementations were conceived to overcome the above drawbacks of locking [1, 2, 3]. A wait-free implementation guarantees that every process completes its operation on the data structure in a bounded number of its steps, regardless of whether other processes are slow, fast, or have crashed. A weaker form of implementation, known as *non-blocking* implementation [2], guarantees that if a process p repeatedly takes steps, then the operation of *some* process

J.H. Anderson, G. Prencipe, and R. Wattenhofer (Eds.): OPODIS 2005, LNCS 3974, pp. 17–31, 2006.
© Springer-Verlag Berlin Heidelberg 2006

- LL($\mathcal{O}$) returns $\mathcal{O}$'s value.
- SC($\mathcal{O}, v$) by process p "succeeds" if and only if no process performed a successful SC on $\mathcal{O}$ since p's latest LL on $\mathcal{O}$. If SC succeeds, it changes $\mathcal{O}$'s value to v and returns *true*. Otherwise, $\mathcal{O}$'s value remains unchanged and SC returns *false*.
- VL($\mathcal{O}$) returns *true* if and only if no process performed a successful SC on $\mathcal{O}$ since p's latest LL on $\mathcal{O}$.

Fig. 1. Definitions of operations LL, SC, and VL

- CAS(X, u, v) behaves as follows: if X's current value is u, X is assigned v and *true* is returned; otherwise, X is unchanged and *false* is returned.

Fig. 2. Definition of the CAS operation

(not necessarily p) will eventually complete. Thus, non-blocking implementations guarantee that the system as a whole makes progress, but admit starvation of individual processes. An even weaker form of implementation, known as *obstruction-free* implementation [4], guarantees that a process completes its operation on the data structure, provided that it eventually executes for a sufficient number of steps without interference from other processes. This progress condition therefore allows for a situation where all processes starve.

It is a well understood fact that whether lock-free algorithms (i.e., wait-free, non-blocking, or obstruction-free) can be efficiently designed depends crucially on what synchronization instructions are available for the task. After more than two decades of experience with different instructions, there is growing consensus among algorithm designers on the desirability of a pair of instructions known as *Load-Link* (LL) and *Store-Conditional* (SC). The LL and SC instructions act like read and conditional-write, respectively. More specifically, the LL instruction by process p returns the value of the memory word, and the SC(v) instruction by p writes v if and only if no process updated the memory word since p's latest LL. A more precise formulation of these instructions is presented in Figure 1.

Despite the desirability of LL/SC, no processor supports these instructions in hardware; instead, they support either *compare&swap*, also known as CAS (e.g., UltraSPARC [5], Itanium [6]) or restricted versions of LL/SC (e.g., POWER4 [7], MIPS [8], Alpha [9]). Although the restrictions on LL/SC vary from one architecture to another, Moir [10] noted that the LL/SC instructions supported by current architectures, henceforth referred to as RLL/RSC, satisfy at a minimum the semantics stated in Figure 3.

Since CAS suffers from the well-known ABA problem [11] and RLL/RSC impose severe restrictions on their use [10], it is difficult to design algorithms based on these instructions. Thus, there is a gap between what algorithm designers want (namely, LL/SC) and what multiprocessors actually support (namely, CAS or RLL/RSC). This gap must be bridged efficiently, which gives rise to the following problem:

Design an algorithm that implements LL/SC objects from memory words supporting either CAS or RLL/RSC operations. To be useful in practice, the time and space complexities must be kept small.

– RLL/RSC are similar to *LL* and *SC*, with two differences [10]: (i) there is a chance of *RSC* failing spuriously: *RSC* might fail even when *SC* would succeed, and (ii) a process must not access any shared variable between its *RLL* and the subsequent *RSC*.

Fig. 3. Definition of operations RLL/RSC

The above problem has been extensively studied in the literature [10, 12, 13, 14, 15, 16, 17, 18, 19]. The most efficient algorithm for implementing LL/SC from CAS is due to Moir [10]. His algorithm runs in constant time and has no space overhead. However, it can only implement small (e.g., 24 to 32 bit) LL/SC objects, which are inadequate for storing pointers, large integers and doubles. This size limitation is due to the fact that Moir's algorithm stores a sequence number along with the object's value in the same memory word. Since sequence number could take up to 32 to 40 bits, only 24 to 32 bits are left for the value field.

Elsewhere, we presented an algorithm that implements a *word-sized* LL/SC object from a word-sized CAS object and registers (e.g., 64-bit LL/SC on a 64-bit machine) [17]. This algorithm stores a value and a sequence number in separate memory words, thus enabling values to be as big as 64 bits. The algorithm implements both LL and SC in $O(1)$ time and uses $O(N)$ space, where N is the maximum number of processes that the algorithm is designed to handle. Although these space requirements are modest when a single LL/SC object is implemented, the algorithm does not scale well when the number of LL/SC objects to be supported is large. In particular, in order to implement M LL/SC objects, the algorithm requires $O(NM)$ space. Furthermore, the algorithm requires that N is known in advance.

The recent algorithms by Doherty, Herlihy, Luchangco, and Moir [14] and Michael [19] have aimed to overcome the above two drawbacks. Doherty et al.'s algorithm [14] uses only $O(N + M)$ space and does not require knowledge of N, but is only non-blocking and not wait-free. Michael's [19] algorithm, on the other hand, is wait-free and does not require knowledge of N, but uses $O(N^2 + M)$ space. The main drawback of this algorithm is the time complexity of the SC operation: although the *expected amortized* running time of SC is only $O(1)$, the *worst-case* running time of SC is $O(N^2)$. The algorithm in this paper overcomes this drawback, as described below.

We design a wait-free algorithm that achieves a space complexity of $O(N^2 + M)$, while still maintaining the $O(1)$ worst-case running time for LL and SC operations. This algorithm too does not require knowledge of N. When constructing a large number of LL/SC objects (i.e., when $M = \omega(N)$), our implementation is the first to be simultaneously (1) wait-free, (2) time optimal, and (3) space efficient. Specifically, the algorithm by Doherty et al. [14], although more space efficient than ours, is not wait-free. Michael's algorithm [19] has the same space complexity as ours and is wait-free, but is not time optimal. Other algorithms are either not space efficient [10, 12, 13, 15, 16, 17], not wait-free [18], or implement small LL/SC objects [10, 13, 15].

We note that the algorithm in this paper, as well as the algorithms by Doherty et al. [14] and Michael [19], implement (the more general) *multiword* LL/SC object, i.e., an LL/SC object whose value spans across multiple machine words (e.g., 512- or 1024-bit LL/SC object). Many existing applications [12, 20, 21, 22] require support for such an object. When implementing a W-word LL/SC object, the time and space complexities increase by a factor of W, which is also the case with the algorithms of [14] and [19]. Specifically, the space complexity of our algorithm becomes $O((N^2 + M)W)$, and the time complexity of LL and SC becomes $O(W)$.

Elsewhere, we presented an algorithm that implements M W-word LL/SC objects using $O(NMW)$ space [16]. This algorithm employs a helping scheme by which processes help each other complete their LL operations. We use a similar helping scheme in the present paper.

1.1   Related Work

The quality of an LL/SC algorithm can be judged by several criteria: (1) the maximum size of the object that the algorithm is capable of implementing (e.g., small, word-sized, or multiword), (2) the strength of the progress condition that the algorithm satisfies (obstruction-free, non-blocking, or wait-free), (3) whether the algorithm requires explicit knowledge of N, and (4) the time and space complexities of the algorithm. With these criteria in mind, we present a comparison of related work in Table 1. We used the following notation: M is the number of implemented LL/SC objects, and N is the number of processes sharing those objects.

1.2   Correctness Condition

The correctness condition that we use in the paper is *linearizability* [23]. Since this correctness condition is well known, we only describe it informally here.

A *shared object is linearizable* if operations applied to the object appear to act instantaneously, even though in reality each operation executes over an interval of time. More precisely, every operation applied to the object appears to take effect at some instant between its invocation and completion [23]. This instant (at which an operation appears to take effect) is called the *linearization point* for that operation. Our algorithms ensure that the implemented object $\mathcal{O}$ is linearizable whenever the primitive objects from which $\mathcal{O}$ is implemented are linearizable.

1.3   Organization for the Rest of the Paper

In the next section, we present the algorithm that implements an array of M LL/SC objects shared by N processes, where N is known in advance. The proof of this algorithm is given in Section 3. The algorithm that does not require knowledge of N is ommitted due to space constraints; it is presented in the full version of the paper [24].

Table 1. A comparison of algorithms that implement LL/SC from CAS

			Worst-case Time Complexity	
Algorithm	Size of LL/SC	Progress Condition	LL	SC
1. This paper	W-word	wait-free	$O(W)$	$O(W)$
2. Israeli and Rappoport [15]	small	wait-free	$O(N)$	$O(N)$
3. Anderson and Moir [13], Figure 1	small	wait-free	$O(1)$	$O(1)$
4. Anderson and Moir [12], Figure 2	W-word	wait-free	$O(W)$	$O(W)$
5. Moir [10], Figure 4	small	wait-free	$O(1)$	$O(1)$
6. Moir [10], Figure 7	small	wait-free	$O(1)$	$O(1)$
7. Luchangco et al. [18][1]	63-bit	obstruction-free	–	–
8. Jayanti and Petrovic [17]	64-bit	wait-free	$O(1)$	$O(1)$
9. Doherty et al. [14]	W-word	non-blocking	–	–
10. Michael [19]	W-word	wait-free	$O(W)$	$O(N^2 + W)^2$
11. Jayanti and Petrovic [16]	W-word	wait-free	$O(W)$	$O(W)$

Algorithm	Space Complexity	Knowledge of N
1. This paper	$O((N^2 + M)W)$	not required
2. Israeli and Rappoport [15]	$O(N^2 + NM)$	required
3. Anderson and Moir [13], Figure 1	$O(N^2 M)$	required
4. Anderson and Moir [12], Figure 2	$O(N^2 MW)$	required
5. Moir [10], Figure 4	$O(N + M)$	not required
6. Moir [10], Figure 7	$O(N^2 + NM)$	required
7. Luchangco et al. [18]	$O(N + M)$	required
8. Jayanti and Petrovic [17]	$O(NM)$	required
9. Doherty et al. [14]	$O((N + M)W)$	not required
10. Michael [19]	$O((N^2 + M)W)$	not required
11. Jayanti and Petrovic [16]	$O(NMW)$	required

[1] This algorithm implements a weaker form of LL/SC in which an LL operation by a process can cause some other process's SC operation to fail.

[2] The *expected amortized* running time for SC is $O(W)$.

2 LL/SC for a Known N

Figure 4 presents an algorithm that implements an array $\mathcal{O}[0..M-1]$ of M W-word LL/SC object shared by N processes. To make the presentation easier to follow, the algorithm is shown for the case when each process has at most one outstanding LL operation. Later, we explain how the algorithm can be trivially modified to handle any number of outstanding LL operations. We provide below an intuitive description of the algorithm.

2.1 The Variables Used

We begin by describing the variables used in the algorithm. BUF$[0..M + (N + 1)N - 1]$ is an array of $M + (N + 1)N$ buffers. Of these, M buffers hold the current values of objects $\mathcal{O}[0], \mathcal{O}[1], \ldots, \mathcal{O}[M-1]$, while the remaining $(N+1)N$ buffers

Types

   valuetype = **array** $[0 .. W]$ of 64-bit value

   xtype = **record** seq: $(64 - \lg(M + (N + 1)N))$-bit number;

              buf: $0 .. M + (N + 1)N - 1$ **end**

   helptype = **record** seq: $(63 - \lg(M + (N + 1)N))$-bit number; $helpme$: $\{0, 1\}$;

              buf: $0 .. M + (N + 1)N - 1$ **end**

Shared variables

   X: **array** $[0 .. M - 1]$ of xtype; Announce: **array** $[0 .. N - 1]$ of $0 .. M - 1$

   Help: **array** $[0 .. N - 1]$ **of** helptype

   BUF: **array** $[0 .. M + (N + 1)N - 1]$ **of** *valuetype

Local persistent variables at each $p \in \{0, 1, \ldots, N - 1\}$

   $mybuf_p$: $0 .. M + (N + 1)N - 1$; Q_p: Single-process queue; x_p: xtype

   $lseq_p$: $(63 - \lg(M + (N + 1)N))$-bit number; $index_p$: $0 .. N - 1$

Initialization

   $X[k] = (0, k)$, for all $k \in \{0, 1, \ldots, M - 1\}$

   $BUF[k]$ = the desired initial value of $\mathcal{O}[k]$, for all $k \in \{0, 1, \ldots, M - 1\}$

   For all $p \in \{0, 1, \ldots, N - 1\}$

       $enqueue(Q_p, M + (N + 1)p + k)$, for all $k \in \{0, 1, \ldots, N - 1\}$

       $mybuf_p = M + (N + 1)p + N$; $Help[p] = (0, 0, *)$; $index_p = 0$; $lseq_p = 0$

---

procedure LL$(p, i, retval)$

1: Announce$[p] = i$
2: Help$[p] = (++lseq_p, 1, mybuf_p)$
3: $x_p = $ X$[i]$
4: **copy** *BUF$[x_p.buf]$ **into** *retval
5: **if** ¬CAS(Help$[p]$, $(lseq_p, 1, mybuf_p)$,
                         $(lseq_p, 0, mybuf_p)$)
6:     $mybuf_p = $ Help$[p].buf$
7:     $x_p = $ BUF$[mybuf_p][W]$
8:     **copy** *BUF$[mybuf_p]$ **into** *retval
9: **return**

procedure VL(p, i) returns boolean

10: **return** $(X[i] = x_p)$

---

procedure SC(p, i, v) returns boolean

11: **copy** *v **into** *BUF$[mybuf_p]$
12: **if** ¬CAS(X$[i]$, x_p, $(x_p.seq + 1, mybuf_p)$)
13:    **return** *false*
14: $enqueue(Q_p, x_p.buf)$
15: $mybuf_p = dequeue(Q_p)$
16: **if** (Help$[index_p] \equiv (s, 1, b)$)
17:    $j = $ Announce$[index_p]$
18:    $x = $ X$[j]$
19:    **copy** *BUF$[x.buf]$ **into** *BUF$[mybuf_p]$
20:    BUF$[mybuf_p][W] = x$
21:    **if** CAS(Help$[index_p]$, $(s, 1, b)$,
                        $(s, 0, mybuf_p)$)
22:      $mybuf_p = b$
23: $index_p = (index_p + 1)$ mod N
24: **return** *true*

Fig. 4. Implementation of $\mathcal{O}[0 .. M - 1]$: an array of M N-process W-word LL/SC objects

are "owned" by processes, $N + 1$ buffer by each process. Each process p, however, uses only one of its $N + 1$ buffers at any given time. The index of the buffer that p is currently using is stored in the local variable $mybuf_p$, and the indices of the remaining N buffers are stored in p's local queue Q_p. Array X$[0 .. M-1]$ holds the tags associated with the current values of objects $\mathcal{O}[0], \mathcal{O}[1], \ldots, \mathcal{O}[M-1]$. A tag in X$[i]$ consists of two fields: (1) the index of the buffer that holds $\mathcal{O}[i]$'s current value, and (2) the sequence number associated with $\mathcal{O}[i]$'s current value. The sequence number increases by 1 with each successful SC on $\mathcal{O}[i]$, and the buffer holding $\mathcal{O}[i]$'s current value is not reused until some process performs at least N more successful SC's (on any $\mathcal{O}[j]$). Process p's local variable x_p maintains the tag corresponding to the value returned by p's most recent LL operation; p will use this tag during the subsequent SC operation to check whether the object still holds the same value (i.e., whether it has been modified). Finally, it turns out that a process p might need the help of other processes in completing its LL operation on $\mathcal{O}$. The shared variables $\text{Help}[p]$ and $\text{Announce}[p]$, as well as p's local variables $lseq_p$ and $index_p$, are used to facilitate this helping scheme. Additionally, an extra word is kept in each buffer along with the value. Hence, all the buffers in the algorithm are of length $W + 1$.[3]

2.2 The Helping Mechanism

The crux of our algorithm lies in its helping mechanism by which SC operations help LL operations. This helping mechanism is similar to that of [16], but whereas the mechanism of [16] requires $O(NMW)$ space, the mechanism in this paper requires only $O((N^2 + M)W)$ space. Below, we describe this mechanism in detail.[4]

A process p begins its LL operation on some object $\mathcal{O}[i]$ by announcing its operation to other processes. It then attempts to read the buffer containing $\mathcal{O}[i]$'s current value. This reading has two possible outcomes: either p correctly obtains the value in the buffer or p obtains an inconsistent value because the buffer is overwritten while p reads it. In the latter case, the key property of our algorithm is that p is helped (and informed that it is helped) before the completion of its reading of the buffer. Thus, in either case, p has a valid value: either p reads a valid value in the buffer (former case) or it is handed a valid value by a helper process (latter case). The implementation of such a helping scheme is sketched in the following paragraph.

Consider any process p that performs a successful SC operation. During that SC, p checks whether a single process—say, q—has an ongoing LL operation that requires help. If so, p helps q by passing it a valid value and a tag associated with that value. (We will see later how p obtains that value.) If several processes try to help, only one will succeed. Process p makes a decision on which process to help by consulting its variable $index_p$: if $index_p$ holds value j, then p helps process j. The algorithm ensures that $index_p$ is incremented by 1 modulo N after every successful SC operation by p. Hence, during the course of N successful SC operations, process p examines all N processes for possible help. Recall the earlier stated property that the buffer holding an $\mathcal{O}[i]$'s current value is not reused until some process performs at least N successful SC's (on any $\mathcal{O}[j]$). As a consequence of the above facts, if a process q begins reading the buffer that holds $\mathcal{O}[i]$'s current value and the buffer happens to be reused while q still reads it (because some process p has since performed N successful SC's), then p is sure to have helped q by handing it a valid value of $\mathcal{O}[i]$ and a tag associated with that value.

---

[3] The only exception are the buffers passed as an argument to procedures LL and SC, which are of length W.

[4] Some of the text to follow has been taken directly from [16].

2.3   The Roles of Help[p] and Announce[p]

The variables Help[p] and Announce[p] play an important role in the helping scheme. Help[p] has three fields: (1) a binary value (that indicates if p needs help), (2) a buffer index, and (3) a sequence number (independent from the sequence numbers in tags). Announce[p] has only one field: an index in the range $0 .. M-1$. When p initiates an LL operation on some object $\mathcal{O}[i]$, it first announces the index of that object by writing i into Announce[p] (see Line 1), and then seeks the help of other processes by writing $(s, 1, b)$ into Help[p], where b is the index of the buffer that p owns (see Line 2) and s is p's local sequence number incremented by one. If a process q helps p, it does so handing over its buffer c containing a valid value of $\mathcal{O}[i]$ to p by writing $(s, 0, c)$. (This writing is performed with a CAS operation to ensure that at most one process succeeds in helping p.) Once q writes $(s, 0, c)$ in Help[p], p and q exchange the ownership of their buffers: p becomes the owner of the buffer indexed by c and q becomes the owner of the buffer indexed by b. (This buffer management scheme is the same as in Herlihy's universal construction [25].) Before q hands over buffer c to process p, it also writes a tag associated with that value into the Wth location of the buffer.

2.4   How the Helper Obtains a Valid Value

We now explain an important feature of our algorithm, namely, the mechanism by which a process p obtains a valid value to help some other process q with. Suppose that process p wishes to help process q complete its LL operation on some object $\mathcal{O}[i]$. To obtain a valid value to help q with, p first attempts to read the buffer containing $\mathcal{O}[i]$'s current value. This reading has two possible outcomes: either p correctly obtains the value in the buffer or p obtains an inconsistent value because the buffer is overwritten while p reads it. In the latter case, by an earlier stated property, p knows that there exists some process r that has performed at least N successful SC operations (on any $\mathcal{O}[j]$). Therefore, r must have already helped q, in which case p's attempt to help q will surely fail. Hence, it does not matter that p obtained an inconsistent value of $\mathcal{O}[i]$ because p will anyway fail in giving that value to q. As a result, if p helps q complete its LL operation on some object $\mathcal{O}[i]$, it does so with a valid value of $\mathcal{O}[i]$.

2.5   Code for LL

A process p performs an LL operation on some object $\mathcal{O}[i]$ by executing the procedure LL($p, i, retval$), where *retval* is a pointer to a block of W-words in which to place the return value. First, p announces its operation to inform others that it needs their help (Lines 1 and 2). It then attempts to obtain the current value of $\mathcal{O}[i]$ by performing the following steps. First, p reads the tag stored in X[i] to determine the buffer holding $\mathcal{O}[i]$'s current value (Line 3), and then reads that buffer (Line 4). While p reads the buffer at Line 4, the value of $\mathcal{O}[i]$ might change because of successful SC's by other processes. Specifically, there are three possibilities for what happens while p executes Line 4: (i) no process performs a successful SC, (ii) no process performs more than $N - 1$ successful SC's, or (iii) some process performs N or more successful SC's. In the first case, it is obvious that p reads a valid value at Line 4. Interestingly, in the second case too, the value read at Line 4 is a valid value. This is because, as remarked earlier, our algorithm does not reuse a buffer until some process performs at least N successful SC's. In the third case, p cannot rely on the value read at Line 4. However, by the helping mechanism described earlier, a helper process would have made available a valid value (and a tag associated with that value) in a buffer and written the index of that buffer in Help[p]. Thus, in each of the three cases, p has access to a valid value as well as a tag associated with that value. Further, as we now explain, p can also determine which of the three cases actually holds. To do this, p performs a CAS on Help[p] to try to revoke its request for help (Line 5). If p's CAS succeeds, it means that p has not been helped yet. Therefore, Case (i) or (ii) must hold, which implies that $retval$ has a valid value of $\mathcal{O}$. Hence, p returns from the LL operation at Line 9.

If p's CAS on Help[p] fails (Line 5), p knows that it has been helped, and that a helper process must have written in Help[p] the index of a buffer containing a valid value U of $\mathcal{O}[i]$ (as well as a tag associated with U). So, p reads U and its associated tag (Lines 7 and 8), and takes ownership of the buffer it was helped with (Line 6). Finally, p returns from the LL operation at Line 9.

2.6 Code for SC

A process p performs an SC operation on some object $\mathcal{O}[i]$ by executing the procedure SC(p, i, v), where v is the pointer to a block of W-words which contain the value to write to $\mathcal{O}[i]$ if SC succeeds. First, p writes the value v into its local buffer (Line 11), and then tries to make its SC operation take effect by changing the value in X[i] from the tag it had witnessed in its latest LL operation to a new tag consisting of (1) the index of p's local buffer and (2) a sequence number (of the previous tag) incremented by one (Line 12). If the CAS operation fails, it follows that some other process performed a successful SC after p's latest LL, and hence p's SC must fail. Therefore, p terminates its SC procedure, returning $false$ (Line 13). On the other hand, if CAS succeeds, then p's current SC operation has taken effect. In that case, p gives up ownership of its local buffer, which now holds $\mathcal{O}[i]$'s current value, and becomes the owner of the buffer B holding $\mathcal{O}[i]$'s old value. To remain true to the promise that the buffer that held $\mathcal{O}[i]$'s current value (B, in this case) is not reused until some process performs at least N successful SC's, p enqueues the index of buffer B into its local queue (Line 14), and then dequeues some other buffer index from the queue (Line 15). Notice that, since p's local queue contains N buffer indices when p inserts B's index into it, p will not reuse buffer B until it performs at least N successful SC's.

Next, p tries to determine whether some process needs help with its LL operation. As we stated earlier, the process to help is $q = index_p$. So, p reads Help[q] to check whether q needs help (Line 16). If it does, p consults variable Announce[q] to learn the index j of the object that q needs help with (Line 17). Next, p reads the tag stored in X[j] to determine the buffer holding $\mathcal{O}[j]$'s current value

(Line 18), and then copies the value from that buffer into its own buffer (Line 19). Then, p writes into the Wth location of the buffer the tag that it read from $X[j]$ (Line 20). Finally, p attempts to help q by handing it p's buffer (Line 21). If p succeeds in helping q, then, by the earlier discussion, the buffer that p handed over to q contains a valid value of $\mathcal{O}[j]$. Hence, p gives up its buffer to q and assumes ownership of q's buffer (Line 22). (Notice that p's CAS at Line 21 fails if and only if, while p executed Lines 16–21, either another process already helped q or q withdrew its request for help.) Regardless of whether process q needed help or not, p increments the $index_p$ variable by 1 modulo N (Line 23) to ensure that in the next successful SC operation it helps some other process (Line 23), and then terminates its SC procedure by returning *true* (Line 24).

The procedure VL is self-explanatory (Line 10). The following theorem summarizes the above discussion. Its proof is presented in Section 3.

Theorem 1. *The algorithm in Figure 4 is a linearizable, wait-free implementation of an array $\mathcal{O}[0 .. M-1]$ of W-word LL/SC objects, shared by N processes. The time complexities of LL, SC and VL operations on any $\mathcal{O}[i]$ are $O(W)$, $O(W)$ and $O(1)$, respectively. The space complexity of the implementation is $O((N^2 + M)W)$.*

2.7 Remarks

Sequence Number Wrap-Around. Each 64-bit variable $X[i]$ stores in it a buffer index and an unbounded sequence number. The algorithm relies on the assumption that during the time interval when some process p executes one LL/SC pair, the sequence number stored in $X[i]$ does not cycle through all possible values. If we reserve 32 bits for the buffer index (which allows the implementation of up to 2^{31} LL/SC objects, shared by up to $2^{15} = 32,768$ processes), we still will have 32 bits for the sequence number, which is large enough that sequence number wraparound is not a concern in practice.

The Number of Outstanding LL Operations. Modifying the code in Figure 4 to handle multiple outstanding LL/SC operations is straightforward. Simply require that each LL operation, in addition to returning a value, also returns the tag associated with that value. Then, when calling an SC operation on some object, the caller p must also provide the tag that was returned by p's latest LL operation on that object.

3   Proof

Let $\mathcal{H}$ be finite execution history of the algorithm in Figure 4. Let OP be some LL operation, OP$'$ some SC operation, and OP$''$ some VL operation on $\mathcal{O}[i]$ in $\mathcal{H}$, for some i. Then, we define the linearization points (LPs) for OP, OP$'$, and OP$''$ as follows. If the CAS at Line 5 of OP succeeds, then LP(OP) is Line 3 of OP. Otherwise, let t be the time when OP executes Line 2, and t' be the time when OP performs the CAS at Line 5. Let v be the value that OP reads from BUF at

1. For any process p, we have $|Q_p| \geq N$.
2. For any process p such that $PC(p) = 15$, we have $|Q_p| \geq N + 1$.
3. For any process p and any value b in Q_p, we have $b \in [0 .. M + (N + 1)N - 1]$.
4. For any processes $p \in \mathcal{P}$, we have $mybuf_p \in [0 .. M + (N + 1)N - 1]$.
5. For any process $p \in \mathcal{P}'$, we have $\mathtt{Help}[p].buf \in [0 .. M + (N + 1)N - 1]$.
6. For any process $p \in \mathcal{P}''$, we have $x_p.buf \in [0 .. M + (N + 1)N - 1]$.
7. For any process $p \in \mathcal{P}'''$, we have $b(p) \in [0 .. M + (N + 1)N - 1]$.
8. For any index $i \in [0 .. M - 1]$, we have $\mathtt{X}[i].buf \in [0 .. M + (N + 1)N - 1]$.
9. Let p and q, (respectively, p' and q', p'' and q'', p''' and q'''), be any two processes in $\mathcal{P}$ (respectively, $\mathcal{P}'$, $\mathcal{P}''$, $\mathcal{P}'''$). Let r be any process and b_1 and b_2 any two values in Q_r. Let i and j be any two indices in $[0 .. M - 1]$. Then, we have $mybuf_p \neq mybuf_q \neq b_1 \neq b_2 \neq \mathtt{X}[i].buf \neq \mathtt{X}[j].buf \neq \mathtt{Help}[p'].buf \neq \mathtt{Help}[q'].buf \neq x_{p''}.buf \neq x_{q''}.buf \neq b(p''') \neq b(q''')$.

Fig. 5. The invariants satisfied by the algorithm in Figure 4

Line 8 of OP. Then, we show that there exists a successful SC operation SC_q on $\mathcal{O}[i]$ such that (1) at some point t'' during (t, t'), SC_q is the latest successful SC on $\mathcal{O}[i]$ to execute Line 12, and (2) SC_q writes v into $\mathcal{O}[i]$. We then set LP(OP) to time t''. We set LP(OP$'$) to Line 12 of OP$'$, and LP(OP$''$) to Line 10 of OP$''$.

In the following, we let $PC(p)$ denote the value of process p's program counter. For any register r at process p, we let $r(p)$ denote the value of that register. We let $\mathcal{P}$ denote a set of processes such that $p \in \mathcal{P}$ if and only if $PC(p) \in \{1, 2, 7 - 13, 16 - 21, 23, 24\}$ or $PC(p) \in \{3 - 5\} \wedge \mathtt{Help}[p] \equiv (*, 1, *)$. We let $\mathcal{P}'$ denote a set of processes such that $p \in \mathcal{P}'$ if and only if $PC(p) \in \{3 - 6\} \wedge \mathtt{Help}[p] \equiv (*, 0, *)$. We let $\mathcal{P}''$ denote a set of processes such that $p \in \mathcal{P}''$ if and only if $PC(p) = 14$. We let $\mathcal{P}'''$ denote a set of processes such that $p \in \mathcal{P}'''$ if and only if $PC(p) = 22$. Finally, we let $|Q_p|$ denote the length of process p's local queue Q_p.

Due to space constraints, we present the next six lemmas without proofs.

Lemma 1. *Let p be some process, and LL_p some LL operation by p in $\mathcal{H}$. Let t and t' be the times when p executes Line 2 and Line 5 of LL_p, respectively. Let t'' be either (1) the time when p executes Line 2 of its first LL operation after LL_p, if such operation exists, or (2) the end of $\mathcal{H}$, otherwise. Then, the following statements hold:*

(S1) During the time interval $(t, t']$, exactly one write into $\mathtt{Help}[p]$ is performed.
(S2) Any value written into $\mathtt{Help}[p]$ during (t, t'') is of the form $(*, 0, *)$.
(S3) Let $t''' \in (t, t']$ be the time when the write from statement (S1) takes place. Then, during the time interval (t''', t''), no process writes into $\mathtt{Help}[p]$.

Lemma 2. *The algorithm satisfies the invariants in Figure 5.*

Lemma 3. *Let $t_0 < t_1 < \ldots < t_K$ be all the times in $\mathcal{H}$ when some variable $\mathtt{X}[i]$ is written to (by a successful CAS at Line 12). Then, for all $j \in \{0, 1, \ldots, K\}$, the value written into $\mathtt{X}[i]$ at time t_j is of the form $(j, *)$.*

Lemma 4. *Let $\mathcal{O}[i]$ be an LL/SC object. Let t be the time when some process p reads $X[i]$ (at Line 3 or 18), and $t' > t$ the first time after t that p completes Line 4 or Line 19. Let OP be the latest successful SC operation on $\mathcal{O}[i]$ to execute Line 12 prior to time t, and v the value that OP writes in $\mathcal{O}[i]$. If there exists some process q such that Help$[q]$ holds value $(*, 1, *)$ throughout (t, t') and doesn't change, then p reads value v from BUF at Line 4 or Line 19 (during (t, t')).*

Lemma 5. *Let $\mathcal{O}[i]$ be an LL/SC object and OP some LL operation on $\mathcal{O}[i]$. Let SC_q be the latest successful SC operation on $\mathcal{O}[i]$ to execute Line 12 prior to Line 3 of OP, and v_q the value that SC_q writes in $\mathcal{O}[i]$. If the CAS at Line 5 of OP succeeds, then OP returns value v_q.*

Lemma 6. *Let $\mathcal{O}[i]$ be an LL/SC object, and OP an LL operation on $\mathcal{O}[i]$ such that the CAS at Line 5 of OP fails. Let p be the process executing OP. Let t and t' be the times, respectively, when p executes Lines 2 and 5 of OP. Let x and v be the values that p reads from BUF at Lines 7 and 8 of OP, respectively. Then, there exists a successful SC operation SC_q on $\mathcal{O}[i]$ such that (1) at some point during (t, t'), SC_q is the latest successful SC on $\mathcal{O}[i]$ to execute Line 12, and (2) SC_q writes x into $X[i]$ and v into $\mathcal{O}[i]$.*

Lemma 7 (Correctness of LL). *Let $\mathcal{O}[i]$ be some LL/SC object. Let OP be any LL operation on $\mathcal{O}[i]$, and OP' be the latest successful SC operation on $\mathcal{O}[i]$ such that $LP(\text{OP}') < LP(\text{OP})$. Then, OP returns the value written by OP'.*

Proof. Let p be the process executing OP. We examine the following two cases: (1) the CAS at Line 5 of OP succeeds, and (2) the CAS at Line 5 of OP fails. In the first case, let SC_q be the latest successful SC operation on $\mathcal{O}[i]$ to execute Line 12 prior to Line 3 of OP, and v_q be the value that SC_q writes in $\mathcal{O}[i]$. Since all SC operations are linearized at Line 12 and since OP is linearized at Line 3, we have $SC_q = \text{OP}'$. Furthermore, by Lemma 5, OP returns value v_q. Therefore, the lemma holds in this case.

In the second case, let t and t' be the times, respectively, when p executes Lines 2 and 5 of OP. Let v be the value that p reads from BUF at Line 8 of OP. Then, by Lemma 6, there exists a successful SC operation SC_r on $\mathcal{O}[i]$ such that (1) at some time $t'' \in (t, t')$, SC_r is the latest successful SC on $\mathcal{O}[i]$ to execute Line 12, and (2) SC_r writes v into $\mathcal{O}[i]$. Since all SC operations are linearized at Line 12 and since OP is linearized at time t'', we have $SC_r = \text{OP}'$. Therefore, the lemma holds. $\square$

Lemma 8 (Correctness of SC). *Let $\mathcal{O}[i]$ be some LL/SC object. Let OP be any SC operation on $\mathcal{O}[i]$ by some process p, and OP' be the latest LL operation on $\mathcal{O}[i]$ by p prior to OP. Then, OP succeeds if and only if there does not exist any successful SC operation OP'' on $\mathcal{O}[i]$ such that $LP(\text{OP}') < LP(\text{OP}'') < LP(\text{OP})$.*

Proof. We examine the following two cases: (1) the CAS at Line 5 of OP' succeeds, and (2) the CAS at Line 5 of OP' fails. In the first case, let t_1 be the time when p executes Line 3 of OP', and t_2 be the time when p executes Line 12 of OP. Then, we show that the following claim holds.

Claim. Process p's CAS at time t_2 succeeds if and only if there does not exist some other SC operation on $\mathcal{O}[i]$ that performs a successful CAS at Line 12 during (t_1, t_2).

Proof. Suppose that no other SC operation on $\mathcal{O}[i]$ performs a successful CAS at Line 12 during (t_1, t_2). Then, $\mathtt{X}[i]$ doesn't change during (t_1, t_2), and hence p's CAS at time t_2 succeeds.

Suppose that some SC operation SC_q on $\mathcal{O}[i]$ does perform a successful CAS at Line 12 during (t_1, t_2). Then, by Lemma 3, $\mathtt{X}[i]$ holds different values at times t_1 and t_2. Hence, p's CAS at time t_2 fails, which proves the claim.   □

Since all SC operations are linearized at Line 12 and since OP' is linearized at time t_1, it follows from the above claim that OP succeeds if and only if there does not exist some successful SC operation OP'' on $\mathcal{O}[i]$ such that LP(OP') < LP(OP'') < LP(OP). Hence, the lemma holds in this case.

In the second case (when the CAS at Line 5 of OP' fails), let t and t' be the times when p executes Lines 2 and 5 of OP', respectively. Let x and v be the values that p reads from BUF at Lines 7 and 8 of OP', respectively. Then, by Lemma 6, there exists a successful SC operation SC_r on $\mathcal{O}[i]$ such that (1) at some time $t'' \in (t, t')$, SC_r is the latest successful SC on $\mathcal{O}[i]$ to execute Line 12, and (2) SC_r writes x into $\mathtt{X}[i]$ and v into $\mathcal{O}[i]$. Therefore, at Line 7 of OP', p reads the value that variable $\mathtt{X}[i]$ holds at time t''. We now prove the following claim.

Claim. Process p's CAS at time t_2 succeeds if and only if there does not exist some other SC operation on $\mathcal{O}[i]$ that performs a successful CAS at Line 12 during (t'', t_2).

Proof. Suppose that no other SC operation on $\mathcal{O}[i]$ performs a successful CAS at Line 12 during (t'', t_2). Then, $\mathtt{X}[i]$ doesn't change during (t'', t_2), and hence p's CAS at time t_2 succeeds.

Suppose that some SC operation SC_q on $\mathcal{O}[i]$ does perform a successful CAS at Line 12 during (t'', t_2). Then, by Lemma 3, $\mathtt{X}[i]$ holds different values at times t'' and t_2. Hence, p's CAS at time t_2 fails, which proves the claim.   □

Since all SC operations are linearized at Line 12 and since OP' is linearized at time t_1, it follows from the above claim that OP succeeds if and only if there does not exist some successful SC operation OP'' on $\mathcal{O}[i]$ such that LP(OP') < LP(OP'') < LP(OP). Hence, the lemma holds.   □

Lemma 9 (Correctness of VL). *Let $\mathcal{O}[i]$ be some LL/SC object. Let OP be any VL operation on $\mathcal{O}[i]$ by some process p, and OP' be the latest LL operation on $\mathcal{O}[i]$ by p that precedes OP. Then, OP returns true if and only if there does not exist some successful SC operation OP'' on $\mathcal{O}[i]$ such that LP(OP'') $\in$ (LP(OP'), LP(OP)).*

Proof. Similar to the proof of Lemma 8.   □

Theorem 2. *The algorithm in Figure 4 is a linearizable, wait-free implementation of an array $\mathcal{O}[0 \ldots M-1]$ of W-word LL/SC objects, shared by N processes. The time complexities of LL, SC and VL operations on any $\mathcal{O}[i]$ are $O(W)$, $O(W)$ and $O(1)$, respectively. The space complexity of the implementation is $O((N^2 + M)W)$.*

Proof. The theorem follows immediately from Lemmas 7, 8, and 9.   □

Acknowledgments

We thank the anonymous OPODIS reviewers for their valuable comments on an earlier version of this paper.

References

1. Herlihy, M.: Wait-free synchronization. ACM TOPLAS **13**(1) (1991) 124–149
2. Lamport, L.: Concurrent reading and writing. Communications of the ACM **20**(11) (1977) 806–811
3. Peterson, G.L.: Concurrent reading while writing. ACM TOPLAS **5**(1) (1983) 56–65
4. Herlihy, M., Luchangco, V., Moir, M.: Obstruction-free synchronization: Double-ended queues as an example. In: Proceedings of the 23rd International Conference on Distributed Computing Systems. (2003)
5. International, S.: (The SPARC Architecture Manual) Version 9.
6. Corporation, I.: Intel Itanium Architecture Software Developer's Manual Volume 1: Application Architecture. (2002) Revision 2.1
7. Group, I.S.: IBM e server POWER4 System Microarchitecture. (2001)
8. Systems, M.C.: MIPS64™Architecture For Programmers Volume II: The MIPS64™Instruction Set. (2002) Revision 1.00
9. Site, R.: Alpha Architecture Reference Manual. Digital Equipment Corporation. (1992)
10. Moir, M.: Practical implementations of non-blocking synchronization primitives. In: Proceedings of the 16th Annual ACM Symposium on Principles of Distributed Computing. (1997) 219–228
11. Center, I.T.W.R.: System/370 Principles of operation. (1983) Order Number GA22-7000
12. Anderson, J., Moir, M.: Universal constructions for large objects. In: Proceedings of the 9th International Workshop on Distributed Algorithms. (1995) 168–182
13. Anderson, J., Moir, M.: Universal constructions for multi-object operations. In: Proceedings of the 14th Annual ACM Symposium on Principles of Distributed Computing. (1995) 184–194
14. Doherty, S., Herlihy, M., Luchangco, V., Moir, M.: Bringing practical lock-free synchronization to 64-bit applications. In: Proceedings of the 23rd Annual ACM Symposium on Principles of Distributed Computing. (2004) 31–39
15. Israeli, A., Rappoport, L.: Disjoint-Access-Parallel implementations of strong shared-memory primitives. In: Proceedings of the 13th Annual ACM Symposium on Principles of Distributed Computing. (1994) 151–160

16. Jayanti, P., Petrovic, S.: Efficient wait-free implementation of multiword LL/SC variables. In: Proceedings of the 25th International Conference on Distributed Computing Systems. (2005)
17. Jayanti, P., Petrovic, S.: Efficient and practical constructions of LL/SC variables. In: Proceedings of the 22nd ACM Symposium on Principles of Distributed Computing. (2003)
18. Luchangco, V., Moir, M., Shavit, N.: Nonblocking k-compare-single-swap. In: Proceedings of the fifteenth annual ACM symposium on Parallel algorithms and architectures. (2003) 314–323
19. Michael, M.: Practical lock-free and wait-free LL/SC/VL implementations using 64-bit CAS. In: Proceedings of the 18th Annual Conference on Distributed Computing. (2004) 144–158
20. Chandra, T., Jayanti, P., Tan, K.Y.: A polylog time wait-free construction for closed objects. In: Proceedings of the 17th Annual Symposium on Principles of Distributed Computing. (1998) 287–296
21. Jayanti, P.: An optimal multi-writer snapshot algorithm. In: Proceedings of the 37th ACM Symposium on Theory of Computing. (2005)
22. Jayanti, P.: f-arrays: implementation and applications. In: Proceedings of the 21st Annual Symposium on Principles of Distributed Computing. (2002) 270 – 279
23. Herlihy, M., Wing, J.: Linearizability: A correctness condition for concurrent objects. ACM TOPLAS **12**(3) (1990) 463–492
24. Jayanti, P., Petrovic, S.: Efficiently implementing a large number of ll/sc objects. Technical Report TR 2005 562, Dartmouth College Computer Science Department (2005)
25. Herlihy, M.: A methodology for implementing highly concurrent data structures. ACM Transactions on Programming Languages and Systems **15**(5) (1993) 745–770

Can Memory Be Used Adaptively by Uniform Algorithms?

Burkhard Englert and Darin Goldstein

California State University Long Beach,
Dept. of Comp. Engr. & Comp. Science,
Long Beach, CA 90840
{englert, daring}@cecs.csulb.edu

Abstract. We introduce a novel term, *memory-adaptive*, that intuitively captures what it means for a distributed protocol to most efficiently make use of its shared memory. We also prove three results that relate to our memory-adaptive model. In our *store/release* protocols processors are required to store a value in shared MWMR memory so that it cannot be overwritten until it has been released by the processor. We show that there do not exist uniformly wait-free store/release protocols using only the basic operations read and write that are memory-adaptive to point contention. We further show that there exists a uniformly wait-free store/release protocol using only the basic operations read and write that is memory-adaptive to total contention. We finally show that there exists a uniformly wait-free store/release protocol using only the basic operations read, write, and write-plus that is memory-adaptive to interval contention and time-adaptive to total contention.

1 Introduction

In order to solve certain well known problems such as collect, atomic snapshot, or renaming, the active processors need to gather information about each other. For example, in the renaming problem, before choosing a new name, processors need to know which names other processors have already chosen. A straightforward way in which information can be communicated is to use an array of Single-Writer Multi-Reader (SWMR) registers such that each processor has a unique array entry assigned to it. Only a single fixed processor is allowed to write to each array location while all processors can read them. A processor can update information about itself by writing into its entry and it can then collect information about the other processors by reading all entries in an arbitrary order. Such a simple algorithm has the property that if a collect by a processor p_j returns a value v for a processor p_i then v is the value of the last update operation by p_i before the beginning of the collect or of an update that is concurrent with the collect. Moreover in two successive collects that do not overlap, the later one will not return for any processor a value that is older than a value returned by the earlier one for the same processor.

Such a collect algorithm with step complexity $O(N)$, however, where N is the total number of processors in the system, is possibly inefficient if only few

J.H. Anderson, G. Prencipe, and R. Wattenhofer (Eds.): OPODIS 2005, LNCS 3974, pp. 32–46, 2006.

of the N processors are actually participating. This motivated researchers to look for *adaptive* algorithms whose step complexity only depends on the number of participating processors. We will call these algorithms *time-adaptive* to distinguish them from algorithms that we call *memory-adaptive* in this paper. In *memory-adaptive* algorithms processors are only allowed to write to a shared MWMR register whose index is a function of the contention during the processors previous shared memory access.

Time-adaptive algorithms have a worst case step complexity that is bounded by a function of the number of concurrently participating, or actually active processors [3]. Motivated by Lamport's MX algorithm [26], many such time-adaptive algorithms have since been designed [1, 3, 4, 5, 6, 7, 9, 11, 13, 14, 15, 17, 18, 20, 21] [22, 24, 25, 27, 29]. The strongest forms of time-adaptiveness in the read/write shared memory model have been defined and achieved in recently presented long-lived time-adaptive collect [7] and renaming [1, 19] algorithms. In these algorithms, called *time-adaptive to point contention* the number of steps taken by a processor executing an operation is a function of the maximum number of processors that were active simultaneously at some point in time during this operations execution interval. Algorithms *time-adaptive to interval contention* have a slightly weaker level of adaptiveness. Here the number of steps taken during a given operation is a function of the total number of different processors active during the operation's execution interval. Finally, an algorithm is time-adaptive to *total contention* if the number of steps taken by a processor is a function of the total number of processors active since the beginning of the execution.

1.1   Background

Though we do not prove any results on the problem, this research is motivated by attempts to prove lower bounds in various settings for collect and related problems. We therefore give a few recent references and outline the current state of research on the collect problem below. (This is not meant to be a comprehensive summary by any means.)

Recently, a number of different time-adaptive collect algorithms were presented [7, 19, 20, 21, 22]. The algorithm presented by Attiya, Fouren and Gafni [20] has an asymptotically optimal $O(k)$ step complexity[1], but it is a one-shot algorithm and the memory consumption is exponential in N. Attiya, Kuhn, Wattenhofer and Wattenhofer [21] presented a new randomized time-adaptive collect algorithm with asymptotically optimal step complexity and polynomial memory overhead. For any constant $\gamma > 1$ they also presented a new deterministic collect algorithm with $O(k^2/((\gamma - 1) \log N))$ step complexity and $O(N^{\gamma+1}/((\gamma-1) \log N))$ memory complexity. However, their algorithms are *one-shot*, not long-lived and hence time-adapt only to total contention with respect to shared memory operations. On the other hand the collect algorithm by Afek,

---

[1] Throughout this paper, we will use the lowercase k to refer to the contention and the uppercase N to refer to the total number of processors that could *potentially* become active. We capitalize N to emphasize that it is to be considered large in comparison to k.

Stupp and Touitou [7] is long-lived and time-adapts to the point contention (and hence to interval contention) k. It is designed for low contention, has step complexity $O(k^3)$ and uses $O(N^3)$ shared memory registers.

Additionally, Afek, Boxer and Touitou [2] showed that the number of Multi-Writer Multi-Reader (MWMR) registers used must be a function of N. They specifically show that for any constant d there is a large enough N_d such that every long-lived time-adaptive (to interval contention, and hence, point contention as well) read/write implementation of collect (and renaming) with N_d processors must use at least d MWMR registers. In their paper they use a simple object called weak test and set [12] to derive their impossibility results. More recently Attiya, Fich and Kaplan [16] significantly improved on [2]. They showed that if a collect algorithm is time-adaptive to total contention, namely, its step complexity is $f(k)$, where k is the number of processors that ever became active during the current execution, then it uses $\Omega(f^{-1}(N))$ MWMR registers, where N is the total number of processors in the system.

1.2 Motivation

What if in a distributed system such as the Internet, we have a potentially huge number of processors that might participate in some protocol but it is known that with very high probability only a small number of processors will be active at any given time. It is unrealistic and wasteful for a system to provide a huge number of shared memory registers for the operation of such a protocol. Algorithms that operate in this setting are not able to use a priori knowledge about a finite upper bound on the number of processors in the system and are called *uniform* algorithms. Aguilera, Englert and Gafni [10] showed that there are single shot tasks such as generalized weak test and set [12] that cannot be solved uniformly with a finite number of MWMR registers. In other words a protocol solving this task with finitely many MWMR registers must know the number of participating processors in advance. Since generalized weak test and set is a one-shot algorithm, this implies that the long lived nature of test and set and the requirement that the step complexity adapt to interval contention are not the only requirements that preclude a solution in finite space.

Consider a setting where no *finite* a priori upper bound on the number of possibly participating processors is known. Ultimately we would like to know if in such a setting it is possible to uniformly implement collect (or any of the other closely related protocol problems) with finitely many MWMR registers. In such a setting an algorithm that implements collect will not be able to rely on and make use of processor id's (such as in [7]) to decide which MWMR registers to write to. With this in mind we present in this paper some new results concerning a new measure of adaptiveness that we call *memory-adaptiveness*. Algorithms that are memory-adaptive strictly only use memory space whose size *at all times* is a function of the contention. We investigate what can be implemented memory adaptively in a system with infinitely many processors and an infinite shared memory. We provide results for algorithms memory-adaptive to point, interval, and total contention. Ultimately we hope that the continuation of this investigation will shed some light on the question of if and, if so, how collect and similar algorithms can be solved uniformly in a system with infinitely many MWMR registers and infinitely many SWMR registers.

Memory-Adaptiveness. For the purposes of investigating uniform protocols on systems with enormous shared memory resources[2], we introduce the notion of *memory-adaptiveness*: each write operation that a processor makes must be close to the "front" of shared memory. Intuitively such a definition is motivated by the fact that, if processors are able to write to registers with "unpredictably large" indices, then the amount of shared memory used by the protocol needs to be at least as "unpredictably large" as the largest index written. Imagine a distributed operating system with essentially infinite memory. If the protocols it runs are allowed to write to any part of memory, then, if pointer-based structures are not used[3], it can only run a single protocol at a time so as to prevent memory collisions between protocols. On the other hand, if it can guarantee that the memory required by each protocol is a bounded function of the contention, then it can allocate large memory blocks to each protocol on an ad hoc basis and, on the rare occasions when it is necessary, increase or decrease the individual allocations as necessary. If the system is guaranteed of an upper bound on the potential index of a register based on the contention, then the memory requirements of each protocol run in the system are clearly much less.

Another reason for investigating memory-adaptiveness is as follows. If processors are allowed to write to arbitrarily large indices (i.e. indices that are independent of the contention) for the first time, later processors will not be able to accurately determine the contention without performing a potentially huge number of reads. Hence they will want to register in a fixed finite subset of the infinite set of MWMR registers that we call "close to the beginning of shared memory."

By way of contrast, consider the renaming problem [1, 5, 17, 19], for example. Each active processor is required to choose a unique name for itself that is as small as possible by storing its index in a shared memory register. Its new "name" becomes the index of this shared register. Processors are allowed to use any shared register during the execution of the protocol, even a register with an extremely large index, but the final result must lie within a bounded distance from the front of shared memory. In our new definition of *memory-adaptiveness*, to capture the notion of having to write close to the front of shared memory *every* time, we require processors to write to a MWMR register whose index is a function of the contention during the previous operation of the same processor.

---

[2] Currently, purchasing a potentially huge amount of memory is possible for a distributed system. Memory is cheap nowadays. However, effectively managing this memory is a serious problem.

[3] Pointer-based structures inherently require numerous small, on-the-fly memory allocations, which usually necessitate the intervention of the operating system and hence greatly slow the computation. As any seasoned programmer knows, operating system interrupts (and hence pointer-based structures) are to be avoided when programming a computationally intensive algorithm.

Our Contributions. We begin by investigating simple tasks, *store* and *release*, that require a given processor to store a value in shared MWMR memory that cannot be overwritten by any other processor and then erasing the value when no longer needed, freeing the memory for other processors to use[4]. We will study whether these simple commands can be implemented memory-adaptively under different assumptions about the contention of the protocol.

We roughly summarize the contributions of our paper here. The rigorous phrasing of the theorems and definitions will come in Section 2.

1. Point contention: (Theorem 1) We show that in a system with *infinitely* many MWMR registers and *infinitely* many SWMR registers, for any constant d, there exists a number N_d such that if N_d processors are allowed to participate in a *memory-adaptive* (to POINT contention) execution of the protocol, then at least one does not make a single uncovered write to a shared register in d writes. In other words we show that under these conditions processors cannot memory-adaptively store a value in shared memory. This implies that any time-adaptive collect or renaming algorithm in this setting that uses only finitely many of the infinitely many MWMR registers (if such an algorithm exists) cannot be built from memory-adaptive building blocks alone.

    Note that Afek, Boxer, and Touitou [7] showed that for any constant d there is a large enough N_d such that every long-lived time-adaptive (to interval contention and hence point contention as well) read/write implementation of collect (and renaming) with N_d processors must use at least d MWMR registers. This result essentially implies that there cannot exist a uniform long-lived time-adaptive (to interval contention) read/write implementation of collect or renaming that uses only a finite number of memory registers. However, their result is not immediately applicable to the case where there are an infinite number of registers available for use. Also, we show that a processor cannot even hope to reliably store its value in a register in the point-contention memory-adaptive model, much less reliably collect all of the values of the other active processors.

    Oddly enough, however, if we relax the type of contention, we get positive results for the very same store and release protocols.

2. Total Contention: (Theorem 2) We show that there does exist a uniform long-lived implementation of store and release in the read-write model that is memory-adaptive to TOTAL contention. Thus, the definition of memory-adaptiveness itself is not one that precludes the possibility of a meaningful protocol for store and release. The proof is constructive and similar to [20].

3. Interval contention: (Theorem 3) Note that if one can implement store and release, then the collect protocol becomes trivial to implement. Unfortunately, given the result in [7], it seems unlikely that a collect protocol

---

[4] Another way to view a *store* and *release* protocol is as a simple renaming protocol where the index of the register in which a value is stored becomes the new name and where *release* simply releases this name. To focus attention on the central components of such a protocol and to avoid confusion with already existing renaming protocols we choose the store/release terminology.

memory-adaptive to interval contention is possible. If we change the model to allow a slightly stronger write command called WRITE-PLUS, then such an algorithm for store/release does exist. Note that the WRITE-PLUS command is much weaker than the standard read-modify-write. We give a thorough description of the command and the algorithm below.

The covering techniques used in our impossibility proofs first appeared in [23] to show some bounds on the number of registers necessary for mutual exclusion. However there they were used to prove an impossibility in a system with finitely many MWMR registers. Here, we modify them to show an impossibility in a system with infinitely many MWMR registers.

2 The Model

We use the standard shared-memory model of distributed computation. There exists a large numbers of processors modeled by infinite-state machines capable of unbounded computation that are allowed to engage in a distributed deterministic asynchronous protocol. Processors are indexed by the positive natural numbers and each knows its own "name." There are two areas of memory: the single-writer multi-reader (SWMR) space and the multi-writer multi-reader (MWMR) space. The former can be thought of as a large array of numbered registers indexed by the positive natural numbers. Each register is associated with a distinct processor and can store an unbounded number of bits. A given processor may only write to its assigned register though it may read the contents of any other SWMR registers. The MWMR registers have all the same properties as the SWMR registers with the exception that any processor may both read *and* write to any register. Intuitively, we think of the SWMR registers as private memory controlled by the individual processors, and the MWMR registers as the memory domain of a separate entity with its own operating system accessible by the all the processors.

Processors interact with the memory space using basic atomic operations. The atomic operations we will allow in this paper are *read, write,* and a new operation we call *write-plus*.

- READ: To execute a read command, a processor specifies a register to be read and upon completion of the read, the processor has gained a snapshot of the contents of the specified register.
- WRITE: A processor specifies which register to write to (in either private or shared memory) and the data to be written. Upon completion of the write command, all previous data is overwritten with the new data specified by the processor. (Note that we do not allow a processor to overwrite "part" of a register.)
- WRITE-PLUS: A write-plus command is similar to a write command except that after the value of the register is written, the processor receives a snapshot of the value that was overwritten. It is a special case of a Read-Modify-Write (RMW). The RMW command allows the unbreakable execution of the following code (where X is a shared variable and f is a mapping):

```
function RMW(X,f)
begin
    temp←X;
    X←f(X);
    return(temp);
end
```

The write-plus command is equivalent to specifying that the function f is required to be a constant independent of X.

A *protocol* is an algorithm that accomplishes a task using basic operations. An *adaptive* protocol is one in which the resources consumed by the protocol are functions of the number of processors that actually participate in the protocol (a.k.a. active processors) rather than the total number of processors. When dealing with adaptive protocols, it is convenient to have definitions that measure the number of active processors in the system at a given time (i.e. the "contention"). *Total contention* refers to the total number of processors that become active during the entire execution of the algorithm. *Interval contention* during a given processor's protocol is defined to be the total number of processors that become active during the execution of a processors protocol. Finally, *point contention* during a given processor's protocol refers to the maximum number of processors that are simultaneously active during the execution of a processors protocol.

There are naturally several different ways to measure the complexity of an adaptive protocol. One says that a protocol is *time-adaptive* to a particular type of contention if the maximum number of basic operations executed during the protocol by any given processor is a bounded function of the contention type. This is another way of saying that the step complexity of the algorithm depends on the contention. This definition is fairly standard in the literature [1, 3, 4, 5, 6, 7, 9, 11, 13, 14, 15, 17, 18, 20, 21, 22, 24, 25, 27, 29].

To obtain our results we are mainly interested in the writes processors make to shared memory (MWMR registers). We hence introduce a new measure of complexity that we call *memory-adaptive*. We say that a command is *memory-adaptive* to a type of contention if and only if the following is true. Whenever a processor executes a basic operation, if the next basic operation will change the state of a shared memory register, the index of the register is a bounded function of the contention at the time of the previous basic operation. (In the asynchronous model, without loss of generality, we may assume that the first basic operation in any protocol is a read, which does not change the state of any register.) In other words, a processor can read wherever it wants, but it can only write to places that are as close to the "front" of shared memory as possible.

Our definition of memory-adaptiveness is not well-established in the literature. The common understanding of the concept of memory-adaptiveness refers to the end result of the computation [1, 3, 4, 5, 6, 7, 9, 11, 13, 14, 15, 17, 18, 20, 21, 22, 24] [25, 27, 29]. The final result must lie within a bounded distance of the "front" of shared memory. For example, in the renaming protocol, each active processor is required to choose a unique name for itself that is as small as possible by storing its index in a shared memory register. Its new "name" becomes the index of this shared register. Processors are allowed to use any shared register during the execution of the protocol, even a register with an extremely large index, but the final result must lie within a bounded distance from the front of shared memory. We justify our new definition based on the following reasoning. Assume that a distributed system has a potentially huge number of processors that might participate in some protocol. (For example, assume that a renaming protocol is executing on a certain subset of the computers connected to the Internet...) It is known that with very high probability only a small number of processors will be active at any given time. It is unrealistic and wasteful for a system to provide a huge number of shared memory registers for the operation of such a protocol. Using the established definition of "memory-adaptiveness," a protocol could be memory-adaptive and yet require unbounded resources for a proper execution. On the other hand, if a protocol is memory-adaptive using our new definition of memory-adaptiveness, one need not have prior knowledge of the *potential* number of active processors before the protocol begins. This new definition seems to better capture the intuitive feel of what memory-adaptiveness should be.

The two protocols that we will focus on in this paper are *store* and *release*.

- STORE: A data value is specified in advance by the processor. The goal is for the processor to store the data value in some shared register in such a way that upon completion the processor knows that the value will not be moved or erased by any other processor until the register is explicitly released. Essentially, this amounts to storing a value in shared memory and locking the location. Ideally, the index of the shared register in question will be as close to the "front" as possible.
- RELEASE: This assumes that the processor has already executed a previous store protocol. Upon completion, the shared register occupied by the processor is released.

Note that these are fundamental commands useful for many distributed protocols (e.g. collect, mutual exclusion, consensus, approximate agreement, and so on).

We call a protocol *uniformly wait-free* if there exists a uniform bound applicable to all processors on the number of basic operations that the protocol requires before termination. All protocols considered in this paper will be uniformly wait-free.

3   Point Contention

Our first major result is the following theorem.

Theorem 1. *There do not exist long-lived uniformly wait-free store/release protocols using only the basic operations read and write that are memory-adaptive to point contention.*

The proof requires a preliminary combinatorial lemma. Throughout this paper, $\mathcal{N}$ represents the set of positive integers.

Lemma 1. *Assume that you are given an infinite collection of sets $S_i \subseteq \mathcal{N}$ such that $|S_i| \leq k$ for some nonnegative constant k. Then $\exists X \subseteq \mathcal{N}$ such that $|X| = \infty$ and such that $\forall x, y \in X, y \neq x \Rightarrow x \notin S_y$.*

Note that it is not enough to make the S_i bounded. They *must* be uniformly bounded. As a counterexample, note that if we let $S_i = \{1, 2, \ldots, i\}$, then $\forall i, |S_i| < \infty$ but for any set such that $|X| = \infty$, if $x < y \in X$, then $x \in S_y$.

Proof. We will induct on the value of k. For the base case, assume that $k = 0$. Then $\forall x \in \mathcal{N}, S_x = \emptyset$ so the claim is trivially true.

Assume inductively that the claim is true for all nonnegative integers up to some nonnegative constant k.

Assume that you are given sets $S_i \subseteq \mathcal{N}$ such that $|S_i| \leq k + 1$. By way of contradiction, assume that $\forall X \subseteq \mathcal{N}$, the condition

$$\forall x, y \in X, y \neq x \Rightarrow x \notin S_y$$

implies that $|X| < \infty$. Choose a set X. Perform the following algorithm repeatedly:

– Determine whether the following statement is true or false: $\exists a \in \mathcal{N} - X, \forall x \in X, x \notin S_a \wedge a \notin S_x$.
  • If the statement is true, then let $X = X \cup \{a\}$. Start again.
  • If the statement is false, stop.

Either the procedure above lasts forever or eventually stops. If the procedure lasts forever, then by the Axiom of Choice, we have found a set X such that $|X| = \infty$ and $\forall x, y \in X, y \neq x \Rightarrow x \notin S_y$ which is a contradiction. So we may assume that the procedure eventually terminates. Then X is a finite-size maximal set such that $\forall x, y \in X, y \neq x \Rightarrow x \notin S_y$. We also know by virtue of the fact that the algorithm above terminated, that

$$\forall a \in \mathcal{N} - X, \exists x \in X, x \in S_a \vee a \in S_x$$

Create a new collection of sets S_i' from the old collection S_i. For each $i \in \mathcal{N}$,

– If $i \in X \vee i \in \bigcup_{a \in X} S_a$, let $S_i' = \emptyset$
– If $i \notin X \wedge i \notin \bigcup_{a \in X} S_a$, let $S_i' = S_i - X$

Our first claim is that $\forall i \in \mathcal{N}, |S_i'| \leq k$. This is clear if $i \in X \vee i \in \bigcup_{a \in X} S_a$. If $i \notin X \wedge i \notin \bigcup_{a \in X} S_a$, then we claim that $\exists x \in X, x \in S_i$ which would prove the claim.

Claim.

$$i \notin X \wedge i \notin \bigcup_{a \in X} S_a \Rightarrow \exists x \in X, x \in S_i$$

Proof of Claim: Assume that $i \notin X \wedge i \notin \bigcup_{a \in X} S_a$. Assume by way of contradiction that $S_i \cap X = \emptyset$. Recall that X is finite and maximal. We claim that

$$\forall x, y \in X \cup \{i\}, y \neq x \Rightarrow x \notin S_y$$

thus violating the maximality of the set X because $i \notin X$. Let $x \in X$. Then we have two things to check: (a) $i \notin S_x$ and (b) $x \notin S_i$. For the condition (a), note that $i \notin \bigcup_{a \in X} S_a \Rightarrow i \notin S_x$. For the condition (b), $S_i \cap X = \emptyset \Rightarrow x \notin S_i$. So we are done. □

Thus, we have new sets $S_i' \subseteq \mathcal{N}$ such that $|S_i'| \leq k$. Using the inductive hypothesis, $\exists X' \subseteq \mathcal{N}$ such that $|X'| = \infty$ and such that $\forall x, y \in X', y \neq x \Rightarrow x \notin S_y'$. Let $X'' \subseteq \mathcal{N}$ be $X' - X - \bigcup_{a \in X} S_a$. We claim that (a) $|X''| = \infty$ and (b) $\forall x, y \in X'', y \neq x \Rightarrow x \notin S_y$.

Condition (a) is trivially true from the fact that $|X'| = \infty$ and $|X| < \infty$ and $|\bigcup_{a \in X} S_a| < \infty$.

To prove condition (b), choose $x, y \in X''$. We want to show that $x \in S_y \Rightarrow x = y$. Assume that $x \in S_y$. Note that $y \in X'' \Rightarrow y \notin X \wedge y \notin \bigcup_{a \in X} S_a \Rightarrow S_y' = S_y - X$. We also have $x \in X'' \Rightarrow x \notin X$ so that $x \in S_y \Rightarrow x \in S_y'$. Finally, $x, y \in X'' \Rightarrow x, y \in X'$ and therefore $x \in S_y' \Rightarrow x = y$. Thus, X'' is the inductive set for $k + 1$ and we are done. □

Proof of Theorem 1: Assume that store and release protocols exist that are uniformly wait-free and memory-adaptive to point contention. Assume that there are an infinite number of potential processors indexed by $\mathcal{N}$, only a finite number of which will ever participate in executing the protocol.

We make the following claim. For all $k \geq 0$, there exists an infinite set of processors P and an execution sequence such that all processors in P satisfy the following statements: $\forall p \in P$, if p is executing a store command from a configuration that is consistent with all processors inactive, then after k writes to shared memory, (a) p has not written a single uncovered write into shared memory and (b) p's current computational transcript is consistent with any positive number of active processors in the system. It is clear that this claim implies the theorem: after k writes, the processor is no better off than at the beginning of its execution. The remainder of the proof proves this claim.

Fix some k. We will build a set $P = P_k$ that satisfies both properties. We will first examine the computational transcripts of our processors just before each is about to make its first shared write. Initially, the system is in a configuration that is consistent with all processors being inactive.

Assuming each processor in $\mathcal{N}$ makes a solo execution, let $S_i^{(0)}$ be the set of single-writer registers read by processor i. Note that by the uniform wait-free nature of the store command, $|S_i^{(0)}| \leq j_0$ for some constant j_0. By Lemma 1, $\exists X_0 \subseteq \mathcal{N}$ such that $|X_0| = \infty$ and such that $\forall x, y \in X_0, y \neq x \Rightarrow x \notin S_y^{(0)}$. Translating this back into English, this implies that there exists an infinite set of processors X_0 such that no processor reads the single-writer register of any other processor in the set. Because we start from an inactive state, the first write must be to within a constant distance from the front of shared memory (by the definition of memory-adaptiveness). By the Pigeonhole Principle, there must exist an infinite number of processors from the set X_0 that cover the same shared register. Call this infinite set P_0. We claim that P_0 satisfies properties (a) and (b). (a) is trivial. Because each processor cannot see any other processor by construction, (b) is also trivial.

Assume that P_m has been constructed and we wish to construct P_{m+1}.

To construct P_{m+1}, we do the following. Choose some $p' \in P_m$. For every $p \in P_m - \{p'\}$, we can construct an execution that happens like this. p finishes its write but the value it writes is immediately overwritten by p'. We allow p' to completely finish its store and then we allow p' to completely finish a release operation. Note that shared memory now looks completely inactive. Index the set $P_m - \{p'\}$ by $\mathcal{N}$. Let $S_i^{(m)}$ be the set of single-writer registers that are read by p_i in a p_i-only execution up until the next shared p_i-write. (Note that $\mathcal{N}$ is only indexing $P_m - \{p'\}$ and so a processor might read some single-writer registers that are not in this set, but we don't care because all other processors are assumed to be inactive.) Once again, note that $|S_i^{(m)}| \leq j_m$ for some constant j_m. By Lemma 1, $\exists X_{m+1} \subseteq \mathcal{N}$ such that $|X_{m+1}| = \infty$ and such that $\forall x, y \in X_{m+1}, y \neq x \Rightarrow x \notin S_y^{(1)}$. So we again get an infinite set of processors that still cannot see each other. Because of condition (b) and the definition of memory-adaptiveness, for each processor, we can only write to within a constant distance from the front of shared memory. Again, by the Pigeonhole Principle, there must be an infinite number of processors covering the same shared memory location. Let this be P_{m+1}. Because all the processors in $P_m - \{p'\}$ were executing covered writes, (a) is trivially true because it was true previously. (b) is also trivial by construction.

We can continue in this way for any number of shared writes.   □

4   Total Contention

Interestingly, it is possible to make an equivalent protocol adaptive to total contention rather than point contention.

Theorem 2. *There exists a long-lived uniformly wait-free store/release protocol using only the basic operations read and write that is memory-adaptive to total contention.*

Proof Sketch. This is very similar to existing algorithms for collect, renaming such as the algorithms presented in [20, 28]. Think of the memory as a two dimensional grid $\mathcal{N} \times (\mathcal{N} \cup \{0\})$. We can easily convert this back to a one-dimensional linear configuration via a simple diagonalization argument. The registers $(i, 0)$ will be the ones that are used to store the actual values. The registers (i, j) for $j \geq 1$ are all splitters [8, 26, 28] and will be the competition space for $(i, 0)$. Initially the spot $(i, 0)$ for all i will consist of a pointer to $(i, 1)$ (i.e. the first "empty splitter") and a flag indicating that the register is empty. When a processor executes a store, it tries for $(i, 0)$ first. If $(i, 0)$ is not occupied with a value, it notes the current round and proceeds to the first empty splitter in the column. The operation of the splitters is as follows:

The processor writes its name into slot #1. It then looks into slot #2. If there is a processor in slot #2, then it proceeds onwards to try for $(i+1, 0)$. If not, the processor writes its name into slot #2. It then checks slot #1. If the processors name is not written in slot #1, then it proceeds to $(i, j + 1)$. If the processors name is in slot #1, then it wins the splitter and the register. In the register, it will note its own value, the fact that the register is "taken", and the value of j that it won from. This will be the "lowest" dirty splitter. Below that are clean splitters; the next processor that tries to claim this register will start from the highest clean splitter. When a release is called, all the processor needs to do is indicate that the register is open.

5 Interval Contention

Oddly enough, there also exists a store/release protocol similar to the one above that is memory-adaptive to interval contention. However, in order to make the protocol memory-adaptive to interval contention, we need to use the somewhat stronger write-plus operation.

Theorem 3. *There exists a long-lived uniformly wait-free store/release protocol using only the basic operations read, write, and write-plus that is memory-adaptive to interval contention and time-adaptive to total contention.*

Proof. Once again, we assume that the memory is arranged in the form of a two-dimensional grid, this time indexed by $\mathcal{N} \times \mathcal{N}$.

Whenever a processor executes a write-plus into shared memory, it notes what was previously written there in its private memory space along with whatever it writes into the register. It therefore always has a complete record of all of its operations from the beginning of time in its private space along with the values that it overwrites. During each store and with each write, the processor keeps track of the number of times it has stored a value in shared memory. Each write will contain a field with this parameter. Also, splitters are able to hold values. Whenever a processor captures a splitter, it uses it to store its value.

Assume for the moment that a processor has the ability to tell whether a splitter is "clean" or "dirty". In other words, the processor is able to tell whether, given a splitter, there exists another processor that has previously written into the splitter's slot #1 and yet has not either written into slot #2 or written into some other shared register. Then we perform the following protocol: Whenever a processor executes a store, it begins at $(1, 1) = (i, j)$. If the splitter is taken with a value, then the processor moves to $(i + 1, 1)$. If the splitter is dirty, it moves to $(i, j + 1)$. If the splitter is clean, it competes. It writes its name into slot #1 and checks slot #2. If there is a "new" name (i.e. a name that has been written in the splitter after the processor started competing) in slot #2, the processor moves to $(i + 1, 1)$. If there is no new name, then the processor writes its name into slot #2 and checks slot #1. If there is a new name in slot #1, then the processor moves to $(i, j + 1)$. If the processor's name is still written in slot #1, then the processor has won the splitter and the right to use its value register. It notes this in the register and writes in its value.

It remains to show that a processor has the ability to tell whether a splitter is clean or dirty. The processor examines the names of the processors in each slot of the splitter. Using this information, it can work backwards to determine all of the processors that have written into the slot previously by examining the private register of each and working backwards recursively. With that information, the processor can determine whether there exists a processor that has written into slot #1 and not #2 or has written into slot #1 and then nowhere else. This is the definition of dirty.

In order to execute a release, the processor simply indicates that the splitter is now clean.

We claim that this protocol is time-adaptive to total contention and memory-adaptive to interval contention. First, we will show the memory-adaptiveness.

We assume that the total number of processors that ever become active during the interval under consideration is k. Consider the protocol restricted to a given column i. Assume that only at most j active processors are ever in the column at any given time. Because all processors are required to start at position $(i, 1)$, note that the furthest downward that any processor could ever move is (i, j). We now claim that in column i, at most $k - i + 1$ processors will ever exist in the column at any given time. Clearly, this is true for $i = 1$. In order for a processor to move to the right, another processor must be "left behind." Thus, there can be at most one fewer active processor in a given column than in the column to the left. Inductively, our claim is therefore proved. The processors are therefore restricted to move in the space above and to the left of the grid points $(i, k - i + 1), 1 \leq i \leq k$. Because the processors are only allowed to move right and down, this restricts the number of moves to at most k before an empty splitter is found. This implies a bound of $O(k^2)$ on the memory-adaptiveness of the protocol.

For the time-adaptive claim, note that the number of reads that is necessary for a given processor to determine the history of a given splitter is proportional to the number of processors that has previously written into the splitter.

6   Open Problems

We leave open the question of whether it is possible to design a store/release protocol that is memory-adaptive to interval contention and does not require the use of the slightly stronger write-plus operation. We conjecture, based on previous results in a slightly different setting, that this will not be possible.

Moreover, the question remains whether a time-adaptive, uniform collect algorithm in an unbounded execution exists that always uses only finitely many registers. We conjecture that it must use infinitely many MWMR registers even if throughout, in this unbounded execution, only finitely many processors appear. We hope that the results in this paper help lead to an eventual proof of this conjecture.

References

1. Y. Afek, H. Attiya, A. Fouren, G. Stupp and D. Touitou. Long-Lived Renaming made adaptive. *Proc. of 18th Annual ACM Symp. on Principles of Distributed Computing*: 91-103, May 1999.
2. Y. Afek, P. Boxer and D. Touitou. Bounds on the shared memory requirements for long-lived and adaptive objects. *Proc. of the 19th Ann. ACM Symp. on Principles of Distributed Computing (PODC 2000)*:81-89, July 2000.
3. Y. Afek, D. Dauber and D. Touitou. Wait-free made fast. *Proc. of the 27th Ann. ACM Symp. on Theory of Computing*: 538-547, May 1995.
4. Y. Afek, H. Attiya, G. Stupp and D. Touitou. Adaptive long-lived renaming using bounded memory. *Proc. of the 40th IEEE Ann. Symp. on Foundations of Computer Science*, pages 262-272, October 1999.
5. Y. Afek and M. Merritt. Fast, wait-free $(2k-1)$-renaming. In *Proc. of the 18th Ann. ACM Symp. on Principles of Distributed Computing*: 105-112, May 1999.
6. Y. Afek, M. Merritt, G. Taubenfeld and D. Touitou. Disentangling multi-object operations. In *Proc. of 16th Annual ACM Symp. on Principles of Distributed Computing*: 111-120, August 1997.
7. Y. Afek, G. Stupp and D. Touitou. Long-lived adaptive collect with applications. *Proc. of the 40th Ann. Symp. on Foundations of Computer Science*: 262-272, October 1999.
8. Y. Afek, G. Stupp and D. Touitou. Long Lived Adaptive Splitter and Applications. *Distributed Computing*, 15(2): 67-86, 2002.
9. Y. Afek, G. Stupp and D. Touitou. Long lived and adaptive atomic snapshot and immediate snapshot. *Proc. of the 19th Ann. ACM Symp. on Principles of Distributed Computing*, pages 71-80, 2000.
10. M. Aguilera, B. Englert and E. Gafni. Uniform Solvability with a finite number of MWMR registers. In *Proc. 17th International Conference DISC 2003*: 16-30, October 2003.
11. J. Anderson and Y.-J. Kim. Adaptive mutual exclusion with local spinning. *Proceedings of the 14th International Conference, DISC 2000*, pages 29-43, October 2000.
12. J. Anderson and J-H. Yang. Time/contention trade-offs for multiprocessor synchronization. *Information and Computation*, 124(1):68-84, 1996.
13. J. Aspnes, G. Shah and J. Shah. Wait free consensus with infinite arrivals. *Proc. of the 34th Annual ACM Symposium on the Theory of Computing*, pages 524-533, May 2002.
14. H. Attiya and V. Bortnikov. Adaptive and efficient mutual exclusion. In *Proceedings of the 19th Annual ACM Symposium on Principles of Distributed Computing (PODC 2000)*, pages 91-100, 2000.
15. H. Attiya and E. Dagan. Universal operations: Unary versus binary. In *Proc. 15th Annual ACM Symp. on Principles of Distributed Computing*: 223-232, May 1996.
16. H. Attiya, F. Fich and Y. Kaplan. Lower bounds for adaptive collect and related objects. In *Proc. 23 Annual ACM Symp. on Principles of Distributed Computing*: 60-70, July 2004.
17. H. Attiya and A. Fouren. Adaptive wait-free algorithms for lattice agreement and renaming. In *Proc. 17th Annual ACM Symp. on Principles of Distributed Computing*: 277-286, June 1998.
18. H. Attiya and A. Fouren. Adaptive long-lived renaming with read and write operations. Technical Report 0956, Faculty of Computer Science, Technion, Haifa, 1999. http://www.cs.technion.ac.il/ hagit/pubs/tr0956.ps.gz.

19. H. Attiya and A. Fouren. Algorithms adaptive to point contention. In *J. ACM*, 50(4): 444-468, July 2003.
20. H. Attiya, A. Fouren and E. Gafni. An adaptive collect algorithm with applications. *Distributed Computing*, 15(2): 87-96, 2002.
21. H. Attiya, F. Kuhn, M. Wattenhofer and R. Wattenhofer. Efficient Adaptive Collect using Randomization. *Proc. 18th Annual Conference on Distributed Computing (DISC)*, October 2004.
22. H. Attiya and I. Zach. Fully adaptive algorithms for atomic and immediate snapshots. WWW.CS.TECHNION.AC.IL/ HAGIT/PUBS/AZ03.PDF, 2003.
23. J. Burns and N. Lynch. Bounds on shared memory for mutual exclusion. *Information and Computation*, 107(2): pp. 171-184, 1993.
24. M. Choy and A.K. Singh. Adaptive solutions to the mutual exclusion problem. *Distributed Computing*, 8(1), pp. 1-17, 1994.
25. M. Inoue, S. Umetani, T. Masuzawa and H. Fujiwara. Adaptive long-lived $O(k^2)$ renaming with $O(k^2)$ steps. *Proceedings of the 15th International Conference on Distributed Computing (DISC 2001)*, pages 123-135, 2001.
26. L. Lamport. A fast mutual exclusion algorithm. *ACM Transactions on Computer Systems*, 5(1): 1-11. February 1987.
27. M. Merritt and G. Taubenfeld. Speeding Lamport's fast mutual exclusion algorithm. *Information Processing Letters*, 45: 137-142, 1993.
28. M. Moir and J. H. Anderson. Wait-free algorithms for fast, long-lived renaming. *Sci. Comput. Programming*, 25(1): pp. 1-39, 1995.
29. G.L. Peterson. Time efficient adaptive mutual exclusion algorithms. Unpublished manuscript, 2001.

Randomized Wait-Free Consensus Using an Atomicity Assumption

Ling Cheung*

Department of Computer Science, University of Nijmegen
P.O. Box 9010, 6500 GL Nijmegen, The Netherlands

Abstract. We present a randomized algorithm for asynchronous wait-free consensus using multi-writer multi-reader shared registers. This algorithm is based on earlier work by Chor, Israeli and Li (CIL) and is correct under the assumption that processes can perform a random choice and a write operation in one atomic step. The expected total work for our algorithm is shown to be $O(N \log(\log N))$, compared with $O(N^2)$ for the CIL algorithm, and $O(N \log N)$ for the best known weak adversary algorithm. We also model check instances of our algorithm using the probabilistic model checking tool PRISM.

Keywords: Asynchronous Consensus, Randomized Algorithms, Wait-Free Termination, Weak Adversary, Probabilistic Model Checking.

1 Introduction

Distributed consensus refers to a class of problems in which a set of parallel processes exchange messages in order to agree on a common preference. Initially, each process is given an input value from a fixed, finite domain and, at the end of the algorithm, each non-faulty process outputs a decision value. Correctness requirements are typically formulated as follows.

- *Validity*: the output of any non-faulty process must have been the input of some process.
- *Agreement*: all non-faulty processes decide on the same value.
- *Termination*: every non-faulty process decides after a finite number of steps.

As shown in [FLP85], there exists no deterministic algorithm that solves distributed consensus in a setting of asynchronous communication with undetected process failure. Nonetheless, many efficient solutions exist under stronger assumptions (e.g. partial synchrony [DLS88] and failure detection [ACT00]) or weaker correctness requirements (e.g. probabilistic termination [CIL87]).

Our algorithm falls into the category of *randomized consensus algorithms*, where processes may use coin tosses to determine their course of actions. In this

* Supported by DFG/NWO bilateral cooperation project Validation of Stochastic Systems (VOSS2).

J.H. Anderson, G. Prencipe, and R. Wattenhofer (Eds.): OPODIS 2005, LNCS 3974, pp. 47–60, 2006.

setting, termination is weakened to a probabilistic statement: the set of all non-terminating executions has probability 0. We refer to [Asp03] for a comprehensive overview on randomized consensus.

The first randomized consensus algorithm was proposed by Chor, Israeli and Li [CIL87, CIL94]. It satisfies the following termination condition.

– *Probabilistic wait-free termination*: with probability 1, each non-faulty process decides after a finite number of steps.

We adopt the same requirement. In fact, the logical structure of our algorithm closely resemble that in [CIL94], while we borrow ideas from [Cha96] to reduce the amount of shared and local data. We shall refer to [CIL94] as the original CIL algorithm and our own as the modified CIL algorithm.

Adversary Models and Work Bounds. To prove probabilistic termination, we must reason about probability distributions on the set of executions. These distributions are induced by the so-called *adversaries*, which are functions from finite histories to available next steps.

The strength of an adversary varies according to the amount of information it can extract from a finite history. The *strong* adversaries have access to complete history of all processes and shared registers. Some weaker forms, such as *write-oblivious* and *value-oblivious*, delay the adversary's knowledge of outcomes of internal coin tosses. Clearly, a stronger adversary model permits more possibilities and therefore renders consensus more difficult. Consensus against strong adversaries is shown to be $\Omega(N^2/\log^2 N)$ in expected total work, where N is the number of processes participating in the algorithm [Asp98]. The best known algorithms achieve expected $O(N^2 \log N)$ total work [BR91] and $O(N \log^2 N)$ per process [AW96]. Against write-oblivious adversaries, one can achieve expected $O(\log N)$ per process work and $O(N \log N)$ total work [Aum97]. Against value-oblivious adversaries, the fastest algorithm is $O(N \log N\, e^{\sqrt{\log N}})$ in a single-writer single-reader (SWSR) setting [AKL99][1].

Our adversary model takes the form of an atomicity assumption: processes can perform a random choice and a write operation in one atomic step. In particular, the process increments its round number if and only if the coin lands heads; then immediately it writes 1 to the memory location $\mathsf{mem}(r, v)$, where r is the round number *after* the coin toss and v is the current preference. This amounts to saying that the adversary cannot distinguish between the two locations $\mathsf{mem}(r, v)$ and $\mathsf{mem}(r + 1, v)$. The original CIL algorithm relies on a similar atomicity assumption[2] and achieves expected $O(N^2)$ total work [CIL94]. In the present paper, we replace the single-writer multiple-reader (SWMR) registers of [CIL94] with multi-writer multi-reader (MWMR) registers, thereby reducing the expected total work to $O(N \log(\log N))$.

---

[1] This is faster than other value-oblivious algorithms because SWSR is a weak primitive. More discussion can be found in Section 7.

[2] The assumption in [CIL94] says that the adversary cannot distinguish between the values r and $r + 1$ as they are written to the same memory location.

Since our adversaries are value-sensitive, every non-faulty process must perform at least one *read* operation, otherwise we can easily construct an execution that violates the agreement property. Therefore, expected total work in this model is $\Omega(N)$, which is almost matched by our upper bound of $O(N \log(\log N))$.

We have adopted the worst case expected total work as our complexity measure, mainly because it is more natural to reason about the collective effect of all processes on the shared memory. In fact, per process work in our case is comparable to total work: if all but one process suffer crash failures, the lone survivor carries the total work burden and performs expected $\Omega(N)$ tosses in order to pull far enough ahead for termination. In this sense, our algorithm is less efficient than [Cha96, Aum97], where polylogarithmic upper bounds are given for per process work.

Probabilistic Model Checking. We model check instances of our algorithm using PRISM, which can check PCTL (*Probabilistic Computation Tree Logic*) formulas against an MDP (*Markov Decision Process*) [PRI, BK98]. This tool has been applied to many randomized algorithms, including the consensus algorithm of Aspnes and Herlihy [AH90, KNS01] and Byzantine agreement [KN02].

Consensus algorithms are often hard to model check, because the state space grows exponentially with the number of participating processes. In [KNS01], PRISM is applied only to a shared-coin subroutine, while full correctness relies on verification using Cadence SMV, as well as higher level manual proofs. Unfortunately, the structure of our algorithm does not provide such convenient isolation of probabilistic reasoning. Nevertheless, we are able to build models of binary consensus with up to 4 processes and verify relevant properties. In Section 6, we briefly describe these models and give a summary of PRISM results. In Section 7, we discuss some prospects in improving feasibility of model checking.

Overview. Section 2 describes in greater detail our computational setting and assumptions. Section 3 presents the algorithm and Sections 4 and 5 outline correctness proofs. Detailed proofs are carried out in [Che05b]. Section 6 is devoted to model checking and Section 7 contains closing discussions.

2   System Model

We consider a system of N processes interacting asynchronously via shared memory objects. Each process P_i is given as input an initial preference p_i^0, which belongs to a fixed, finite domain. Without loss of generality, this preference domain is assumed to be $\mathbb{Z}_K$ for some natural number constant $K \geq 2$. As a convention, we write $\mathbb{Z}_K$ for $\{0, \ldots, K-1\}$ and $\mathbb{Z}_K^+$ for $\{1, \ldots, K-1\}$.

We take a state-based view of our system. The *local state* of a process is determined by a valuation of all of its local variables, plus a program counter indicating the next line of code to be executed. The *global state* is then de-termined by local states of all N processes, together with contents of shared MWMR atomic registers.

A process executes a possibly infinite sequence of discrete steps, each consist-ing of a change in local state and/or a memory operation. It may also exhibit a limited form of non-deterministic behavior: crashing at any point of its execution. A crashed process may never recover and re-enter the algorithm.

An execution of the entire system is obtained by interleaving executions of individual processes, where scheduling among processes is determined by an adversary that satisfies the atomicity assumption stated in Section 1. That is, if a process is scheduled to toss a coin, it must be allowed to write to the memory before another process is given a turn. The worst-case complexity is measured in terms of the expected number of *read* and *write* operations taken by all processes, quantifying over all admissible adversaries.

3   Modified CIL Algorithm

As in many other consensus algorithms (e.g. [BO83, CIL94, AH90, Cha96]), we make use of a *round* structure. During each round, a process goes through a possibly infinite sequence of *phases*, each of which is a complete pass through the main **while**-loop.

In original CIL, the shared memory is configured into an array of N many SWMR registers, one for every process. Each register$_i$ contains two pieces of information: round number r_i and preference value p_i. At the beginning of each phase, process P_i copies the contents of all register$_j$ $(i \neq j)$ and stores them locally. These entries are then examined to decide the next action of P_i: output a decision value and terminate, toss a coin to advance to the next round, or jump to a higher round.

The initial copying of each phase is the main source of inefficiency in original CIL: copied data contain more information than necessary for decision making. For example, P_i need not know exactly which P_j is in a higher round, as long as it knows *some* P_j is. This observation is precisely the motivation of our move from SWMR memory to MWMR memory. Thus, instead of a *race among processes*, we envision a *race among preference values*. In this way, processes participate anonymously and the number of *read* operations in the main loop is reduced from $O(N)$ to $O(1)$. Moreover, consensus is achieved with high probability using only $O(\log N)$ registers containing one bit each.

Following [Cha96], our MWMR shared memory is configured into K arrays of bits, each of length $R + 2$, where $R := 2\lceil \log N \rceil$. In other words, we have mem $: \mathbb{Z}_{R+2} \times \mathbb{Z}_K \to \{0, 1\}$. (Recall that K is the size of the preference domain and is a constant, while N is the number of participating processes.) These bits can be interpreted as follows.

- For all $r \in \mathbb{Z}_{R+1}^+$ and $v \in \mathbb{Z}_K$, mem$(r, v) = 1$ if and only if value v has reached round r (i.e., some process holds/held preference v while in round r). These entries are initialized to 0.

- We assume every value v participates in the race from round 0, therefore $\mathsf{mem}(0, v)$ is initialized to 1. This prevents a process from deciding (erroneously) in round 1 before all processes "wake up" and join the protocol[3].
- Round-$(R + 1)$ entries are initialized to 0 and are used for marking decision values. That is, if a process decides on value v, it writes 1 to $\mathsf{mem}(R + 1, v)$.

Each process P_i maintains a current preference p_i and a round number r_i. Intuitively, P_i "believes" that p_i is a leading value and r_i is the highest round reached by p_i. If P_i detects any value v in a round higher than r_i, it updates its "belief" by running a subroutine Jump. In this way, lagging values are quickly abandoned by active processes and are eventually *eliminated* from the race. (This notion is made precise in Definition 1 in Section 4.) Therefore the number of contending preference values never increases and the algorithm terminates when that number decreases to 1. If P_i sees p_i at least two rounds ahead in the race, the algorithm guarantees that every other contending value has been eliminated, therefore P_i can safely terminate with p_i.

Notice, biased coin tosses are used to break ties in the lead pack, so that with probability 1 the number of contending preferences eventually reaches 1. This technique is used in [CIL94] and is quite different from the more common approach of shared coin subroutines, in which processes cast randomly generated votes to obtain a weak shared-coin (e.g. [AH90, BR91]).

Although every non-faulty process is guaranteed (with probability 1) to terminate after a finite number of steps, the round in which it terminates can become arbitrarily high. This requires an unbounded number of registers and is infeasible. Therefore we stop our algorithm when it reaches a certain round without successful termination, in which case we switch to a slower algorithm that requires bounded memory. We call this the *exit* algorithm. For convenience, the original CIL algorithm is chosen for this purpose[4]. We will show that any exit algorithm is invoked with probability at most $\frac{1}{N}$, therefore the higher cost of original CIL does not affect overall expected complexity.

Figure 1(a) contains the pseudocode for process P_i. The numbered lines can be described informally as follows.

(1) Check if some process has decided.
(2) If so, decide for the same value.
(3) Check if a value other than p_i has reached round $r_i - 1$.
(4) If not, write 1 to $\mathsf{mem}(R + 1, p_i)$ and terminate with output p_i.
(5) Otherwise, if round R is reached, run the original CIL algorithm.
(6) Otherwise, check if some value has reached round $r_i + 1$.
(7) If not, advance p_i to the next round with probability $\frac{1}{2N}$.
(8) Otherwise, run subroutine Jump to find a leading value.

---

[3] As noted in [CH05], original CIL contains this initialization error.
[4] Technically, original CIL requires registers with unbounded size. However, according to [CIL94], the probability of non-termination is already extremely small (2^{-56}) when each register is 128 bits.

ModifiedCIL(i, p_i^0)
local variables
  // round number
  $r_i \in \mathbb{Z}_{R+2}$,
  // preference
  $p_i \in \mathbb{Z}_K$,
  // decision value
  $d_i \in \mathbb{Z}_{K+1}$,
  // values read from memory
  $ahead_i, behind_i \in \mathbb{Z}_{K+1}$
begin
  $p_i := p_i^0; \quad r_i := 0;$
  while $r_i \leq R$ **do**
(1) $d_i := \mathsf{ReadMem}(R+1, K);$
(2)   **if** $d_i \neq K$ **then return** $d_i;$
    if $r_i > 0$ **then** {
(3) $behind_i := \mathsf{ReadMem}(r_i - 1, p_i);$
(4)   **if** $behind_i = K$ **then** {
        $mem(R+1, p_i) := 1;$
        return p_i
      }
(5)   **elseif** $r_i = R$ **then return**
        OriginalCIL(i, p_i)
    }
(6) $ahead_i := \mathsf{ReadMem}(r_i + 1, K);$
    if $ahead_i = K$ **then** {
(7)   **with probability** $\frac{1}{2N}$ **do**
        $r_i := r_i + 1;$
        $mem(r_i, p_i) := 1$
      }
(8)   **else** $\langle r_i, p_i \rangle := \mathsf{Jump}(r_i + 1, ahead_i)$
  od
end

(a) Main Algorithm.

ReadMem(r, p)
local variables
  // counter
  $k \in \mathbb{Z}_K$,
  // preference value found
  $v \in \mathbb{Z}_{K+1}$,
begin
  $k := 0; \quad v := K;$
  while $k < K$ **and** $v = K$ **do**
    if $mem(r, k) = 1$ **and** $k \neq p$ **then**
      $v := k;$
    $k := k + 1$
  od
  return v
end

(b) Subroutine ReadMem.

Jump(r, p)
local variables
  // confirmed round and preference
  $r' \in \mathbb{Z}_{R+1}, \; p' \in \mathbb{Z}_K$,
  // current round and preference
  $l \in \mathbb{Z}_{R+1}^+, u \in \mathbb{Z}_{K+1}$,
  // counter
  $c \in \mathbb{Z}_{R+1}$,
begin
  if $r \geq R$ **then return** $\langle r, p \rangle;$
  $r' := r; \quad p' := p; \quad c := \lceil \log(R - r) \rceil;$
  while $c > 0$ **do**
    $l := r' + 2^{c-1};$
    if $l \leq R$ **then** {
      $u := \mathsf{ReadMem}(l, K);$
      if $u \neq K$ **then** {
        $r' := l; \quad p' := u$
      }
    }
    $c := c - 1$
  od
  return $\langle r', p' \rangle$
end

(c) Subroutine Jump.

Fig. 1. Modified CIL Algorithm

Notice that the atomicity assumption discussed in Section 1 applies at Line (7). This prevents the adversary from selectively delaying *write* operations of processes who are ready to advance its preference to the next round.

Figures 1(b) and 1(c) contain the subroutines ReadMem and Jump, respectively. The former is used to read from the shared memory, while the later is used to find a faster value. When called with parameters r and p, ReadMem scans one-by-one the r-th entry of every bit vector, except for the p-th. In other words, we would like to know if any process has reached round r with preference other than p. It returns the first k such that both $k \neq p$ and, at the time of *read* access, $\text{mem}(r, k) = 1$. If no such k is encountered, ReadMem returns K.

In every pass through the **while**-loop of Figure 1(a), ReadMem is called with at most three round numbers: $R + 1$, $r_i - 1$, and $r_i + 1$. This does not reveal the highest round ever reached by any value. Therefore, a separate subroutine Jump is run when the process sees itself behind. This is a key difference between our algorithm and original CIL: in exchange for fewer *read* operations in the main loop, more work is needed for slower processes to catch up.

The subroutine Jump can be implemented in various ways. The version presented here is essentially a binary search on mem. This involves $O(\log(\log N))$ operations per invocation of Jump, but a process can correctly locate a fastest value in one complete phase (provided no further progress is made in the mean time).

4   Validity and Agreement

In this section, we treat all coin tosses as non-deterministic choices. Let s_0 denote the initial state of our system, where all N processes as well as the shared memory have been properly initialized. A *path* of the system is a finite sequence of states $s_0 s_1 \dots s_m$ where, for all $j \in \mathbb{Z}_m$, s_{j+1} can be obtained from s_j by allowing exactly one non-faulty process to execute its next instruction. A state s is *reachable* if there is a path ending in s. Finally, a value $k \in \mathbb{Z}_K$ is said to be *valid* if there is $i \in \mathbb{Z}_N$ such that k equals the input p_i^0 to process P_i.

We use record notation to indicate valuation of variables. For example, $s.r_i$ denotes the round number of P_i in state s. If P_i is running a subroutine (e.g. ReadMem), we add subscript i to variables of that subroutine (e.g. $s.k_i$ and $s.v_i$).

First we state some properties about mem and subroutines ReadMem and Jump. Lemma 1 says that an entry in mem never changes from 1 to 0. Lemma 2 says that the return value of ReadMem is correct (although it may be out-of-date). Similarly, Lemma 3 states the correctness of Jump.

Lemma 1. *Let $r \in \mathbb{Z}_{R+2}$, $v \in \mathbb{Z}_K$ and a path $s_0 \dots s_m$ be given. Suppose there is $j \in \mathbb{Z}_{m+1}$ with $s_j.\text{mem}(r, v) = 1$. Then $s_{j'}.\text{mem}(r, v) = 1$ for all $j \leq j' \leq m$.*

Lemma 2. *Let $r \in \mathbb{Z}_{R+2}$, $p, v \in \mathbb{Z}_{K+1}$ and a path $s_0 \dots s_m$ be given. If the last step is $\text{ReadMem}(r, p)$ returning $v \neq K$, then $s_m.\text{mem}(r, v) = 1$.*

Lemma 3. *Let $r, r'' \in \mathbb{Z}_{R+1}$, $p, p'' \in \mathbb{Z}_K$ and a path $s_0 \dots s_m$ be given. Suppose the last step is $\text{Jump}(r, p)$ returning $\langle r'', p'' \rangle$. If $\text{mem}(r, p) = 1$ when $\text{Jump}(r, p)$ is called, then $s_m.\text{mem}(r'', p'') = 1$.*

Proof (Sketch). This follows from the fact that $\text{mem}(r', p') = 1$ is an invariant of the **while**-loop in Jump.   □

Lemma 4 below states that mem correctly reflects the preference history of participating processes. Validity is then proven to be an invariant (Theorem 1).

Lemma 4. *Let a path $s_0 \ldots s_m$ be given.*

(i) *For all $i \in \mathbb{Z}_N$, $s_m.r_i \leq R$ implies $s_m.\text{mem}(s_m.r_i, s_m.p_i) = 1$.*

(ii) *For all $r \in \mathbb{Z}_{R+2}^+$ and $v \in \mathbb{Z}_K$, $s_m.\text{mem}(r, v) = 1$ implies there exist $i \in \mathbb{Z}_N$ and $j \in \mathbb{Z}_{m+1}$ such that $s_j.p_i = v$.*

Theorem 1. *The following claims hold in every reachable state s.*

(i) *For every $i \in \mathbb{Z}_N$, $s.p_i$ is valid.*

(ii) *For every $r \in \mathbb{Z}_{R+2}^+$ and $v \in \mathbb{Z}_K$, $s.\text{mem}(r, v) = 1$ implies v is valid.*

(iii) *For every $i \in \mathbb{Z}_N$, if $s.d_i \neq K$ then $s.d_i$ is valid. Similarly for $s.\text{ahead}_i$ and $s.\text{behind}_i$.*

Corollary 1. *The modified CIL algorithm in Figure 1 is valid, assuming the exit algorithm (in this case, the original CIL algorithm) is valid.*

Next we prove agreement. A key ingredient is a predicate Φ on global states.

Definition 1. *Let $v, v' \in \mathbb{Z}_K$ and $r \in \mathbb{Z}_{R+1}^+$ be given. We say that v eliminates v' in round r in global state s (denoted $s \models \Phi(v, v', r)$) just in case $s.\text{mem}(r, v) = 1$ and $s.\text{mem}(r - 1, v') = 0$.*

We state a string of lemmas leading to the claim that no two processes terminating by Line (4) do so with conflicting decision values (Lemma 8). First, if an entry $\text{mem}(r, v)$ is marked 1, then every entry $\text{mem}(r', v)$ with $r' \leq r$ is also marked 1 (Lemma 5). Second, if v' is eliminated by v in round r, then no process subsequently reaches round r with preference v' (Lemma 6). Finally, if a process P_i terminates by Line (4) with value v in round r, then every other v' must have been eliminated by v in round r at some earlier state (Lemma 7).

Lemma 5. *Let s be a reachable state. For all $r \in \mathbb{Z}_{R+1}$ and $v \in \mathbb{Z}_K$, if $s.\text{mem}(r, v) = 1$ then $s.\text{mem}(r', v) = 1$ for all $r' \leq r$.*

Lemma 6. *Let $v, v' \in \mathbb{Z}_K$ and $r \in \mathbb{Z}_{R+1}^+$ be given. Consider a path $s_0 \ldots s_m$ such that $s_j \models \Phi(v, v', r)$ for some $j \in \mathbb{Z}_{m+1}$. Then, for all $j' \in \{j, \ldots, m\}$, $s_{j'}.\text{mem}(r, v') = 0$.*

Proof (Sketch). If the claim doesn't hold, then some process P_i must have written 1 to $\text{mem}(r, v')$ by executing Line (7) between s_j and s_m. This leads to a contradiction because the definition of Φ implies that P_i does not reach Line (7).

Lemma 7. *Consider a path $s_0 \ldots s_{m+1}$. Suppose that in the last step some process P_i terminates by executing Line (4). Let r denote $s_m.r_i$ and v denote $s_m.p_i$. For every $v' \neq v$, there is $j' \in \mathbb{Z}_{m+1}$ such that $s_{j'} \models \Phi(v, v', r)$.*

Proof (Sketch). Set $s_{j'}$ to be the state from which the last invocation of ReadMem in Line (3) reads from $\text{mem}(r - 1, v')$. □

Lemma 8. *Let a path $s_0 \ldots s_m$ and $j, j' \in \mathbb{Z}_{m+1}$ be given. Assume that process P_i terminates by Line (4) with output v from state s_j and some other process $P_{i'}$ does the same with output v' from state $s_{j'}$. Then $v = v'$.*

Proof (Sketch). From the assumptions we prove that v and v' have eliminated each other, which by Lemma 6 is a contradiction.   □

It remains to consider termination by Line (2). Lemma 9 below implies that every process terminating by Line (2) must be preceded by a process terminating by Line (4) with the same decision.

Lemma 9. *Let $v \in \mathbb{Z}_K$ and a path $s_0 \ldots s_m$ be given. Assume that $s_m.\text{mem}(R + 1, v) = 1$. There is $j \in \mathbb{Z}_{m+1}$ such that some process P_i terminates with decision value v by executing Line (4) from s_j.*

Theorem 2. *Let a path $s_0 \ldots s_m$ be given. Assume that process P_i terminates by executing either Line (2) or Line (4) from state s_j ($j \in \mathbb{Z}_{m+1}$) and its decision value is v. Similarly for $P_{i'}$, $s_{j'}$ and v'. Then $v = v'$.*

Proof (Sketch). Applying Lemma 9, we find a process that has terminated by Line (4) with v. Similarly for v'. The claim is then reduced to Lemma 8.   □

5   Probabilistic Termination and Expected Complexity

Let us first consider the amount of work required during each phase of the algorithm. (Recall that a phase is an entire pass through the **while**-loop in Figure 1(a)). Notice each phase involves at most (i) three calls to ReadMem, (ii) one *write* operation and (iii) one call to Jump. Each call to ReadMem requires $O(1)$ *read* operations, because the size K of the preference domain is a constant in our analysis. Therefore, aside from Jump, each phase involves constant work.

Consider the **while**-loop in Jump. Each pass through this loop involves at most one call to ReadMem. Furthermore, this loop is executed at most $\log R + 1$ times. Since $R = 2\lceil \log N \rceil$ by definition, each call to Jump requires $O(\log(\log N))$ *read* operations. This is then also the cost of a complete phase. Later on, we will prove that the expected number of complete phases until at least one process terminates successfully is $O(N)$ and hence the expected number of *read/write* operations is $O(N \log(\log N))$ (Lemma 13).

For any state s, let $s.r_{\max}$ denote the highest round reached by any process in state s. In other words, $s.r_{\max} := \max_{i \in \mathbb{Z}_N} s.r_i$. Since the two updates in Line (7) of Figure 1(a) are performed in a single step, $s.r_{\max}$ is also the largest r such that $s.\text{mem}(r, v) = 1$ for some value $v \in \{0, \ldots, K - 1\}$. Lemma 10 below says, if no value advances to round $r_{\max} + 1$, a lagging process can catch up to round $r_{\max}$ in one complete phase. Lemma 11 then shows, whenever $r_{\max}$ is at most $R - 2$, the probability of at least one process terminating successfully within the next two rounds is bounded below by a constant. Moreover, this termination takes place before $15N$ complete phases are executed.

Lemma 10. *Let $s_0 \ldots s_m \ldots s_{m'}$ be a path with $m < m'$. Assume that $s_j.r_{\max} = s_m.r_{\max}$ for every $j \in \{m, \ldots, m'\}$. Moreover, assume that P_i completes a phase between s_m and $s_{m'}$ without crashing, successfully terminating or switching to the exit algorithm. Then $s_{m'}.r_i = s_m.r_{\max}$.*

Proof (Sketch). First we argue that P_i reaches Line (8) in its first complete phase after s_m. Then, based on the **while**-loop in Jump, we construct a nested sequence of intervals shrinking to the singleton $\{s_m.r_{\max}\}$. Therefore $s_m.r_{\max}$ is the round number returned by Jump.   □

Lemma 11. *Suppose* ModifiedCIL *starts from a reachable state* s*. Let* r *denote* $s.r_{\max}$ *and suppose* $r \leq R - 2$*. Then, with probability greater than* 0.511*, at least one process terminates successfully in a round no higher than* $r + 2$*. Moreover, at most* $15N$ *complete phases are executed between* s *and the successful termination.*

Proof (Sketch). Consider two events: E_1 is "a success occurs before $5N$ attempts to move from r to $r + 1$ are made and all subsequent such attempts fail" and E_2 is "a success occurs before $5N$ attempts to move from $r + 1$ to $r + 2$ are made." We argue that the conjunction of E_1 and E_2 implies at least one process terminates successfully in round $r + 2$ before $15N$ complete phases are executed. Moreover, the probability of both E_1 and E_2 occurring is at least 0.511, using the fact that $\{(1 - \frac{1}{n})^n\}_{n=2}^{\infty}$ increases to the limit $\frac{1}{e}$.   □

Notice Lemma 11 applies only to executions starting in round $R - 2$ or lower. The next lemma covers rounds $R - 1$ and R, assuming a decision is reached without switching to the exit algorithm.

Lemma 12. *Suppose* ModifiedCIL *starts from a reachable state* s*. Let* r *denote* $s.r_{\max}$ *and suppose* $R - 2 < r \leq R$*. Assuming the exit algorithm is not invoked, the (conditional) probability that at least one process terminates successfully before* $15N$ *complete phases are executed after* s *is greater than* 0.511*.*

Theorem 3. *If the exit algorithm is wait-free and satisfies probabilistic termination, the same holds for* ModifiedCIL*.*

Proof. By correctness of the exit algorithm, we may focus on the case in which the exit algorithm is not invoked. Consider execution blocks of $15N$ complete phases each. By Lemma 11 and Lemma 12, the probability of successful termination within each block is at least 0.511. Thus, with probability 1, the algorithm terminates successfully after a finite number of blocks. Since we have made no assumption on the number of surviving processes, the algorithm is wait-free.   □

We now turn to complexity considerations. Again, we make a case distinction based on whether the exit algorithm is invoked.

Lemma 13. *Assume that the exit algorithm is not invoked. The expected number of elementary read/write operations until at least one process terminates successfully is* $O(N \log(\log N))$*.*

Proof (Sketch). Again we consider blocks of $15N$ complete phases and argue that the expected number of blocks is at most 2. Hence the expected number of complete phases is $O(N)$. Since each phase involves $O(\log(\log N))$ elementary operations, the expected number of elementary operations $O(N \log(\log N))$.   □

Lemma 14. *Suppose the exit algorithm is the original CIL algorithm and is invoked. The expected number of elementary read/write operations until at least one process terminates successfully is $O(N^2 \log(\log N))$.*

Proof (Sketch). The expected number of elementary operations before switching is shown to be $O(N(\log N)(\log(\log N)))$. Using results of [CIL94], the expected complexity after switching is $O(N^2)$. Therefore, the overall expected complexity is $O(N^2 \log(\log N))$. □

Lemma 15. *Suppose the ModifiedCIL starts from the initial state s_0. The probability of failing to reach a decision in or before round R is at most $1/N$.*

Proof (Sketch). By Lemma 11, this probability is at most $(1 - 0.511)^{\frac{R}{2}} \leq \frac{1}{N}$. □

Putting together Lemmas 13, 14, and 15, we conclude that the expected complexity of ModifiedCIL is $O(N \log(\log N))$.

Theorem 4. *Suppose ModifiedCIL starts from the initial state s_0 and the exit algorithm is original CIL. The expected number of elementary read/write operations until at least one process terminates successfully is $O(N \log(\log N))$.*

6   Model Checking

It is quite straightforward to specify our algorithm in PRISM's state-based input language. Each process is modeled as a *module* and the shared memory is modeled using global variables. Two more global variables are used to keep track of process failures and the number of completed phases.

We consider binary consensus (i.e., $K = 2$) with $N = 2, 3, 4$ processes. Processes are assumed to disagree initially, therefore validity is trivial. Agreement is satisfied in all models constructed. For probabilistic termination, we ask PRISM to compute the (exact) minimum probability of at least one process terminating successfully, given an allowance of $R = 2\lceil \log N \rceil$ rounds and $15N \cdot \frac{R}{2} = 15N\lceil \log N \rceil$ complete phases. This result is compared against our analytic lower bound of $1 - \frac{1}{N}$.

In the case of $N = 4$, the model becomes too complex (with $2\lceil \log N \rceil = 4$ rounds and $15N\lceil \log N \rceil = 120$ complete phases). However, we discover that the analytic bound of $1 - \frac{1}{N} = 0.750$ is already met when we restrict to 40 complete phases. This suggests that we have made some overly conservative estimates while deriving the analytic bound.

The table below summarizes our results. We use PRISM version 2.1, running on a 1.4 GHz Pentium M machine with 500 Mb memory under Linux 2.6. The MTBDD engine is used with a CUDD memory limit of 400 Mb. Other parameters remain at default settings. All relevant files, including model checking logs, can be found in [Che05a].

N	R	#Phases	Model		Agreement	Termination		
			#States	Time(s)	Time(s)	Time(s)	MinProb	AnalyticBd
2	2	30	42,320	4	0.025	6	0.745	0.511
3	4	90	12,280,910	213	0.094	2,662	0.971	0.667
4	2	60	45,321,126	429	0.078	602	0.755	0.511
4	4	40	377,616,715	5224	3.926	55,795	0.765	0.750

7   Conclusions

We have given a simple algorithm that solves asynchronous wait-free consensus in expected $O(N \log(\log N))$ total work. We follow a value-based (as opposed to process-based) approach and make use of MWMR atomic registers. This strategy, also adopted in [Cha96, Aum97], leads to a significant reduction in data handling and hence more efficient consensus algorithms. As a pleasant side-effect, the reduction in both global and local data makes model checking significantly more feasible, for it helps to avoid the typical state explosion problem.

MWMR memory is often regarded as a stronger primitive than SWMR memory. Indeed, there are optimal implementations of MWMR from physical SWMR registers using linear time and logarithmic space [IS92]. However, if one makes comparisons from the basis of SWSR, then MWMR and SWMR become roughly the same: when implemented from SWSR, both require linear time and logarithmic space. Moreover, it is argued in [BPSV00] that SWMR memory requires the hidden assumption of *naming*: existence of distinct identifiers known to all. In that sense, MWMR is a weaker primitive compared to SWMR. This idea is echoed by the fact that, unlike the original CIL algorithm, our version allows processes to participate anonymously.

The MWMR strategy has another advantage, namely, flexibility in memory usage. We have shown that, with high probability, consensus can be reached using $O(\log N)$ many single-bit MWMR registers. (That is, the main algorithm succeeds and thus the exit algorithm is not invoked.) This can be seen as a temporary reprieve from the lower bound of $\Omega(\sqrt{N})$ for the space requirement of randomized consensus [FHS98]. In practice, one may be willing to accept a small probability of failing to reach consensus, in which case we can remove the exit algorithm altogether. The main algorithm can be repeated to increase the success probability, and memory is allocated only as needed.

For future work, we want to improve the per process work bound of our algorithm. In [AW96], a similar improvement is achieved by allowing fast processes to cast votes of increasing weights. However, their proofs rely on properties of Martingale processes and cannot be adapted immediately to our setting. At this time, we do not know if per process work is inherently high in our setting (e.g. $\Omega(\frac{N}{f(N)})$, where f is a polylogarithmic function).

Finally, we comment on model checking using PRISM. Although the current limit seems to be 4 processes, we conjecture a vast improvement using a symmetry reduction option, which is under development by the PRISM team. Before symmetry reduction is available, manual abstraction can be used to increase feasibility. That is, we manually construct an abstraction that captures core ideas of an algorithm, while significantly decreasing the model size. We experimented with such an abstraction of original CIL, by focusing on the shared memory and filtering out local states of processes. Having done so, we were in fact able to handle up to 10 processes. However, it is non-trivial to prove soundness of the abstraction. Standard techniques such as probabilistic simulation are available for this purpose, but substantial investment of time is required.

Overall, PRISM allows us to conduct experiments during the development stage of an algorithm, with minimal learning effort. Although in most cases it still cannot handle large instances of a full algorithm, it is perfectly feasible to model check a subroutine or an abstract version. This already provides valuable information, especially to those who simply wish to gain more insight into an algorithm.

Acknowledgment. We thank James Aspnes for his inspiring article [Asp03] and many helpful comments, as well as David Parker for support in using PRISM. Also we thank Jaap-Henk Hoepman and the anonymous referees at OPODIS'05 for their useful suggestions.

References

[ACT00]   M.K. Aguilera, W. Chen, and S. Toueg. Failure detection and consensus in the crach recovery model. *Distributed Computing*, 13(2):99–125, 2000.

[AH90]   J. Aspnes and M. Herlihy. Fast randomized consensus using shared memory. *Journal of Algorithms*, 11(3):441–461, 1990.

[AKL99]   Y. Aumann and A. Kapah-Levy. Cooperative sharing and asynchronous consensus using single-read single-writer registers. In *Proceedings of the 10th ACM-SIAM Anuual Symposium on Discrete Algorithms (SODA)*, pages 61–70, 1999.

[Asp98]   J. Aspnes. Lower bounds for distributed coin-flipping and randomized consensus. *Journal of the ACM*, 45(3):415–450, 1998.

[Asp03]   J. Aspnes. Randomized protocols for asynchronous consensus. *Distributed Computing*, 16(2-3):165–175, 2003.

[Aum97]   Y. Aumann. Efficient asynchronous consensus with the weak adversary scheduler. In *Proceedings of the Sixteenth Annual ACM Symposium on Principles of Distributed Computing*, pages 209–218, 1997.

[AW96]   J. Aspnes and O. Waarts. Randomized consensus in expected $O(n \log^2 n)$ operations per process. *SIAM Journal on Computing*, 25(5):1024–1044, 1996.

[BK98]   C. Baier and M. Kwiatkowska. Model checking for a probabilistic branching time logic with fairness. *Distributed Computing*, 11(3):125–155, 1998.

[BO83]   M. Ben-Or. Another advantage of free choice: completely asynchronous agreement protocols. In *Proceedings of the Second Annual ACM Symposium on Principles of Distributed Computing*, pages 27–30, 1983.

[BPSV00] H. Buhrman, A. Panconesi, R. Silvestri, and P.M.B. Vitányi. On the importance of having an identity or is consensus really universal? In *Proceedings of the 14th International Conference on Distributed Computing*, volume 1914 of *LNCS*, pages 134–148. Springer-Verlag, 2000.

[BR91]   G. Bracha and O. Rachman. Randomized consensus in expected $O(n^2 \log n)$ operations. In *Proceedings of the 5th International Workshop on Distributed Algorithms*, volume 579 of *LNCS*, pages 143–150, 1991.

[CH05]   L. Cheung and M. Hendriks. Causal dependencies in parallel composition of stochastic processes. Technical Report ICIS-R05020, Institute for Computing and Information Sciences, University of Nijmegen, 2005.

[Cha96]   T.D. Chandra. Polylog randomized wait-free consensus. In *Proceedings of the 15th Annual ACM Symposium on Principles of Distributed Computing*, pages 166–175, 1996.

[Che05a] L. Cheung. Collection of PRISM models of the modified CIL algorithm, 2005. Available at `http://www.niii.ru.nl/~lcheung/mcil/`.

[Che05b] L. Cheung. Randomized wait-free consensus using an atomicity assumption. Technical Report ICIS-R05035, Institute for Computing and Information Sciences, University of Nijmegen, 2005. Available at `http://www.niii.ru.nl/~lcheung/cilTR.pdf`.

[CIL87]   B. Chor, A. Israeli, and M. Li. On processor coordination using asynchronous hardware. In *Proceedings PODC'87*, pages 86–97, 1987.

[CIL94]   B. Chor, A. Israeli, and M. Li. Wait-free consensus using asynchronous hardware. *SIAM Journal on Computing*, 23(4):701–712, 1994.

[DLS88]   C. Dwork, N. Lynch, and L. Stockmeyer. Consensus in the presence of partial synchrony. *Journal of the ACM*, 35(2):288–323, 1988.

[FHS98]   F. Fich, M. Herlihy, and N. Shavit. On the space complexity of randomized synchronization. *Journal of the ACM*, 45(5):843–862, September 1998.

[FLP85]   M. Fischer, N.A. Lynch, and M.S. Paterson. Impossibility of distributed consensus with one faulty process. *Journal of the ACM*, 32(2):374–382, 1985.

[IS92]   A. Israeli and A. Shaham. Optimal multi-writer multi-reader atomic register. In *Proceedings of the 11th Annual ACM Symposium on Principles of Distributed Computing*, pages 71–82, 1992.

[KN02]   M. Kwiatkowska and G. Norman. Verifying randomized Byzantine agreement. In *Proc. Formal Techniques for Networked and Distributed Systems (FORTE'02)*, volume 2529 of *LNCS*, pages 194–209, 2002.

[KNS01]   M. Kwiatkowska, G. Norman, and R. Segala. Automated verification of a randomized distributed consensus protocol using Cadence SMV and PRISM. In *Proceedings CAV'01*, volume 2102 of *LNCS*, pages 194–206, 2001.

[PRI]   PRISM web site. `http://www.cs.bham.ac.uk/~dxp/prism`.

Optimal Randomized Fair Exchange
with Secret Shared Coins

Felix Freiling[1], Maurice Herlihy[2,*], and Lucia Draque Penso[3,**]

[1] Computer Science Department, University of Mannheim,
D-68131 Mannheim, Germany
`freiling@informatik.uni-mannheim.de`
[2] Computer Science Department, Box 1910, Brown University,
Providence, RI 02912, USA
`mph@cs.brown.edu`
[3] Computer Science Department, RWTH Aachen University,
D-52056 Aachen, Germany
`lucia@i4.informatik.rwth-aachen.de`

Abstract. In the *fair exchange* problem, mutually untrusting parties must securely exchange digital goods. A fair exchange protocol must ensure that no combination of cheating or failures will result in some goods being delivered but not others, and that all goods will be delivered in the absence of cheating and failures.

This paper proposes two novel randomized protocols for solving fair exchange using simple trusted units. Both protocols have an optimal expected running time, completing in a constant (3) expected number of rounds. They also have optimal resilience. The first one tolerates any number of dishonest parties, as long as one is honest, while the second one, which assumes more agressive cheating and failures assumptions, tolerates up to a minority of dishonest parties.

The key insight is similar to the idea underlying the *code-division multiple access* (CDMA) communication protocol: outwitting an adversary is much easier if participants share a common, secret pseudo-random number generator.

1 Introduction

In the *fair exchange* problem, a set of parties want to trade an item which they have for an item of another party (for a survey of fair exchange see [11]). Fair exchange is a fundamental problem in domains with electronic business transactions since (1) items can be any type of electronic asset (electronic money, documents, music files, etc.) and (2) fairness is especially important in rather

---

* Maurice Herlihy was supported by Deutsche Forschungsgemeinschaft (DFG) when visiting RWTH Aachen University.
** Lucia Draque Penso was supported by Deutsche Forschungsgemeinschaft (DFG) as part of the Graduiertenkolleg "Software for Mobile Communication Systems" at RWTH Aachen University.

J.H. Anderson, G. Prencipe, and R. Wattenhofer (Eds.): OPODIS 2005, LNCS 3974, pp. 61–72, 2006.

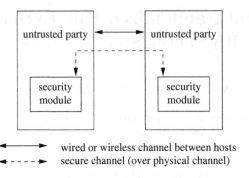

Fig. 1. Untrusted parties and security modules

anonymous environments without means to establish mutual trust relationships. Briefly spoken, fair exchange guarantees that (1) every honest party eventually either delivers its desired item or aborts the exchange, (2) the exchange is successful if no party misbehaves and all items match their descriptions, and (3) the exchange should be fair, i.e., if the desired item of any party does not match its description, then no party can obtain any (useful) information about any other item. Fair exchange algorithms must guarantee these properties even in the presence of arbitrary (malicious) misbehavior of a subset of participants.

Fair exchange, a security problem, can be reduced [2] to a fault-tolerance problem, namely a special form of *uniform consensus*. In the (non-uniform) consensus problem [13], each process in a group starts with a private input value, and after some communication, each non-faulty process is required to decide (termination) on the same private output value (agreement), so that all processes that decide choose some process's private input value (validity). In its uniform version, however, agreement requires all processes that decide (faulty or non-faulty) to decide the same value. Only non-faulty processes are required to terminate.

The reduction from fair exchange to consensus [2] holds in a synchronous model where each participating party is equipped with a trusted unit, that is, a tamper-proof security module like a smart card (see Fig. 1). Security modules have recently been advocated by key players in industry to improve the security of computers in the context of *trusted computing* [15]. Today, products exist which implement such trusted devices (see for example [7]). Roughly speaking, a security module is a certified piece of hardware executing a well-known algorithm. Security modules can establish confidential and authenticated channels between each other. However, since they can only communicate by exchanging messages through their (untrusted) host parties, messages may be intercepted or dropped. Overall, the security modules form a *trusted subsystem* within the overall (untrusted) system. The integrity and confidentiality of the algorithm running in the trusted subsystem is protected by the shield of tamper proof hardware. The integrity and confidentiality of data sent across the network is protected by standard cryptographic protocols. These mechanisms reduce the type and nature of adversarial behavior in the trusted subsystem to message loss and process self-destruction, two standard fault-assumptions known under the names of *omission* and *crash* in the area of fault-tolerance.

This paper proposes two novel randomized protocols for solving uniform consensus with binary inputs (and hence fair exchange) using such trusted units. Our protocols are time optimal, completing in a constant (3) expected number of rounds. They are also optimal in terms of resilience. The key insight is similar to the idea underlying the *code-division multiple access* (CDMA) communication protocol [16]: outwitting an adversary is much easier if participants share a common, secret pseudo-random number generator. In a multi-round protocol, each trusted unit can flip a coin, and take action secure in the knowledge that every other trusted unit has flipped the same value, and is taking a compatible action in that round. Because messages are encrypted, coin flip outcomes can be hidden, so dishonest parties can neither observe past coin flips nor predict future ones. (Of course, the pseudo-random algorithm itself need not be secret as long as the trusted units' common seed is kept secret, just like their common cryptographic key.) We believe that this approach is both efficient and practical.

The presentation is structured as follows. In section 2 we describe the model of computation considered, whereas in section 3 we show how to reduce fair exchange to uniform consensus. Section 4 displays related work. Optimal randomized uniform consensus protocols for binary inputs with a constant (3) expected number of rounds are introduced in sections 5 and 6. Note that both protocols may be generalized to a larger set of k values with an extra factor cost of $\log(k)$. However, we concentrate on the binary case, since we are mainly interested in solving fair exchange efficiently. Finally, we conclude with section 7, where a summary and work future directions are exhibited.

2   Model of Computation

Our model of computation is essentially synchronous: participants exchange messages in synchronous rounds. Of course, real distributed systems are not synchronous in the classical sense, but it is reasonable to assume an upper bound on how long one can expect a non-faulty processor to take before responding to a message. A processor that takes too long to join in a round is assumed to be faulty or malicious.

The system is logically structured into an untrusted system (including the untrusted parties and their communication channels) and the trusted subsystem consisting of the parties' individual trusted units, that is, their tamper-proof security modules (see Fig. 2). The untrusted parties can interact with their trusted units through a well-defined interface, but they cannot in any other form influence the computation within the trusted unit.

As noted, communication among the trusted units is confidential and authenticated, so malicious parties cannot interpret or tamper with these messages. Because each trusted unit sends the same encrypted message to every other trusted unit, we have receiver anonymity and so a cheating party cannot learn who is communicating to who from traffic analysis. An untrusted party can,

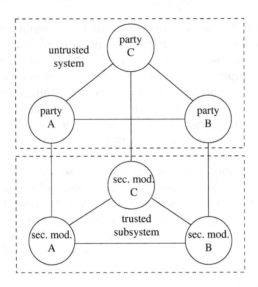

Fig. 2. The untrusted system and the trusted subsystem

however, prevent outgoing messages from being sent (called a *send omission*), or incoming messages from being received (called a *receive omission*) or destroy its trusted unit (called a *crash*). The effects of a crash can be regarded as a permanent send (and receive) omission.

Define a party as *cheating* if it causes send or receive omissions of its trusted unit. A party which does not cheat is *honest*. A fair exchange protocol must ensure that under no circumstances will goods be delivered to a cheating party but not to all honest parties. It is, however, acceptable to deliver the goods to all honest parties, but not to some cheating parties. Cheating may cause the exchange to *fail*, so that no goods are delivered to any party. In the absence of cheating, the exchange should *succeed*, causing goods to be delivered to all participants. For brevity, we refer to processes when we really mean untrusted processes equipped with trusted units. With a *process failure* we mean either a crash, a send message omission or a receive message omission.

3 Fair Exchange as Consensus

The reduction from fair exchange to uniform consensus works as follows. In the first round of the protocol, each party applies its acceptance test to the encrypted digital goods received from the others (in special cases this test can also be performed within the trusted unit). It then informs its trusted unit whether the goods passed the test. The trusted units broadcast this choice (using confidential and authenticated messages) within the trusted subsystem. Each unit that receives unanymous approvals starts the consensus protocol with input 1, and each trusted unit that either observes a disapproval or no message from a trusted unit starts the consensus protocol with input 0. At the end of the protocol, each trusted unit delivers the goods if the outcome of the protocol is 1, and refuses to do so if the outcome is 0.

It is easy to see that in the absence of failures or cheating all goods will be delivered. The uniform consensus protocol ensures that all honest parties agree on whether to deliver the goods, and its uniformity ensures that no trusted unit residing at a cheating party will deliver the goods if any trusted unit at an honest party decides not to. (Recall that it is acceptable if the honest processes deliver the goods after deciding 1, even if a cheating process fails to deliver the goods after deciding 0.)

As noted, the protocols considered in this paper are *randomized*, in the sense that they rely on the assumption that trusted units generate pseudo-random values that cannot be predicted by an adversary. These protocols always produce correct results, but their running time is a random variable, the so-called *Las Vegas* model. (It is straightforward to transform these protocols into *Monte-Carlo* protocols that run for a fixed number of rounds, and produce correct results with very high probability.)

To simplify the presentation, we first present an uniform consensus protocol that works in a failure model that permits send, but not receive omissions. This protocol is slightly simpler and more robust: it tolerates $f < n$ cheating processes, while the full send/receive omissions model protocol tolerates $f < n/2$ failures. Both resilience levels are optimal for their respective models [12]. Presenting the protocol in two stages illustrates how assumptions about the model affect the protocol's complexity and resilience.

4   Related Work

We build on work of Parvédy and Raynal [12]. They derive optimal early stopping deterministic uniform consensus algorithms for synchronous systems with send or send/receive omission failures. However, our algorithms are more efficient in most cases (if the number of failures is not constant) and at least comparable (otherwise).

Feldman and Micali [8] exhibit optimal consensus algorithms for Byzantine agreement, which in principle could also be used in omission failure models. Despite having also an optimal expected running time, our algorithms outperform theirs both on resilience and on the probability of not having termination violated.

Avoine, Gärtner, Guerraoui and Vukolic [2] show how to reduce the fair exchange problem in a system where processes are provided with security modules to the consensus problem in omission failure models. A solution to the fair exchange problem is presented by use of the algorithms of Parvédy and Raynal [12]. In the same context, Delporte, Fauconnier and Freiling [6] investigate solutions to consensus for *asynchronous* systems which are equipped with unreliable failure detectors. They exhibit a weak failure detector in the spirit of previous work by Chandra, Hadzilacos and Toueg [4] that allows to solve asynchronous consensus in omission failure environments.

Aspnes [1] presents a survey of randomized consensus algorithms for the shared memory model where processes are prone to crashes. These results are particularly interesting, since consensus cannot be solved deterministically in a pure asynchronous distributed system, as proved in [9] by Fischer, Lynch and Paterson.

Finally, Chaudhuri [5] introduces the k-set agreement problem, a generalization of the consensus problem, and proves it to be harder. Later, Borowsky and Gafni [3], Herlihy and Shavit [10], and Saks and Zaharoglou [14] would demonstrate that there is no wait-free protocol for k-set agreement (or consensus) in asynchronous message-passing or read/write memory models.

5   Optimal Protocol for Send Omissions

The *ConsensusS* algorithm in Figure 3 solves uniform consensus with binary inputs in optimal 3 expected synchronous rounds tolerating an optimal number of up to $f < n$ failures - send message omissions as well as process crashes.

As noted, all processes share a common secret seed and pseudo-random number generator. We denote the r-th such pseudo-random binary number by $flip(r)$. For each r, every process computes the same value for $flip(r)$.

In ConsensusS, each process broadcasts its binary input (line 1). In each subsequent round, the process waits to hear each process's *preference*. If they disagree (line 3), the process broadcasts a message informing the others. When receiving

```
1   send prefer (binary preference) to all ;
2   for each round r {
3     if (both prefer(0) and prefer(1) received) {
4       send disagreement(r) to all ;
5     }
6     on (receipt of disagreement(r) for the first time) {
7       send disagreement(r) to all ;
8     }
9     if (all received preferences are prefer(v)) and (no disagreement(r) received){
10      if ( flip (r) == v) {
11        send decide(v) to all and return(v);
12      } else {
13        send prefer (v) to all ;
14      }
15    } else {
16      send prefer ( flip (r)) to all ;
17    }
18    if (any decide(v) received) {
19      return(v)
20    }
21  }
```

Fig. 3. Uniform consensus for send message omissions and process crashes

such a broadcast for the first time (line 6), every process relays it. Hence, if any non-faulty process receives mixed preferences or a *disagreement*(r) message, then all processes receive a *disagreement*(r) message and will change preference according to the coin flip. If they agree (line 9) and no message communicating disagreement seen by another process is received, then the process checks whether that preference agrees with the common pseudo-random binary number for that round. If so, it is safe to decide that value (line 11). If not, the process simply rebroadcasts the preference (line 13). If the preferences disagree or the process is informed so, then the process uses the common pseudo-random binary number to choose a new preference (line 16). If any process announces that it has decided, then the process decides on the same value (line 18).

Very informally, this protocol exploits in an essential way the observation that each process (but not the adversary) can predict the others' next coin flips. If a process receives v from all processes, then v was sent by at least one good process, so every other process will either receive all v preferences or both preferences. Any processes that receive either mixed preferences or *disagreement*(r) messages will change preference according to the coin flip. If the coin flip is the same as v, then all processes will prefer v, and it is safe to decide.

Lemma 1. *If $f < n$, for every process the expected number of rounds of ConsensusS is 3, and the protocol terminates with probability 1.*

Proof. Think of an execution as a tree, where the root node represents the initial round and the children of a node represent the following round possibilities. Let $E(n)$ be the expected number of rounds from node n. If n has children $n.1$ and $n.2$, chosen by coin flip, then $E(n) = (1/2)(1 + E(n.1)) + (1/2)(1 + E(n.2))$. Each child contributes one plus its expected running time, but with probability one-half. Now let

- $E(n) = E_1(n)$ if at node n some non-faulty processes sent *prefer*(0) and some non-faulty processes sent *prefer*(1),
- $E(n) = E_2(n)$ if at node n all non-faulty processes sent *prefer*(v) and some non-faulty processes receive a disagreement message or both *prefer*(0) and *prefer*(1),
- $E(n) = E_3(n)$ if at node n all non-faulty processes sent *prefer*(v) and all non-faulty processes receive no disagreement messages and only *prefer*(v).

Note that if $E(n) = E_z(n)$ and $E(n.1) = E_w(n.1)$, it may be that $z \neq w$. However, it is always the case that if $E(n.1) = E_z(n.1)$ then $E(n.2) = E_z(n.2)$. The reason is that from one round to the other the values that the non-faulty processes send and receive may change. However, if the non-faulty processes behave in a way at one children, then they should behave the same way at the other, since both children just differ in the coin flip. Hence, executions differing themselves by the values sent and received by non-faulty processes may generate distinct execution trees.

Now let e be the root of an execution tree. Consider that

- $E(e) = E_1(e)$: If there are non-faulty processes that sent $prefer(0)$ and other non-faulty processes that sent $prefer(1)$ in round r, then at round $r+1$ every process receives at least one message $prefer(0)$ and one message $prefer(1)$, and thus, from round $r+1$ on, all preference messages sent by every process (and all received as well) will be $prefer(flip(r+1))$. Hence, all processes will decide on $flip(r+1)$ in the first round t such that $flip(t) = flip(r+1)$, and the probability that any process (and thus, a non-faulty one) violates termination is the same as the probability that such a round t never happens, that is, zero. Besides, the expected number of rounds to achieve a round t such that $flip(t) = flip(r+1)$ is 2. Thus, the expected number of rounds of ConsensusS is $3 = E_1(e) = (1/2)(1+2) + (1/2)(1+2)$.
- $E(e) = E_2(e)$: If all non-faulty processes sent $prefer(v)$ in round r and part of the non-faulty processes receive a disagreement message or both messages $prefer(0)$ and $prefer(1)$ in round $r+1$, then all processes receive disagreement messages and from round $r+1$ on, all preference messages sent by every process (and all received as well) will be $prefer(flip(r+1))$. Thus, all processes will decide on $flip(r+1)$ in the first round t such that $flip(t) = flip(r+1)$, and the probability that any process (and thus, a non-faulty one) violates termination is the same as the probability that such a round t never happens, that is, zero. Besides, the expected number of rounds to achieve a round t such that $flip(t) = flip(r+1)$ is 2. Thus, the expected number of rounds of ConsensusS is $3 = E_2(e) = (1/2)(1+2) + (1/2)(1+2)$.
- $E(e) = E_3(e)$: If all non-faulty processes sent $prefer(v)$ and receive no disagreement messages and only $prefer(v)$ in round $r+1$, then if $flip(r+1) = v$, all non-faulty processes send $decide(v)$ messages and then decide by returning v themselves. Moreover, on receipt of $decide(v)$, all remaining processes decide by returning v. If $flip(r) \neq v$, then we fall again into the case that all non-faulty processes send $prefer(v)$. That is, $E_3(e.2) = E_2(e.2) or E_3(e.2)$. Thus, the probability that any process (and thus, a non-faulty one) violates termination is zero and the expected number of rounds of ConsensusS is $3 = E_3(e) = (1/2)(1+1) + (1/2)(1+3)$.

In short, in all cases, if $f < n$, the probability that any process (and thus, a non-faulty one) violates termination is zero. Moreover, the expected number of rounds of ConsensusS is 3 for all processes.   □

Lemma 2. *If $f < n$, each decided value is some process's input.*

Proof. Any decided value v is either an original input or the result of a shared coin flip. Consider the first $prefer(flip(r))$ statement to be executed, if any. In this case, there must have been a process received both $prefer(0)$ and a $prefer(1)$ messages, which means that some process had input value 0 and another had input value 1. It follows that either value is some process's input.   □

Lemma 3. *If $f < n$, no two processes decide differently.*

Proof. Consider the first round r in which a process decides v. It must be the case that at round r, $flip(r) = v$ and all preference messages received by the process are $prefer(v)$. As the messages from all non-faulty processes are received by all processes and there is at least one non-faulty process, all processes receive at least one $prefer(v)$ message, and either decide on v at the same round r or send $prefer(v) = prefer(flip(r))$. It follows that from the next round $r + 1$ on, all messages sent from all processes (and thus, also all received ones) will be $prefer(v)$. Henceforth, no process can decide a value different from v.   □

Theorem 1. ConsensusS *solves uniform consensus with binary inputs in a synchronous system prone to crashes and send message omissions, with a probability zero of termination violation, and both an optimal constant (3) expected rounds and an optimal $n - 1$ resilience (that is, up to $n - 1$ processes may be faulty: $f < n$).*

Proof. Follows directly from Lemmas 1, 2 and 3.   □

6 Optimal Protocol for Send and Receive Omissions

The *ConsensusSR* algorithm in Figure 4 solves uniform consensus with binary inputs in optimal 3 expected synchronous rounds tolerating an optimal number of up to $f < n/2$ failures - send message omissions and receive message omissions as well as process crashes.

In ConsensusSR, all processes start by broadcasting their inputs (line 2). Whenever one process does not receive a message from another, it decides that process must be faulty, and ignores it from that point on (line 6). Even so, all non-faulty processes send and receive messages from one another. Moreover, a live faulty process always receives messages from at least one non-faulty process, since otherwise, it would have less than $n/2+1$ messages and it would halt before reaching a decision (line 7).

On each round, every process checks if all received messages contain the same preferred value v (line 9). If so, it broadcasts a message that it wants to decide on v (line 10). When receiving this message for the first time (line 12), processes relay it. If a process receives such message from a majority of processes (line 15) or if it receives a message to decide on v (line 18), then it sends messages to all processes to decide on v and retuns v. Note that if a non-faulty process relays the message, all non-faulty processes will relay the message as well, so all non-faulty processes will receive the message from a majority of processes. As every process needs a non-faulty process to relay the message in order to decide on v, if any process decides on v, then every non-faulty process does as well. If a decision is not reached, then the process either sends a message with v as its current preference (line 22), if it received a majority of preferences v, or sends a message containing $flip(r)$ (line 24), otherwise.

Lemma 4. *On any single round after initialization (sending the binary private input), only one value is preferred or chosen deterministically.*

```
1    Recipients = set of all processes;
2    send prefer(binary preference) to all ;
3    foreach round r {
4       Received(r) = set of processes from which messages were received in round r
5       Recipients = Recipients intersection Received(r);
6       Messages(r) = set of messages received in round r which were sent by Recipients;
7       if (|Messages(r)|<n/2+1) {
8          halt; // too many failures
9          if ( all in Messages(r) are prefer(v)) {
10            send want_decide(v) to Recipients;
11         }
12         on (receipt of want_decide(r,v) for the first time) {
13            send want_decide(r,v) to Recipients;
14         }
15         if (want_decide(r,v) received from majority of processes) {
16            send decide(v) to all and return(v);
17         }
18         on (receipt of decide(v)) {
19            send decide(v) to all and return(v);
20         }
21         if (majority in Messages(r) are prefer(v)) {
22            send prefer(v);
23         } else {
24            send prefer(\ flip (r ));
25         }
26   }
```

Fig. 4. Uniform consensus for send and receive message omissions and process crashes

Proof. A process prefers or decides v deterministically only if it sees a majority for v.   □

Lemma 5. *If $f < n/2$, for every process the expected number of rounds of ConsensusSR is 3, and the protocol terminates with probability 1.*

Proof. After initialization (sending the binary private input), if all live processes send $prefer(flip(r))$ or if all live processes send $prefer(v)$, they agree right away, by Lemma 4. If some send $prefer(v)$ and some send $prefer(flip(r))$, again by Lemma 4, then all live processes will agree in the first round t such that $v = flip(r)$, and the probability that any non-faulty process violates termination is the same as the probability that such a round t never happens, that is, zero. Besides, the expected number of rounds to achieve a round t such that $v = flip(r)$ is 2.

Once agreement by all live processes is achieved, non-faulty processes will receive a majority of $want_decide(r, v)$, send decide(v) and return(v), immediately in the same round. This is because they always receive messages from each other, that is, they always belong to the *Recipients* of non-faulty processes, so once a non-faulty process sends a $want_decide(r, v)$ message, all non-faulty processes will send $want_decide(r, v)$ messages to (and receive them from) all non-faulty processes and guarantee a majority of $want_decide(r, v)$.

In short, in all cases, if $f < n/2$, the probability that a non-faulty process violates termination is zero. Moreover, the expected number of rounds of ConsensusSR is 3 for all processes. □

Lemma 6. *If $f < n/2$, all processes in ConsensusSR decide some process's input.*

Proof. A decided value v, from $decide(v)$, is just obtained from a $prefer(v)$. Now, by induction, a v from $prefer(v)$ has to be either an input or a $flip(r)$ for some r. However, take the first $prefer(flip(r))$ to occur, if any do. In this case, a process received both a $prefer(0)$ and a $prefer(1)$, which means that there should be a proposed input value equal to 0 and another equal to 1, as the particular $prefer(flip(r))$ was the first one to take place. Otherwise, either there would be a majority of $prefer(v)$ or Hence, $flip(r)$ must be a proposed input value if any $prefer(flip(r))$ occurs, and v must also be one of the proposed values. □

Lemma 7. *If $f < n/2$, agreement is never violated in ConsensusSR: no two processes decide differently.*

Proof. Consider the first round r when a process decides by returning v. Then, it must be the case that a majority of $want_decide(r, v)$ is received by the process. However, because each process deciding has to receive a $want_decide(r, v)$ from a non-faulty process and non-faulty processes always receive messages from each other, when any process has a majority of $want_decide(r, v)$, it must be the case that all non-faulty processes have a majority of $want_decide(r, v)$, that is, all non-faulty processes decide by returning v as well. □

Theorem 2. *ConsensusSR solves uniform consensus with binary inputs in a synchronous system prone to crashes, send message omissions and receive message omissions, with a probability zero of termination violation, and both an optimal constant (3) expected number of rounds and an optimal $n/2 - 1$ resilience (that is, up to $n/2 - 1$ processes may be faulty: $f < n/2$).*

Proof. Follows directly from Lemma 5, 6 and 7. □

7   Conclusions

The key idea in this paper is that if secure coprocessors can share secret cryptographic keys (as they do), then they can also share secret seeds for secure pseudo-random number generators. Such shared coins enable randomized (Las Vegas) algorithms for fair exchange and uniform consensus that are optimal in terms of expected running time and resilience.

Both the ConsensusS and ConsensusSR binary consensus protocols can be extended to a larger set of k values in $3\log(k)$ rounds via bit-by-bit consensus. It is an open question whether faster protocols exist (perhaps by doing bit-by-bit consensus in parallel).

References

1. James Aspnes. Randomized protocols for asynchronous consensus. *Distributed Computing*, 16(2–3):165–175, September 2003.
2. Gildas Avoine, Felix Gärtner, Rachid Guerraoui, and Marko Vukolic. Gracefully degrading fair exchange with security modules. In *Proceedings of the Fifth European Dependable Computing Conference*, pages 55–71. Springer-Verlag, April 2005.
3. Elizabeth Borowsky and Eli Gafni. Generalized FLP impossibility result for t-resilient asynchronous computations. In *Proceedings of the Twenty-Fifth ACM Symposium on Theory of Computing*, pages 91–100. ACM Press, May 1993.
4. Tushar Deepak Chandra, Vassos Hadzilacos, and Sam Toueg. The weakest failure detector for solving consensus. *J.ACM*, 43(4):685–722, July 1996.
5. Soma Chaudhuri. Agreement is harder than consensus: Set consensus problems in totally asynchronous systems. In *Proceedings of the Ninth Annual ACM Symposium on Principles of Distributed Computing*, pages 311–234. ACM Press, August 1990.
6. Carole Delporte-Gallet, Hugues Fauconnier, and Felix C. Freiling. Revisiting failure detection and consensus in omission failure environments. In *Proceedings of the International Colloquium on Theoretical Aspects of Computing (ICTAC05)*, Hanoi, Vietnam, October 2005.
7. Joan G. Dyer, Mark Lindemann, Ronald Perez, Reiner Sailer, Leendert van Doorn, Sean W. Smith, and Steve Weingart. Building the IBM 4758 secure coprocessor. *IEEE Computer*, 34(10):57–66, October 2001.
8. Paul Feldman and Silvio Micali. Optimal algorithms for byzantine agreement. In *Proceedings of the Twentieth Annual ACM Symposium on Theory of Computing*, pages 148–161. ACM Press, May 1988.
9. Michael Fischer, Nancy Lynch, and Michael Paterson. Impossibility of distributed consensus with one faulty process. *Journal of the ACM (JACM)*, 32(2):374–382, April 1985.
10. Maurice Herlihy and Nir Shavit. The topological structure of asynchronous computability. *Journal of the ACM (JACM)*, 46(6):858–923, November 1999.
11. Henning Pagnia, Holger Vogt, and Felix C. Gärtner. Fair exchange. *The Computer Journal*, 46(1), 2003.
12. Philippe Raïpin Parvédy and Michel Raynal. Optimal early stopping uniform consensus in synchronous systems with process omission failures. In *Proceedings of the Sixteenth Annual ACM Symposium on Parallelism in Algorithms and Architectures*, pages 302–310. ACM Press, June 2004.
13. Marshall Pease, Robert Shostak, and Leslie Lamport. Reaching agreements in the presence of faults. *Journal of the ACM (JACM)*, 27(2):228–234, April 1980.
14. Michael Saks and Fotios Zaharoglou. Wait-free k-set agreement is impossible: The topology of public knowledge. *SIAM Journal on Computing*, 29(5):1449–1483, March 2000.
15. Trusted Computing Group. Trusted computing group homepage. Internet: https://www.trustedcomputinggroup.org/, 2003.
16. Andrew J. Viterbi. *CDMA : Principles of Spread Spectrum Communication*. Prentice Hall, 1995. ISBN 0201633744.

Two Abstractions for Implementing Atomic Objects in Dynamic Systems

Roy Friedman[1], Michel Raynal[2], and Corentin Travers[2]

[1] Computer Science Department, Technion, Haifa 32000, Israel
[2] IRISA, Université de Rennes 1, Campus de Beaulieu, 35042 Rennes, France
roy@cs.technion.ac.il, {raynal, ctravers}@irisa.fr

Abstract. Defining appropriate abstractions is one of the main challenges in computer science. This paper investigates two matching abstractions for implementing read/write objects in a dynamic server system prone to crash failures. The first abstraction concerns dynamic quorum systems. The second is a persistent reliable broadcast communication primitive. These two abstractions capture the essence of basic mechanisms allowing the implementation of atomic objects in a distributed system where servers can dynamically enter and leave the system (or crash). A read protocol and a write protocol based on these abstractions are described and proved correct. The properties defining these abstractions can be seen as requirements that are sufficient for implementing a dynamic storage service, while the feasibility conditions that are stated can be seen as necessary requirements. Instantiating the proposed abstractions in different contexts (e.g., settings defined by specific assumptions on failures, synchrony, message delays and processing times) provides as many system specific protocols.

Keywords: Atomic object, Communication primitive, Crash failures, Distributed system, Dynamic system, Quorum, Server, Shared memory.

1 Introduction

This paper is on the implementation of atomic read/write objects in a dynamic server system. More precisely, the general context that is considered is the following:

- There is an a priori infinite number of clients accessing shared objects. A client can sequentially issue read and write operations. It can also crash while executing an operation. A crash outside an operation is irrelevant.
- Each read or write operation on an object issued by a client is considered as an "atomic interaction" that accesses copies of the object. From an internal structure point of view, each operation follows the two phase pattern introduced in [5]. The first phase obtains control information, while the second phase ensures data persistence and consistency. This internal structure is unknown to the clients. From a client point of view, a read or write operation is a "primitive".
- Each object is supported by a set of servers. The server model is the infinite arrival model with finite concurrency [27]. This means that each run can have an infinite number of servers (i.e., an infinite number of servers can join and leave the system), but in each finite time interval there are finitely many servers. So intuitively, the only source of "infinitely" is the passage of time [1].

J.H. Anderson, G. Prencipe, and R. Wattenhofer (Eds.): OPODIS 2005, LNCS 3974, pp. 73–87, 2006.

This model is very general, and matches many types of long lived dynamic applications, as we elaborate in Section 6. In this paper, we are interested in implementing an atomic read/write object.

If servers join and leave the system arbitrarily fast, it is possible that no server remains long enough in the system for completing any read or write operations. So, implementing read and write operations requires some form of stability. This stability could be obtained by considering *duration assumptions* on the time a server process remains in the system, on message delays and on processing times. We consider here a more high level approach based only on the statement of *abstract properties* (in that sense our approach is similar to the failure detector approach introduced in [6]). Of course, implementing these properties can be done in dynamic systems satisfying some synchrony and durations assumptions (e.g., when there is a sliding time period of known and long enough duration during which some fixed and known number of non-faulty servers are continuously present).

So, instead of relying on specific low-level assumptions, the approach we propose to implement atomic shared objects in a dynamic distributed system is based on two complementary abstractions. The aim of these abstractions is to capture the relevant properties that facilitate the design of read and write protocols that focus on solving the problem rather than being overloaded with system specific implementation details. More precisely, we consider the following matching abstractions:

- The first defines quorums suited for read/write operations in a dynamic server system.[1] Each phase of an operation uses a particular type of quorum, and only some quorums have to intersect. More precisely, only the quorums of different types and belonging to consecutive operations have to intersect. Interestingly, the abstract properties defining these dynamic quorums can be interpreted as sufficient conditions when one wants to implement a dynamic reliable storage service. Feasibility conditions are also associated with these properties; those can be seen as necessary requirements for such implementations.
- The second abstraction, which we call *persistent reliable broadcast*, concerns communication. The primitives we propose allow an operation to broadcast a message uniformly to a sufficient subset of servers in a dynamic server model.

A read protocol and a corresponding write protocol that are based only on these abstractions are then presented and proved correct. Their correctness depends only on the properties of the abstractions. As those are defined as a set of abstract properties independent of a particular system or given technology, they can be implemented differently in different systems[2]. This modular approach favors the proof of the upper layer protocols, and cleanly separates between the properties we want to benefit from and their implementation [12].

---

[1] By definition, an object type that allows solving the Consensus problem despite process failures in otherwise asynchronous environment cannot be implemented purely by intersecting quorums. In particular, read-modify-write semantics is too strong to be supported by intersecting quorums without additional synchrony assumptions or failure detection capabilities.

[2] A trivial case being a static system with a majority of correct servers.

2   Application and System Model

An *application* is made up of clients processes that enter and leave the system (or crash). These processes can access read/write shared data objects. A client is not aware of other clients; it only knows that other clients can concurrently coexist. There is no global time notion accessible to the clients or the objects. This section defines the corresponding computation model.

To simplify the presentation, we assume the existence of a discrete global clock. This clock, whose domain is the set of integers denoted $\mathbb{N}$, is a fictional device that is known neither by the clients, nor by the objects.

2.1   Client Processes

From the application's point of view, the system consists of a possibly infinite set of sequential processes (called clients) that access a pool of shared read/write objects. The client process model we consider is sometimes called the *infinite arrival process with finite concurrency* [27]: the system has infinitely many processes, each run can have infinitely many clients, but in each finite time interval only finitely many processes can take steps [1].

Each client has an identity. These identities are such that no two clients have the same identity, and any two identities can be compared. A client knows its identity, but does not know the identities of the other clients. In the following we consider that a client identity is an integer, yet the client identities are not necessarily consecutive integers. The interested reader may refer to [1] for a protocol to "name the anonymous".

A client process can crash. In that case it stops its execution. A crashed process does not recover. Let us note that practically, this means that a process that recovers can re-enter the system as a new process, i.e., with a new identity. As a client process is not aware of the other clients, it has to terminate its operations (if it does not crash) whatever the behavior of the other clients. This means that the operations provided to the client processes have to be *wait-free* [20] (with respect to other clients).

2.2   Shared Objects

Each object x of the shared memory can be accessed by two operations denoted READ (x) and WRITE (x, v). They allow the invoking process to obtain the value of x, or define the new value v of x, respectively. Each object x is *atomic*. This means that, from an external observer point of view, all the operations accessing x can be totally ordered in such a way that (1) this order respects their real-time occurrence order, and (2) each read obtains the value written by the last write that precedes it in this total order [23]. Atomicity is a fundamental concept as it allows us to reason sequentially despite concurrency.

Let us note that in the context of concurrent objects, i.e., objects that can be concurrently accessed by several processes, the *atomicity* concept has initially been formalized and investigated for read/write shared objects [23]. It has then been extended under the name *linearizability* to any object that has a sequential specification [21].

Interestingly, it has been shown that a run that satisfies the atomicity (linearizability) consistency criterion with respect to each shared object considered separately, also satisfies this criterion when we consider the whole set of atomic objects as a single (bigger) variable [21]. This property is called *locality*. Thus, atomic consistency is *local*. However, sequential consistency and causal consistency are not [21]. That is, merging a protocol providing sequential consistency on a single object x with a protocol providing sequential consistency on another object y does not provide a protocol providing sequential consistency on the composite object $X = [x, y]$.[3]

Locality is significant for both theory and practice. From a theoretical point of view, it allows us to reason sequentially on the combined set of all objects as if it was a single object. From an implementation and software engineering point of view, this property enables scalable composable realizations. That is, as soon as we have a protocol implementing atomic consistency for one object, we can run multiple independent instantiations of this protocol, one for each object, and the entire system will behave correctly without any additional control or synchronization.

2.3   Shared Memory: A Set of Servers

We consider a shared memory service consisting of read/write objects that are implemented on top of a distributed message-passing system made up of a set of server processes, denoted $s_1, s_2, \ldots$ As indicated in the introduction, this system may have an infinite number of servers. Yet (as for clients), in each finite time interval there is only a finite number of servers (*infinite arrival model with finite concurrency*). A server s_j can enter the shared memory service (event $init_j$). It can later crash (event $fail_j$) or leave the system (event $leave_j$). As we noted earlier, this means that a process that crashed or left the system can re-enter the system, each time with a new identity. Each object is implemented by a subset of servers. Practically, this allows us to assume that the subset of servers implementing a single object at any given finite time interval is reasonably small, even though the system as a whole might include a huge number of servers. Due to the locality property of *atomicity* (recall the discussion in Section 2.2), in the rest of the paper we consider a single object x without losing generality.

Let $up(t)$ denote the set of servers (implementing object x) that joined the system before time t and have neither crashed nor left at t. We assume that $\forall t : up(t) \neq \emptyset$. This is a *feasibility* condition necessary to obtain *live* quorums, i.e., quorums that can prevent from definitive blocking the read and write operations that use them.

2.4   Operations as Intervals

As we have seen, an application process can only invoke a read or a write operation on a shared object. These operations are abstract for it in the sense that it can use them as primitives but it does not know how these primitives and the atomic objects are implemented at the underlying level.

Let us consider the ath READ () or WRITE () operation invoked by the same client process p_i. The beginning of the execution of that operation at the client defines an

---

[3] The bounds of the locality property with respect to various consistency criteria have been investigated in [33].

event that we denote $start_i^a$. Similarly, its termination at the client defines an event that we denote end_i^a. The crash of a client p_i while it is executing a read or write operation defines an event that we denote $crash_i$ (let us note that the crash of p_i outside an operation is irrelevant). On the application side, these are the only relevant events.

The invocations of read and write operations by a client p_i defines its local history. The subsequence of events between $start_i^a$ and end_i^a (or $crash_i$) defines what we call the *interval* I_i^a [18]. Let us stress that an interval is defined with respect to events at the client only, regardless of any events and operations taken by the servers or other clients. An execution of a set of processes sharing a set of atomic objects can be represented by a history h that is the sequence of events issued by these processes (if two or more events are "simultaneous", they can be arbitrarily ordered [22]).

Interestingly, the history h defines a natural partial order on the intervals. $I_i^a \rightarrow_h I_j^b$ (*precedes*) if end_i^a (or $crash_i$) appears in h before $start_j^b$. I_i^a is an *immediate predecessor* of I_j^b if $I_i^a \rightarrow_h I_j^b$ and there is no interval I such that $I_i^a \rightarrow_h I$ and $I \rightarrow_h I_j^b$. Finally, $im\_pred(I1, I2)$ is a predicate that is true if and only if $I1$ is an immediate predecessor of $I2$.

Let I be an interval whose start and end events occur at time t_b^I and t_e^I, respectively (if there is no end event for I, let $t_e^I = +\infty$). The following set of servers is associated with each interval I:

$$STABLE(I) = \{s \mid \exists t \in [t_b^I, t_e^I] : \forall t' : t \leq t' \leq t_e^I : s \in up(t')\}.$$

Another feasibility condition necessary to obtain live quorums is to have, for any interval I, $STABLE(I) \neq \emptyset$.

3   A Dynamic Read/Write Quorum Abstraction

3.1   Quorum Oracle

A quorum oracle is a device that provides the processes with a single primitive, namely a query. Moreover, we consider here that such a query can only be issued at a client due to a READ () or a WRITE () operation on a shared object inside the corresponding interval. Each query returns a set of servers. To be meaningful, the sets of servers returned by the queries have to satisfy some properties. A given set of such properties defines the type of the corresponding quorum oracle.

3.2   Dynamic Read/Write Quorums

We are now in order to define a class of quorum oracles that can be used to implement an atomic object in a dynamic server system. This class, denoted $\mathcal{RW}_{dyn}$, allows a process to issue two types of queries. As elaborated below, the goal of the first type is to obtain a "consistent" timestamp (associated with the value read or written), so we denote it CD (for control data). The second is to ensure that "enough" servers will have an up to date copy of the last value of the object, so we denote it VAL. $\mathcal{RW}_{dyn}$ is defined by the following properties:

- Progress property.

  Let $Q(t)$ be the quorum obtained by a query issued at time t during an interval I (whatever the type CD or VAL of the query).

  $$\exists t \in [t_b^I, t_e^I]: \quad \forall t' : t \leq t' \leq t_e^I : \ Q(t') \subseteq STABLE(I).$$

  This property states that, by repeatedly querying its quorum oracle, an operation (that does not crash) eventually obtains a quorum of servers that have joined the system and have neither crashed nor left the system.

- Typed Bounded Lifetime Intersection property.

  This property involves the two types of queries and their associated intervals. It states that the quorums returned by two such queries have a non empty intersection only if these queries (1) have different types and (2) belong to consecutive intervals. Let Q_{cd} (resp., Q_{val}) denote both the quorum returned by a query whose type is CD (resp., VAL), and the corresponding query event. Let $I1$ and $I2$ be the intervals associated with these queries. We have:

  $$[(Q_{val} \in I1) \wedge (Q_{cd} \in I2) \wedge im\_pred(I1, I2)] \Rightarrow Q_{val} \cap Q_{cd} \neq \emptyset.$$

3.3   Related Quorum Systems

When comparing $\mathcal{RW}_{dyn}$ with traditional quorum systems [14, 15, 32], a noteworthy difference lies in the limited period during which quorums (of different types) have to intersect[4]. Interestingly, this intersection requirement allows all the servers that are alive and participate in a quorum at a given time to later crash or leave the system. In contrast, the *quorum failure detectors* introduced in [7, 8] require that all quorums will intersect in at least one process that never crashes. The generalization of quorum failure detectors in [11] only requires intersections between concurrent and immediately consecutive quorums, but does not allow all the servers that are alive at some point to later crash.

Herlihy's work describe a scheme that allows processes to switch between quorums, e.g., due to partitions [19]. The work of Herlihy concentrates on the mechanisms for performing such transformations and assumes a finite set of servers. Our work, on the other hand, concentrates on the formal framework and definitions of quorums in a dynamic system. In our approach, the change in the set of servers is inherently decided by the environment and cannot be controlled by the processes.

The class $\mathcal{RW}_{dyn}$ differs also from the quorums as defined in the seminal work on RAMBO [24]. RAMBO is a reconfigurable atomic memory service for dynamic networks. A key notion in RAMBO is the concept of *configuration* that is a set of members plus sets of read quorums and write quorums. RAMBO requires that any read quorum and any write quorum of the same configuration do intersect. Moreover, this intersection requirement is independent of the actual pattern of read and write operations (in

---

[4] One server that has the latest value of the object (it appears in the Q_{val} quorum) has to survive until the next operation (that obtains the quorum Q_{cd}), so that the previous intersection property can be satisfied.

our case, only consecutive operations require typed quorums to intersect). Thus, our intersection requirement may allow for more continuous evolution of the system.

The notion of a Byzantine quorum system, i.e., one that is resilient to Byzantine failures, was introduced in [25]. An extension that allows dynamically modifying the resilience threshold, yet with a constant set of servers, was introduced in [3]. The work of [29] describes a method that allows to dynamically change the set of servers by running Byzantine consensus to decide on the next configuration of the system, and thus can be thought as a kind of a Byzantine RAMBO like system. A somewhat similar approach of switching quorum systems using views was taken in [26]. However, in [26], a view change is performed by having an external entity notify a quorum of the current view to stop accepting requests in that view, and then notifying all members of the new view of its existence and initial state.

Finally, the idea of implementing a distributed shared memory in a dynamic system based on a group communication system was introduced in [10]. Rather than using quorums, that work relies on the virtual synchrony and total ordering mechanisms of the underlying group communication toolkit to obtain total ordering of operations and state continuity.

3.4 The Static Case

The static case is when the server system is statically defined with $m = 2f + 1$ servers, and up to f of them can crash. Moreover, the bound f is known by the processes. In this system, the classical quorum definition as sets of $f + 1$ servers trivially satisfies the two requirements of the previous definition. It is important to notice that if, incidentally, a run has more than $f + 1$ servers that crash, the Progress property can no longer be ensured, and operations based on such quorums can block forever. This means that, be the system dynamic or static, there are assumptions for the operations to terminate correctly. Here the implicit assumption is that "no more than f servers crash" (even when this assumption is embedded into the model, it may or may not be satisfied during a particular run).

4   A Communication Abstraction

In addition to the classical one-to-one reliable *send* and *receive* communication primitives, the underlying system offers two communication primitives prst_broadcast() and prst_deliver(). The first is to allow a read or a write operation to send a message to the set of servers. The second allows a server s to be delivered the corresponding message.

These primitives assume that each message m has a type $type(m)$ and a sequence number $sn(m)$. When a process executes prst_broadcast(m) (resp., prst_deliver()), we say that it "broadcasts" (resp., "delivers") m. The *persistent reliable broadcast* communication abstraction is defined by the following properties:

- Validity. If a message m is delivered by a server, it has been broadcast as part of the execution of a read or a write operation.
- Integrity. A message m is delivered at most once by each server.

- Server/server Termination. If a message m is broadcast during an interval I and is delivered by a server, then any server $s \in STABLE(I)$ eventually delivers a message m' such that $type(m) = type(m')$ and $sn(m') \geq sn(m)$.[5]
- Client/server Termination. If the client process does not crash while it is executing the read or write operation defining the interval I that gave rise to the broadcast of m, the message m is delivered eventually by at least one server.

The validity and integrity properties are *safety* properties. The first states that no spurious message is created, while the second states that no message is duplicated. The two other properties address the *liveness* of message deliveries. The client/server termination property states that if the application process that executes a read or write operation does not crash while it is executing that operation, each message it broadcasts (during that operation) is not lost in the sense that it is eventually delivered by at least one server. Due to asynchrony and the fact that servers can crash, or dynamically join/leave the system, it is not possible to require that all the servers that are active when a message m is broadcast will deliver the message. Hence the rationale for the server/server termination property that states that if a message is delivered by a server, then all the servers that have entered or will enter the system and neither leave it nor crash by the end of the operation (the servers defining the set denoted $STABLE(I)$), will deliver this message or a message of the same type sent later[6].

When all the messages have different types, the type notion disappears and sequence numbers become useless. If additionally the number of servers is statically defined, and all the events define a single interval [18], the primitives prst_broadcast() and prst_deliver() then boil down to the classical uniform reliable broadcast primitives [17].

An implementation of the *persistent reliable broadcast* abstraction can be done according to the following lines. When a server receives a message m, the server first forwards m to all the other processes, and only then delivers the message to itself (the way message forwarding is ensured depends on the underlying overlay network and the associated routing [28, 30, 31] – see also discussion in Section 6). Moreover, a new server that joins the system has first to broadcast (using the underlying routing) an inquiry message to the servers currently present in the system. When a server receives such a message, the server sends back its state and, for each message type, the sequence number of the last message it has delivered.

5 An Atomic Object Service

Assuming the previous dynamic quorum and persistent reliable broadcast abstractions, this section presents and proves correct a simple and general protocol implementing read and write operations suited to dynamic server systems.

---

[5] Notice that unlike uniform delivery, here the message m' that is eventually delivered by the servers in $STABLE(I)$ can be different from m, as long as the types of m and m' is the same and $sn(m') \geq sn(m)$.

[6] The underlying idea is here the following. A message m' that is causally affected by a message m (hence $sn(m') > sn(m)$) "includes" m from a causality point of view, and consequently the delivery of m' implicitly contains the delivery of m.

5.1   Structure of the Implementation

Each client p_i has a local variable sn_i that it uses to generate local sequence numbers. This allows p_i to give a unique identity to each read and write operation it invokes. In the following we consider an application process p_i and a read/write object x.

As a side comment, let us note that in some systems, an application process communicates only with a proxy, and several processes can share the same proxy. The proxy plays the role of the process with respect to the server processes. As an example, we have the following correspondence with transaction systems: transaction $\leftrightarrow$ operations, transaction manager $\leftrightarrow$ proxy, data managers $\leftrightarrow$ servers, and data $\leftrightarrow$ shared object copy. Here we could envisage a similar architecture, but as our focus is on atomic consistency, we do not detail the architectural issues of the whole system. Intuitively, the reader can think that the sequence numbers may be managed by the proxies and not by the processes themselves (as done, e.g., in [9]).

Back to our model, the protocol uses a classical timestamping mechanism [22]. It associates a timestamp ts, which consists of a pair made up of an integer denoted $ts.clock$ plus a process id denoted $ts.proc$, with each value that has been successfully written. Using lexicographic ordering, this allows us to obtain a total order on all the values that have been written. This total order is used to enforce atomic consistency. This basic principle is used in most atomic consistency protocols we are aware of.

The protocols implementing write and read operations are described in Figure 1 and Figure 2, respectively. They are based on the principles used in [5], namely, they are two-phase protocols. We first describe the write protocol, and then the read protocol.

5.2   Implementing a WRITE (x, v) Operation

When an application process p_i wants to write a new value, its first phase consists of defining a correct timestamp for the value v. The second phase is for p_i to ensure that the new pair (value, timestamp) is known by enough servers so that atomic consistency can be achieved. Each phase obeys the same algorithmic pattern, involving both abstractions, namely, a persistent broadcast followed by a quorum-based synchronization. Thus, the phases proceed as follows.

– Phase 1. First, p_i builds an identity for its requests concerning this write. This identity is the pair (i, sn_i). Then, it broadcasts a request to the servers with the goal of obtaining the timestamp associated with the last value of the object. This corresponds to line 2, where the field "no" in the message means that p_i does not need the last value of the object.

   The type of this first broadcast is defined by the pair (cd_req, i) where cd_req is the message tag, and i the sender id. Then, p_i waits until it receives acknowledgments from the processes defining a CD quorum (lines 3–6). Due to the bounded lifetime intersection property of quorums (as can be seen in the proof in the full version of this paper [13]), p_i can then define the new timestamp ts associated with the value v it wishes to write. This timestamp is greater than all the timestamps associated with values previously written.

– Phase 2. During this phase, p_i broadcast to the servers a new request carrying the pair (ts, v) (line 8). This request is tagged *write_req* and its type is the pair (*write_req,i*). Next, p_i waits until it has received acknowledgments from the processes defining a VAL quorum (lines 10–13). When this occurs, it knows (see the proof in [13]) that "enough" servers have received the write request and, consequently, the current write can terminate (line 14).

---

operation WRITE$_i$ (x, v)
    % Phase 1 (lines 1-7): synchronization to obtain consistent information %
(1) $sn_i \leftarrow sn_i + 1; ans_i \leftarrow \emptyset;$
(2) **prst_broadcast** $cd\_req(i, sn_i, \text{no});$
(3) **repeat**
(4)   **wait for** a message $cd\_ack(sn_i, ts)$ received from $s;$
(5) $ans_i \leftarrow ans_i \cup \{s\}$
(6) **until** $\left(Q_{cd} \subseteq ans_i\right);$
(7) $ts.clock \leftarrow$ max of the $ts.clock$ fields received $+1; ts.proc \leftarrow i;$
    % Phase 2 (lines 8-14): synchronization to ensure atomic consistency %
(8) **prst_broadcast** $write\_req(i, sn_i, ts, v);$
(9) $ans_i \leftarrow \emptyset;$
(10) **repeat**
(11)   **wait for** a message $write\_ack(sn_i)$ received from $s;$
(12) $ans_i \leftarrow ans_i \cup \{s\}$
(13) **until** $\left(Q_{val} \subseteq ans_i\right);$
(14) return()

Fig. 1. Implementing a WRITE () operation

---

operation READ$_i$ (x)
    % Phase 1 (lines 1-7): synchronization to obtain consistent information %
(1) $sn_i \leftarrow sn_i + 1; ans_i \leftarrow \emptyset;$
(2) **prst_broadcast** $cd\_req(i, sn_i, \text{yes});$
(3) **repeat**
(4)   **wait for** a message $cd\_ack(sn_i, ts, value)$ received from $s;$
(5) $ans_i \leftarrow ans_i \cup \{s\}$
(6) **until** $\left(Q_{cd} \subseteq ans_i\right);$
(7) $ts \leftarrow$ max of the ts received; $v \leftarrow value$ field associated with $ts;$
    % Phase 2 (lines 8-14): synchronization to ensure atomic consistency %
(8) **prst_broadcast** $write\_req(i, sn_i, ts, v);$
(9) $ans_i \leftarrow \emptyset;$
(10) **repeat**
(11)   **wait for** a message $write\_ack(sn_i)$ received from $s;$
(12) $ans_i \leftarrow ans_i \cup \{s\}$
(13) **until** $\left(Q_{val} \subseteq ans_i\right);$
(14) return(v)

Fig. 2. Implementing a READ () operation

5.3   Implementing a READ (x) Operation

The protocol for a read operation is structurally the same, and semantically nearly the same, as the write protocol. It has two phases with exactly the same meaning, as described in Figure 2. The only noteworthy difference with respect to the write protocol lies in the fact that the last field of the message $cd\_req()$ broadcast at line 2 carries the value "yes". This is to demand each server that sends back an acknowledgment to provide not only its last timestamp but also the associated value. This is required because a read has to return a value when it terminates (line 14).

The second phase of the read protocol is to ensure atomicity. It prevents two sequential read operations from obtaining inconsistent values. More precisely, let $R1$ and $R2$ be two read operations such that $R2$ starts after $R1$ is finished, and both $R1$ and $R2$ are concurrent with a write operation W that updates the object x from $v1$ to $v2$. The second phase prevents what is called "new/old" inversion, namely, it is not possible for $R1$ to read $v2$ while $R2$ would obtain $v1$. The prevention of new/old inversions is what makes an "atomic" object distinct from a "regular" object [23][7].

5.4   Read/Write Protocol: The Server Side

Each server s manages two local variables, ts_s and $value_s$, that contain the highest timestamp value that s has ever received, and the associated value, respectively.

As we have seen, only messages of the type (cd_req,i) or $(write\_req,i)$ can be delivered to a server s. These messages have been broadcast by p_i during the first phase (line 2) or the second phase (line 8) of the write or the read protocol.

- When a server receives $cd\_req(i, sn, bool)$, it sends back to p_i an acknowledgment (carrying the same sequence number sn so that p_i does not confuse all acks it receives), plus the required control information (local timestamp) with the associated value if it is required.
- When a server s receives $write\_req(i, sn, ts, v)$, is first updates its local data if they are out of date. In all cases, s sends back an acknowledgment to the process p_i that initiated the broadcast.

It is interesting to notice that an application process communicates anonymously with the set of servers using the persistent reliable broadcast primitives. That is, an application process sees only a service and does not know the servers on an individual basis. Differently, a server works on a responsive mode, and can always send back an acknowledgment to the sender of the message it receives. The acknowledgments are one-to-one. The broadcasts are one-to-all.[8]

5.5   Another Implementation for a READ (x) Operation

There are distinct ways to implement the second phase of the read protocol. An alternative approach consists of asking the servers to inform the reader p_i when they have

---

[7] The interested reader can find an elaborate discussion on this difference in [16].

[8] Let us remind the reader that when we say "all the servers", we mean the set of alive servers that currently implement the desired object.

```
(1)  when cd_req(i, sn, bool) is delivered:
(2)      if (bool = yes) then val_to_send ← value_s else val_to_send ← ⊥ end_if;
(3)      send cd_ack(sn, ts, val_to_send) to i

(4)  when write_req(i, sn, ts, v) is delivered:
(5)      if (ts > ts_s) then ts_s ← ts; value_s ← v end_if;
(6)      send write_ack(sn) to i
```

Fig. 3. Processing by a server s of the messages it receives

stored a value whose timestamp is equal to or higher than ts (the timestamp of the value read by p_i). When p_i learns that a VAL type quorum of servers have stored such a timestamp, it can terminate the read operation and return v (the value associated with ts). Protocols based on a similar approach are described in [1, 2] to implement atomic variables from a fixed set of crash-prone disks.

Adapting this idea to our context can be done as follows. A new message tag is used by a read operation and its lines 8-13 are replaced by the following lines:

```
8'   prst_broadcast read_req(i, sn_i, ts, v);
9'   ans_i ← ∅;
10'  repeat
11'      wait for a message read_ack(sn_i) received from s;
12'      ans_i ← ans_i ∪ {s}
13'  until (Q_val ⊆ ans_i)
```

The code of a server is modified accordingly, namely, it additionally includes the following statement to process $read\_req$ () messages:

```
(7)  when read_req(i, sn, ts) is delivered:
(8)      wait until (ts_s ≥ ts);
(9)      send read_ack(sn) to i
```

Proof: Due to space limitation, the proof appears in the full version of this paper [13].

6 Practical Instantiations

Read/write objects are a general abstraction that can be used to implement various distributed services. These include, e.g., distributed shared memory, maintaining distributed files, distributed directory lookup services, shared bulletin boards, etc.

With proper assumptions about the rate of failures (process crashes), joins, and leaves, it is possible to implement the required quorum oracles with many existing *distributed hash tables*-based *peer-to-peer* systems (e.g., CAN [28], Chord [31], Pastry [30], Tapestry [34], to name a few). Specifically, most of these peer-to-peer systems provide a service that enables implicit routing of messages to servers without the application ever knowing the identifiers of the servers. The way these services operate is that the application passes an object identifier to the service. The service calculates a hashed identifier, and gradually forwards the message between some of the servers until it reaches the server whose hashed identifier value is closest, under some metric, to the hashed object identifier.

When there are no changes in the system (i.e., no failures, no joins, and no leaves), the service ensures that all requests to route a message with the same object identifier x will reach the same server. In the rest of this section, we refer to such a server as the *responsible server for object* x. Moreover, asymptotically, these systems provide with high probability good load balancing for the division of object identifiers to corresponding responsible servers. That is, when there are "enough" servers and "enough" object identifiers, each server is responsible for roughly the same number of objects. Moreover, two slightly different object identifiers (e.g., the Hamming distance between their binary representation is small) have different responsible servers.

If we assume that the rate of change in the system is low, we can employ the following scheme, similar to what is done in [4]: for a given object identifier x and constant k, we define the following *set of derived object identifiers* $\{1\_x, 2\_x, \ldots, k\_x\}$. This set of derived object identifiers implies a corresponding set of *derived responsible servers*. Thus, the set of servers that implement a shared object x now becomes the set of derived responsible servers for x.

Let us further assume that the rate of change, the latency of messages, and the speed of processes are such that there exist constants k and f so that for every set of derived servers whose size is k, at most f fail during an interval (an execution of a read or write operation). With these assumptions, $STABLE(I)$ becomes the set of derived responsible servers for object x that do not fail or leave during I. Moreover, an implementation of the oracle can periodically use the peer-to-peer service to find the current set of derived responsible servers for x, and return any subset of them of size at least $(k - f)$.

Note that the choice of k and f, as well as the assumptions about the rate of change in the systems are dependent on the specific peer-to-peer system used, as well as other external environmental assumptions. This highlights the benefits of our approach, since we have identified generic abstractions and devised a generic protocol based on them. The specification of the protocol is independent of the low level assumptions needed to implement the abstractions. Similarly, the proof of correctness only relies on the functional properties of the abstractions, and does not rely on system dependent parameters.

7 Conclusion

This paper has investigated two matching abstractions suited to the implementation of atomic objects in a dynamic distributed system where servers can dynamically enter and leave the system (or crash). One of these abstractions concerns quorum systems, the other one communication. Both abstractions are complementary in the sense they address the two basic problems encountered when implementing atomic objects (data persistence and data consistency). Their conceptual simplicity is a great advantage that allows coping with and mastering the complexity of dynamic systems. As their definition is based on abstract properties (and not on low-level assumptions), they are problem-oriented and versatile.

A read protocol and a write protocol based on these abstractions have been described and proved correct. The properties defining these abstractions can be seen as requirements that are sufficient for implementing a dynamic storage service. Instantiating the proposed abstractions in different contexts (e.g., settings defined by specific assumptions on failures, synchrony, message delays and processing times) provides as many system specific protocols. It has also been shown that these abstractions can be realized in dynamic peer-to-peer systems satisfying appropriate requirements.

As a server has to return values and execute *Compare-&-Swap*-like operations (i.e., store a value only if its timestamp is newer than the existing one) , it can actually be either a process node or an active disk. It is consequently possible to envisage a hybrid dynamic server system made up of nodes and active disks.

References

1. Aguilera M.K., A Pleasant Stroll Through the Land of Infinitely Many Creatures. *ACM SIGACT News, Distributed Computing Column*, 35(2):36-59, 2004.
2. Aguilera M.K. and Gafni E., On Using Network Attached Disks as Shared Memory. *Proc. 21th ACM PODC*, ACM Press, pp. 315-324, 2003.
3. Alvisi L., Malkhi D., Pierce E., Reiter M and Wright R.N., Dynamic Byzantine Quorum Systems, *Proc. IEEE Conf. on Depend. Syst. and Networks (DSN'00)*, pp. 283-392, 2000.
4. Anceaume E., Friedman R., Gradinariu M. and Roy M., An Architecture for Dynamic Scalable Self-managed Transactions. *Proc. 6th International Symposium on Distributed Objects and Applications*, LNCS # 3291, pp. 1445-1462, 2004.
5. Attiya H., Bar-Noy A. and Dolev D., Sharing Memory Robustly in Message Passing Systems. *Journal of the ACM*, 42(1):121-132, 1995.
6. Chandra T.D. and Toueg S., Unreliable Failure Detectors for Reliable Distributed Systems. *Journal of the ACM*, 43(2):225-267, 1996.
7. Delporte-Gallet C., Fauconnier H. and Guerraoui R., Shared memory *vs* Message Passing. *Tech Report* IC/2003/77, EPFL, Lausanne, December 2003.
8. Delporte-Gallet C., Fauconnier H. and Guerraoui R., Hadzilacos V., Kouznetsov P. and Toueg S., The Weakest Failure Detectors to Solve Certain Fundamental Problems in Distributed Computing. *Proc. 23rd ACM PODC*, pp. 338-346, 2004.
9. Ezhilchelvan P., Helary J.-M. and Raynal M., Building TMR-Based Reliable Servers Despite Bounded Input Lifetime. *Proc. 7th European Parallel Computing Conference (Europar'01)*, Manchester (UK), LNCS # 2150, pp. 482-485, 2001.
10. Friedman R., Using Virtual Synchrony to Develop Efficient Fault Tolerant Distributed Shared Memories. Technical Report 95-1506, Dept. of Computer Science, Cornell University, 1995.
11. Friedman R., Mostefaoui A. and Raynal M., Asynchronous Bounded Lifetime Failure Detectors. *Information Processing Letters*, 94:85-91, 2005.
12. Friedman R. and Raynal M., On the Benefits of the Functional Modular Approach in Distributed Data Management Systems. *Proc. SRDS'04 IEEE satellite Workshop on Dependable Distributed Data Management (WDDDM'04)*, IEEE Computer Press, pp. 1-6, 2004.
13. Friedman R., Raynal M. and Travers C., Two Abstractions for Implementing Atomic Objects in Dynamic Systems. *Tech Report #1692*, IRISA, University of Rennes 1 (France), 2005.
14. Garcia-Molina H. and Barbara D., How to Assign Votes in a Distributed System. *Journal of the ACM*, 32(4):841-860, 1985.
15. Gifford D.K., Weighted Voting for Replicated Data. *Proc. 7th ACM Symposium on Operating Systems Principles (SOSP'79)*, ACM Press, pp. 150-162, 1979.
16. Guerraoui R. and Raynal M., Fault-Tolerance Techniques for Concurrent Objects. *Tech Report # 1667*, 22 pages, IRISA, Université de Rennes 1 (France), December 2004.
17. Hadzilacos V. and Toueg S., Reliable Broadcast and Related Problems. In *Distributed Systems*, ACM Press (S. Mullender Ed.), New-York, pp. 97-145, 1993.

18. Helary J.-M., Mostefaoui A. and Raynal M., Interval Consistency of Asynchronous Distributed Computations. *Journal of Computer and System Sciences,* 64(2):329-349, 2002.
19. Herlihy M.P., Dynamic Quorum Adjustment for Partitioned Data. *ACM Transactions on Database Systems,* 12(2):170-194, 1987.
20. Herlihy M.P., Wait-Free Synchronization. *ACM TOPLAS,* 13(1):124-149, 1991.
21. Herlihy M.P. and Wing J.L., Linearizability: a Correctness Condition for Concurrent Objects. *ACM Transactions on Programming Languages and Systems,* 12(3):463-492, 1990.
22. Lamport, L., Time, Clocks and the Ordering of Events in a Distributed System. *Communications of the ACM,* 21(7):558-565, 1978.
23. Lamport L., On Interprocess communication. Part I: Formalism. Part II: Algorithms. *Distributed Computing,* 1-2(2):87-103, 1986.
24. Lynch N.A. and Shvartsman A.A., RAMBO: a Reconfigurable Atomic Memory Service for Dynamic Networks. *Proc. 16th Int'l Symposium on Distributed Computing (DISC'02),* Springer-Verlag LNCS #2508, pp. 173-190, 2002.
25. Malkhi D. and Reiter M., Byzantine Quorums Systems, *Dist. Comp.,* 11(4):203-213, 1998.
26. Martin J.-P. and Alvisi L., A Framework for Dynamic Byzantine Storage, *Proc. IEEE Conf. on Dependable Systems and Networks (DSN'04),* pp. 325-334, 2004.
27. Merritt M. and Taubenfeld G., Computing Using Infinitely Many Processes. *Proc. 14th Int'l Symposium on Distributed Computing (DISC'00),* LNCS #1914, pp. 164-178, 2000.
28. Ratnasamy S., Handley M., Francis P. and Karp R., A Scalable content-Addressable Network. *Proc. ACM SIGCOMM Conf. on Applications, Technologies, Architectures, and Protocols for Computer Communication,* ACM Press, pp. 161-172, 2001.
29. Rodrigues R and Liskov B., Reconfigurable Byzantine Fault-tolerant Atomic Memory. Brief annoucement in *Proc. 24th ACM PODC,* ACM Press, p. 386, 2004.
30. Rowstron A. and Druschel P., Pastry: Scalable, Distributed Object Location and Routing for Large Scale peer-to-Peer Systems. *Proc.18th IFIP/ACM Int'l Conf. on Distributed Systems Platforms (Middleware 2001),* Springer-Verlag LNCS #2218, pp. 329-350, 2001.
31. Stoica I., Morris R., Liben-Nowell D., Karger D., Kaashoek M.F., Dabek F. and Balakrishnan H., Chord: A Scalable Peer-to-Peer Lookup Protocol for Internet Applications. *ACM/IEEE Transactions on Networking,* 11(1):17-32, 2003.
32. Thomas R.H., A Majority Consensus Approach to Concurrency Control for Multiple Copy Database. *ACM Transactions on Database Systems,* 4(2):180-229, 1979.
33. Vitenberg R. and Friedman R., On the Locality of Consistency Conditions. *Proc. 17th Int'l Symposium on Distributed Computing (DISC'03),* LNCS #2848, pp. 92-105, 2003.
34. Zhao B., Kubiatowicz J. and Joseph A., Tapestry: An Infrastructure for Fault-Tolerant Wide-area Location and Routing. *Technical Report UCB/CSD-01-1141,* U.C. Berkeley, 2001.

Parsimonious Asynchronous Byzantine-Fault-Tolerant Atomic Broadcast

HariGovind V. Ramasamy* and Christian Cachin

IBM Zurich Research Laboratory, CH-8803 Rüschlikon, Switzerland
hvr@zurich.ibm.com, cca@zurich.ibm.com

Abstract. Atomic broadcast is a communication primitive that allows a group of n parties to deliver a common sequence of payload messages despite the failure of some parties. We address the problem of asynchronous atomic broadcast when up to $t < n/3$ parties may exhibit Byzantine behavior. We provide the first protocol with an amortized expected message complexity of $\mathcal{O}(n)$ per delivered payload. The most efficient previous solutions are the BFT protocol by Castro and Liskov and the KS protocol by Kursawe and Shoup, both of which have message complexity $\mathcal{O}(n^2)$. Like the BFT and KS protocols, our protocol is optimistic and uses inexpensive mechanisms during periods when no faults occur; when network instability or faults are detected, it switches to a more expensive recovery mode. The key idea of our solution is to replace reliable broadcast in the KS protocol by consistent broadcast, which reduces the message complexity from $\mathcal{O}(n^2)$ to $\mathcal{O}(n)$ in the optimistic mode. But since consistent broadcast provides weaker guarantees than reliable broadcast, our recovery mode incorporates novel techniques to ensure that safety and liveness are always satisfied.

1 Introduction

Atomic broadcast is a fundamental communication primitive for the construction of fault-tolerant distributed systems. It allows a group of n parties to agree on a set of payload messages to deliver and also on their delivery order, despite the failure of up to t parties. A fault-tolerant service can be constructed using the state machine replication approach [1] by replicating the service on all n parties and propagating the state updates to the replicas using atomic broadcast.

In this paper, we present a new message-efficient atomic broadcast protocol that is suitable for building highly available and intrusion-tolerant services in the Internet [2, 3]. Since the Internet is an adversarial environment where an attacker can compromise and completely take over nodes, we allow the corrupted parties to deviate arbitrarily from the protocol specification thereby exhibiting so-called *Byzantine faults*. We work in an asynchronous system model for two reasons: (1) it best reflects the loosely synchronized nature of nodes in the Internet, and (2) not relying on synchrony assumptions for correctness also eliminates a potential vulnerability of the system that the adversary can exploit, for example, through denial-of-service attacks.

Any asynchronous atomic broadcast protocol must use randomization, since deterministic solutions cannot be guaranteed to terminate [4]. Early work focused on the

---

* Work done at University of Illinois at Urbana-Champaign, USA.

J.H. Anderson, G. Prencipe, and R. Wattenhofer (Eds.): OPODIS 2005, LNCS 3974, pp. 88–102, 2006.

polynomial-time feasibility of randomized agreement [5,6,7] and atomic broadcast [8], but such solutions are too expensive to use in practice. Many protocols have followed an alternative approach and avoided randomization completely by making stronger assumptions about the system model, in particular by assuming some degree of synchrony (like Rampart [9], SecureRing [10], and ITUA [11]). However, most of these protocols have an undesirable feature that makes them inapplicable for our purpose: they may violate safety if synchrony assumptions are not met.

Only recently, Cachin et al. proposed a practical asynchronous atomic broadcast [12] protocol that has optimal resilience $t < n/3$, relying on a trusted initialization process and on public-key cryptography. The protocol involves one randomized Byzantine agreement [13] per round of atomically delivered payload messages.

The BFT protocol by Castro and Liskov [14] and the protocol by Kursawe and Shoup [15] (the *KS protocol* for short) take an optimistic approach for providing more efficient asynchronous atomic broadcast while never violating safety. The motivation for such optimistic protocols is the observation that conditions are *normal* during most of a system's operation. Normal conditions refer to a stable network and no intrusions. Both protocols proceed in *epochs*, where an epoch consists of an *optimistic phase* and a *recovery phase*, and expect to spend most of their time operating in the optimistic phase which uses an inexpensive mechanism that is appropriate for normal conditions. The protocols switch to the more expensive recovery phase under unstable network or certain fault conditions. In every epoch, a designated party acts as a *leader* for the optimistic phase, determines the delivery order of the payloads, and conveys the chosen delivery order to the other parties through Bracha's reliable broadcast protocol [16], which guarantees delivery of a broadcast payload with the same content at all correct parties. Bracha's protocol is deterministic and involves $\mathcal{O}(n^2)$ messages; it is much more efficient than the most efficient randomized Byzantine agreement protocol [12], which requires expensive public-key cryptographic operations in addition. Consequently, both the BFT and KS protocols communicate $\mathcal{O}(n^2)$ messages per atomically delivered payload under normal conditions, i.e., they have *message complexity $\mathcal{O}(n^2)$*.

No protocol for asynchronous atomic broadcast with message complexity less than $\Theta(n^2)$ was known prior to our work. Our protocol for asynchronous atomic broadcast is the first to achieve optimal resilience $t < n/3$ and $\mathcal{O}(n)$ amortized expected message complexity. We call our protocol *parsimonious* because of this significant reduction in message complexity. Linear message complexity appears to be optimal for atomic broadcast because a protocol needs to send every payload to each party at least once and this requires n messages (assuming that payloads are not propagated to the parties in batches). Like the BFT and KS protocols, our protocol is *optimistic* in the sense that it progresses very fast during periods when the network is reasonably behaved and a party acting as designated *leader* is correct. Unlike the BFT protocol (and just like the KS protocol), our protocol guarantees both *safety* and *liveness* in asynchronous networks by relying on randomized agreement. The reduced message complexity of our protocol comes at the cost of introducing a digital signature computation for every delivered payload. But in a wide-area network (WAN), the cost of a public-key operation is small compared to message latency. And since our protocol is targeted at WANs, we expect the advantage of lower message complexity to outweigh the additional work incurred by the signature computations. A comparison of our protocol with the asynchronous atomic broadcast protocols mentioned above is given in Table 1.

Our Approach. The starting point for the development of our protocol, which we call **PABC**, is the BFT protocol [14]. In the BFT protocol, a leader determines the delivery order of payloads and conveys the order using reliable broadcast to other parties. The parties then atomically deliver the payloads in the order chosen by the leader. If the leader appears to be slow or exhibits faulty behavior, a party switches to the recovery mode. When enough correct parties have switched to recovery mode, the protocol ensures that all correct parties eventually start the recovery phase. The goal of the recovery phase is to start the next epoch in a consistent state and with a new leader. The difficulty lies in determining which payloads have been delivered in the optimistic phase of the past epoch. The BFT protocol delegates this task to the leader of the new epoch. But since the recovery phase of BFT is also deterministic, it may be that the new leader is evicted immediately, before it can do any useful work, and the epoch passes without delivering any payloads. This denial-of-service attack against the BFT protocol violates liveness but is unavoidable in asynchronous networks.

The KS protocol [15] prevents this attack by ensuring that at least one payload is delivered during the recovery phase. It employs a round of randomized multi-valued Byzantine agreement (MVBA) to agree on a set of payloads for atomic delivery, much like the asynchronous atomic broadcast protocol of Cachin et al. [12]. During the optimistic phase, the epoch leader conveys the delivery order through reliable broadcast as in BFT, which leads to an amortized message complexity of $\mathcal{O}(n^2)$.

Our approach is to replace reliable broadcast in the KS protocol with a consistent broadcast protocol, also known as *echo broadcast* [17]. The replacement directly leads to an amortized message complexity of only $\mathcal{O}(n)$. But consistent broadcast is weaker than reliable broadcast and guarantees agreement only among those correct parties that actually deliver the payload. Therefore, a corrupted leader may cause the fate of some payloads to be undefined in the sense that there might be only a single correct party that has delivered a payload from consistent broadcast, but no way for other correct parties to learn about this fact. We solve this problem by delaying the atomic delivery of a payload delivered from consistent broadcast until more payloads have been delivered from consistent broadcast. However, the delay introduces an additional problem of payloads getting "stuck" if no further payloads arrive. We address this by having the leader generate *dummy* payloads when no further payloads arrive within a certain time window.

The recovery phase in our protocol has a structure similar to that of the KS protocol, but is simpler and more efficient. At a high level, a first MVBA instance ensures that all correct parties agree on a synchronization point. Then, the protocol ensures that all correct parties atomically deliver the payloads up to that point; to implement this step, every party must store all payloads that were delivered in the optimistic phase, together with information that proves the fact that they were delivered. A second MVBA instance is used to atomically deliver at least one payload, which guarantees that the protocol makes progress in every epoch.

Organization of the Paper. The rest of the paper is organized as follows. Section 2 introduces preliminaries, some protocol primitives on which our algorithm relies, and the

Table 1. Comparison of Efficient Byzantine-Fault-Tolerant Atomic Broadcast Protocols

Protocol	Sync. for Safety?	Sync. for Liveness?	Public-key Operations?	Message Complexity	
				Normal	Worst-case
Rampart [9]	yes	yes	yes	$\mathcal{O}(n)$	unbounded
SecureRing [10]	yes	yes	yes	$\mathcal{O}(n)$	unbounded
ITUA [11]	yes	yes	yes	$\mathcal{O}(n)$	unbounded
Cachin et al. [12]	no	no	yes	exp. $\mathcal{O}(n^2)$	exp. $\mathcal{O}(n^2)$
BFT [14]	no	yes	no	$\mathcal{O}(n^2)$	unbounded
KS [15]	no	no	yes	$\mathcal{O}(n^2)$	exp. $\mathcal{O}(n^2)$
Protocol PABC	no	no	yes	$\mathcal{O}(n)$	exp. $\mathcal{O}(n^2)$

definition of atomic broadcast. The protocol is presented in Section 3, and its practical significance is discussed in Section 4. For lack of space, the details of the formal system model and the analysis of our protocol are contained in the full version [18].

2   Preliminaries

2.1   System Model

This section contains an overview of the system model. We consider an asynchronous distributed system model equivalent to the one of Cachin et al. [12], in which there are no bounds on relative processing speeds and message delays. The system consists of n parties $P_1, \ldots, P_n$ and an *adversary*. Up to $t < n/3$ parties are controlled by the adversary and are called *corrupted*; the other parties are called *correct*. We use a *static* corruption model, and there is an initialization algorithm run by a trusted *dealer* for system setup. All computations by the parties, the adversary, and the dealer are probabilistic, polynomial-time algorithms. Since our model is based on the formal approach in cryptography, we allow for a negligible probability of failure in the specification of our protocols. The system model includes a digital signature scheme that is secure against existential forgery using adaptive chosen-message attacks [19].

Each pair of parties is linked by an *authenticated asynchronous channel* that provides message integrity. Messages on the channels are scheduled by the adversary. However, we assume that every message on a channel between two correct parties is *eventually* delivered. Every protocol instance is identified by a unique string ID, called the *tag*. Formally, the local interface to our protocols consists of *input actions*, which are messages of the form $(ID, \text{in}, type, \ldots)$ and *output actions*, which are messages of the form $(ID, \text{out}, type, \ldots)$. The parties receive and generate *protocol messages* of the form $(ID, type, \ldots)$, which are delivered to other parties over the channels. Before a party starts to process messages for an instance ID, the instance with that ID must be *initialized*.

2.2   Protocol Primitives

Our atomic broadcast protocol relies on a consistent broadcast protocol with special properties and on a Byzantine agreement protocol.

Strong Consistent Broadcast. We enhance the notion of consistent broadcast found in the literature [12] to develop the notion that we call *strong consistent broadcast.* Ordinary consistent broadcast provides a way for a designated sender P_s to broadcast a payload to all parties and requires that any two correct parties that deliver the payload agree on its content.

The standard protocol for implementing ordinary consistent broadcast is Reiter's *echo broadcast* [17]; it involves $\mathcal{O}(n)$ messages, has a latency of three message flows, and relies on a digital signature scheme. The sender starts the protocol by sending the payload m to all parties; then it waits for a quorum of $\lceil \frac{n+t+1}{2} \rceil$ parties to issue a signature on the payload and to "echo" the payload and the signature to the sender. When the sender has collected and verified enough signatures, it composes a final protocol message containing the signatures and sends it to all parties.

With a faulty sender, an ordinary consistent broadcast protocol permits executions in which some parties fail to deliver the payload when others succeed. Therefore, a useful enhancement of consistent broadcast is a transfer mechanism, which allows any party that has delivered the payload to help others do the same. For reasons that will be evident later, we introduce another enhancement and require that when a correct party terminates a consistent broadcast and delivers a payload, there must be a quorum of at least $n - t$ parties (instead of only $\lceil \frac{n+t+1}{2} \rceil$) who participated in the protocol and approved the delivered payload. We call consistent broadcast with such a transfer mechanism and the special quorum rule *strong consistent broadcast.*

Formally, every broadcast instance is identified by a tag *ID*. At the sender P_s, strong consistent broadcast is invoked by an input action of the form $(ID, \text{in}, \text{sc-broadcast}, m)$, with $m \in \{0, 1\}^*$. When that occurs, we say P_s *sc-broadcasts m with tag ID.* Only P_s executes this action; all other parties start the protocol only when they initialize instance *ID* in their role as receivers. A party terminates a consistent broadcast of m tagged with *ID* by generating an output action of the form $(ID, \text{out}, \text{sc-deliver}, m)$. In that case, we say P_i *sc-delivers m with tag ID.*

For the transfer mechanism, a correct party that has *sc-delivered* m with tag *ID* should be able to output a bit string M_{ID} that *completes* the *sc-broadcast* in the following sense: any correct party that has not yet *sc-delivered* m can run a *validation algorithm* on M_{ID} (this may involve a public key associated with the protocol), and if M_{ID} is determined to be *valid*, the party can also *sc-deliver* m from M_{ID}.

Definition 1 (Strong consistent broadcast). *A protocol for strong consistent broadcast satisfies the following conditions except with negligible probability.*

Termination: If a correct party sc-broadcasts *m with tag ID, then all correct parties eventually* sc-deliver *m with tag ID.*

Agreement: If two correct parties P_i and P_j sc-deliver *m and m' with tag ID, respectively, then $m = m'$.*

Integrity: Every correct party sc-delivers *at most one payload m with tag ID. Moreover, if the sender P_s is correct, then m was previously* sc-broadcast *by P_s with tag ID.*

Transferability: After a correct party has sc-delivered *m with tag ID, it can generate a string M_{ID} such that any correct party that has not* sc-delivered *a message with tag ID is able to* sc-deliver *some message immediately upon processing M_{ID}.*

Strong unforgeability: For any ID, it is computationally infeasible to generate a value M that is accepted as valid by the validation algorithm for completing ID unless $n - 2t$ correct parties have initialized instance ID and actively participated in the protocol.

Given the above implementation of consistent broadcast, one can obtain strong consistent broadcast with two simple modifications. The completing string M_{ID} for ensuring transferability consists of the final protocol message; the attached signatures are sufficient to allow for any other party to complete the *sc-broadcast*. Strong unforgeability is obtained by setting the signature quorum to $n - t$.

With signatures of size K bits, the echo broadcast protocol has communication complexity $\mathcal{O}\big(n(|m| + nK)\big)$ bits, where $|m|$ denotes the bit length of the payload m. By replacing the quorum of signatures with a threshold signature [20], it is possible to reduce the communication complexity to $\mathcal{O}\big(n(|m| + K)\big)$ bits [12], under the reasonable assumption that the lengths of a threshold signature and a signature share are also at most K bits [21].

Multi-valued Byzantine Agreement. We use a protocol for multi-valued Byzantine agreement (MVBA) as defined by Cachin et al. [12], which allows agreement values from an arbitrary domain instead of being restricted to binary values. Unlike previous MVBA protocols, their protocol does not allow the decision to fall back on a *default* value if not all correct parties propose the same value, but uses a protocol-external mechanism instead. This so-called *external validity condition* is specified by a global, polynomial-time computable predicate Q_{ID}, which is known to all parties and is typically determined by an external application or higher-level protocol. Each party proposes a value that contains certain validation information. The protocol ensures that the decision value was proposed by at least one party, and that the decision value satisfies Q_{ID}.

When a party P_i starts an MVBA protocol instance with tag *ID* and an input value $v \in \{0,1\}^*$ that satisfies predicate Q_{ID}, we say that P_i *proposes v for multi-valued agreement with tag ID and predicate Q_{ID}*. Correct parties only propose values that satisfy Q_{ID}. When P_i terminates the MVBA protocol instance with tag *ID* and outputs a value v, we say that it *decides v for ID*.

Definition 2 (Multi-valued Byzantine agreement). *A protocol for* multi-valued Byzantine agreement *with predicate Q_{ID} satisfies the following conditions except with negligible probability.*

External Validity: Any correct party that decides for ID decides v such that $Q_{ID}(v)$ holds.

Agreement: If some correct party decides v for ID, then any correct party that decides for ID decides v.

Integrity: If all parties are correct and if some party decides v for ID, then some party proposed v for ID.

Termination: All correct parties eventually decide for ID.

We use the MVBA protocol of Cachin et al. [12], which has expected message complexity $\mathcal{O}(n^2)$ and expected communication complexity $\mathcal{O}\big(n^3 + n^2(K + L)\big)$, where K is the length of a threshold signature and L is a bound on the length of the values that can be proposed.

2.3   Definition of Atomic Broadcast

Atomic broadcast provides a "broadcast channel" abstraction [22], such that all correct parties deliver the same set of messages broadcast on the channel in the same order. A party P_i *atomically broadcasts* (or *a-broadcasts*) a payload m with tag *ID* when an input action of the form $(ID, \text{in}, \text{a-broadcast}, m)$ with $m \in \{0, 1\}^*$ is delivered to P_i. Broadcasts are parameterized by the tag *ID* to identify their corresponding broadcast channel. A party *atomically delivers* (or *a-delivers*) a payload m with tag *ID* by generating an output action of the form $(ID, \text{out}, \text{a-deliver}, m)$. A party may *a-broadcast* and *a-deliver* an arbitrary number of messages with the same tag.

Definition 3 (Atomic broadcast). *A protocol for atomic broadcast satisfies the following properties except with negligible probability.*

Validity: If $t + 1$ correct parties a-broadcast *some payload m with tag ID, then some correct party eventually* a-delivers *m with tag ID.*

Agreement: If some correct party has a-delivered *m with tag ID, then all correct parties eventually* a-deliver *m with tag ID.*

Total Order: If two correct parties both a-delivered *distinct payloads m_1 and m_2 with tag ID, then they have* a-delivered *them in the same order.*

Integrity: For any payload m, a correct party P_j a-delivers *m with tag ID at most once. Moreover, if all parties are correct, then m was previously* a-broadcast *by some party with tag ID.*

The above properties are similar to the definitions of Cachin et al. [12] and of Kursawe and Shoup [15]. We do not formalize their *fairness* condition, although Protocol **PABC** satisfies an equivalent notion.

3   The Parsimonious Atomic Broadcast Protocol

We now describe Protocol **PABC** in detail. The line numbers refer to the detailed protocol description in Figures 1–3.

3.1   Optimistic Phase

Every party keeps track of the current epoch number e and stores all payloads that it has received to *a-broadcast* but not yet *a-delivered* in its *initiation queue $\mathcal{I}$*. An element x can be appended to $\mathcal{I}$ by an operation $append(x, \mathcal{I})$, and an element x that occurs anywhere in $\mathcal{I}$ can be removed by an operation $remove(x, \mathcal{I})$. A party also maintains an array log of size B that acts as a buffer for all payloads to *a-deliver* in the current epoch. Additionally, a party stores a set $\mathcal{D}$ of all payloads that have been *a-delivered* so far.

Normal Protocol Operation. When a party receives a request to *a-broadcast* a payload m, it appends m to $\mathcal{I}$ and immediately forwards m using an `initiate` message to the leader P_l of the epoch, where $l = e \mod n$ (lines 12–14). When this happens, we say P_i *initiates* the payload.

initialization:

1: $e \leftarrow 0$ {current epoch}
2: $\mathcal{I} \leftarrow []$ {initiation queue, list of *a-broadcast* but not *a-delivered* payloads}
3: $\mathcal{D} \leftarrow \emptyset$ {set of *a-delivered* payloads}
4: *init_epoch*()

function *init_epoch*():

5: $l \leftarrow (e \bmod n) + 1$ {P_l is leader of epoch e}
6: $log \leftarrow []$ {array of size B containing payloads committed in current epoch}
7: $s \leftarrow 0$ {sequence number of next payload within epoch}
8: $complained \leftarrow \texttt{false}$ {indicates if this party already complained about P_l}
9: $start\_recovery \leftarrow \texttt{false}$ {signals the switch to the recovery phase}
10: $c \leftarrow 0$ {number of $\texttt{complain}$ messages received for epoch leader}
11: $\mathcal{S} \leftarrow \mathcal{D}$ {set of *a-delivered* or already *sc-broadcast* payloads at P_l}

upon $(ID, \texttt{in}, \texttt{a-broadcast}, m)$:

12: send $(ID, \texttt{initiate}, e, m)$ to P_l
13: $append(m, \mathcal{I})$
14: $update_{\mathcal{F}_l}(\texttt{initiate}, m)$

forever: {optimistic phase}

15: **if** $\neg complained$ **then** {leader P_l is not suspected}
16:     initialize an instance of strong consistent broadcast with tag $ID|\texttt{bind}.e.s$
17:     $m \leftarrow \bot$
18:     **if** $i = l$ **then**
19:         **wait for** $timeout(T)$ **or** receipt of a message $(ID, \texttt{initiate}, e, m)$
              such that $m \notin \mathcal{S}$
20:         **if** $timeout(T)$ **then**
21:             $m \leftarrow \text{dummy}$
22:         **else**
23:             $\mathcal{S} \leftarrow \mathcal{S} \cup \{m\}$
24:             $stop(T)$
25:         *sc-broadcast* the message m with tag $ID|\texttt{bind}.e.s$
26:     **wait for** $start\_recovery$ **or** *sc-delivery* of some m with tag $ID|\texttt{bind}.e.s$
          such that $m \notin \mathcal{D} \cup log$
27:     **if** $start\_recovery$ **then**
28:         $recovery()$
29:     **else**
30:         $log[s] \leftarrow m$
31:         **if** $s \geq 2$ **then**
32:             $update_{\mathcal{F}_l}(\texttt{deliver}, log[s-2])$
33:             $deliver(log[s-2])$
34:         **if** $i = l$ **and** $(log[s] \neq \text{dummy}$ **or** $(s > 0$ **and** $log[s-1] \neq \text{dummy}))$ **then**
35:             $start(T)$
36:         $s \leftarrow s + 1$
37:         **if** $s \bmod B = 0$ **then**
38:             $recovery()$

Fig. 1. Protocol PABC for party P_i and tag ID (Part I)

---

function $deliver(m)$:

    39: **if** $m \neq$ dummy **then**

    40:     $remove(m, \mathcal{I})$

    41:     $\mathcal{D} \leftarrow \mathcal{D} \cup \{m\}$

    42:     output $(ID, \text{out}, \text{a-deliver}, m)$

upon receiving message $(ID, \text{complain}, e)$ from P_j for the first time:

    43: $c \leftarrow c + 1$

    44: **if** $(c = t + 1)$ **and** $\neg complained$ **then**

    45:     $complain()$

    46: **else if** $c = 2t + 1$ **then**

    47:     $start\_recovery \leftarrow$ true

function $complain()$:

    48: send $(ID, \text{complain}, e)$ to all parties

    49: $complained \leftarrow$ true

predicate $Q_{ID|\text{watermark}.e}\Big(\big[(s_1, C_1, \sigma_1), \ldots, (s_n, C_n, \sigma_n) \big] \Big) \equiv$

    $\big($for at least $n - t$ distinct j, $s_j \neq \bot \big)$ **and**

    $\big($for all $j = 1, \ldots, n$, it holds $(s_j = \bot)$ **or**

        $(\sigma_j$ is a valid signature by P_j on $(ID, \text{committed}, e, s_j, C_j)$ **and** $(s_j = -1$

        or the value C_j completes the *sc-broadcast* with tag $ID|\text{bind}.e.s_j)))$

predicate $Q_{ID|\text{deliver}.e}\Big(\big[(\mathcal{I}_1, \sigma_1), \ldots, \mathcal{I}_n, \sigma_n) \big] \Big) \equiv$

    for at least $n - t$ distinct j,

        $(\mathcal{I}_j \cap \mathcal{D} = \emptyset$ **and** σ_j is a valid signature by P_j on $(ID, \text{queue}, e, j, \mathcal{I}_j))$

Fig. 2. Protocol PABC for party P_i and tag ID (Part II)

The leader binds a sequence number to every payload that it receives in an initiate message, and conveys the binding to the other parties through strong consistent broadcast. For this purpose, all parties execute a loop (lines 15–38) that starts with an instance of strong consistent broadcast (lines 15–26). The leader acts as the sender of strong consistent broadcast and the tag contains the epoch e and a sequence number s. Here, s starts from 0 in every epoch. The leader *sc-broadcasts* the next available initiated payload, and every party waits to *sc-deliver* some payload m. When m is *sc-delivered*, P_i stores it in *log*, but does not yet *a-deliver* it (line 30). At this point in time, we say that P_i has *committed* sequence number s to payload m in epoch e. Then, P_i *a-delivers* the payload to which it has committed the sequence number $s - 2$ (if available, lines 31–33). It increments s (line 36) and returns to the start of the loop.

Delaying the *a-delivery* of the payload committed to s until sequence number $s + 2$ has been committed is necessary to prevent the above problem of payloads whose fate is undefined. However, the delay results in another problem if no further payloads, those with sequence numbers higher than s, are *sc-delivered*. We solve this problem by instructing the leader to send dummy messages to eject the original payload(s) from the buffer. The leader triggers such a dummy message whenever a corresponding timer

function *recovery*():

    {*Part 1: agree on watermark*}

50: compute a signature σ on $(ID, \texttt{committed}, e, s - 1)$

51: send the message $(ID, \texttt{committed}, e, s - 1, C, \sigma)$ to all parties, where C denotes
      the bit string that completes the *sc-broadcast* with tag $ID|\texttt{bind}.e.(s - 1)$

52: $(s_j, C_j, \sigma_j) \leftarrow (\bot, \bot, \bot) \qquad (1 \le j \le n)$

53: **wait for** $n - t$ messages $(ID, \texttt{committed}, e, s_j, C_j, \sigma_j)$ from distinct P_j s.t.
      C_j completes the *sc-broadcast* instance $ID|\texttt{bind}.e.s_j$ and σ_j is a valid
      signature on $(ID, \texttt{committed}, e, s_j)$

54: $W \leftarrow [(s_1, C_1, \sigma_1), \ldots, (s_n, C_n, \sigma_n)]$

55: propose W for MVBA with tag $ID|\texttt{watermark}.e$ and predicate $Q_{ID|\texttt{watermark}.e}$

56: **wait for** MVBA with tag $ID|\texttt{watermark}.e$ to decide
      some $\bar{W} = [(\bar{s}_1, \bar{C}_1, \bar{\sigma}_1), \ldots, (\bar{s}_n, \bar{C}_n, \bar{\sigma}_n)]$

57: $w \leftarrow \max\{\bar{s}_1, \ldots, \bar{s}_n\} - 1$

    {*Part 2: synchronize up to watermark*}

58: $s' \leftarrow s - 2$

59: **while** $s' \le \min\{s - 1, w\}$ **do**

60:    **if** $s' \ge 0$ **then**

61:      *deliver*($log[s']$)

62:    $s' \leftarrow s' + 1$

63: **if** $s > w$ **then**

64:    **for** $j = 1, \ldots, n$ **do**

65:      $u \leftarrow \max\{s_j, \bar{s}_j\}$

66:      $\mathcal{M} \leftarrow \{M_v\}$ for $v = u, \ldots, w$, where M_v completes the *sc-broadcast*
        instance $ID|\texttt{bind}.e.v$

67:      send message $(ID, \texttt{complete}, \mathcal{M})$ to P_j

68: **while** $s \le w$ **do**

69:    **wait for** a message $(ID, \texttt{complete}, \bar{\mathcal{M}})$ such that $\bar{M}_s \in \bar{\mathcal{M}}$ completes
      sc-broadcast with tag $ID|\texttt{bind}.e.s$

70:    use $\bar{M}_s$ to *sc-deliver* some m with tag $ID|\texttt{bind}.e.s$

71:    *deliver*(m)

72:    $s \leftarrow s + 1$

    {*Part 3: deliver some messages*}

73: compute a digital signature σ on $(ID, \texttt{queue}, e, i, \mathcal{I})$

74: send the message $(ID, \texttt{queue}, e, i, \mathcal{I}, \sigma)$ to all parties

75: $(\mathcal{I}_j, \sigma_j) \leftarrow (\bot, \bot) \qquad (1 \le j \le n)$

76: **wait for** $n - t$ messages $(ID, \texttt{queue}, e, j, \mathcal{I}_j, \sigma_j)$ from distinct P_j s.t. σ_j is a
      valid signature from P_j and $\mathcal{I}_j \cap \mathcal{D} = \emptyset$

77: $Q \leftarrow [(\mathcal{I}_1, \sigma_1), \ldots, (\mathcal{I}_n, \sigma_n)]$

78: propose Q for MVBA with tag $ID|\texttt{deliver}.e$ and predicate $Q_{ID|\texttt{deliver}.e}$

79: **wait for** MVBA $ID|\texttt{deliver}.e$ to decide some $\bar{Q} = [(\bar{\mathcal{I}}_1, \bar{\sigma}_1), \ldots, (\bar{\mathcal{I}}_n, \bar{\sigma}_n)]$

80: **for** $m \in \bigcup_{j=1}^{n} \bar{\mathcal{I}}_j \setminus \mathcal{D}$, in some deterministic order **do**

81:    *deliver*(m)

82: *init_epoch*()

83: **for** $m \in \mathcal{I}$ **do**

84:    send $(ID, \texttt{initiate}, e, m)$ to P_l

Fig. 3. Protocol PABC for party P_i and tag ID (Part III)

T expires (lines 20–21); T is activated whenever one of the current or the preceding sequence numbers was committed to a non-dummy payload (lines 34–35), and T is disabled when the leader sc-broadcasts a non-dummy payload (line 24). Thus, the leader sends at most two dummy payloads to eject a non-dummy payload.

Failure Detection and Switching to the Recovery Phase. There are two conditions under which the protocol switches to recovery phase: (1) when B payloads have been committed (line 38) and (2) when the leader is not functioning properly. The first condition is needed to keep the buffer *log* bounded and the second condition is needed to prevent a corrupted leader from violating liveness.

To determine if the leader of the epoch performs its job correctly, every party has access to a leader failure detector $\mathcal{F}_l$. For simplicity, Figures 1–3 do not include the pseudocode for $\mathcal{F}_l$. The protocol provides an interface *complain*(), which $\mathcal{F}_l$ can asynchronously invoke to notify the protocol about its suspicion that the leader is corrupted. Our protocol synchronously invokes an interface $update_{\mathcal{F}_l}$ of $\mathcal{F}_l$ to convey protocol-specific information (during execution of the $update_{\mathcal{F}_l}$ call, $\mathcal{F}_l$ has access to all variables of Protocol **PABC**).

An implementation of $\mathcal{F}_l$ can check whether the leader is making progress based on a timeout and protocol information as follows. Recall that every party maintains a queue $\mathcal{I}$ of initiated but not yet *a-delivered* payloads. When P_i has initiated some m, it calls $update_{\mathcal{F}_l}(\texttt{initiate}, m)$ (line 14); this starts a timer $T_{\mathcal{F}_l}$ unless it is already activated. When a payload is *a-delivered* during the optimistic phase, the call to $update_{\mathcal{F}_l}(\texttt{deliver}, m)$ (line 32) checks whether the *a-delivered* payload is the first undelivered payload in $\mathcal{I}$, and if it is, disables $T_{\mathcal{F}_l}$. When $T_{\mathcal{F}_l}$ expires, $\mathcal{F}_l$ invokes *complain*().

When P_i executes *complain*(), it sends a `complain` message to all parties (line 48); it also sets the *complained* flag (line 49) and stops participating in the sc-broadcasts by not initializing the next instance. When a correct party receives $2t + 1$ `complain` messages, it enters the recovery phase. There is a complaint "amplification" mechanism by which a correct party that has received $t + 1$ `complain` messages and has not yet complained itself joins the complaining parties by sending its own `complain` message. Complaint amplification ensures that when some correct party enters the recovery phase, all other correct parties eventually enter it as well.

3.2   Recovery Phase

The recovery phase consists of three parts: determining a watermark sequence number, synchronizing all parties up to the watermark, and delivering some payloads before entering the next epoch.

Part 1: Agree on Watermark. The first part of the recovery phase determines a *watermark* sequence number w with the properties that (a) at least $t + 1$ correct parties have committed all sequence numbers less than or equal to w in epoch e, and (b) no sequence number higher than $w + 2$ has been committed by a correct party in epoch e.

Upon entering the recovery phase of epoch e, a party sends out a signed `committed` message containing $s - 1$, the highest sequence number that it has committed in this epoch. It justifies $s - 1$ by adding the bit string C that completes the *sc-broadcast* instance with tag e and $s-1$ (lines 50–51). Then, a party receives $n-t$ such committed messages with valid signatures and valid completion bit strings. It collects the received committed messages in a *watermark proposal vector* W and proposes W for MVBA. Once the agreement protocol decides on a *watermark decision vector* $\bar{W}$ (lines 52–56), the watermark w is set to the maximum of the sequence numbers in $\bar{W}$ minus 1 (line 57).

Consider the maximal sequence number $\bar{s}_j$ in $\bar{W}$ and the corresponding $\bar{C}_j$. It may be that P_j is corrupted or that P_j is the only correct party that ever committed $\bar{s}_j$ in epoch e. But the values contain enough evidence to conclude that at least $n - 2t \geq t + 1$ correct parties contributed to this instance of strong consistent broadcast. Hence, these parties have previously committed $\bar{s}_j - 1$. This ensures the first property of the watermark above.

Although one or more correct parties may have committed $w + 1$ and $w + 2$, none of them has already *a-delivered* the corresponding payloads, because this would contradict the definition of w. Hence, these sequence numbers can safely be discarded. The discarding also ensures the second property of the watermark above. It is precisely for this reason that we delay the *a-delivery* of a payload to which sequence number s was committed until $s+2$ has been committed. Without it, the protocol could end up in a situation where up to t correct parties *a-delivered* a payload with sequence number $w + 1$ or $w + 2$, but it would be impossible for all correct parties to learn about this fact and to learn the *a-delivered* payload.

Part 2: Synchronize Up to Watermark. The second part of the recovery phase (lines 58–72) ensures that all parties *a-deliver* the payloads with sequence numbers less than or equal to w. It does so in a straightforward way using the *transferability* property of strong consistent broadcast.

In particular, every correct party P_i that has committed sequence number w (there must be at least $t + 1$ such correct parties by the definition of w) computes *completing strings* M_s for $s = 0, \ldots, w$ that complete the *sc-broadcast* instance with sequence number s. It can do so using the information stored in *log*. Potentially, P_i has to send $M_0, \ldots, M_w$ to *all* parties, but one can apply the following optimization to reduce the communication. Note that P_i knows from at least $n - t$ parties P_j their highest committed sequence number s_j (either directly from a committed message or from the watermark decision vector); if P_i knows nothing from some P_j, it has to assume $s_j = 0$. Then P_i simply sends a complete message with $M_{s_j+1}, \ldots, M_w$ to P_j for $j = 1, \ldots, n$. Every party receives these completing strings until it is able to *a-deliver* all payloads committed to the sequence numbers up to w.

Part 3: Deliver Some Messages. Part 3 of the recovery phase (lines 73–84) ensures that the protocol makes progress by *a-delivering* some messages before the next epoch starts. In an asynchronous network, implementing this property must rely on randomized agreement or on a failure detector [4]. This part uses one round of MVBA and is derived from the atomic broadcast protocol of Cachin et al. [12].

Every party P_i sends a signed queue message with all undelivered payloads in its initiation queue to all others (lines 73–74), collects a vector Q of $n - t$ such messages with valid signatures (lines 75–77), and proposes Q for MVBA. Once the agreement protocol has decided on a vector $\bar{Q}$ (lines 78–79), party P_i delivers the payloads in $\bar{Q}$ according to some deterministic order (lines 80–81).

Then P_i increments the epoch number and starts the next epoch by re-sending `initiate` messages for all remaining payloads in its initiation queue to the new leader (lines 82–84).

3.3 Analysis

Theorem 1. *Given a digital signature scheme, a protocol for strong consistent broadcast, and a protocol for multi-valued Byzantine agreement, Protocol* **PABC** *provides atomic broadcast for* $n > 3t$.

The proof can be found in the full version [18].

To analyze the complexity of Protocol **PABC**, we assume that strong consistent broadcast is implemented by the echo broadcast protocol using threshold signatures and that MVBA is implemented by the protocol of Cachin et al. [12], as described in Section 2.2.

For a payload m that is *a-delivered* in the optimistic phase, the message complexity is $\mathcal{O}(n)$, and the communication complexity is $\mathcal{O}(n(|m| + K))$, where the length of a threshold signature and a signature share are at most K bits.

The recovery phase incurs higher message and communication complexities because it exchanges the *log* of the epoch and involves Byzantine agreement. Parts 1 and 3 use MVBA with proposal values of length $\mathcal{O}(n|m|)$; hence, the expected message complexity is $\mathcal{O}(n^2)$ and the expected communication complexity is $\mathcal{O}(n^3|m|)$. In part 2, $\mathcal{O}(n^2)$ `complete` messages are exchanged; each of the $w \le B$ completing strings in a `complete` message may be $\mathcal{O}(|m| + K)$ bits long, where m denotes the longest *a-delivered* payload in the epoch; this leads to a communication complexity of $\mathcal{O}(n^2 B(|m| + K))$.

Hence, for a payload that is *a-delivered* in the recovery phase, the cost is dominated by the MVBA protocol, resulting in an expected message complexity of $\mathcal{O}(n^2)$ and an expected communication complexity of $\mathcal{O}(n^2(n + B)(|m| + K))$. Assuming that the protocol stays in the optimistic mode as long as possible and *a-delivers* B payloads before executing recovery, the *amortized* expected complexities per payload over an epoch are $\mathcal{O}(n + \frac{n^2}{B})$ messages and $\mathcal{O}(\frac{n^3}{B}(|m| + K))$ bits. It is reasonable to set $B \gg n$, so that we achieve amortized expected message complexity $\mathcal{O}(n)$ as claimed.

3.4 Optimizations

Both the BFT and KS protocols process multiple sequence numbers in parallel using a sliding window mechanism. For simplicity, our protocol description does not include this optimization and processes only the highest sequence number during every iteration of the loop in the optimistic phase. However, Protocol **PABC** can easily be adapted to process Ω payloads concurrently. In that case, up to Ω *sc-broadcast* instances are active in parallel, and the delay of two sequence numbers between *sc-delivery* and *a-delivery* of a payload is set to 2Ω. In part 1 of the recovery phase, the watermark is set to the maximum of the sequence numbers in the watermark decision vector minus Ω, instead of the maximum minus 1.

In our protocol description, the leader *sc-broadcasts* one initiated payload at a time. However, Protocol **PABC** can be modified to process a *batch* of payload messages at a time by committing sequence numbers to batches of payloads, as opposed to single payloads. The leader *sc-broadcasts* a batch of payloads in one instance, and all payloads in an *sc-delivered* batch are *a-delivered* in some deterministic order. This optimization has been shown to increase the throughput of the BFT protocol considerably [14].

Although the leader failure detector described in Section 3.1 is sufficient to ensure liveness, it is possible to enhance it using protocol information as follows. The leader in the optimistic phase will never have to *sc-broadcast* more than two dummy messages consecutively to evict non-dummy payloads from the buffer. The failure detector oracle can maintain a counter to keep track of and restrict the number of successive dummy payloads *sc-broadcast* by the leader. If m is a non-dummy payload, the call to $update_{\mathcal{F}_l}(\texttt{deliver}, m)$ upon *a-delivery* of payload m resets the counter; otherwise, the counter is incremented. If the counter ever exceeds 2, then $\mathcal{F}_l$ invokes the *complain*() function.

4   Practical Significance

In our formal system model, the adversary controls the scheduling of messages and hence the timeouts; thus, the adversary can cause parties to complain about a correctly functioning leader resulting in unnecessary transitions from the optimistic phase to the recovery phase. In contrast to the formal model, the network in a real-world setting will not always behave in the worst possible manner. The motivation for Protocol **PABC** — or any optimistic protocol such as the BFT and KS protocols for that matter — is the hope that timing assumptions based on stable network conditions have a high likelihood of being accurate. Practical observations indicate that unstable network conditions are the exception rather than the norm. During periods of stability and when no new intrusions are detected, our protocol will make fast progress, but both safety and liveness are still guaranteed even if the network is unstable.

Acknowledgments

We are grateful to Bill Sanders for support, interesting discussions, and comments on improving the quality of the paper. We also thank Jenny Applequist for her editorial comments.

This work was supported in part by NSF under Grant No. CNS-0406351 and in part by the European Commission through the IST Programme under Contract IST-2002-507932 ECRYPT.

References

1. Schneider, F.B.: Implementing fault-tolerant services using the state machine approach: A tutorial. ACM Computing Surveys **22**(4) (1990) 299–319
2. Cachin, C.: Distributing trust on the Internet. In: Proc. Intl. Conf. Dependable Systems and Networks. (2001) 183–192

3. Schneider, F.B., Zhou, L.: Distributed trust: Supporting fault-tolerance and attack-tolerance. Technical Report TR 2004-1924, Cornell University (2004)
4. Fischer, M.J., Lynch, N.A., Paterson, M.S.: Impossibility of distributed consensus with one faulty process. Journal of the ACM **32**(2) (1985) 372–382
5. Rabin, M.O.: Randomized Byzantine generals. In: Proc. 24th Symp. Foundations of Computer Science. (1983) 403–409
6. Canetti, R., Rabin, T.: Fast asynchronous Byzantine agreement with optimal resilience. In: Proc. 25th Symp. Theory of Computing. (1993) 42–51
7. Berman, P., Garay, J.A.: Randomized distributed agreement revisited. In: Proc. 23th Intl. Symp. Fault-Tolerant Computing. (1993) 412–419
8. Berman, P., Bharali, A.A.: Quick atomic broadcast. In: Proc. 7th Intl. Workshop on Distributed Algorithms. Volume 725 of Lecture Notes in Computer Science. (1993) 189–203
9. Reiter, M.K.: The Rampart toolkit for building high-integrity services. In: Theory and Practice in Distributed Systems. Volume 938 of Lecture Notes in Computer Science. (1995) 99–110
10. Kihlstrom, K.P., Moser, L.E., Melliar-Smith, P.M.: The SecureRing protocols for securing group communication. In: Proc. 31st Hawaii Intl. Conf. on System Sciences. (1998) 317–326
11. Ramasamy, H.V., Pandey, P., Lyons, J., Cukier, M., Sanders, W.H.: Quantifying the cost of providing intrusion tolerance in group communication systems. In: Proc. Intl. Conf. Dependable Systems and Networks. (2002) 229–238
12. Cachin, C., Kursawe, K., Petzold, F., Shoup, V.: Secure and efficient asynchronous broadcast protocols (extended abstract). In: Advances in Cryptology: CRYPTO 2001. Volume 2139 of Lecture Notes in Computer Science. (2001) 524–541
13. Cachin, C., Kursawe, K., Shoup, V.: Random oracles in Constantinople: Practical asynchronous Byzantine agreement using cryptography. Journal of Cryptology **18**(3) (2005)
14. Castro, M., Liskov, B.: Practical Byzantine fault tolerance and proactive recovery. ACM Transactions on Computer Systems **20**(4) (2002) 398–461
15. Kursawe, K., Shoup, V.: Optimistic asynchronous atomic broadcast. In: Proc. 32nd International Colloquium on Automata, Languages and Programming (ICALP). Volume 3580 of Lecture Notes in Computer Science. (2005) 204–215
16. Bracha, G.: An asynchronous $[(n-1)/3]$-resilient consensus protocol. In: Proc. 3rd Symp. Principles of Distributed Computing. (1984) 154–162
17. Reiter, M.K.: Secure agreement protocols: Reliable and atomic group multicast in Rampart. In: Proc. 2nd ACM Conference on Computer and Communications Security. (1994) 68–80
18. Ramasamy, H.V., Cachin, C.: Parsimonious asynchronous Byzantine-fault-tolerant atomic broadcast. Cryptology ePrint Archive, Report 2006/082 (2006) http://eprint.iacr.org/.
19. Goldwasser, S., Micali, S., Rivest, R.L.: A digital signature scheme secure against adaptive chosen-message attacks. SIAM Journal on Computing **17**(2) (1988) 281–308
20. Desmedt, Y.: Society and group oriented cryptography: A new concept. In: Advances in Cryptology: CRYPTO '87. Volume 293 of Lecture Notes in Computer Science. (1988) 120–127
21. Shoup, V.: Practical Threshold Signatures. In: Advances in Cryptology: EUROCRYPT 2000. Volume 1087 of Lecture Notes in Computer Science. (2000) 207–220
22. Hadzilacos, V., Toueg, S.: Fault-tolerant broadcasts and related problems. Distributed Systems (2nd Ed.) (1993) 97–145

Self-stabilizing Population Protocols

Dana Angluin, James Aspnes*, Michael J. Fischer, and Hong Jiang**

Yale University, Department of Computer Science

Abstract. Self-stabilization in a model of anonymous, asynchronous interacting agents deployed in a network of unknown size is considered. Dijkstra-style round-robin token circulation can be done deterministically with constant space per node in this model. Constant-space protocols are given for leader election in rings, local-addressing in degree-bounded graphs, and establishing consistent global direction in an undirected ring. A protocol to construct a spanning tree in regular graphs using $O(\log D)$ memory is also given, where D is the diameter of the graph. A general method for eliminating nondeterministic transitions from the self-stabilizing implementation of a large family of behaviors is used to simplify the constructions, and general conditions under which protocol composition preserves behavior are used in proving their correctness.

1 Introduction

In some practical scenarios, a large (and sometimes unknown) number of devices are deployed over a region without fine control of their locations, communication and movement patterns. The devices are all indistinguishable and have only a few bits of memory each. Such scenarios are modeled by the *population protocols* introduced in [1], where families of predicates computable in this model are explored. Graph properties computable in the same model are discussed in [2]. Communication in population protocols occurs through pairwise interaction of anonymous finite-state agents. The number of agents is finite but unbounded. A communication graph describes which pairs of nodes may interact.

In the theoretical literature on distributed computing, a weak fairness condition is usually assumed. Informally, in an infinite fair execution each process or node is given a turn infinitely often. We call this definition *local fairness*. The environment/scheduler is viewed as a powerful adversary who can strategically determine the sequence in which processes are activated, as long as local fairness is preserved. Many impossibility results rely on this assumption. For instance, the impossibility of deterministic self-stabilizing token circulation in uniform rings [3] follows from the assumption that the scheduler can activate the nodes in a round-robin fashion, preserving symmetry and achieving local fairness.

However, in practical distributed systems, such a powerful scheduler seldom exists. The global ordering of computational steps depends on a variety of elements. Temperature and power-supply affect the efficiency of electronic devices.

* Supported in part by NSF grants CNS-0305258 and CNS-0435201.
** Supported by the PORTIA project (NSF grant ITR-0331548).

J.H. Anderson, G. Prencipe, and R. Wattenhofer (Eds.): OPODIS 2005, LNCS 3974, pp. 103–117, 2006.

Local clock frequency influences the progress of each node. For ad hoc networks, the movement of nodes determines possible sequences of interactions. Random delay is usually used in practical leader election and collision detection protocols, which can be viewed as a way to randomize the scheduling of the system.

In the model of population protocols, an alternative fairness condition is assumed, *global fairness*, which better reflects the scheduling properties of many distributed systems. Global fairness puts more constraints on the scheduler, so problems proved impossible under global fairness are also impossible under local fairness. Global fairness also provides a simple conceptual framework for protocol design. For instance, once a task is known to be possible in our model, randomization techniques can be applied to make the protocol work under some weaker fairness conditions.

The responsibility of many systems is to meet certain specifications for well-behavedness such as avoidance of deadlock, fairness among processes, fault tolerance, and other global system properties that cannot be simply modeled as I/O behavior. We extend the model of population protocols to accommodate such tasks. We focus on *self-stabilizing* systems that can start in any global configuration and achieve behavior meeting the task specification by itself. Such systems can tolerate worst-case transient faults.

1.1   Other Related Work

Self-stabilizing systems were first introduced by Dijkstra [3]. In his seminal paper, Dijkstra gives three protocols to achieve process mutual-exclusion in rings in a self-stabilizing way. Leader election and token management are fundamental problems in self-stabilization and have been extensively studied in various other models. Each of these result differs from our work in at least one of these aspects: there is an external timeout mechanism to detect deadlocks [4]; each node can access the states of all neighbors at the same time to determine its next state [5]; the protocol is randomized [6, 7, 8], knows the size of the network [6], or has per-node space or message size in $O(\log n)$ [6, 9]; or nodes have unique IDs [10].

Herman [8] proposed a probabilistic synchronous self-stabilizing token-circulation algorithm for identical nodes in an odd ring. Johnen [7] presents a randomized self-stabilizing token circulation protocol on unidirectional anonymous rings. Fairness is enforced by randomization and the fair circulation of *privileges*. The scheduler can only choose nodes that hold a privilege token to make the next step. In our model, nodes are deterministic, and the nondeterminism in the environment (scheduler) is utilized to break symmetry.

Itkis and Levin [11] present a self-stabilizing leader-election protocol for asynchronous networks of identical nameless nodes with arbitrary topology. In their model, each node can set points to neighbors whose state satisfies given properties. Our impossibility result for leader election in connected interaction graphs with arbitrary topology in Section 5.5 shows that their model and ours differ. However, it is an open problem whether our model can simulate theirs in some special classes of interaction graphs.

Distance-2 coloring, also known as neighborhood unique naming, was defined in [12] as the graph labeling problem with conditions at distance 2. The communication networks community have studied variants of this problem, for applications such as assigning radio frequency ranges or time slots to wireless-signal transmitters to avoid interference. The existing results are different from ours in the following aspects: nodes have unique IDs [13] or have the ability to associate incoming messages with their sources [14, 15]; and the protocol has probabilistic rules [13, 14, 15]. We impose a strong anonymity condition: A node does not have innate ability to distinguish different neighbors. To our knowledge no existing protocol is applicable in this model.

2   Basic Model

We represent a network by a directed graph $G = (V, E)$ with n vertices numbered 0 through $n - 1$ and no multi-edges or self-loops. Each vertex represents a finite-state sensing device, and an edge (u, v) indicates the possibility of a communication between u and v in which u is the *initiator* and v is the *responder*.[1] An "undirected" communication graph refers to a network in which for every edge (u, v), interactions of the forms (u, v) and (v, u) are both possible.

A *protocol* $P(Q, C, X, Y, O, \delta)$ consists of a finite set of *states* Q, a set of *initial configurations* C, a finite set X of *input symbols*, an *output function* $O : Q \rightarrow Y$, where Y is a finite set of *output symbols*, and a *transition function* δ mapping each element of $(Q \times X) \times (Q \times X)$ to a nonempty subset of $Q \times Q$. If $(p', q') \in \delta((p, x), (q, y))$, we call $((p, x), (q, y)) \rightarrow (p', q')$ a *transition*. The transition function, and the protocol, is *deterministic* if $\delta((p, x), (q, y))$ always contains just one pair of states. The inputs provide a way for a protocol to interact with an external entity, be it the environment, a user, or another protocol.

A *configuration* is a mapping $C : V \rightarrow Q$ specifying the state of each device in the network, and an *input assignment* is a mapping $\alpha : V \rightarrow X$. A *trace* $T_G(Z)$ on a graph $G(V, E)$ is an infinite sequence of assignments from V to the symbol set Z: $T_G = \lambda_0, \lambda_1, \ldots$ where λ_i is an assignment from V to Z. Z is called the alphabet of T_G. If $Z = X$, we say T_G is an *input trace* of the protocol. Let C and C' be configurations, α be an input assignment, and u, v be distinct nodes. We say that (C, α) goes to C' via pair $e = (u, v)$, denoted $(C, \alpha) \xrightarrow{e} C'$, if the pair $(C'(u), C'(v))$ is in $\delta((C(u), \alpha(u)), (C(v), \alpha(v)))$ and for all $w \in V - \{u, v\}$ we have $C'(w) = C(w)$. We say that (C, α) can go to C' in one step, denoted $(C, \alpha) \rightarrow C'$, if $(C, \alpha) \xrightarrow{e} C'$ for some edge $e \in E$. Given an input trace $IT = \alpha_0, \alpha_1, \ldots$ we write $C \xrightarrow{*} C'$ if there is a sequence of configurations $C = C_0, C_1, \ldots, C_k = C'$, such that $(C_i, \alpha_i) \rightarrow C_{i+1}$ for all i, $0 \leq i < k$, in which case we say that C' is *reachable* from C given input trace IT.

An *execution* is an infinite sequence of configurations and input assignments $(C_0, \alpha_0), (C_1, \alpha_1), \ldots$ such that $C_0 \in C$ and for each i, $(C_i, \alpha_i) \rightarrow C_{i+1}$. An

---

[1] The distinct roles of the two devices in an interaction is a fundamental assumption in our model.

execution is *fair* if for every α, C and C' such that $(C, \alpha) \rightarrow C'$, if (C, α) occurs infinitely often in the execution, then C' also occurs infinitely often in the execution. We extend the output function O to take a configuration C and produce an *output assignment* $O(C)$ defined by $O(C)(v) = O(C(v))$. Let $E = (C_0, \alpha_0), (C_1, \alpha_1), \ldots, (C_i, \alpha_i), \ldots$ be an execution of P. We define the *output trace* of an execution as $OT(E) = O(C_0), O(C_1), \ldots, O(C_i), \ldots$.

A self-stabilizing system can start at an arbitrary configuration and eventually exhibit "good" behavior. We define a *behavior* B on a network $G(V, E)$ to be a set of traces on G that have the same alphabet. We write $B(Z)$ to be explicit about the common alphabet Z. A behavior B is *constant* if every trace in B is constant. If given the constraint that every input trace is contained in some behavior $B_{in}(X)$, the output trace of every fair execution of a protocol $P(Q, C, X, Y, O, \delta)$ starting from any configuration in C is in some behavior $B_{out}(Y)$, we say P is an *implementation* of output behavior B_{out} given input behavior B_{in}. If P does not have any restriction on inputs, we simply say P is an implementation of B_{out}. Given a behavior $B(Z)$, we define the corresponding *stable behavior* $B^s(Z)$: $T \in B^s$ if and only if Z is T's alphabet, and there exists $T' \in B$ such that T' is a suffix of T. Thus, an execution in a stable behavior may have a completely arbitrary finite prefix followed by an execution with the desired properties. If $P(Q, C, X, Y, O, \delta)$ is an implementation of B^s, and C is the set of all possible configurations, we say that P is a *self-stabilizing implementation* of B.

3   Nondeterministic Protocols

In [2], we showed that nondeterminism in the transition function does not increase the class of stably computable predicates. In this section, we extend the result to self-stabilizing algorithms.

We define the *repetition closure* of a sequence t to be set of sequences obtainable from t by repeating each element one or more times. In other words, given any sequence $t = a_1 a_2 \ldots a_i \ldots$, the repetition closure $R(t)$ is $a_1^+ a_2^+ \ldots a_i^+ \ldots$ in regular expression notation. We extend the definition of R to a behavior B by taking the union of $R(t)$ for all $t \in B$. We say a behavior B is *elastic* if $B = R(B)$.

Theorem 1. *If a nondeterministic protocol P is a self-stabilizing implementation of a behavior B, there exists a deterministic protocol P' that is a self-stabilizing implementation of $R(B)$.*

Proof. The proof is similar to that of the theorem in [2] corresponding to computations. We construct a compiler using a nondeterminizer to convert every nondeterministic protocol to a deterministic one. For the compiler to preserve self-stabilization, the nondeterminizer itself must be self-stabilizing.

Let P_1 be a nondeterministic protocol with states Q, input alphabet X, and transition function δ. We describe a simulation of P_1 that works in graphs with at least 3 vertices. Let m be the maximum cardinality of any of the sets $\delta((q, x), (q', x'))$ for $q, q' \in Q$ and $x, x' \in X$. For each $q, q' \in Q$ and $x, x' \in X$, select an arbitrary surjective function $f_{(q,x),(q',x')}$ mapping $\{0, 1, \ldots, m - 1\}$ to $\delta((q, x), (q', x'))$.

We describe a protocol P_2 to simulate each step of P_1 by multiple deterministic steps. and the state components used in P_1 only change in the last of the corresponding steps in P_2. The state consist of three components: (1) a nondeterminizer mark $\circ$ or its absence $-$, (2) a state $q \in Q$, (3) a choice counter, consisting of an integer between 0 and $m - 1$ inclusive. The transitions are:

1. $((\circ qc, x), (\circ q'c', x')) \rightarrow (-qc, \circ q'c')$
2. $((\circ qc, x), (-q'c', x')) \rightarrow (-qc, \circ q'(c' + 1))$
3. $((-q'c', x), (\circ qc, x')) \rightarrow (\circ q'(c' + 1), -qc)$
4. $((-qc, x), (-q'c', x')) \rightarrow (-rc, \circ r'c')$

where the increments are made modulo m and the pair of states (r, r') is the element of $\delta((q, x), (q', x'))$ selected by the function $f_{(q,x),(q',x')}(c)$. Thus, in transitions of type 4, the value of the choice counter of the initiator is used to make a deterministic choice of an element of $\delta((q, x), (q', x'))$. The role of the nondeterminizers is to hop around the graph incrementing choice counters as they go. accomplish this purpose. Transitions of type 4 ensure that deadlock is impossible: even if we start from a configuration with no nondeterminizers, the rule will generate new nondeterminizers. Transitions of type 1 ensure that the nondeterminizers have room to move around by merging two adjacent nondeterminizers.

□

If B is an elastic behavior, $B = R(B)$. The following corollary is immediate:

Corollary 1. *If a nondeterministic protocol P is a self-stabilizing implementation of an elastic behavior B, there exists a deterministic protocol P' that is a self-stabilizing implementation of B.*

4   Protocol Composition

It is desirable to be able to combine protocols to obtain new protocols. Parallel execution of protocols is easily achieved by taking the Cartesian product of their state sets and updating the states for each protocol independently when a transition occurs. In this section we introduce one technique of protocol composition in our model. We want to compose protocols $P_1, P_2, \ldots, P_n$, so that the self-stabilizing behavior of $P_1, P_2, \ldots, P_i$ is used as an assumption in P_{i+1}.

For $n = 2$, assuming P_1 and P_2 access different components of the node's state, we run P_1 and P_2 in parallel, except that whenever P_2 is executed, it uses the current output of P_1 as its current input. When an edge is fired, it is nondeterministically determined which protocol gets the chance to execute. Recall that a behavior is constant if it contains only constant traces.

Theorem 2. *Suppose B_1 is a constant behavior. If P_2 is a self-stabilizing implementation of an elastic behavior B_2 given input behavior B_1, and P_1 is a self-stabilizing implementation of B_1, the composition of P_1 and P_2 (written as $P_1 \circ P_2$) is a self-stabilizing implementation of B_2.*

Proof. Let $S = C_0, C_1, \ldots$ be any fair execution of $P_1 \circ P_2$. Define the projection $\Pi_1(C)$ of a configuration C to be the sub-configuration produced by taking each node's state components that are accessed by P_1. Π_2 is defined similarly for P_2. Define $S' = C'_0, C'_1, \ldots$ the maximal subsequence of S in which for each i, the transition immediately after C'_i is defined in P_1. $S'' = C''_0, C''_1, \ldots$ is defined similarly for P_2. Because P_1 is self-stabilizing, and $\Pi_1(C'_0), \Pi_1(C'_1), \ldots$ is a fair execution of P_1, there exists some i such that the output trace of $\Pi_1(C'_i), \Pi(C'_{i+1}), \ldots$ satisfies B_1. Let C''_j be any configuration that appears after C'_i in S, and let $C''_j, C''_{j+1}, \ldots$ be the sequence starting from C''_j in S''. Because the output trace of P_1 in $C''_j, C''_{j+1}, \ldots$ is constant and satisfies B_1, $\Pi_2(C''_j), \Pi_2(C''_{j+1}), \ldots$ is a fair execution of P_2 whose output trace satisfies B_2. Because B_2 is elastic, the output trace of $P_1 \circ P_2$ in the subsequence of S starting from C''_j satisfies B_2. Therefore $P_1 \circ P_2$ is a self-stabilizing implementation of B_2. $\square$

5   Self-stabilizing Protocols

5.1   Token-Circulation in a Directed Ring

As an simple example, we discuss the token circulation problem in an interaction graph whose topology is a directed ring. The protocol uses the same idea as in Dijkstra's first algorithm in [3], but we only use 2 colors (0 and 1). Readers from the self-stabilization community will find the protocol familiar.

The *token-circulation behavior* TC on graph $G(V, E)$ is the set of all traces $t = \beta_0, \beta_1, \ldots$ with alphabet $\{T, \phi\}$ such that:

1. For all $m \geq 0$, $\exists v \in V$ such that $\beta_m(v) = T$ and $\forall u \in V - \{v\}$, $\beta_m(u) = \phi$.
2. For all $0 \leq m < k < n$, if $\exists v, v' \in V$ $(v \neq v')$ such that $\beta_m(v) = \beta_k(v') = \beta_n(v) = T$, then $\forall u \in V - \{v\}$, $\exists l$ such that $m < l < n$ and $\beta_l(u) = T$.
3. For all $v \in V$, $\beta_k(v) = T$ for infinitely many k.

A node owns a token in a configuration if its output is T. For any trace in TC, exactly one node has a token in each configuration, and after a node releases a token, it does not obtain a token again until every other node has obtained a token once.

We describe a self-stabilizing implementation of TC given the *leader-election behavior* LE. The description of a self-stabilizing implementation of LE is postponed to Section 5.5. LE on graph $G = (V, E)$ is the set of all constant traces $\beta, \beta, \ldots$ such that for some $v \in V$, $\beta(v) = L$ and for all $u \neq v$, $\beta(u) = N$. Informally, there is a static node with the leader mark L, and all other nodes have the nonleader mark N in every configuration. Given the LE input behavior, the leader receives input L and all other nodes receive input N.

Node states are pairs in $\{-, +\} \times \{0, 1\}$. "+" indicates the presence of a token and "−" indicates the absence of token. The second component of a node is called the *label* of that node. The interaction rules are:

1. $((*b, N), (*b, L)) \rightarrow (-b, +\bar{b})$;
2. $((*b, *), (*\bar{b}, N)) \rightarrow (-b, +b)$.

We use the convention that $*$ on the left side of a rule matches any value for the component, that b on the left side matches either 0 or 1, and $\bar{b}$ means the complement of b. The output rules are $+* \to T$ and $-* \to \phi$. (Output T if and only if the first component is "+".)

Because of space limitation and the simplicity of the protocol, we state the following theorem without giving the proof.

Theorem 3. *There exists a constant-space self-stabilizing implementation of output behavior TC given input behavior LE in a directed ring.*

This protocol does not need a non-constant number of colors as in [3] or randomized transition rules as in [7], because of the stronger fairness condition.

5.2   Distance-2 Coloring in Bounded-Degree Graphs

To extend the token circulation algorithm to undirected rings, we need a protocol that imposes direction on the ring. A necessary condition is that each node be able to recognize its two different neighbors. Here we describe a more general algorithm that enables each node in a degree bounded graph to distinguish between its neighbors.

Suppose an undirected graph has a degree bound d and we want to color the graph such that any two nodes whose distance is 2 have different colors. After a graph is properly colored, the neighbors of any node bear different colors and thus are distinguishable. It is not difficult to see that $d(d-1)+1$ colors suffice for a distance-2 coloring of a graph with degree bound d.

The *distance-2 coloring behavior* $D2C$ on graph $G = (V, E)$ with color set C is defined as the set of constant traces $\lambda, \lambda, \ldots$ where the alphabet of λ is C and whenever $u, v, w \in V$ are such that $(u, v) \in E$ and $(v, w) \in E$ and $u \neq w$, we have $\lambda(u) \neq \lambda(w)$.

A node i has the following state components:

$color_i$ An integer encoding the color of node i; its value is between 0
   and $d(d-1)$.
F_i A boolean array whose size is $d(d-1)+1$, indexed by colors.

Each node i outputs the current value of its $color_i$ component.

In this and the following sections, we describe our algorithms by specifying the interaction between two adjacent nodes i and j when the edge (i, j) is activated. The intuition behind the protocol is that if a node i has only one neighbor j with a given color and vice versa, then interactions between i and j will flip the bits $F_i[color_j]$ and $F_j[color_i]$ synchronously. If there is a second neighbor j' with the same color as j, then an interaction with j' will set the bit at i to the opposite value of the bit at j; this will be detected in a later interaction between i and j, causing a recoloring of either i or j and a resynchronization of the bits i and j use to follow each other. After enough nondeterministic recolorings, the protocol will eventually reach a state in which all distance-2 neighbors have distinct colors and all alternating bits are properly synchronized.

Protocol 1. Distance-2 coloring with degree bound d

1: **if** $F_i[color_j] \neq F_j[color_i]$ **then**		▷ possibly conflicting colors
2: $color_i \leftarrow color_i'$		▷ nondeterministic coloring
3: $F_i[color_j] \leftarrow F_j[color_i]$		
4: **else**		▷ valid coloring
5: $F_i[color_j] \leftarrow \overline{F_i[color_j]}$		
6: $F_j[color_i] \leftarrow \overline{F_j[color_i]}$		
7: **end if**		

For a formal argument, we define the *safe configurations* to be the set of configurations that satisfy the following conditions:

1. Let (u, v) and (v, w) be any two edges in the network, it holds that $color_u \neq color_w$.
2. Let u and v be any two adjacent nodes, $F_u[color_v] = F_v[color_u]$.

Lemma 1. *The trace of any execution of Protocol 1 starting from a safe configuration is in D2C.*

Proof. Let C_0 be a safe configuration and (u, v) be any edge. Suppose $C_0 \xrightarrow{(u,v)} C_1$. Because $F_u[color_v] = F_v[color_u]$, no change of color occurs. Because both $F_u[color_v]$ and $F_v[color_u]$ complemented in the interaction, it still holds that $F_u[color_v] = F_v[color_u]$. Notice that if the first safety condition holds, among u's neighbors only v has the color $color_v$, and u is the only one of v's neighbor with $color_u$, therefore $F_u[color_v]$ and $F_v[color_u]$ cannot be changed unless (u, v) is activated. Therefore both requirements of safety are preserved. Because C_0 and (i, j) are chosen arbitrarily, we can conclude that the coloring does not change in any execution starting from any safe configuration.   □

Lemma 2. *Starting from an arbitrary configuration, there exists a finite execution fragment that reaches a safe configuration.*

Proof (sketch). Suppose the second safety condition is violated in the starting configuration. There exists an edge (u, v) such that $F_u[color_v] \neq F_v[color_u]$. When (u, v) is activated, node v will change its color and ensure that $F_u[color_v] = F_v[color_u]$ holds for the new value of $color_u$.

If the first safety condition is violated, there exist two edges (u, v) and (v, w) such that $color_u = color_w$. For any initial states of u, v, and w, there is a sequence of activations of (u, v) and (w, v) which will cause the second condition to be violated and either u or w to change its color.

Therefore the coloring cannot stabilize until a safe configuration is reached. By fairness, the nondeterministic coloring rule will eventually choose colors that lead to a safe configuration.

According to Corollary 1, there is a deterministic version of this protocol. We remark without proof that one way to turn the nondeterministic protocol to a deterministic one is to change line 2 to $color_i \leftarrow (color_i + 1) \bmod (d(d-1) + 1)$.   □

The following theorem follows from the lemmas and establishes the correctness of the protocol.

Theorem 4. *For each d, there exists a constant-space self-stabilizing implementation of the distance-2 coloring behavior in communication graphs of degree bounded by d.*

5.3   Directing an Undirected Ring

Given a graph colored by Protocol 1, Protocol 2 gives a sense of direction to each edge on an undirected ring and guarantees global consistency.

Formally, the *ring direction behavior* RD on $G(V, E)$ is defined as the set of all constant traces $t = \lambda, \lambda, \ldots$ over an alphabet $C \times C \times C$, where we denote $\lambda(v)$ by $(c_v, c_{v,0}, c_{v,1})$, satisfying the conditions:

1. For all $v \in V$, $c_{v,0} \neq c_{v,1}$.
2. For all $(u, v) \in E$, there exists $b \in \{0, 1\}$ such that $c_v = c_{u,b} \wedge c_u = c_{v,\bar{b}}$.

We think of c_v as the color of node v, $c_{v,0}$ as the color of its left neighbor and $c_{v,1}$ as the color of its right neighbor, and the conditions ensure global consistency.

In the protocol, each node i has the following components:

$color_i$ the color of node i (we assume this value is provided by the input
behavior $D2C$.)
$color_{i,0}$ the color of the left neighbor
$color_{i,1}$ the color of the right neighbor

Node i outputs $(color_i, color_{i,0}, color_{i,1})$. A configuration is safe if its output assignment satisfies the requirement of RD.

Protocol 2. Directing an undirected ring

1: **if** $color_j = color_{i,0}$ and $color_j \neq color_{i,1}$ **then**
2:     $color_{j,1} \leftarrow color_i$
3: **else if** $color_j = color_{i,1}$ and $color_j \neq color_{i,0}$ **then**
4:     $color_{j,0} \leftarrow color_i$
5: **else**
6:     $color_{i,0} \leftarrow color_j$
7:     $color_{j,1} \leftarrow color_i$
8: **end if**

Lemma 3. *In the executions of Protocol 2, given input behavior D2C, all reachable configurations from any safe configuration are also safe configurations.*

Proof. Let C be a safe configuration, that is, for all $(i, j) \in E$, there exists $b \in \{0, 1\}$ such that $color_j = color_{i,b}$ and $color_i = color_{j,\bar{b}}$, and for all i, $color_{i,0} \neq color_{i,1}$. Depending on the value of b, the condition in either line 1 or line 3 is true, and the assignments in line 2 and 4 do not modify the states, since the components already have the assigned values. Therefore, starting from a safe configuration, the state of each node does not change.   □

Lemma 4. *Starting from an arbitrary unsafe configuration given input behavior D2C, there exists a finite execution fragment of Protocol 2 that ends at a safe configuration.*

Proof (sketch). Starting from an arbitrary configuration, after each edge is activated once, all dangling pointers are eliminated, which means the "left neighbor" pointer and "right neighbor" pointer of each node points to its actual neighbors. Under this assumption, consider an arbitrary node and label it 0. Label the ring sequentially in a direction such that $color_{0,0} = color_1$. If the scheduler activates $(0,1)$, it must hold afterwards that $color_{0,0} = color_1$ and $color_{1,1} = color_0$, because either of the conditions on line 1 or line 5 applies. Let the scheduler activate $(0,1), (1,2), \ldots, (n-1,0)$ sequentially. Each activation $(i, (i+1) \bmod n)$ ensures that $color_{i,0} = color_{(i+1) \bmod n}$ and $color_{((i+1) \bmod n),1} = color_i$. After this sequence of activations, all edges are directed consistently and a safe configuration is reached.   □

Theorem 5. *Given the distance-2-coloring input behavior, there exists a constant-space self-stabilizing implementation of ring direction.*

5.4 Self-stabilizing Spanning Trees in Regular Graphs

Assuming the existence of a special node and the local addresses assigned by the distance-2 coloring protocol, a spanning tree rooted at the special node can be constructed in a self-stabilizing fashion in a regular graph of degree d. Our protocol uses $O(\log D)$ bits of memory, where D is the diameter of the graph.

Let N be a set of labels and $\phi \notin N$ be a special element. The *spanning tree behavior ST* on graph $G(V, E)$ consists of all constant traces $t = \lambda, \lambda, \ldots$ such that:

1. For $v \in V$, $\lambda(v)$ is a pair (c, p) where $c \in N$ and $p \in N \cup \{\phi\}$, and there exists a unique $r \in V$ such that the second component of $\lambda(r)$ is ϕ.
2. For all $v_0 \neq r$, there exists $v_0, v_1, \ldots,$ and $v_k = r$, where $v_i \in V$, $\lambda(v_i) = (c_i, p_i)$ and $p_i = c_{i+1}$ for all $0 \leq i < k$.

Informally, N is the set of possible colors of nodes. If $\lambda(v) = (c, p)$, c is the color of v and p is the color of its parent in the spanning tree. For the root node r in the spanning tree, $p = \phi$.

We define the *first spanning tree* of a distance-2-colored graph with a unique leader to be the spanning tree satisfying the following conditions:

1. The root of the tree is the leader.
2. The parent of each node is the neighbor closest to the root. Ties are broken by an ordering of the colors.

It is easy to see that the first spanning tree is unique, if the coloring and the leader is fixed. Due to space limitations, we leave the detailed specification of the protocol to the full version of the paper and only informally describe the protocol to construct the first spanning tree.

The protocol consists of two parts. Each node keeps a *neighbors* queue of size d which records the distinct colors of the nodes it interacts with. When the queue is full and the node interacts with a node whose color is not in the queue, the oldest value is removed from the queue and the new value is recorded. After the coloring protocol stabilizes, each node will eventually have the d distinct colors of all its neighbors.

When node i interacts with node j, if i is the root, j sets its state variable $dist_j$ to 1, which records the length of the shortest path from j to the root that has been discovered, and it sets the *parent* variable $parent_j$ to $color_i$, the color of node i. Otherwise, if $parent_j$ is undefined or if $parent_j \neq color_i$ and $dist_i < dist_j - 1$, j sets $parent_j$ to $color_i$ and $dist_j$ to $dist_i + 1$. If $dist_i = dist_j - 1$ but $color_i < parent_j$, j also sets $parent_j$ to $color_i$. If $parent_j = color_i$, j sets $dist_j$ to $dist_i + 1$.

Theorem 6. *Given input behaviors LE and D2C, the above protocol is a self-stabilizing implementation of output behavior ST for all regular graphs of degree d.*

Proof. Given input behaviors $D2C$ and LE, we may assume that the interaction graph G is properly distance-2 colored with one node marked L and all other nodes marked N. Let T denote the unique first spanning tree of G. Starting from an arbitrary configuration, after every edge has been activated in each direction, the queue of neighbors of each node consists of the d colors of its neighbors, and the parent pointer of every node except the root points to some neighbor of the node. Define graph H to be: (i, j) is in H if $parent_i = j$. We look at each edge that is in H but not in T and show each such edge will be corrected. For ease of description, we associate a number N_i with each node i: the higher bits of N_i gives the distance from the root (the real distance in G, not the current value of $dist_i$), and the lower bits give i's color.

Let i be the node such that:

1. $parent_i = j$ $((i, j) \in H)$, but $(i, j) \notin T$.
2. N_i has the smallest value among those that satisfy 1.

Let k be the node such that $(i, k) \in T$. That is, i's parent should be k, but i currently thinks j is his parent. There are two cases:

1. In graph H, the root is reachable from j. The scheduler activates the edges on the path from the root to k in H sequentially. These edges are in both T and H. Because each node will set its distance variable to be the distance variable of its parent plus one, $dist_k$ will be the real distance of k from the root. The scheduler then activates the edges on the path from the root to j in H sequentially. After that it must holds that $dist_j > dist_k$ or the distances are equal but the color of k precedes the color of j. Then (i, k) is activated, and i will set $parent_i = k$.
2. In graph H, the root is not reachable from j. Let's only look at H, and let C consist of j and the nodes reachable from it. C does not contain the root. Because all nodes in C have out-degree one, there must be a directed cycle in C. By the definition of H, every node in the cycle think the next node is its

parent. By letting the scheduler keep activating the edges in the cycle, the *dist* values of the nodes in that cycle can be increased to become arbitrarily large. By activating the edges on the path from j to any of the nodes on the cycle in the reversed order, the large *dist* value will be propagated back to j. Thus i will switch the *parent* pointer to another node which has a smaller *dist* component than j. If the root is reachable from the new parent, do (1), otherwise repeat (2).

The process is repeated until $H = T$.   □

We remark that a traversal of the tree can simulate a directed ring. Therefore, token-circulation can be done in a regular graph by running the ring token-circulation protocol in parallel with the distance-2 coloring protocol and the spanning tree protocol.

5.5   Leader Election

Two of the above protocols assume a pre-designated special node. In our model, self-stabilizing leader election is possible in some classes of interaction graphs and impossible in others. In this section, we first describe a family of leader-election protocols in directed rings. We also present an impossibility result for leader election in general graphs. The formal definition of the leader-election behavior (LE) is given in Section 5.1.

We first consider rings of odd size. Supposing each node has a *label* bit, we call a maximal sequence of alternating labels a *segment*. Since the size of the ring is odd, there is at least one pair of adjacent nodes with the same label. We define the *head* and *tail* of a segment in the natural way according to the direction of the ring. One edge of the form $(0, 0)$ or $(1, 1)$ connects the tail of one segment to the head of another segment. We call such edges *barriers*.

The protocol consists of several parts. At the base is the "unstable clock" protocol, in which the barriers move forward around the ring (which we call "clockwise"). When two barriers collide, one of them is eliminated. There exists a sequence of activations that remove all but one barrier. By fairness, eventually there is a single barrier which rotates clockwise around the ring forever.

The remainder of the protocol manipulates the leader marks and two kinds of tokens, *bullet* and *probe*. Probes move faster than barriers. Probes are sent out by the barrier in a clockwise direction and absorbed by any leader they run into. If a probe makes it all the way back to the barrier, it is converted to leader. Leaders fire bullets counterclockwise around the ring. Bullets are absorbed by the barrier, but they kill any leaders they encounter along the way.

Call a configuration "clean" if it contains exactly one barrier, exactly one leader, and there are no *bullet* or *probe* marks on any node in the interval starting from the leader and proceeding clockwise to the barrier. Thus, any *bullet* and *probe* marks are confined to the interval starting from the barrier and proceeding clockwise to the leader. As the barrier rotates, this region gets squeezed smaller and smaller until finally the barrier passes leader, at which point there are no *bullet* or *probe* marks at all. We leave the pseudocode specification of the protocol to the full version, and only give proof sketches of correctness according to the description above.

Lemma 5. *All configurations reachable from a clean configuration are also clean, and the same node is marked leader in each.*

Proof. No *probe* ever encounters the barrier, because there are no *probe* marks anywhere in the region between leader and the barrier, hence, no new leader is created. No *bullet* ever encounters the leader because there are no *bullet* marks anywhere in the region starting from the barrier and going counterclockwise to the barrier, hence the leader is never killed. Newly created *bullet* and *probe* marks are both confined to the region from the barrier to the leader.   □

Lemma 6. *For any configurations C there exists a clean configuration C' reachable from C.*

Proof. It follows from our fairness condition that every fair computation contains a clean configuration. From the above claim, all configurations following the first clean configuration are also clean and have the same node marked as leader.

Here's how to reach a clean configuration starting from an arbitrary configuration C. First, pick a barrier edge and rotate the barrier once around the ring as described above. This eliminates any other barriers that might have been present. Next, take any bullet in the forbidden region starting from the barrier and proceeding counterclockwise to the first leader (or the entire ring if no node is marked leader) and propagate the bullets counterclockwise around the ring until they are absorbed by the barrier. Some or all leaders may die in the process. If any leader remains, take the farthest leader from the barrier (in the counterclockwise direction), fire a bullet, and propagate it until it is absorbed by the barrier. Now at most one leader remains. Next, let the barrier create a *probe* mark, then propagate all *probe* marks clockwise around the ring until they are absorbed by the leader or they encounter the barrier and are converted to leader. At this point, we have a ring with one barrier, one leader, and no other marks, so it is clean.   □

Lemmas 5 and 6 complete the proof of correctness.

This protocol is a special case of a family of protocols. For any ring of size n, we can pick an integer $k > 1$ that is relatively prime to n. Each node is labeled by an integer between 0 and $k-1$ inclusive. Call an edge a "barrier" if it is (i, j) where $i + 1 \not\equiv j \pmod{k}$. Because k is relatively prime to n, there is at least one barrier. The barrier advancement rule would be $(i, j) \rightarrow (i, i + 1 \bmod k)$, where $i + 1 \not\equiv j \pmod{k}$. Calling this protocol P_k, then the protocol we detailed in this section is P_2. We thus have a family of protocols P_2, P_3, ... such that for any ring, P_k accomplishes self-stabilizing leader election whenever k does not divide the size of the ring.

Theorem 7. *For each integer $k \geq 2$, there exists a constant-space self-stabilizing implementation of the leader-election behavior on all rings whose sizes are not multiples of k.*

Finally, we present the following impossibility result:

Theorem 8. *There does not exist a self-stabilizing protocol for leader election in interaction graphs with general topology.*

Proof. Assuming such a protocol A exists, we consider how it would behave in directed lines. Let e be an arbitrary edge. If e were removed, the interaction graph would become two directed lines, and by the correctness assumption of A, the two shorter lines would each elect a leader. Therefore from any configuration C there is a reachable configuration C' in which there are two leaders, because from C the scheduler just stops activating e and only activates other edges for a certain amount of time to reach C'. By fairness, in any fair execution of A, some configuration C' with two leaders occurs infinitely often. Therefore the output trace of any fair execution of A cannot have a suffix in the behavior LE. $\square$

A class C of graphs is *simple* if there does not exist a graph in C which contains two disjoint subgraphs that are also in C. Notable simple classes of graphs include rings, or, more generally, connected degree-d regular graphs. Directed lines, connected graphs with a certain degree bound and strongly connected graphs are non-simple classes of graphs. The proof above shows that there is no self-stabilizing leader election protocol that works for all the graphs in any non-simple class.

6   Conclusion and Open Problems

In this paper, we extended the population protocol model of [1] to allow for inputs at each step, and we defined general classes of behaviors. We studied self-stabilization protocols for token-circulation, distance-2 coloring, ring orientation, spanning tree, and leader election in this extended model.

We remark that one of the applications of the self-stabilizing protocols is to combine them with the protocols in [1, 2] to compute algebraic predicates or graph properties, with the additional benefit of transient-fault tolerance. For instance the token-circulation protocol could be augmented to compute predicates such as $n > k$ or expressions like $n \bmod k$ in regular graphs in which n is the size of the network and k is a constant. We leave the detailed discussion to the full version of the paper.

The leader election protocol we presented in this paper depends on the size of the ring. There are impossibility results and space bounds on self-stabilizing leader election in general rings in various other models [3, 10]. Because of the difference between our model and that of the previous papers, those results cannot be easily extended to our model. The existence of a uniform constant-space leader election protocol on the class of all rings or on the class of regular communication graphs of degree $d > 2$ is still open for future research.

References

1. Angluin, D., Aspnes, J., Diamadi, Z., Fischer, M.J., Peralta, R.: Computation in networks of passively mobile finite-state sensors. In: Twenty-Third ACM Symposium on Principles of Distributed Computing. (2004) 290–299

2. Angluin, D., Aspnes, J., Chan, M., Fischer, M.J., Jiang, H., Peralta, R.: Stably computable properties of network graphs. In Prasanna, V.K., Iyengar, S., Spirakis, P., Welsh, M., eds.: Distributed Computing in Sensor Systems: First IEEE International Conference, DCOSS 2005, Marina del Rey, CA, USE, June/July, 2005, Proceedings. Volume 3560 of Lecture Notes in Computer Science., Springer-Verlag (2005) 63–74

3. Dijkstra, E.W.: Self-stabilizing systems in spite of distributed control. Communications of the ACM **17**(11) (1974) 643–644

4. Mayer, A., Ofek, Y., Ostrovsky, R., Yung, M.: Self-stabilizing symmetry breaking in constant-space (extended abstract). In: Proc. 24th ACM Symp. on Theory of Computing. (1992) 667–678

5. Itkis, G., Lin, C., Simon, J.: Deterministic, constant space, self-stabilizing leader election on uniform rings. In: Workshop on Distributed Algorithms. (1995) 288–302

6. Higham, L., Myers, S.: Self-stabilizing token circulation on anonymous message passing rings. Technical report, University of Calgary (1999)

7. Johnen, C.: Bounded service time and memory space optimal self-stabilizing token circulation protocol on unidirectional rings. In: Procedings of the 18th International Parallel and Distributed Processing Symposium. (2004) 52a

8. Herman, T.: Probabilistic self-stabilization. Information Processing Letters **35**(2) (1990) 63–67

9. Dolev, S., Israeli, A., Moran, S.: Uniform dynamic self-stabilizing leader election. IEEE Transactions on Parallel and Distributed Systems **8** (1997) 424–440

10. Beauquier, J., Gradinariu, M., Johnen, C.: Memory space requirements for self-stabilizing leader election protocols. In: Eighteenth ACM Symposium on Principles of Distributed Computing. (1999) 199–207

11. Itkis, G., Levin, L.A.: Fast and lean self-stabilizing asynchronous protocols. In: Proceeding of 35th Annual Symposium on Foundations of Computer Science, IEEE Press (1994) 226–239

12. Griggs, J.R., Yeh, R.K.: Labeling graphs with a condition at distance two. Journal of Discrete Mathematics **5** (1992) 586–595

13. Herman, T., Tixeuil, S.: A distributed TDMA slot assignment algorithm for wireless sensor networks. Lecture Notes in Computer Science **3121** (2004) 45–58

14. Gradinariu, M., Johnen, C.: Self-stabilizing neighborhood unique naming under unfair scheduler. Lecture Notes in Computer Science **2150** (2001) 458–465

15. Moscibroda, T., Wattenhofer, R.: Coloring unstructured radio networks. In: Procedings of the 17th annual ACM symposium on Parallelism in algorithms and architectures, ACM Press (2005) 39–48

A Self-stabilizing Link-Coloring Protocol Resilient to Unbounded Byzantine Faults in Arbitrary Networks

Toshimitsu Masuzawa[1] and Sébastien Tixeuil[2]

[1] Osaka University, Japan
masuzawa@ist.osaka-u.ac.jp
[2] LRI-CNRS UMR 8623 & INRIA Grand Large, France
tixeuil@lri.fr

Abstract. Self-stabilizing protocols can tolerate any type and any number of transient faults. However, in general, self-stabilizing protocols provide no guarantee about their behavior against permanent faults. This paper proposes a self-stabilizing link-coloring protocol resilient to (permanent) Byzantine faults in arbitrary networks. The protocol assumes the central daemon, and uses $2\Delta - 1$ colors where Δ is the maximum degree in the network. This protocol guarantees that any link (u, v) between non faulty processes u and v is assigned a color within $2\Delta + 2$ rounds and its color remains unchanged thereafter. Our protocol is Byzantine insensitive in the sense that the subsystem of correct processes remains operating properly in spite of unbounded Byzantine faults.

Keywords: distributed protocol, self-stabilization, link-coloring, Byzantine fault, fault tolerance, fault containment.

1 Introduction

Self-stabilization [4] is one of the most effective and promising paradigms for fault-tolerant distributed computing [5]. A self-stabilizing protocol is guaranteed to achieve its desired behavior eventually regardless of the initial network configuration (*i.e.*, global state). This implies that a self-stabilizing protocol is resilient to any number and any type of transient faults since it converges to its desired behavior from any configuration resulting from transient faults. However the convergence to the desired behavior is guaranteed only under the assumption that no further fault occurs during convergence.

The problem of vertex or link coloring has important applications related to resource allocation in distributed systems (*e.g.* frequency or time slot allocation in wireless networks), and has been largely studied in the self-stabilizing area. Self-stabilizing algorithms for distance one vertex coloring have been studied in [7,10,11,13,18,19,20], and for distance two vertex coloring in [9,12]. To our knowledge, [17] is the only known self-stabilizing link-coloring algorithm, and is further discussed thereafter.

J.H. Anderson, G. Prencipe, and R. Wattenhofer (Eds.): OPODIS 2005, LNCS 3974, pp. 118–129, 2006.

There exists several researches on self-stabilizing protocols that are also resilient to permanent faults [1,2,3,8,14,15,16,21]. Most of those consider only crash faults, and guarantee that each non faulty process achieves its intended behavior regardless of the initial network configuration. Nesterenko *et al.* [16] provide solutions that are self-stabilizing and tolerate unbounded Byzantine faults. The main difficulty in this setting is caused by arbitrary and unbounded state changes of the Byzantine process: processes around the Byzantine processes may change their states in response to the state changes of the Byzantine processes, and processes next to the processes changing their states may also change their states. This implies that the influence of the Byzantine processes could expand to the whole system, preventing every process from conforming to its specification forever. In [16], the protocols manage to contain the influence of Byzantine processes to only processes near them, the other processes begin able to eventually achieve correct behavior. The complexity measure they introduce is the *containment radius*, which is the maximum distance between a Byzantine process and a processor affected by the Byzantine process. They also propose self-stabilizing protocols resilient to Byzantine faults for the vertex coloring problem and the dining philosophers problem. The containment radius is one for the vertex coloring problem and two for the dining philosophers problem. In [17], the authors consider a self-stabilizing link-coloring protocol resilient to Byzantine faults in oriented tree networks, achieving a containment radius of two. Link-coloring of the distributed system is an assignment of colors to the communication links such that no two communication links with the same color share a process in common. Link-coloring has many applications in distributed systems, *e.g.*, scheduling data transfer and assigning frequency band in wireless networks.

When the network is uniform (all nodes execute the same code) and anonymous (nodes have no possibility to distinguish from one another), a self-stabilizing coloring algorithm cannot make the assumption that the color of a link is determined by a single node. Indeed, since nodes are uniform, it could be that two nodes have decided (differently) on the color of the link. As a result, the color of a link must come from some kind of coordination between at least two nodes. In this paper, we make the realistic assumption that a link color is decided only by its adjacent nodes. In this context, it follows that, from a Byzantine containment point of view, link coloring is harder than vertex coloring and dining philosophers for the following reason: while the two latter problems require only one process to take an action to correct a single fault (and the aforementioned papers make that assumption), link colors result from an agreement of two neighboring nodes, and thus can result in the update of two nodes to correct a single failure.

In this paper, we present a self-stabilizing link-coloring protocol resilient to unbounded Byzantine faults. Unlike the protocol of [17], we consider arbitrary anonymous networks, where no pre-existing hierarchy is available. As it was proved necessary in [17] to achieve constant containment radius, we assume the central daemon, *i.e.* exactly one process can execute an action at a given time. We use $2\Delta - 1$ colors, where Δ is the maximum degree in the network. Our protocol guarantees that any link (u, v) between non faulty processes u and v is assigned a color within $2\Delta + 2$ rounds and its color remains unchanged thereafter. As far as fault containment is considered, our protocol is optimal, since the influence of Byzantine processors is limited to themselves. Thus, our protocol also trivially achieves Byzantine-fault containment with containment radius of one.

2   Preliminaries

2.1   Distributed System

A *distributed system* $S = (P, L)$ consists of a set $P = \{v_1, v_2, \ldots, v_n\}$ of processes and a set L of bidirectional communication links (simply called links). A link is an unordered pair of distinct processes. A distributed system S can be regarded as a graph whose vertex set is P and whose link set is L, so we use some graph terminology to describe a distributed system S.

A *subsystem* $S' = (P', L')$ of a distributed system $S = (P, L)$ is such that $P' \subseteq P$ and $L' = \{(u, v) \in L | u \in P', v \in P'\}$.

Processes u and v are called *neighbors* if $(u, v) \in L$. The set of neighbors of a process v is denoted by N_v, and its cardinality (the *degree* of v) is denoted by $\Delta_v (= |N_v|)$. The degree Δ of a distributed system $S = (P, L)$ is defined as $\Delta = \max\{\Delta_v \mid v \in P\}$. We do not assume existence of a unique identifier of each process. Instead we assume each process can distinguish its neighbors from each other by locally arranging them in some arbitrary order: the k-th neighbor of a process v is denoted by $N_v(k)$ $(1 \leq k \leq \Delta_v)$.

Each process is modeled by a state machine that can communicate with its neighbors through link registers. For each pair of neighboring processes u and v, there are two link registers $r_{u,v}$ and $r_{v,u}$. Message transmission from u to v is realized as follows: u writes a message to link register $r_{u,v}$ and then v reads it from $r_{u,v}$. The link register $r_{u,v}$ is called an *output register* of u and is called an *input register* of v. The set of all output (resp. input) registers of u is denoted by Out_u (resp. In_u), i.e., $Out_u = \{r_{u,v} \mid v \in N_u\}$ and $In_u = \{r_{v,u} \mid v \in N_u\}$.

The variables that are maintained by processes denote their states. Similarly, the values of the variables stored in each register denote the state of these registers. A process may take actions during the execution of the system. An action is simply a function that is executed in an atomic manner by the process.

A global state of a distributed system is called a *configuration* and is specified by a product of states of all processes and all link registers. We define C to be the set of all possible configurations of a distributed system S. For each configuration $\rho \in C$, $\rho|u$ and $\rho|r$ denote the process state of u and the state of link register r in configuration ρ respectively. For a process u and two configurations ρ and ρ', we denote $\rho \overset{u}{\mapsto} \rho'$ when ρ changes to ρ' by executing an action of u. Notice that ρ and ρ' can be different only in the states of u and the states of output registers of u.

A *schedule* of a distributed system is an infinite sequence of processes. Let $Q = u^1, u^2, \ldots$ be a schedule. An infinite sequence of configurations $e = \rho_0, \rho_1, \ldots$ is called an *execution* from an initial configuration ρ_0 by a schedule Q, if e satisfies

$\rho_i \overset{u^{i+1}}{\mapsto} \rho_{i+1}$ for each i ($i \geq 0$). In this paper, process action are executed atomically, and we also assume that a *locally central daemon* schedules the actions of our processes, *i.e.*, no two neighboring processes may execute their actions at the same time. In the literature, the central daemon is mostly used in conjunction with a shared memory model [5], where a process is able to read the whole state of its neighboring processes. Our scheme uses shared registers instead, in order to narrow the communication capabilities to what is actually needed to solve the problem.

The set of all possible executions from an initial configuration $\rho_0 \in C$ is denoted by E_{ρ_0}. The set of all possible executions is denoted by E, that is, $E = \bigcup_{\rho \in C} E_\rho$. We consider *asynchronous* distributed systems where we can make no assumption on schedules except that any schedule is *weakly fair*: every process appears in the schedule infinitely often.

In this paper, we consider (permanent) *Byzantine faults*: a Byzantine process (i.e., a Byzantine-faulty process) can arbitrarily behave independently from its actions. If v is a Byzantine process, v can repeatedly change its variables and its output registers arbitrarily.

Let $BF = \{f_1, f_2, \ldots, f_c\}$ be the set of Byzantine processes. We call a process v ($\notin BF$) a *correct process*. In distributed systems with Byzantine processes, execution by a schedule $Q = u^1, u^2, \ldots$ is an infinite sequence of configurations $e = \rho_0, \rho_1, \ldots$ satisfying the following conditions.

- When u^{i+1} is a correct process, $\rho_i \overset{u^{i+1}}{\mapsto} \rho_{i+1}$ holds (possibly $\rho_i = \rho_{i+1}$).
- When u^{i+1} is a Byzantine process, $\rho_{i+1}|u^{i+1}$ and $\rho_{i+1}|r$ ($r \in Out_{u^{i+1}}$) can be arbitrary states. For any process v other than u^{i+1}, $\rho_i|v = \rho_{i+1}|v$ and $\rho_i|r = \rho_{i+1}|r$ ($r \in Out_v$) hold.

In asynchronous distributed systems, time is usually measured by *asynchronous rounds* (simply called *rounds*). Let $e = \rho_0, \rho_1, \ldots$ be an execution from configuration ρ_0 by a schedule $Q = u^1, u^2, \ldots$. The first round of e is defined to be the minimum prefix of e, $e' = \rho_0, \rho_1, \ldots, \rho_k$, such that $\{u^i \mid 1 \leq i \leq k\} = P$. Round t ($t \geq 2$) is defined recursively, by applying the above definition of the first round to $e'' = \rho_k, \rho_{k+1}, \ldots$. Intuitively, every process has a chance to update its state in every round.

2.2 Self-stabilizing Protocol Resilient to Byzantine Faults

The *link coloring problem* considered in this paper is a so-called *static problem*, *i.e.*, once the system reaches a desired configuration, the configuration remains unchanged forever. For example, the spanning-tree construction problem is a static problem, while the mutual exclusion problem is not [5]. Some static problems can be defined by a *specification predicate*, $spec(v)$, for each process v, which specifies the condition that v should satisfy at the desired configuration. A specification predicate $spec(v)$ is a boolean expression consisting of the variables of $P_v \subseteq P$ and link registers $R_v \subseteq R$, where R is the set of all link registers.

A self-stabilizing protocol is a protocol that guarantees each process v satisfies $spec(v)$ eventually regardless of the initial configuration. By this property, a self-stabilizing protocol can tolerate any number and any type of transient faults. However, since we consider permanent Byzantine faults, faulty processes may not satisfy $spec(v)$. In addition, non faulty processes near the faulty processes can be influenced by the faulty processes and may be unable to satisfy $spec(v)$. Nesterenko and Arora [16] define a *strictly stabilizing protocol* as a self-stabilizing protocol resilient to Byzantine faults. Informally, the protocol requires each process v more than ℓ away from any Byzantine process to satisfy $spec(v)$ eventually, where ℓ is a constant called *stabilization radius*. A *strictly stabilizing protocol* is defined as follows.

Definition 1. *A configuration ρ_0 is a BF-stable configuration with stabilizing radius ℓ if and only if, for any execution $e = \rho_0, \rho_1, \ldots$ and any process v, the following condition holds:*

> *If the distance from v to any Byzantine process is more than ℓ, then for any i ($i \geq 0$) (i) v satisfies $spec(v)$ in ρ_i, (ii) $\rho_i|v = \rho_{i+1}|v$ holds, and (iii) $\rho_i|r = \rho_{i+1}|r$ ($r \in Out_v$) holds.*

Definition 1 states that, once the system reaches a stable configuration, a process v more than ℓ away from any Byzantine process satisfies $spec(v)$ and never changes the states of v and r ($r \in Out_v$) afterwards.

Definition 2 ([16]). *A protocol A is a strictly stabilizing protocol with stabilizing radius ℓ if and only if, for any execution $e = \rho_0, \rho_1, \ldots$ of A starting from any configuration ρ_0, there exists ρ_i that is a BF-stable configuration with radius ℓ. We say that the stabilizing time of A is k for the minimum k such that the last configuration of the k-th round is a BF-stable configuration in any execution of A.*

Definition 3. *A protocol A is Byzantine insensitive if and only if every process eventually satisfies its specification in $S' = (P', L')$, the subsystem of all correct processes.*

Notice that if a protocol is Byzantine insensitive, it is also strictly stabilizing with stabilizing radius of 1, but the converse is not necessarily true. So, the former property is strictly stronger than the latter.

2.3   Link-Coloring Problem

The *link-coloring problem* consists in assigning a color to every link so that no two links with the same color are adjacent to the same processor. In the following, let $CSET$ be a given set of colors, and let $Color(u, v) \in CSET$ be the color of link (u, v).

Definition 4. *In the link-coloring problem, the specification predicate $spec(v)$ for a process v is given as follows:*

$$\forall x, y \in N_v : x \neq y \implies Color(v, x) \neq Color(v, y)$$

In the following, we denote a link-coloring protocol with b colors as a *b-link-coloring protocol*.

3 Link-Coloring Protocol

3.1 Link-Coloring Protocol on Arbitrary Networks

Our protocol is presented as Algorithms 3.1 and 3.2. It is informally described as follows: each process maintains a list of colors assigned to its incident links and periodically exchanges the list with each neighboring process. From the list received from its neighbor v, a processor u can propose a color for the link (u, v). This proposed color must not appear in the set of incident colors of u or v. The system is scheduled by the central daemon, so no two neighboring processes can propose a color at the same time. Since the set of colors is of size $2\Delta - 1$, u can choose a color that is not used at u or v. If both u and v are correct, once they settle on a color c for link (u, v), this color is never changed.

In case of a Byzantine process, it may happen however, that a Byzantine process keeps proposing colors conflicting with other neighbors proposals. If the color proposed by the Byzantine process conflict with a color on which two neighbors u and v have settled on, the proposition is ignored. The remaining case is when a node u has two neighbors v and w (where u and v are correct processes and w is Byzantine), and has not settled on any color with either v or w. The Byzantine process w may continuously proposed colors that conflict with v to u, and u could always chose the color proposed by w. To ensure that this behavior may not occur infinitely often, we use a priority list so that neighbors of a particular node u get round robin priority when proposing conflicting colors. Then, once u and v (the two correct processes) settle on a color for the link (u, v), the following proposals from w (the Byzantine process) are ignored by u.

3.2 Correctness Proof

Let u and v be neighboring processes, and let v be the k-th neighbor of u. We say that register $r_{u,v}$ is consistent (with the state of u) if $PC_{u,v} = outCol_u(k)$ and $USET_{u,v} = \{outCol_u(m) \mid 1 \le m \le \Delta_u, m \ne k\}$ hold.

Lemma 1. *Once a correct process executes an action, its output registers become consistent and remain so thereafter.*

Proof. By the code of the algorithm (see the last three lines).

Corollary 1. *In the second round and later, all output registers of correct processes are consistent.*

The following lemma also holds clearly.

Lemma 2. *Once a correct process v executes an action, $outCol_v(k) \ne outCol_v(k')$ holds for any k and k' $(1 \le k < k' \le \Delta_v)$ at any time (except that $outCol_v(k) = outCol_v(k') = \perp$ holds temporarily during execution of an action).*

Algorithm 3.1. The SS link-coloring protocol (Part 1: constants and variables)

constants

    $\Delta =$ the maximum degree of the network
    $\Delta_v =$ the degree of v
    $N_v(k)$ $(1 \leq k \leq \Delta_v) =$ the k-th neighbor of v
    $CSET = \{1, 2, \ldots, 2\Delta - 1\}$ // set of all colors

local variables of node v

    $outCol_v(x)$ $(1 \leq x \leq \Delta_v)$;
        // color proposed by v for the x-th incident link
        // We assume $outCol_v(x)$ takes a value from $CSET \cup \{\bot\}$
        // The value $\bot$ is used temporarily only during execution of an atomic step
    $Decided_v :$ subset of $\{1, 2, \ldots, \Delta_v\}$;
        // the set of neighbor u such that the color of (u, v) is accepted
        // (or finally decided)
    $UnDecided_v :$ ordered subset of $\{1, 2, \ldots, \Delta_v\}$;
        // the ordered set of neighbor u such that the color of (u, v) is not accepted
        // We assume $Decide_v \cup UnDecided_v = \{1, 2, \ldots, \Delta_v\}$ holds
        // in the initial configuration

variables in shared register $r_{v,u}$

    $PC_{v,u}$;
        // color proposed by v for the link (v, u)
    $USET_{v,u}$;
        // colors of links incident to v other than (v, u)
        // in-register $r_{u,v}$ has $PC_{u,v}$ and $USET_{u,v}$

Proof. The lemma clearly holds from the following facts:

- When $outCol_v(k) = outCol_v(k')$ and $\{k, k'\} \subseteq Decided_v$ hold, then either $outCol_v(k)$ or $outCol_v(k')$ is reset to $\bot$. ($outCol_v(k) = outCol_v(k')$ and $\{k, k'\} \subseteq Decided_v$ may hold in the initial configuration.)
- v assigns a color c to $outCol_v(k)$ only when $outCol_v(k') \neq c$ holds for any k' $(k' \neq k)$.

Let u and v be any neighboring processes, and let v be the k-th neighbor of u. In the followings, we say that process u *accepts* a color c for a link (u, v) if $k \in Decided_u$ and $outCol_u(k) = c$ holds.

Lemma 3. *Let u and v be any correct neighboring processes, and let v be the k-th neighbor of u and u be the k'-th neighbor of v.*

Once v accepts a color of (u, v) in the second round or later, $outCol_u(k)$ and $outCol_v(k')$ never change afterwards. Moreover, u accepts the color of (u, v) in the next round or earlier.

Proof. When process v completes its action at which v accepts a color c of (u, v),

$$outCol_u(k) = PC_{u,v} = outCol_v(k') = PC_{v,u} = c$$
$$\wedge\, outCol_u(k) \notin \{outCol_u(m) \mid 1 \leq m \leq \Delta_u, m \neq k\}$$
$$\wedge\, outCol_v(k') \notin \{outCol_v(m) \mid 1 \leq m \leq \Delta_v, m \neq k'\}$$

holds.

Algorithm 3.2. The SS link-coloring protocol (Part 2: the LINKCOLORING function)

```
function LINKCOLORING {
```
// check the conflict on the accepted color
// This is against that a Byzantine process changes the accepted color.
// Also, this is against the initial illegitimate configuration
// (meaningful only in the first two rounds)
for each $k \in Decided_v$ {
   if $(PC_{N_v(k),v} \neq outCol_v(k))$
     or $(outCol_v(k) = outCol_v(k'))$ **for some** $k'(\neq k))$
     then { // something strange happens
       $outCol_v(k) := \perp$;
       remove k **from** $Decided_v$;
       append k **to** $UnDecided_v$ **as the last element**;
       // if this occurs in the third round or later, $N_v(k)$ is a Byzantine
       // process
     }
}
// check whether v's previous proposals were accepted by neighbors
for each $k \in UnDecided_v$ {
   if $PC_{N_v(k),v} = outCol_v(k)$
     then { // v's previous proposed was accepted by $N_v(k)$
       remove k **from** $UnDecided_v$;
       append k **to** $Decided_v$;
     }
     else // v's previous proposed was rejected by $N_v(k)$
       $outCol_v(k) := \perp$;
}
// check whether v can accept the proposal made by neighbors
for each $k \in UnDecided_v$ **in the order in** $UnDecided_v$ {
   // the order in $UnDecided_v$ is important to avoid infinite obstruction of
   // Byzantine processes
   if $PC_{N_v(k),v} \notin \{outCol_v(m) \mid 1 \leq m \leq \Delta_v\}$
     then { // accept the color proposed by $N_v(k)$
       $outCol_v(k) := PC_{N_v(k),v}$;
       remove k **from** $UnDecided_v$;
       append k **to** $Decided_v$;
     }
     else // make proposal of a color for undecided links
       $outCol_v(k) := min(CSET \backslash$
          $((\{outCol_v(m) \mid 1 \leq m \leq \Delta_v\} - \{\perp\}) \cup USET_{N_v(k),v}))$
     // at least one color is available (remark that $outCol_v(k) = \perp$ holds)
}
for $k := 1$ **to** Δ_v { // write to its own link registers
   $PC_{v,N_v(k)} := outCol_v(k)$;
   $USET_{v,N_v(k)} := \{outCol_v(m) \mid 1 \leq m \leq \Delta_v, m \neq k\}$;
}
}

Process u or v never accepts a proposal c for any other incident link, and never makes a proposal c for any other incident link, as long as $outCol_u(k) = outCol_v(k') = c$ holds. This implies that $outCol_u(m) \neq c$ (for each $m \neq k$) and $outCol_v(m) \neq c$ (for each $m \neq k'$) hold as long as $outCol_u(k) = outCol_v(k') = c$ holds.

Now we show that $outCol_u(k) = outCol_v(k') = c$ remains holding once $outCol_u(k) = outCol_v(k') = c$ holds. We assume for contradiction that either $outCol_u(k)$ or $outCol_v(k')$ changes. Without loss of generality, we can assume that $outCol_u(k)$ changes first. This change of the color occurs only when $outCol_u(m) = c$ holds for some m such that $m \neq k$. This contradicts the fact that $outCol_u(m) \neq c$ ($m \neq k$) remains holding as long as $outCol_u(k) = c$ holds.

It is clear that u accepts the color c for the link (u, v) when u is activated and $outCol_u(k) = PC_{v,u} = c$ holds. Thus, the lemma holds.

Lemma 4. *Let u and v be any correct neighboring processes. Process u accepts a color for the link (u, v) within $2\Delta_u + 2$ rounds.*

Proof. Let v be the kth neighbor of u. Let t_1, t_2 and t_3 ($t_1 < t_2 < t_3$) be the steps (i.e., global discrete times) when u, v and u are activated respectively, and u is never activated between t_1 and t_3. We consider the following three cases of the configuration immediately before u executes an action at t_3. In what follows, let c be the color such that $outCol_u(k) = c$ holds immediately before u executes an action at t_3.

1. If $PC_{v,u} = c$ holds: Process u accepts the color c for (u, v) in the action at t_3.
2. If $PC_{v,u}(= c') \neq c$ holds and v is the first process among processes w such that $PC_{w,u} = c'$ in $UnDecided_u$: Process u accepts the color c' of $PC_{v,u}$ for (u, v) in the action at t_3.
3. If $PC_{v,u}(= c') \neq c$ holds and v is not the first process among processes w such that $PC_{w,u} = c$ in $UnDecided_u$: Process u cannot accept color c' for (u, v) in the action at t_3. Process u accepts the color c' for the link (u, w) such that w is the first process among processes x such that $PC_{x,u} = c'$ in $UnDecided_u$.

In the third case, Process w is removed from $UnDecided_u$. From Lemma 3, w is never appended to $UnDecided_u$ again when w is a correct process. When w is a Byzantine process, w may be appended to $UnDecided_u$ again but its position is after the position of u. This observation implies that the third case occurs at most $\Delta - 1$ times for the pair of u and v before u accepts a color for (u, v).

Now we analyze the number of rounds sufficient for u to accept a color of the link (u, v). Consider three consecutive rounds. Let t be the time when u is activated last in the first round of the three consecutive rounds, and let t' be the time when u is activated first in the last round of the three consecutive rounds. It is clear that v is activated between t and t'. This implies that we have at least one occurrence of the t_1, t_2 and t_3 described above between t and t'. We repeat this argument by regarding the last round of the three consecutive rounds as the first round of the three consecutive rounds we consider next. Thus, u accepts a color of (u, v) within $2\Delta_v + 2$ rounds.

From Lemma 4, we can obtain the following theorem.

Theorem 1. *The protocol is a Byzantine insensitive link-coloring protocol for arbitrary networks. The stabilization time of the protocol is $2\Delta + 2$ rounds.*

4   Conclusion

In this paper, we presented the first self-stabilizing link-coloring algorithm that can be used on uniform anonymous and general topology graphs. In addition to being self-stabilizing, it is also Byzantine insensitive, in the sense that the subsystem of correct processes resumes correct behavior in finite time regardless of the number and placement of potentially malicious (so called Byzantine) processes.

The system hypothesis that we assumed (central daemon scheduling) are necessary to ensure bounded fault-containment of Byzantine processes (as proved in [17]). However, we assumed that the number of link colors that is available is $2\Delta - 1$, where Δ is the maximum degree of the graph. It is well known that $\Delta + 1$ colors are sufficient for link coloring general graphs. Recently, a distributed (non-stabilizing and non fault tolerant) solution [6] that uses only $\Delta + 1$ colors was provided. There remains the open question of a possible tradeoff between the number of colors used for link coloring and the fault-tolerance properties of distributed solutions.

Acknowledgements

This work is supported in part by MEXT: "The 21st Century Center of Excellence Program", JSPS: Grant-in-Aid for Scientific Research ((B)15300017), MEXT: Grant-in-Aid for Scientific Research on Priority Areas (16092215) and MIC: Strategic Information and Communications R&D Promotion Programme (SCOPE). This work is also supported in part by the FRAGILE and SR2I projects of the ACI "Sécurité et Informatique" of the French Ministry of Research.

References

1. E. Anagnostou and V. Hadzilacos. Tolerating transient and permanent failures. *Lectures Notes in Computer Science, Vol 725 (Springer-Verlag)*, pages 174–188, 1993.
2. J. Beauquier and S. Kekkonen-Moneta. Fault-tolerance and self-stabilization: impossibility results and solutions using self-stabiling failure detectors. *International Journal of Systems Science*, 28(11):1177–1187, 1997.

3. J. Beauquier and S. Kekkonen-Moneta. On ftss-solvable distributed problems. In *Proceedings of the 6th Annual ACM Symposium on Principles of Distributed Computing*, page 290, 1997.
4. E. W. Dijkstra. Self stabilizing systems in spite of distributed control. *Communications of the Association of the Computing Machinery*, 17:643–644, 1974.
5. S. Dolev. *Self-Stabilization*. MIT Press, 2000.
6. Shashidhar Gandham, Milind Dawande, and Ravi Prakash. Link scheduling in sensor networks: Distributed edge coloring revisited. In *Proceedings of Infocom 2005*. IEEE Press, 2005.
7. Sukumar Ghosh and Mehmet Hakan Karaata. A self-stabilizing algorithm for coloring planar graphs. *Distributed Computing*, 7(1):55–59, 1993.
8. A. S. Gopal and K. J. Perry. Unifying self-stabilization and fault-tolerance. In *Proceedings of the 12th Annual ACM Symposium on Principles of Distributed Computing*, pages 195–206, 1993.
9. Maria Gradinariu and Colette Johnen. Self-stabilizing neighborhood unique naming under unfair scheduler. In *Euro-Par 2001: Parallel Processing, 7th International Euro-Par Conference Manchester, UK August 28-31, 2001, Proceedings*, pages 458–465, 2001.
10. Maria Gradinariu and Sébastien Tixeuil. Self-stabilizing vertex coloration and arbitrary graphs. In *Procdings of the 4th International Conference on Principles of Distributed Systems, OPODIS 2000, Paris, France, December 20-22, 2000*, pages 55–70, 2000.
11. Stephen T. Hedetniemi, David Pokrass Jacobs, and Pradip K. Srimani. Linear time self-stabilizing colorings. *Inf. Process. Lett.*, 87(5):251–255, 2003.
12. Ted Herman and Sébastien Tixeuil. A distributed tdma slot assignment algorithm for wireless sensor networks. In *Algorithmic Aspects of Wireless Sensor Networks: First International Workshop, ALGOSENSORS 2004, Turku, Finland, July 16, 2004. Proceedings*, pages 45–58, 2004.
13. Shing-Tsaan Huang, Su-Shen Hung, and Chi-Hung Tzeng. Self-stabilizing coloration in anonymous planar networks. *Information processing letters*, 95(1):307–312, 2005.
14. T. Masuzawa. A fault-tolerant and self-stabilizing protocol for the topology problem. In *Proceedings of the 2nd Workshop on Self-Stabilizing Systems*, pages 1.1–1.15, 1995.
15. H. Matsui, M. Inoue, T. Masuzawa, and H. Fujiwara. Fault-tolerant and self-stabilizing protocols using an unreliable failure detector. *IEICE Transactions on Information and Systems*, E83-D(10):1831–1840, 2000.
16. M. Nesterenko and A. Arora. Tolerance to unbounded byzantine faults. In *Proceedings of 21st IEEE Symposium on Reliable Distributed Systems*, pages 22–29, 2002.
17. Yusuke Sakurai, Fukuhito Ooshita, and Toshimitsu Masuzawa. A self-stabilizing link-coloring protocol resilient to byzantine faults in tree networks. In *8th International Conference on Principles of Distributed Systems, Grenoble, France, December 15-17*, pages 196–206, 2004.
18. S. Shukla, D. Rosenkrantz, and S. Ravi. Developing self-stabilizing coloring algorithms via systematic randomization. In *Proceedings of the International Workshop on Parallel Processing*, pages 668–673, Bangalore, India, 1994. Tata-McGrawhill, New Delhi.

19. S. Shukla, D. Rosenkrantz, and S. Ravi. Observations on self-stabilizing graph algorithms for anonymous networks. In *Proceedings of the Second Workshop on Self-stabilizing Systems (WSS'95)*, pages 7.1–7.15, 1995.

20. Sumit Sur and Pradip K. Srimani. A self-stabilizing algorithm for coloring bipartite graphs. *Inf. Sci.*, 69(3):219–227, 1993.

21. S. Ukena, Y. Katayama, T. Masuzawa, and H. Fujiwara. A self-stabilizing spanning tree protocol that tolerates non-quiescent permanent faults. *IEICE Transaction*, J85-D-I(11):1007–1014, 2002.

Timed Virtual Stationary Automata
for Mobile Networks

Shlomi Dolev[1,*] Seth Gilbert[2,**] Limor Lahiani[1,*] Nancy Lynch[2,**],
and Tina Nolte[2,**]

[1] Dep. of Computer Science, Ben-Gurion University of the Negev, Beer-Sheva, 84105, Israel
{dolev, lahiani}@cs.bgu.ac.il
[2] MIT CSAIL, Cambridge, MA 02139, USA
{sethg, lynch, tnolte}@theory.csail.mit.edu

Abstract. We define a programming abstraction for mobile networks called the *Timed Virtual Stationary Automata* programming layer, consisting of mobile clients, virtual timed I/O automata called virtual stationary automata (VSAs), and a communication service connecting VSAs and client nodes. The VSAs are located at prespecified regions that tile the plane, defining a static virtual infrastructure. We present a self-stabilizing algorithm to emulate a timed VSA using the real mobile nodes that are currently residing in the VSA's region. We also discuss examples of applications whose implementations benefit from the simplicity obtained through use of the VSA abstraction.

Keywords: Ad-hoc networks, mobile computing, location-aware distributed computing, fault tolerance/availability, virtual infrastructure, state replication, virtual machine.

1   Introduction

The task of designing algorithms for constantly changing networks is difficult. Highly dynamic networks, however, are becoming increasingly prevalent, especially in the context of pervasive and ubiquitous computing, and it is therefore important to develop new techniques to simplify this task. Here we focus on mobile ad-hoc networks, where mobile processors attempt to coordinate despite minimal infrastructure support. This paper develops new techniques to cope with this dynamic, heterogeneous, and chaotic environment.

We mask the unpredictable behavior of mobile networks by defining and emulating a *virtual* infrastructure, consisting of *timing-aware* and *location-aware* machines at fixed locations, that mobile nodes can interact with. The static virtual infrastructure allows application developers to use simpler algorithms — including many previously developed for fixed networks.

There are a number of prior papers that take advantage of geography to facilitate the coordination of mobile nodes. For example, the GeoCast algorithms [19, 1], GOAFR

* Partially supported by IBM faculty award, NSF grant and the Rita Altura chair in computer sciences.
** Supported by DARPA contract F33615-01-C-1896, NSF ITR contract CCR-0121277, and USAF, AFRL contract FA9550-04-1-0121.

J.H. Anderson, G. Prencipe, and R. Wattenhofer (Eds.): OPODIS 2005, LNCS 3974, pp. 130–145, 2006.
© Springer-Verlag Berlin Heidelberg 2006

[13], and algorithms for "routing on a curve" [18] route messages based on the location of the source and destination, using geography to delivery messages efficiently. Other papers [14, 10, 21] use geographic locations as a repository for data. These algorithms associate each piece of data with a region of the network and store the data at certain nodes in the region. This data can then be used for routing or other applications. All of these papers take a relatively ad-hoc approach to using geography and location. We suggest a more systematic approach; many algorithms presented in these papers could be simplified by using a fixed, predictable timing-enabled infrastructure.

In industry there have been a number of attempts to provide specialized applications for ad-hoc networks by organizing some sort of virtual infrastructure over the mobile nodes. PacketHop and Motorola envision mobile devices cooperating to form mesh networks to provide communication in areas with wireless-broadcast devices but little fixed infrastructure [15,26]. These virtual infrastructures could allow on-the-fly network formation that can be used at disaster sites, or areas where fixed infrastructure does not exist or has been damaged. BMW and other car manufacturers are developing systems that allow cars to communicate about local road or car conditions, aiding in accident avoidance [25, 17, 11, 22].

Each of the above examples tackles very specific problems, like routing or distribution of sensor data. A more general-purpose virtual infrastructure, that organizes mobile nodes into general programmable entities, can make a richer set of applications easier to provide. For example, with the advent of autonomous combat drones [24], the complexity of algorithms coordinating the drones can make it difficult to provide assurance to an understandably concerned public that these firepower-equipped autonomous units are coordinating properly. With a formal model of a general and easy-to-understand virtual infrastructure available, it would be easier to both provide and prove correct algorithms for performing sophisticated coordination tasks.

Virtual Stationary Automata programming layer. The programming abstraction we introduce in this paper consists of a static infrastructure of fixed, timed virtual machines with an explicit notion of real-time, called *Virtual Stationary Automata* (VSAs), distributed at known locations over the plane, and emulated by the real mobile nodes in the system. Each VSA represents a predetermined geographic area and has broadcast capabilities similar to those of the mobile nodes, allowing nearby VSAs and mobile nodes to communicate with one another. This programming layer provides mobile nodes with a virtual infrastructure with which to coordinate their actions. Many practical algorithms depend significantly on timing, and many mobile nodes have access to reasonably synchronized clocks. In the VSA programming layer, the virtual automata also have access to *virtual* clocks, guaranteed to not drift too far from real-time. These virtual automata can then run programs whose behaviour might be dependent on the continuous evolution of timing variables.

Our virtual infrastructure differs in key ways from others that have previously been proposed for mobile ad-hoc networks. The GeoQuorums algorithm [6,7] was the first to use virtual nodes; the virtual nodes in that work are atomic objects at fixed geographical locations. More general virtual mobile automata were suggested in [5]; our automata are stationary, and are arranged in a connected pattern that is similar to a traditional wired network. Our automata also have more powerful computational capabilities than those in [5] in that ours include timing capabilities, which are important for many applications. Finally, we use a different implementation stategy for virtual nodes than in [5], incurring less communication cost and enabling us to provide virtual clocks that are never far from real-time.

Emulating the virtual infrastructure. Our clock-enabled VSA layer is emulated by the real mobile nodes in the network. Each mobile node is assumed to have access to a GPS service informing it of the time and region it is currently in. A VSA for a geographic region is then emulated by a subset of the mobile nodes populating its region: the VSA state is maintained in the memory of the real nodes emulating it, and the real nodes perform VSA actions on behalf of the VSA. The emulation is shared by the nodes while one leader node is responsible for performing the outputs of the VSA and keeping the other emulators consistent. If no mobile nodes are in the region, the VSA fails; if mobile nodes later arrive, the VSA restarts.

An important property of our implementation is that it is self-stabilizing. Self-stabilization [3, 4] is the ability to recover from an arbitrarily corrupt state. This property is important in long-lived, chaotic systems where certain events can result in unpredictable faults. For example, transient interference may disrupt the wireless communication, violating our assumptions about the broadcast medium. This might result in inconsistency and corruption in the emulation of the VSA. Our self-stabilizing implementation, however, can recover after corruptions to correctly emulate a VSA.

Applications. We present in this paper an overview of some applications that are significantly simplified by the VSA infrastructure. We consider both low-level services, such as routing and location management, as well as more sophisticated applications, such as motion coordination, tracking, traffic management, and traffic coordination. The key idea in all cases is to locate data and computation at timed VSAs throughout the network, thus relying on the virtual infrastructure to simplify coordination in ad-hoc networks. This infrastructure can be used to implement services such as routing that are oftentimes thought of as the lowest-level services in a network.

2 Datatypes and System Model

The system consists of a finite collection of mobile client processes moving in a closed, connected, and bounded region of the 2D plane called R. Region R is partitioned into predetermined connected subregions called *tiles* or *regions*, labeled with unique ids from the set of tile identifiers U. In practice it may be convenient to restrict tiles to be regular polygons such as squares or hexagons. We define a neighbor relation $nbrs$ on ids from U: two tiles u and v are neighbors iff the supremum distance between points in $tile(u)$ and $tile(v)$ is bounded by a constant r_{virt}.

Each mobile node C_p, $p \in P$, the set of mobile node ids, is modeled as a mobile timed I/O automaton whose location in R at any time is referred to as $loc(p)$. Mobile node speed is bounded by a constant v_{max}. We assume each node occasionally receives information about the time and its current region u; a GPSupdate$(u, now)_p$ happens every ϵ_{sample} time. While GPS is not entirely accurate in reality, as long as an error bound is known, its effects here are small. We assume the node's local clock now progresses at the rate of real-time.

Each client is equipped with a local broadcast communication service called P-bcast, with a minimum broadcast radius of r_{real} and a message delay d. This service allows each client C_p to broadcast a message to all nearby clients through $\mathsf{bcast}(m)_p$ and receive messages broadcast by other clients through $\mathsf{brcv}(m)_p$ actions. We assume that a local broadcast service guarantees two properties: integrity and reliable local delivery. *Integrity* guarantees that every message received was previously broadcast. *Reliable local delivery* (roughly) guarantees that a transmission will be received by nearby nodes: If client C_p broadcasts a message, then every client C_q within r_{real} distance of C_p's transmission location during the transmission interval of length d receives the message before the end of the interval.

Clients are susceptible to stopping and corruption failures. After a stopping failure, a client performs no additional local steps until restarted. If restarted, it starts operating again from an initial state. If a node is corrupted, it suffers from a nondeterministic change to its program state.

Additional arbitrary external interface actions and local state used by algorithms running at the client are allowed. For simplicity local steps are assumed to take no time.

3   Virtual Stationary Automata Programming Layer

Here we describe the *Virtual Stationary Automata* programming layer. This abstraction includes the real mobile nodes discussed in the last section, the virtual stationary automata (VSAs) that the real nodes emulate, and a local broadcast service, V-bcast, between them (see Figure 1). The layer allows developers to write programs for both mobile clients and stationary tiles of the network as though broadcast-equipped virtual machines exist in those tiles. We begin by describing the properties of VSAs and then describe the V-bcast service.

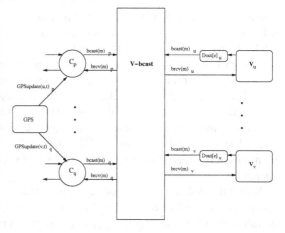

Fig. 1. Virtual Stationary Automata abstraction. VSAs and clients communicate using the V-bcast service. VSA bcasts may be delayed in Dout buffers.

3.1   Virtual Stationary Automata

An abstract VSA is a timing-capable virtual machine. We formally describe such a timed machine for a tile u, V_u, as a TIOA whose program can be referred to as a tuple of its action signature, sig_u, valid states, $states_u$, a start state function, $start_u$, mapping clock values to appropriate start states, a discrete transition function, δ_u, and a set of valid trajectories of the machine, τ_u. Trajectories [12] describe state evolution over intervals of time.

A virtual automaton V_u's external interface is restricted to include only stopping failure, corruption, and restart inputs and the ability to broadcast and receive messages (the restriction guarantees the VSA can be emulated by mobile nodes). Corruptions result in a nondeterministic change to any portion of V_u's state, $vstate$, including the virtual clock $vstate.now$. As with mobile clients, this now value is assumed to progress at the rate of real-time and, outside of failure, equal real-time. Since a VSA is emulated by physical nodes (corresponding to clients) in its region, its failures are defined in terms of client movements and failures in its region: (1) If no clients are in the region, the VSA is crashed, (2) If V_u is failed but a client C_p enters the region and remains for at least $t_{restart}$ time, then in that interval of time V_u restarts, (3) If no client failure (corruption or stopping) occurs in an alive VSA's region over some interval, the VSA does not suffer a failure during that interval, and (4) A VSA may suffer a corruption only if a mobile client in its region suffers a corruption; our self-stabilizing implementation of a VSA guarantees that starting from an arbitrary configuration of the emulation, the emulation's external trace will eventually look like that of the abstract VSA, starting from a corrupted abstract state.

3.2   V-bcast Service

The V-bcast service is a "virtual" broadcast communication service with transmission radius r_{virt}. It is similar to that of the real nodes' P-bcast service and implemented using the P-bcast service. It allows broadcast communication between neighboring VSAs, between VSAs and nearby clients, and between clients through bcast and brcv actions, as before. V-bcast guarantees the integrity property described for P-bcast, as well as a similar reliable local delivery property. The *reliable local delivery* property for V-bcast is as follows: If a client or VSA in a region u transmits a message, then every client or VSA in region u or neighboring regions during the entire time interval starting at transmission and ending d later receives the message by the end of the interval. (For this definition, due to GPSupdate lag, a client is still said to be "in" region u even if it has just left region u but has not yet received a GPSupdate with the change.)

Notice that V-bcast's broadcast radius is different from that of P-bcast; since virtual broadcasts are performed using real broadcasts, the virtual transmission radius cannot be larger than the real. Recall r_{virt} is the supremum distance between points in two neighboring tiles. V-bcast then allows a real node p and a VSA for tile u to communicate as long as the node is at most r_{virt} distance from any point in tile u and a VSA to communicate with another VSA as long as they are in neighboring tiles. The implementation of the V-bcast service using the mobile clients' P-bcast service introduces the requirement that $r_{virt} \leq r_{real} - 2\epsilon_{sample} \cdot v_{max}$. The $2\epsilon_{sample} \cdot v_{max}$ adjustment guarantees that two nodes emulating VSAs for tiles they have just left (because they have not yet received GPSupdates that they've change tiles) can still receive messages transmitted to each other. If GPS error is considered, we would compensate by further decreasing r_{virt} by twice the error bound.

3.3 Delay Augmentation

The overhead of emulating V_u may introduce additional delays in the broadcasting of messages. The emulation of V_u is then called a *delay-augmented TIOA*, an augmentation of V_u with timing perturbations composed with V_u's output interface. These timing perturbations are represented with a buffer Dout$[e]_u$, composed with V_u's bcast output. The buffer delays delivery of messages by some nondeterminstic time $[0, e]$. Program actions of V_u must be written taking into account the emulation parameter e, just as it must the message delay factor d. A discussion of the value of e is in Section 4.4.

4 Implementation of the VSA Layer

We describe the implementation of a VSA by mobile clients in its tile in the network. At a high level, the individual mobile clients in a tile share emulation of the virtual machine through a deterministic state replication algorithm while also being coordinated by a leader. We begin by describing a totally-ordered broadcast service and leader election service for individual regions, also implemented using the underlying real mobile nodes, that we will use in our replication algorithm. We then focus on describing the core emulation algorithm, briefly sketch correctness, and analyze emulation overhead.

4.1 TOBcast Service

In order to keep emulators' state consistent, emulators must process the same sets of messages in the same order. We accomplish this by using the emulators' clocks and P-bcast service to implement a TOBcast service for each region and client. This service allows a client C_p in tile u to broadcast m, TOBcast$(m)_{u,p}$, and to have the message be received, TOBrcv$(m, u)_{v,q}$, by clients in $tile(u)$ and neighboring tiles exactly d time later. To implement this service, when a client wants to TOBcast m from itself or its tile, it tags m with its current tile, time, message sequence number (incremented when the client sends multiple messages at once), and the client id, and broadcasts it using P-bcast. When a client receives such a message from a client in its tile or a neighboring tile it holds the message in a queue until exactly d time has passed since the message's timestamp. Messages that are exactly d old are then TOBrcved in order of sender id and sequence number, ordering the messages. Timestamps are also used to ensure self-stabilization; this is similar to the use of GPS oracles in [9]. To avoid the use of shared variables, we include input and output actions so the TOBcast service can inform the client whether all messages sent up to d time ago have been received. Most complications in the use of these actions come from self-stabilization.

4.2 Leader Election Service

Here we describe the specification for a leader election service required for our emulator implementation. We divide time up into segments of length t_{slice} called timeslices, that begin on multiples of t_{slice}. Assume $t_{slice} \geq 4d$. When there are no corruption failures, the leader election service for a region u guarantees:

(1) There is at most one leader of a region at a time, and the leader is in the region (or within $\epsilon_{sample} \cdot v_{max}$) distance,

(2) If a process p becomes leader of region u at some time, then at that time either:
  (a) there was a prior leader of region u during an interval starting at least d after p entered u and ending after some multiple of t_{slice} at least $2d$ later, or
  (b) there is no process in u where a prior leader such as in (a) can be found,

(3) If a process ceases being leader at time t then it will be at least d time before a new leader is chosen,

(4) For any two consecutive timeslices such that at least one process is alive in u for both timeslices and no failures occur in the latter timeslice, there will be a leader in one of the two timeslices from at least $2d$ time before the end of the timeslice to the end of the timeslice.

Property (2) guarantees that either the process that is chosen as a leader has been in the region long enough to have interacted with a prior leader, or there are no processes for which that is true. Property (3) provides a time gap between leaders that will later be useful in guaranteeing that a new leader had heard all prior leader broadcasts before it became a leader.

One example of a self-stabilizing heartbeat implementation of this leader election specification is as follows: if a process is leader, it broadcasts a leaderhb message every t_{slice} amount of time. Once it fails or leaves the tile, the other processes in the region will synchronously timeout the heartbeat and send restart messages, from which the lowest id process that had previously heard a heartbeat from the leader at least $3d$ time after entering the tile is chosen as leader; this ensures that property (2a) holds. If there is no such process, then the lowest id process becomes leader. This simplistic strategy ignores issues of network contention or power management. We briefly discuss alternative leader election strategies in Section 6.

4.3   Emulator Implementation

Here we describe a fault-tolerant implementation of a VSA emulator. We first describe how our leader-based emulation generally works and then address details in the emulation. The signature, state, and trajectories for the algorithm are in Figure 2 and the actions are in Figure 3. Line numbers refer to lines in Figure 3.

Leader-based virtual machine emulation. In our virtual machine emulation, at most one of the mobile nodes in a VSA's tile is a leader (chosen by the leader election service), with primary responsibility for emulating the VSA and performing VSA outputs. A leader stores and updates the state of the VSA (including the VSA's clock value) locally, simulating all actions of the VSA based on it. When the leader receives a TOBcast message, it places the message in a local saved message queue (lines 33-37) from which it simulates the VSA brcving (processing) the message (lines 39-45). If the VSA is to perform a local action, the leader simulates its effect on the VSA state (lines 47-54). If the VSA action is to bcast a message, the leader places the message in an outgoing VSA queue (lines 53-54), to be removed and TOBcasted with the tile as the source by the leader, in the VSA's stead (lines 56-61).

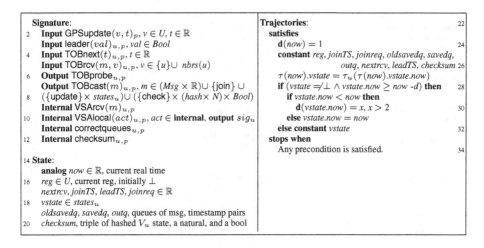

Fig. 2. $\text{VSAE}_{u,p}$, emulator at p of $\mathbf{V}_u = \langle sig_u, states_u, start_u, \delta_u, \tau_u \rangle$ - signature, state, trajectories

For fault-tolerance and load balancing reasons, it is necessary to have more than just the leader maintaining a VSA. In our multiple emulator approach, a VSA is maintained by several emulators, including at most one leader, each maintaining and updating its local copy of the VSA state and saved message queue as above. However, non-leader emulators, unlike leaders, do not transmit messages for the VSA from their outgoing VSA queues, preventing multiple transmission of messages from the VSA. To keep emulators consistent, the emulation trajectories are based on a determinized version of the VSA trajectories.

Emulation details. There are several complications in VSA emulation that arise due to both message delays and process failure:

Joining: When a node discovers it is in a new region, it TOBcasts a join message (lines 23-31). Any process that receives this message stores the timestamp of the message as the latest join request (lines 63-65). If a leader has processed all messages in its saved message queue and TOBcasted all messages in its outgoing VSA queue, it answers outstanding join requests by TOBcasting an update message, containing a copy of the leader's current emulated VSA state (lines 67-75). The leader holds off on performing any additional VSA-related transmissions until it receives this message (line 75). When any process that has been in the region at least $2d$ time receives the update, it adopts the attached VSA state as its own local VSA state and erases its outgoing VSA queue (lines 77-91). (If it has not been in the region $2d$ time, its saved message queue may not have all messages that were too recent to be reflected in the update.)

Catching up to real time: After receipt of an update message, the VSA's clock (and state) can be d behind real time. Intuitively, the VSA emulation is "set back" whenever an update message is received. To guarantee the VSA emulation satisfies the specifications from Section 3 (bounding the time the output trace of the emulation may be behind that of the VSA being emulated), the virtual clock must catch up to real time.

Output TOBprobe$_{u,p}$	**Output** TOBcast($\langle$update, $vstate'\rangle$)$_{u,p}$

Output TOBprobe$_{u,p}$
2 **Precondition:**
  $nextrcv \leq now$ -d
4

Input TOBnext(t)$_{u,p}$
6 **Effect:**
  $nextrcv \leftarrow t$
8

Input GPSupdate(v,t)$_p$
10 **Effect:**
  $now \leftarrow t$
12 **if** $reg \neq v$ **then**
  $reg \leftarrow v$
14 $joinTS \leftarrow \infty$

16 **Input** leader(val)$_{u,p}$
Effect:
18 **if** (! $val \lor joinTS > now$ -d) **then**
  $leadTS \leftarrow \infty$
20 **else if** $leadTS > now + d$ **then**
  $leadTS \leftarrow now$
22

Output TOBcast(join)$_{u,p}$
24 **Precondition:**
  $reg = u \land joinTS > now$
26 **Effect:**
  $joinTS \leftarrow now$
28 $nextrcv \leftarrow now$ -d
  $leadTS, joinreq \leftarrow \infty$
30 $savedq, oldsavedq, outq \leftarrow \emptyset$
  $vstate, checksum \leftarrow \perp$
32

Input TOBrcv(m,s)$_{u,p}$, $m.\textbf{first} \notin$ {check,update,join}
34 **Effect:**
  $savedq \leftarrow \textbf{append}(savedq, \langle m.\textbf{first}, now$ -$d\rangle)$
36 **if** ($s = u \land \exists x,y$:[$outq = \textbf{append}(\textbf{append}(x, m), y)$])
  then $outq \leftarrow y$
38

Internal VSArcv(m)$_{u,p}$
40 **Precondition:**
  $vstate \neq \perp \land \langle m, t\rangle = \textbf{head}(savedq)$
42 **Effect:**
  $vstate \leftarrow \delta_u(vstate, \textbf{brcv}(m))$
44 $oldsavedq \leftarrow \textbf{append}(oldsavedq, \textbf{head}(savedq))$
  $savedq \leftarrow \textbf{tail}(savedq)$
46

Internal VSAlocal(act)$_{u,p}$
48 **Precondition:**
  $vstate \neq \perp \neq \delta_u(vstate, act) \land savedq = \emptyset$
50 $nextrcv > now$ -$d \land act = \textbf{next}(vstate, \delta_u)$
Effect:
52 $vstate \leftarrow \delta_u(vstate, act)$
  if $act = \textbf{bcast}(m)$ **then**
54 $outq \leftarrow \textbf{append}(outq, \langle m, vstate.now\rangle)$

56 **Output** TOBcast(m)$_{u,p}$
Precondition:
58 $reg = u \land leadTS \leq now < nextrcv + d \land vstate \neq \perp$
  $vstate.now \geq now$ -$d \land \forall\langle m, t\rangle \in outq: t \geq now$ -e
60 $m = \textbf{head}(outq)$
Effect: $outq \leftarrow \textbf{tail}(outq)$
62

Input TOBrcv(join, u)$_{u,p}$
64 **Effect:**
  $joinreq \leftarrow now$ -d

Output TOBcast($\langle$update, $vstate'\rangle$)$_{u,p}$
Precondition: 68
  $reg = u \land leadTS \leq now < nextrcv + d$
  ($vstate' = vstate \land [vstate = \perp \lor (vstate.now = now$ 70
  $\land outq = \emptyset = savedq \land joinreq =/\infty)]) \lor (vstate' = \perp$
  $\land [vstate.now < now$ -$d \lor \exists \langle m, t\rangle \in outq: t < now$ -$e])$72
Effect:
  $joinreq \leftarrow \infty$ 74
  $leadTS \leftarrow now + d$
76

Input TOBrcv($\langle$update, $vstate'\rangle$, u)$_{u,p}$
Effect: 78
  if $joinreq \leq now$ -$2d$ **then**
    $joinreq \leftarrow \infty$ 80
  if ($joinTS \leq now$ -$2d \land vstate' = \perp$) **then**
    $vstate \leftarrow start_u(now)$ 82
    $savedq \leftarrow \emptyset$
  else if $joinTS \leq now$ -$2d$ **then** 84
    if $vstate = \perp$ **then**
      $oldsavedq \leftarrow \emptyset$ 86
    $vstate \leftarrow vstate'$
    $savedq \leftarrow \textbf{append}(oldsavedq, savedq)$ 88
      $- \{\langle m, t\rangle: t \leq now$ -$2d\}$ 90
    $oldsavedq, outq \leftarrow \emptyset$
    $checksum \leftarrow \perp$
92

Internal correctqueues$_{u,p}$
Precondition: 94
  $\exists \langle m,t\rangle \in oldsavedq \cup savedq: t > now$ -d
  $\lor \exists \langle m,t\rangle \in outq: t > now$ 96
Effect:
  $savedq, oldsavedq - = \{\langle m, t\rangle: t > now$ -$d\}$ 98
  $outq - = \{\langle m, t\rangle: t > now\}$ 100

Internal checksum$_{u,p}$
Precondition: 102
  $vstate.now \textbf{ mod } ttl_{update} = 0 \land nextrcv > now$ -d
  $savedq = \emptyset \land \forall act \in sig_u$-$\{\textbf{brcv}(m)\}:\delta_u(vstate,act)= \perp$ 104
  $checksum =/\langle\textbf{checksum}(vstate),vstate.now/ttl_{update},*\rangle$ 106
Effect:
  $checksum \leftarrow$
    $\langle\textbf{checksum}(vstate), vstate.now / ttl_{update}, \textbf{false}\rangle$ 108
  if ($joinreq \neq \infty \land joinreq > now$ -d) **then**
    $joinreq \leftarrow now$ -d 110

Output TOBcast($\langle$check, $\langle csum, t\rangle, jr\rangle$)$_{u,p}$ 112
Precondition:
  $reg = u \land leadTS \leq now < nextrcv + d \land outq = \emptyset$ 114
  $now + d \leq (t + 1)\cdot ttl_{update}$
  $checksum = \langle csum, t, \textbf{false}\rangle \land jr = = (joinreq \neq \infty)$ 116
Effect:
  $checksum \leftarrow \langle csum, t, \textbf{true}\rangle$ 118

Input TOBrcv($\langle$check, $\langle csum', t'\rangle, jr\rangle$, u)$_{u,p}$ 120
Effect:
  $outq - = \{\langle m, t\rangle: t \leq t' \cdot t_{slice}\}$ 122
  if ($jr \land joinreq = \infty$) **then**
    $joinreq \leftarrow now$ -$2d$ 124
  if ([$vstate = \perp \land joinTS \leq now$ -$2d \land ! jr$]
    $\lor [vstate \neq \perp \land checksum \neq \langle csum', t', *\rangle]$) **then** 126
    $joinTS \leftarrow \infty$
  else $checksum \leftarrow \langle csum', t', \textbf{true}\rangle$ 128

Fig. 3. VSAE$_{u,p}$, emulator at p of $V_u = \langle sig_u, states_u, start_u, \delta_u, \tau_u\rangle$ - actions

This is done by having the virtual clock advance more than twice as fast as real time until both are equal, after which they increase at the same rate. This is formally described in Figure 2, lines 28-32. To guarantee that the virtual clock can catch up before d time, we require a leader to only transmit an update message once its virtual clock is caught up to real time (line 70).

Message processing: Messages to be received by the VSA are placed in a saved message queue from which emulators simulate receiving the messages. If an update message is received, setting back the state of the VSA, emulators must be able to resimulate receiving messages that were sent up to d time before the update was sent. In order to guarantee this, whenever an emulator processes a message from the saved message queue for the VSA, it moves the message into an old saved message queue (line 44); if a process receives an update message, it moves all messages in that queue that were received after the update was sent back into its saved message queue to be reprocessed (line 88-89).

Making up leader broadcasts: If a leader is supposed to perform broadcasts on the VSA's behalf, but fails or leaves before sending them, the next leader needs to transmit the messages. Since emulators store outgoing VSA messages in a local outgoing queue, the new leader just transmits any messages stored in its outgoing queue (lines 56-61) and removes them. To prevent messages from being rebroadcast by future leaders, emulators that receive a VSA message broadcast by the leader remove it from their own outgoing queues (lines 36-37).

Restarting a VSA: If a process is leader and has no value for the VSA state or has messages in its outgoing queue with timestamps older than the delay augmentation parameter e, it restarts the emulation. It does this by sending an update message with attached state of $\bot$ and then waiting to receive the message (lines 67-75). When processes that have been in the region $2d$ time receive the message d later, they initialize the VSA state and messaging queues and begin emulating a restarted VSA (lines 77-91).

Self-stabilization. Our implementation is self-stabilizing through the use of local correction and update and checksum messages. The update messages sent by a leader contain state information which overwrites any VSA state information at other emulators, bringing emulators into agreement about VSA state. In the event that join requests do not occur very often, if the virtual clock is divisible by ttl_{update}, the emulators calculate and store a checksum of the VSA state. The leader is then responsible for sending out checksum messages with the attached checksum. Emulators, when they receive this message, compare the attached checksum to the version that they have stored. If the versions differ, they re-join. This ensures that emulators will have state consistent with the leader's.

4.4 Correctness and Performance Evaluation

Correctness roughly consists of guaranteeing liveness of the emulation under certain circumstances and guaranteeing that emulations of an abstract VSA implement the VSA.

We say a VSA emulation is *failed* if no process in the region has VSA state $vstate \neq \bot$ such that $vstate.now \geq now - d$ and its outgoing queue has no messages with timestamps more than e before real-time.

Assume that as a parameter of the system, there is some positive integer k such that if a process is alive in a region from the beginning of any timeslice t through the end of timeslice $t + k$, then there is at least one timeslice in $t + 1 \ldots t + k$ where no failures or leaves of processes occur in the region. We can then show the following:

Lemma 1. *For any non-failed VSA emulation, VSA outputs are not delayed by more than $e = (k + 1) \cdot t_{slice} - d$ time, and as long as from the beginning of any timeslice there is at least one alive process in the VSA's region with $vstate \neq \bot$, $vstate.now \geq now - d$, and an outgoing queue without messages that are older than e that remains alive in the region through the following k timeslices, the VSA emulation does not fail or restart.*

Lemma 2. *If a VSA is failed in some timeslice but there is an alive process in the VSA's region from the beginning of the timeslice through the following k timeslices, then the VSA will be restarted within e time.*

Theorem 1. *The VSA emulator and client implementation (S) correctly implement the VSA abstraction (A): timed-traces(S) $\subseteq$ timed-traces(A).*

Proof sketch: We introduce an intermediate layer, and describe a (simple) simulation relation [12] between this layer and the abstract layer. We then describe a simulation relation from our implementation to the intermediate layer. Together, this shows the implementation implements the abstract layer.

The intermediate layer is similar to the abstract layer, except that VSAs may have clocks that are behind real-time and have incoming delay buffers that hold each message bound for the VSA until the VSA's clock passes the message's timestamp. This layer captures the idea that VSA state in the emulation can be behind what the corresponding abstract VSA state would be. A simulation relation is then defined to show that this intermediate layer implements the abstract layer, by relating the state of a VSA, its incoming message buffer, and outgoing message buffer in the intermediate layer to what will be the state of that VSA and its delayed outgoing message buffer in the abstract layer, once its virtual clock equals the current real-time.

We then describe a forward simulation relation between the implementation and the intermediate VSA abstraction for non-failed VSA emulations. There are several parts, relating state of emulators to the state of the abstract VSA and state of message buffers in the implementation to those of the abstract system:

(1) For any process where $vstate \neq \bot$, the value of $vstate$ is equivalent to $V_u.vstate$ unless there is an **update** message in transit, in which case $V_u.vstate$ is equal to the attached state in the **update** message.

(2) If m is a message either in transit to p or in p's saved message queue, then m is in virtual transmission to u. If there is an **update** message in transit and m is in p's old saved message queue and if m was sent less than d before the **update**, then it is in virtual transmission to u.

(3) If m is a message in transit to p and was sent by V_u, then the message is in virtual transmission to p.

(4) If m is a message in the outgoing queue and not currently in transit, and no **update** message is in transit then m is in Dout[e].   □

Message complexity. There are two parts to the message overhead introduced by this algorithm. The first is that of the overhead in normal operation introduced over that of the virtual machine if it was real. This is just one checksum-sized message every ttl_{update} time (used for self-stabilization). The second is that of the overhead from dealing with processes joining the emulation. In this case, when a successful join occurs it results in a broadcast of the VSA state and saved message queue, which could contain as many messages as could be received in d time. If M' is the number of messages that can be received in d time, then the bit overhead of a join is $O(|vstate| + |msg| \cdot M')$.

5 Applications for the VSA Layer

We believe the VSA layer will be helpful for many applications, including some of the more difficult coordination problems for nonhomogenous networks oftentimes desired in true mobile ad-hoc deployments. It allows application developers to re-use many algorithms originally designed for the fixed network or base station setting, and to design different services for different regions. Here we list several applications whose implementations would benefit from use of the VSA abstraction.

Geo-routing. One important application is to allow arbitrary regions to communicate. This can be easily implemented by VSAs that utilize the fixed tiling of the network to forward messages [9]. Each VSA chooses a neighboring VSA to forward a message to according to criteria of shortest path to destination or greedy DFS as suggested in [8]. The VSA layer offers a fixed tiled infrastructure to depend on, rather than the ad-hoc imaginary tiling used in that algorithm. Retransmissions along greedy DFS explored links can be used to cope with repeated crashes and recoveries [9]. The GOAFR algorithm [13], combining greedy routing and face routing, can be used to give efficient routing in the face of "holes" in the VSA tiling.

Location management and end-to-end routing. Location management is a difficult task in ad-hoc networks, as many algorithms assume fixed infrastructure and raise difficult-to-analyze concerns about data consistency. However, *home location* algorithms are easily implemented using the VSA layer [9]. Each client's id can be hashed to a set of VSAs (home locations) that would store the client's location. The client would occasionally inform its local VSA of its presence. That local VSA would then inform the client's home locations, using a Geo-routing service, of the region. Anyone searching for the client would have their local VSA query the client's home location VSAs, again using the a Geo-routing service, for the client's location.

The home location service can then be used to provide tracking services or end-to-end communication between individual clients [9]. A message is sent to a client by looking up its location using the home location service and then using Geo-routing to send the message to VSAs close to the returned location. Those VSAs that receive the message broadcast it to local clients for delivery by the intended recipient.

Distributed coordination. VSAs corresponding to geographic regions can be a source of on-line information and coordination, directing mobile clients to help them complete distributed systemwide missions. The virtual infrastructure can make it easier to handle coordination of many clients when tasks are complex. Also, many coordination problems can tolerate a VSA in an empty region failing since such regions have no clients to coordinate. The use of a virtual infrastructure to enable mobile clients to coordinate and equally space themselves along a target curve was recently demonstrated in [16]. The paper provides a simple framework for coordinating client nodes through interaction with virtual nodes. It also demonstrates a simplistic "emulator-aware" approach to maintenance of virtual automata; a VSA makes decisions about target destinations for participating clients based partly on information about local population density in an attempt to keep the VSA alive. The approach could be extended to take into account more client or network factors and even to provide active recruitment, where virtual automata can request emulator aid from distant virtual automata regions.

An example of a timed coordination application is that of a *virtual traffic light*. A VSA for a region corresponding to the intersection of roads in a remote area can provide a virtual traffic light that keeps the light green in each direction for a specific amount of time, providing a substitute for the fixed infrastructure lacking in the region. The VSA would be emulated by computers on vehicles approaching the intersection. Multiple traffic VSAs can also coordinate to facilitate optimal movement of mobile clients.

Another coordination application is the Virtual Air-Traffic Controller [20]. The VSA controller uses detailed knowledge of time in order to plan where and when airborne planes should fly. The burden of regulating lateral separation of aircraft could be allocated in a distributed fashion by VSAs, where VSAs assign local planes different time separations and altitudes based on aircraft type and heading. By devolving some decision-making to aircraft, we can both alleviate ground-based bottlenecks and allow for more local control of flight plans, resulting in optimized routes and better fuel economy [23]. Airspace VSAs are easy to envision, given positioning, long-range communications, and computing resources increasingly available on commercial aircraft.

Data collection and dissemination. A VSA could maintain a summary database of information about its local conditions and those of other regions. Clients could then query their local VSA to get recent information about a location. The history is complete as long as the VSA's tile remains occupied. Resiliency can be built in by using techniques already designed for static but failure-prone networks, such as automatically backing up data at neighboring VSAs or sending data to a central, reliable location by a background convergecast algorithm executed by the VSA network.

Hierarchical distributed data structures. Here, tile size is constrained by the broadcast range of the underlying nodes. An hierarchical emulation of the model, where multiple nodes coordinate to emulate larger tiles, can provide a more general infrastructure. The VSA layer can be a basic building block to implement hierarchies in a network that could, for example, be used to allow clients to register and query attributes.

6   Current and Future Work

The system model assumed so far abstracts away details of the underlying physical layer in order to clearly describe algorithmic issues. Here we discuss some implementation issues and extensions. We also hope that current work simulating this layer and implementing it will guide improvements in our layer implementation.

Non-synchronized clocks. The VSA layer model and implementation could be extended to allow for a known bound on mobile node clock drift. This results in the addition of incoming message delay buffers for VSAs in the abstract model, in addition to the outgoing ones already present.

Emulation strategies to accommodate message collisions. Our work is being extended to a communication model allowing message collisions [2]. One approach is to relax the physical and VSA layer broadcast models to allow message loss in the presence of contention, but guarantee the VSA emulation is reliable by taking advantage of the fact that leader election effectively defines an orderly timeslicing of a communication channel for at least one process. Consider two channels per tile in the network, provided either through frequency allocation or additional timeslicing. Assuming a leader election service for this setting, whichever process is leader can have one channel to itself, allowing it to perform VSA related broadcasts without interference from other processes. The other channel could be used by nodes trying to communicate with the VSA; message loss on this channel would be possible since there could be contention. The leader can then become the arbiter of which messages are actually received by the VSA, by rebroadcasting received messages; other emulators adopt these as the incoming messages for the VSA. Alternatively, a more state transmission heavy approach could be adopted, where non-leader emulators are passive, and the leader periodically broadcasts up-to-date state to them.

Leader election algorithms. Our emulation algorithm utilizes a basic leader election service with a simple interface. Alternative leader election strategies can be considered. For example, a round-robin strategy can help relieve network congestion. Such a strategy could periodically select a new leader from a k-bounded vector of mobile nodes in a region called *guards*. This is done by defining globally known *timeslices* of length t_{slice} and rotating the *guards* vector each timeslice, defining revolving responsibility for leadership. Whichever process's id and join timestamp pair is currently at the head of the rotating vector is the leader. Processes trying to join the *guards* vector are appended to it if there is room while leaders that fail to transmit during their timeslice are subsequently dropped from the vector.

A promising area for further research is into region-based leader election algorithms for mobile networks that are designed to produce stable outputs that take into account factors such as location, speed, power constraints, and reliability of individual nodes. Improved leader election guarantees can lead to improved emulation guarantees.

In addition, a leader election service could be extended to inform client nodes if they should participate in emulation at all. Some clients could be told they are not needed for emulation for some period, allowing them to conserve power.

Extensions to non-homogenous networks. In many cases, there are portions of a deployment area that have fixed infrastructure or sensing capabilities and portions that do not. While the model we introduced here does not take into account the fact that some deployments may have some access to fixed infrastructure, the model in this paper should easily be extended to accommodate these mixed deployments.

References

1. Camp, T. and Liu, Y., "An adaptive mesh-based protocol for geocast routing", *Journal of Parallel and Distributed Computing: Special Issue on Mobile Ad-hoc Networking and Computing*, pp. 196–213, 2002.
2. Chockler, G., Demirbas, M., Gilbert, S., Newport, C., and Nolte, T., "Consensus and Collision Detectors in Wireless Ad Hoc Networks", *Proceedings of the 24th Annual ACM Symposium on Principles of Distributed Computing (PODC)*, 2005.
3. Dijkstra, E.W., "Self stabilizing systems in spite of distributed control", *Communications of the ACM*, 1974.
4. Dolev, S., *Self-Stabilization*, MIT Press, 2000.
5. Dolev, S., Gilbert, S., Lynch, N., Schiller, E., Shvartsman, A., and Welch, J., "Virtual Mobile Nodes for Mobile Ad Hoc Networks", *International Conference on Principles of Distributed Computing (DISC)*, 2004.
6. Dolev, S., Gilbert, S., Lynch, N., Shvartsman, A., and Welch, J., "GeoQuorums: Implementing Atomic Memory in Ad Hoc Networks", *17th International Conference on Principles of Distributed Computing (DISC)*, Springer-Verlag LNCS:2848, 2003.
7. Dolev, S., Gilbert, S., Lynch, N., Shvartsman, A., and Welch, J., "GeoQuorums: Implementing Atomic Memory in Ad Hoc Networks", Technical Report MIT-LCS-TR-900, MIT Laboratory for Computer Science, Cambridge, MA, 02139, 2003.
8. Dolev, S., Herman, T., and Lahiani, L., "Polygonal Broadcast, Secret Maturity and the Firing Sensors", *Third International Conference on Fun with Algorithms (FUN)*, pp. 41-52, May 2004. Also to appear in *Ad Hoc Networks Journal*, Elseiver.
9. Dolev, S., Lahiani, L., Lynch, N., and Nolte, T., "Self-Stabilizing Mobile Node Location Management and Message Routing", Symposium on Self Stabilizing Systems (SSS), 2005.
10. Hubaux, J.P., Le Boudec, J.Y., Giordano, S., and Hamdi, M., "The Terminodes Project: Towards Mobile Ad-Hoc WAN", *Proceedings of MOMUC*, 1999.
11. Kan, M., Pande, R., Vinograd, P., and Garcia-Molina, H., "Event Dissemination in High-Mobility Ad-hoc Networks", Technical Report, 2005.
12. Kaynar, D., Lynch, N., Segala, R., and Vaandrager, F., "The Theory of Timed I/O Automata", Technical Report MIT-LCS-TR-917a, MIT LCS, Cambridge, MA, 2004.
13. Kuhn, F., Wattenhofer, R., Zhang, Y., and Zollinger, A., "Geometric Ad-Hoc Routing: Of Theory and Practice", *Proceedings of the 22nd Annual ACM Symposium on Principles of Distributed Computing (PODC)*, 2003.
14. Li, J., Jannotti, J., De Couto, D.S.J., Karger, D.R., and Morris, R., "A Scalable Location Service for Geographic Ad Hoc Routing", *Proceedings of Mobicom*, 2000.
15. Lok, C., "Instant Networks: Just Add Software", *Technology Review*, June, 2005.
16. Lynch, N., Mitra, S., and Nolte, T., "Motion coordination using virtual nodes", To appear: IEEE Conference on Decision and Control, 2005.
17. Morris, R., Jannotti, J., Kaashoek, F., Li, J., and Decouto, D., "CarNet: A Scalable Ad Hoc Wireless Network System", 9th ACM SIGOPS European Workshop, Kolding, Denmark, September 2000.
18. Nath, B. and Niculescu, D., "Routing on a curve", *ACM SIGCOMM Computer Communication Review*, 2003.
19. Navas, J.C. and Imielinski, T., "Geocast- geographic addressing and routing", *Proceedings of the 3rd MobiCom*, 1997.
20. Neogi, N., "Designing Trustworthy Networked Systems: A Case Study of the National Airspace System", International System Safety Conference, Ottawa, Canada, 2003.

21. Ratnasamy, S., Karp, B., Yin, L., Yu, F., Estrin, D., Govindan, R., and Shenker, S., "GHT: A Geographic Hash Table for Data-Centric Storage", *First ACM International Workshop on Wireless Sensor Networks and Applications (WSNA)*, 2002.

22. Sun, Q., and Garcia-Molina, H., "Using Ad-hoc Inter-vehicle Networks for Regional Alerts", Technical Report, 2004.

23. Talbot, D., "Airborne Networks", *Technology Review*, May, 2005.

24. Talbot, D., "The Ascent of the Robotic Attack Jet", *Technology Review*, March, 2005.

25. Vasek, T., "World Changing Ideas: Germany", *Technology Review*, April, 2005.

26. Woolley, S., "Backwater Broadband", *Forbes*, 2005.

Asynchronous and Fully Self-stabilizing
Time-Adaptive Majority Consensus

Janna Burman[1], Ted Herman[2], Shay Kutten[1,*], and Boaz Patt-Shamir[3]

[1] Dept. of Industrial Engineering & Management
Technion, Haifa 32000, Israel
bjanna@tx.technion.ac.il, kutten@ie.technion.ac.il
[2] Dept. of Computer Science
University of Iowa, Iowa City, Iowa 52242, USA
herman@cs.uiowa.edu
[3] Dept. of Electrical Engineering
Tel-Aviv University, Tel Aviv 69978, Israel
boaz@eng.tau.ac.il

Abstract. We study the scenario where a batch of transient faults hits an asynchronous distributed system by corrupting the state of some f nodes. We concentrate on the basic *majority consensus* problem, where nodes are required to agree on a common output value which is the input value of the majority of them. We give a fully self-stabilizing adaptive algorithm, i.e., the output value stabilizes in $O(f)$ time at all nodes, for any unknown f. Moreover, a state stabilization occurs in time proportional to the (unknown) diameter of the network. Both upper bounds match known lower bounds to within a constant factor. Previous results (stated for a slightly less general problem called "persistent bit") assumed the synchronous network model, and that $f < n/2$.

1 Introduction

We consider protocols that can withstand *state-corrupting faults* that flip the bits of the volatile memory in a system arbitrarily. A system that reaches a legitimate state starting from an arbitrary state is called *self-stabilizing* [14] or *fully self-stabilizing*.[1] The *stabilization time* is the time that elapses since the protocol starts executing (with arbitrary states at the corrupted nodes) until the system reaches a legal state. Classical self-stabilizing protocols were designed to minimize worst-case stabilization time regardless of the number of nodes whose state was corrupted by the faults. More recently, it has been recognized that if the faults hit only a few nodes, then a much faster stabilization is possible, see e.g. [25, 2, 29, 30]. In [29, 30] a system is called *time-adaptive* or *fault-local* if its stabilization time is proportional to the number of nodes whose state was corrupted.

---

* This research was partially supported by the Israel Science Foundation (Grant 4005/02).
[1] We use the qualifier "fully" to emphasize that the state can be arbitrarily corrupted. We mention some weaker forms of stabilization later.

J.H. Anderson, G. Prencipe, and R. Wattenhofer (Eds.): OPODIS 2005, LNCS 3974, pp. 146–160, 2006.

The *Majority Consensus* problem is a basic problem in distributed computing: each node has an input, and it is required that the output at each node stabilizes to the majority of these inputs. In this paper it is assumed that the input can be changed by transient faults, by the environment, or by the stabilizing algorithm. This problem is a simple form of the general consensus problem [20], which is fundamental to fault tolerant distributed applications.

Our Results. We present a fully self-stabilizing, optimal time-adaptive solution for the majority consensus problem for asynchronous networks. The output of our algorithm stabilizes in time proportional to f, the number of nodes hit by faults. The state stabilization time is proportional to the network diameter. In other words, our algorithm is optimal in both output and state stabilization (see [29]). These properties hold even in the case that $f \geq n/2$ (where n is the number of nodes). This should be contrasted with previous results that were only for $f < n/2$.

As a corollary, our solution solves the *Persistent Bit* problem [30, 29] whenever such a solution is possible. "Persistent Bit" is the task of remembering the value of a replicated bit in the face of state corruptions. The time adaptive solution in [29] was only for *synchronous* networks, while we solve it time adaptively for asynchronous networks.

The algorithm utilizes some known techniques, namely the self-stabilizing synchronization [6] and the power-supply method [1]. We use a new version of the power-supply method. The time-adaptivity we prove for power-supply is stronger than the self-stabilization proven in [1]; this new property may be useful for other applications of power supply.

For simplicity, we present the algorithm as one maintaining only 0/1 values, but it can easily be adapted for any range of values.

Related Work. The study of self-stabilizing protocols was initiated by Dijkstra [14]. *Reset-based* approaches to self-stabilization are described in [27, 3, 7, 6, 16, 5]. One of the main drawbacks of this approach is that the detection mechanism triggers a system-wide reset in the face of the slightest inconsistency.

Fast stabilization of the output variables are demonstrated in a number of algorithms [26, 24, 2, 22, 4, 11, 32, 8]. Some general methods to achieve time adaptivity are discussed in [29, 17, 21]. The distinction between output stabilization and state stabilization (see definitions in Sec. 2) is used and discussed in a number of papers [29, 31, 15, 25, 23].

We use the self stabilizing synchronizer with a counter (sometimes called *phase clock*) of [6]. Other phase clocks in the literature, such as [10, 18, 13, 23], may also be useful.

Papers most closely related to our work are [6, 25, 2, 29, 30, 22, 11, 32]. A preliminary brief announcement [28] at the PODC'98 symposium announces results that appear in the current paper.

Paper Organization. In Sec. 2, we formalize the model and introduce a few notations. In Sec. 3, we present the problems and explain the overall structure of the solution. The new algorithm is presented in Sec. 4 and 5 dealing with output and state stabilization respectively.

2   Model and Notations

System Model. The system topology is represented by an undirected graph $G = (V, E)$, where nodes represent processors and edges represent communication links. The number of the nodes is denoted by $n = |V|$. The diameter of the graph is denoted by **diam**. We assume that there is a known upper bound on the diameter of the network, denoted by D. This upper bound serves only for the purpose of having finite space protocols. For $i \in V$, we define $N(i) = \{j \mid (i, j) \in E\}$, called the *neighbors* of i. We do not assume that the set of edges in the network is known in advance, i.e., algorithms are required to work on any topology. We consider an *asynchronous message passing network* model. In a message passing network, processors may exchange values only by transmitting *packet*s. In our model, a packet consists of a set of *messages*. The packet delivery time can be arbitrary, but for the purpose of time analysis only, we assume that each packet is delivered in at most one time unit.

The number of packets that may be in transit on any link in each direction and at the same time is bounded by some parameter B (independent of the network size). We adopt this assumption from [1]; it is necessary, as shown in [19], for solving problems in a self-stabilizing manner. For simplicity, we assume that $B = 1$, i.e., there is at most one outstanding packet on each link at any given time (see [7] for more details). A packet may contain any number of messages. Each message contains information (a node identity and more) related to some specific node. In our algorithm, we distinguish between two types of messages, called *strong* and *weak* (Sec. 4.1). Each node maintains two buffers for each link: one for the incoming packets and another one for the outgoing packets. Each buffer contains at most one message for each type and for each node: for each type and node, only the most recent message is stored in the buffer (cf. [1]). If a new message arrives, the previous one is discarded.

We adopt the usual definitions of the following: a local state of a node (an assignment of values to the local variables and the location counter); a global state of a system of nodes (the cross product of the local states of its constituent nodes, plus the contents of the links); the semantics of protocol actions (possible atomic steps and their associated state changes); an execution sequence of protocol P (a possibly infinite sequence of global states in which each element follows from its predecessor by execution of a single atomic step of P).

Fault Model. We follow the terminology of [29]. We assume that each protocol has a *legality predicate* over the set of global states. Informally, a legal global state of our protocol is a state in which the protocol is ready to get a new batch of faults in the sense that following these faults the protocol satisfy all its claimed execution properties (in particular, time adaptivity; as for state stabilization, our protocol stabilizes from any finite number of faults that occur anytime). A formal definition of the legality predicate of our protocol is deferred to the full paper. A *faulty node* is defined as in [6]. We define two global states: a *start state* s_0 that exists at time $t_0 = 0$, right after the faults hit, and a *reference state* s_{-1}, where s_{-1} is legal; a node is called faulty if its local state is different in s_0 and s_{-1}. Note that every part of the state (except for the ID of the node) can be changed by the adversary and this is considered a fault. Without loss of generality, a fault that corrupts a packet over a link is considered a fault in the node that receives that packet eventually. A *fault number* is the number of faulty nodes at the start state s_0.

A protocol is called f-*stabilizing* if starting from a state with fault number at most f, it reaches a legal state eventually and remains in a legal state thereafter. A protocol is called *self-stabilizing* or *fully self-stabilizing* if it is f-stabilizing for $f = n$. We distinguish between *output stabilization* and *state stabilization*: output stabilization is said to occur once the externally observable portion of the state becomes (and stays) legal, and state stabilization is said to occur when the entire state becomes (and stays) legal. The maximum number of time units that takes to reach the state stabilization (respectively, output stabilization) is called the *state stabilization time* of the protocol (resp., *output stabilization time*). If the output stabilization time of an algorithm depends only on the fault number then the algorithm is said to be *fault local*, or *time-adaptive*.

Typographical Convention. Protocol variables are represented using `teletype font`, with a subscript indicating the node in which the variable is located. For example, $\texttt{dist}_i$ denotes the "distance" variable at node i, whose value may be arbitrary. Graph properties are represented using a **boldface font**, as in $\mathbf{dist}(i, j)$, which denotes the true distance in the graph between nodes i and j.

3   The Majority Consensus Problem

A node is said to be *internally legal* if its local state can be reached in an execution with no faults.

Our main target is the following problem.

Definition 1. *In the Majority Consensus problem, each node has an* input bit *that can be changed by the environment and an externally observable* output bit. *The bits satisfy the following requirements.*

- Eventual Agreement: *eventually, all output and input bits must be equal.*
- Majority Consensus: *If there is a majority of internally legal nodes having a common value b in all the input and output bits at the start state, then the eventual common value of all the output and input bits is b.*

Let us also define the Persistent Bit problem that was dealt with previously in [30, 29]. In this problem, each node has an *input bit* that can be changed by the environment and an externally observable *output bit*. It is assumed that all input bits were assigned a common value b, and then a fault may have occurred. The "Eventual Agreement" requirement is identical to that of the Majority Consensus problem. However, the *Persistence* requirement (which replaces the "Majority Consensus" requirement) is that all output and input bits eventually stabilize to the original value b. It is not hard to see that Persistence is impossible if

$f \geq n/2$. In the case of $f < n/2$, the Persistent Bit problem can be reduced to the Majority Consensus problem, since in this case there is a majority of non-faulty nodes in the start state.

In [29], an algorithm was presented for which the following result was proven.

Theorem 1. *There exists a protocol for the **Persistent Bit** problem in the synchronous network model such that if the local states of $f < n/2$ of the nodes are changed arbitrarily, then the output bits are restored everywhere in $O(f)$ time units, and the state stabilization occurs in $O(\mathbf{diam})$ time units, where $\mathbf{diam}$ denotes the actual unknown diameter of the network.*

Here we prove the following strictly stronger result.

Theorem 2. *There exists a protocol for the **Majority Consensus** problem in the asynchronous network model such that if the local states of $f \leq n$ of the nodes are changed arbitrarily, then the output bits stabilize everywhere in $O(f)$ time units, and the state stabilization occurs in $O(\mathbf{diam})$ time units, where $\mathbf{diam}$ denotes the actual unknown diameter of the network.*

As explained above, a solution to the majority consensus problem is a solution to the persistent bit problem. Thus, the improvement in our result is twofold: first, the algorithm presented here is for the strictly weaker model of asynchronous communication; and second, our algorithm can withstand any number of faults (i.e. it is fully self-stabilizing for the majority consensus problem).

3.1   Overview of the Protocol

The high-level structure of the new protocol is identical to that of the algorithm presented in [29]. The protocol has two parts: the *output stabilization* (OS) protocol and the *input fixing* (IF) protocol. The input is given replicated at all the nodes. Then, if faults corrupt a minority of the input bits, they can be repaired by adopting the value of the majority. Here, if the majority is corrupted, the correct minority is brought to agree with the majority if a majority exists for some input value in internally legal nodes. Otherwise, the protocol chooses some legal value - the same at all the nodes. To perform this repair, the input bit of each node is disseminated to all the other nodes using a protocol called *power-supply regulated broadcast* (PS-RB) [29]. The (externally observable) output bit is computed at each node by taking the majority of the values received by PS-RB. For the input fixing part we design an algorithm that works independently from the output stabilization algorithm and stabilizes the input bits to legal values in $O(\mathbf{diam})$ time units.

While the high-level structure of the solution resembles the one in [29], component sub-protocols had to be changed. First, OS was changed because of the asynchrony. In [29], the propagation of broadcasted input values was slowed down. The idea was to allow fault detection messages to catch up with faulty broadcast messages and stop them. Slowing down is easy in a synchronous model: say, by forwarding slow messages every other clock "tick" (called *pulse*). This method cannot be used in asynchronous systems. Instead, we use the Power Supply technique [1]. This change enables the use of OS in asynchronous networks. No change to OS was needed to ensure full stabilization, i.e., to allow for the case $f \geq n/2$. This is because, even if $f \geq n/2$, the new Input Fixing makes sure that complete state stabilization occurs in $O(\textbf{diam})$ and hence, in $O(n)$ time. Note that for $f \geq n/2$, the time adaptivity requirement is vacuous since in that case, $f = \Theta(n)$, and hence, an output stabilization time of $O(n)$ is good enough.

Second, the new IF is a fully-stabilizing protocol for any f. To design the IF algorithm, we first construct a fully-stabilizing algorithm which solves the case of $f \leq n$ for the *synchronous* network model. We then combine it with the self-stabilizing synchronizer to make it work in the asynchronous network model. Such a use of a synchronizer was not possible for OS, since known synchronizers are not time adaptive. The use of a synchronizer is possible for IF, since IF cannot be time adaptive anyway [29].

4   Output Stabilization

4.1   The Output Stabilization Protocol

The main tool of the OS protocol is that each node has faithful replicas of all input values in the system. These replicas, called *estimates,* are used to compute the local output bit by a majority rule. For now, assume that for $f < n/2$, input bits at non-faulty nodes never change (we prove this later). Under this assumption, it is sufficient for time-adaptivity that (1) in $O(f)$ time all unfaithful estimates (those damaged by the faults) disappear, and (2) at each node there are at least $f + 1$ (a majority) faithful estimates of non-faulty nodes. In this way, after $O(f)$ time, the majority vote at each node outputs the original value that was at the nodes at the reference state s_{-1} before the faults (Theorem 3).

In the case that $f \geq n/2$, the output stabilization is achieved in two stages: first, input bits of all nodes stabilize (by the IF protocol) in $O(\textbf{diam})$ time (Sec. 5); second, output bits stabilize to the common value of the input bits (by the OS protocol) in $O(\textbf{diam})$ time too (Theorem 4).

We now introduce some terms used in the following description of the OS protocol. The term *estimate* is used to describe not only the replica of some input value, but also any other broadcast piece of information (like distance or parent pointer values used by PS-RB). Given a node $k \in V$, an estimate is said to be *faithful w.r.t. k* if: (1) it is an input value estimate and its value is identical to the input value that is broadcast by the source k, or (2) it is a distance or a parent pointer estimate and its value conforms with the graph properties. An *erased estimate* means an estimate the value of which is its default value, e.g. $\perp$ is a default value for an input bit estimate (**null** and ∞ are the default values of parent pointer and distance estimates (resp.)). An *unfaithful estimate* is one that is both not faithful and not erased. The term *unfaithful message/node w.r.t k* refers to a message/node that contains an unfaithful estimate for node k.

Let us explain the mechanism of the OS protocol. As in the algorithm presented in [29], to disseminate the input values through the system in the regulated manner, OS builds a Bellman-Ford (BF) [9] minimal hop spanning tree rooted at each node, which is "regulated" by the power-supply technique as explained below. Thus, each node $r \in V$ maintains multiple (n) BF trees: one tree to broadcast its own input value and the rest $n-1$ trees for participating in broadcasts of other nodes' input values. The invocation of the algorithm that builds such a spanning tree is independent from those that build the other trees. We term this algorithm *power-supply regulated broadcast* (PS-RB). The following description of OS applies to *one* PS-RB tree, rooted at some node r.

A fault can create at some node i an unfaithful estimate of the input of r. Moreover, a careless protocol could have disseminated the unfaithful estimate to other nodes, causing them to behave as if they were faulty too. This would have rendered time adaptive stabilization impossible. To avoid that situation, the power supply technique presented in [1] is used to regulate the broadcast of the input values. That is, the OS algorithm uses two types of messages: *strong* and *weak*. Each node i sends to its neighbors a set of *weak* messages periodically. Each weak message contains node's current estimates for every other node. Weak messages are not forwarded. The goal of the exchange of weak messages is to detect faults in nodes' states as fast as possible by detecting an *inconsistency* in states of neighbors. An inconsistency (w.r.t. node r) in some node $i \neq r$ is checked by evaluating the local predicate $inconsis_{i,p}(r)$ (given in Fig. 1) whenever a message (either weak or strong) arrives from neighbor $p \in N(i)$ (Def. 4). The predicate is local in the sense that it is computed only on variables of node i, and variables of its neighbors, received by messages from them. When an inconsistency w.r.t. r is detected at node i, i initiates a *reset wave*. This is a broadcast wave that is forwarded over the subtree (for r's broadcast) rooted at i. The reset erases all the estimates of r and r's tree structure (the subtree rooted at i) as it goes. Note that a reset in r's tree does not harm the other trees in the same nodes.

Strong messages are generated originally by each PS-RB tree root r to broadcast its own input value. They are the only messages that can propagate estimates of a particular root r. A strong message of r propagates from the broadcast tree root r to the leaves. To "adopt" new estimates for r, the following must happen for node i: (a) i must receive two identical consecutive strong messages (m_1 and m_2) containing these new estimates; (b) m_1 and m_2 must arrive on the same path from r; (c) weak messages received from the same neighbor p on that path in between m_1 and m_2 must be consistent in the sense that they do not cause the local predicate $cand\_inconsis_{i,p}(r)$ (given in Fig. 1) to be true. Node i that receives a candidate estimate (in a strong massage) for the first time, does not propagates this estimate. Instead, i "consumes" that strong message and initiates a reset wave down the tree. Only on the second receive of the same candidate estimate, node i can "adopt" and propagate this estimate. Note that new estimate "adoption" can occur only if the explained above Constrains (a)-(b) holds true.

The described mechanism ensures that unfaithful strong messages eventually disappear from the network, since: (a) strong messages cannot flow in a cycle

(Obs. 2 [1]), (b) although nodes can forward unfaithful strong messages, no node can generate such messages, and (c) the number of unfaithful strong messages is reduced by each node that "consumes" it. This, in turn, prevents unfaithful strong messages from propagating unfaithful estimates too far. Thus, a reset wave eliminates the effect of unfaithful estimates on the majority function as fast as possible (in $O(f)$ time). Meanwhile, in $O(f)$ time too (for $f < n/2$), a majority (at least $f + 1$) of faithful (and correct) input value estimates of non-faulty nodes arrive (by the broadcast of faithful strong messages) and are "adopted" by each node i. Now, the majority function outputs a legal value at each i.

Pseudo-code for the output stabilization is presented in Fig. 2. Definitions for the pseudo-code are presented separately in Fig. 1. For every pair of nodes i, j, $\mathtt{val}_i[j]$ is the current estimate of node i for the input value of node j, and $\mathtt{val}_i[i]$ is the input value of node i. The majority function ignores the $\perp$ values and outputs 0 in the case of a tie. Variable $\mathtt{dist}_i[j]$ is the current estimate of i for the shortest distance from i to j. Variable $\mathtt{par}_i[j]$ is the current estimate of i for the parent pointer to the neighbor leading to j on the shortest path. Variables with the prefix $\mathtt{cand}$ are used to store candidate values for newly arrived estimates in strong messages. $\mathtt{Strong}_{i,p}(j)$ and $\mathtt{Weak}_{i,p}(j)$ are strong and weak messages received at node i from neighbor p and contain estimates for node j. Each message contains three elements: an identity of a node j, an estimate for the input value of node j and an estimate for the shortest distance between p and j.

4.2   Analysis of the Output Stabilization Protocol

To analyze the OS part of the new algorithm we use the structure of the analysis used for the synchronous algorithm in [29]. To benefit from the work that was already performed, we conform to definitions, notations and the proof sequence as much as possible while emphasizing the differences. First, we concentrate on proofs of the output stabilization for the case of $f < n/2$.

Since the regulated broadcast on any BF tree in the system works independently of the others, we consider a single representative tree rooted at a non-faulty node j. For the case of $f < n/2$, trees rooted at faulty nodes are ignored, since they can distribute an arbitrary value.

Definition 2. *Let $i \in V$. The* depth *of i is* $\mathbf{depth}(i) \stackrel{\text{def}}{=} \max \{\mathbf{dist}(i,j) \mid j \in V\}$.

Definition 3. *Let $j \in V$, and fix a global state.*

- *A node i is* faithful with respect to $j \neq i$ *if* $(\mathtt{val}_i[j] = \mathtt{val}_j[j]) \wedge (\mathtt{dist}_i[j] = \mathbf{dist}(i,j))$ *and there exist path of nodes* $(x_1 = j, x_2, ..., x_l, i)$, *such that* $x_l = \mathtt{par}_i[j]$ *and the length of the path is* $\mathbf{dist}(i,j)$.
- *A node i is* faithful w.r.t. itself *if* $\mathtt{dist}_i[i] = 0$ *and* $\mathtt{par}_i[i] = \mathtt{null}$.
- *A strong or a weak message $(j, value, dist)$ is* faithful w.r.t. j *if the following condition holds:* $(value = \mathtt{val}_j[j]) \wedge (dist = \mathbf{dist}(i,j))$.

Constants
      V : the set of nodes
      D : an upper bound on **diam**
      $N(i)$: the set of neighbors of i

State for node i
                                   (* local estimates and candidates for the local estimates *)
      $\text{val}_i[V]$, $\text{cand\_val}_i[V]$: array of $\{0, 1, \bot\}$, except for $\text{val}_i[i]$ that is in $\{0, 1\}$
      $\text{par}_i[V]$, $\text{cand\_par}_i[V]$: array of $N(i) \cup \{\text{null}\}$
      $\text{dist}_i[V]$, $\text{cand\_dist}_i[V]$: array of $\{1, \dots, D\} \cup \{\infty\}$
      output_i $\in \{0, 1\}$

Messages at node i (* received from $p \in N(i)$ with estimates for node v *)
      $\text{Weak}_{i,p}(v)$, $\text{Strong}_{i,p}(v)$ $\in$ $\{$ $[V, \{0, 1, \bot\}, \{1, \dots, D\} \cup \{\infty\}]$ $\}$

Shorthand   (* $value$ and $dist$ are estimates for node j received from $p \in N(i)$ *)
      $inconsis_{i,p}(j, value, dist) \equiv inconsis_{i,p}(j) \equiv$
            $\equiv [i \neq j] \wedge [(value \neq \text{val}_i[j] \wedge p = \text{par}_i[j]) \vee$
            $(dist + 1 < \text{dist}_i[j]) \vee$
            $(dist + 1 \neq \text{dist}_i[j] \wedge p = \text{par}_i[j]) \vee$
            $(\text{par}_i[j] = \text{null} \wedge \text{dist}_i[j] \neq \infty) \vee$
            $(\text{par}_i[j] \neq \text{null} \wedge \text{dist}_i[j] = \infty) \vee$
            $(\text{par}_i[j] = \text{null} \wedge \text{dist}_i[j] = \infty \wedge \text{val}_i[j] \neq \bot) \vee \text{par}_i[j] \notin N(i)]$
      $cand\_inconsis_{i,p}(j, value, dist) \equiv cand\_inconsis_{i,p}(j) \equiv$
      (* obtained by applying the $inconsis_{i,p}(j)$ on node i variables with prefix cand *)
      $is\_candidate_{i,p}(j, value, dist) \equiv (\text{cand\_val}_i[j] = value \neq \bot) \wedge$
            $(\text{cand\_dist}_i[j] = dist + 1 \wedge dist \neq \infty) \wedge (\text{cand\_par}_i[j] = p)$

Fig. 1. Definitions at node i

Definition 4. *Let $j, i \in V$ such that $i \neq j$ and fix a global state.*

- *Let $p \in N(i)$. Node i is* inconsistent *with p with respect to j if Predicate $inconsis_{i,p}(j, \text{val}_p[j], \text{dist}_p[j])$, given in Fig. 1 holds true.*
- *A node i is* inconsistent *w.r.t. j if for some $p \in N(i)$ $inconsis_{i,p}(j)$ holds.*

Note that there is a subtle, but important, difference between the definition of the inconsistency between nodes i and p (Def. 4) and the definition of Predicate $inconsis_{i,p}(j)$. The predicate is computed by the algorithm, hence it uses the variables of i and the values of the message received from p, in the buffer of i. On the other hand, Def. 4 applies to the variables of i versus the variables of p. The algorithm at i cannot access the variables of p, so it cannot know immediately whether i and p are inconsistent. However, in at most an additional (fault-free) time unit, an additional weak message that is originated in p arrives at i and the true inconsistency may be detected.

We ignore the case of inconsistency w.r.t. the node itself, since it is easy to see that the algorithm ensures a permanent consistency in this case (see the first two actions in the *Do forever* loop and in the procedures dealing with the receive of weak and strong messages in Fig. 2).

Procedure send_weak()   (* sending a set of weak messages *)
   for each $j \in V$ **do**
      Send [$j, \mathtt{val}_i[j], \mathtt{dist}_i[j]$] as a weak message to $N(i)$

Upon receiving $\mathtt{Strong}_{i,p}(v) \equiv (v,\ msg\_value,\ msg\_dist)$ *message:*
                                         (* the following is executed atomically *)
   $\mathtt{par}_i[i] \leftarrow \mathtt{null}$, $\mathtt{dist}_i[i] \leftarrow 0$ (* i is the root of its tree *)
   if $inconsis_{i,p}(\mathtt{Strong}_{i,p}(v))$ **then**
      if $is\_candidate_{i,p}(\mathtt{Strong}_{i,p}(v))$ **then**
         $\mathtt{val}_i[v] \leftarrow msg\_value$
         $\mathtt{par}_i[v] \leftarrow p$
         $\mathtt{dist}_i[v] \leftarrow msg\_dist + 1$
         Send [$v, \mathtt{val}_i[v], \mathtt{dist}_i[v]$] as a strong message to $N(i)$
      else   (* new information received *)
         $\mathtt{cand\_val}_i[v] \leftarrow msg\_value$
         $\mathtt{cand\_par}_i[v] \leftarrow p$
         $\mathtt{cand\_dist}_i[v] \leftarrow msg\_dist + 1$
         $\mathtt{val}_i[v] \leftarrow \perp$ (* generate reset on inconsistency *)
         $\mathtt{par}_i[v] \leftarrow \mathtt{null}$
         $\mathtt{dist}_i[v] \leftarrow \infty$
         Send [$v, \mathtt{val}_i[v], \mathtt{dist}_i[v]$] as a weak message to $N(i)$
   else   (* if consistent, just forward *)
      if $p = \mathtt{par}_i[v]$ **then**
         Send [$v,\ \mathtt{val}_i[v], \mathtt{dist}_i[v]$] as a strong message to $N(i)$

   $output_i \leftarrow$ majority $\{\mathtt{val}_i[j] \mid j \in V\}$

Upon receiving $\mathtt{Weak}_{i,p}(v) \equiv (v,\ msg\_value,\ msg\_dist)$ *message:*
                                         (* the following is executed atomically *)
   $\mathtt{par}_i[i] \leftarrow \mathtt{null}$, $\mathtt{dist}_i[i] \leftarrow 0$ (* i is the root of its tree *)
   if $inconsis_{i,p}(\mathtt{Weak}_{i,p}(v))$ **then**   (* generate reset on inconsistency *)
      $\mathtt{val}_i[v] \leftarrow \perp$
      $\mathtt{par}_i[v] \leftarrow \mathtt{null}$
      $\mathtt{dist}_i[v] \leftarrow \infty$
      Send [$v, \mathtt{val}_i[v], \mathtt{dist}_i[v]$] as a weak message to $N(i)$
   if $cand\_inconsis_{i,p}(\mathtt{Weak}_{i,p}(v))$ **then**
      $\mathtt{cand\_val}_i[v] \leftarrow \perp$
      $\mathtt{cand\_par}_i[v] \leftarrow \mathtt{null}$
      $\mathtt{cand\_dist}_i[v] \leftarrow \infty$

Do forever: (* each iteration of the loop executes atomically *)
   $\mathtt{par}_i[i] \leftarrow \mathtt{null}$, $\mathtt{dist}_i[i] \leftarrow 0$ (* i is the root of its tree *)
   Send [$i, \mathtt{val}_i[i], \mathtt{dist}_i[i]$] as a strong message to $N(i)$
   send_weak()

Fig. 2. Code for output stabilization at node i

The importance of the following property of PS-RB is that it holds even before stabilization. A similar lemma was used also in [29] for the synchronous algorithm. The proof is deferred to the full paper.

Lemma 1. *Let $i, j \in V$, and let $t \geq t_0(= 0)$. Assume that no faults occur in the time interval $[0, t]$. Then, at time $t + 1$, $\text{dist}_i[j] \geq \min(t, \text{dist}(i, j))$.*

The following lemma implies that faithful estimates of input values that do not change, are established quickly.

Lemma 2. *Let $i, j \in V$, and let $t \geq 0$. If $\text{val}_j[j]$ does not change in a (fault-free) time interval $[0, 3t+3]$, then for every node i with $\text{dist}(i, j) \leq t$, i is faithful w.r.t j at time $3t + 3$.*

Proof Sketch: By induction on t. The basis for $t = 0$ is trivial. For the induction step we assume that the lemma holds for some $t = k$. We now prove the lemma for $t = k + 1$. Let x_{k+1} be a node, such that $\text{dist}(x_{k+1}, j) = k + 1$.

Starting at a time (at $3k + 3$), some neighbor x_k becomes faithful w.r.t j by the induction hypothesis. This x_k provides faithful w.r.t. j distance estimate value k. Thus, starting at time $(3k + 3) + 1$, any distance estimate, which is *higher* than $k + 1$, cannot be "adopted" at x_{k+1}. This is correct due to the BF minimal hop tree construction scheme used by the algorithm. See the definition of predicate $inconsis_{x_{k+1}, x_k}(j)$ (Fig.1). Moreover, by Lemma 1, starting at time $k + 2$, $\text{dist}_{x_{k+1}}[j] \geq k + 1$. This implies the following:

(*) Starting at time $(3k + 3) + 1$, $\text{dist}_{x_{k+1}}[j] = k + 1$ is the only candidate distance estimate value that can be "adopted" at x_{k+1}.

If starting at time $(3k + 3) + 1$, node x_{k+1} adopts (faithful) estimates from some node z_k, such that $\text{dist}(z_k, j) = k$, then the lemma holds by the induction hypothesis (and the assumption that this is a fault free interval). Let us assume, by way of contradiction, that at some time after $(3k + 3)$ the estimates at node x_{k+1} are not faithful w.r.t. j. Consider the first time $\tau > 3k + 3$ that this happens. First, note that if just before time τ, node x_{k+1} is not consistent w.r.t. j then x_{k+1} resets it variables for the tree of j. Hence, at time τ, node x_{k+1} adopts unfaithful estimates from some node y, such that $\text{dist}_y[j] = dist_y > k$. On the other hand, if just before time τ node x_{k+1} does not reset its estimates, then there exists a neighbor y such that x_{k+1} is consistent with y w.r.t. j. As before, by our assumption that the estimates are unfaithful, and by the induction hypothesis, $\text{dist}_y[j] = dist_y > k$.

By Lemma 1, starting at time $dist_y + 1$ ($> k + 1$), $\text{dist}_y[j] > k$. If x_{k+1} either adopts estimates from y, or is consistent with y w.r.t. j, it follows that $\text{dist}_{x_{k+1}}[j] = dist_y + 1 > k + 1$. However, this is impossible by statement (*) above. A contradiction. ∎

Let us now describe the ideas behind the following lemma Lem. 3 informally. Note that if a node v_0 is inconsistent w.r.t. some j, then v_0 resets its estimates for j. Unfortunately, it is possible for a node to be unfaithful w.r.t. j, while not being inconsistent. For example, consider an unfaithful w.r.t. j node v_1 that is a neighbor of v_0, such that $\text{par}_{v_1}[j] = v_0$, $\text{dist}_{v_1}[j] = \text{dist}_{v_0}[j] + 1$, and $\text{val}_{v_1}[j] = \text{val}_{v_0}[j]$. (Moreover, assume that $\text{dist}_{v_0}[j]$ is the smallest among the distances estimates for j received from v_1's neighbors.). Clearly, node v_1 is consistent with v_0 w.r.t. j. Hence, no resetting of the estimates for j will take place until different estimates are received.

We say that v_0 and v_1 are in an *unfaithful parent chain* (w.r.t. j). The definition of a parent chain is deferred to the full paper. It takes into account the facts that the chain can change in time, and that it can be based on cand_par, cand_val, and cand_dist, not just on par, val, and dist.

The first crucial observation is that the maximum length of an unfaithful parent chain immediately after the faults is $O(f)$. Moreover, the first node v_0 in an unfaithful parent chain is always inconsistent, hence it leaves the parent chain within $O(1)$ time, since it resets its estimates for j. Every child of v_0 (in the tree of j) now becomes a first node in an unfaithful parent chain, and hence inconsistent. Thus, it leaves the parent chain in $O(1)$ time, and so forth.

The second observation is that the number of unfaithful w.r.t. j strong messages in buffers or over links of the parent chain immediately after the faults is $O(f)$ too. Moreover, no new unfaithful w.r.t j strong messages can be created (unless additional faults occur), since j is the only node who can generate its strong messages. Moreover, for a node not in the parent chain to join a parent chain, the number of unfaithful strong messages must decrease by one (the first such message to be received by such a node is consumed, not forwarded; this is the essence of Power Supply). The end result is that some nodes may join and leave a chain several times. Nevertheless, the total number of such joins (total over of all the nodes, for a given chain) is bounded by $O(f)$. Moreover, the total number of nodes' joins, plus the original length of the chain is $O(f)$.

Finally, it is easy to observe that chains cannot merge, nor can a chain contain a cycle at any given time. The end result of these three observations is that an unfaithful parent chain disappears in $O(f)$ time. The above argument is used in the proof of the following lemma. The formal proof is deferred to the full paper.

Lemma 3. *Let $i \in V$ be any node. Let $j \in V$ be non-faulty, and assume that* $\text{val}_j[j]$ *does not change for $t \geq 3 \cdot \min(\textbf{depth}(i) + 1, f + 1)$ time (since a start state s_0 in $t_0 = 0$). Assume that no faults occur in the time interval $[0, t]$. Then, at time t, we have that* $\text{val}_i[j] \in \{\text{val}_j[j], \bot\}$.

We note that one of the main by-products of the lemma's proof is the basic property of the power supply: unfaithful estimates are forwarded only a few times (depending on f). The dependence on f, we prove, is required for the time-adaptive solution. Although [1] concentrated on the worst case stabilization time complexities (rather than time adaptivity), the proofs of [1] already hints of time adaptivity.

We can now prove that the output stabilizes quickly, provided that the non-faulty input bits remain fixed (we prove this in Theorem 5, [12]). The proof follows directly from the last two lemmas.

Theorem 3. *Starting from an arbitrary state with a fault number $f < n/2$, if non-faulty input values do not change, then starting at time $\min(3 \cdot \mathbf{diam}, 6f) + 3$ the output stabilizes, i.e., all output values are equal to the input values of non-faulty nodes.*

The following theorem implies the required output stabilization time in the case of $f \geq n/2$, provided that input values stabilize in $O(\mathbf{diam})$ time (Sec. 5). The proof is easily implied by Lemma 2.

Theorem 4. *Starting from an arbitrary state with a fault number $f \leq n$, if input values do not change, then starting at time $3 \cdot \mathbf{diam} + 3$ the output stabilizes, i.e., all output values are equal to the majority value of the input values.*

The complete state stabilization time of PS-RB is larger than $O(f)$. We have shown above that this does not harm the $O(f)$ output stabilization time. We note that the complete stabilization time of PS-RB is $O(\mathbf{diam})$ [1]. Hence, this does not harm the state stabilization time of the combined OS-IF algorithm either.

5   Input Fixing and Full Stabilization

Due to lack of space, we only give a brief outline of the IF protocol. For the details, see the extended version of this abstract ([12]). First, consider the Input fixing protocol of [29]. Recall that every node has two variables. The output variable must stabilize quickly, and hence it may change its value several times before stabilization (see [29]). The input variable, on the other hand, retains its value for a long time. In [29] it was *corrected* by the algorithm only when it was certain that this correction will not change a correct value to an incorrect one.

To ensure that a correct value will not be changed "too soon," [29] uses the assumption that only a minority of the processes are faulty. When coming to ensure the full stabilization, we need to change the input fixing protocol such that the reliance on a correct majority is removed. (The changes of the output stabilization described in Sec. 4 were due only to the asynchronous network model and assume an appropriate behavior of the IF.) The new IF protocol with the adaptation for the case of $f \geq n/2$ is given below.

Suppose that the majority of the nodes suffered faults, such that the input value in the majority was changed to some new value maj. The first idea is to view nodes with input $=$ maj as correct nodes, and then use the output stabilization algorithm as is. The idea above needs some refinements, though. For example: had maj really been the value of a correct node v, then the output (not just the input) at v would have also equaled maj at the start state. We addressed this point (together with some related points) by being more careful in the definition of the Majority Consensus requirement (Def. 1) and requiring a node to be internally legal (Sec. 3) to be considered a part of the majority.

The main difficulty is raised by the need to ensure the assumption used in Sec. 4 that if the input value at a node is the majority value, then it is not changed, or, more precisely, it is assumed that this value is not changed for a sufficiently long time.

The new Input Fixing protocol ensures this property even when the majority input value belongs to faulty nodes. First, we use a self stabilizing synchronizer, which allows us to design the new IF for synchronous networks and than adopt this solution to work in asynchronous networks as desired. (Recall that Input Fixing cannot be time adaptive anyway [29], so a non-adaptive synchronizer does not harm its time complexity.) We then use a self stabilizing phase clock algorithm: this is a kind of a synchronizer that also keeps and advances a counter of the passing time.[2] Moreover, the phase clock algorithm ensures that time counter values at different nodes differ by at most the nodes' distance. Now, if a node either fixes its input, or finds an inconsistency, it resets its time counter to zero, and so do all the other nodes within diameter time. On the other hand, in order to fix an input, the time counter value must be much larger than the diameter. Hence, a long time passes (after the resetting) with no node fixing its input. Actually, this is somewhat more involved: after fixing its input, a node does not reset the counters immediately, but rather continues counting for a long time and only then resets, to give the other nodes the opportunity to reach the maximum of their counters and fix their inputs too.

References

1. Y. Afek and A. Bremler-Barr. Self-stabilizing unidirectional network algorithms by power-supply. In the 8th SODA, pp. 111-120, 1997.
2. Y. Afek and S. Dolev. Local stabilizer. In *Proceedings of the 5th Israel Symposium on Theory of Computing and Systems*, June 1997.
3. Y. Afek, S. Kutten, and M. Yung. Memory-efficient self-stabilization on general networks. In the 4th WDAG, pp. 15-28, 1990.
4. A. Arora and H. Zhang. LSRP: Local stabilization in shortest path routing. In *IEEE-IFIP DSN*, 2003.
5. A. Arora and M. G. Gouda. Distributed reset. *IEEE Transactions on Computers*, 43:1026-1038, 1994.
6. B. Awerbuch, S. Kutten, Y. Mansour, B. Patt-Shamir, and G. Varghese. Time optimal self-stabilizing syncronization. In the 25th STOC, pp. 652-661, 1993.
7. B. Awerbuch, B. Patt-Shamir, and G. Varghese. Self-stabilization by local checking and correction. In the 32nd FOCS, pages 268-277, Oct. 1991.
8. J. Beauquier and T. Hérault. Fault Local Stabilization : the shortest path tree. In SRDS'02, pp. 62-69, 2002
9. D. Bertsekas and R. Gallager. *Data Networks*. Prentice Hall, Englewood Cliffs, New Jersey, second edition, 1992.
10. C. Boulinier, F. Petit, V. Villain. When graph theory helps self-stabilization. In the 23rd PODC, pp. 150-159, 2004
11. A. Bremler-Barr, Y. Afek, and S. Schwarz. Improved BGP Convergence via Ghost Flushing. In *IEEE J. on Selected Areas in Communications*, 22:1933–1948, 2004.

---

[2] Indeed, we use two synchronizers; but we use only the phase clock property of the phase clock synchronizer. We do not use it as a synchronizer.

12. J. Burman, T. Herman, S. Kutten, and B. Patt-Shamir. Asynchronous and Fully Self-Stabilizing Time-Adaptive Majority Consensus (extended version), http://tx.technion.ac.il/~bjanna/.

13. J. M. Couvreur, N. Francez, and M. Gouda. Asynchronous unison. In the ICDCS'92, pp. 486-493, 1992.

14. E. W. Dijkstra. Self-stabilizing systems in spite of distributed control. In *Comm. ACM*, 17(11):643-644, November 1974.

15. S. Dolev, M. Gouda, and M. Schneider. Memory requirements for silent stabilization. In the 15th PODC, pp. 27-34, 1996.

16. S. Dolev and T. Herman. SuperStabilizing Protocols for Dynamic Distributed Systems. *Chicago Journal of Theoretical Computer Science*, 4, pp. 1-40, 1997.

17. S. Dolev and T. Herman. Parallel composition of stabilizing algorithms. In *WSS99 Proc. 1999 ICDCS Workshop on Self-Stabilizing Systems*, pp. 25-32, 1999.

18. S. Dolev. Self-Stabilization. *The MIT Press*, 2000.

19. S. Dolev, A. Israeli, and S. Moran. Resource bounds for self stabilizing message driven protocols. In the 10th PODC, pp. 281-294, 1991.

20. M. Fischer, N. A. Lynch, and M. S. Paterson. Impossibility of distributed consensus with one faulty process. *J. ACM* 32, 2, pages 374-382, Apr. 1985.

21. C. Genolini and S. Tixeuil. A lower bound on dynamic k-stabilization in asynchronous systems. In SRDS'02, pp. 211-221, 2002.

22. T. Herman. Observations on time-adaptive self-stabilization. *Technical Report* TR 97-07.

23. T. Herman. Phase clocks for transient fault repair. *IEEE Transactions on Parallel and Distributed Systems*, 11(10):1048-1057, 2000.

24. S. Ghosh and A. Gupta. An exercise in fault-containment: self-stabilizing leader election. *Inf. Proc. Let.*, 59:281-288, 1996.

25. S. Ghosh, A. Gupta, T. Herman, and S. V. Pemmaraju. Fault-containing self-stabilizing algorithms. In the 15th PODC, 1996.

26. S. Ghosh, A. Gupta, and S. V. Pemmaraju. A fault-containing self-stabilizing algorithm for spanning trees. *J. Computing and Information*, 2: 322-338, 1996.

27. S. Katz and K. Perry. Self-stabilizing extensions for message-passing systems. In the 10th PODC, 1990.

28. S. Kutten and B. Patt-Shamir. Asynchronous time-adaptive self stabilization. In the 17th PODC, p. 319, 1998.

29. S. Kutten and B. Patt-Shamir. Time-Adaptive self-stabilization. In the 16th PODC, pp. 149-158, 1997.

30. S. Kutten and D. Peleg. Fault-local distributed mending. In the 14th PODC, 1995.

31. G. Parlati and M. Yung. Non-exploratory self-stabilization for constant-space symmetry-breaking. In 2nd ESA, pp. 26-28, 1994.

32. H. Zhang, A. Arora, Z. Liu. A Stability-Oriented Approach to Improving BGP Convergence. In SRDS'04, pp. 90-99, 2004.

Stable Predicate Detection in Dynamic Systems[*]

Donald Darling[1], Jean Mayo[2], and Xinli Wang[2]

[1] Texas Instruments, 12203 Southwest Freeway, Stafford, TX 77477 USA
`ddarling@ti.com`
[2] Michigan Technological University, Houghton, MI 49931 USA
{`jmayo, xinlwang`}`@mtu.edu`

Abstract. Detection of stable predicates is fundamental to distributed application development and control. Stable predicates are distinguished by the fact that once they are true in some consistent global state, they remain true indefinitely. We present a protocol for the detection of stable predicates within dynamic systems (in which process membership may not be static). Unlike existing protocols, the presented protocol is not restricted to the detection of distributed termination and is based upon the use of approximately synchronized clocks. When clocks are approximately synchronized, the difference between the readings of any two clocks at an instant of time is kept within some known bound. Although clocks are assumed to be synchronized, temporary loss of synchronization is tolerated. The use of a global time base facilitates detection of predicates that remain true only after becoming true at some instant of time, while correctly detecting predicates that remain true upon becoming true in some consistent global state.

1 Introduction

The ability to evaluate stable predicates over the global state of a distributed system is fundamental to application development, including debugging, monitoring, and control. Stable predicates are characterized by the fact that once they become true, they remain true indefinitely (or until the predicate is detected and action is taken). Examples include program termination, deadlock, and token loss.

Modern system architectures, including peer-to-peer systems, ad hoc networks, and computational grids, have given rise to a class of applications in which process membership is not permanent. In these *dynamic systems* processes may enter and leave as the computation progresses.

Existing protocols for the detection of stable predicates in dynamic systems are restricted to the problem of detecting distributed termination [1, 2, 3]. In this paper, we present a decentralized protocol for the detection of stable predicates in dynamic systems. We assume the existence of at least one permanent process.

---

[*] This material is based upon work supported by the National Science Foundation under Grant No. CCR-9984862.

J.H. Anderson, G. Prencipe, and R. Wattenhofer (Eds.): OPODIS 2005, LNCS 3974, pp. 161–175, 2006.
© Springer-Verlag Berlin Heidelberg 2006

Other processes may initiate entry into, or exit from, the system at any time during the computation.

The algorithm is structured around the use of approximately synchronized clocks, for which the difference between the readings of any two system clocks at a single instant of time is within a known bound. Clocks may be synchronized in hardware, software, and hybrid combinations of hardware and software [4, 5]. Global Positioning System (GPS) based hardware has become available that allows physically dispersed systems to be synchronized within a few microseconds of each other via their mutual synchronization to Coordinated Universal Time (UTC). The clocks of processors world-wide can then be kept within a few milliseconds of each other via an inexpensive combination of hardware and software [6].

The motivation behind the use of a global time base is twofold. First, it provides significant leverage for both designing simple protocols and reasoning about protocol correctness. Second, a global time base provides support for systems in which changes in the truth of a predicate are rooted in time; predicate truth is not affected by the communication in the system. This is common within distributed systems that monitor and control physical systems [7].

The presented protocol asserts the truth of the stable predicate only once it is true at a point in time during the computation. Hence, predicates that remain true only upon becoming true at a point in time during the computation are correctly detected. Stable predicates, which remain true upon becoming true in some consistent global state, will always eventually be true at a point in time. Hence, these predicates are also correctly detected. While our protocol assumes the existence of approximately synchronized clocks, temporary loss of synchronization is tolerated.

In the following section we give a brief overview of existing work on the detection of stable predicates. In section 3, we present our system model. The protocol is presented in section 4. We discuss the performance of the protocol in section 5. Conclusions and directions for future work are presented in section 6.

2   Related Work

The detection of stable predicates is a well-studied problem. Algorithms for collection of a consistent global state [8, 9, 10, 11] can be run repeatedly in order to detect stable predicates. A significant amount of work has been focused on exploiting the unique characteristics of certain stable predicates, such as distributed termination [12] and distributed deadlock [13], to develop more efficient protocols for detection of these predicates.

Time-based protcols exist for the detection of stable predicates in systems with constant process membership [14, 15, 16]. These protocols all are decentralized. Work has also been done on time-based detection of unstable predicates in static systems [17, 18, 19, 20]. Both centralized [17, 18, 19] and decentralized [20] approaches have been developed. Stoller uses timestamps (from approximately synchronized real-time clocks) to define two orderings on events: "definitely occurred before" and "possibly occurred before". He then develops algorithms to detect a global predicate Φ under three modalities based on these orderings. Stoller's algorithm for detecting predicates under the modality $\mathrm{Inst}(\Phi)$ correctly detects predicates that remain true upon becoming true at a point in time.

Existing predicate evaluation protocols for dynamic systems are restricted to detection of distributed termination [1, 2, 3]. The contribution of this paper is an algorithm for detection of stable predicates in dynamic systems. We assume the predicate can be expressed as the conjunction of predicates over the local process states. The protocol is decentralized and has constant process state and protocol message size complexity. Processes may initiate entry into the system at any node. The protocol uses approximately synchronized clocks and tolerates temporary loss of clock synchronization. The protocol correctly detects predicates that remain true only upon becoming true at a point in time during the computation. A stable predicate remains true indefinitely once it becomes true in a consistent global state, and then will eventually be true at some instant of time. Hence, our protocol facilitates detection of these predicates as well.

3   System Model

A distributed system is represented as a finite set of reliable processes. Let SYS denote the set of all processes that are ever present in the system before the global predicate is detected. Also, for $t \geq 0$, let $SYS(t)$ denote the subset of SYS containing the processes in the system at real time t.

Processes in SYS share no common memory and can only communicate via message passing. It is assumed that all protocol control messages are delivered correctly after an arbitrary but finite amount of time. No restriction is placed on message delivery order or on communication within the underlying computation.

Distributed systems are *dynamic* if processes can be created or destroyed during execution. It is assumed that at least one process in a dynamic system is *permanent*. Permanent processes exist in the system from the time of system creation until system termination. Non-permanent processes may leave the system at any time.

Each process P_j, $P_j \in SYS$, is assumed to have access to a local clock. The clock at P_j is represented by the function C_j, where $C_j(t) = T$ is the time on the clock of P_j at real time t. Throughout the paper, real times are denoted by lowercase letters, and process clock values are denoted by uppercase letters.

The clock of an arbitrary permanent process is designated as the master clock, and is denoted C_M. Other process clocks can be either in synchrony or out of synchrony with the master clock. No assumptions are made about the behavior of a clock when it is not synchronized. A synchronized process clock value is assumed to be within a known bound of the master clock value. While synchronized, C_j is assumed to be nondecreasing. Further, any clock that falls out of synchrony will eventually regain synchronization. These assumptions are formally stated in the following *clock axioms*.

Clock Axiom 1. *For all $P_j \in SYS$, there exists a nonempty set Σ_j such that $|C_j(t) - C_M(t)| < \epsilon/2$ for all $t \in \Sigma_j$.*

Clock Axiom 2. *For each $t \notin \Sigma_j$, $P_j \in SYS$, there exists $t' > t$ such that $t' \in \Sigma_j$.*

Clock Axiom 3. *For all $P_j \in SYS$ and $t, t' \in \Sigma_j$, $C_j(t) \geq C_j(t')$ iff $t \geq t'$.*

The following corollaries follow trivially from the clock axioms.

Corollary 1. *For all $t > 0, t \in \Sigma_M$.*

Corollary 2. *For all $P_i, P_j \in SYS$ and $t \in \Sigma_i \cap \Sigma_j$, $|C_i(t) - C_j(t)| < \epsilon$.*

The inverse of the clock function $C_j^{-1}(T)$ returns the set of instants in Σ_j at which C_j read T. *Inf* $C_j^{-1}(T)$ and *sup* $C_j^{-1}(T)$ return the earliest and latest real time instants, respectively, in Σ_j at which C_j read T.

Selection of the master clock is arbitrary from the perspective of the stable predicate detection protocol. In a system where clocks are synchronized to some external reference signal, this reference signal can assume the role of master clock. Assuming the existence of a reference clock simplifies reasoning about the protocol, but the protocol remains correct without this assumption. In section 4.5 we present modifications to the clock axioms that eliminate this assumption.

We assume that process P_i is able to detect when it is in approximate synchrony with the other process clocks. P_i need not know whether a given instant of time t is in Σ_i. However, P_i is assumed to be able to measure intervals delimited

Table 1. Protocol State and Supported Functions for Process P_j

Name	Functionality
$state_j$	indicates P_j's state; initially *refuse*
TS_j	value of P_j's timestamp; initially 0
Γ_j	set of all tokens received by P_j during the current *transition* state; initially empty; the operator *tsmax* applied to Γ_j returns the token with the largest timestamp value; *tsmax*($\emptyset$) returns *Token*(0, 0)
$Token(TS_i, i)$	received token, initiated by P_i with timestamp TS_i
$Cmd(P_i, msg, P_k)$	received command message, initiated by P_i with message *msg* and optional argument P_k; *msg* can be one of *enter*, *exit*, *accept*, *reject*, *pred*, or *ack*
R_j	P_j's predecessor in the logical cycle of processes
S_j	P_j's successor in the logical cycle of processes
$SynchTimer_j(\epsilon)$	signals P_j after an interval $[t_1, t_2]$, where $t_1, t_2 \in \Sigma_j$, $C_j(t_2) - C_j(t_1) \geq \epsilon$, and t_1 is a point in real time that occurs no earlier than the point at which the function was invoked; $SynchTimer_j(0)$ cancels the timer
$SynchTime_j()$	returns $C_j(t_1)$ for the most recently expired timer interval $[t_1, t_2]$

by instants of time known to be in Σ_i. P_i then must be able to detect instants when the clock is synchronized. This is achievable with certain probabilistic clock synchronization protocols [21].

The predicate to be detected is expressed as the conjunction of predicates over the local process states at some moment in time. For some $t \geq 0$, the predicate is denoted $\mathcal{A}(t)$, where $\mathcal{A}(t) = \wedge_{j:P_j \in SYS(t)} \mathcal{A}_j$. Each predicate $\mathcal{A}_j$ represents a local predicate over the state of P_j, $P_j \in SYS(t)$, and is evaluated by P_j [1]. Detection of predicates over the channel states is discussed in section 4.4.

If the global predicate becomes true at time pt, then $\mathcal{A}(t)$ is true for all $t \geq pt$ since the predicate is stable. The protocol insures that for all $t \geq pt$, $SYS(t) \subseteq SYS(pt)$. That is, no process can enter the system once the global predicate becomes true. This is necessary to prevent processes from entering that may change the value of the global predicate from true to false. Since every process in $SYS(pt)$ has a true local predicate that will remain true forever, then any subset of $SYS(pt)$ will also consist only of processes with true local predicates.

4   Protocol

Detection of the predicate is token-based. Each token contains information about the process that created it, as well as a timestamp associated with that process. The tokens in the system circulate through a logical cycle of the processes. Processes initiate a token when their local predicates become true. When a process receives a token, it either discards it or propagates it to the next process in the cycle, depending on the timestamp on the token, the timestamp of the receiving process, and the current state of the receiving process.

In addition to tokens, processes can also send *command messages*. Command messages are used to restructure the logical cycle of processes when processes enter or leave the system. Processes can only send and forward command messages to their predecessors or successors, with the exception of entering processes. Since entering processes do not initially have a successor or predecessor, they may send an entry request to an arbitrary system process. (It is assumed that the address of at least one system process is known to all entering processes.) The protocol is fully distributed. In support of the protocol, process P_j, $P_j \in SYS$, maintains the state data given in Table 1. It is assumed that each process is capable of supporting a timer function $SynchTimer_j(\epsilon)$ which measures intervals of time instants in Σ_j. If the input interval is ϵ, then the timer will signal P_j after C_j has passed through an interval of at least ϵ, as measured when C_j is synchronized with the other process clocks. Minimally, C_j is synchronized at the real time instants corresponding to the interval endpoints.

Discussion of the protocol is divided into two parts. Static systems will be discussed first, followed by the entry and exit mechanisms needed to support dynamic systems.

---

[1] The local predicates may also vary over time, if whenever all local predicates become true, the global predicate is true and remains true indefinitely. We have specified time-invariant local predicates to simplify the presentation.

Table 2. Conjunctive Stable Predicate Detection Protocol for Process P_j (Static Systems)

$state_j$	Event	Action
refuse	$\mathcal{A}_j$ becomes true	$SynchTimer_j(\epsilon)$; $\Gamma_j \leftarrow \emptyset$; $state_j \leftarrow transition$
	receive $Token(TS_i, i)$	discard $Token(TS_i, i)$
transition	$SynchTimer_j$ expires	$TS_j \leftarrow SynchTime_j()$
		$Token(TS_i, i) \leftarrow$ tsmax (Γ_j)
		if $TS_i > TS_j$ **then**
		$\quad$ propagate $Token(TS_i, i)$
		else
		$\quad$ initiate $Token(TS_j, j)$
		$state_j \leftarrow agree$
	receive $Token(TS_i, i)$	$\Gamma_j \leftarrow \Gamma_j \cup \{Token(TS_i, i)\}$
	$\mathcal{A}_j$ becomes false	$SynchTimer_j(0)$; $state_j \leftarrow refuse$
agree	$\mathcal{A}_j$ becomes false	$state_j \leftarrow refuse$
	receive $Token(TS_i, i)$	**if** $(j = i)$ **then**
		$\quad$ declare $\mathcal{A}$ true
		else if $(TS_j \leq TS_i)$ **then**
		$\quad$ propagate $Token(TS_i, i)$
		else if $TS_j > TS_i$ **then**
		$\quad$ discard $Token(TS_i, i)$

4.1 Static Systems

In static systems, $SYS(t) = SYS$ for all $t \geq 0$. While attempting to detect the global predicate, processes are in one of three states: *refuse*, *transition*, or *agree*.

The protocol for static systems is given in Table 2. It is specified as a set of rules for the way that P_j reacts to events when it is in a given state. We assume that all actions associated with an event are executed before another event is processed. If no action is specified for a given event, then no action is taken.

Each process P_j in the system initially starts out in the *refuse* state. When a process is in this state, it is waiting for its local predicate to become true. All tokens received in the *refuse* state are discarded. Upon satisfaction of the local predicate, the *transition* state is entered.

The *transition* state is essentially a pause prior to releasing a token to account for the clock skew. Prior to entering this state, $SynchTimer_j()$ is set to signal P_j after a synchronized interval of ϵ has elapsed. When P_j is signaled, the first time instant in the synchronized interval becomes the timestamp for P_j. A new token is initiated by P_j at this time, and the *agree* state is entered. If the local predicate becomes false before the timer expires, the *refuse* state is restored.

While in the *agree* state, a process is waiting for receipt of its own token. Received tokens that were not initiated by P_j are forwarded to S_j if they have timestamps greater than P_j's, and are discarded otherwise. Upon receiving its own token, P_j declares detection of the global stable predicate.

Table 3. The Entry and Exit Mechanisms for Process P_j

$state_j$	Event	Action
refuse	receive $Cmd(P_i, enter)$	send $Cmd(P_j, accept, S_j)$ to P_i; block until $Cmd(P_i, ack)$ is received; $S_j \leftarrow P_i$

	receive $Cmd(P_i, exit, P_k)$	**if** $P_i = S_j$ **then**
		   send $Cmd(P_j, pred)$ to P_k;
		   send $Cmd(P_j, accept, nil)$ to S_j;
		   $S_j \leftarrow P_k$
		 else
		   discard Cmd

	receive $Cmd(P_k, pred)$	$R_j \leftarrow P_k$
transition	receive $Cmd(P_i, enter)$	forward $Cmd(P_i, enter)$ to S_j

	receive $Cmd(P_i, exit, P_k)$	**if** $P_i = S_j$ **then**
		   send $Cmd(P_j, pred)$ to P_k;
		   send $Cmd(P_j, accept, nil)$ to S_j;
		   $S_j \leftarrow P_k$;
		   $SynchTimer_j(0)$;
		   $SynchTimer_j(\epsilon)$; $\Gamma_j \leftarrow \emptyset$
		 else
		   discard Cmd

	receive $Cmd(P_k, pred)$	$R_j \leftarrow P_k$
agree	receive $Cmd(P_i, enter)$	forward $Cmd(P_i, enter)$ to S_j

	receive $Cmd(P_i, exit, P_k)$	**if** $P_i = S_j$ **then**
		   send $Cmd(P_j, pred)$ to P_k;
		   send $Cmd(P_j, accept, nil)$ to S_j;
		   $S_j \leftarrow P_k$;
		   $SynchTimer_j(\epsilon)$; $\Gamma_j \leftarrow \emptyset$;
		   $state_j \leftarrow transition$
		 else
		   discard Cmd

	receive $Cmd(P_k, pred)$	$R_j \leftarrow P_k$
exit	receive $Cmd(R_j, accept, nil)$	P_j exits the system
	receive $Cmd(P_i, enter)$	forward $Cmd(P_i, enter)$ to S_j
	receive $Cmd(S_j, exit, P_k)$	discard Cmd
	receive $Cmd(P_i, pred)$	$R_j \leftarrow P_i$; send $Cmd(P_j, exit, S_j)$ to R_j
	receive $Token(TS_i, i)$	discard $Token(TS_i, i)$

4.2 Dynamic Systems

In dynamic systems, command messages are used to communicate information that is necessary for processes to enter and exit the system. Five different command messages are used, which have the following meanings when received by a process P_j:

$Cmd(P_i, enter)$: P_i is requesting entry into the system immediately following P_j in the logical cycle.

$Cmd(P_i, exit, P_k)$: P_i is requesting to leave the system; if P_j accepts this request, then all subsequent tokens will be sent to P_k.

$Cmd(P_i, accept, P_k)$: In response to $Cmd(P_j, enter)$, P_j has been allowed to join the system following P_i, and should send all tokens to P_k; in response to $Cmd(P_j, exit, S_j)$, P_j is free to leave the system.

$Cmd(P_i, pred)$: A process has entered or exited the system immediately preceding P_j; P_i is the new predecessor of P_j in the cycle.

$Cmd(P_i, ack)$: P_i has finished restructuring the logical cycle of processes.

Processes in a dynamic system must execute the state machine given for static systems, and additionally handle the protocol events and actions concerning entry and exit of processes given in table 3.

Process Entry. Processes are allowed to enter the system at any time in the logical cycle following a process with a false local predicate. A new process P_{new} sends $Cmd(P_{new}, enter)$ to a process P_j in the system, and if A_j is false, then P_{new} becomes the new successor of P_j in the logical cycle. If A_j is true, then P_j forwards the request to the next process in the cycle, until the request reaches a process with a false local predicate. As long as the global predicate is not true, there exists at least one process in the system whose local predicate is false.

It is possible that the truth of the local predicates will oscillate in such a manner that an entry request never reaches a process with a false local predicate, even when the global predicate is not true. However, such an occurrence is expected to be very rare. Rather than complicating the protocol with the details of handling such an occurrence, it is assumed that a process will never need to forward a specific entry request more than once. A simple solution to this problem would be to require that upon receiving a particular entry request a second time, a process P_j keeps the request, and allows the process to enter the next time A_j becomes false.

If a process P_j accepts a request for entry from P_{new}, then P_j must be in the *refuse* state. When P_j accepts the request, it sends $Cmd(P_j, accept, S_j)$ to P_{new} to inform P_{new} that it can enter the system between processes P_j and S_j. P_j then blocks (on activity related to the detection protocol) until receiving $Cmd(P_{new}, ack)$. This is to insure that P_j does not exit the system until restructuring is complete, and that no command messages or tokens are sent to P_{new} until P_{new} has finished entering the system. Upon receiving acknowledgment from P_{new}, P_j sets its successor to P_{new}.

When P_{new} receives notification that it can enter the system, it sets its predecessor to P_j, its successor to S_j, and then sends $Cmd(P_{new}, pred)$ to S_j to inform S_j that P_{new} now precedes it. If S_j attempts to exit before receiving this message, the exit request will be received and ignored by P_j. S_j will attempt to exit again when it is notified that it has a new predecessor. Finally, P_{new} sends $Cmd(P_{new}, ack)$ to P_j to announce that the restructuring of the logical cycle is complete. Pseudo code that P_j executes to enter the system is depicted in Figure 1.

```
send Cmd(P_new, enter) to P_i;
block until Cmd(P_j, accept, P_k) is received;
R_new ← P_j;
S_new ← P_k;
send Cmd(P_new, pred) to S_new;
send Cmd(P_new, ack) to P_j;
state_new ← refuse
```

Fig. 1. Pseudocode for Entry by Process P_j

Process Exit. To exit the system, a process P_j sends $Cmd(P_j, exit, S_j)$ to its predecessor, R_j. If R_j accepts the exit request, it sends $Cmd(R_j, pred)$ to S_j, to notify S_j that it is now the predecessor of S_j in the cycle. If R_j is in the *transition* or *agree* state when it receives the exit request, it will re-start or re-enter the *transition* state, update its timestamp, and initiate another token. This is to account for any tokens that may have been en route to P_j that will be lost. Also, by updating its timestamp, R_j will discard any token that would have been discarded by P_j. R_j then sends $Cmd(R_j, accept)$ to P_j, and sets its successor to S_j. When P_j receives this message, it is free to leave the system.

The only time a process is not allowed to exit the system is when its predecessor is in the process of exiting. In this case, the predecessor R_j will simply discard the exit request, or the request will be lost if R_j exits before receiving it. At some point while R_j is exiting, P_j will receive a notification that its predecessor has changed. When this occurs, P_j sends a new exit request to its new predecessor. Any tokens that are received by a process that is waiting to leave the system are discarded.

Pseudo code that P_j executes in order to exit the system is depicted in figure 2. Note that upon execution of this code, P_j enters the *exit* state, where it remains until it receives notification that it can leave:

```
send Cmd(P_j, exit, S_j) to R_j
state_j ← exit
```

Fig. 2. Pseudocode for Exit by Process P_j

4.3 Correctness

The following results are useful in establishing the correctness of our protocol.

Lemma 1. *Suppose $C_j(t_j) \geq TS_j + \epsilon$ for some $t_j \in \Sigma_j$, and that $t_i \geq t_j$ for some $t_i \in \Sigma_i$. Then $C_i(t_i) > TS_j$.*

Proof. By clock axiom 1, $C_M(t_j) > TS_j + \epsilon/2$. Then by clock axiom 3 and corollary 1, $C_M(t_i) > TS_j + \epsilon/2$. Finally, by clock axiom 1, $C_i(t_i) > TS_j$. □

Lemma 2. *Suppose P_j initiates $Token(TS_j, j)$ at time tp_j. If any process $P_i \in SYS(tp_j)$ has a false local predicate at time tp_j, then some process will discard the token.*

Proof. If $\mathcal{A}_i$ is false at tp_j, then P_i will be in the *refuse* state at that time. If P_i remains in the *refuse* state, then it will clearly discard the token. If P_i has entered the *transition* state since the token was initiated, then it will either re-enter the refuse state and discard the token, or it will generate a timestamp at some real instant $tt_i \in \Sigma_i, tt_i > tp_j$. By the protocol, $tp_j \geq \inf C_j^{-1}(TS_j + \gamma)$ for some $\gamma \geq \epsilon$. Then by our assumption and Lemma 1, $C_i(tt_i) > TS_j$. By the protocol, P_i will discard the token from both the *transition* and *agree* states since $TS_i > TS_j$.

If P_i exits the system before receiving the token, then R_i will discard the token. This is clearly true if R_i receives the token while in the *refuse* state. If R_i was in the *transition* or *agree* state when P_i exited, then by the protocol, R_i will re-start or re-enter the *transition* state when P_i exits, and will generate a new timestamp. Then, when R_i receives the token, it will have a timestamp greater than TS_j by the same argument given above. Thus, R_i will discard the token.   □

To establish the correctness of the protocol, we must first establish that if some process detects the global stable predicate, then the predicate was in fact true (safety). Secondly, we must establish that if the global stable predicate becomes true, then some process will detect it (liveness).

Theorem 1 (Safety). *If some process P_i detects the global stable predicate, then the predicate was true at some real time instant.*

Proof. If P_i declares detection of the global stable predicate, then it must have received its own token containing its current timestamp value. It follows from Lemma 2 that if P_i received its own token, then every process had a true local predicate when the token was initiated. The global stable predicate was also true at this time.   □

Theorem 2 (Liveness). *If at some time $t \geq 0$, the global stable predicate $\mathcal{A}(t) = \wedge_{j:P_j \in SYS(t)} \mathcal{A}_j$ becomes true, then some process will detect it.*

Proof. When the global predicate becomes true, the local predicate of every process is true. By the protocol, no process can enter the system after this point. Also, after some point, no more processes will exit, since at least one process is required to remain in the system permanently.

Once all of the local predicates have become true, and no more processes will exit the system, then by the protocol every process has entered the *transition* state a final time. By assumption, any process clock that falls out of synchronization eventually regains synchronization. Then all processes in the *transition* state will eventually generate some final timestamp and enter the *agree* state.

Let TS_{max} be the highest-valued timestamp generated, and let P_{max} be a process that generates a token with this timestamp. When $Token(TS_{max}, max)$ is initiated, another process can be in the *refuse, transition*, or *agree* state. By the protocol, C_{max} reads at least $TS_{max} + \epsilon$ when the token is initiated. Then by Lemma 1, a process in the *refuse* state would eventually generate a timestamp greater than TS_{max}, contradicting the definition of TS_{max}.

Thus, when $Token(TS_{max}, max)$ is initiated, every other process must be in either the *transition* or the *agree* state. No process in the *agree* state discards a token with a timestamp greater than or equal to its own. A process in the *transition* state may discard a token with a timestamp equal to its own, but will then initiate a token of its own with this same timestamp. Hence, the last token initiated with timestamp TS_{max} will circulate completely and the predicate will be detected. □

4.4 Predicates over the Channel States

Many stable predicates, such as distributed termination [22], require evaluation of the state of the communication channels.

The protocol can be easily modified to evaluate channel states. It follows from Lemma 2 that if a process receives its own token, then every process in the system had a true local predicate at the time the token was initiated. Further, by the protocol, the predicate of each process $P_j \in SYS$ remained true from the time the token was initiated until P_j propagated the token. If the state of the channels incident to P_j is constant throughout this same interval, then P_j can append channel state information to the token, which can be evaluated by a process receiving its own token.

To evaluate channel states, the protocol could be modified as follows. Each process P_j records the state of all incident channels that can affect the truth of the global predicate. The channel state is recorded via a message history, the set of all messages sent and received, as described in [9]. A collection of these message histories can be used to accurately reconstruct the state of any channel. When the state of a channel changes while P_j is in the *transition* or *agree* state, P_j will enter the *refuse* state if its local predicate is no longer true, otherwise it will enter or re-start the *transition* state and generate a new timestamp. Hence, the state of the channels incident to P_j remains constant throughout the time P_j is in the *transition* and *agree* states. P_j appends this state information on the circulating token. A process that receives its own token evaluates the collected state of all channels in order to determine the truth of the global predicate.

It must be noted that this approach is based on an assumption that the state of the channels related to the truth of the predicate does not vary continuously. This is true for many stable predicates. For example, distributed termination requires that the channels be empty of application messages. In this case, each process can track the number of messages it has sent, minus the number received, and append this count to circulating tokens. Receipt of an application message in the *transition* or *agree* state will cause process P_j to re-enter the *refuse* state.

Once the global predicate becomes true, application messages will no longer be received, processes will remain in the *agree* state, and eventually a token reflecting empty channels will circulate completely.

4.5   Eliminating the Master Clock

The notion of a master clock makes reasoning about the synchronization of a set of clocks more intuitive. Further, it does not significantly restrict the set of clock synchronization protocols over which the predicate detection protocol may run. In a system in which clocks are synchronized to each other, the role of the master clock can be assumed by any process clock. However, the stable predicate detection protocol does not require the existence of a master clock. Intuitively, clock axiom 1 only need be replaced by corollary 2. However, consider lemma 1, on which the correctness arguments are based. Clock axiom 3 only requires that synchronized clock readings be nondecreasing for a given clock. It is then possible for clock C_j to read T after another clock C_i $(i \neq j)$ has read $T + \epsilon$, and lemma 1 will not hold. For example, suppose some subset S_α of the system clocks is synchronized during an initial interval of system operation. Then all clocks fall out of synchrony for a following interval. Let S_{sys} denote the set of all system clocks. Finally, the clocks that were initially unsynchronized, $S_{sys} - S_\alpha$, acquire synchronization, while the clocks in S_α remain unsynchronized. Then, according to corollary 2 and clock axioms 2 and 3 (which comprise the remaining axioms on clock behavior), there is no restriction on the values of the clocks in $S_{sys} - S_\alpha$ during the interval in which they are synchronized, relative to the values of the clocks in S_α during the interval in which they were synchronized.

In addition to replacing clock axiom 1 with corollary 2, we then make an additional restriction which ensures that no synchronized clock can read T after another synchronized clock reads $T + \epsilon$. Let $M(t)$ represent the minimum synchronized clock value at real time instant t. More formally, $M(t) = min\{C_i(t) : t \in \Sigma_i, i \in SYS\}$. We then require that:

Clock Axiom 4. *For all t_j in Σ_j, $j \in SYS$, $C_j(t_j) \geq max\{M(t) : t < t_j\}$.*

We now restate lemma 1 and show that it still holds.

Suppose $C_j(t_j) \geq TS_j + \epsilon$ for some $t_j \in \Sigma_j$, and that $t_i \geq t_j$ for some $t_i \in \Sigma_i$. Then $C_i(t_i) > TS_j$.

Proof. The lemma holds by corollary 2 when $t_i = t_j$. Suppose that $t_i > t_j$. By corollary 2, $M(t_j) > TS_j$. Then by our additional restriction, given by clock axiom 4, $C_i(t_i) \geq M(t_j) > TS_j$.   □

5   Performance

In this section we will analyze the additional network traffic introduced by the protocol and the amount of communication for detecting a true global predicate.

5.1   Total Cost

Suppose the global predicate becomes true at time pt. Let $M = |SYS(pt)|$, and let $N = |SYS|$. We will consider worst-case scenarios for process entry, global predicate detection, and process exit separately.

By assumption, if a process requests entry to the system, the request will be forwarded to at most N processes (see section 4.2). Other messages involved with process entry are negligible, since their number is fixed for each entering process. Suppose all but one process in SYS requests entry to the system at some point, and let D be the total number of processes that request entry after the global predicate is satisfied. Then $O(N^2 + ND)$ messages are required for process entry.

The cost of the predicate detection depends on the number of times each local predicate oscillates between true and false before the global predicate becomes true. For each $P_i \in SYS$, let $\mathcal{F}_i$ be equal to the total number of times that $\mathcal{A}_i$ changed from false to true before the global predicate is satisfied, and let $\mathcal{F} = \mathcal{F}_0 + \mathcal{F}_1 + \cdots + \mathcal{F}_{N-1}$.

Tokens are potentially initiated by a process P_i whenever $\mathcal{A}_i$ becomes true, and whenever S_i exits the system. Thus, no more than $\mathcal{F} + N$ tokens will ever be initiated. Each of these tokens may be propagated by every process in the system. If each token propagation is considered a separate message, then $O(N\mathcal{F} + N^2)$ messages will be generated.

Suppose all but one process in SYS exits the system at some point before the predicate is detected. By the protocol, an exit request made by P_{ex} may be discarded if R_{ex} is already exiting the system, in which case P_{ex} will eventually make a new request to its new predecessor. Thus, P_{ex} may send exit requests to every other process in the system. As with entry messages, other messages concerning process exit are negligible, since their number is fixed for each exiting process. Then $O(N^2)$ messages are required for process exit.

Overall, the communication cost of our protocol is $O(N\mathcal{F} + N^2 + ND)$. This reduces to $O(N\mathcal{F})$ for static systems, since $D = 0$ and $\mathcal{F} \geq N$ in this case. (The only time $\mathcal{F} < N$ is when one or more processes exit the system before their local predicate ever becomes true.)

5.2   Detection Cost

We will now consider the number of messages required to detect the global predicate once it becomes true. There are only three differences when measuring the cost of detecting a true global predicate as opposed to the total communication cost. First, we are only dealing with entry requests from D processes, rather than $N - 1 + D$ processes. Secondly, since no processes enter the system after satisfaction of the predicate, we need only consider a system of at most M processes, rather than N. Lastly, at most $2M - 1$ tokens will be initiated after the global predicate becomes true. The first M tokens can be initiated when the local predicates of all M processes become true simultaneously, and the second $M - 1$ tokens are initiated when all but one process exits. The number of messages required for process exits is then $O(M^2)$. This gives an overall detection cost of $O(M^2 + MD)$ messages, which reduces to $O(M^2)$ for static systems.

6   Conclusions

We have proposed a decentralized time-based protocol for detecting global stable predicates within dynamic systems. The protocol is structured around the use of a global time base, but tolerates temporary loss of clock synchronization. The use of time allows detection of predicates that remain true only upon becoming true at a point in time during the execution, in addition to predicates that remain true upon becoming true in some consistent global state. A process entering the system needs only the address of one process currently in the system. A process may initiate exit from the system at any time; exit is achieved after a protocol that is $O(N^2)$, where N is a count of the number of processes that were in the system before its termination.

References

1. Lai, T.H.: Termination detection for dynamically distributed systems with non-first-in-first-out communication. Journal of Parallel and Distributed Computing **3**(4) (1986) 577–599
2. Dhamdhere, D.M., Iyer, S.R., Reddy, E.K.K.: Distributed termination detection for dynamic systems. Parallel Computing **22**(14) (1997) 2025–2045
3. Wang, X., Mayo, J.: A general model for detecting distributed termination in dynamic systems. In: Proceedings of 18th International Parallel and Distributed Symposium, IEEE Press (2004) 84–90
4. Welch, B.S.J., Lynch, N.: An overview of clock synchronization. In Simons, B., Spector, A., eds.: Fault-Tolerant Distributed Computing. Volume 448 of Lecture Notes in Computer Science. Springer-Verlag (1990) 84–96
5. Ramanathan, P., Shin, K.G., Butler, R.W.: Fault-tolerant clock synchronization in distributed systems. IEEE Computer **23**(10) (1990) 33–44
6. Birman, K.: Building Secure and Reliable Network Applications. Manning Publications Co. (1996)
7. Marzullo, K., Neiger, G.: Detection of global state predicates. In Toueg, S., Spirakis, P.G., Kirousis, L.M., eds.: Distributed Algorithms, 5th International Workshop. Volume 579 of Lecture Notes in Computer Science., Delphi, Greece, Springer, 1992 (1991) 254–272
8. Chandy, K.M., Lamport, L.: Distributed snapshots: Determining global states of distributed systems. ACM Transactions on Computer Systems **3**(1) (1985) 63–75
9. Lai, T.H., H.Yang, T.: On distributed snapshots. Information Processing Letters **25**(3) (1987) 153–158
10. Mattern, F.: Efficient algorithms for distributed snapshots and global virtual time approximation. Journal of Parallel and Distributed Computing **18**(4) (1993) 423–434
11. Spezialetti, M., Kearns, J.: Efficient distributed snapshots. In: Proceedings of the Sixth International Conference on Distributed Computing Systems. (1986) 382–388
12. Matocha, J., Camp, T.: A taxonomy of distributed termination detection algorithms. J. Syst. Softw. **43**(3) (1998) 207–221

13. Knapp, E.: Deadlock detection in distributed databases. ACM Computing Surveys **19**(4) (1987) 303–328
14. Rana, S.P.: A distributed solution of the distributed termination problem. Information Processing Letters **17**(1) (1983) 43–46
15. Mayo, J., Kearns, P.: Distributed termination detection with roughly synchronized clocks. Information Processing Letters **52**(2) (1994) 105–108
16. Darling, Jr., D., Mayo, J.: Stable predicate detection with probabilistically synchronized clocks. In: Proceedings of the ISCA 13th International Conference on Parallel and Distributed Computing Systems. (2000) 574–579
17. Mayo, J., Kearns, P.: Global predicates in rough real time. In: Proceedings of the Seventh IEEE Symposium on Parallel and Distributed Processing. (1995) 17–24
18. Stoller, S.D.: Detecting global predicates in distributed systems with clocks. In Mavronikolas, M., ed.: Proc. 11th International Workshop on Distributed Algorithms (WDAG '97). Volume 1320 of Lecture Notes in Computer Science., Spring-Verlag (1997) 185–199
19. Stoller, S.D.: Detecting global predicates in distributed systems with clocks. Distributed Computing **13** (2000) 85–98
20. Bansod, S., Mayo, J.: A distributed algorithm for unstable global predicate evaluation with approximately synchronized clocks. Stud. Inform. Univ. **3**(2) (2004) 151–168
21. Cristian, F.: Probabilistic clock synchronization. Distributed Computing **3**(3) (1989) 146–158
22. Lynch, N.: Distributed Algorithms. Morgan Kaufmann Publishers (1997)

MTcast: Robust and Efficient P2P-Based Video Delivery for Heterogeneous Users

Tao Sun[1], Morihiko Tamai[1], Keiichi Yasumoto[1], Naoki Shibata[2],
Minoru Ito[1], and Masaaki Mori[2]

[1] Graduate School of Information Science,
Nara Institute of Science and Technology, Ikoma, Nara 630-0192, Japan
{song-t, morihi-t, yasumoto, ito}@is.naist.jp
[2] Department of Information Processing and Management, Shiga University,
Hikone, Shiga 522-8522, Japan
{shibata, mori}@biwako.shiga-u.ac.jp

Abstract. In this paper, we propose a new video delivery method called *MTcast (Multiple Transcode based video multicast)* which achieves efficient simultaneous video delivery to multiple users with different quality requirements by relying on user nodes to transcode and forward video to other user nodes. In MTcast, each user specifies a quality requirement for a video consisting of bitrate, picture size and frame rate based on the user's environmental resource limitation. All users can receive video with the specified quality (or near this quality) along a single delivery tree. The main characteristics of MTcast are in its scalability, high user satisfaction degree in received video quality, short startup latency and robustness against node failure. Through simulations, we have confirmed that MTcast can achieve much higher user satisfaction degree and robustness against node failure than the layered multicast method.

Keywords: video multicast, transcode, QoS, service overlay networks.

1 Introduction

There is a demand for an efficient video delivery method for *heterogeneous user nodes* which have different computation powers, display sizes and available bandwidths. There are several approaches for simultaneously delivering video to multiple users with different quality requirements. In the multiversion technique [1], multiple versions of a video with different bitrates are prepared in advance so that the best one can be delivered to each user, within resource limitation. In the online transcoding method [2], an original video is transcoded at a server or an intermediate node (i.e. proxy) to videos with various quality, according to receivers' preferences, and forwarded to the receivers. In the layered multicast method [3, 4], video is encoded with layered coding techniques such as in [5] so that each user can decode the video by receiving arbitrary number of layers. Since each layer is delivered as an independent multicast stream, each user can receive as many layers as possible within his/her resource limitation. In this method, as the number of users increases, more layers are required in order to improve user satisfaction degree. However, decoding video from many layers consumes large processing

J.H. Anderson, G. Prencipe, and R. Wattenhofer (Eds.): OPODIS 2005, LNCS 3974, pp. 176–190, 2006.

power and buffers. In [3], a method for optimizing bitrate of each layer to maximize user satisfaction degree is proposed. In the multiversion method, the control mechanism is simple, but not efficient in terms of server storage and network bandwidth usage. In the multiversion and layered multicast methods, there can be a large gap between the requested quality and the delivered quality if there are not enough number of versions or layers. The online transcoding method can satisfy all the above requirements since it can transcode original video to arbitrary quality video. But, large computation power required for transcoding can be a problem.

There are many studies on video streaming in peer to peer networks. [6] has proposed the Overlay Multicast Network Infrastructure (OMNI). In OMNI, each user node works as a service provider as well as a service user, and a multicast tree is composed of user nodes so that the video delivery service is provided to all the user nodes through the tree. OMNI can adapt to the change of the user node distribution and the network conditions. [7] has proposed CoopNet where traditional client-server based streamings are augmented when the load of the video server exceeds it's limit. In CoopNet, user nodes cache parts of stream data, and deliver them through multiple diverse distribution trees to the user nodes while the server load is high. OMNI and CoopNet aim at adapting the video delivery service depending on the dynamic change of network conditions, server load and so on. However, they do not treat video delivery to user nodes with different quality requirements.

We propose a new video delivery method called *MTcast (Multiple Transcode based video multicast)* which achieves efficient simultaneous video delivery to multiple heterogeneous users by relying on user nodes to transcode and forward video to other user nodes. In MTcast, each user specifies a quality requirement for a video consisting of bitrate, picture size and frame rate based on the user's environmental resource limitation. All users can receive video near specified quality along a delivery tree. Each user can change the quality requirement each time segment or each video shot.

We have considered the following criteria : (1) *high scalability* for accommodating a large number of users, (2) *high user satisfaction* in the sense that the delivered quality is close to the required quality, (3) *small resource consumption* within available resource of each user node, (4) *short startup latency* to start playing back video quickly, (5) *reasonable number of transcoding times* for keeping good video quality as well as short delivery latency, and (6) *high robustness* for continuing video delivery service even with node/link failures.

In order to achieve the above (1) to (3), a delivery tree called *transcode tree* whose root is the sender of a video content, is constructed as a variation of a perfect n-ary tree, where user nodes with higher quality requirements are located near the root of the tree, and nodes with lower quality requirements are located near leaves. Nodes are placed according to their computation power, available downstream and upstream bandwidths. Each node in the tree receives a video stream, transcodes it to lower quality video in real time and forwards it to its children nodes. In order to achieve the above (4) to (6), nodes are grouped so that each group has k members with similar quality requirements. These groups are called *layers*. All nodes in a layer receives the video with the same quality from their parent nodes along the transcode tree. We let the representative node of each layer keep the complete information of the tree. This allows a new receiver to easily find the layer which has the closest quality to its own quality requirement and to quickly send a request to the node in the layer to start delivery of the video. In order to accommodate new receivers or to replace faulty nodes with normal ones, we let each layer keep a certain amount of extra computation power and available upstream bandwidth (computed from the value of k). In general, if we use a large number for k, we can improve performance of the above (4) to (6). However, user satisfaction degree may be reduced since the received video quality is averaged over k members. So, in the proposed method, we adopted an approach to dynamically increase the value of k as the total number of receivers increases. When the number of receivers is sufficiently large, we can keep both user satisfaction and system robustness high.

After certain time elapses, extra resources at a layer might have been exhausted. So, our method reconstructs the transcode tree periodically or at each time boundary between subsequent video shots. When video delivery requests and failures occur after extra resources of a layer have been exhausted, they are processed at the next tree reconstruction.

We have investigated performance of MTcast by simulations using network topologies generated by Inet3.0 [8]. As a result, we have confirmed that MTcast can achieve both higher user satisfaction degree and higher robustness than the layered multicast method.

2   Target Environment

In this paper, we deal with a method for simultaneously delivering a video content to multiple *heterogeneous users* who have different available bandwidths, different computation power, and different display resolutions. Here, we assume the following types of user terminals, types of communication infrastructures and target contents.

- user terminal: desktop PC, laptop PC, PDA, cellular phone, etc.
- communication infrastructure: Either fixed broadband (leased lines, ADSL, CATV, etc.) or wireless network (wireless LAN, W-CDMA, Bluetooth, GSM/PDC, etc.).
- the total number of users: 500 to 100,000
- target contents: video (both recorded and live)

We target a video delivery service which starts to transmit a video content to all receivers at the same starting time like TV broadcast. Even after the starting time of the video, users can start to receive the video anytime, but the video can be watched from the scene currently in transmission.

We assume that user nodes are connected to each other through overlay links, and that each node uses overlay multicast to transmit/receive streams to/from the other node.

In the multicast tree, we let each user node except leaf nodes transcode a video stream and forward it to its children nodes, playing back the stream.

From the above discussion, the main purpose of this paper is to build and manage the multicast tree which satisfies criteria (1) to (6) in Sect. 1 and to devise the efficient video delivery method using the tree.

3   MTcast

In this section, first we briefly define notations used in our MTcast algorithm, and then explain the details of MTcast.

3.1   Definitions

Let s denote a video server, and $U = \{u_1, ..., u_N\}$ denote a set of user nodes. We assume that for each $u_i \in U$, available upstream (i.e., node to network) bandwidth and downstream (i.e., network to node) bandwidth are known in advance. We denote them by $u_i.upper\_bw$ and $u_i.lower\_bw$, respectively. Let $u_i.q$ denote u_i's video quality requirement. In general, as $u_i.q$, multiple video parameters such as bitrate, picture size and frame rate are specified. In this paper, we assume that $u_i.q$ represents only bitrate of video[1]. Let $u_i.n_{trans}(q)$ denote the maximum number of simultaneous transcoding which can be executed by u_i for videos with quality q. Let $u_i.n_{link}(q)$ denote the maximum number of simultaneous forwarding of videos with quality q which can be performed by u_i. $u_i.n_{trans}(q)$ and $u_i.n_{link}(q)$ are calculated from computation power of u_i, $u_i.upper\_bw$ and video quality.

In the proposed method, we construct a multicast tree where s is the root node and user nodes in U are intermediate (internal) or leaf nodes. Hereafter, this multicast tree is called the *transcode tree*.

3.2   Structure of Transcode Tree

Internal nodes in the transcode tree transmit a video stream to children nodes. In the proposed method, we assume that fanout (degree) of each node is basically a constant (denoted by n). As we will explain in Sect. 3.3, we decide the value of n depending on available resources of user nodes.

In order to reduce the number of transcoding between the root node and each leaf node, we construct the transcode tree as a variation of complete n-ary tree where degree of the root node is changed to k instead of n (k is a constant, and explained later). In the transcode tree, for each node $u_i \in U$ and each of its children nodes u_j, $u_i.q \geq u_j.q$ holds.

In order to tolerate node failures and to shorten startup delay of video delivery, every k nodes in U are bunched up into one group. We call each group a *layer*, where k is a predetermined constant, as shown in Fig. 1. We let user nodes in the same layer receive video with the same quality. This quality is called the *layer quality*. A representative node is selected for each layer. Parent-child relationship among all layers on the transcode tree is called the *layer tree*.

An example of the transcode tree with $n = 2$ and $k = 6$ is shown in Fig. 1. Here, small circles and big ovals represent nodes and layers, respectively. Each bitrate (e.g., 500kbps) represents the layer quality.

3.3   Construction of Transcode Tree

In our method, the transcode tree is calculated in a centralized way by one of the nodes. The way of deciding the calculation node u_c is explained later. We assume that u_c has

---

[1] A method to treat a parameter vector as quality is discussed in [9].

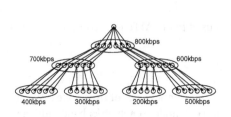

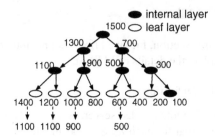

Fig. 1. Example of Transcode Tree, where $n = 2, k = 6$

Fig. 2. Tree construction in order of depth-first search

information of a video server s and user nodes $U' \subseteq U$ who have requested video. Our tree construction algorithm consists of the following three steps.

In the first step, our algorithm divides U into the set of candidate internal nodes U_I and the set of leaf nodes U_L. We always put s into U_I.

$$u.n_{trans}(u.q) \geq 1 \qquad (1)$$
$$u.n_{link}(u.q) \geq n + 1 \qquad (2)$$

For each node $u \in U$, the algorithm checks if the above inequalities hold or not. If they hold for u, then u is put into U_I, otherwise put into U_L. The above inequalities (1) and (2) represent whether node u can perform transcoding of one or more videos and whether u can forward $n + 1$ video streams, respectively.

After that, if $|U_I| < \frac{1}{n}|U|$, quality requirements of $|U_L| - \frac{n-1}{n}|U|$ nodes in U_L with larger upstream bandwidths are reduced so that the inequalities (1) and (2) hold. Then, those nodes are moved to U_I. By the above procedure, $|U_I| \geq \frac{1}{n}|U|$ always holds.

In the second step, the algorithm assigns the set of all nodes U to layers. Elements of U_I are sorted in decreasing order of their quality requirements and every bunch of k elements is packed to an internal layer. Here, we select the first node of each layer as the representative node of the layer. The average value of quality requirements is assigned as the layer quality. For the set of leaf nodes U_L, elements are similarly packed to leaf layers.

In the last step, the transcode tree is constructed. The algorithm sorts internal layers in decreasing order of layer quality, and constructs a complete n-ary tree of those internal layers so that the layer quality of each layer does not exceeds that of its parent layer. Next, the algorithm attaches each leaf layer L to the internal layer whose layer quality is closest to L. If the layer quality of L exceeds that of L's parent layer, the layer quality of L is adjusted to that of L's parent. The order of assigning internal layers to n-ary tree could be depth-first, breadth-first, or so on. Example using depth-first is shown in Fig. 2.

Finally, the transcode tree is obtained by assigning internal nodes and leaf nodes to internal layers and leaf layers in decreasing order of their required quality, respectively.

Adaptation to Available Bandwidth Between Nodes
In our method, after constructing the layer tree, each node which belongs to the child layer selects an actual delivery node from k nodes in the parent layer. Whether each

child node can receive the video with the requested quality or not depends on the available bandwidth on the path, that is, links on a physical network connecting the child node to the parent node. Below, we describe how to decide the parent nodes by taking into consideration of the physical topology of the network and available bandwidths on paths in the network. Here, we also consider the case that two or more overlay links share the same physical links and thus compete the available bandwidths on those links.

Let C and P be the sets of nodes which belong to a layer and its parent layer, respectively. We suppose that, for each pair of nodes between a child layer and its parent layer, the physical path and the available bandwidth can be obtained with tools such as *traceroute* and *pathload*[10], respectively. Let $bw(c,p)$ and $L(c,p)$ denote the available bandwidth measured with a tool like pathload (called *measured available bandwidth*, hereafter) and the set of links between $c \in C$ and $p \in P$ except for links attached to nodes c and p, respectively. Next, we estimate the worst-case available bandwidth of each overlay link (called *estimated available bandwidth*, hereafter) by considering some of links which are shared among multiple overlay links. Initially, for each pair of nodes $(c,p) \in C \times P$, the estimated available bandwidth of each link $l \in L(c,p)$ is set to $bw(c,p)$. The estimation is done based on the *link stress* of each link (i.e., the number of overlay links which use the same physical link for the same data transmission) as follows. (1) The initial link stress is set to 0 for each physical link. (2) For each pair $(c,p) \in C \times P$ and for each link $l \in L(c,p)$, the link stress of l is incremented. However, once the link stress has been already incremented by node c, we do not let other paths including c increment the link stress of the same link to avoid duplicate counting. Based on the measured available bandwidth and the link stress of each physical link, we decide the parent node of each child node as follows.

- (i) For each $c \in C$, the following step (ii) is examined in increasing order of node ID.
- (ii) For each $p \in P$, whether node p can deliver the video with the specified bitrate to node c or not is decided based on the estimated available bandwidth on path $L(c,p)$. If there is no parent node which has enough available bandwidth for the video delivery to node c, node c is moved to a lower quality layer. If only a node can deliver video to c with required bitrate, this node is selected as the parent node of c, and the following step (iv) is executed. If there are multiple nodes which can deliver video to node c with the required bitrate, the following step (iii) is applied to selecting the parent node of c.
- (iii) For each node $p \in P$ which can deliver video to c with the required bitrate, the new estimated available bandwidth for each link in $L(c,p)$ is calculated by dividing the current estimated bandwidth by the link stress. One node with the largest estimated available bandwidth is selected as the parent node of c.
- (iv) Once node p is selected as the parent of c, we re-calculate the link stress of each link $l \in L(c,p)$ without incrementing it by the paths including c and subtract the bitrate of the video from the estimated available bandwidth of l. If some bandwidth is still remaining in l, it can be used for another overlay link.

We compared our bandwidth adaptation method with hop count first method where each node greedily selects a parent node which has the minimum hop count. From experiment, we confirmed that our bandwidth adaptation method can achieve higher successful rate ($\approx$ 1.0) of finding parent node which has enough bandwidth to stream video than that of the hop count first method ($\approx$ 0.65) in the similar environment described in Sect. 4.

How to decide appropriate values of n and k

In our method, the transcode tree is constructed as a variation of a complete n-ary tree. So, as the value of n becomes large, the tree height (i.e., the number of transcoding) also decreases. Since the required upstream bandwidth of each node increases in proportion to n's value, the value of n must be carefully decided considering upstream bandwidth limitation of each node. We can decide the maximum value of n so that the number of nodes satisfying inequality $u.n_{link}(q) \geq n + 1$ is equal to $\frac{1}{n}|U|$. If f nodes may leave from a layer at the same time before the transcode tree is reconstructed, the remaining $k - f$ nodes in the current layer must transmit video streams to $n \cdot k$ children nodes. So, the following inequalities must hold in order to recover from f simultaneous failures in each layer. Thus, the appropriate value of k can be decided from values of n and f.

$$(k - f)u.n_{link}(q) \geq n \cdot k \land (k - f)u.n_{trans} \geq \lceil \frac{k}{u.n_{link}(q)} \rceil n \qquad (3)$$

3.4   Behavior of MTcast

Startup Behavior

Let t denote the time of video delivery. Each user who wants to receive video stream sends a video delivery request to the video server s before time $t - \delta$. At time $t - \delta$, s calculates the transcode tree with the algorithm explained in Sect. 3.3. Here, δ is the time to calculate the transcode tree and distribute the necessary information to all nodes. s also decides the node u_c which calculates the transcode tree next time. u_c is selected from representative nodes of layers which have sufficient downstream bandwidths. Next, s distributes the information which is necessary for video delivery to all nodes in T.

For information distribution, s composes data I which contains the complete information on T, its layer tree, representative nodes and quality of layers, and u_c. Then, it sends I to the representative node of the root layer. Then, the node forwards the information to its children layers' representative nodes. Data I is propagated until all leaf layers' representative nodes receive it. When each representative node receives the data I, it sends part of the information in I to member nodes of the same layer. We let each representative node keep (a) the whole layer tree with each layer's layer quality and representative node's address, and (b) its responsible layer and addresses of the layer's member nodes. We also let each node keep (1) addresses and layer quality of children nodes, (2) current layer's quality and responsible node's address, (3) parent node's layer and its responsible node's address, and (4) node u_c to calculate the transcode tree next time. By the above steps, information of the transcode tree is shared among all nodes and video gets ready to be delivered.

How to cope with new delivery requests and node failures

As explained in Sect. 3.3, each node in an internal layer has an extra upstream bandwidth for forwarding one more video stream. A user node u_{new} who has requested video delivery after time t can use this extra bandwidth to receive a video stream. Here, the fanout of the forwarding node u_f which sends a stream to u_{new} is allowed to be $n + 1$ tentatively. The forwarding node u_f does not need to transcode a video stream for u_{new}, since u_f is already transmitting a video stream to n children nodes and it transmits the same stream to u_{new}.

If one or more nodes in a layer fail or suddenly leave from the transcode tree, all of their descendant nodes will not be able to receive video streams. Our method allows children nodes of the failure nodes to find alternative nodes in the same layer as those failure nodes and to ask them to forward video streams. Therefore those alternative nodes use their extra upstream bandwidths similarly to the case of processing new delivery requests.

As we will explain later, the transcode tree is reconstructed periodically, the fanout of each stream is reduced to n or less than n and the consumed extra upstream bandwidth is regained after reconstruction.

If the representative node of a layer fails, children nodes of the representative node cannot find new parent nodes. Thus, one of other nodes in the layer becomes sub representative node, and nodes in children layers keep addresses of these nodes. When the representative node fails, one of children nodes of the representative node sends a switch request to the sub representative node so that the sub representative node becomes the new representative node. If a sub representative node fails before the representative node fails, one of other nodes becomes a sub representative node.

Procedure for new delivery requests

We assume that a new user node u_{new} knows at least one node u^* in the transcode tree which is already receiving a video stream. u_{new} tries to find the best node in the transcode tree which can be u_{news}'s parent node in the following procedure. (1) u_{new} sends a query with its quality requirement $u_{new}.q$ and its address to u^*. (2) If u^* is not a responsible node of any layer, it forwards the received query to the responsible node u_r of u^*'s current layer. (3) When u_r receives the query, it sends the information of the layer tree to u_{new}. (4) When u_{new} receives the layer tree, it finds the layer which has the layer quality closest to $u_{new}.q$ and sends a video delivery request to the responsible node u_r' of the layer. (5) u_r' selects a node u' and forwards the request to u' which has the required extra upstream bandwidth. (6) Finally, u' starts to deliver a video stream to u_{new}.

Recovery from node failure

We let each node u monitor status of data receiving in real-time, and u thinks that node failure happened when it does not receive any data (or the average data reception rate is much less than the expected one) during a specified time period. When u detects failure of its parent node u_p, u sends a video forwarding request to the representative node of u_p's layer. Then, similarly to the case of a new video delivery request, the video stream is forwarded from an alternative node if it has an extra upstream bandwidth. At u, video can be played back seamlessly by buffering certain time of video data during the above switching process.

Reconstruction of Transcode Tree

User node u_c reconstructs the transcode tree in the following steps. We assume that all nodes know the time t_r when the reconstructed transcode tree is in effect.

Before time $t_r - \delta'$, each node u sends a new quality requirement which will be effective after t_r to the representative node of $u's$ current layer, if u wants to change video quality. Here, δ' is the time to gather quality requirements from all nodes, calculate the transcode tree and distribute the necessary information to (part of) nodes. When the representative node u_L of each layer L receives quality requirements from all members of L and those from representative nodes of L's children layers (if L has children layers), u_L sends the unified list of quality requirements to L's parent layer's representative node. Finally, the representative node of the root layer sends the received list of quality requirements to node u_c. Finally, u_c has quality requirements of all nodes which will be effective after time t_r.

Then, node u_c calculates the transcode tree with the algorithm in Sect. 3.3 and distribute to all nodes the information for the new transcode tree and the node u'_c which calculates the tree next time, as explained in Sect. 3.3.

At time t_r, all nodes stop receiving streams from current parent nodes and the nodes in the root layer of the new transcode tree starts to deliver video streams. Nodes in internal layers also forward video streams after receiving them. The video stream transmitted along the new transcode tree arrives after a certain time lag due to transcode and link latency. So, during the time lag, each node plays back video from its buffer to avoid blank screen.

For the next reconstruction of the transcode tree, the buffer of each node must be filled with video data of the above time lag. This process is done by transmitting the video stream slightly faster than its playback speed. This fast transmission requires more computation power for transcoding and more bandwidth for forwarding video data. Let α denote the ratio of the above time lag over the time period between two subsequent tree reconstructions. α is a real constant number between 0 and 1. Then this fast transmission requires computation power and upstream/downstream bandwidths $(1 + \alpha)$ times as much as the normal transmission.

Reconstruction of the transcode tree may greatly change positions of nodes in the tree. So, we let nodes closer to the root node play back video with larger delay by buffering certain time of video data. Data amount to be buffered can be decided with statistic information calculated from received video streams.

Validity of assumptions

As described in Sect.3.2, if there are not enough number of candidate internal nodes, part of leaf nodes which have larger upstream bandwidths are transformed into internal nodes by decreasing their quality requirements. This could be the largest factor of users' unsatisfaction. Thus, the proposed technique is especially effective if (i) there are many users who have larger bandwidths compared to quality requirements. Also, our technique is effective if (ii) users' quality requirements are distributed widely, since the proposed technique can flexibly adjust video quality by transcoding, compared to layered multicast techniques.

Hereafter, we give some typical environments where the above conditions (i) and (ii) hold. Under the following three example environments, condition (i) holds. (1) A video delivery system in which users pay fee according to video quality. (2) An environment where user's available network bandwidth is much larger than bitrate of video. (3) An environment where video quality is restricted by display resolution rather than bandwidth. Regarding (1), even if a user has large available network bandwidth, the user may want to keep video quality low to save on fee. Regarding (2), if a user is connecting to the Internet through the optical fiber network, available network bandwidth is usually much larger than bitrate of video, and thus there can be many users with large unused network bandwidth if such a network becomes popular. Regarding (3), it is possible that a user watches video using a portable game console or a PDA. These devices normally have screens with resolutions smaller than VGA, and it is quite unlikely that users of these devices request larger resolution than that, even if plenty of network bandwidth is available.

Next, we give three examples under which condition (ii) holds. (1) Watching multiple videos simultaneously on a single screen. (2) Recording video under restriction of disk space. (3) Watching multi-object video with adjusted quality of objects according to importance of each object. Regarding (1), contents such as news and stock prices are displayed on PC screen, and watched when the user is doing other jobs on another window. Users set window size according to their interests, and thus there would be various quality requirements. Regarding (2), users may want to record received video in bitrate according to importance of the video. In this case, quality requirement varies depending on user's interest and the size of disk space. Regarding (3), multi-object video is played back under constraints of network bandwidth. Users may want to watch important objects in higher bitrate. Quality requirements of objects would vary depending on importance of objects.

Thus, we can say that users' quality requirements can widely be distributed.

4 Evaluation

In order to show usefulness of MTcast, we have conducted several experiments for measuring (1) required computation power for transcoding (2) overhead of transcode tree construction and (3) the user satisfaction degree on received quality.

4.1 Required Computation Power for Transcoding

In our method, since transcoding is processed on user nodes, the load of transcoding should not influence the playback of video. So, we examined the load of transcoding while playing back a video using a desktop PC, a laptop PC, and a PDA. In the experiment, we measured maximum processing speed of transcoding (in fps) while playing back a video and compared it with the actual playback speed of the video. If the maximum processing speed is sufficiently larger than the actual playback speed, it can be said that the load of the transcoding doesn't influence playback of the video. We measured the maximum processing speed by changing the transcoding degree (i.e., the number of simultaneous transcode processing) from 1 to 3. In the experiment, we used mpeg2dec 0.4.0b as the decoder and ffmpeg 0.4.9-pre1 as the encoder. The experimental parameters and results are shown in Table 1. The specifications of the devices in Table 1 are as follows: desktop PC (CPU: Pentium4 2.4GHz, 256MB RAM, Linux2.6.10), laptop PC (CPU: Celeron 1GHz, 384MB RAM, Linux 2.4.29), and PDA (SHARP Zaurus SL-C700, CPU: XScale PXA250 400MHz, 32MB RAM, Linux 2.4.28). The original frame rate of all videos is 24 fps.

Table 1. Maximum processing speed while playing back a video

device	original video		transcoded video		transcoding degree		
	picture size	bit rate (kbps)	picture size	bit rate(kbps)	1	2	3
Desktop PC	640x480	3000	480x360	2000	35.66	20.03	14.84
Desktop PC	480x360	2000	352x288	1500	61.60	36.40	25.89
Laptop PC	352x288	1500	320x240	1000	49.90	30.65	21.84
PDA	320x240	1000	208x176	384	10.12	6.04	4.33

Table 1 shows that common desktop PCs and laptop PCs have enough computation power to simultaneously transcode one or more videos with 3000Kbps (640x480 pixels) and with 1500 Kbps (352x288 pixels) in real-time, respectively.

In MTcast, each internal node needs computation power more than one transcoding degree. Table 1 shows that this requirement is not hard to be achieved. However, PDA's maximum processing speed is 10.12 fps even if the transcoding degree is 1. It shows that PDAs and smaller computing devices cannot be used as internal nodes of the transcode tree.

4.2 Overhead of Tree Reconstruction

In our method, the transcode tree is reconstructed periodically and/or when a new video segment starts. The overhead of the tree reconstruction consists of (i) aggregation of quality requirements for the new video segment from (part of) user nodes, (ii) calculation of the new transcode tree, and (iii) distribution of the new transcode tree to representative nodes of all layers.

For the above (i), even when the number of nodes is 100,000 [2] and each node sends a 50 Byte packet for quality requirement directly to the computation node u_c, 5 MByte information is sent to the node u_c which computes the transcode tree. If we assume that this information is sent in 10 seconds (it should be less than the period of the tree reconstruction), the average transmission speed becomes 4 Mbps. Since only the node with enough downstream bandwidth can be selected as u_c, this would not be a bandwidth bottleneck.

In order to investigate the impact of the above (ii) and (iii), we measured the size and the computation time of the transcode tree with the number of nodes from 1,000 to 100,000. Here, we assumed that $n = 2$ and $k = 5$, where n and k are the fanout of each internal node and the number of layer members, respectively. The experimental result is shown in Table 2. According to Table 2, the computation time was within 2 seconds even when the number of nodes is 100,000 (Pentium 4 2.4GHz with 256MB RAM on Linux2.6.10). So, computation time would not be a bottleneck.

The size of the transcode tree was 30 Kbyte when the number of all nodes is 10,000. The information of the tree is sent to representative nodes of all layers along the layer tree. If we assume that this is sent in 10 seconds, each representative node needs 24Kbps extra bandwidth. Even when the number of nodes is 100,000, the required bandwidth

---

[2] This number is actually much smaller since only the nodes which want to change their quality requirements for the next video segment send the messages.

Table 2. Size and Computation Time of Transcode Tree

number of nodes	computation time (sec)	size of tree (byte)
1000	0.016	3K
10000	0.140	30K
100000	1.497	300K

would be 240Kbps. Also, the tree size can be further reduced with the general compression algorithm like `gzip`.

4.3 User Satisfaction

In this section, we compare MTcast with the layered multicast method in terms of the user satisfaction degree for the quality requirements.

Similarly to [3], the satisfaction degree of user u ($0 \leq S_u \leq 1$) is defined as follows.

$$S_u = 1 - \frac{|u.q - u.q'|}{u.q} \tag{4}$$

Here, $u.q$ represents u's required quality and $u.q'$ represents the quality of the received video. When $u.q'$ is closer to $u.q$, S_u gets closer to 1.

The experiment has been conducted as follows: The physical network topology with 6000 nodes is generated with Inet3.0 [8] and 1000 nodes are selected as user nodes. Links directly connected to those user nodes are regarded as LANs. Links attached to LAN links are considered as MAN links, and other links are considered as WAN links. We assume that there are the following four types of user nodes: (1) user nodes with cell phone networks whose available downstream bandwidths are 100 to 500 Kbps; (2) user nodes with wireless LAN (2 Mbps to 5 Mbps); and (3) user nodes with wired broadband networks (10 Mbps to 20 Mbps). We assume that each user node has the same amount of available upstream bandwidth as the downstream bandwidth.

We selected the quality requirement of each user node according to one of the following three distributions within the available bandwidth: (a) uniform distribution from 300 Kbps to 3 Mbps; (b) sum of two normal distributions with 300 Kbps average and 50Kbps standard deviation and with 3 Mbps average and 1 Mbps standard deviation. On the other hand, the total sum of bandwidths of LAN links connected to each MAN link was used as the bandwidth of the MAN link. 6 Gbps was used as bandwidths for WAN links.

In the above simulation configuration, we measured the average user satisfaction degree ($\frac{1}{|U|} \sum_{u \in U} S_u$, U is the set of all users). We changed the number of user nodes

Table 3. Configuration of Available Bandwidth

	100k to 500k	2M to 5M	10M to 20M
case1	33%	33%	33%
case2	5%	33%	62%
case3	45%	10%	45%
case4	62%	33%	5%

Table 4. Relationship of $u.n_{transcode}$, $u.n_{link}$, f

	$p.n_{transcode}$	$p.n_{link}$	k	f
pref. 1	2	4	2	1
pref. 2	1	3	3	1
pref. 3	1	3	6	2
pref. 4	1	3	9	3

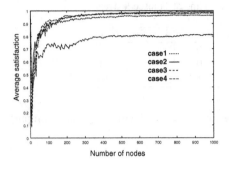
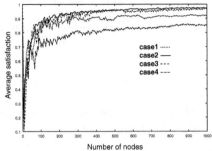

Fig. 3. Average User Satisfaction by require- **Fig. 4.** Average User Satisfaction by requirement (a)   ment (b)

from 1 to 1000 and measured the average satisfaction degree for the combination of the above quality requirement distributions (a), (b) and four different types of populations of user nodes shown in Table 3. The experimental results are shown in Fig. 3, Fig. 4. In the figures, X-axis and Y-axis represent the number of nodes and the average satisfaction degree, respectively.

In Fig. 3 and Fig. 4 , we see that MTcast can achieve pretty high satisfaction degree for various distribution of quality requirements from user nodes, when the number of user nodes are more than 100. The satisfaction degree is lower in case4 than other cases. This is because the percentage of user nodes with higher bandwidth is much smaller in case 4. However, even in such a case, MTcast achieved more than 70% user satisfaction.

In order to measure variation of user satisfaction degree depending on the value of k, we measured average user satisfaction degrees for $k = 2, 3, 6$ and 9 which are derived when applying four different combinations of $u.n_{trans}(u.q)$ and $u.n_{link}(u.q)$ in Table 4. From Table 4, when $k = 2$ or $k = 3$, the system can be recovered from one node failure per layer, and when $k = 6$ or $k = 9$, the system can be recovered from two and three simultaneous node failures per layer, respectively (these are calculated by equation (3). However, as the value of k increases, the average user satisfaction degree might decrease since the delivered quality is averaged among k members of each layer. The experimental result is shown in Fig. 5.

From Fig. 5, while the number of nodes is relatively small (i.e., less than 300), the average user satisfaction degree decreases as the value of k increases. However, as the number of user nodes increases, the decrease gets smaller. From the result, while the number of user nodes is small, we should keep the value of k small in order to keep the average user satisfaction degree high, and we should increase the value of k gradually to improve robustness against node failure as the number of users increases.

For comparison, we also measured the average user satisfaction degree when using the layered multicast method. The average user satisfaction degree depends largely on the proportion of bitrates among multiple layers. So, we used the following way for allocating bitrates of layers: The average user satisfaction degree was considered as the evaluation function, and the optimal allocation of encoding rates were calculated for basic and extension layers using the Simulated Annealing method (the number of repetition times were 10,000).

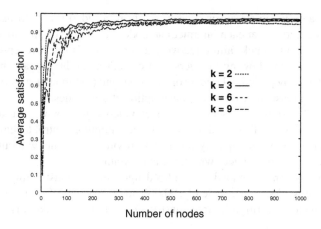

Fig. 5. User Satisfaction vs. Allowable Failures per Layer

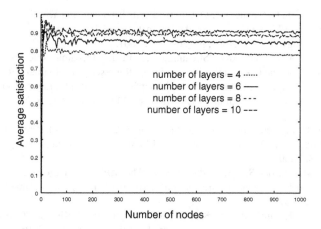

Fig. 6. Average User Satisfaction by Layered Multicast

With this optimization technique, we measured the average user satisfaction degrees. The results are shown in Fig. 6. From Fig. 5 and Fig. 6, when the number of user nodes is small (less than 200), and we use $k = 6$ or $k = 9$ with MTcast for two failure recovery per layer, the layered multicast achieves higher satisfaction degree than MTcast. On the other hand, when the number of nodes is sufficient (more than 200), MTcast achieves much higher satisfaction degree than the layered multicast with less than 10 layers (when the number of layers is higher than 10, the computational complexity may exceed the power of an ordinary PC [3]).

5   Concluding Remarks

In this paper, we proposed a new video delivery method called MTcast to achieve efficient simultaneous video delivery to multiple heterogeneous users. In the proposed method, the same video stream is transmitted from a video server to user nodes by step-by-step transcoding at each intermediate node. The main contributions of MTcast are the following: (1) quick failure recovery and new user's quick reception of video streams can be achieved owing to layers of user nodes, (2) the size and height of the tree are kept small by periodical tree reconstruction, and (3) higher user satisfaction can be achieved with reasonable resource consumption at user nodes.

The above (2) also allows users to play back video segments with various different quality. When we use MTcast with our energy consumption control technique in [11], users can increase playback quality for preferred video segments without shortening playable time at portable devices within the battery amount.

In this paper, we only provided a centralized algorithm for constructing the transcode tree, although it works for the scale of 100,000 nodes. As part of future work, we will design a distributed algorithm for tree construction to improve scalability further.

References

1. G.J. Conklin, G.S. Greenbaum, K.O. Lillevold, A.F. Lippman, and Y.A. Reznik, "Video Coding for Streaming Media Delivery on the Internet," IEEE Trans. on Circuits and Systems for Video Technology, Vol. 11, No. 3, pp. 269–281, 2001.
2. S. Jacobs and A. Eleftheriadis, "Streaming Video using Dynamic Rate Shaping and TCP Flow Control," Visual Communication and Image Representation Journal, 1998.
3. J. Liu, B. Li, and Y. Zhang, "An End-to-End Adaptation Protocol for Layered Video Multicast Using Optimal Rate Allocation," IEEE Trans. on Multimedia, Vol. 6, No. 1, pp. 87–102, 2004.
4. B. Vickers, C. Albuquerque, and T. Suda, "Source-Adaptive Multilayered Multicast Algorithms for Real-Time Video Distribution," IEEE/ACM Trans. on Networking, Vol. 8, No. 6, pp. 720–733, 2000.
5. H. Radha, M. van der Schaar, and Y. Chen, "The MPEG-4 Fine-Grained-Scalable video coding method for multimedia streaming over IP," IEEE Trans. on Multimedia, Vol. 3, No. 1, pp. 53–68, 2001.
6. S. Banerjee, C. Kommareddy, K. Kar, B. Bhattacharjee, and S. Khuller, "Construction of an Efficient Overlay Multicast Infrastructure for Real-time Applications," Proc. of IEEE Infocom 2003, pp. 1521–1531, 2003.
7. V. Padmanabhan, H. Wang, P. Chou, and K. Sripanidkulchai, "Distributing streaming media content using cooperative networking," Proc. of the 12th Int'l. Workshop on Network and Operating Systems Support for Digital Audio and Video (NOSSDAV 2002), pp. 177–186, 2002.
8. J. Winick and S. Jamin, "Inet-3.0: Internet Topology Generator," Tech. Report UM-CSE-TR-456-02 (http://irl.eecs.umich.edu/jamin/), 2002.
9. S. Yamaoka, T. Sun, M. Tamai, K. Yasumoto, N. Shibata, and M. Ito, "ResourceAware Service Composition for Video Multicast to Heterogeneous Mobile Users" to appear in 1st Int'l. Workshop on Multimedia Service Composition, 2005.
10. R.S. Prasad, M. Murray, C. Dovrolis, and K.C. Claffy, "Bandwidth Estimation: Metrics, Measurement Techniques, and Tools," IEEE Network, Vol. 17, No. 6, pp. 27–35, 2003.
11. M. Tamai, T. Sun, K. Yasumoto, N. Shibata, and M. Ito, "Energy-aware Video Streaming with QoS Control for Portable Computing Devices," Proc. of the 14th Int'l. Workshop on Network and Operating Systems Support for Digital Audio and Video (NOSSDAV 2004), pp. 68–73, 2004.

Towards a Theory of Self-organization

Emmanuelle Anceaume[1], Xavier Défago[2], Maria Gradinariu[1],
and Matthieu Roy[3]

[1] IRISA, Campus de Beaulieu, 35042 Rennes CEDEX, France
[2] JAIST and PRESTO, JST, Japan
[3] LAAS-CNRS, France

Abstract. This paper aims at providing a rigorous definition of *self-organization*, one of the most desired properties for dynamic systems, such as peer-to-peer systems, sensor networks, cooperative robotics, or ad-hoc networks. We propose a framework in order to prove the self-organization of dynamic systems with respect to generic criteria (e.g., similarity, load balancing, geographical neighborhood, battery level) that can be composed in order to construct more complex criteria. We illustrate our theory with a case study that consists in proving the self-organization of CAN, a representative peer-to-peer system.

1 Introduction

Self-organization is an evolutionary process in which the effects of the environment are present. Natural phenomena, living forms, or social systems (e.g., growing crystals, cells aggregation, ant colonies) are examples of self-organizing systems in which a global order of the system emerges from local interactions.

In the newly emerging fields of distributed systems (p2p, ad-hoc networks, sensor networks, cooperative robotics), self-organization became one of the most desired properties.

The major feature of all recent scalable distributed systems is their extreme dynamism in terms of structure, content, and load. In p2p networks, nodes continuously join and leave the system. In large scale sensor, ad-hoc or robot networks, the energy fluctuation of batteries and the inherent mobility of nodes induce a dynamic aspect of the system (the system size and the topology may change) that must be addressed. In all these systems there is no central entity in charge of their organization and control, and there is an equal capability, and responsibility entrusted to each of them to own data [10]. To cope with such characteristics, these systems must be able to spontaneously organize toward desirable global properties. In peer-to-peer systems, self-organization is handled through protocols for node arrival and departure, based either on a fault-tolerant overlay network, such as in CAN, Chord, Pastry [7, 14, 16, 18], or on some localization and routing infrastructure, such as in OceanStore [11, 22]. Recent peer-to-peer applications exploit the natural self-organization of peers in semantic communities (clusters) [9, 12, 17]. In ad-hoc networks, solutions have been proposed for a self-organizing public-key management system that allows users to create, store, distribute, and revoke their public keys without the help of

J.H. Anderson, G. Prencipe, and R. Wattenhofer (Eds.): OPODIS 2005, LNCS 3974, pp. 191–205, 2006.

any trusted authority or fixed server [4]. Self-organization was also used in order to cluster ad-hoc nodes [21]. Self-organizing algorithms have also been developed that arrange mobile robots into predefined geometric patterns (e.g., [19]). Inspired from crystal growth, Fujibayashi et al. [8] simulations self-organizing heuristics for the shape formation of a group of mobile robots. Their work uses the notion of virtual spring—a virtual link between neighboring nodes. The global shape is obtained by tuning the parameters of the springs.

Informal definitions for self-organization, or the related self* properties (e.g., self-configuration, self-healing or self-reconfiguration) have been proposed previously [3, 20, 21]. Babaoğlu et al. [3] propose a platform, called Anthill, aimed at the design of peer-to-peer applications based on self-organized colonies and swarms of agents. Anthill offers a bottom-up opportunity to understand the emergent behavior of complex adaptive systems. Walter et al. [20] focus on the concept of reconfiguration of a metamorphic robotic system with respect to a goal configuration. One of the problems left open in this work is the specification of admissible and non-admissible configurations, key notions in proving the correctness of the proposed solutions. Zhang and Arora [21] propose the concepts of self-healing and self-configuration in wireless ad-hoc networks, and propose self-stabilizing [5] solutions for self* clustering in ad-hoc networks.

The correctness proofs for all previously mentioned self-organizing systems should be based on a well-founded theoretical model, able to encapsulate the dynamic behavior of these systems. Dynamic systems must cope with frequent changes in topology and size. Hence, the characterization of the self-organizing aspects of these systems cannot solely focus on the non-dynamic periods, since they may be absent or very short. Moreover, defining self-organization as a simple convergence process towards a stable predefined set of admissible configurations is inadequate for two reasons. First, it may be impossible to clearly characterize the set of admissible configurations since, in dynamic systems, a configuration should include the state of some key parameters that have a strong influence on the dynamicity of the system. These parameters can seldom be quantified *a priori* (e.g., the status of batteries in sensor networks, or the data stored within p2p systems). Second, due to the dynamic behavior of nodes, it may happen that no execution of the system converges to one of the predefined admissible configurations.

The main contribution of this paper is to propose a formal specification of the self-organization notion which, to the best of our knowledge, has never been formalized in the area of scalable and dynamic systems, in spite of an overwhelming use of the term. Our specification is based on the principles that govern dynamic systems. The first one relates to the exchange of information or resources within the system (components are possibly capable to infinitely often retrieve new information/resources from components around them). The second one is the dynamics of these systems (components have the ability to move around, to leave or to join these systems based on local knowledge). The third principle is the specificity of the components: Among all components of the system, some have huge computation resources, some have large memory space, some are highly dynamic, some have broad centers of interest. In contrast, seeing such systems as a simple mass of components completely obviates the differences that may exist between individual components; those very differences that make the richness of these systems. The tenets mentioned above share as a common seed the locality principle, i.e., the fact that interactions and knowledge are both limited in range. We formalize this idea, leading first to the notion of *local self-organization*. Intuitively, a locally self-organizing system should reduce locally the entropy of the system. For example, a locally self-organized p2p system forces components to be adjacent to components that improve, or at least maintain, some property or evaluation criterion. We then formalize the notion of *self-organization* by imposing the system to be locally self-organizing at all its nodes and by ensuring that despite its dynamicity, the system entropy progressively reduces. Using our framework we prove the weak self-organization of CAN, a well known peer-to-peer overlay. The proof of the self-organization of Pastry is proposed in [1].

The remaining of this paper is organized as follows: Section 2 proposes a model for dynamic and scalable systems. Section 3 formalizes the local and global self-organization properties. In Section 4, we propose the study of CAN, a dynamic peer-to-peer overlay. Section 5 concludes and discusses open issues.

2   Model

2.1   Dynamic System Model

Communication Graph. The physical network is described by a weakly connected graph. Its nodes represent processes of the system and its edges represent established communication links between processes. The graph is referred in the following as the communication graph. We assume that the communication graph is subject to frequent and unpredictable changes: processes can leave or join the system arbitrarily often, and they can fail temporarily (transient faults) or permanently (crash failures). Communication links can commit transient failures (e.g., messages loss).

Data Model. Nearly all modern applications in the dynamic distributed systems are based on *the principle of data independence*—the separation of data from the programs that use the data. This concept was first developed in the context of database management systems. In dynamic systems, in particular in P2P systems, data stored locally at each node, organized in flat or hierarchical structures (e.g., XML trees), play a crucial role in creating semantic based communities (logical links between processes that store or query similar data). Note that system data is subject to frequent and unpredictable changes adjusting to nodes connections and disconnections. Data also suffers modifications like replication, aggregation, removal and can be subject to permanent or transient failures.

Logical Overlay. We consider the network plus the data stored in the network represented by a logical multi-layer overlay, each logical layer l being a weakly connected graph, also referred to as the logical communication graph at layer l. In order to connect to a particular layer l, a process executes an underlying connection protocol. A process p is called *active* at a layer l if there exists at least one process q which is connected at l and aware of p. The set of logical *neighbors* of a process p at a layer l is the set of processes q such that the logical link (p, q) is up (p and q are aware of each other) and is denoted $\mathcal{N}^l(p)$. Notice that a process p may belong to several layers simultaneously. Thus, p may have different sets of neighbors at different logical layers. Can, Pastry or Chord ([14, 15, 18]) are logical overlays using DHTs as design principle. In sensors or ad-hoc networks, connected coverings (such as trees, weakly connected maximal independent sets or connected dominating sets) can also be seen as logical overlays.

2.2   State Machine-Based Framework

To rigorously analyze the execution of the dynamic systems, we use the dynamic I/O automata introduced by Attie and Lynch [2]. This model allows the modeling of individual components, their interactions and their changes. The external actions of a dynamic I/O automata are classified in three categories, namely the actions that modify data (by replication, aggregation, removal, or writing), the input-output actions (I/O actions), and dynamic actions (C/D actions for Connection-Disconnection actions) describing the mobility within the system. A configuration is the system state at time t altogether with the communication graph and data stored in the system. A *fragment* of an execution e is a finite subsequence of e. Its size is the length of this subsequence. A *static fragment* is a maximal-sized fragment that does not contain C/D actions. Let $f = (c_i, \ldots, c_j)$ be a fragment in a dynamic I/O automaton execution. We denote as $\text{begin}(f)$ and $\text{end}(f)$ the configurations c_i and c_j respectively. In the sequel, all the referred fragments are static and are denoted by f or f_i. Thus, an execution of a dynamic I/O automaton is a infinite sequence of fragments $e = (f_0, \ldots, f_i, \ldots f_j, \ldots)$ interleaved with dynamic actions.

3   Self-organization

In this section we propose to formally define the notion of self-organization in the context of scalable and dynamic systems (in particular p2p systems) altogether with tools for proving their self-organization.

3.1   Local Self-organization

Intuitively, a locally self-organizing system should force processes to improve or at least maintain some criterion. In the following we restrict our attention to *insensitive criterion*, that is criterion whose evaluation at a process is not modified by the internal actions of other processes. A typical example of such criterion is the proximity metric in the nodeId space. Let $\mathcal{C}$ be a $[0, 1]$-valued function defined on the local neighborhood of a process (the local neighborhood of a process p includes both the state of p and the state of p's neighbors). In the following C_p denotes an evaluation criterion in the local neighborhood of a process p. Let γ_p be a $[0,1]$ function defined for a process p, a configuration c and an evaluation criterion C_p. $\gamma_p(c, C_p)$ is the aggregate of the $C_p(q)$ values in the configuration c for all one hop neighbors q of p. In the following $\gamma_p(c, C_p)$ is referred as the local aggregate criterion. In order to define local self-organization, we introduce the notion of *stable configurations*. Informally, a configuration c is *p-stable* for a given evaluation criterion in the neighborhood of a process p if the local aggregate criterion has reached a local maximum in c.

Definition 1 (*p*-stable configuration). *Let c be a configuration of a system S and p be a process, C_p be an evaluation criterion and $\gamma_p(c, C_p)$ the local aggregate of C_p at the configuration c. Configuration c is p-stable for γ_p if, for any configuration c' reached from c after one action executed by p, $\gamma_p(c, C_p) \geq \gamma_p(c', C_p)$.*

Definition 2 (local self-organization). *Let S be a system, p a process, C_p an evaluation criterion of p and γ_p the aggregate of C_p. S is locally self-organizing for γ_p if S eventually reaches a p-stable configuration. S is locally self-organizing if $\forall p \in S$, S is locally self-organizing for γ_p.*

In p2p systems local self-organization should force processes to be logical neighbors with processes which improve the evaluation criterion. Module 1 executed by a process p, referred in the following LSA, proposes a local self-organizing generic algorithm for an arbitrary insensitive criterion C. Note that existing DHT-based peer-to-peer systems (see Section 4) execute similar algorithms to ensure self-organization with respect to specific criteria (e.g., geographical proximity). The nice property of our generic algorithm is its adaptability to unstructured networks.

LSA is based on a greedy technique, which reveals to be a well adapted technique for function optimization. Its principle follows the here above intuition: Let q such that $q \in \mathcal{N}^C(p)$, and r such that $r \in \mathcal{N}^C(q)$ but $r \notin \mathcal{N}^C(p)$, where $\mathcal{N}^C(p)$ and $\mathcal{N}^C(q)$ are the logical neighborhoods of p and q respectively with respect to the criterion C. If p notices that r improves the evaluation criterion previously computed for q, then p replaces q by r in $\mathcal{N}^C(p)$. Inputs of this algorithm are the evaluation criterion C and the set of p's neighbors for C, that is $\mathcal{N}^C(p)$. The output is the updated view of $\mathcal{N}^C(p)$. Given a criterion C, a p-stable configuration, in this context, is a configuration where for any neighbor q of p, there is no neighbor r of q ($r \neq p$) that strictly improves C, formally $\forall q \in \mathcal{N}^C(p), \forall r \in \mathcal{N}^C(q) \setminus \mathcal{N}^C(p)$, $C_p(r) < C_p(q)$. Note that, because of the partial view that a component has on the global state of the system (due to the scalability and dynamism of the system), only a heuristic algorithm can be found under these assumptions.

Theorem 1 (Local Self-organization of LSA). *Let S be a system and C be an insensitive evaluation criterion. If S executes the LSA algorithm with C, then S is a locally self-organizing system for any strictly monotonic local aggregation of C.*

Module 1. Local Self-Organization Algorithm for Criteria $\mathcal{C}$ Executed by p (LSA)

Inputs :

   $\mathcal{C}_p$: the evaluation criterion used by p;

   $\mathcal{N}^{\mathcal{C}}(p)$: p neighbors for the evaluation criterion $\mathcal{C}$;

Actions :

   $\mathcal{R}$: if $\exists q \in \mathcal{N}^{\mathcal{C}}(p), \exists r \in \mathcal{N}^{\mathcal{C}}(q) \setminus \mathcal{N}^{\mathcal{C}}(p), \mathcal{C}_p(q) < \mathcal{C}_p(r)$
      then $\mathcal{N}^{\mathcal{C}}(p) = \mathcal{N}^{\mathcal{C}}(p) \bigcup \{r_{max}\} \setminus q$;
         where $r_{max} \in \mathcal{N}^{\mathcal{C}}(q)$, $\mathcal{C}_p(r_{max}) = \max_{r' \in \mathcal{N}^{\mathcal{C}}(q), \mathcal{C}_p(q) < \mathcal{C}_p(r')}(\mathcal{C}_p(r'))$

Proof. Let p be a processor in the system executing the LSA algorithm. Assume that $\mathcal{S}$ does not locally self-organize in the neighborhood of p. That is, there is an execution of $\mathcal{S}$, say e, that does not include a p-stable configuration.

Assume first that e is a static execution (i.e., no connection/disconnection action is executed during e). Let c be the first configuration in e. By assumption of the proof, c is not p-stable. Thus there is a neighbor of p, say q, that has itself a neighbor improving the evaluation criterion. Hence, rule $\mathcal{R}$ (Module 1) can be applied which makes r replacing q in the neighbors table of p. By applying the assumption of the proof again, the obtained configuration is not stable, hence there is at least one neighbor of p which has a neighbor which improves the evaluation criteria. Since the evaluation criteria is bounded and the replacement of a neighbor is done only if there is a neighbor at distance 2 which strictly improves the evaluation criteria, then either the system converges to a configuration c_{end} where the evaluation criteria reaches its maximum for some neighbors of p, or the evaluation criterion cannot be improved. There are two cases:

- The system has a finite number of nodes. Following the execution of the algorithm LSA at nodes p, we can exhibit the following finite maximal chain:

$$\mathcal{C}_p(q_0) < \mathcal{C}_p(q_1) < \ldots < \mathcal{C}_p(q_m)$$

  where q_0 is the p's neighbor replaced by the algorithm and $q_i, i \in \{0, 1, \ldots, m\}$ are the nodes which will successively replace nodes in the neighborhood of p. Let c_{end} be the configuration where the node q_m is added to the neighbors table of p. Since the chain is finite and maximal (due to the finite number of nodes), in c_{end} the value of $C_p(q_m)$ is also maximal hence, either c_{end} is stable, or no neighbor of q_m improves the evaluation criteria. Thus, there exists a configuration in e, namely c_{end}, that is p-stable.
- The number of processes in the system is infinite. Similar to the previous case we can exibit the following chain:

$$\mathcal{C}_p(q_0) < \mathcal{C}_p(q_1) < \ldots < \mathcal{C}_p(q_m) < \ldots$$

where q_0 is the node q and q_i, $i \in \{0, 1, \ldots, m \ldots\}$ are the nodes which will successively replace nodes in the p's neighborhood. By hypothesis, $\mathcal{C}_p$ is bounded and by construction, the generated chain is monotonic strictly increasing. Therefore, the chain converges to its supremum. That is, there exists a configuration c_{end} in e where the criteria cannot be further improved or the criteria reached its supremum. In both cases any configuration reached from c_{end} in e after one action executed by p cannot improve the criteria. Thus, the system reached a p-stable configuration.

Assume now that the execution e is dynamic, hence the system size and topology may be modified by nodes connection and disconnection. Assume that node p joins the system. This case is similar to the previous one, where p executes the rule $\mathcal{R}$ of Module 1 until it reaches a p-stable configuration.

Now, let us study the case where the system is in a p-stable configuration and, due to the connection/disconnections the p neighbors set changes. That is, in the p neighbors set a node r appears, and the new node r is improving the criterion. Once p is aware of the new configuration of it neighbor it restarts the convergence period by applying rule $\mathcal{R}$. The system reaches eventually a p-stable configuration.

3.2   Self-organization Through Local Self-organization

As previously said, self-organization strongly relies on the local self-organization property, as well as on the effect of connection/disconnection actions and data modifications on the system. According to this effect, the system guarantees different levels of self-organization, namely, from weak to strong self-organization. Before defining these properties, we introduce the notion of *global evaluation criterion*, denoted in the following γ. The global evaluation criterion evaluates the global organization of the system at a given configuration. More precisely, the global evaluation criterion is the aggregate of all local criteria. For instance, if the evaluation criterion is logical proximity (i.e., the closer a process, the higher the evaluation criterion), then optimizing the global evaluation criterion γ will result in all processes being connected to nearby processes.

Let $\mathcal{C}_p$ be an evaluation criterion and let γ_p be its local aggregation for any p process in the system. In the sequel we focus only on global evaluation criteria γ that exhibit the following property :

$$\forall f, \forall c_1, c_2 \in f, \ \gamma(c_1) < \gamma(c_2) \text{ if } \exists p, \ \gamma_p(c_1, \mathcal{C}_p) < \gamma_p(c_2, \mathcal{C}_p) \text{ and}$$
$$\forall t \neq p, \ \gamma_t(c_1, \mathcal{C}_t) \leq \gamma_t(c_2, \mathcal{C}_t)$$

Intuitively, the increase of the value of a local criterion will determine the increase of the global criterion if the other local criteria increase their values or remain constant. An example of criterion that meets such a requirement is the union/intersection of local criteria. Namely, γ is the sum of a local aggregation criterion γ: $\gamma(c) = \sum_{p \in \mathcal{S}} \gamma_p(c)$.

The weak self-organization is defined in terms of two properties. The *weak liveness* property says that for each static fragment f_i, either (1) f_i is stable, or (2) there exists some fragment f_j, in the future of f_i, during which the global evaluation criteria strictly improves (see Fig. 1). The *safety* property requires that the global evaluation criteria never decreases during a static fragment. Formally, we have:

Definition 3 (Weak Self-organization). *Let S be a system and γ be a global evaluation criterion defined on the configurations of S. A system is weakly self-organizing for γ if the following two properties hold (recall that $(f_0, \ldots, f_i, \ldots)$ stand for static fragments):*

Weak Liveness Property

$$\forall e = (f_0, \ldots, f_i, \ldots, f_j, \ldots), \forall f_i \in e, \exists f_j \in e, j \geq i : \ \gamma(end(f_j)) > \gamma(begin(f_j))$$
$$or \ \forall p \in S, begin(f_j) \ is \ p\text{-}stable$$

Safety Property: $\forall e = (f_0, \ldots, f, \ldots), \forall f \in e : \gamma(end(f)) \geq \gamma(begin(f))$

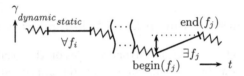

Fig. 1. Illustration of the Weak liveness property

The following theorem gives a sufficient condition to build a weakly self-organizing system:

Theorem 2 (Weak Self-organization). *Let S be a system and γ be an insensitive global evaluation criterion. S is weakly self-organizing for γ if for any process p, S locally self-organizes in p's neighborhood.*

Proof. Let e be an execution of S. We first prove that the sufficient part.

Safety proof. Let f be a static fragment in e. Since S is locally self-organizing then for any p node in the system there are two situations: (1) p is executing some actions in f, and thus $\gamma_p(begin(f)) < \gamma_p(end(f))$ or (2) p does not execute any action and, in this case $\gamma_p(begin(f)) \leq \gamma_p(end(f))$. Overall, $\gamma(end(f)) \geq \gamma(begin(f))$.

Weak liveness proof. Let p be a process. Let f_i be an arbitrary static fragment in e. S is locally self-organizing hence there is a static fragment f_j, $i \leq j$ in e such that p executes self-organizing actions in f_j hence $C_p(begin(f_j)) < C_p(end(f_j))$. Overall, for any f_i there is a fragment f_j such that $\gamma(end(f)) > \gamma(begin(f))$.

The weak self-organization definition applies to static fragments. Nothing is guaranteed during dynamic ones (i.e., fragments in which connections / disconnections occur or data are modified). For example, Pastry self-organization protocol may cause the creation of multiple, isolated Pastry overlay networks during periods of IP routing failures. Because Pastry relies almost exclusively on information exchange within the overlay network to self-organize, such isolated overlays may persist after full IP connectivity resumes [7].

The following definition proposes a characterization of the system during both static and dynamic fragments. This definition is characterized by the safety property as defined above and a liveness property. This property says that either (1) infinitely often, there are static fragments during which the knowledge of the system enriches (see Fig. 2), or (2) all the processes have reached a stable state.

Definition 4 (Self-organization). *Let S be a system and γ be a global evaluation criterion defined on the configurations of S. A system is self-organizing for γ if both safety (defined here above) and liveness hold, with the liveness property defined as follows:*

Liveness Property

$$\forall e = (f_0, \ldots, f_i, \ldots, f_j, \ldots), \forall f_i \in e, \exists f_j \in e, \quad j \geq i : \gamma(end(f_j)) > \gamma(end(f_i))$$
$$or \ \forall p \in S, begin(f_j) \ is \ p\text{-}stable$$

Fig. 2. Illustration of the liveness property

Note that none of these properties forbid processes to reset their neighbors lists after each connection/disconnection. To prevent the system from "collapsing" during dynamic fragments, we need to specify a stronger property guaranteeing that for all the processes whose neighborhood has not changed, information is maintained. Specifically, this ensures the existence of a non-empty group of processes for which local information has been maintained between the end of a static fragment and the beginning of the subsequent one. We can see this group of processes as the kernel of the system. More precisely, given two successive configurations c_i and c_{i+1} with their associated graphs G_i and G_{i+1}, the static common core of G_i and G_{i+1} is the sub-graph common to G_i and G_{i+1} minus all nodes for which the neighborhood has changed. Formally, let $G1$ and $G2$ be two graphs, and $\Gamma_{G_i}(a)$ the set of neighbors of a in G_i. We define the topological static common core of $(G1, G2)$ as:

Notation 1 (Topological Kernel). $KerT(G1, G2) = G1 \cap G2 \setminus \{a : \Gamma_{G1}(a) \neq \Gamma_{G2}(a)\}$.

Since we study systems where the self-organization may be data-oriented (typically the peer-to-peer systems), we propose a data oriented definition of the static core of the system. That is, given two successive configurations c_i and c_{i+1}, the data static common core of c_i, c_{i+1} is:

Notation 2 (Data Kernel). $KerD(c_i, c_{i+1}) = D_i \cap D_{i+1}$, where D_i is the system data in c_i.

This leads to the following property:

Definition 5 (Kernel Preservation). *Let S be a system and γ be a global evaluation criterion defined on the configurations of S. Let $e = (f_0, \ldots, f_i, f_{i+1}, \ldots)$ be an execution of S and let $K_i = Ker^*(end(f_i), begin(f_{i+1}))$ (where Ker^* denotes either $KerT$ or $KerD$). S verifies the kernel preservation property for γ if the following property holds:*

Kernel Safety. $\forall i, \gamma(Proj_{|K_i}(end(f_i))) \leq \gamma(Proj_{|K_i}(begin(f_{i+1})))$ *where* $Proj_{|K_i}(c)$ *is the sub-configuration of c corresponding to the kernel K_i.*

This leads to a stronger version of self-organization defined as follows:

Definition 6 (Strong Self-organization). *Let S be a system and γ be a global evaluation criterion defined on the configurations of S. S is strongly self-organizing for γ if it is self-organizing and it verifies the kernel preservation property defined here above.*

The concept of self-organization can be easily extended to a finite set of criteria. In the following we show that when criteria are not interfering, i.e., when they are independent, then one can build a self-organizing system for a complex criterion by using simple criteria as building blocks. Using the previous example where the local evaluation criterion was proximity, a second global evaluation criterion is needed to decrease the number of hops of a lookup application. For instance, we may want to use a few long links to reduce the lookup length.

Definition 7 (Independent Criteria). *Let S be a system and let γ_1 and γ_2 be two global criteria defined on the configurations of S. Let c be a configuration of S and sc and sc' the sub-configurations of c spanned by γ_1 and γ_2. γ_1 and γ_2 are independent with respect to c if $sc \neq sc'$. γ_1 and γ_2 are independent with respect to S if for any configuration c in S, γ_1 and γ_2 are independent with respect to c.*

Definition 8 (Monotonic Composition). *Let S be a system and let $\gamma_i \in I$ a set of criteria on the S configurations. $\gamma = \times_{i \in I} \gamma_i$ is a monotonic composition of the criteria $\gamma_i, i \in I$ if the following property is verified: $\forall c_1, c_2, \gamma(c_1) < \gamma(c_2)$ iff $\exists i \gamma_i(c_1) < \gamma_i(c_2)$ and $\forall j \neq i \in I, \gamma_j(c_1) \leq \gamma_j(c_2)$.*

Theorem 3 (Multi-criteria Self-orgnization). *Let S be a system and let $\gamma_1 \ldots \gamma_m$ be a set of independent evaluation criteria. If S is weakly, resp. strongly, self-organizing for each γ_i, $i \in [1..m]$ then S is weakly, resp. strongly, self-organizing for $\gamma_1 \times \ldots \times \gamma_m$.*

Proof. Let e be a configuration of S and let e_i be the projection of e on the sub-configurations modified by γ_i. Since, S is self-organizing with respect to γ_i then e_i is self-organizing with respect to γ_i.

Safety Proof. Let f be a static fragment in e and let f_i be the projection of f on the sub-configurations spanned by γ_i. From the hypothesis, $\gamma_i(\text{begin}(f_i)) \leq \gamma_i(\text{end}(f_i))$ $\forall i$ hence $\gamma_i(\text{begin}(f)) \leq \gamma_i(\text{end}(f))$. So, $\gamma(\text{begin}(f)) \leq \gamma(\text{end}(f))$.

Weak Liveness Proof. Let f_i be a fragment. There is f_j and γ_k such that $\gamma_k(\text{begin}(f_j)) < \gamma_k(\text{end}(f_j))$. Using the safety for all $\gamma_j, j \neq k$ it follows $\gamma(\text{begin}(f_j)) < \gamma(\text{end}(f_j))$.

Overall, S is weak self-stabilizing for γ. The proof for strong self-organization follows using a similar reasoning.

Theorem 4 (Self-organization Hierarchy). *Weak self-organization $\subset$ self-organization $\subset$ strong self-organization.*

Proof. Straigtforward from the definitions.

4   Case Study: Self-organization of CAN

We now prove the self-organization of CAN. CAN [14, 13] is a scalable content-addressable network, the principle of which is to use a single namespace—the d-dimensional torus $[0, 1]^d$—for both data and nodes. Data and CAN nodes are assigned a physical volume in the torus. Each zone has associated a virtual indentifier - a binary string. The insertion of a new node in the torus is done by splitting an existing zone in two halves, one of which is assigned to the new node. At the insertion each node has assigned a virtual indentifier (VID) which is the identifier of its reposponsability zone. Each existing zone can be seen as a leaf of a virtual binary tree. The internal vertices in the tree represent zones that no longer exist, but were split at some previous time. The children of a tree vertex are the two zones into which it was split. Each edge in the virtual tree has a binary label. The VID of a CAN-node is the binary string labeling the path from the root to the corresponding leaf zone in the virtual tree. CAN-nodes does not maintain the virtual tree structure however, each node maintains pointers to the immediate successor and predecessor VIDs. This linked list guaranties the connectivity between any two CAN-nodes.

The distributed algorithms executed on a node arrival or departure ensures that the complete torus volume is uniquelly partitioned between all participating CAN nodes. These algorithms are crucial for the self-organization of the system, since the topology of CAN changes only when nodes enter or leave the system. In the following, we show how CAN fits into our self-organization framework. Let us consider the following evaluation criterion:

$$C_p^{cart-dist}(q) = \frac{1}{1 + dist(p, q)}, \text{where } dist \text{ is the cartesian distance in the torus.}$$

Theorem 5. *CAN is weak self-organizing for $C_p^{cart-dist}$.*

Proof. We first show that CAN protocols for node insertion and node removal perform actions that leave the system in a locally stable configuration. Then, we show that, if static fragments are too short, the system may not reach a locally stable configuration. To this end, we first assume that the system is in a locally stable configuration, and prove that after a join or a leave the system reaches again a locally stable configuration. Finally, we address the high churn case.

Nodes Insertion. The insertion of a node is a two-step operation. In the first step, the node p that wants to join the system computes a Cartesian point, id, in the d-torus, then obtains the IP address of some CAN node q_0. The second step is the actual insertion: (1) q_0 sends a message to the node q_1 responsible for the volume containing the id computed by p, then (2) p contacts q_1 which, in turn, contacts its neighbors and splits its volume in order to maximize the uniform distribution of nodes within the torus, and finally (3) p enters the system with a volume defined by q_1.

  The key point here is that, for any node r in the torus, when a new node p is inserted in CAN, it becomes a neighbor of r only if p is closer to r than one of r's previous neighbors. Hence, the Cartesian distance from r to its neighbors is either identical or reduced, when compared to the situation before the insertion: the evaluation criterion for every node in the system is improved by an insertion. The insertion of a node is a finite process since the number of nodes in the system is finite. Once the insertion process finishes, the system is again in a locally stable configuration.

Nodes Departure. When a node p leaves the systems, every neighbor of p will have its evaluation function decreased, and will start a recovery process, that is, the replacement of the departing neighbor by an active node. The reponsability zone of p is taken over by the node t the virtual identifier (VID) of which is numerically closest to p. The important point here is that, for any node r which has lost a neighbor p, node t becomes r's neighbor only if t is the closest to p in terms of VID distance. Node r finds the location of node t by querying one of its neighbors having the closest VID to p's VID. If this neighbor has no neighbor with VID closer to p's VID than its own VID, it becomes responsible for p's zone, otherwise the query is forwarded to the neighbor closest to p's VID. Eventually, the recovery returns the node closest to p's VID. This node replaces p in the neighbors list of r and becomes new owner of p's zone. In order to ensure that every neighbor of p reaches the same node, each CAN-node maintains pointers to the next and previous nodes in the VIDs space using a protocol similar to Chord ([18]).

  Once every neighbor of the departing node finishes the recovery protocol, the topology of CAN remains unchanged unless another insertion or departure occurs. Hence, the departure protocol leaves the system in a locally stable configuration.

The main problem occurs in systems with high churn. That is, if during the recovery process a node experiences concurrent departures, the locally stable configuration may never be reached. Nevertheless, during each static fragment that follows a dynamic period, the criteria is improved or else, a locally stable configuration is reached. Thus, CAN is a weak self-organizing system.

Observation 1. *When CAN experiences only connections the evaluation criterion $C_p^{cart-dist}$ in the common core is unchanged, while its value increases for the new connected nodes and their neighborhood. Therefore in dynamic systems where only connections are experienced CAN is strong self-organizing for $C_p^{cart-dist}$.*

Multi-layering in CAN. Another feature of CAN is its ability to support multiple *realities* [14, 13]: several coordinate spaces can be used in parallel, in a layered form. For example, in a scenario where three different realities coexist in CAN, every node of the system has three different coordinates and, correspondingly, three lists of neighbors, one for each layer. These realities are completely independent, and hence Theorem 3 can be used to show that multi-realities CAN is an example of a multi-criteria self-organizing system.

5   Conclusion and Open Problems

In this paper, we have proposed a framework for proving the self-organizing properties of dynamic systems. Self-organization is a key feature for the newly emerging dynamic networks (peer-to-peer, ad-hoc, robot or sensor networks). Our framework includes formal definitions for self-organization, altogether with sufficient conditions for proving the self-organization of a dynamic system. We have illustrated our theory by proving the self-organization of two p2p overlays: Pastry and CAN.

We have also provided a generic algorithm that ensures the self-organization of a system with respect to a given input criterion. Our algorithm is based on the greedy technique, and relies solely on the local knowledge provided by the direct neighborhood of each process. This algorithm can be used as building-block in the construction of any self-organized DHT-based or unstructured peer-to-peer system.

Several problems are left open for future investigation. The first one is the design of a probabilistic extension to our model. This study is motivated by the fact that connection/disconnection actions are well-modeled by probabilistic laws. Essentially, the liveness property could be redefined using the Markov chains model for probabilistic dynamic I/O automata. Moreover, since our generic algorithm for self-organization uses a greedy deterministic strategy, it may reach just a local maximum for the global criterion. Adding randomized choices could be a way to converge (with high probability) to a global maximum.

Another interesting research direction is to prove or refute our conjecture that the selfish self-organizing generic strategy (Algorithm LSA) is optimal among all the self-organizing local strategies. Games and economic mechanisms theories are rich in tools adequate to this study.

We also intend to extend our framework towards a unified theory of the self* (self-healing, self-configuration, self-reconfiguration, self-repairing) properties of dynamic systems. To this end, we need to extend our case study to other dynamic systems like robots networks and large scale ad-hoc or sensor networks, that may offer complementary insides for understanding the rules that govern complex adaptive systems.

Finally, we would like to study the relationship between the self-organization and super-stabilization [6]. Note that CAN and Pastry are not self-stabilizing or super-stabilizing (direct consequence of Theorem 1, [1]). We conjecture that self-organization and super-stabilization are two complementary notions.

Acknowledgment

We thank Lisa Higham for her valuable comments on an earlier version of this paper. Her suggestions are at the origin of the Case Study section. We thank also Joffroy Beauquier for pointing us the super-stabilization work [6].

References

1. E. Anceaume, X. Défago, M. Gradinariu, and M. Roy. Towards a theory of self-organization. Technical Report 1694, IRISA, 2005.
2. P. Attie and N. Lynch. Dynamic input/output automata: a formal model for dynamic systems. In *Proc. of the 20st Annual ACM Symposium on Principles of Distributed Computing (PODC'01)*, pages 314–316, July 2001.
3. O. Babaoglu, H. Meling, and Montresor A. Anthill: A framework for the developments of agent-based peer-to-peer systems. *ICDCS 2002*, 2002.
4. S. Capkun, L. Buttyan, and J. P. Hubaux. Self-organized public-key management for mobile ad-hoc networks. *Transactions on Mobile Computing*, January-March 2003.
5. S. Dolev. *Self-Stabilization*. The MIT Press, 2000.
6. Shlomi Dolev and Ted Herman. Superstabilizing protocols for dynamic distributed systems. *Chicago J. Theor. Comput. Sci.*, 1997.
7. P. Druschel and A. Rowstron. Past: A large-scale, persistent peer-to-peer storage utility. In *HotOS VIII*, May 2001.
8. K. Fujibayashi, S. Murata, K. Sugawara, and M. Yamamura. Self-organizing formation algorithm for active elements. *SRDS'02*, pages 416–422, October 2002.
9. L. Garcés-Erice, E. W. Biersack, and P. Felber. Multi+: Building topology-aware overlay multicast trees. In *QofIS*, pages 11–20, 2004.
10. G. Kan. *Harnessing the benefits of a disruptive technology*. O'Reilley & Associates, March 2001.
11. J. Kubiatowicz, D. Bindel, Y. Chen, S. Czerwinski, P. Eaton, D. Geels, R. Gummadi, R. Rhea, H. Weatherspoon, W. Weimer, C. Wells, and B. Zhao. Oceanstore: An architecture for global-scale persistent storage. In *Proc. of the 9th International Conference on Architectural Support for Programming Languages and Operating Systems (ASPLOS 2000)*, November 2000.
12. Alberto Montresor, Márk Jelasity, and Özalp Babaoğlu. Robust aggregation protocols for large-scale overlay networks. In *Proc. DSN*, pages 19–28, June 2004.

13. S. Ratnasamy, P. Francis, M. Handley, R. Karp, and S. Shenker. A scalable content-addressable network. In *Proc. SIGCOMM'01*, pages 161–172. ACM press, 2001.

14. Sylvia Paul Ratnasamy. *A Scalable Content-Addressable Network*. PhD thesis, University of California at Berkeley, 2002.

15. A. Rowstron and P. Druschel. Pastry: Scalable, distributed object location and routing for large-scale peer-to-peer systems. In *Proc. of the 4th IFIP/ACM Middleware Conference (Middleware '01)*, pages 329–350, 2001.

16. A. Rowstron and P. Druschel. Storage management and caching in past, a large-scale, persistent peer-to-peer storage utility. In *Proc. of the 17th ACM Symposium on Operating Systems Principles (SOSP)*, pages 188–201, 2001.

17. K. Sripanidkulchai, B. Maggs, and H. Zhang. Efficient content location using interest-based locality in p2p systems. *Proc. Infocom'03*, 2003.

18. I. Stoica, R. Morris, D. Karger, M. F. Kaashoek, and H. Balakrishnan. Chord: A scalable peer-to-peer lookup service for internet applications. In *Proc. of the ACM SIG/COMM*, pages 149–160, aug 2001.

19. I. Suzuki and M. Yamashita. Distributed anonymous mobile robots: formation of geometric paterns. *SIAM Journal of Computing*, 28:1347–1363, 1999.

20. J. E. Walter, J. L. Welch, and N. M. Amato. Distributed reconfiguration of metamorphic robot chains. *Proc. of the 19th Annual ACM Symposium on Principles of Distributed Computing (PODC'00)*, pages 171–180, 2000.

21. H. Zhang and A. Arora. Gs3 : Scalable self-configuration and self-healing in wireless networks. *Proc. of the 21st Annual ACM Symposium on Principles of Distributed Computing (PODC'02)*, pages 58–67, 2002.

22. B. Zhao, J. Kubiatowicz, and A. Joseph. Tapestry: An infrastructure for fault-tolerant wide-area location and routing. Technical Report UCB/CSD-01-1141, Computer Science Division, U. C. Berkeley, April 2001.

Node Discovery in Networks[*]

Kishori M. Konwar[1], Dariusz Kowalski[3], and Alex A. Shvartsman[1,2]

[1] Department of Computer Science & Engineering, University of Connecticut, Storrs, CT, USA
kishori@cse.uconn.edu
[2] CSAIL, Massachusetts Institute of Technology, Cambridge, MA, USA
alex@theory.csail.mit.edu
[3] Instytut Informatyki, Uniwersytet Warszawski, Warszawa, Poland
D.R.Kowalski@csc.liv.ac.uk

Abstract. This paper abstracts the problem of network nodes discovering one another in a network of unknown size using all-to-all gossip. The problem is studied in terms of evolving directed graphs where vertices represent the participating nodes and an edge represents one node's knowledge about another. Ideally, such a graph has diameter one, i.e., each node knows all others. Nodes share their knowledge by sending gossip messages. Gossip among the nodes allows them to discover one another, decreasing the diameter of the graph. Here this problem is considered in several synchronous settings under different assumptions about the ability of the participating nodes to communicate. Specifically, the following aspects of communication are considered: (1) the ability of the nodes to multicast gossip messages, and (2) the size of the messages. The results describe the lower and upper bounds on the number of synchronous rounds required for the participants to discover each other. A particular question of interest is if the network size is unknown, how does a node know that it has discovered all other nodes? Given a weakly-connected graph describing the initial knowledge of the nodes, every node in our algorithm can stop the discovery process knowing that there are no unknown nodes—this is done without any prior knowledge of the total number of nodes participating in the computation.

Keywords: Distributed algorithms, resource discovery.

1 Introduction

In distributed systems it is often the case that a large subset of machines want to cooperate with one another to accomplish a common task. For example, the machines may want to perform a distributed computation or to implement a distributed file system. A first step in such an application would be to discover the available relevant resources that are distributed across the network. This first step is referred to as the *Resource Discovery Problem* [3]. The most interesting metrics used in evaluating the efficiency of message-passing algorithms are (a) time and (b) message complexity that counts the number of elementary transmissions performed by the communicating processes. A resource discovery algorithm must be efficient with respect to time and cost of messaging.

[*] This work is supported in part by the NSF Grants 9984778, 9988304, 0121277, 0311368.

J.H. Anderson, G. Prencipe, and R. Wattenhofer (Eds.): OPODIS 2005, LNCS 3974, pp. 206–220, 2006.

In particular, the machines participating in the computation should be able to terminate the algorithm upon the completion of the discovery task. Solutions to such problems often rely on gossip and broadcast, both of which are among the basic communication patterns in network computing (e.g., [4, 9, 6, 2]). The goal of *broadcasting* is to deliver information known at one node to all other known nodes, while in the case of *gossiping* one is interested in all nodes exchanging their local information. Depending on the setting, resource discovery algorithms may have to be constrained based on the allowable message size and the availability of efficient broadcast.

Konwar et al. [5] considered dynamic settings where the set of participants can change over time as new participants join, and as failures and voluntary departures remove those who have joined previously. The question they posed for these settings is: how soon can newly joined nodes discover each other by means of gossiping? They abstracted the problem, called the Join Problem, and studied it for dynamic systems that use all-to-all gossip. The problem is studied in terms of join-connectivity graphs where vertices represent the participants and where each edge represents one participant's knowledge about another. Ideally, such a graph has diameter one, i.e., all participants know each other. The diameter can grow as new participants join, and as failures remove edges from the graph. Gossip helps participants discover one another, decreasing the diameter. The results in [5] describe the lower and upper bounds on the number of communication rounds such that the participants who have previously joined discover one another, under a variety of assumptions about joining and failures. The problem is defined for an asynchronous setting, but for the performance analysis, certain additional timing assumptions are made. The protocols considered in [5] have high message and communication complexity. They also make a less-than-realistic assumption that a node can broadcast arbitrary information to arbitrary number of other nodes: the number of messages sent out concurrently could be $O(n)$ and each message can be of size $O(n \log n)$, where n is the number of participants. The current work considers a somewhat similar problem in the synchronous setting. However, in the current work the set of participating nodes remains the same throughout the computation. i.e., there are no failures or joining of new nodes. On the other hand, we introduce limitations on the ability of the nodes to multicast and also on the size of the messages that can be transmitted.

Motivation and Contributions. In this work we consider a more general version of the Resource Discovery Problem. We model our problem as a directed graph with processors at the vertices, where a directed edge from node u to node v means that u knows v and thus can transmit a message to v. Initially, we assume that the graph is at least weakly connected. Nodes share their knowledge by sending gossip messages. Gossip among the nodes allows them to discover one another, decreasing the diameter of the graph. We are interested in protocols that achieve the state where every node knows about every other node participating in the computation. We refer to this problem as the *Node Discovery in Graphs* problem (NDIG).

An important goal is for the nodes to be able to decide when to terminate the algorithm, i.e., once a node realizes that it has discovered all the nodes participating in the computation it can stop within some constant number of local steps. However, such termination should not affect the liveness of the protocol. The need for the participating nodes to detect the completion of the resource discovery without prior knowledge of the number of participants is mentioned in [3,7]. The resource discovery problem stated in [3,7] aims to guarantee the existence of a unique node, called the *root*, that knows every other node participating in the computation. However, in a practical system it is often not enough for one node to know the identities of all other nodes. Firstly, the root is a bottleneck when the number of participating nodes is large. Secondly, the root may be a single point of failure. The algorithms presented in this paper aim to make every node aware of every other node participating in the computation. Another aspect of the problem, often overlooked, is the maximum allowable message size and the limitation on the number of destinations a node can simultaneously send (multicast) messages to. Here this problem is considered in several synchronous settings under different assumptions about the ability of the participating nodes to communicate. Specifically, the following aspects of communication are examined: (1) the ability of the nodes to multicast gossip messages, and (2) the size of the messages. The results describe the lower and upper bounds on the number of synchronous rounds required for all the participants to discover each other. One of the algorithms, viz., algorithm A, has the property that the nodes can detect the discovery of all the nodes, and decide when to terminate the algorithm without knowing the number of participating nodes *a priori*. For this algorithm we do not assume any bound on message size, or the number of concurrent messages that can be sent in a single step. As a result, this algorithm suffers from high message and communication complexities, although its complexity matches the lower bound in the model.

In more detail, the contributions in this paper are as follows. Let n be the number of processes participating in the computation. We consider four message passing models depending on multicast ability and size of messages, viz., model M_A—multicast with message size $O(n \log n)$ (each node identifier can have $O(\log n)$ bits); model M_B—multicast and messages of size $O(\log n)$; model M_C—unicast and message size $O(\log n)$; and model M_D—unicast with message size $O(n \log n)$.

In model M_A we provide an algorithm that has the ability to detect the termination without any vertex knowing the number of participating processes *a priori*, i.e., any node can tell if it has discovered all the nodes without knowing how many nodes were participating in the computation *a priori*. It is noteworthy, that this algorithm is inferior to the algorithms proposed in [7] in terms of message and communication complexities but the fact that it can detect termination makes it distinctive.

For model M_C, we show that any algorithm that runs on model M_B can be simulated in model M_C at the cost of increasing the running time by a factor of n (Theorem 3). This shows a structural relation between these models, and is a result of independent interest. Using this result we provide an algorithm for model M_C by simulating the algorithm for model M_B. The time, message, and communication complexities of the simulated algorithm are close to the respective lower bounds.

For model M_D we provide algorithm D with time complexity $O((\max_{C \in \mathscr{C}} diam(C) + |\mathscr{C}|) \log n)$, where $\mathscr{C}$ is the set of strongly connected components of the initial weakly-connected graph. For this model there is still a large gap between the lower and upper bounds. We also show that any algorithm that can be used with model M_D can be simulated in the more restrictive model M_C. Table 1 summarizes the complexity bounds.

Table 1. Summary results, where $\Delta = diam(G)$ and $L = (\max_{C \in \mathscr{C}} diam(C) + |\mathscr{C}|$ where $\mathscr{C}$ is the set of strongly connected components of the initial weakly-connected graph. In model M_A the bounds are based on the fact the algorithm that can detect termination.

Model	Time Complexity		Message Complexity		Communication Complexity	
	Upper	Lower	Upper	Lower	Upper	Lower
M_A^*	$O\left(\log \Delta\right)$	$\Omega\left(\log \Delta\right)$	$O\left(n^2 \log \Delta\right)$	$\Omega(n)$	$O\left(n^3 \log \Delta \log n\right)$	$\Omega(n^2 \log n)$
M_B	$O(\log^2 n)$	$\Omega(\log n)$	$O(n^2 \log^2 n)$	$\Omega(n)$	$O(n^2 \log^3 n)$	$\Omega(n^2 \log n)$
M_C	$O\left(n \log^2 n\right)$	$\Omega\left(n\right)$	$O\left(n^2 \log^2 n\right)$	$\Omega\left(n^2\right)$	$O\left(n^2 \log^3 n\right)$	$\Omega(n^2 \log n)$
M_D	$O(L \log n)$	$\Omega\left(\log n\right)$	$O(nL \log n)$	$\Omega\left(n\right)$	$O(n^2 L \log n)$	$\Omega(n^2 \log n)$

Related Problems. The problem of resource discovery was formalized by Harchol-Balter, Leighton, and Lewin in [3]. Several algorithms were proposed in [3] in the synchronous setting assuming that the initial logical network is a weakly connected graph. However, the best algorithm they used was a randomized algorithm. Following [3], Kutten, Peleg, and Vishkin [7] proposed a deterministic algorithm. In this algorithm the time complexity has been reduced, in comparison to [3], from $O(\log^2 n)$ to $O(\log n)$; the message complexity from $O(n \log^2 n)$ to $O(n \log n)$; and the communication complexity from $O(n^2 \log^3 n)$ to $O(|E_0| \log^2 n)$, where E_0 is the number of edges in the initial graph. In [3], the the cost of communication is measured using two complexity measures called "connection" complexity and "pointer" complexity. However, optimizing these measures is equivalent to optimizing the usual message and communication complexity. The deterministic algorithm in [7] does not impose limits on the message size. Furthermore, any number of messages can be sent by a node in a given step.

A dynamic version of gossiping, called *perpetual gossiping*, has been proposed by Liestman and Richards [8]. Here the new information is generated continuously and the goal is to update the received information, hence the gossiping-like protocol must be repeated. Another related problem is maintaining consistency among the sites in the face of updates in the replicated database. Demers *et al.* [1] developed randomized algorithms for distributing updates and driving the replicas toward consistency. They use epidemic-like approach to model and analyze the performance of designed protocols.

Document Structure. The rest of the paper is structured as follows. Section 2 describes the models of computation and measures of efficiency. Section 3 provides an algorithm that can detect termination. In Section 4 we provide an efficient algorithm that solves the NDIG problem introduced in this paper. Section 5 shows a method for simulating any algorithm for the model of computation considered in Section 4 under the model of computation considered in Section 6. Section 6 gives an algorithm for the fourth model in this paper. We conclude in Section 7. An online technical report [10] contains the omitted proofs.

2 Models and Complexity Measures

System model. We consider a system of n processes, with unique identifiers, able to communicate over a fully connected synchronous network. Initially, a process may not be aware of all other processes participating in the computation, and also may not know the value of n. We define *step* to be a standard constant period of time sufficient for a processor to accept any incoming messages, to perform some local computation, or to send/broadcast any outgoing messages. We assume that the nodes do not fail and that messages are not lost. By vertex we denote a process and also we use the words vertices and nodes synonymously.

Modeling Knowledge. We model the knowledge in the system by a directed graph whose vertices represent processors and whose edges represent the knowledge of one processor about another. We denote by V the set of vertices, where $|V| = n$. For each vertex v we denoted by $world(v)$ the set of adjacent vertices of v and clearly $world(v) \subseteq V$. We call this graph the connectivity graph:

Definition 1. *Given a set V and for each $v \in V$ the set $world(v) \subseteq V$, we define the* **connectivity graph** *as the directed graph, denoted as $G = (V, E)$, where $E = \{(u, v) : u, v \in V, v \in world(u)\}$.*

We assume that any connectivity graph is at least *weakly-connected* which is a reasonable assumption to guarantee that eventually any node can possibly know any other node. Next we define an undirected version of the graph.

Definition 2. *The* **induced connectivity graph**, $\mathcal{G} = (\mathcal{V}, \mathcal{E})$ *of the connectivity graph $G = (V, E)$, is the undirected graph such that $\mathcal{V} = V$ and $\mathcal{E} = \{(u, v) : ((u, v) \in E) \vee ((v, u) \in E)\}$.*

Problem Definition. Now, we give a relatively formal definition of the problem of node discovery in graphs as follows. Given the initial connectivity graph $G = (V, E)$ the node discovery in graphs problem (NDIG) is to use a distributed protocol, under the given message passing model of computation, to evolve the initial connectivity graph to a fully connected connectivity graph.

Algorithmic Template. We will consider iterative algorithms, where each iteration consists of a constant, fixed at "compile-time", number of steps, i.e. the number of synchronous steps involved in an iteration is known or decided *a priori*. We number iterations using natural numbers. We define the following algorithmic template. At some step within an iteration, a node v chooses a set of nodes $send(v) \subseteq world(v)$. It then sends messages $M_{v,u}$, for $u \in send(v)$. Here, $M_{v,u}$ denotes the content of message sent to node u from v. Each message contain a set of identifiers, such that $M_{v,u} \subseteq world(v)$. When a message reaches the destination u, the set $world(u)$ is updated as follows: $world(u) \leftarrow world(u) \cup M_{v,u}$. Thus the connectivity graph may evolves after every iteration.

Now let $G_0 = (V_0, E_0)$ and $\mathcal{G}_0 = (V_0, \mathcal{E}_0)$ to be the connectivity graph and induced connectivity graph corresponding to the initial state. At the end of each iteration $i > 0$, we define $G_i = (V_i, E_i)$ and $\mathcal{G}_i = (V_i, \mathcal{E}_i)$ to be the resulting connectivity graph and induced connectivity graph, respectively. Clearly, $V_0 = V_i, i \geq 0$.

We consider several algorithms that are instantiated from the above algorithmic template by constraining, in each round, the cardinality of the sets of destinations and the size of the messages. Our problem is to study the conditions under which the connectivity graph becomes fully connected. We analyze the upper and lower bounds on the number of iterations required to achieve that. Specifically, we examine four models defined by imposing the following constraints on each communication round:

- Model M_A: multicast and message size is $O(n \log n)$ where n is the total number of nodes
- Model M_B: multicast is at most linear in the total number of nodes and message size is $O(\log n)$
- Model M_C: unicast and messages are of size $O(\log n)$
- Model M_D: unicast and message size at most $O(n \log n)$

Complexity Measures. In this paper we measure the performance of the algorithms presented in terms of time complexity, and commonly used measures of communication cost in terms of message complexity and communication complexity. Given an initial connectivity graph G_0 and an algorithm to solve the NDIG problem we define the time complexity as the number of synchronous steps of the algorithm executed in solving the NDIG problem, i.e., to evolve the connectivity graph into a fully connected graph.

The message complexity of an algorithm that solves the NDIG problem on an initial connectivity graph G_0 is the total number of messages sent during the execution of the algorithm to solve the NDIG problem.

The communication complexity of an algorithm is the total number of bits sent during the execution of the algorithm until it solves the NDIG problem. Below we provide a lower bound on the communication complexity of the NDIG problem valid for all the four models. These lower bounds are proved under the assumption that the algorithms are polynomial time complexity.

Lemma 1. *The lower bound the communication complexity to solve the NDIG model, under the models M_A, M_B, M_C and M_D is $\Omega\left(n^2 \log n\right)$, where n is the number of vertices in the connectivity graph.*

3   Multicast and Message Size $O(n \log n)$

In this section we consider the least constrained model where each node v is able to multicast in one step messages to all other nodes it is aware of, i.e, all nodes in $world(v)$. The size of the messages can be linear in the number of nodes times the logarithm of the number of nodes (i.e., $O(n \log n)$). We give an algorithm solving the problem and analyze its complexity and provide lower bounds.

Algorithm A, at any node v, is given in Fig. 1 which can detect the discovery of all the nodes and also decide termination. On the other hand, it suffers from high message and communication complexities. A natural question in resource discovery arises: *how will a vertex know how to stop?* That is, how can a processor know that it discovered all resources? First we describe the resource discovery problem as in [7]: a distributed algorithm is said to solve the *Resource Discovery Problem* if the following applies to every initially weakly connected component C in the directed graph G when the algorithm terminates:

(i) there exists a root vertex $v \in C$ so that for every other vertex $u \in C$, G contains a directed edge (v, u).

(ii) every vertex $u \in C$ recognizes v as the root vertex.

With this we explain the question as follows: given a resource discovery problem on a weakly connected graph, where each edge represents the knowledge of the tail vertex about the head vertex, is there a distributed protocol where each node can detect the termination condition, and thus terminate the protocol ?

RECEIVE-PHASE:

Step 1. Receive all the messages sent to v, denote by $\mathcal{M}_v$ the set of messages received.

Step 2. $world_i(v) \leftarrow world_{i-1}(v) \cup \left(\bigcup_{M_{u,v} \in \mathcal{M}_v} M_{u,v} \right)$.

Step 3. if node v determines that $i \geq 2 \wedge world_i(v) \setminus world_{i-2}(v) = \emptyset$ then it STOPS

SEND-PHASE:

Step 4. Prepare outgoing message M such that $M = world_i(v)$.

Step 5. Prepare a set of destinations D such that $D \subseteq world_i(v)$.

Step 6. Send messages $M_{v,u}$ to destinations u, such that $M_{v,u} = M$ and $u \in D$.

Fig. 1. Algorithm A: Structure of the iteration number i, at node v

In algorithm A every vertex can detect the termination condition and thereby know the identities of every other vertex when it terminates. Choosing the vertex with the least identifier as the root solves the resource discovery problem.

In algorithm A each node broadcasts all of its current knowledge to every other node it knows. We show that this algorithm has message complexity $O(n^2)$ and communication complexity $O(n^3 \log n)$. We show that eventually all nodes terminate the execution once they know about every other node in the graph, i.e., without any prior knowledge of the total number of nodes participating in the computation.

The algorithm iterates through a *receive phase* and a *send phase* (for convenience we start with the receive phase). Each phase consists of three steps. We refer to the six steps iterated by the algorithm as the *iteration* of the algorithm, and we number the iterations starting with 0. For phase 0, $M_0 = world_0(v)$ and $D_0 = world_0(v)$. For $i > 0$, $M_i = world_i(v)$ and $D_i = \{u : u \in world_i(v) \wedge u \notin world_{i-1}(v)\}$. If the node at vertex v terminates the algorithm in iteration i, we define $world_j(v) = world_i(v)$ for every $j > i$.

Lemma 2. *Algorithm A, for model M_A, with the initial connectivity graph $G_0 = (V_0, E_0)$, every vertex $v \in V_0$ eventually reaches termination.*

Lemma 3. *Algorithm A, in model M_A, with the initial connectivity graph $G_0 = (V_0, E_0)$, for any two $u, v \in V_0$ we have $v \in world(u)$ and $u \in world(v)$ at termination.*

Lemma 4. *For model M_A, the number of iterations required to solve NDIG problem on the connectivity graph $G_0 = (V_0, E_0)$ is lower bounded by $\Omega(\log diam(G))$, where $diam(G) = $ diameter of the graph G_0.*

Lemma 5. *Algorithm A, for model M_A, the number of iterations required to solve the NDIG problem on the initial connectivity graph is $G_0 = (V_0, E_0)$ is $O\left(\log diam(G)\right)$, where $diam(G) = diameter of the graph $\mathcal{G}_0$.*

Lemma 6. *The message and communication complexities of Algorithm A, for model M_A, to solve the NDIG problem in the initial connectivity graph $G_0 = (V_0, E_0)$ are $O\left(n^2 \log diam(G)\right)$ and $O\left(n^3 \log diam(G) \log n\right)$, respectively, where $n = |V|$ and $diam(G)$ is the diameter of the graph $\mathcal{G}_0$.*

In algorithm A, each of the vertices can detect termination, i.e., they know whether there are any more vertices to be discovered or not. Intuitively, the termination condition can be realized in the following observation. In algorithm A, in any node until all nodes are discovered by it then in each consecutive iterations its aware of at least one new node. This leads us to conclude that it is possible to detect termination in this problem without knowing the number of vertices by any vertex *a priori*. However, although algorithm A has running time matching with the lower bound for the model M_A and reasonable message complexity, it suffers from very high communication complexity.

4   Multicast and Messages of Size $O(\log n)$

In this model we assume that a vertex at any step can multicast messages of constant size. Recall the fact that we assume that the connectivity graph is weakly connected. We provide an algorithm (viz., algorithm B) that solves the NDIG problem with closely matching lower and upper bounds on time complexity, message complexity and communication complexity. The algorithm progresses with the aim of reaching two main objectives, viz, (1) produce a vertex that knows the names of all the vertices in the connected component to which it belongs to, and (2) concurrently spread the knowledge of such a vertex to other vertices. Recall that *the number of vertices participating in the computation is not known in advance to any of the vertices*. As a result we cannot assure the completion of the first part, i.e., to produce a vertex that knows the names of all the vertices in the connected component it belongs to. Therefore, we run these two parts of the algorithm concurrently. For the clarity of presentation we present these two aspects of the same algorithm as two separate algorithms, viz., algorithm B_1 and algorithm B_2. An iteration of algorithm B consists of the execution of the steps of algorithm B_1 followed by the steps corresponding to algorithm B_2.

Notations and Definitions.   Now we define the data structure required for the algorithm. Each vertex v has the following variables associated with it, viz., ptr, $world$, as follows. The variable ptr associated with vertex v is such that $ptr(v) \in V$.

First, we explain both parts of the algorithm independently for clarity of presentation. Then we will put together both the parts to get the final algorithm and show that our algorithm solve the NDIG problem. Since each vertex $v \in V$ has a unique identifier, which we denote as $id(v)$, we can always assume that the set of possible identifiers is well-ordered. Hence, for any $v \in V$ we can always have a linear ordering of the set of nodes in $world_t(v)$, for any $t > 0$.

4.1 Algorithm B_1

Notations and Definitions. One of the data structures is the *pointer graph*, (i) at any time of the algorithm every vertex v points to another vertex (possibly itself) through its variable $ptr(v)$, and (ii) the graph formed by the pointers (edges induced by the pointers) is a forest. As the algorithm progresses these invariants are maintained. For any $v \in V$ if we have $ptr(v) = v$ we call such a vertex a root vertex of the tree rooted at v. As the algorithm proceeds the final emergence of exactly one star with all the vertices in V is anticipated by: (i) merging trees and, (ii) shortening height of the trees.

As a result, messages are sent to communicate with other vertices. All messages are of size at most $O(\log n)$, where n is the maximum number of participating nodes. A message can consist of identifiers of vertices, or control messages such as a **join** invitation. The initial contents of $world(v)$ are the vertices at the tail of the outgoing edges of G_0; also, any new vertex v comes to know about, during the execution of the protocol, are added to $world(v)$. In the algorithm in Fig. 2, the data structure"children" is updated in Step 6.

Initially, every vertex $v \in V$ is a root, i.e., sets $ptr(v) \leftarrow v$. An iteration i (beginning with $i \leftarrow 0$) in v consists of the following steps.

Step 1. Every root vertex v sends **join** invitations to all edges in G_i.
Step 2. For a root vertex v, suppose r_{min} is the vertex with the minimum identifier among all the vertices from which a **join** invitation is received. If $id(r_{min}) < id(v)$ then inform r_{min} about it and set $ptr(v) \leftarrow r_{min}$.
Step 3. Every vertex v sends its $ptr(v)$ to its "children".
Step 4. The children point their pointers to the pointers received from their parents, i.e., set $ptr(v) \leftarrow ptr(ptr(v))$
Step 5. Every vertex v sends its $ptr(v)$ to all its neighbors in G_i.
Step 6. The vertices receiving messages from Step 5 send their id (i.e. $id(v)$) to each of the $ptr(v)$'s.
Step 7. Any vertex v receiving messages from Step 6 adds the vertex id's received to its $world(v)$.

Fig. 2. Algorithm B_1: The main steps during iteration i

Correctness and liveness. We want to prove if we run algorithm B_1 the pointer graph will always be a forest and eventually consist of one root and within a finite number of iterations every vertex would know any other vertex, i.e., *safety* and *liveness*.

Lemma 7. *In algorithm B_1, under the model M_B, for a given initial connectivity graph $G_0 = (V_0, E_0)$, the pointer graph is a forest during any iteration.*

Lemma 8. *In $O(\log^2 n)$ iterations there exists a vertex v such that each vertex $v \in V$ is in $world(v)$.*

4.2 Algorithm B_2

Notations and Definitions. In this algorithm the main data structure is the $world(v)$ variable as already described. Initially, for every vertex $v \in V_0$, we have $count \leftarrow 0$. Algorithm B_2 carries out a "circular binary broadcasting" on a logical ring of vertices. This logical ring is induced by the identifiers of the vertices known to a root index (through its $world$ variable). Each root vertex perpetually tries to disseminate its knowledge of the vertices in its $world$ variable to each of the vertices in its $world$ variable to form a all-to-all logical connection. In order to do so, assume the following: *given a set of vertex IDs, every vertex should be able have a commonly agreed circular ordering of these IDs*. We can do this by defining this order by comparison of the IDs. In order to carry out the "circular binary broadcasting" we use a function f to determine, locally by a vertex v, the target vertex given the information about which vertex started the current broadcast and when the current broadcast (called the *initiator*) was started (by the $count$ variable).

Suppose $U = \{u_1, u_2, \cdots, u_k\}$ where $U \subseteq W$ and suppose $id(u_1) < id(u_2) < \cdots < id(u_k)$ and denote by $ord(u_i) = i$. Next, define a function as $f : U \times \mathbb{N} \times \mathbb{N} \to V$, such that, $f(u, i, j) = (ord(u) + 2^i + j) \mod k + 1$

Each vertex is equipped with the following additional variables: *broadcaster* - a binary variable set to true or false to indicate if a vertex is taking part as a broadcaster in some iteration or not; *count* - every broadcaster counts the number of iterations that have passed since the beginning of the current broadcasting round; and *initiator* - the identity of the root vertex that started the current circular binary broadcast.

Initially, every vertex $v \in V$ sets $broadcaster \leftarrow$ true

Step 1. If $broadcaster$ then
$\qquad count \leftarrow count + 1$
$\qquad$ if new known are added to $world(v)$ or $count > \lceil \log_2 n \rceil$ then
$\qquad\qquad$ if v is a root vertex then
$\qquad\qquad\qquad count \leftarrow 0, initiator \leftarrow id(v)$
$\qquad\qquad$ else
$\qquad\qquad\qquad broadcaster \leftarrow$ false
Step 2. If $broadcaster$ then
$\qquad\qquad target \leftarrow f(initiator, count, v)$
$\qquad$ and send the message $\langle initiator, count, target \rangle$ to each vertex in $world(v)$
Step 3. Receive messages from Step 2 and send all the vertices collected as $target$'s of the messages.
Step 4. Receive messages from Step 3 and include all the identifiers into $world(v)$ and set $count \leftarrow$ count, $initiator \leftarrow$ initiator, $broadcaster \leftarrow$ true with the values "count" and "initiator" received from the messages.

Fig. 3. Algorithm B_2: At vertex v for iteration i

Initially, every vertex $v \in V$ is a root, i.e., sets $ptr(v) \leftarrow v$ and $broadcaster \leftarrow$ true. An iteration of the algorithm consists of the following. If a root vertex already sent join messages to all the vertices in its $world$ and its $world$ did not change during the last $\lceil \log_2 |world| \rceil$ consecutive iterations then it does not send any message until it receives from other vertices.

Phase I: Execute one iteration (all the steps 1-7) of algorithm B_1.
Phase II: Execute one iteration (all the steps 1-4) of algorithm B_2.

Fig. 4. Algorithm B: At vertex v for iteration i

Correctness and Liveness of Algorithm B_2. We want to show that if the algorithm B_2 is run on a connectivity graph such that there is exactly one root vertex that has all other vertices in its $world$ variable then in $O(\log n)$ iterations the connectivity graph will evolve to a fully connected graph, i.e., the NDIG problem will be solved. We state the algorithm B as in Fig. 4.

Lemma 9. *Consider an initial connectivity graph G such that it has exactly one root vertex such that all other vertices are in its world variable then algorithm B_2, under model M_B, solves the the NDIG problem in $O(\log n)$ iterations.*

Complexity of the algorithm. We now state and prove the performance measures for the Algorithm B, in model M_B, with the initial connectivity graph $G_0 = (V_0, E_0)$ for solving the NDIG problem.

Theorem 1. *Algorithm B, in model M_B, with the initial connectivity graph $G_0 = (V_0, E_0)$, solves the NDIG problem with the initial connectivity graph $G_0 = (V_0, E_0)$ in $O\left(\log^2 n\right)$ iterations, where $n = |E_0|$.*

Theorem 2. *Under the M_B model the lower bound on the number of iterations required to solve the NDIG problem on is $\Omega(\log n)$, where n is the number of vertices on the connectivity graph.*

Lemma 10. *The message and communication complexities of Algorithm B, under the M_B model, with the initial connectivity graph $G_0 = (V_0, E_0)$, to solve the NDIG problem are $O\left(n^2 \log^2 n\right)$ and $O\left(n^2 \log^3 n\right)$ respectively, where $n = |V|$.*

Lemma 11. *The lower bound on the message complexity to solve the NDIG problem in model M_B is $\Omega\left(n^2\right)$, where $n = |V|$.*

Above we provided an algorithm (we call it algorithm B) for model M_B that has an upper bound on its running time of $O(\log^2 n)$ which is only a $\log n$ factor higher than the lower bound of $O(\log n)$.

5   Unicast and Message Size $O(\log n)$

In this model we assume that a vertex at any step can send only a constant number of messages and of size $O(\log n)$, where n is the number of vertices participating in the computation. Although this is a very stringent model, in this section we show that any computation that can be carried out in model M_B can be simulated in the model M_C. However, we can show a stronger result: any computation that can be carried out in model M_B can be simulated in the model *unicast and messages of size $O(1)$* . In the latter model messages can be of size $O(1)$ bits.

For our problem of node discovery we can use the above mentioned result to construct an algorithm that gives closely matching upper and lower bound.

Theorem 3. *Any algorithm that can be run in model M_B in $O(g(n))$ iterations can be simulated in model "unicast and message size $O(1)$" in $O(ng(n)\log n)$ iterations, where $g(n)$ is some function $g : \mathbb{N} \to \mathbb{R}^{+}$.*

Proof. We will show this proof by simulating any algorithm for model M_B by an algorithm for model M_C. We assume that each vertex has enough local memory to store the local history of the computation, i.e., as seen by the vertex. Since we are in a deterministic message passing model the progress of the execution at a node is dependent on the messages received from other nodes. When we refer to an iteration of algorithm in model M_B we refer to it as *phase*. The intuition behind the simulation algorithm, in model "unicast and message size $O(1)$", is that the algorithm, for model M_B, is simulated by keeping track of its phase numbers. We call the algorithm for model M_B the *simulated algorithm* and the algorithm, in model M_C, that carries out the simulation as the *simulating algorithm*. Any message sent, in the simulated algorithm, by a vertex v to vertex u in model M_B is now simulated, in the simulating algorithm, by having v send from v at most $O(n \log n)$ consecutive messages of size $O(1)$ over consecutive synchronous steps. At any step of the simulating algorithm it has no way of figuring out if it has received all the messages corresponding to a phase in the simulated algorithm. Since the number of participants n is not known *a priori* therefore the simulating algorithm does not wait expecting messages. But it simulates the steps of the simulated algorithm in whatever messages it received up to that point. However, if a computation is already carried out for a particular *phase* and a message corresponding to this or a earlier phase arrives, then the computation for such phases are re-computed (or re-simulated) with the new information. So, this requires sending (or re-sending) messages to some nodes–which might even include certain "ignore" messages–so that the computation can be repeated or corrected in some relevant nodes.

We present in Fig. 5 the main steps of the simulating algorithm. Every message has a *tag* associated with that that contains the *phase number* of the simulated algorithm, we denote it by $tag(i, u, v)$, where u is the sender and v is the receiving vertex.

Now, we want to show the correctness of the simulation algorithm as follows. Suppose we run the simulated algorithm (i.e. algorithm for the model "multicast is at most linear in the total number of nodes and message size is $O(\log n)$") and the simulating algorithm (i.e. algorithm for the model "unicast and constant message size $O(1)$") with the same initial connectivity graph G. Now, given any phase $k \in \mathbb{N}$ of the simulated algorithm there exists an $\ell \in \mathbb{N}$, so that, for any iteration $i > \ell$ of the simulating algorithm

RECEIVE MESSAGES PHASE: Receive all the messages and choose the earliest or smallest *phase i* that comes from the *tags*. We denote by i_v the iteration number of the simulating algorithm at vertex/node v.

> Case $i_v > i + 1$ *or message with $tag(i, u, v)$ was already received before:* Include new information and ignore old information. Recompute the step with the logged data structure values beginning with the phase $i + 1$.
>
> Case $i_v < i + 1$: Store this information that is to used in the context of *phase $i + 1$*.
>
> Case $i_v = i + 1$: Simulate for *phase i_v*.

SEND MESSAGES PHASE: If re-computation was done, then send to the newly decided destinations the re-computed results starting from the earliest phase i. This train of messages is sent in consecutive steps until a new re-computation is started. If in the earlier phase i some message was sent, then send *ignore/cancel* messages.

Fig. 5. Algorithm to simulate an algorithm in model M_B at vertex v for iteration i

---

the simulated data structure values (*world, initiator*, etc) for phases $0, 1, \cdots, k$ are similar to those of the simulated algorithm. We show this by induction on k (i.e. phase).

Base case $k = 0$: Since the first phase depends on the initial connectivity graph G and the initialized values the claim is clearly held for $k = 0$ and $\ell = 0$.

Induction hypothesis: Suppose our claim is true for some phase k and hence there exists an ℓ as defined above.

Induction step: Observe that for iterations i, $i > \ell$ the simulated data structures are similar to those of the simulated algorithm's. Therefore, after $O(n \log n)$ iterations, since there are at most $O(n)$ nodes to send messages each of size at most $O(\log n)$, all the messages from phase k will arrive at their destinations in the simulating algorithm, and hence this will have the simulated data structures hold values similar to the simulated algorithm. Also, no re-computing will be done for phase $k + 1$ since all messages have arrived. So, after $\ell + O(n)$ iterations all the phases $0, 1, \cdots, k + 1$ have the property as claimed. Also, if the simulated algorithm takes $O(g(n))$ phases to evolve the connectivity graph to a fully connected graph, from the above argument the simulating algorithm would achieve the same in $O(ng(n) \log n)$ iterations.

Theorem 4. *Any algorithm that can be run in model M_B in $O(g(n))$ iterations can be simulated in the model M_C in $O(ng(n))$ iterations.*

Theorem 5. *In the model M_C the lower bound on the number of iterations required to solve the NDIG problem on the initial connectivity graph $G_0 = (V_0, E_0)$ is $\Omega(n)$, where $n = |V|$.*

5.1   The Algorithm C

From Lemma 4 we have seen above that if there is an algorithm for the model M_B we can simulate the algorithm to work for the model M_C. We have already seen an algorithm, viz., algorithm B, that runs on the first model. Therefore, we can simulate this algorithm in the latter model as given in the proof of Lemma 3 that would evolve the initial connectivity graph G to a fully connected graph. We call this simulated algorithm "Algorithm C". By Lemma 4 the running time of the simulated algorithm in $O(n \log^2 n)$ iterations. Hence, we state the following theorem.

Theorem 6. *Algorithm C, under model M_C, with the initial connectivity graph $G_0 = (V_0, E_0)$, solves the NDIG problem in $O\left(n \log^2 n\right)$ iterations, where $n = |E_0|$.*

Lemma 12. *The message and communication complexities of Algorithm C, for model M_C, with any initial connectivity graph $G_0 = (V_0, E_0)$, to solve the NDIG problem are $O\left(n^2 \log^2 n\right)$ and $O\left(n^2 \log^3 n\right)$, respectively, where $n = |V|$.*

Lemma 13. *For model M_C, the lower bound for the message complexity of any algorithm that solves NDIG on any given initial connectivity graph $G_0 = (V_0, E_0)$ is $\Omega\left(n^2\right)$, where $n = |V|$.*

6   Unicast and Message of Size $O(n \log n)$

In this model we assume that a vertex at any step can send only constant number of messages but the message size is $O(n \log n)$, where $n = |V|$. Recall, we only assume that the connectivity-graph is weakly connected. Let $\mathscr{C}$ be the set of strongly connected components of G_0. For this model (i.e. model M_D) we present an algorithm, viz., algorithm D in Fig. 6 that solves the NDIG problem in $O((\max_{C \in \mathscr{C}} diam(C) + |\mathscr{C}|) \log n)$, where n is the number of vertices in G_0. We again use a "circular binary broadcasting"

Initially, every vertex $v \in V$ we set $broadcaster \leftarrow$ true, $count \leftarrow 0$, $root \leftarrow$ true. If a root vertex's $world$ did not change during the last $\lceil \log_2 |world| \rceil$ consecutive iterations then it does not send any messages until it receives a message from other vertex.

Step 1. If $broadcaster$ then
    $count \leftarrow count + 1$
    if new known are added to $world(v)$ or $count > \lceil \log_2 |world| \rceil$ then
        if v is a root vertex then
            $count \leftarrow 0$, $initiator \leftarrow id(v)$
        else
            $broadcaster \leftarrow$ false
Step 2. If $broadcaster$ then
        $target \leftarrow f(initiator, count, v)$
    and send the message $\langle initiator, count, world \rangle$ to vertex corresponding to $target$.
Step 3. Receive messages from Step 2 and include $world(initiator)$ in $world(v)$. If multiple initiators are received choose the one with the smallest id. If there is any $u \in world(v)$ such that $id(u) < id(v)$, then $broadcaster \leftarrow$ false and $root \leftarrow$ false

---

Fig. 6. Algorithm D: At vertex v for iteration i

to spread the content of the *world* variable of a root vertex. For this purpose we use the same function $f : U \times \mathbb{N} \times \mathbb{N} \to V$ as in Section 4.2.

Theorem 7. *Algorithm D, for model* M_D, *takes* $O((\max_{C \in \mathscr{C}} diam(C) + |\mathscr{C}|) \log n)$ *iterations to solve the NDIG problem for the initial weakly connected graph* $G_0 = (V_0, E_0)$, *where* $n = |V|$.

Theorem 8. *The message and communication complexities of Algorithm D, for model* M_D, *with the initial weakly connected graph* $G_0 = (V_0, E_0)$, *to solve the NDIG problem are* $O(n(\max_{C \in \mathscr{C}} diam(C) + |\mathscr{C}|) \log n)$ *and* $O(n^2(\max_{C \in \mathscr{C}} diam(C) + |\mathscr{C}|) \log n)$, *respectively, where* $n = |V|$.

7 Conclusion

In this paper we considered the NDIG problem in four message passing models depending on multicast ability and size of message sent by any vertex, in each synchronous step, viz., models M_A, M_B, M_C and M_D. One natural question arises about the lower bounds on message and communication complexities whether the termination detection is always possible. Certainly, in such a situation there is a trade-off between the running time, and message and communication complexities. Another issue is to design algorithm with fault-tolerant capabilities.

References

1. A. Demers *et. al.*, "Epidemic Algorithms for Replicated Database Maintenance", in *Proc. of the Sixth Symposium on Principles of Distributed Computing (PODC'87)*, pp. 1–12, (1987).
2. Ch Georgiou, D. Kowalski and A. Shvartsman, "Robust distributed cooperation using inexpensive gossip", in *Proc. of 17th International Symposium on Distributed Computing*, pp. 224-238, (2003).
3. M. Harchol-Balter, F.T. Leighton and D. Lewin, " Resource Discovery in Distributed Networks", in *Proc of 18th Symposium on Principles of Distributed Computing*, pp. 229-237 (1999).
4. S. M. Hedetniemi, T. Hedetniemi, and A. L. Liestman., "A Survey of Gossiping and Broadcasting in Communication Networks", *Networks*, Vol 18, pp. 319-349 (1988).
5. K.M. Konwar, D.R. Kowalski, and A.A. Shvartsman, "The Join Problem in Dynamic Network Algorithms". *Proc. of the International Conference on Dependable Systems and Networks*, pp. 315-324 (2004).
6. D. Kowalski and A. Pelc, Deterministic broadcasting time in radio networks of unknown topology, *Proc. 43rd Ann. IEEE Symp. on Foundations of Computer Science*, pp 63-72 (2002).
7. S. Kutten, D. Peleg and U. Vishkin, " Deterministic resource discovery in distributed networks", *Thirteenth ACM Symposium on Parallel Algorithms and Architectures*, pp. 77-83 (2001).
8. A.L. Liestman and D.S. Richards, "Perpetual Gossiping", *Parallel Processing Letters*, Vol 3, pp. 347-355, (1993).
9. A. Pelc, "Fault-tolerant Broadcasting and Gossiping in Communication Networks", *Networks*, Vol. 28, pp. 143-156 (1996).
10. K.M. Konwar, D. Kowalski and A.A. Shvartsman, "Node Discovery in Networks", Technical Report, http://www.cse.uconn.edu/~kishori/TR-KKS.pdf (2005).

Optimal Clock Synchronization Under Energy Constraints in Wireless Ad-Hoc Networks
(Extended Abstract)

Hagit Attiya[1], David Hay[1], and Jennifer L. Welch[2]

[1] Computer Science Department, Technion, Israel
[2] Computer Science Department, Texas A&M University, USA

Abstract. Clock synchronization is a crucial service in many distributed systems, including wireless ad-hoc networks. This paper studies *external* clock synchronization, in which nodes should bring their clocks close to the value of some external reference time, which is provided in the system by one or more *source* clocks.

Reference broadcast synchronization (RBS) is a known approach that exploits the broadcast nature of wireless networks for a single hop. However, when networks are large in physical extent, additional mechanisms must be employed.

Using multi-hop algorithms that re-broadcast time information to short distances reduces the energy consumed for clock synchronization. The reason is that energy costs grow more than linearly with the broadcast distance. On the other hand, the quality of the clock synchronization, as measured in the closeness of the clocks, deteriorates as the number of hops increases.

This paper shows how to balance these two contradictory goals, achieving optimal clock synchronization while adhering to an energy budget at each node. In particular, a distributed algorithm is presented that uses multi-hop broadcasting over a shallow infrastructure to synchronize the clocks. The closeness of clock synchronization achieved by the algorithm is proved to be optimal for the given energy constraints.

Keywords: Clock Synchronization, Wireless Networks, Ad-hoc Networks, Multi-hop Broadcasts.

1 Introduction

Multi-hop ad-hoc networks consist of a collection of computing devices (called *nodes*) communicating by wireless broadcast. Their simplicity and the fact they do not require a pre-existing, wired infrastructure, have made them very popular. A broadcast transmission reaches all nodes within a specific *range* of its source; in order to reach a node outside this range, one or more intermediate broadcast transmissions are used. The transmission range of a broadcast is determined by the power used by the node: the power needed to broadcast to distance d is γd^β,

J.H. Anderson, G. Prencipe, and R. Wattenhofer (Eds.): OPODIS 2005, LNCS 3974, pp. 221–234, 2006.
© Springer-Verlag Berlin Heidelberg 2006

where $\beta \geq 1$ is the *distance-power gradient*, which depends on the environmental conditions of the network, and $\gamma > 0$ is the *transmission quality parameter*.

Many applications in distributed systems need synchronized clocks to work correctly. Such applications need to relate the local occurrence time of events to some reference time that is provided in the system by (possibly multiple) *sources*, which are perfectly synchronized with each other (e.g., by relying on UTC [32]). *Reference broadcast synchronization* (RBS) [12] is a known approach for clock synchronization in wireless ad-hoc networks, which broadcasts reference time on a single hop. When networks are large in physical extent, RBS is extended to use multi-hop re-broadcasting [23].

An important parameter for evaluating clock synchronization algorithms is the *clock skew* it provides, namely, the maximal (absolute) difference between the reading of a local clock and the reference time. The theory of clock synchronization [3,18,25,28] indicates that clock skew depends on the *uncertainty* about the accumulated delay of delivering messages between the nodes. For example, in case the uncertainty about the delay experienced by each broadcast message is the same, the clock skew increases as the number of intermediate hops increases.

In wireless ad-hoc networks, energy is typically a scarce resource, which should be used sparingly. Additionally, the likelihood of interference among transmissions increases with their transmission power [19]. In the common case, where $\beta > 1$, the energy costs grow super-linearly with the broadcast distance, making it more energy-economic to broadcast information in several hops, rather than transmitting at the maximum power and reaching far away nodes in a single broadcast hop.

This paper considers clock synchronization in multi-hop ad-hoc networks from a new angle, relating the energy constraints on a clock synchronization algorithm with the optimal skew it may obtain. Given individual energy budgets indicating how much a node is willing to spend on each message transmission for clock synchronization, we give exact bounds on the optimal skew that can be achieved, as a function of the uncertainty in message delays.

As we show, the optimal skew is the minimal depth of a particular *spanning forest*—whose trees are rooted at the time sources—of the topology graph induced by respecting the energy budgets. For the upper bound, we describe how to construct a *shallow* spanning forest, whose depth is minimal with respect to the accumulated uncertainty. This is done by applying simple (centralized or distributed) algorithms for finding *breath-first search* trees from multiple sources. Then, the source time is propagated down the trees. The skew attained by this simple algorithm is the sum of the uncertainties along the path from a source to a node. The matching lower bound is shown using well-known shifting techniques.

This paper considers *external* clock synchronization, in which there is at least one node in the system with access to the reference, or source, time. Applications sometimes require only *internal* (or *mutual*) clock synchronization, in which the local clocks of the nodes are brought close to each other but with no necessary relation to a reference time. Clearly, by invoking an external clock synchronization algorithm **A** in which an arbitrary node plays the role of the time source, it is possible to achieve internal clock synchronization with skew that is at most twice the skew of **A**.

Theoretical study of the clock synchronization problem dates back to the early 1980's. In particular, Lundelius and Lynch [20], and later Halpern et al. [18], proved tight bounds on the best skew achieved by *internal* clock synchronization algorithms. Interestingly, our bound is a simple expression depending on the (weighted) depth of the tree, no matter how complicated the topology is. This stands in contrast to the result in [18] for internal synchronization, in which the tight bound on clock skew is only characterized as the solution to a particular linear program. Later work [3, 25, 28] considered the issue of internal and external clock synchronization algorithms that exploit specific assumptions on message delay. Recently, Fan and Lynch proved lower [16] and upper [15] bounds on clock skew for the problem of *gradient* clock synchronization, in which the skew between nodes' clocks should be smaller if they are closer to each other.

Clock synchronization in wireless ad-hoc networks has been the topic of extensive research over the last few years (see the survey papers [30, 31] as well as surveys in Elson and Römer [14] and in Cao's thesis [9]). RBS [12], mentioned above, broke new ground by exploiting the nature of wireless broadcasts to get improved performance. Römer's algorithm [29] assigns timestamps to events, which can be compared to estimate the relative times at which events occurred; it was designed for systems with mobile nodes. The local nature of gradient clock synchronization [16, 15] makes it particularly well-suited to sensor networks.

Much of the previous work is not directly comparable to the results in this paper, by focusing, for instance, on one-hop networks, on internal clock synchronization, on how neighboring nodes estimate each other's clock values, or by evaluating the performance solely through experiments or simulation. Here we discuss more related papers, in which either the approach or algorithm is similar to ours or some notion of optimality is proved.

Several papers have addressed the issue of trading off energy and accuracy of the clock synchronization. For instance, PalChaudhuri et al. [26] describe a probabilistic version of RBS [12] and provide an analysis that gives the number of messages and synchronization overhead required to achieve a certain accuracy in the synchronization. van Greunen and Rabaey [33] have a way to devise an algorithm with minimum number of messages to achieve a certain accuracy. Finally, in the context of RBS-style algorithms, Elson et al. [13] show how to achieve an optimal tradeoff between energy consumption and accuracy. In all these papers, the energy usage is equated with the number of messages sent.

Several papers (e.g., [17, 33]) contain algorithms for clock synchronization that work by constructing and using a spanning tree of the network, preferably one of low depth, and propagating time information down the tree. These papers measure the depth of the trees by hop-count, in contrast to our work, which measures depth based on the accumulated uncertainty; since we allow non-uniform uncertainties on links, the two measures are not equivalent. Our matching lower bound shows that uncertainties must be taken into account when constructing the spanning forest to achieve optimality. Thus, our approach yields more accurate clock synchronization when uncertainties are non-uniform.

The Network Time Protocol (NTP) [22], used to synchronize clocks in the Internet, also uses a spanning forest rooted at time sources to broadcast synchronization messages. This spanning forest is built in an ad-hoc manner, and it minimizes the message delay, while our algorithm minimizes message uncertainty.

A few papers provide lower bounds on some complexity measures, which can be used to show that various algorithms are optimal in that regard. Blum et al. [8] prove a lower bound on the size of the interval for algorithms in which each node keeps an interval in which the real time should lie. Meier et al. [21] present an algorithm for internal synchronization that uses the data in a communication pattern optimally in order to obtain the best synchronization.

2   The System Model

Next we sketch a model of computation that captures our assumptions about nodes and their communication. The formalism is based on that in [4, 7].

We consider a set of n nodes $V = \{v_1, \ldots, v_n\}$, located in the Euclidean plane $\mathbb{R}^2$, that communicate with each other through wireless broadcasts. We assume that nodes are not mobile.

Associated with each broadcast is a distance d; we define the *recipients* of a broadcast performed by node v_i to be the set of nodes whose Euclidean distance from v_i is at most d. The power required for broadcasting to distance d is γd^β, where $\beta \geq 1$ is the *distance-power gradient*, which depends on the environmental conditions of the network, and $\gamma > 0$ is the *transmission quality parameter*; typically, $1 \leq \beta \leq 8$ and γ is normalized to one. We assume messages are of a fixed size, therefore γd^β is proportional to the energy consumed when broadcasting to distance d.

Various *events* can occur at a node, including the arrival of a message as well as internal happenings, e.g., internal timers going off.

Each node v_i has a *hardware clock*, denoted HC_i, which is a function from real time to hardware clock time of the form $HC_i(t) = t + o_i$, where o_i is the *offset* of the hardware clock from real time. This form of the hardware clock corresponds to the situation when hardware clocks have no drift, i.e., these clocks run at the same rate as real time.

Each node is modelled as a deterministic state machine, with a set of states, including subsets of initial and final states, and a transition function. The transition function takes as input the current state of the node, the current value of the hardware clock, and the current event, and produces as output a new state and possibly a message to be broadcast to a certain distance (equivalently, with a certain power). The hardware clock cannot be modified by the node. The state machine encodes the local algorithm executed by the node.

A *history* of a node is an infinite sequence of alternating states and pairs, where each pair consists of an event ϕ and a hardware clock value T. The first state must be an initial state of the node and each subsequent state must follow correctly, according to the node's transition function, from the previous state and pair. Furthermore, the hardware clock values must form a strictly increasing sequence that is unbounded.

A *timed history* of a node v_i is a history together with an assignment of a real time to each pair such that for each pair (ϕ, T), the time t assigned to it satisfies $HC_i(t) = T$. The value of a node's variable at real time t is the value of the variable in the latest state whose preceding pair is assigned a real time at most t. If t is less than the real time assigned to the first pair in the history, then the value of the variable is that in the first state of the history.

An *execution* is a set of n timed histories, one for each node. For each pair appearing in one timed history, say that of v_i, which causes a message to be broadcast, there must be exactly one pair appearing in the timed history of each broadcast recipient v_j whose event is the receipt of v_i's broadcast. Furthermore, for each pair appearing in a timed history whose event is the receipt of a broadcast, there must be a pair containing the corresponding broadcast. Here we are modelling reliable communication via the broadcasts.

The *delay* of a message (received by a node in an execution) is the difference between the real time when the message is received by the node and the real time when the message is broadcast. Specific instances of the model restrict the *admissible* executions, by making assumptions on message delay. These assumptions can vary from one node to another or even from one broadcast to another.

3   Problem Statement

Our goal is to synchronize the clocks of the non-source nodes as closely as possible without using too much energy.

We start by explaining how nodes adjust their clocks. Each node v_i has an *adjustment variable* adj_i as part of its state whose value it adds to its hardware clock to produce its *logical clock*, denoted LC_i. That is, $LC_i(t) = HC_i(t) + adj_i(t)$ for all real times t.

There is a set $S \subseteq V$ of distinguished *source* nodes that have perfectly synchronized clocks; call this *source time*, denoted $ST(t)$. Thus, $LC_i(t) = ST(t) = t$ for all $v_i \in S$ and all real times t, i.e., the source time is the real time.

The non-source nodes have arbitrary logical and hardware clock values initially.

Informally, every node should set the value of its logical clock so as to minimize the difference between its clock and the source time. More formally, we say a system solves the *external clock synchronization problem* if there exists a value ϵ such that in every admissible execution there exists a real time t_f such that for each node v_i and every real time $t \geq t_f$, v_i is in a final state at time t and $|ST(t) - LC_i(t)| \leq \epsilon$. We call the quantity $|ST(t) - LC_i(t)|$ the *skew* of v_i's logical clock.

The way we model energy constraints and how they affect the clock synchronization problem is explained next.

Each node v_i has a value, denoted $energy_i$, which bounds the amount of energy it is allowed to use for each transmission. This constraint translates to a bound on the power with which each node is allowed to broadcast. We denote this bound by $power_i$; note that for fixed-size messages, $power_i = c \cdot energy_i$, for some constant c. For a node v_i, let its *neighborhood*, denoted $N(v_i)$, be the set of nodes that can correctly receive a message sent from v_i and send a message to v_i without violating the energy constraints, that is, the set of nodes within Euclidean distance $\frac{1}{\gamma^{1/\beta}} \left(\min\{power_i, power_j\} \right)^{\frac{1}{\beta}}$ from v_i.

The neighborhoods induce a *topology graph*, $TG = \langle V, E \rangle$, such that $\langle v_i, v_j \rangle \in E$ if and only if $v_j \in N(v_i)$. Since the neighborhoods are *bidirectional*, the topology graph is in fact undirected (i.e., $\langle v_i, v_j \rangle \in E$ if and only if $\langle v_j, v_i \rangle \in E$).

We also assume that the energy constraints are "feasible", in particular, that they allow each node to communicate (perhaps indirectly) with every other node. This means that TG is strongly-connected.

We assume that for each pair of neighboring nodes v_i and v_j, the behavior of the link from v_i to v_j is the same as that of the link from v_j to v_i regarding the median message delay and the uncertainty in the message delays. Therefore, we associate with each link e in the topology graph, real numbers δ_e and u_e, with $\delta_e > u_e \geq 0$, such that each message on the link e has delay in the range $[\delta_e - u_e, \delta_e + u_e]$, regardless of its direction.

The relationship to the definition of external clock synchronization is that we now consider *admissible* executions to be executions in which the recipients of a broadcast by node v_i are all the neighbors of v_i in TG, and every message on link e has delay within the range $[\delta_e - u_e, \delta_e + u_e]$.

Crucial to our analysis of clock synchronization algorithms is the *weighted* variant of TG, denoted WTG, in which the weight of each edge e is u_e. Consider any path Π in WTG. Let the *uncertainty* of Π, denoted $u(\Pi)$, be $\Sigma_{e \in \Pi} u_e$, that is, the sum of the weights on all the edges in Π. Let $u_{i,j}$ be the minimum, over all paths Π in WTG between v_i and v_j, of the uncertainty $u(\Pi)$ of the path. A path between v_i and v_j that achieves the minimum uncertainty is called a *minimum-uncertainty* path. We define u_i^{min} to be the minimum, over all source nodes v_s, of $u_{s,i}$, i.e., the shortest (weighted) distance from v_i to any source.

We conclude this section with a few observations about our problem statement.

Since the clocks do not drift, we are considering a "one-shot" problem: the nodes execute some algorithm during which they can reset their adjustment variables. Eventually each node finishes the algorithm and makes no further changes to its adjustment variable. After this point, the relative values of their logical clocks stay the same, no further resynchronization takes place, and the skew of a node is unchanged thereafter.

As we have defined the problem, the goal of a clock synchronization algorithm is to minimize the maximum, over all nodes v_i, of the skew of v_i's clock. In fact, in this paper we introduce clock synchronization algorithms that achieve even stronger property: Not only do they minimize the maximum clock skew over all nodes, but in addition they minimize the clock skew for each node v_i separately.

The assumption of bidirectional links in the topology graph is common in protocols for ad-hoc networks, e.g., the *temporally-ordered routing algorithm*

(TORA) [27]. The IEEE 802.11 specification also requires bidirectional signaling. The justification for the assumption that the message delays and uncertainties are symmetric is that variation in the delay is mostly due to processing in the nodes and contention in the physical layer. We assume that nodes are roughly the same and running the same software. Since the number of neighbors affects the level of contention and the number of neighbors of a node v_i is approximately the same as the number of neighbors of any neighbor v_j of v_i, we expect the uncertainty of messages from v_i to v_j to be about the same as that of messages from v_j to v_i.

Note that we measure the delay of a specific message as the time elapsing from when the transmitting node starts broadcasting until the time the recipient finishes its processing. Therefore, this quantity includes processing time in both transmitting and recipient nodes, and the accumulated delays of any retransmissions of the message necessary in case the message is not successfully transmitted at first. This implies that the delay of messages corresponding to the same broadcast may be significantly different, and therefore, *receiver-to-receiver synchronization* [12, 31], which exploits the fact that the propagation delay of such correlated messages is about the same, cannot be applied in our model.

4   Multi-hop Broadcast-Based Clock Synchronization

In this section, we present algorithms for clock synchronization in the presence of multiple sources. First, we describe a generic algorithm for clock synchronization which assumes that there is a spanning forest of the topology graph TG, with each source being the root of a tree in the spanning forest. We prove that the clock skew achieved by the generic algorithm, depends linearly on the *depth* of the forest, namely, the maximum weighted distance of a path from a leaf to a root. (Recall that edge weights are their uncertainties.) Then, we discuss simple methods to construct a shallow spanning forest. Finally, we present an algorithm that synchronizes clocks while constructing the spanning forest.

4.1   A Generic Synchronization Algorithm

We assume there is a spanning forest of TG such that each source is the root of a separate tree, called its *broadcast tree*. Each source wakes up at some time and sends its current clock value over its broadcast tree. When a node gets the message, it adopts that clock value, after adding D to account for the message delay, where D is the sum of the median delays along the path the message has travelled so far. The detailed pseudocode is omitted from this version due to space limitations.

Specifically, the spanning forest is represented by storing in each node v_i an indication of its parent, $parent_i$; if v_i is a source node, we have $parent_i = \perp$. Non-source nodes also keep in a local variable $delay_i$ the sum of the median delays on all the edges in the path in the broadcast tree between the node and the source. Broadcasts received from a non-parent node are ignored. All broadcasts by node v_i are performed with power level $power_i$.

It is easy to see that the largest error that a neighbor v_i of a source can make is u_e, where e is the edge between v_i and the source. The largest error occurs if the message from the source took the minimum time $\delta_e - u_e$, or the maximum time $\delta_e + u_e$, to arrive. This maximum error propagates linearly with the (weighted) distance, as the wave of messages moves down the tree away from the source.

Clearly, the clock skew of the algorithm is minimized when the spanning forest is *shallow*, namely, when the maximum (weighted) depth over all the trees is minimized. It is straightforward to prove the next theorem:

Theorem 1. *In every admissible execution of the generic algorithm over a shallow spanning forest, the clock skew of each node v_i is eventually at most u_i^{min}.*

4.2   Pre-computing a BFS Forest

It is simple to construct a shallow spanning forest of the topology graph TG, needed for the generic clock synchronization algorithm. The spanning forest complies with the energy constraints, since it is a subgraph of TG.

One option is to use a *centralized* algorithm to compute the topology graph TG, and then run a generalization of Dijkstra's algorithm [10,11] to construct a *shortest paths* forest from the sources.

Another option is to use a *distributed* algorithm to compute the spanning forest. Here we describe a two-step process. A simple distributed algorithm constructs the topology graph TG, by computing the neighborhood $N(v_i)$ of each node v_i; the latter task is achieved by broadcasting a message and waiting for acknowledgments. Once the neighborhoods are computed, we can construct the spanning forest by invoking well-known distributed algorithms for finding a Breadth-First Search (BFS) forest rooted at multiple sources (e.g., [1,5] or OSPF [24]). These algorithms require a node to send messages using its maximal power under the energy restrictions. The reason is to ensure that the calculated communication links actually "exist".

4.3   Computing the BFS Forest On-the-Fly

In this section, we describe an algorithm that does not rely on pre-processing for constructing the broadcast forest. Instead, the forest is built *on the fly*, while doing the clock synchronization for the first time. The broadcast forest constructed by the algorithm can be used in future computations, including, for instance, clock resynchronizations to handle clock drift.

The code is presented in Algorithm 1. Each node has a local variable *uncertainty* which keeps track of the uncertainty associated with the path to a source that has the smallest uncertainty discovered so far. Each node keeps a local variable *parent* indicating which neighbor is its parent in the spanning forest. The local variable *updated* is used to control when the node sends broadcasts. Each node knows the median delay δ_e and the uncertainty u_e on each edge e adjacent to it.

The algorithm uses a ⟨sync⟩ message with the following fields:

time: the logical time at the sender when the message is sent.
sender: the originator of the message.
uncertainty: the value of the *uncertainty* variable of the sender.

Algorithm 1. Clock synchronization without a predefined spanning forest; code for node v_i

---

Initialization
    $parent_i \leftarrow \bot$
    $updated_i \leftarrow false$
    if $v_i \in S$ then $uncertainty_i \leftarrow 0$ // a source
    else $uncertainty_i \leftarrow \infty$

Upon beginning the algorithm: // only performed by a source
    broadcast $\langle sync, ST, i, 0 \rangle$

Upon receiving $\langle sync, T, j, u \rangle$ on an edge e:
    if $uncertainty_i > u + u_e$ then   // u_e is the uncertainty over edge e
        $adj_i \leftarrow (T + \delta_e) - HC_i$ // δ_e is the median delay on the edge e
        $uncertainty_i \leftarrow u + u_e$
        $parent_i \leftarrow j$
        $updated_i \leftarrow true$

Upon a trigger causing a node to broadcast   // depends on heuristics
    if $updated_i$ then
        $updated_i \leftarrow false$
        broadcast $\langle sync, LC_i, i, uncertainty_i \rangle$

The algorithm is initiated by having each source $s \in S$ send $\langle sync, ST(t), s, 0 \rangle$, at some time t. Each time a node v_i receives a $\langle sync \rangle$ message m with uncertainty u on edge e such that $u + u_e$ is smaller than v_i's current uncertainty, v_i has discovered a shorter path to one of the sources. In this case, v_i updates its adjustment variable based on the time in the message m and the median delay for that link, its current parent to be the originator of message m, and its current uncertainty to be $u + u_e$. At some later time, controlled by the *update* variable, v_i broadcasts a new $\langle sync \rangle$ message with the current value of its logical clock.

We show that the algorithm achieves the same properties as the generic clock synchronization scheme. Namely, every node v_i ultimately adopts the clock value $t + D$, where t is the real time at which the message is sent from some source s, and D is the median delay on a path with minimum weight from s to v_i.

The next lemma says that the *uncertainty* variable of a node is the uncertainty of some path to that node from a source and the clock skew is the same value. The proof, which is omitted in this version, follows by induction on prefixes of the execution.

Lemma 1. *For all admissible executions, all nodes v_i, and all times t, if $uncertainty_i(t) < \infty$, then there exists a path Π from some source node v_s to v_i such that $uncertainty_i(t) = u(\Pi)$, $parent_i(t)$ is the predecessor of v_i in Π, and $|ST(t) - LC_i(t)| \leq u(\Pi)$.*

The next lemma, whose proof is omitted, says that the *uncertainty* variable of each node continues to decrease until reaching the uncertainty of a minimum-uncertainty path.

Lemma 2. *For every admissible execution, each source node v_s, and each node v_i, eventually uncertainty$_i \leq u_{s,i}$.*

Theorem 2. *For each admissible execution of Algorithm 1 and each node v_i, eventually the clock skew of v_i is u_i^{min}, and parent$_i$ is the predecessor of v_i in the (weighted) path to the closest source.*

Proof. Lemma 2 implies that eventually v_i's *uncertainty* variable is at most that of a minimum-uncertainty path to a closest source. Let v_s be this closest source. Lemma 1 states that v_i's uncertainty always corresponds to some path to a source, so once v_i's uncertainty is at most $u_{s,i}$, it actually is exactly $u_{s,i}$, never gets any smaller, and the clock skew is $u_{s,i} = u_i^{min}$. Lemma 1 also implies that *parent$_i$* is the predecessor of v_i in the (weighted) path to v_s.   ∎

The worst-case message complexity of Algorithm 1 depends on the frequency with which ⟨sync⟩ messages are transmitted. It is possible to apply heuristics proposed by Banerjee and Khuller [6], and delay sending ⟨sync⟩ messages for a certain time; this creates the effect of waiting for messages on paths with less uncertainty that encounter higher total delay. A careful inspection of our correctness proof reveals that doing so does not compromise the *eventual* convergence of the tree. As Banerjee and Khuller show, careful choice of parameters in this heuristic can significantly reduce the message complexity.

5   Optimality

We prove that the synchronization achieved over a shallow spanning forest is optimal for the topology graph. This implies that our algorithms achieve optimal clock skew for the given energy budget. More specifically, we prove a lower bound of u_i^{min} on the skew of a node v_i. Recall that in our model, nodes may "overhear" any message that is broadcast within their reception distance, namely, by their neighbors in the topology graph. Potentially, overhearing may yield algorithms that provide lower skew than our spanning-forest-based algorithm, in which a broadcast by a node is only used by its children; our lower bound shows that this is not the case.

The intuition for this result is to think of lifting up a piece of cloth from the table, holding the sources pinned to the table. The node of interest is some point on the cloth. We pinch the cloth at that location and lift it up by u_i^{min}. The nodes in the neighborhood of the node of interest correspond to points on the cloth that will be lifted by smaller amounts; these amounts form a gradient. Using the fact that u_i^{min} is the shortest distance from a source, we can show that the cloth will not tear, namely, the timing at adjacent nodes remains consistent.

The detailed proof relies on a well-known *shifting argument* [20]: Given an execution α and an n-vector $\mathbf{x}$ of real numbers, we define a new execution, denoted $\alpha' = shift(\alpha, \mathbf{x})$, by adding x_i to the real time associated with each event of node v_i's history in α, for all i. Shifting an execution affects the hardware clocks and the message delays, in ways that are quantified in the next lemma.

Lemma 3 (Shifting [4,20]). *Let α be an execution with hardware clocks HC_i, and let $\mathbf{x}$ be an n-vector of real numbers. Then $\alpha' = shift(\alpha, \mathbf{x})$ is an execution with hardware clocks HC_i', where*

(a) $HC_i'(t) = HC_i(t) - x_i$ for all t, and
(b) if the delay of a message in α from v_i to v_j is d, then the delay of this message in α' is $d - x_i + x_j$.

Theorem 3. *For any external clock synchronization algorithm that complies with the energy constraints and every node v_i, there exists an admissible execution in which the final skew of v_i's clock is at least u_i^{min}.*

Proof. Fix an arbitrary external clock synchronization algorithm. Consider the admissible execution α of the algorithm in which the delay of each broadcast on each edge e of TG is the median delay δ_e. Choose any node v_i and let t_f be the real time when v_i has finished the algorithm.

Let σ be the skew of v_i at time t_f in α, i.e., $|ST(t_f) - LC_i(t_f)| = \sigma$. We first assume that $ST(t_f) - LC_i(t_f) \geq 0$.

We build execution α' by shifting execution α such that every node v_j is shifted by u_j^{min}, that is, $\alpha' = shift(\alpha, \mathbf{x})$ where $x_j = u_j^{min}$ for every j. Since the sources are at distance 0 (from themselves), they are not shifted (and they should not be, since they must have the real time).

We must verify that message delays are within the bounds so that α' is admissible. Consider a message m sent from node v_j to node v_k on an edge e in the topology graph TG. We distinguish between three cases:

If $u_j^{min} = u_k^{min}$, then the delay of m is are unaffected, since sender and receiver are shifted by the same amount.

If $u_j^{min} < u_k^{min}$, then since there is an edge between v_j and v_k, the fact that u_k^{min} is a shortest path distance implies that $u_k^{min} \leq u_j^{min} + u_e$ (recall that u_e is the uncertainty in message delay over the edge e). In α, the delay of m is δ_e; hence, by part (b) of Lemma 3, the delay of m in α' is $\delta_e + u_k^{min} - u_j^{min}$. This implies that the delay of m in α' is between δ_e and $\delta_e + u_e$, since $0 < u_k^{min} - u_j^{min} \leq u_e$.

If $u_j^{min} > u_k^{min}$, then since the weighted graph WTG is undirected, we have that $u_j^{min} \leq u_k^{min} + u_e$, and a similar argument shows that the delay of m in α' is between $\delta_e - u_e$ and δ_e.

We conclude that α' is admissible.

Consider what happens to v_i's skew in α'. At real time $t_f' = t_f + u_i^{min}$ in α', v_i has finished the algorithm. In α' we have:

$$|ST'(t'_f) - LC'_i(t'_f)| = |ST(t'_f) - LC'_i(t'_f)| \text{source clocks do not change}$$
$$= |ST(t'_f) - (LC_i(t'_f) - u_i^{min})| \text{by part (a) of Lemma 3}$$
$$= |ST(t_f) - LC_i(t_f) + u_i^{min}|$$
$$\text{skew does not change after } t_f < t'_f$$
$$\geq u_i^{min}   ST(t_f) - LC_i(t_f) \text{ and } u_i^{min} \text{ are positive}$$

In the symmetric case where $ST(t_f) - LC_i(t_f)$ in α is negative, we shift execution α by negative amounts instead of positive to produce α'. Namely, $\alpha' = shift(\alpha, \mathbf{x})$, where $x_j = -u_j^{min}$ for each j. The skew of node v_i in execution α' is $|ST(t_f) - LC_i(t_f) - u_i^{min}|$. Since $ST(t_f) - LC_i(t_f)$ is negative and u_i^{min} is positive, the skew is at least u_i^{min}.   ∎

6   Discussion

In this section we discuss generalizations of our approach, especially to make it more practical, as well as alternative approaches.

Our algorithm proposes a specific way to *estimate* clock readings over one hop (in a single broadcast), and a simple method to *combine* the estimations over several hops (re-broadcasts). However, we consider our key contribution to be the approach of picking the multi-hop broadcasts in a way that minimizes the worst-case accumulated uncertainty, while complying with the energy constraints. It is reasonable to apply other estimation and combination methods over shallow spanning forests of the topology, for example, methods that are geared towards optimizing the expected skew [26]. It would be interesting to prove that shallow energy-constrained spanning forests are optimal under these measures as well, as experimentally observed by van Greunen and Rabaey [33]. It would also be interesting to extend our results to deal with the more theoretical approach of optimizing the skew on a per-execution basis [3, 25, 28].

In this paper, we fixed the energy constraints and found algorithms that achieve optimal skew, under this budget. A complementary approach is to fix the desired skew and look for the minimal-energy algorithm achieving this skew. With uniform uncertainties, our techniques easily translate the desired skew into a desired number of hops, reducing the problem to the task of constructing a *minimal-energy* forest with this depth. For a constant depth and a single source, the tree can be approximated using an algorithm of Ambühl et al. [2]. It would be interesting to handle multiple sources and arbitrary depths.

Our approach can also be extended to apply when the sources are only approximately synchronized, as is the case when sources are in a wired network and run a separate algorithm to synchronize with each other. The approach can also accommodate clock *drift*; this requires clock synchronization to be invoked repeatedly and not only once. Once a shallow spanning forest is constructed, later resynchronization can use the same infrastructure. We leave the development of these ideas, and their analysis, as a topic for future research.

Finally, it is interesting to remove (at least some of) the assumptions we have made, most notably, the immobility of nodes and the reliability of communication links as well as their bidirectionality.

Acknowledgments. We would like to thank Siva Subramanian for his useful comments.

References

1. Y. Afek and M. Ricklin. Sparser: A paradigm for running distributed algorithms. *Journal of Algorithms*, 14:316–328, 1993.
2. C. Ambühl, A. E. F. Clementi, M. D. Ianni, N. Lev-Tov, A. Monti, D. Peleg, G. Rossi, and R. Silvestri. Efficient algorithms for low-energy bounded-hop broadcast in ad-hoc wireless networks. In *Proceedings of the 21st Annual Symposium on Theoretical Aspects of Computer Science (STACS)*, pages 418–427, 2004.
3. H. Attiya, A. Herzberg, and S. Rajsbaum. Optimal clock synchronization under different delay assumptions. *SIAM Journal on Computing*, 25(2):369–389, 1996.
4. H. Attiya and J. L. Welch. *Distributed Computing: Fundamentals, Simulations and Advanced Topics.* John Wiley& Sons, second edition, 2004.
5. B. Awerbuch and R. G. Gallager. A new distributed algorithm to find breadth first search trees. *IEEE Transactions on Information Theory*, 33(3):315–322, 1987.
6. S. Banerjee and S. Khuller. A clustering scheme for hierarchical control in multi-hop wireless networks. In *Proceedings of the 20th Annual Joint Conference of the IEEE Computer and Communications Societies (IEEE INFOCOM)*, pages 1028–1037, 2001.
7. S. Biaz and J. L. Welch. Closed form bounds for clock synchronization under simple uncertainty assumptions. *Information Processing Letters*, 80:151–157, November 2001.
8. P. Blum, L. Meier, and L. Thiele. Improved interval-based clock synchronization in sensor networks. In *Proceedings of the 3rd International Symposium on Information Processing in Sensor Networks (IPSN)*, pages 349–358, April 2004.
9. G. Cao. *Distributed Services in Mobile Ad Hoc Networks.* PhD thesis, Texas A&M University, April 2005.
10. T. H. Cormen, C. E. Lieserson, and R. L. Rivest. *Introduction to Algorithms.* MIT Press, 1990.
11. N. Deo and C. Pang. Shortest path algorithms: Taxonomy and annotation. *Networks*, 14(2):275–323, 1984.
12. J. Elson, L. Girod, and D. Estrin. Fine-grained network time synchronization using reference broadcasts. In *Proceedings of the 5th Symposium on Operating System Design and Implementation (OSDI)*, 2002.
13. J. Elson, R. Karp, C. Papadimitriou, and S. Shenker. Global synchronization in sensornets. In *Proceedings of the 6th Latin American Symposium on Theoretical Informatics (LATIN'04)*, pages 609–624, Buenos Aires, Argentina, 2004.
14. J. Elson and K. Römer. Wireless sensor networks: a new regime for time synchronization. *Computer Communication Review*, 33(1):149–154, 2003.
15. R. Fan, I. Chakraborty, and N. Lynch. Clock synchronization for wireless networks. In *Proceedings of the 8th International Conference on Principles of Distributed Systems (OPODIS)*, 2004.

16. R. Fan and N. Lynch. Gradient clock synchronization. In *Proceedings of the 23rd ACM Symposium on Principles of Distributed Computing (PODC)*, pages 320–327, 2004.

17. S. Ganeriwal, R. Kumar, and M. B. Srivastava. Timing-sync protocol for sensor networks. In *Proceedings of the 1st International Conference on Embedded Networked Sensor Systems (SenSys)*, pages 138–149, 2003.

18. J. Y. Halpern, N. Megiddo, and A. A. Munshi. Optimal precision in the presence of uncertainty. In *Proceedings of the 17th ACM Symposium on Theory of Computing (STOC)*, pages 346–355, 1985.

19. L. Li, J. Y. Halpern, P. Bahl, Y.-M. Wang, and R. Wattenhofer. Analysis of a cone-based distributed topology control algorithm for wireless multi-hop networks. In *Proceedings of the 20th ACM Symposium on Principles of Distributed Computing (PODC)*, pages 264–273, 2001.

20. J. Lundelius and N. A. Lynch. An upper and lower bound for clock synchronization. *Information and Control*, 62(2/3):190–204, 1984.

21. L. Meier and L. Thiele. Gradient clock synchronization in sensor networks. In *Proceedings of the 24th ACM Symposium on Principles of Distributed Computing (PODC)*, page 238, July 2005.

22. D. L. Mills. Internet time synchronization: The Network Time Protocol. *IEEE Transactions on Communications*, 39(10):1482–1493, Oct. 1991.

23. S. Mitra and J. Rabek. Energy efficient connected clusters for mobile ad hoc networks. In *3rd Annual Mediterranean Ad Hoc Networking Workshop (MEDHOC-NET)*, 2004.

24. J. Moy. RFC 2328 - OSPF version 2, April 1998.

25. R. Ostrovsky and B. Patt-Shamir. Optimal and efficient clock synchronization under drifting clocks. In *Proceedings of the 18th ACM Symposium on Principles of Distributed Computing (PODC)*, pages 3–12, 1999.

26. S. PalChaudhuri, A. K. Saha, and D. B. Johnson. Adaptive clock synchronization in sensor networks. In *Proceedings of the 3rd International Symposium on Information Processing in Sensor Networks (IPSN)*, pages 340–348, 2004.

27. V. D. Park and M. S. Corson. A highly adaptive distributed routing algorithm for mobile wireless networks. In *Proceedings of the Conference on Computer Communications (IEEE INFOCOM)*, pages 1405–1413, 1997.

28. B. Patt-Shamir and S. Rajsbaum. A theory of clock synchronization. In *Proceedings of the 26th ACM Symposium on Theory of Computing (STOC)*, pages 810–819, 1994.

29. K. Römer. Time synchronization in ad hoc networks. In *Proceedings of the 2nd ACM International Symposium on Mobile Ad Hoc Networking & Computing (MobiHoc)*, pages 173–182, 2001.

30. F. Sivrikaya and B. Yener. Time synchronization in sensor networks: A survey. *IEEE Network*, pages 45–50, July/August 2004.

31. B. Sundararaman, U. Buy, and A. D. Kshemkalyani. Clock synchronization for wireless sensor networks: A survey. *Ad Hoc Networks*, 3(3):281–323, May 2005.

32. The Official U.S. time. http://www.time.gov/.

33. J. van Greunen and J. Rabaey. Lightweight time synchronization for sensor networks. In *Proceedings of the 2nd ACM International Conference on Wireless Sensor Networks and Applications (WSNA)*, pages 11–19, 2003.

Half-Space Proximal: A New Local Test for Extracting a Bounded Dilation Spanner of a Unit Disk Graph

Edgar Chavez[1], Stefan Dobrev[2], Evangelos Kranakis[3], Jaroslav Opatrny[4],
Ladislav Stacho[5], Héctor Tejeda[1], and Jorge Urrutia[6]

[1] Escuela de Ciencias Físico-Matemáticas de la Universidad Michoacana, México.
Partially supported by CONACyT grant 36911-A
[2] School of Information Technology and Engineering (SITE), University of Ottawa,
800 King Eduard, Ottawa, Ontario, Canada, K1N 6N5
[3] School of Computer Science, Carleton University, Ottawa. Research supported in
part by NSERC and MITACS
[4] Department of Computer Science, Concordia University, Montréal. Research
supported in part by NSERC
[5] Department of Mathematics, Simon Fraser University, 8888 University Drive,
Burnaby, British Columbia, Canada, V5A 1S6
[6] Instituto de Matemáticas, Universidad Nacional Autónoma de México. Research
partially supported by CONACYT grant no. 37540-A, and PAPIIT UNAM

Abstract. We give a new local test, called a *Half-Space Proximal* or *HSP test*, for extracting a sparse directed or undirected subgraph of a given unit disk graph. The HSP neighbors of each vertex are unique, given a fixed underlying unit disk graph. The HSP test is a fully distributed, computationally simple algorithm that is applied independently to each vertex of a unit disk graph. The directed spanner obtained by this test is shown to be strongly connected, has out-degree at most six, its dilation is at most $2\pi + 1$, contains the minimum weight spanning tree as its subgraph and, unlike the Yao graph, it is rotation invariant. Since no coordinate assumption is needed to determine the HSP nodes, the test can be applied in any metric space.

1 Introduction

An *ad-hoc network* is a network consisting of transmitters, often called *hosts*, that is established as needed, typically without any assistance from a fixed infrastructure. It is assumed that each host can communicate with all the hosts within its transmission range with a single transmission, called a hop. Typically, not all hosts are within the transmission range of each other and the transmission ranges of all hosts are identical. We will additionally assume that each host knows its location, its coordinates in the plane, obtained by a low energy GPS device or by other means.

Such an ad-hoc network can be represented by a *unit disk graph* (UDG) in which the vertices are points in the Euclidean plane at coordinates corresponding

J.H. Anderson, G. Prencipe, and R. Wattenhofer (Eds.): OPODIS 2005, LNCS 3974, pp. 235–245, 2006.

to the geographical location of the hosts. Two nodes are connected by an edge if their Euclidean distance is less than a given unit, where the unit represents the common transmission range of the hosts. Due to the use of unit disk graphs for ad-hoc network representations, computations in the UDG are of interest in computer science.

A subgraph of the UDG is called a *geometric graph*. The length of an edge $[u, v]$ between adjacent vertices u and v of a geometric graph is defined to be the Euclidean distance between u and v. Given a path p in a geometric graph G the length of the path is the sum of the Euclidean lengths of the edges of p. Thus, for any pair of vertices u, v of a geometric graph G we define the distance $d_G(u, v)$ to be the length of the shortest path between u and v in G. Let G be a geometric graph and G' be a spanning subgraph of G. If two vertices of G are connected by an edge e in G and the distance of these vertices in G' is equal to k then we say that the dilation of e is equal to k. We call G' a $t-spanner$ of G if the dilation of any pair of adjacent vertices of G is at most t. A geometric graph is planar if no two of its edges represented by the straight line segments intersect each other.

When a UDG contains regions with many vertices, the graph may contain a large number of edges, or in an extreme case it may contain a complete subgraph (all the nodes are reachable). For many applications, like routing, energy efficient broadcast, power optimizations, etc., it is often preferable to extract from a given UDG a subgraph having some specific properties, e.g., being planar, or close in weight to a minimal spanning tree, or a $t-$spanner [7, 17, 4, 13]. In an ad-hoc network the topology of the whole network is typically not available in the nodes of the network due to the lack of a central infrastructure, the reduced amount of memory available and the possible mobility of the hosts. Thus, in these situations, the extraction of a suitable geometric subnetwork must be done in a distributed manner in the network using local information. Ideally, there should be a simple algorithm that is executed by each node of the network using only information on nodes reachable within a fixed number of hops, called a fixed-hop neighborhood. This algorithm would determine which edges of the UDG incident with the node are retained for the suitable geometric subgraph. Such algorithms are called *tests* and the geometric graphs which are obtained in this manner are usually called *local proximity graphs* [9].

For extracting a planar subgraph of a given UDG one can use the *Relative Neighborhood test* [17], the *Gabriel test* [7], or the *Morelia test* [3]. Given a UDG G, the spanner $RNG(G)$ is obtained by applying the RNG test to every edge of the UDG: edge $[u, v]$ is retained in $RNG(G)$ if there is no vertex z such that $\max\{d_G(u, z), d_G(v, z)\} < d_G(u, v)$. The Gabriel and the Morelia tests have a different condition to retain edges for the spanner and the graphs produced by applying the tests are denoted $G(G)$ and $M(G)$, respectively. Given a UDG G we have $RNG(G) \subseteq G(G) \subseteq M(G)$, but none of the graphs is a $t-$spanner for any fixed number t.

For extracting a spanner of a given UDG having a bounded dilation of edges, one can use a *Yao test* [18] that is defined as follows. Let k be an integer greater or equal to 6. From each vertex v of a unit disk graph G draw rays separated by $2\pi/k$ angles, starting with a ray in the horizontal line. A cone is defined as the space between two rays and including one of the rays so that the plane is partitioned into k cones. Yao test retains in each cone the shortest edge $[u, v]$ of G, if any exists. The collection of these oriented edges form the *directed Yao graph* $\overrightarrow{Y}_k$ (G). The *undirected Yao graph* $Y_k(G)$ is obtained by omitting the direction of edges. It has been shown [10] that the Yao graph is a $\frac{1}{1-2\sin \pi/k}$-spanner and, clearly, its out-degree is at most k. Unlike the spanners obtained by the RNG, Gabriel, or Morelia test, the graph $Y_k(G)$ depends on the exact position of the cones. Thus if G' is obtained by a rotation of a unit disk graph G then, in general, $Y_k(G)$ is not a rotation of $Y_k(G')$.

In this paper we propose a new local test for constructing a t-spanner of a UDG, called the Half-Space Proximal test, or HSP test for short. In Section 2, we give a definition of the HSP test and show that, similarly to the Yao test, the spanner obtained by the HSP test has a bounded dilation, out-degree at most 6, and is strongly connected, and it contains the minimum weight spanning tree as its subgraph. However, unlike the Yao test, the HSP test applied to a rotation of the UDG G yields a rotation of the HSP spanner of G. Thus, the graph properties of the HSP spanner are independent of the orientation of the unit disk graph in the plane. Section 3 contains experimental results involving HSP and Yao spanners of randomly generated unit disk graphs of different densities.

2   Half-Space Proximal Spanner and Its Properties

We assume that graph $G = (V, E)$ is a unit geometric graph where each node v has the coordinates v_x, v_y in the Euclidean plane and each vertex is assigned a unique integer label.

2.1   HSP Test

Input: a vertex u of a geometric graph and a list L_1 of edges incident with v.

Output: A list of directed edges L_2 which are retained for the $\overrightarrow{HSP}$ (G) graph.

1. Set the forbidden area $F(u)$ to be $\oslash$.
2. Repeat the following while L_1 is not empty.
   (a) Remove from L_1 the shortest edge, say $[u, v]$, (any tie is broken by smaller end-vertex label) and insert in L_2 directed edge (u, v) with u being the initial vertex.
   (b) Add to $F(u)$ the open half-plane determined by the line perpendicular to the edge $[u, v]$ in the middle of the edge and containing the vertex v. (Notice that the points of the line do not belong to the forbidden area)
   (c) Scan the list L_1 and remove from it any edge whose end-vertex is in $F(u)$.

An illustration of the HSP test applied to an UDG is given in Figure 1, zooming is applied to a selected node and the forbidden area is shaded.

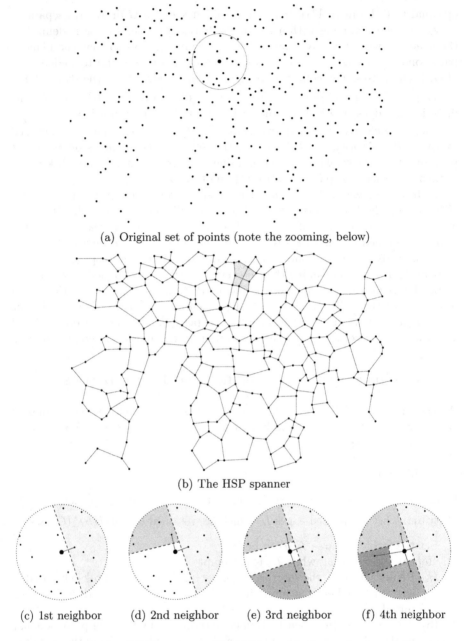

(a) Original set of points (note the zooming, below)

(b) The HSP spanner

(c) 1st neighbor   (d) 2nd neighbor   (e) 3rd neighbor   (f) 4th neighbor

Fig. 1. Applying the HSP test to an UDG. The original set of points (a) and the resulting indirected graph (b). A zooming around the vicinity of a selected node (c) ⋯ (e). Notice the crossing (shaded area) in (b).

We stated the test using the forbidden half space due to its easy visualization. Computationally, the elimination of edge $[u, z]$ by an edge $[u.v]$ is done when the Euclidean distance from z to v is less than the Euclidean distance from z to u. Furthermore notice that the proximity test can be done without any explicit use of the coordinates, the test can be accomplished in any metric space. The HSP test is a local test since all we need to know in each vertex is the set of edges incident with it.

Definition 1. *Let G be a UDG with vertex set V. The oriented graph $\overrightarrow{HSP}$ (G) is defined to be the graph with vertex set V whose edges are obtained by applying the HSP test to each vertex in V. The undirected graph $HSP(G)$ is obtained from $\overrightarrow{HSP}(G)$ by omitting the directions of edges.*

Theorem 1. *If G is a connected UDG then the digraph $\overrightarrow{HSP}(G)$ has out-degree at most 6 and is strongly connected.*

Proof. Let u be a vertex of G and $[u, v]$ be an edge that is selected for $\overrightarrow{HSP}$ (G) by the above algorithm. The forbidden area generated by $[u, v]$ is a half-plane determined by the line perpendicular to the edge $[u, v]$ at the middle of the edge $[u, v]$. Furthermore, the next edge selected from u for $\overrightarrow{HSP}(G)$ cannot be shorter than $[u, v]$. This implies that the end-vertex v' of the next edge selected from u for $\overrightarrow{HSP}(G)$ is in the area outside the circle around u of radius equal to the length of $[u.v]$ and inside the half-plane containing u. This means that angle vuv' is at least $\pi/3$. Since the angle between any two edges selected from u for $\overrightarrow{HSP}(G)$ is at least $\pi/3$, the out-degree of u is at most 6. Notice that the degree 6 would be possible only if the selected edges form a regular hexagon.

We show the strong connectivity of $\overrightarrow{HSP}(G)$ by showing that if $[u, v]$ is an edge of G than there is a directed path from u to v in $\overrightarrow{HSP}(G)$. Assume that there exist edges in G such that there is no directed path between the end-vertices of the edges in $\overrightarrow{HSP}(G)$. Let $[u, v]$ be the shortest edge of G such that there is no directed path from u to v in $\overrightarrow{HSP}(G)$. According to the construction, one possibility for $[u, v]$ not being in $\overrightarrow{HSP}(G)$ is that there exists an edge $[u, z]$ in $\overrightarrow{HSP}(G)$ such that $[u, z]$ is of length shorter or equal to the length of $[u, v]$ and v is in the forbidden area generated by the edge $[u, z]$. This implies that the vertices u, v, z form a triangle with the angle vuz being at most $\pi/3$. Since G is a UDG and the distance between z and v is strictly less than the distance between u and v, edge $[z, v]$ is in G, and furthermore, there exists a directed path from z to v in $\overrightarrow{HSP}(G)$. Since $[u, z]$ is an edge in $\overrightarrow{HSP}(G)$, there is a directed path from u to v in $\overrightarrow{HSP}(G)$. □

One can lower the highest out-degree of any HSP−spanner to 5. As mentioned in the proof, the list L_2 contains 6 edges after the execution of the HSP−test on vertex v when v is the center of a regular hexagon. In this case we may always remove from the list the directed edge closest to, say the vertical line drawn through vertex v in the clockwise direction. It is easy to check that this results in a strongly connected spanner of degree at most 5. Since there is a sense of orientation for this edge deletion, this out-degree at most 5 spanner depends on the rotation of the graph. In cases when the degree reduction is more important, one can use the degree reduction to 5 using the above test.

One can ask whether or not the degree of the spanning subgraph could be further improved. The answer is negative, by considering a star graph of degree 5 in which all edges are of length 1 and the angles between two consecutive edges is $2\pi/5$. This is a UDG and the only spanning subgraph is equal to G and thus the degree is necessarily 5 in some cases.

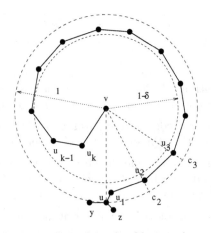

Fig. 2. Upper bound on the dilation of an edge

Theorem 2. *Let G be a geometric UDG and $\overrightarrow{HSP}(G)$ be the digraph constructed from G by the above algorithm. Then the stretch factor of $\overrightarrow{HSP}(G)$ is at most $2\pi + 1$.*

Proof. Let u be a vertex of G and $[u, v]$ be an edge of G of length $r \leq 1$ such that the edge is not selected by u for $\overrightarrow{HSP}(G)$. Then there exist an edge $[u, u_1]$ in G which is selected by u for $\overrightarrow{HS}(G)$ such that $[u, u_1]$ is shorter than $[u, v]$ and the angle u_1uv is less than $\pi/2$. Thus the edge $[u, u_1]$ makes the vertex v to be in the forbidden area (see Figure 1). If the edge $[u_1, v]$ is in $\overrightarrow{HSP}(G)$ than the stretch factor is less than 3, else we can argue inductively that there exists a sequence of vertices $u_0 = u, u_1, u_2, u_3, \ldots, u_{k+1} = v$ such that (see Figure 2):

1. for every i, $0 \leq i \leq k$, there is an edge $[u_i, u_{i+1}]$ in $\overrightarrow{HS}(G)$,
2. for every i, $0 \leq i \leq k - 1$, the length of $[u_i, u_{i+1}]$ is less than the Euclidean distance between u_i and v,

3. for every i, $0 \leq i \leq k - 1$, the angle $u_{i+1}u_i v$ is less than $\pi/2$,
4. for every i, $0 \leq i \leq k-1$, the vertices $u_0, u_1, u_2, \ldots, u_k$ are in either clockwise or anticlockwise order around v,
5. for every i, $0 \leq i \leq k - 1$, the Euclidean distance between u_{i+1} and v is smaller than the Euclidean distance between u_i and v,
6. the sum of the angles $\sum_{i=0}^{k} u_i v u_{i+1} < 2\pi$

The items 1, 2 and 3 are due to the fact that the edge $[u_i, v]$ is not chosen for $\overrightarrow{HSP}(G)$ by u_i. If the vertices $u_0, u_1, u_2, \ldots, u_k$ are not all in clockwise or anticlockwise order then let i be the index of a vertex such that both, u_1 and u_{i+1} are both say anticlockwise from the edge $[u_1, v]$. If the distance between u_{i-1}, u_{i+1} is not more than the distance between u_i, u_{i+1} then the edge $[u_{i-1}, u_{i+1}]$ exists in G since G is a UDG and we can argue that there is a path from u to v in $\overrightarrow{HSP}(G)$ that is even shorter than the sequence $u_0 = u, u_1, u_2, u_3, \ldots, u_{k+1} = v$. If the distance between u_{i-1}, u_{i+1} is greater than the distance between u_i, u_{i+1} then by considering the angles between $[u_i, u_{i+1}]$ and $[u_i, v]$ we can argue that there is a configuration of vertices that follows a clockwise path from u to v in $\overrightarrow{HSP}(G)$ that is even shorter than the sequence $u_0 = u, u_1, u_2, u_3, \ldots, u_{k+1} = v$. The item 5 follows directly from item 3.

If $\sum_{i=0}^{k} u_i v u_{i+1} \geq 2\pi$ then there exist integers i and j, $0 \leq i < j - 1$ such that the vertex u_j is in the triangle u_i, v, u_{i+1}. Since G is a UDG, either there is a path from u to v in $\overrightarrow{HSP}(G)$ that omits some of the edges between u_{i+1} and u_j and hence is shorter than the sequence $u_0 = u, u_1, u_2, u_3, \ldots, u_{k+1} = v$, or the vertices of the path must be inside a circle of radius $[u_{[i} + 1], u_j]$, also leading to a shorter path.

Consider the circle with center v of diameter r and denote by c_i the point of intersection of the line segment from v through vertex u_i (see Figure 2). By the triangular inequality, the Euclidean length of the edge $[u_i, u_{i+1}]$ is bounded from above by $s_i + r_i - r_{i+1}$ where s_i denotes the length of the circle segment from c_i to c_{i+1} and r_i denotes the Euclidean distances between u_i and v. Thus the Euclidean length of the path specified by the sequence $u_0 = u, u_1, u_2, u_3, \ldots, u_{k+1} = v$ is at most $\sum_{i=0}^{k} s_i + r_i - r_{i+1} \leq 2\pi r + r$. Thus the stretch factor is at most $2\pi + 1$. □

The dilation given in the theorem is an upper bound on the maximal dilation of an edge in an HSP spanner. A lower bound on the maximal dilation can be obtained from graph G in Figure 3. Consider edge $[u, v]$ in this graph. Due to either edge $[u, u_1]$ or the distance from u, there is no edge from u to $v, u_2, u_3, \ldots, u_k$ in the HSP spanner of G. Thus the path length from u to v in the HSP spanner of the graph is at least $5\pi/3(1 - \delta) + (1 - \delta) = 5\pi/3 + 1 - \delta(5\pi/3 + 1)$. Since δ can be an arbitrarily small positive number, the dilation can be arbitrarily close to $5\pi/3 + 1$. Thus $5\pi/3 + 1$ gives a lower bound on the maximum dilation of an edge in an HSP spanner. We conjecture that the maximum dilation of an HSP spanner is close to this lower bound.

For a comparison, the upper bound of $\frac{1}{1 - 2\sin \pi/k}$ of Yao spanners is valid for $k \geq 7$ and this bound is larger than $2\pi + 1$ when $k = 7$. It is clear that the

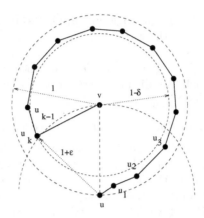

Fig. 3. HSP-spanner with edge dilation $5\pi/3 + 1$

configuration in Figure 3 is unlikely to occur in a UDG that represents an ad-hoc network and thus the dilation of the HSP spanner of a UDG graph corresponding to an ad-hoc network should be substantially smaller.

Theorem 3. *If G is a connected unit disk graph then a geometric minimum spanning tree of G is a subgraph of $HSP(G)$.*

Proof. Let G be a geometric unit disk graph and T be the geometric minimum spanning tree of G that contains the maximum number of edges of $HSP(G)$. Assume that there is an edge $[u,v] \in T$ which is not in $HSP(G)$. Since the edge $[u,v]$ is not in $HSP(G)$, there exist an edge $[u,w]$ in $HSP(G)$ and either $[u,w]$ and $[w,v]$ are shorter than $[u,v]$ or $d_G[u,v] = d_G[u,w]$ and $[w,v]$ is shorter than $[u,v]$. Clearly, for one of u and v there is a path p to w in T that does not contain edge $[u.v]$. If such a path exists from v then removing $[u,v]$ from T and adding $[u,w]$ we obtain a spanning tree of the same or lower cost containing one more edge of $HSP(G)$, a contradiction. If such a path p exists from u then removing $[u,v]$ from T and adding edge $[w,v]$ instead we obtain a spanning tree of lower cost, a contradiction.   □

It should be noted that, like in a Yao graph, the in-degree of $\overrightarrow{HSP}(G)$ is not bounded by any constant, and $\overrightarrow{HSP}(G)$ is not necessarily a planar graph (see Figure 1(f), shaded area). If a low in-degree is needed, one can apply to HSP spanners the technique from [1] that has been used to lower the in-degree of Yao graphs.

3   Experimental Results

In our experiments we used a UDG with 50 nodes randomly placed in a grid area of size varying between 500 and 2000 units. The transmission radius is 250 units in all of these graphs. Thus, as the grid size becomes larger the UDG density

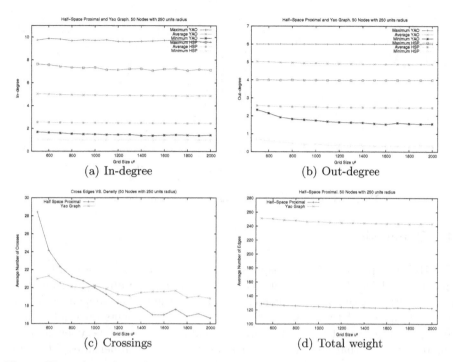

(a) In-degree   (b) Out-degree

(c) Crossings   (d) Total weight

Fig. 4. We performed some experiments to compare the Yao graph, in several parameters, against the HSP graph. The in-degree and out-degree of the HSP graph is smaller for the HSP for minimum, average and maximum, (a) and (b). The number of crossings for HSP spanner is smaller than Yao spanner for more sparse graphs, and for denser graphs is exactly the reverse. For dense graphs the HSP spanner have more crosses (c). The total weigth of the HSP spanner is about half the total weigth of the Yao spanner, consistently through the density (d).

gets smaller. For each unit disk graph HSP spanner and YAO spanner (with 6 cones) were generated both directed and undirected versions.

We measured the dependence of the following parameters of the HSP and Yao spanners on the density of UDG:

1. Minimum, maximum and average in-degree,
2. Minimum, maximum ans average out-degree,
3. The number of edges that cross each other,
4. The total weight of spanners,
5. Average Euclidean distance in the spanner,
6. The average number of hops.

See the results of experiments in Figures 3,5(a) and 5(b). The in-degree and out-degree of HSP spanners is lower that those of Yao spanners and so is the total weight of the spanners. As far as the number of crossing edges is concerned, it is higher for HSP spanners when the density is higher, but is lower for smaller densities. Due to the significantly lower in and out-degrees of HSP spanners, the average distances in HSP spanners are higher.

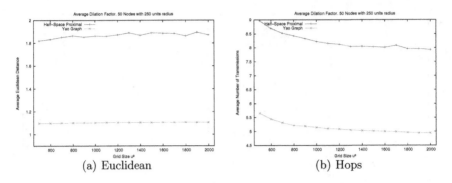

Fig. 5. The average dilation as a function of the density

4   Conclusion

The HSP test proposed in this paper is a distributed test that gives a $(2\pi + 1)-$
spanner of a UDG. The computation of the test is simple, it obviously generalizes
to any metric space, and the spanner obtained by the test is independent of the
exact placement of the graph in the plane. The experiments on random unit
disk graphs show that the average in-degree of the spanner is very low and the
number of edges that cross each other is very low for small densities. The total
weight is small and a high in-degree in unlikely to occur.

Thus, HSP spanner could be very convenient in network applications where
the use of spanners having these properties is needed. At present, we are investigating a generalization of the HSP test to ad-hoc networks with irregular
transmission ranges [2].

References

1. S. Arya, G. Das, D. M. Mount, J. S. Salowe, M. Smid, Euclidean spanners: short,
   thin, and lanky, Proceedings of the twenty-seventh annual ACM symposium on
   Theory of computing, p.489-498, 1995.
2. L. Barriere, P. Fraignaud, L. Narayanan, and J. Opatrny, Robust position-based
   routing in wireless ad hoc networks with unstable transmission ranges, In the Proceedings of the 5th International Workshop on Discrete Algorithms and Methods
   for Mobile Computing and Communications (DIALM), pp. 19–27, 2001.
3. P. Boone, E. Chavez, L. Gleitzky, E. Kranakis, J.Opatrny, G. Salazar, J. Urrutia,
   Morelia Test: Improving the Efficiency of the Gabriel Test and Face Routing in
   Ad-hoc Networks, Proceedings of SIROCCO 2004, LNCS 3104, pp. 23-34, 2004.
4. P. Bose, P. Morin, I. Stojmenovic, and J. Urrutia. Routing with guaranteed delivery
   in ad hoc wireless networks. In the Proceedings of the 3rd International Workshop
   on Discrete Algorithms and Methods for Mobile Computing and Communications
   (DIALM), pp. 48–55, 1999.
5. J. Broch, D. Maltz, D. Johnson, Y.-C. Hu, and J. Jetcheva. A performance comparison of multi-hop wireless ad hoc network routing protocols. In Mobile Computing
   and Networking, pp. 85–97, 1998.

6. S. Datta, I. Stojmenovic, and J. Wu. Internal node and shortcut based routing with guaranteed delivery in wireless networks. In Proc. IEEE Int. Conf. on Distributed Computing and Systems Workshops; Cluster Computing, pp. 461–466, 2001.
7. K. Gabriel and R. Sokal. A new statistical approach to geographic variation analysis. Systematic Zoology, 18:259–278, 1969.
8. J. Gao, L. Guibas, J. Hershberger, L. Zhang, A. Zhu, Geometric Spanner for Routing in Mobile Networks, Proceedings of the 2nd ACM International Symposium on Mobile Ad hoc Networking and Computing, pp. 45–55, 2001.
9. J. W. Jaromczyk and G. T. Toussaint, Relative neighborhood graphs and their relatives, Proc. IEEE, vol. 80, No. 9, pp. 1502-1517, 1992.
10. J.M. Keil and C.A. Gutwin, Classes of Graphs which approximate the complete euclidean graph, Discrete Comp. Geom., vol 7, pp 13-28, 1992.
11. E. Kranakis, H. Singh, and J. Urrutia, Compass Routing on Geometric Networks, In Proceedings of 11th Canadian Conference on Computational Geometry, pp. 51–54, Vancouver, August, 1999.
12. F. Kuhn, R. Wattenhofer, and A. Zollinger, Asymptotically Optimal Geometric Mobile Ad-Hoc Routing. In Proc. of the 6th International Workshop on Discrete Algorithms and Methods for Mobile Computing and Communications (DIALM), pp. 24–33, 2002.
13. X.-Y. Li, P.-J. Wan, Y. Wang, and O. Frieder, Sparse Power Efficient Topology for Wireless Networks, HICSS '02: Proceedings of the 35th Annual Hawaii International Conference on System Sciences (HICSS'02)-Volume 9, 296.2, 2002.
14. X. Li and Y. Wang, Efficient construction of low weight bounded degree planar spanner, in COCOON 2003, 2003.
15. Localized Delaunay Triangulation with Application in Ad Hoc Wireless Networks X.-Y. Li, G. Calinescu, and P.-J. Wan, Distributed construction of planar spanner and routing for ad hoc wireless networks In IEEE INFOCOM, 2002.
16. C. E. Perkins, editor, Ad Hoc Networking, Addison Wesley, 2001.
17. G. Toussaint, The relative neighbourhood graph of a finite planar set, Pattern Recognition, 12(4):261–268, 1980.
18. A.C.-C. Yao, On constructing minimum spanning trees in k- dimensional spaces and related problems, SIAM Journal on Computing 11(4) (1982) 721–736.

A State-Based Model of Sensor Protocols

Mohamed G. Gouda and Young-ri Choi*

Department of Computer Sciences, The University of Texas at Austin,
1 University Station C0500, Austin, Texas 78712-0233, U.S.A.
{gouda, yrchoi}@cs.utexas.edu

Abstract. We introduce a state-based model that can be used in specifying sensor network protocols. This model accommodates several features that are common in sensor networks. Examples of these features are 1-step local broadcast, probabilistic delivery of messages, asymmetric communication, and message collision. We propose a three-step method for verifying sensor protocols that are specified in this model. In the first step, the specified protocol is shown to be "nondeterministically correct" under the assumption that message delivery is assured and message collision is guaranteed not to occur. In the second step, the protocol is proven "probabilistically correct" under the assumption that message delivery is probabilistic but message collision is guaranteed not to occur. In the third step, the correctness of the protocol is proven by a simulation where message delivery is probabilistic and message collision may occur (when two or more neighboring sensors happen to send messages at the same time). To demonstrate the utility of our model, we discuss an example protocol that can be used by a sensor to identify its strong neighbors in the network, and apply the verification method to the protocol.

Keywords: Sensor network, State-based model, Formal model, Protocol specification, Protocol verification.

1 Introduction

A sensor is a battery-operated small computer with an antenna and a sensing board that can sense magnetism, sound, heat, etc. Sensors in a network can use their antennas to communicate in a wireless fashion by broadcasting messages over radio frequency to neighboring sensors in the network. Due to the limited range of radio transmission, sensor networks are usually multi-hop. Sensor networks can be used for military, environmental or commercial applications such as intrusion detection [1], disaster monitoring [2] and habitat monitoring [3].

Sensor networks and their protocols have several characteristics that make them hard to specify formally and even harder to verify. Examples of these characteristics are

i. *Unavoidable local broadcast:* When a sensor sends a message, even one that is intended for a particular neighboring sensor, a copy of the message is received by every neighboring sensor.

---

* Young-ri Choi is the corresponding author of this paper.

J.H. Anderson, G. Prencipe, and R. Wattenhofer (Eds.): OPODIS 2005, LNCS 3974, pp. 246–260, 2006.

ii. *Probabilistic message transmission:* When a sensor sends a message, the message reaches the different neighboring sensors (and can be received by each of them) with different probabilities.

iii. *Asymmetric communication:* Let u and v be two neighboring sensors in a network. The probability that a message sent by u is received by v can be different from the probability that a message sent by v is received by u.

iv. *Message collision:* If two neighboring sensors send messages at the same time, then neither sensor receives the message from the other sensor. Moreover, if two (not necessarily neighboring) sensors send messages at the same time, then any sensor that is a neighbor of both sensors will not receive any of the two messages. In this case, the two messages are said to have collided.

v. *Timeout actions and randomization steps:* Given the above characteristics of a sensor network, it seems logical that sensor protocols need to heavily depend on timeout actions and randomization steps to perform their functions.

The above characteristics of sensor protocols are far from common in the literature of distributed systems. Thus, one is inclined to believe that the "standard model" of distributed systems is not suitable for sensor protocols. The search for a suitable model for sensor protocols is an obligatory first step towards formal specification, verification, and design of these protocols.

There have been earlier efforts to model the software of sensor networks. Examples of these efforts are [4], [5], [6], and [7]. We review these and other efforts in the related work section of this paper. Nevertheless, it is important to state here that all these efforts are not directed towards modeling sensor protocols; rather they are directed toward modeling sensor network applications. Clearly, sensor protocols are quite different from sensor applications in terms of their functions and in terms of how they accomplish these functions. For instance, sensor protocols need to deal with the intricate characteristics of sensor networks, as they attempt to hide these characteristics from the sensor applications. Thus, whereas a sensor protocol has to deal with unavoidable local broadcast, probabilistic message transmission, asymmetric communication, and message collision, a sensor application can view the sensor network as a reliable medium for communicating sensing data. Also whereas a sensor protocol depends heavily on timeout actions and randomization steps, a sensor application rarely needs to resort to these devices.

2   Topology of Sensor Networks

The *topology* of a sensor network is a directed graph where each node represents a distinct sensor in the network and where each directed edge is labeled with some probability. A directed edge (u,v), from a sensor u to a sensor v, that is labeled with probability p indicates that if sensor u sends a message, then this message arrives at sensor v with probability p (provided that neither sensor v nor any "neighboring sensor" of v sends another message at the same time). There are two probabilities that label the edges in the topology of a sensor network. These two probabilities are 0.95 and 0.5 in this work. (Below we discuss some experiments that we have carried out on sensors and led us to this choice of probabilities in the topology of a sensor network [8].)

In the topology of a sensor network, an edge that is labeled with the large probability 0.95 is called a *strong edge*, and an edge that is labeled with the small probability 0.5 is called a *weak edge*.

Let u and v be two distinct sensors in a network. Sensors u and v are called *strong neighbors* iff there are two strong edges between them in the network topology. The two sensors are called *middle neighbors* iff there are one strong edge and one weak edge between them in the network topology. Sensors u and v are called *weak neighbors* iff there is exactly one edge between them, or there are two weak edges between them in the network topology. They are called *non-neighbors* iff there are no edges between them in the network topology. If there is an edge from u to v in the network topology, then u is called an *in-neighbor* of v and v is called an *out-neighbor* of u.

As an example, Fig. 1 shows the topology of a sensor network that has four sensors. In this network, sensors u and v are weak neighbors, sensors u and v' are strong neighbors, sensors u and v'' are middle neighbors, and sensors v and v'' are non-neighbors. Sensor u has three out-neighbors, namely sensors v, v', and v''. Also sensor u has two in-neighbors, namely sensors v', and v''.

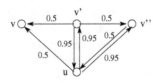

Fig. 1. Topology of a sensor network

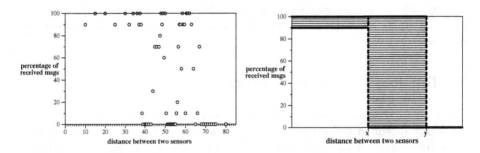

Fig. 2. Percentage of received messages   **Fig. 3.** Idealized percentage of received messages

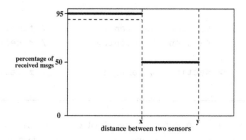

Fig. 4. The probability label of an edge

In [8], we describe some experiments that we have carried out using Mica sensors [9]. In these experiments, a sensor u sends a sequence of messages at the rate of one message per 5 seconds, and another sensor v attempts to receive all the sent messages. The results of these experiments are summarized in Fig. 2 where each point represents the result of one experiment. (Similar results are reported in [10] and [11].)

We observe that from Fig. 2 if the distance between two sensors u and v is in the range 0 .. 38 inches, v receives between 90% and 100% of the messages sent by u. One the other hand, if the distance between sensors u and v is in the range 38 .. 67 inches, v receives anywhere between 0% and 100% of the messages sent by u. Finally, the distance between sensors u and v is longer than 67 inches, v receives 0% of the messages sent by u. From these observations, the diagram in Fig. 2 can be "idealized" as shown in Fig. 3.

Let u and v be distinct sensors in the topology of a sensor network, and assume there is a directed edge from u to v in the network topology. According to the idealized diagram in Fig. 3, if the distance between u and v is in the range 0 .. x, then v receives between 90% and 100% of the messages sent by u. Thus, the directed edge from u to v can be labeled with a probability 0.95, and the edge is strong. If the distance between u and v is in the range x .. y, then v receives between 0% and 100% of the messages sent by u. Thus, the directed edge from u to v can be labeled with a probability 0.5, and the edge is weak. Fig. 4 shows how the probability label of an edge from one sensor to another in the network topology is chosen based on the distance between the two sensors.

3   Sensor Network Execution

A sensor is specified as a program that has global constants, local variables, and one or more actions. In general, a sensor is specified as follows:

```
sensor <sensor name>

const <const name> : <const type>, ... , <const name> : <const type>
var   <var name> : <var type>, ... , <var name> : <var type>
```

```
begin
   timeout-expires   -> <action statements>        // timeout action
[] rcv <msg.0>        -> <action statements>        // receiving action
   ...                   ...
[] rcv <msg.k-1>      -> <action statements>        // receiving action
end
```

Note that the actions of a sensor consist of exactly one timeout action and zero or more receiving actions. Before we can discuss the execution of sensor actions, we need to explain our model of real-time.

We assume that the real-time passes through discrete time instants: instant 1, instant 2, instant 3, and so on. The time periods between consecutive instants are equal. Executions of the different actions of a sensor occur only at the time instants, and not during the time periods between instants. We refer to the time period between two consecutive instants t and $t+1$ as the *time unit* $(t, t+1)$. (The value of a time unit is not critical to the current presentation, but we estimate that the value of the time unit is around 100 milliseconds.)

At a time instant t, if the timeout of a sensor u expires, then u executes its timeout action (at t). Executing the timeout action of sensor u at t causes u to update its local variables, and to send at most one message at t. It also causes u to execute the statement "timeout-after <expression>" which causes the timeout of u to expire (again) after k time units, where k is the value of <expression> at the time unit $(t, t+1)$. The timeout action of sensor u is of the following form:

```
timeout-expires -> <update local variables of u>;
                   <send at most one message>;
                   <execute timeout-after <expression>>
```

To keep track of its timeout, each sensor u has an implicit variable named "timer.u". In each time unit between two consecutive instants, timer.u has a fixed positive integer value. The value of "timer.u" is determined by the following two rules:

i. If the value of timer.u is k, where $k > 1$, in a time unit $(t-1, t)$, then the value of timer.u is $k-1$ in the time unit $(t, t+1)$.

ii. If the value of timer.u is 1 in a time unit $(t-1, t)$, then sensor u executes its timeout action at instant t. Moreover, since sensor u executes the statement "timeout-after <expression>" as part of executing its timeout action, the value of timer.u in the time unit $(t, t+1)$ is the value of <expression> in the same time unit.

If a sensor u executes its timeout action and sends a message at an instant t, then an out-neighbor v of u receives a copy of the message at t, provided that the following three conditions hold.

i. A random integer number is uniformly selected in the range 0 .. 99, and this selected number is less than $100 * p$, where p is the probability label of edge (u,v) in the network topology.

ii. Sensor v does not send any message at instant t.

iii. For each in-neighbor w of v, other than u, if w sends a message at t, then a random integer number is uniformly selected in the range 0 .. 99, and this selected number is at least $100 * p'$, where p' is the probability label of edge (w,v) in the network topology.

If a sensor u receives a message <msg.i> at an instant t, then u executes the following receiving action at t.

```
rcv <msg.i> -> <update local variables of u>;
                <may execute timeout-after <expression>>
```

Note that executing the receiving action of sensor u causes u to update its own local variables. It may also cause u to execute the statement "timeout-after <expression>" which causes the timeout of u to expire after k time units, where k is the value of <expression> in the time unit $(t, t + 1)$. Note that executing the receiving action of sensor u does not cause u to send any message.

Let us summarize how the execution of a sensor network proceeds during one time instant t. First, the value of timer.u for every sensor u in the network is decremented by one at t. Second, if the value of any timer.u becomes 0 at t, then sensor u executes its timeout action at t. Execution of the timeout action of a sensor u at t assigns a new value to timer.u and may cause u to send one message at t. Third, if a sensor u sends a message at t, then any out-neighbor v of u may receive the message at t. Even if an out-neighbor v of u has executed its timeout action but sent no message at t, v can still receive u's message at t. In other words, a sensor may execute its timeout action followed by a receiving action at the same time instant provided that the sensor does not send a message during its execution of the timeout action. It follows from the above discussion that at a time instant, a sensor u executes exactly one of the following:

i. u sends one message, but receives no message.
ii. u receives one message, but sends no message.
iii. u sends no message and receives no message.

In the remainder of the paper, we use this model to specify an example protocol and to prove the protocol correct utilizing our verification method described in the next section.

4 Three-Step Verification Method

The model of sensor network protocols presented in the previous sections is rather complicated. Thus, the correctness of a sensor protocol specification, that is based on this model, is better verified in steps, in fact three steps. In the first step, the correctness of the protocol specification is verified under two assumptions: idealized message transmission and no message collision. In the second step, the effect of relaxing the first assumption on the established correctness in the first step is analyzed. In the third step, the effect of relaxing the second assumption on the established correctness in the second step is analyzed.

We refer to the first step as *nondeterministic analysis*, to the second step as *probabilistic analysis*, and to the third step as *simulation*.

In the next two sections, we present an example of a sensor protocol specification, and then verify the correctness of this specification using our verification method.

The two assumptions, of idealized message transmission and no message collision, upon which our verification method is based are stated as follows.

i. *Idealized message transmission:* In the topology of a sensor network, the probability label of each strong edge is 1 (instead of 0.95), and the probability label of each weak edge is 0 (instead of 0.5).

ii. *No message collision:* For every two distinct sensors u and v in a sensor network, if u is a (in- or out-) neighbor of v, or if the network has a third sensor w that is an out-neighbor for both u and v, then timer.u and timer.v have distinct values at every instant during the execution of the sensor network.

Some explanations concerning these two assumptions are in order. The first assumption has the effect of removing all the weak edges from the topology of a sensor network. It also has the effect of strengthening all the strong edges in a network topology.

To explain the second assumption, recall that a sensor u can send a message only during an execution of its timeout action, and that the timeout action of sensor u can be executed at an instant t iff the value of timer.u is 1 in the time unit $(t-1, t)$. Thus, the assumption of no message collision ensures that any two sensors, whose messages would collide if they were sent at the same instant, are guaranteed never to send messages at the same instant during any execution of the sensor network.

In order to make the second assumption, of no message collision, more acceptable, it is recommended that each statement "timeout-after x" in a sensor u be written as "timeout-after random(x, y)" where $x > 0$ and $x \leq y$. Thus, any new value assigned to timer.u is chosen uniformly from the range $x \,..\, y$. Because the new values of the timer variables are chosen uniformly from a reasonably large range, it is unlikely that any two timer variables will ever have the same value.

Next, we describe in some detail the three steps of our verification method.

i. Nondeterministic analysis:
   This analysis is used to verify that a protocol is guaranteed to reach, from a given initial state, a desirable target state under the two assumptions of idealized message transmission and no message collision. For this analysis, we generate a state transition diagram of the protocol. In the diagram, each protocol state has one or more outgoing edges, since the protocol is specified using randomization steps of the form "timeout-after random(x,y)". From this diagram, we can verify that the protocol nondeterministically satisfies the desired reachability property.

ii. Probabilistic analysis:
   This analysis is used to verify that a protocol will reach, from a given initial state, a desirable target state with a high probability, under the assumption

of no message collision. For this analysis, we generate a probabilistic state transition diagram of the protocol, where each edge in the diagram is labeled with a probability. Note that the probabilities that label the edges in the probabilistic state transition diagram are computed from the probability labels in the network topology of the protocol. From this diagram, we can verify that the protocol probabilistically satisfies the desired reachability property.

iii. Simulation:
The nondeterministic and probabilistic analyses (in the first two steps) of a protocol can be carried out without specifying the values of x and y in the randomization steps "timeout-after random(x,y)" in the protocol specification. In choosing the values of x and y in these steps, one needs to observe two restrictions. First, the difference $y - x$ should be large enough to ensure that the probability of message collision is reasonably small (and so the nondeterministic and probabilistic analyses of the protocol are reasonably accurate). Second, the difference $y - x$ should be small enough to ensure that the protocol reaches its desirable target state in a reasonably short time. To determine the appropriate values of x and y in the randomization steps, one can simulate the protocol for many value combinations of x and y and select the most appropriate values of x and y.

5   A Protocol Specification Example

In this section, we use the above model to specify a sensor protocol that can be used by any sensor in order to identify the strong neighbors of that sensor in its network. We refer to this protocol as the neighbor computation protocol. (Recall that two sensors in a network are strong neighbors iff there are two strong edges between them in the network topology.)

To identify the strong neighbors of a sensor u, sensor u sends three request messages. Whenever a sensor v receives a request message sent by sensor u, sensor v sends a reply message. If sensor u receives two or more reply messages sent by the same sensor v, then sensor u concludes that sensor v is one of its strong neighbors.

Assume that the time period between two successive request messages sent by the same sensor is fixed. Under this assumption, if two neighboring sensors u and u' start to send their request messages at the same time, then the request messages sent by u will collide with the request messages sent by u' and both u and u' may end up concluding wrongly that they have no strong neighbors. Therefore, the time period between two successive request messages should be uniformly selected from a "large enough" range 1 .. x. (In the next section, we discuss how to choose a value for x.)

If every sensor v, that receives a request message from a sensor u, sends a reply message immediately after it receives the request message, then all the reply messages will collide with one another and u may end up receiving no reply messages. Thus, when a sensor v receives a request message from a sensor u, v

should wait a random period of time before it sends a reply message. The length of this time period should be uniformly selected from the range 1 .. x.

Consider the scenario where a sensor v receives a request message from a sensor u and decides to wait for some random period before it sends a reply message to u. It is possible that before v sends its reply to u, v receives another request message from another sensor u'. In this case, v should send one reply message to both u and u'. This requires that sensor v maintains a reply set, called $rset$, that contains the identifier of every sensor u from which v has received a request message and to which v has not yet sent a corresponding reply message. At the end of the above scenario, $rset$ in sensor v has the value $\{u, u'\}$.

Note that sensors u and u' in the above scenario can be the same sensor u. Thus, $rset$ in each sensor is a multiset rather than a set. For example, at the end of the above scenario, $rset$ in sensor v has the value $\{u, u\}$.

Consider the scenario where a sensor u sends a request message and decides to wait for a random period before it sends its second request message. It is possible that before u sends its second request message, u receives a request message from another sensor u'. In this case, u should send one composite message that consists of the second request message and a reply message to sensor u'. We refer to this composite message as a request-reply message. In fact, every message in our protocol, whether a request message, a reply message, or a request-reply message, can be viewed as a request-reply message.

Each message in the neighbor computation protocol has three fields:

$$(v,b,s)$$

The first field v is the identifier of sensor v that sent this message. The second field b has two possible values: 0 and 1. If $b = 0$, then the message is a pure reply message. If $b = 1$, then the message is either a request message or a request-reply message. The third field s is the current value of $rset$ in sensor v. Note that if the message is a pure request message, then $s =$ empty set.

Each sensor u has one constant x and eight variables as follows.

```
sensor u        // sensor u where 0=< u < n

const x    : integer
var   nghs : set {u' | 0<= u' < n},     // strong ngh set
      rcvd : array [0 .. n-1] of 0..3,  // rcvd replies
      rset : set {u' | 0<= u' < n},     // reply set
      rm   : 0..3,                       // remaining request msgs
      done : boolean,                    // computation done or not
      v    : 0..n-1,                     // received sensor id
      b    : 0..1,                       // received request bit
      s    : set {u' | 0<= u' < n}       // received reply set
```

Variable $nghs$ is the set of strong neighbors that sensor u needs to compute periodically. An element $rcvd[v]$ in variable $rcvd$ contains the number of replies that sensor u has received from sensor v after u has sent its first request message (in the current round of request messages). Variable *rm* stores the number of request messages that sensor *u* still needs to send (in the current round of request messages). Variable *rset* is the multiset of all the replies that sensor *u* needs to include in its next request-reply message. Variable *done* is a boolean variable whose value is true when and only when the current computation of the strong neighbors of sensor *u* is completed.

Initially, the value of *nghs* is the empty set, the value of every element in variable *rcvd* is 0, the value of variable *rm* is 0, the value of variable *rset* is the empty set, the value of variable *done* is true, and the value of implicit variable timer.u is any value in the range 1 .. *x*.

Each sensor *u* has two actions that are specified as follows.

```
sensor u       // sensor u where 0=< u < n

begin
   timeout-expires ->
       if rm=0 -> if rset != {} -> send (u,0,rset); rset := {}
                  [] rset = {}  -> skip
                  fi;
                  if done   -> skip              // no new round
                  [] done   -> nghs := {};       // start new round
                               rcvd := 0;
                               rm := 3;
                               done := false
                  [] !done -> COMPNGH(in rcvd, out nghs);
                               rcvd := 0;
                               done := true
                  fi; timeout-after random(1,x)
       [] rm>0 -> send (u,1,rset); rset := {};
                  rm := rm-1;
                  if rm>0 -> timeout-after random(1,x)
                  [] rm=0 -> timeout-after random(x+1,x+1)
                  fi
       fi
[] rcv (v,b,s) -> if !done -> rcvd[v] := rcvd[v] + NUM(u,s)
                  [] done  -> skip
                  fi;
                  if b=1 -> rset := rset+{v}
                  [] b=0 -> skip
                  fi
end
```

Sensor *u* executes its first action when the value of its timer.u becomes zero. The execution of this action starts by checking the value of *rm*. On one hand, if the value of *rm* is 0, then *u* recognizes that it does not need to send a request message, but it needs to send a reply message in case *rset* is non-empty. Thus, the sent message is of the form (u,0,rset). Also if the value of *done* is true, then sensor u chooses arbitrarily whether it starts to compute its strong neighbors or not. If the value of *done* is false, sensor u invokes a procedure named COMPNGH that computes the strong neighbors of sensor u from array *rcvd* and adds them to the set *nghs*. (In COMPNGH, a sensor v is computed to be a strong neighbor of u if $rcvd[v] \geq 2$.) On the other hand, if the value of *rm* is larger than 0, then u recognizes that it needs to send a request-reply message of the form (u,1,rset).

Sensor u executes the second action when u receives a (v,b,s) message sent by a neighboring sensor v. The execution of this action starts by checking the value of *done*. If the value of *done* is false, then the value of the element $rcvd[v]$ is incremented by $NUM(u, s)$, the number of times u occurs in the multiset s. Then sensor u checks the value of b in the received message. If the value of b is 1, then v is added to the multiset *rset*.

6   A Protocol Verification Example

In this section, we use the verification method outlined in Section 4 to verify the correctness of the neighbor computation protocol in Section 5. Recall that the verification method consists of three steps: nondeterministic analysis, probabilistic analysis, and simulation. We apply each of these steps to the neighbor computation protocol in order.

Nondeterministic analysis is used to show that the neighbor computation protocol satisfies some desirable progress property under the two assumptions of idealized message transmission and no message collision, discussed above. The analysis is carried out from the point of view of a sensor u that needs to compute its strong neighbors.

From the assumption of idealized message transmission, each non-neighbor, weak neighbor or middle neighbor of u cannot receive any message sent by u, or cannot send any message to be received by u. Thus, non-neighbors, weak neighbors and middle neighbors of u have no effect on the computation carried out by u to identify its strong neighbors.

It remains to analyze the interaction between sensor u and each strong neighbor v of u. Fig. 5 shows the state transition diagram that describes the interaction between sensor u and its strong neighbor v. Each node in this diagram represents a state of the two sensors u and v. Each dashed edge represents the passing of

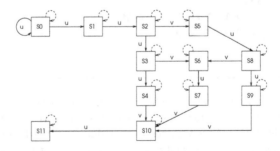

Fig. 5. State Transition Diagram

S0:		rcvd(v).u=0 ∧ rm.u=0 ∧ done.u=T ∧ NUM(u, rset.v)=0
S1:	nghs.u=∅ ∧	rcvd(v).u=0 ∧ rm.u=3 ∧ done.u=F ∧ NUM(u, rset.v)=0
S2:	nghs.u=∅ ∧	rcvd(v).u=0 ∧ rm.u=2 ∧ done.u=F ∧ NUM(u, rset.v)=1
S3:	nghs.u=∅ ∧	rcvd(v).u=0 ∧ rm.u=1 ∧ done.u=F ∧ NUM(u, rset.v)=2
S4:	nghs.u=∅ ∧	rcvd(v).u=0 ∧ rm.u=0 ∧ done.u=F ∧ NUM(u, rset.v)=3
S5:	nghs.u=∅ ∧	rcvd(v).u=1 ∧ rm.u=2 ∧ done.u=F ∧ NUM(u, rset.v)=0
S6:	nghs.u=∅ ∧	rcvd(v).u=2 ∧ rm.u=1 ∧ done.u=F ∧ NUM(u, rset.v)=0
S7:	nghs.u=∅ ∧	rcvd(v).u=2 ∧ rm.u=0 ∧ done.u=F ∧ NUM(u, rset.v)=1
S8:	nghs.u=∅ ∧	rcvd(v).u=1 ∧ rm.u=1 ∧ done.u=F ∧ NUM(u, rset.v)=1
S9:	nghs.u=∅ ∧	rcvd(v).u=1 ∧ rm.u=0 ∧ done.u=F ∧ NUM(u, rset.v)=2
S10:	nghs.u=∅ ∧	rcvd(v).u=3 ∧ rm.u=0 ∧ done.u=F ∧ NUM(u, rset.v)=0
S11:	nghs.u∋v ∧	rcvd(v).u=0 ∧ rm.u=0 ∧ done.u=T ∧ NUM(u, rset.v)=0

Fig. 6. Specifying the states in the state transition diagram in Fig. 5

real-time by one time unit. Each solid edge labeled u represents the execution of the timeout action in sensor u and the execution of the corresponding receiving action, if any, in sensor v. Each solid edge labeled v represents the execution of the timeout action in sensor v and the execution of the corresponding receiving action, if any, in sensor u.

Each of the states S0 through S11 in the state transition diagram is specified by a predicate in Fig. 6. Note that $rcvd[v].u$ is the value of element $rvcd[v]$ in array $rcvd$ in sensor u, $rm.u$ is the value of variable rm in sensor u, $done.u$ is the value of variable $done$ in sensor u, and $NUM(u, rset.v)$ returns the number of times u occurs in the multiset $rset$ in sensor v.

From the state transition diagram, we conclude that the interaction between sensors u and v satisfies the following progress property.

State S1 eventually leads to state S11.

Therefore, the protocol is correct under the two assumptions of idealized message transmission and no message collision.

Probabilistic analysis is used to analyze the effect of relaxing the first assumption of idealized message transmission on the correctness and performance of the protocol. Under the assumption of idealized message transmission, the middle neighbors and weak neighbors of a sensor u play no role in u's computation of its strong neighbors. When this assumption is relaxed, this is no longer true. Let u and v are distinct sensors in a network. If there are no edges or if there is exactly one edge between u and v in the network topology, then v has no effect on u's computation of its strong neighbors. Otherwise, let there be two edges between u and v in the network topology. Moreover, let p be the probability label of edge (u,v) and q be the probability label of edge (v,u). In this case, the probability that u identifies v as one of its strong neighbors depends on the probability labels of edges (u,v) and (v,u), p and q.

Simulation is used to analyze the effect of relaxing the two assumptions of idealized message transmission and no message collision on the correctness and performance of the protocol. In order to run the simulation of the protocol, we need to choose the value of x. There are two contradictory concerns that can affect our choice of x. If x is large, the probability of message collision becomes small, and consequently the probability of correctly identifying a strong neighbor, as measured from the simulation, becomes close to the same probability, as estimated from the probabilistic analysis. On the other hand, if x is large, the average execution time of the protocol, which is around $2 * x + 1$ time units, becomes large. Thus, the simulation is used to evaluate the performance of the protocol over various values of x and choose the most appropriate value for x.

As we relax the two assumptions one by one, the probability for a sensor u to identify a strong neighbor v is decreased. Moreover, middle neighbors and weak neighbors of u affect u's computation of its strong neighbors. The details of probabilistic analysis and simulation can be found in [12].

7   Related Work

Several models for sensor applications have been proposed [5], [6], [4], [7]. In general, the purpose of these models is to hide application programmers from low-level details such as routing, group management, resource management, etc. EnvioTrack [5] provides a high-level programming abstraction for tracking applications in sensor networks. Newton and Welsh proposed a functional language to specify the global behavior of a sensor application [6]. Liu et al. presented a state-centric programming model for sensor networks [4]. Database approach was proposed in TAG [7]. Unlike these models, our proposed model is to describe sensor protocols (that are responsible for routing, group management, etc). Thus, our model deals with the intricate characteristics of wireless sensor networks described in Section 1.

Levis et al. developed a communication-centric virtual machine for sensor networks called Maté [13]. Using Maté's high-level interfaces, sensor applications can be composed in a very short code.

The Abstract Protocol notation was developed earlier to specify network protocols in traditional networks [14]. Gracanin et al. proposed a model that focuses on services provided by wireless sensor networks [15]. Volgyesi et al. proposed a model to describe interface specification of components for sensor networks [16]. This model allows us to check the compatibility of components and to verify the design and composition of components based on their interfaces. In [17], antireplay protocols for sensor networks were proposed. Also it was shown that the proposed protocols satisfy desirable properties (such as corruption detection, replay detection, and freshness detection) under some assumption. In this paper, we investigate what a model should be to describe sensor protocols and how sensor protocols specified in this model can be verified.

Several simulation frameworks have been developed for sensor networks [18], [19], [20]. TOSSIM [18] is a simulator for TinyOS wireless sensor networks. Prowler [19] is a MATLAB-based simulator that can simulate not only network protocol stacks but also radio transmission phenomena. Downey et al. [20] developed a flexible simulation framework, where a new model can be added or substituted easily. Note that the simulator used in this paper is to simulate the execution of a protocol based on our model.

8   Concluding Remarks

In this paper, we presented a state-based model of sensor network protocols. This model accommodates several characteristics of sensor networks, such as unavoidable local broadcast, probabilistic message transmission, asymmetric communication, message collision, and timeout actions and randomization steps. We also proposed a three step verification method that consists of nondeterministic analysis, probabilistic analysis, and simulation. Using this verification method, we can verify and analyze the correctness and performance of a sensor protocol specified in this state-based model.

Although the probability label of a strong edge is chosen to be 0.95 and the probability label of a weak edge is chosen to be 0.5 in this work, different values can be chosen for these probability labels for different setting of sensor networks.

The neighbor computation protocol in Section 5 is suitable for a resource limited sensor network, since each sensor needs to send a small number of messages to compute its strong neighbors. This protocol can be used to calibrate the model such that the estimated performance from the model is correlated to the observed performance from an actual prototype of the protocol.

There are several directions to extend our model for sensor protocols. First, our model assumes that sensors in a sensor network are stationary. The model can be extended to support a sensor network with mobile sensors. Second, energy models of sensors can be added to our model to estimate the lifetime of a sensor network or measure the amount of energy consumed by a sensor.

Acknowledgment

This work was supported by the Defense Advanced Research Projects Agency (DARPA) Contract F33615-01-C-1901.

References

1. Arora, A., Dutta, P., Bapat, S., Kulathumani, V., Zhang, H., Naik, V., Mittal, V., Cao, H., Demirbas, M., Gouda, M., Choi, Y., Herman, T., Kulkarni, S., Arumugam, U., Nesterenko, M., Vora, A., Miyashita, M.: A Line in the Sand: A Wireless Sensor Network for Target Detection, Classification, and Tracking. Computer Networks (Elsevier), Special Issue on Military Communications Systems and Technologies **46**(5) (2004) 605–634
2. Akyildiz, I.F., Su, W., Y.Sankarasubramaniam, Cayirci, E.: Wireless Sensor Networks: A Survey. Computer Networks, Elsevier Science **38**(4) (2002) 393–422
3. Mainwaring, A., Polastre, J., Culler, R., Anderson., J.: Wireless Sensor Networks for Habitat Monitoring. In: Proceedings of the ACM International Workshop on Wireless Sensor Networks and Applications (WSNA'02), Atlanta, GA (2002)
4. Liu, J., Chu, M., Liu, J., Reich, J., Zhao, F.: State-Centric Programming for Sensor-Actuator Network Systems. Pervasive Computing (2003) 50–62

5. Abdelzaher, T., Blum, B., Cao, Q., Chen, Y., Evans, D., George, J., George, S., Gu, L., He, T., Krishnamurthy, S., Luo, L., Son, S., Stankovic, J., Stoleru, R., Wood, A.: EnvioTrack: Towards an Environmental Computing Paradigm for Distributed Sensor Networks. In: Proceedings of the 24th International Conference on Distributed Computing Systems, Tokyo, Japan (2004)
6. Newton, R., Welsh, M.: Region Streams: Functional Macroprogramming for Sensor Networks. In: International Workshop on Data Management for Sensor Networks, DMSN (VLDB 2004). (2004)
7. Madden, S., Franklin, M.J., Hellerstein, J.M., Hong, W.: TAG: a Tiny AGgregation service for ad-hoc sensor networks. ACM SIGOPS Operating Systems Review 36(Winter) (2002) 131–146
8. Choi, Y., Gouda, M.G., Kim, M.C., Arora, A.: The Mote Connectivity Protocol. In: Proceedings of 12th International Conference on Computer Communications and Networks (ICCCN 2003), Dallas, TX (2003) 533–538
9. Wireless Embedded Systems. (http://webs.cs.berkeley.edu/)
10. Woo, A., Tony, T., Culler, D.: Taming the Underlying Challenges of Reliable Multihop Routing in Sensor Networks. In: Proceedings of ACM SenSys, Los Angeles, CA (2003)
11. Cerpa, A., Busek, N., Estrin, D.: SCALE: A tool for Simple Connectivity Assessment in Lossy Environments. CENS Technical Report 21 (2003)
12. Gouda, M., Choi, Y.: A State-based Model of Sensor Protocols. Technical Report TR-05-46, Department of Computer Sciences, The University of Texas at Austin (2005)
13. Levis, P., Culler, D.: Maté: A Tiny Virtual Machine for Sensor Networks. In: International Conference on Architectural Support for Programming Languages and Operating Systems. (2002)
14. Gouda, M.G.: Elements of Network Protocol Design. John Wiley and Sons, Inc, New York, New York (1998)
15. Gracanin, D., Eltoweissy, M., Olariu, S., Wadaa, A.: On Modeling Wireless Sensor Networks. In: Proceedings of the 18th International Parallel and Distributed Processing Symposium (IPDPS 2004). (2004)
16. Volgyesi, P., Maroti, M., Dora, S., Osses, E., Ledeczi, A., Paka, T.: Software Composition and Verification for Sensor Networks. Science of Computer Programming (Elsevier) 56(1-2) (2005) 191–210
17. Gouda, M., Choi, Y., Arora, A.: Antireplay Protocols for Sensor Networks. Handbook on Theoretical and Algorithmic Aspects of Sensor, Ad Hoc Wireless, and Peer-to-Peer Networks, (ed. Jie Wu), CRC (2005)
18. Levis, P., Lee, N., Welsh, M., Culler, D.: TOSSIM: Accurate and Scalable Simulation of Entire TinyOS Applications. In: Proceedings of the First ACM Conference on Embedded Networked Sensor Systems (SenSys 2003). (2003)
19. Simon, G., Volgyesi, P., Maroti, M., Ledeczi, A.: Simulation-based optimization of communication protocols for large-scale wireless sensor networks. In: Proceedings of the IEEE Aerospace Conference. (2003)
20. Downey, P., Cardell-Oliver, R.: Evaluating the Impact of Limited Resource on Performance of Flooding in Wireless Sensor Networks. In: Proceedings of the International Conference on Dependable Systems and Networks, Florence (2004)

Approximation Bounds for Black Hole Search Problems*

Ralf Klasing[1], Euripides Markou[2], Tomasz Radzik[3], and Fabiano Sarracco[4]

[1] LaBRI - Université Bordeaux 1, 351 cours de la Libération, 33405 Talence cedex, (France)
klasing@labri.fr
[2] Department of Informatics and Telecommunications,
National and Kapodistrian University of Athens
emarkou@softlab.ece.ntua.gr
[3] Department of Computer Science, King's College London, London, WC2R 2LS, UK
Tomasz.Radzik@kcl.ac.uk
[4] Dipartimento di Informatica e Sistemistica, Università di Roma "La Sapienza"
Fabiano.Sarracco@dis.uniroma1.it

Abstract. A black hole is a highly harmful stationary process residing in a node of a network and destroying all mobile agents visiting the node without leaving any trace. The Black Hole Search is the task of locating all black holes in a network, through the exploration of its nodes by a set of mobile agents. In this paper we consider the problem of designing the fastest Black Hole Search, given the map of the network, the starting node and, possibly, a subset of nodes of the network initially known to be safe. We study the version of this problem that assumes that there is at most one black hole in the network and there are two agents, which move in synchronized steps. We prove that this problem is not polynomial-time approximable within $\frac{389}{388}$ (unless **P=NP**). We give a 6-approximation algorithm, thus improving on the 9.3-approximation algorithm from [3]. We also prove **APX**-hardness for a restricted version of the problem, in which only the starting node is initially known to be safe.

Keywords: approximation algorithm, black hole search, graph exploration, mobile agent, inapproximability.

1 Introduction

The Background and the Problem. The problem of protecting mobile agents from malicious hosts, i.e., nodes of a network which store harmful processes in them, has been widely studied ([8, 9, 11, 12]). Even though various countermeasures have been proposed, the general belief (see [8, 13]) is that it is very hard (when not virtually impossible) to fully protect mobile agents from malicious hosts attacks.

We consider here malicious hosts of a particularly harmful nature, called *black holes* [3, 2, 4, 5, 6]. A black hole is a node in a network which contains a stationary process

---

* Research supported in part by the European projects IST FET AEOLUS and COST Action TIST 293 (GRAAL), the Royal Society Grant ESEP 16244, and the ACI Masses de données. Part of this work was done while T. Radzik and F. Sarracco were visiting the LaBRI (Laboratoire Bordelais de Recherche en Informatique) in Bordeaux.

J.H. Anderson, G. Prencipe, and R. Wattenhofer (Eds.): OPODIS 2005, LNCS 3974, pp. 261–274, 2006.
© Springer-Verlag Berlin Heidelberg 2006

destroying all mobile agents visiting this node, without leaving any trace. Since agents cannot prevent being annihilated once they visit a black hole, the only way of protection against such processes is identifying the hostile nodes and avoiding further visiting them. In order to locate a black hole, at least one agent must visit it. In the model we considered, the agents communicate only when they are in the same node (and not, e.g., by leaving messages at nodes). Therefore, the black hole can be identified by scheduling a meeting between the agents after any visit of an unknown node. If such node is a black hole, then the agent which visits that node gets destroyed and cannot turn up at a node where the other agents expect it. This allows the surviving agents to infer the existence and location of a black hole.

In this paper we investigate the case in which there are exactly two agents, starting from the same node s, to which at least one agent has to report back the exact locations of the black holes. We assume that there is at most one black hole in the network. We consider the problem of designing a black hole search scheme for a given network, a given starting node s, and a given subset $S \supseteq \{s\}$ of nodes which are initially known to be safe. The black hole, if present, is at any node not in S. It is interesting to observe that the assumption of having at most one black hole in the network does not make the algorithm presented here unsuitable for the general case. A (single black hole) search can be restarted for each new black hole found, on the network obtained by removing all the black holes already found and by inserting into S the nodes already explored. This can be iterated until all the network nodes become explored. Obviously, even if at most two agents can simultaneously coexist in the network, the total number of agents needed is related to the total number of black holes in the network.

The issue of efficient black hole search was extensively studied in [4, 5, 6] under the scenario of totally asynchronous networks, i.e., while every edge traversal by a mobile agent requires finite time, there is no upper bound on this time. To solve the problem in this setting, the network must be 2-connected. Moreover, in an asynchronous network it is impossible to answer the question of whether a black hole actually exists, hence it is assumed in [4, 5, 6] that there is exactly one black hole and the task is to locate it. Due to the asynchronous setting, it is not possible to provide a simple and easy to compute measure of the time needed by the agents to find the black hole. Hence, the complexity measure taken into account for the algorithms is the total number of moves performed by the agents. In the general case, the authors show that $\Theta(n \log n)$ moves are necessary and sufficient.

In this paper we study the problem under the scenario of synchronous networks, previously considered in [3, 2, 10]. In this scenario it is possible to fix the time needed by an agent for traversing any edge. This assumption makes dramatic changes to the problem. First, the black hole can be located by two agents in any network and the agents can decide if there is a black hole or not. Moreover, it is possible in this case to compute exactly the time needed by the agents to find the black hole. With respect to the total number of moves, this is a more relevant measure in the cases in which there is no cost associated with each agent's traversal, but the target is to determine as quickly as possible the location of the black hole. In order to measure the efficiency of a black hole search, we assume that each agent takes exactly one time unit (one synchronized step) to traverse one edge (and to make all necessary computations associated with this move). Then the cost of a given black hole search (scheme) is defined as the total number of time units the search takes under the worst-case location of the black hole in the network, or when the network contains no black hole.

Previous Results. In [3] the authors prove that the Black Hole Search problem is **NP**-hard, and show a 9.3-approximation algorithm. The restricted case of this problem, when the starting node is the only node initially known to be safe ($S = \{s\}$), is considered in [2] and [10]. In [10] the authors prove that this restricted case is also **NP**-hard, and give a $\frac{7}{2}$-approximation algorithm. In [2] the problem is studied in tree topologies, and the main results are an exact linear-time algorithm for some sub-class of trees and a $5/3$-approximation algorithm for arbitrary trees. The existence of an exact polynomial-time algorithm for arbitrary trees is left open.

Our Results. We show that the Black Hole Search problem is not approximable in polynomial time within a $1 + \varepsilon$ factor for any $\varepsilon < \frac{1}{388}$, unless **P=NP**. Moreover, we give a 6-approximation algorithm for this problem, i.e., a polynomial time algorithm which, for any input instance, produces a black hole search scheme with cost at most 6 times the best cost of a black hole search scheme for this input. This improves on the 9.3-approximation algorithm shown in [3]. Finally we prove that the restricted case in which only the starting node is initially known to be safe is also **APX**-hard.

2   Model and Terminology

We represent a network as a connected undirected graph $G = (V, E)$, without multiple edges or self-loops, where nodes denote hosts and edges denote communication links.[1] The two agents, called *Agent*-1 and *Agent*-2, start the black hole search from a STARTING NODE $s \in V$ and explore graph G by traversing its edges. Together with the starting node s, a subset of nodes S which are initially known to be safe is given. Let $U = V \setminus S$, and let $B \subseteq U$, $|B| \leq 1$, denote the (unknown) set of nodes containing a black hole (we have either $B = \emptyset$ or $B = \{b\}$). We recall the formalization of the Black Hole Search problem given in [10], extending it to the case of S containing more nodes than only s, in the following way.

(General) Black Hole Search problem (gBHS)

Instance: a connected undirected graph $G = (V, E)$, a subset of nodes $S \subset V$ and a node $s \in S$.

Solution: a feasible EXPLORATION SCHEME $\mathcal{E}_{G,S,s} = (\mathbb{X}, \mathbb{Y})$ for (G, S, s), where $\mathbb{X} = \langle x_0, x_1, \ldots, x_T \rangle$ and $\mathbb{Y} = \langle y_0, y_1, \ldots, y_T \rangle$ are two equal-length sequences of nodes in G. The feasibility of $\mathcal{E}_{G,S,s}$ is determined by constraints 1–4 given below. The length of $\mathcal{E}_{G,S,s}$ is defined to be T.

Measure: the cost of the Black Hole Search (BHS) based on $\mathcal{E}_{G,S,s}$.

Goal: minimization.

---

[1] In the following we will use the terms graph and network, host and node, and link and edge interchangeably, although we tend to use the term graph to mean an abstract representation of a network.

When the BHS based on a given exploration scheme $\mathcal{E}_{G,S,s}$ is performed in G, *Agent*-1 follows the path defined by $\mathbb{X}$ while *Agent*-2 follows the path defined by $\mathbb{Y}$. At the end of the i-th step of the search (at time i), *Agent*-1 is in node x_i while *Agent*-2 is in node y_i. As soon as an agent deduces the value of B, it "aborts" the exploration and returns to the starting node s by traversing nodes in $V \setminus B$. The cost of the BHS based on $\mathcal{E}_{G,S,s}$ is defined later in this section.

If $\mathbb{X} = \langle x_0, x_1, \ldots, x_T \rangle$ and $\mathbb{Y} = \langle y_0, y_1, \ldots, y_T \rangle$ are two equal-length sequences of nodes in G, then $\mathcal{E}_{G,S,s} = (\mathbb{X}, \mathbb{Y})$ is a feasible exploration scheme for the input (G, S, s) (and can be effectively used as a basis for a BHS in G) if the constraints 1–4 stated below are satisfied.

Constraint 1: $x_0 = y_0 = s$, $x_T = y_T$.

Constraint 2: for each $i = 0, \ldots, T-1$, either $x_{i+1} = x_i$, or $(x_i, x_{i+1}) \in E$; and similarly either $y_{i+1} = y_i$ or $(y_i, y_{i+1}) \in E$.

Constraint 3: $U \subseteq \bigcup_{i=0}^{T} \{x_i\} \cup \bigcup_{i=0}^{T} \{y_i\}$.

Constraint 1 corresponds to the fact that both agents start from the given starting node s. The requirement that the sequences $\mathbb{X}$ and $\mathbb{Y}$ end at the same node provides a convenient simplification of the reasoning without loss of generality. Constraint 2 models the fact that during each step, each agent can either WAIT in the node v where it was at the end of the previous step, or traverse an edge of the network to move to a node adjacent to v. Constraint 3 assures that each node in U is visited by at least one agent during the exploration. We need additional definitions to state Constraint 4.

Given an exploration scheme $\mathcal{E}_{G,S,s} = (\mathbb{X}, \mathbb{Y})$, for each $i = 0, 1, \ldots, T$, we call the EXPLORED TERRITORY at step i the set S_i defined in the following way:

$$S_i = \begin{cases} S \cup \bigcup_{j=0}^{i} \{x_j\} \cup \bigcup_{j=0}^{i} \{y_j\}, & \text{if } x_i = y_i; \\ S_{i-1}, & \text{otherwise.} \end{cases}$$

Thus $S_0 = S$ by Constraint 1, $S_T = V$ by Constraint 1 and Constraint 3, and $S_{j-1} \subseteq S_j$ for each step $1 \le j \le T$. A node v is EXPLORED at step i if $v \in S_i$, or UNEXPLORED otherwise. An unexplored node v may have been already visited by one of the agents, but it will become explored only when the agents meet, and communicate, next time (the agents communicate with each other, exchanging their full knowledge, when and only when they meet at a node). If both agents are alive at the end of step i, then the explored nodes at this step are all nodes which are known to *both* agents to be safe. Note that the explored territory is defined for an exploration scheme $\mathcal{E}_{G,S,s}$, not for the BHS based on $\mathcal{E}_{G,S,s}$, and does not take into account the possible existence of the black hole. This is taken into account in the definition of the cost of the BHS based on $\mathcal{E}_{G,S,s}$.

A MEETING STEP (or simply MEETING) is the step 0 and every step $1 \le j \le T$ such that $S_j \ne S_{j-1}$. Observe that, for each meeting step j, we must have $x_j = y_j$, but not necessarily the opposite, and we call this node a MEETING POINT. The meeting steps are the steps when the agents meet and add at least one new node to the explored territory. A sequence of steps $\langle j+1, j+2, \ldots, k \rangle$ where j and k are two consecutive meetings is called a PHASE of length $k-j$. We give now the last constraint on a feasible exploration scheme.

Constraint 4: for each phase with a sequence of steps $\langle j + 1, j + 2, \ldots, k \rangle$,
  (a) $|\{x_{j+1}, \ldots, x_k\} \setminus S_j| \leq 1$ and $|\{y_{j+1}, \ldots, y_k\} \setminus S_j| \leq 1$; and
  (b) $\{x_{j+1}, \ldots, x_k\} \setminus S_j \neq \{y_{j+1}, \ldots, y_k\} \setminus S_j$.

Constraint 4(a) means that during each phase, one agent can visit at most one unexplored node. If it visited two or more unexplored nodes and one of them was a black hole, then the other, surviving, agent would not know where exactly the black hole is. Constraint 4(b) says that the same unexplored node cannot be visited by both agents during the same phase, or otherwise they both may end up in a black hole (see [2] for a formal proof of this fact). From now on an exploration scheme means a feasible exploration scheme. We recall from [10] the next two simple observations.

Lemma 1. *If $k \geq 1$ is a meeting step for an exploration scheme $\mathcal{E}_{G,S,s}$, then $x_k = y_k \in S_{k-1}$.*

Lemma 2. *Each phase of an exploration scheme $\mathcal{E}_{G,S,s}$ has length at least 2.*

Any phase $\langle j + 1, j + 2 \rangle$ of length 2 which expands the explored territory by 2 nodes has to have the following structure. Let m be the meeting point at step j. During step $j + 1$, *Agent*-1 visits an unexplored node v_1 adjacent to m, while *Agent*-2 visits an unexplored node v_2 adjacent to m as well, and $v_1 \neq v_2$. In step $j + 2$, the agents meet in a node which has been already explored and is adjacent to both v_1 and v_2. This node can be either m, and in this case we denote the phase as **b-split**(m, v_1, v_2), or a different node $m' \neq m$, and in this case the phase is denoted as **a-split**(m, v_1, v_2, m').

For an exploration scheme $\mathcal{E}_{G,S,s} = (\mathbb{X}, \mathbb{Y})$ and a location of a black hole B, the EXECUTION TIME is defined as follows. If $B = \emptyset$, then the execution time is equal to the length T of the exploration scheme, plus the shortest path distance from $x_T (= y_T)$ to s. In this case the agents must perform the full exploration (spending one time unit per step) and then get back to the starting node to report that there is no black hole in the network. If $B = \{b\} \subseteq U$, then let j be the first step in $\mathcal{E}_{G,S,s}$ such that $b \in S_j$. Observe that j must be a meeting step and $1 \leq j \leq T$, since $S_0 = S$ and $S_T = V$. The execution time in this case is equal to j plus the length of the shortest path from $x_j (= y_j)$ to s not including b. In this case one agent, say *Agent*-1, vanishes into the black hole during the phase ending at step j, so it does not show up to meet *Agent*-2 at node $x_j = y_j$. Since, by Constraint 4, *Agent*-1 has visited only one unexplored node during the phase, the surviving *Agent*-2 learns the exact location of the black hole and thus it goes back to s, obviously omitting the black hole.

The COST of the BHS based on an exploration scheme $\mathcal{E}_{G,S,s} = (\mathbb{X}, \mathbb{Y})$ is denoted by $cost(\mathcal{E}_{G,S,s})$ and defined as the worst (maximum) execution time of $\mathcal{E}_{G,S,s}$ over all possible values of B (including $B = \emptyset$). The target of the black hole search problem is to find an exploration scheme $\mathcal{E}_{G,S,s}$ which yields a minimum cost BHS over all possible exploration schemes for (G, S, s).

The following lemma helps to simplify, at least in some cases, the computation of the cost of the BHS based on a given exploration scheme.

Lemma 3. *Let (G, S, s) be an input instance for the gBHS problem, and let U be the set of initially unexplored nodes ($U = V \setminus S$). The case $B = \emptyset$ yields the maximum execution time for any exploration scheme in (G, S, s), if and only if, by removing any node $u \in U$ from G, each node in $V \setminus \{u\}$ either becomes disconnected from s, or maintains its shortest path distance from s.*[2]

3 Approximation Lower Bound for the General BHS Problem

In this section we provide an explicit lower bound on the approximability of the General Black Hole Search problem by showing an approximation preserving reduction from a particular subcase of the Traveling Salesman Problem, presented in [7], and defined in the following way.

(1,M)-Traveling Salesman Problem (TSP(1,M))

Instance: a pair (G, d), where $G = (V, E)$ is a complete graph (with $n = |V|$) and $d: V^2 \to \{1, \ldots, M\}$ is a distance function associating to each pair of nodes (v, u) a positive integer length $d(v, u)$ between 1 and M (where M is a constant). Function d is symmetric (i.e., $d(u, v) = d(v, u)$) and satisfies the triangle inequality (i.e., $d(i, j) + d(j, k) \geq d(i, k), \forall i, j, k \in V$).
Solution: a tour τ of G, i.e., a permutation $\tau = \langle v_{\pi(1)}, v_{\pi(2)}, \ldots, v_{\pi(n)} \rangle$ of the nodes in V.
Measure: the *length* (or *cost*) of the tour, i.e., $cost(\tau) = \sum_{i=1}^{n-1} d(v_{\pi(i)}, v_{\pi(i+1)}) + d(v_{\pi(n)}, v_{\pi(1)})$.
Goal: minimization.

In [7] it is also presented a lower bound on the approximability of such problem.

Lemma 4. *It is NP-hard to approximate TSP(1,8) within $1 + \varepsilon$ for any $\varepsilon < \frac{1}{388}$.*

Reduction from instances (G, d) of TSP(1,M) to instances (G', S, s) of gBHS.
Let (G, d) be an instance of TSP(1,M). We define the graph $G' = (V', E')$, the set $S \subset V'$, and the starting node s, in the following way. Let v_1 be an arbitrary node in V. We add v_1 to V' and to S, and we define $s = v_1$. For each node v_i ($2 \leq i \leq n$) in V, we add to V' a pair of nodes v_i', v_i''. We denote node v_1 as the ISLAND I_1, and each pair of nodes v_j', v_j'' as the ISLAND I_j. For each edge (v_i, v_j) in E of length $d(v_i, v_j)$, we add to V' (and to E') a path of $2 \cdot d(v_i, v_j) - 1$ nodes (BRIDGE $i \leftrightarrow j$), whose endpoints are adjacent respectively to v_i', v_i'' (or v_1 if $i = 1$) and to v_j', v_j'' (or v_1 if $j = 1$). We add all the nodes of the bridge to S. We call as $b_{i,j}$ and as $b_{j,i}$ the endpoints of bridge $i \leftrightarrow j$ adjacent respectively to island I_i and island I_j (note that if $d(v_i, v_j) = 1$, then $b_{i,j} \equiv b_{j,i}$). Each bridge is composed by at least one (safe) node, and $|V' \setminus S| = 2(n-1)$. An example of reduction is given in Figure 1.

Lemma 5. *The distance in G' between any node of island I_i and any node of island I_j (where $i \neq j$ and $i, j = 1, \ldots, n$) is equal to $2 \cdot d(v_i, v_j)$.*

The following lemma gives a useful characterization of G'.

---

[2] Due to space constraints, the proofs of some lemmas have been omitted in this extended abstract.

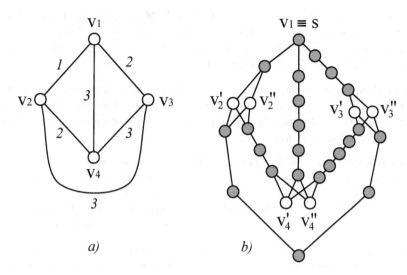

Fig. 1. An example of the reduction from an instance (G, d) (in a)) to an instance (G', S, s) (in b)). The nodes in S are filled with gray color.

Lemma 6. *Let G' be a graph produced with the above mentioned construction. The case $B = \emptyset$ yields the maximum execution time for any exploration scheme in G'.*

Now we define an exploration scheme on G' which explores the islands in G', in the order defined by a tour on G. In the following definition we introduce a new keyword: **walk**. By **walk**(b) we mean that both agents (which are supposed to be already in the same node w), move to b by following a shortest (safe) path from w to b. Actually, the walk is not a complete phase (no new nodes are explored), but it is the initial part of a phase.

Let $\tau = \langle v_{\pi(1)}, v_{\pi(2)}, \ldots, v_{\pi(n)} \rangle$ be a tour on G of length l. We assume w.l.o.g. that $\pi(1) = 1$. A τ-BASED EXPLORATION SCHEME $\mathcal{E}^{\tau}_{G',S,s}$ on G' consists of the following sequence of steps:

1. **walk**($b_{1,\pi(2)}$), where $b_{1,\pi(2)}$ is the node adjacent to s on the bridge $1 \leftrightarrow \pi(2)$;
2. for each $i = 2, \ldots, n$:
   (a) **walk**($b_{\pi(i),\pi(i-1)}$), where $b_{\pi(i),\pi(i-1)}$ is the node adjacent to $I_{\pi(i)}$ on the bridge $\pi(i-1) \leftrightarrow \pi(i)$;
   (b) **a-split**($b_{\pi(i),\pi(i-1)}, v'_{\pi(i)}, v''_{\pi(i)}, b_{\pi(i),\pi(i+1)}$), where $b_{\pi(i),\pi(i+1)}$ is the node adjacent to $I_{\pi(i)}$ on the bridge $\pi(i) \leftrightarrow \pi(i+1)$ (or bridge $\pi(n) \leftrightarrow 1$ if $i = n$).

Given the tour τ in G, the τ-based exploration scheme $\mathcal{E}^{\tau}_{G',S,s}$ can be obviously constructed in linear time. In the following lemma we compute the cost of the Black Hole Search based on $\mathcal{E}^{\tau}_{G',S,s}$.

Lemma 7. *Given a tour $\tau = \langle v_{\pi(1)}, v_{\pi(2)}, \ldots, v_{\pi(n)} \rangle$ on G of length l, the τ-based exploration scheme $\mathcal{E}^{\tau}_{G',S,s}$ satisfies $\mathrm{cost}(\mathcal{E}^{\tau}_{G',S,s}) = 2 \cdot l$.*

Corollary 1. *Let (G, d) be an instance of the* TSP(1,M) *problem, and let (G', S, s) be the corresponding instance of the* BHS *problem where the graph G' is constructed as explained before. Moreover, let τ^* be an optimal solution for (G, d) and let $\mathcal{E}^*_{G', S, s}$ be an optimal solution for (G', S, s). Then* $\text{cost}(\mathcal{E}^*_{G', S, s}) \leq 2 \cdot \text{cost}(\tau^*)$.

In what follows we show a method to modify an exploration scheme without altering its properties (i.e., feasibility, length, sequence of explored territories and the cost of the BHS based on it). We then use this technique to impose a characteristic of "regularity" to any exploration scheme on G'.

Definition 1. *Let $\mathcal{E}_{G, S, s} = (\mathbb{X}, \mathbb{Y})$ be an exploration scheme for (G, S, s), and let $\phi = (\mathbb{X}_\phi, \mathbb{Y}_\phi)$ be a phase in $\mathcal{E}_{G, S, s}$. Let $\mathcal{E}'_{G, S, s}$ be the exploration scheme obtained from $\mathcal{E}_{G, S, s}$ by swapping the paths of the two agents in phase ϕ, i.e., $\phi' = (\mathbb{Y}_\phi, \mathbb{X}_\phi)$. We call this operation a* PHASE-SWAP. *Two exploration schemes are* EQUIVALENT *if and only if one is obtained from the other by applying a finite sequence of phase-swaps.*

Lemma 8. *Let $\mathcal{E}_{G, S, s} = (\mathbb{X}, \mathbb{Y})$ be an exploration scheme for (G, S, s). Let $\mathcal{E}'_{G, S, s}$ be the exploration scheme obtained from $\mathcal{E}_{G, S, s}$ by applying a phase swap on $\mathcal{E}_{G, S, s}$. Then, the exploration scheme $\mathcal{E}'_{G, S, s}$ is feasible, has exactly the same meeting points, the same sequence of explored territories and the same length as $\mathcal{E}_{G, S, s}$. Moreover, $\text{cost}(\mathcal{E}'_{G, S, s}) = \text{cost}(\mathcal{E}_{G, S, s})$.*

Corollary 2. *Two equivalent exploration schemes have exactly the same meeting points, the same sequence of explored territories and the same length. Moreover the cost of the BHS based on them is the same.*

We now turn back our focus to instances (G', S, s) constructed by reduction from instances (G, d). We give a classification of each phase of any exploration scheme in G'. A phase ϕ is a *2s-phase* if the two nodes of the same island are explored during ϕ. It is a *2d-phase*, if two nodes in two distinct islands are explored during ϕ. Finally, it is a *1-phase* if only one node is explored during ϕ.

Definition 2. *Given an exploration scheme $\mathcal{E}_{G', S, s}$, we define the* PHASE GRAPH *of $\mathcal{E}_{G', S, s}$, the following directed multigraph $P(\mathcal{E}_{G', S, s})$. The graph $P(\mathcal{E}_{G', S, s})$ has the nodes $v_2, \dots, v_n$ corresponding to the islands $I_2, \dots, I_n$ in G', plus one further node which we call x. The following edges are added to $P(\mathcal{E}_{G', S, s})$:*

- *a directed edge $\langle v_i, x \rangle$ ($\langle x, v_i \rangle$) is added for each node in island I_i which is explored during a 1-phase by Agent-1 (Agent-2);*
- *a directed edge $\langle v_i, v_j \rangle$ is added for each 2d-phase exploring a node of island I_i with Agent-1 and a node of island I_j with Agent-2;*
- *a directed self-loop $\langle v_i, v_i \rangle$ is added if the nodes of island I_i are explored by a 2s-phase.*

Lemma 9. *Given any exploration scheme $\mathcal{E}_{G', S, s}$, each node of the phase graph $P(\mathcal{E}_{G', S, s})$ has degree (= in-degree + out-degree) equal to 2.*

The graph $P(\mathcal{E}_{G', S, s})$ is thus a set of connected components. In the underlying undirected multigraph, these components are either cycles or isolated nodes. Now we give a new characterization of an exploration scheme in G'.

Definition 3. *An exploration scheme $\mathcal{E}_{G',S,s}$ is REGULAR if and only if each agent explores exactly one node of each island I_j, with $j = 2, \ldots, n$.*

Notice that any τ-based exploration scheme is regular; we can observe that each node in $P(\mathcal{E}_{G',S,s}^{\tau})$ is an isolated node (the only adjacent edge is a self-loop). Indeed, we can prove a tighter relation between regular exploration schemes and their corresponding phase graph.

Lemma 10. *An exploration scheme $\mathcal{E}_{G',S,s}$ is regular if and only if, in the corresponding phase graph $P(\mathcal{E}_{G',S,s})$, for each node v_i, $indeg(v_i) = 1$ and $outdeg(v_i) = 1$.*

Lemma 11. *For any exploration scheme $\mathcal{E}_{G',S,s}$ there is an equivalent regular one that can be found in linear time.*

Proof. We want to prove that we can find in linear time a finite sequence of phase-swaps in $\mathcal{E}_{G',S,s}$, which transforms $\mathcal{E}_{G',S,s}$ into a regular exploration scheme. By Lemma 10, this means transforming $P(\mathcal{E}_{G',S,s})$ into a graph where, for each node v_i, $indeg(v_i) = 1$ and $outdeg(v_i) = 1$. We can observe that each phase-swap in $\mathcal{E}_{G',S,s}$ produces a change in the orientation of the corresponding edge in $P(\mathcal{E}_{G',S,s})$. Since $P(\mathcal{E}_{G',S,s})$ is composed by a set of cycles and isolated nodes, we can swap the edges in the cycles according to a fixed orientation (e.g., clockwise orientation), and thus make regular the graph $P(\mathcal{E}_{G',S,s})$, and the corresponding exploration scheme. □

Lemma 12. *Given an exploration scheme $\mathcal{E}_{G',S,s}$, we can find in linear time a tour τ on G such that, for the τ-based exploration scheme $\mathcal{E}_{G',S,s}^{\tau}$, $cost(\mathcal{E}_{G',S,s}^{\tau}) \leq cost(\mathcal{E}_{G',S,s})$.*

Proof. By Corollary 2 and Lemma 11, we can assume w.l.o.g. that $\mathcal{E}_{G',S,s}$ is a regular exploration scheme. By regularity, *Agent*-1 explores a node of each island in G'. Let $I_X = \langle I_{\pi(2)}, \ldots, I_{\pi(n)} \rangle$ be the sequence of the islands in G' in the order they are explored by *Agent*-1. Let τ be the tour in G corresponding to I_X (i.e., $\tau = \langle v_1, v_{\pi(2)}, \ldots, v_{\pi(n)} \rangle$), and let $l = cost(\tau)$. We show that the τ-based exploration scheme $\mathcal{E}_{G',S,s}^{\tau}$ is such that $cost(\mathcal{E}_{G',S,s}) \geq cost(\mathcal{E}_{G',S,s}^{\tau})$. Consider the case $B = \emptyset$ (Lemma 6). *Agent*-1 starts from s, visits islands in I_X and then gets back to s. By Lemma 5, the length of this tour is at least $2 \cdot l$. The execution time of $\mathcal{E}_{G',S,s}$ cannot be shorter than $2 \cdot l$. Therefore, $cost(\mathcal{E}_{G',S,s}) \geq 2 \cdot l \geq cost(\mathcal{E}_{G',S,s}^{\tau})$. □

Lemma 13. *Let G be an instance of the TSP(1,M) problem, and let G' be the corresponding instance of the gBHS problem. Moreover, let τ^* be an optimal tour in G, and let $\mathcal{E}_{G',S,s}^*$ be an optimal exploration scheme for G'. Let $\varepsilon > 0$. If we can find in polynomial time an exploration scheme $\mathcal{E}_{G',S,s}$ such that $cost(\mathcal{E}_{G',S,s}) \leq cost(\mathcal{E}_{G',S,s}^*)(1 + \varepsilon)$, then we can find in polynomial time a tour τ in G such that $cost(\tau) \leq cost(\tau^*)(1 + \varepsilon)$.*

Proof. Suppose that, given a graph G', we can construct in polynomial time an exploration scheme $\mathcal{E}_{G',S,s}$ such that its cost is at most $1 + \varepsilon$ times the cost of an optimal exploration scheme. By Lemma 12, we can find an exploration scheme $\mathcal{E}_{G',S,s}^{\tau}$, based on a tour τ in G, such that $cost(\mathcal{E}_{G',S,s}^{\tau}) \leq cost(\mathcal{E}_{G',S,s}) \leq cost(\mathcal{E}_{G',S,s}^*)(1 + \varepsilon)$. Supposing that the length of the tour τ is l, then, by Lemma 7: $cost(\mathcal{E}_{G',S,s}^{\tau}) = 2 \cdot l$. Supposing that the length of the optimal tour τ^* is l^*, then, by Corollary 1: $cost(\mathcal{E}_{G',S,s}^*) \leq 2 \cdot l^*$. Therefore, by hypothesis: $2 \cdot l = cost(\mathcal{E}_{G',S,s}^{\tau}) \leq cost(\mathcal{E}_{G',S,s}^*)(1 + \varepsilon) \leq 2 \cdot l^*(1 + \varepsilon)$, and hence, $l \leq l^*(1 + \varepsilon)$. □

The main theorem immediately follows from Lemma 4 and Lemma 13.

Theorem 1. *The* gBHS *problem is not approximable in polynomial time within a factor of* $1 + \varepsilon$ *for any* $\varepsilon < \frac{1}{388}$, *unless* **P=NP***.*

4 The Restricted BHS Problem Is APX-Hard

In this section we consider the restricted version of the BHS problem in which $S = \{s\}$, i.e., the starting point is the only node initially known to be safe (we denote it as rBHS). We show that the BHS problem with this restriction remains **APX**-hard. The input of rBHS is fully specified by providing a graph G and the starting node s. We will hence use now the notation $\mathcal{E}_{G,s}$ to refer to an exploration scheme.

We will prove **APX**-hardness of the rBHS problem using **APX**-hardness of the TSP(1,2) problem. We first recall Lemma 6.3 from [1]:

Lemma 14. *Assume we are given an instance of* TSP(1,2) *on the n-node complete graph* $\overline{G}$, *in the form of the subgraph* G *of* $\overline{G}$ *containing the edges of weight 1. Assume that* G *has max degree* 3. *Assume that we know that its minimum cost TSP tour is either of cost* n *or at least* $(1 + \varepsilon_0)n$, *for some fixed* ε_0. *Then there exists such a constant* ε_0 *for which it is* **NP***-hard to decide which of the two cases holds. The claim holds for* $\varepsilon_0 = \frac{1}{786}$. *If* G *is cubic then the claim holds for* $\varepsilon_0 = \frac{1}{1290}$.

We show a polynomial-time reduction algorithm $\mathcal{A}$ from TSP(1,2) to rBHS, which takes as input an instance G of TSP(1,2), computes an instance (G', s) of rBHS, and has the following property.

Lemma 15. *Let* $0 < \varepsilon < \varepsilon_0/7$, *let* G *be an n-node cubic graph (an instance of* TSP(1,2)), *and let* (G', s) *be the corresponding instance of* rBHS *computed by the reduction algorithm* $\mathcal{A}$. *Then the following two conditions hold.*

1. *If the optimal cost of a tour in* G *is equal to* n, *then the optimal cost of an exploration scheme for* (G', s) *is at most* $\frac{7}{2}n + 1$.
2. *There exists* $n_0 = n_0(\varepsilon_0, \varepsilon)$ *such that for* $n \geq n_0$, *if the optimal cost of a tour in* G *is at least* $n(1 + \varepsilon_0)$, *then the optimal cost of an exploration scheme for* (G', s) *is greater than* $\left(\frac{7}{2}n + 1\right)(1 + \varepsilon)$.

This lemma implies that for $0 < \varepsilon < \varepsilon_0/7$ and $n \geq n_0$, if we have an n-node cubic graph G and we know that the optimal cost of a tour in G either is equal to n or is at least $n(1 + \varepsilon_0)$, then we can decide which of these two cases happens, if we have an $(1 + \varepsilon)$-approximation of the optimal cost of an exploration scheme for (G', s). Thus Lemmas 14 and 15 imply the following theorem.

Theorem 2. *It is* **NP***-hard to compute* $(1+\varepsilon)$-*approximate exploration schemes for the* rBHS *problem for any* $\varepsilon < \frac{1}{9030}$.

Description of the Reduction Algorithm $\mathcal{A}$. Let an n-node graph $G = (V, E)$ be the input instance of TSP(1,2). The construction of the instance (G', s) of rBHS proceeds as follows. We pick an arbitrary node in G (say v_1) as the starting node ($s \equiv v_1$) and we add it to G' (as before, this is island I_1). For each node v_i in G, $2 \le i \le n$, we add in G' a pair of unexplored nodes v_i', v_i'' (as before, we denote this pair as island I_i). For each edge (v_i, v_j) in G, we put in G' an unexplored node $b_{i,j}$ (*bridge node*), connected to v_i', v_i'' (if $i > 1$), to v_j', v_j'' (if $j > 1$) and to s. If the number of bridge nodes (that is, the number of edges in G) is odd, then we add another unexplored node b_s adjacent to s (to ensure that s is adjacent to an even number of unexplored nodes). Node s is adjacent to all bridge nodes and is not adjacent to any "island" nodes.

Sketch of Proof of Lemma 15. Let G be an n-node cubic graph. Since G has $m = \frac{3}{2}n$ edges, the total number of nodes in G' is $\frac{7}{2}n - 1 + odd(m)$, and all of them but one are initially unexplored. For an integer k, $odd(k)$ is equal to 1, if k is odd, and to 0 otherwise. As in Section 3, we define for a tour $\tau = \langle v_1, v_{\pi(2)}, \ldots, v_{\pi(n)} \rangle$ in G, the exploration scheme $\mathcal{E}_{G',s}^\tau$ for (G', s), which explores two by two the nodes of each island in the order $\langle I_{\pi(2)}, \ldots, I_{\pi(n)} \rangle$. Here, however, the scheme first explores the bridge nodes.

More formally, the scheme $\mathcal{E}_{G',s}^\tau$ has the following sequence of steps.

1. While there are two unexplored nodes b', b'' adjacent to s: **b-split**(s, b', b'').
2. For each $i = 2, \ldots, n$:
   (a) **walk**(b'), where b' is either the bridge node $b_{\pi(i-1), \pi(i)}$, if nodes $v_{\pi(i-1)}$ and $v_{\pi(i)}$ are adjacent in G, or any bridge node adjacent to I_i otherwise.
   (b) **a-split**$(b', v_{\pi(i)}', v_{\pi(i)}'', b'')$, where b'' is either the bridge node $b_{\pi(i), \pi(i+1)}$, if $i < n$ and nodes $v_{\pi(i)}$ and $v_{\pi(i+1)}$ are adjacent in G, or any bridge node adjacent to I_i otherwise.

The first **walk** operation, for $i = 2$, has length 1. For each $3 \le i \le n$, the **walk** operation has length either 0, if nodes $v_{\pi(i-1), \pi(i)}$ are adjacent in G, or 2, if nodes $v_{\pi(i-1), \pi(i)}$ are not adjacent in G. Therefore, if the tour τ has cost $n + d$ (that is, contains d edges of weight 2), then the exploration scheme $\mathcal{E}_{G',s}^\tau$ has length at most $\frac{3}{2}n + odd(m) + 1 + 2d + 2(n-1) \le \frac{7}{2}n + 2d$. The execution time for the case $B = \emptyset$ is at most $\frac{7}{2}n + 2d + 1$, since $\mathcal{E}_{G',s}^\tau$ ends in a bridge node, which is adjacent to s. This is also the cost of the BHS based on $\mathcal{E}_{G',s}^\tau$. When an agent realizes that there is a black hole, then this agent must be at a meeting point, and each meeting point is either node s or a bridge node, which is adjacent to s. Hence, if the cost of tour τ is n, then $d = 0$ and the cost of $\mathcal{E}_{G',s}^\tau$ is at most $\frac{7}{2}n + 1$, so the first part of Lemma 15 holds.

To prove the second part of Lemma 15, consider an arbitrary exploration scheme $\mathcal{E}_{G',s}$. By using a similar approach as in Section 3, we can find, through a sequence of phase swaps, a "regular" exploration scheme $\mathcal{E}_{G',s}'$, equivalent to $\mathcal{E}_{G',s}$, where each agent explores exactly one node of each island I_j for $j = 2, \ldots, n$, and $cost(\mathcal{E}_{G',s}') = cost(\mathcal{E}_{G',s})$. We assume by symmetry that scheme $\mathcal{E}_{G',s}'$ is such that *Agent*-1 explores nodes v_j', $j = 2, \ldots, n$, and that $\langle v_{\pi(2)}', \ldots, v_{\pi(n)}' \rangle$ is the order in which *Agent*-1 explores these nodes. We consider the tour $\tau = \langle v_1, v_{\pi(2)}, \ldots, v_{\pi(n)} \rangle$ in G.

Let d be the number of weight 2 edges in τ. Thus the number of indices i, $2 \le i \le n - 1$, such that $(v_{\pi(i)}, v_{\pi(i+1)})$ is not an edge in G is at least $d - 2$. Consider any of these indices i and two consecutive phases ϕ_{j_i} and ϕ_{j_i+1} in $\mathcal{E}_{G',s}'$, where ϕ_{j_i} is the phase during which node $v_{\pi(i)}'$ is explored by *Agent*-1. It can be shown that at least one of the two phases ϕ_{j_i} and ϕ_{j_i+1} is not a split, so at least $(d-2)/2$ phases in scheme $\mathcal{E}'_{G',s}$ are not splits.

The cost of any exploration scheme is at least the number of unexplored nodes plus the number of phases other than splits. Therefore, we have $cost(\mathcal{E}'_{G',s}) \geq \frac{7}{2}n - 3 + \frac{d}{2}$. This implies that if $cost(\mathcal{E}'_{G',s}) \leq \left(\frac{7}{2}n + 1\right)(1 + \varepsilon)$, then $d \leq 7\varepsilon n + 2(4 + \varepsilon)$, and

$$cost(\tau) = n + d \leq n + 7\varepsilon n + 2(4+\varepsilon) \leq n(1+\varepsilon_0) - (\varepsilon_0 - 7\varepsilon)n + 2(4+\varepsilon) < n(1+\varepsilon_0),$$

provided that $\varepsilon < \varepsilon_0/7$ and $n \geq n_0 = \lceil 2(4+\varepsilon)/(\varepsilon_0 - 7\varepsilon) + 1 \rceil$.

5   A 6-Approximation Algorithm for the General BHS Problem

Let G, S and U be defined as in Section 2. We define the distance graph $\widehat{G}$ as the complete weighted graph in which the set of nodes corresponds to the nodes in $U \cup \{s\}$ and the weight of edge (v_i, v_j) is the shortest path distance from v_i to v_j in G (considering both safe and unexplored nodes). Weights in $\widehat{G}$ satisfy triangle inequality. Let T be the minimum spanning tree of $\widehat{G}$ rooted at s, and let $cost(T)$ be its cost, i.e., the sum of the weights of all its edges. Let $L_T = \langle v_0 \equiv s, v_1, \ldots, v_u \rangle$ be the depth-first ordering of the nodes in T, and let L_G be the sequence obtained from L_T by replacing each pair of adjacent nodes v_i, v_{i+1} with the shortest path in G from v_i to v_{i+1}. Since the distance from v_i to v_{i+1} is at most the (weighted) cost of path $v_i, \ldots, v_{i+1}$ in T, the length of L_G is at most $2cost(T) - d(v_u, s)$.

We now construct the exploration scheme $\mathcal{E}_{G,S,s} = (\mathbb{X}, \mathbb{Y})$ for G. Initially $\mathbb{X} = \mathbb{Y} = L_G$. Then, the pairs of adjacent steps $\langle x_i, x_{i+1} \rangle$ and $\langle y_i, y_{i+1} \rangle$ are considered from $i = 1, \ldots, k$. If $x_i = y_i = v'$ and $x_{i+1} = y_{i+1} = v''$, where v'' is an unexplored node occurring for the first time in the sequences, we replace $\langle v', v'' \rangle$ in $\mathbb{X}$ with the sequence $\langle v', v'', v', v'' \rangle$ and we replace $\langle v', v'' \rangle$ in $\mathbb{Y}$ with the sequence $\langle v', v', v', v'' \rangle$. This is to assure that each time the agents have to visit an unexplored node, *Agent-1* first explores it by using the technique of *probing*. Since $|U|$ is the number of unexplored nodes, $2|U|$ steps are added to exploration scheme $\mathcal{E}_{G,S,s}$. The length of $\mathcal{E}_{G,S,s}$ is therefore at most $2cost(T) - d(v_u, s) + 2|U|$, while the execution time in the case $B = \emptyset$ is at most $2cost(T) + 2|U|$ since the surviving agents have to get back from v_u to s. Observing that $B = \emptyset$ yields the worst case for the execution time since we are operating on a tree, we can derive the following lemma.

Lemma 16. *The exploration scheme $\mathcal{E}_{G,S,s}$ is feasible and* $cost(\mathcal{E}_{G,S,s}) \leq 2cost(T) + 2|U|$.

Consider now an optimal exploration scheme $\mathcal{E}^*_{G,S,s} = (\mathbb{X}^*, \mathbb{Y}^*)$. In computing $cost(\mathcal{E}^*_{G,S,s})$ we consider, as lower bound, the execution time of $\mathcal{E}^*_{G,S,s}$ in the case $B = \emptyset$. Let $L' = (x_k, \ldots, s)$ be the shortest path in G from the last node x_k in $\mathbb{X}^*$ to the starting node, excluding the endpoints x_k and s. Let $L'' = \mathbb{X}^* \circ L' \circ \mathbb{Y}^* \circ L' \circ \langle s \rangle$. The sequence L'' starts from s, visits all the nodes in U and ends in s. The length of L'' (we denote it as $|L''|$) is at most twice the execution time of $\mathcal{E}^*_{G,S,s}$ in the case $B = \emptyset$, since L'' is the concatenation of the paths the two agents follow during the exploration in such case; hence $2cost(\mathcal{E}^*_{G,S,s}) \geq |L''|$. Let L^* be the minimum (shortest) tour in G starting from s and visiting all the nodes in U, and let $|L^*|$ be its length; obviously, $|L''| \geq |L^*|$.

Due to its optimality, L^* has the following structure: $L^* = \langle s \rangle \circ P(s, u_1) \circ P(u_1, u_2) \circ \ldots \circ P(u_u, s)$ where $\langle u_1, \ldots, u_u \rangle$ is the sequence of unexplored nodes in the order they are visited for the first time in L^*, and $P(x, y)$ is the shortest path from node x (excluded) to node y in G. Since weights in G satisfy triangle inequality, the length of L^* is equal to the length of the minimum traveling salesman tour in $\widehat{G}$, which is at least the cost of the minimum spanning tree T of $\widehat{G}$. Therefore, $|L^*| \geq cost(T)$, and $cost(\mathcal{E}^*_{G,S,s}) \geq \dfrac{cost(T)}{2}$. Moreover, the trivial lower bound holds: $cost(\mathcal{E}^*_{G,S,s}) \geq |U|$. We compute the approximation ratio of the algorithm presented in this section, by choosing a suitable balance for the two bounds on the optimal cost. Therefore:

$$\frac{cost(\mathcal{E}_{G,S,s})}{cost(\mathcal{E}^*_{G,S,s})} \leq \frac{2\,cost(T) + 2\,|U|}{\frac{2}{3}\dfrac{cost(T)}{2} + \frac{1}{3}|U|} = 6\,.$$

Theorem 3. *The* gBHS *problem is approximable within* 6.

6 Conclusions

We showed that the problem of computing an optimal exploration scheme for a BHS with two agents (the gBHS problem) is not approximable within $\frac{389}{388}$ (unless **P=NP**). We also showed that for the restricted version of this problem (the rBHS problem), when initially only one, starting node is known to be safe, approximating within any factor less than $\frac{9031}{9030}$ is **NP**-hard. We have presented a polynomial-time 6-approximation algorithm for the gBHS problem (while a polynomial-time $3\frac{1}{2}$-approximation algorithm for the rBHS problem was previously shown in [10]).

It seems very difficult to reduce significantly the gap between the upper and lower bounds on the approximation ratios for the gBHS and rBHS problems. However, some small improvements can be achieved, for example, by showing, with a more detailed analysis, that Lemma 15 holds also for $0 < \varepsilon < 2\varepsilon_0/7$ and for graphs G of maximum degree 3. This improves the constant in the lower bound for the rBHS problem to $\frac{2752}{2751}$. Since our lower bounds are based on reductions from problems TSP(1,8) and TSP(1,2), any improvements of the inapproximability results for those problems will directly lead to improved lower bounds for our problems.

We believe that we can improve the 6 approximation ratio, by a more detailed analysis of the bad case, when the two lower bounds on the optimal cost of an exploration scheme are similar. More precisely, if the ratio $cost(T)/2|U|$ is in the range $[1-\delta, 1+\delta]$, for some small constant $\delta > 0$, then one should be able to derive a lower constant than 6 for the bound (5) using a similar analysis as in [10]. If $cost(T)/2|U|$ is outside of this range, then the left-hand side of (5) is less than $6 - \delta$. This approach would however lead most likely only to a small improvement, while requiring substantial expansion and refinement of technical details.

As already observed in Section 1, it would be interesting to investigate how one could model and analyse the more practical and more general case of multiple black holes search, possibly performed by more than two agents.

References

1. B. Csaba, M. Karpinski, and P. Krysta. Approximability of dense and sparse instances of minimum 2-connectivity, TSP and path problems. In *SODA '02: Proceedings of the thirteenth annual ACM-SIAM Symposium on Discrete algorithms*, pages 74–83, Philadelphia, PA, USA, 2002.
2. J. Czyzowicz, D. Kowalski, E. Markou, and A. Pelc. Searching for a black hole in tree networks. In *Proc. 8th Int. Conf. on Principles of Distributed Systems (OPODIS 2004)*, Springer LNCS vol.3544, pages 67–80, 2004.
3. J. Czyzowicz, D. Kowalski, E. Markou, and A. Pelc. Complexity of searching for a black hole. *Fundamenta Informaticae*, (To appear), 2006.
4. S. Dobrev, P. Flocchini, R. Kralovic, G. Prencipe, P. Ruzicka, and N. Santoro. Black hole search by mobile agents in hypercubes and related networks. In *Proc. 6th Int. Conf. on Principles of Distributed Systems (OPODIS 2002)*, pages 169–180, 2002.
5. S. Dobrev, P. Flocchini, G. Prencipe, and N. Santoro. Mobile agents searching for a black hole in an anonymous ring. In *Proc. 15th Int. Symposium on Distributed Computing (DISC 2001)*, Springer LNCS vol. 2180, pages 166–179, 2001.
6. S. Dobrev, P. Flocchini, G. Prencipe, and N. Santoro. Searching for a black hole in arbitrary networks: Optimal mobile agents protocols. In *Proc. 21st ACM Symposium on Principles of Distributed Computing (PODC 2002)*, pages 153–161, 2002.
7. L. Engebretsen and M. Karpinski. TSP with bounded metrics: stronger approximation hardness. Technical Report 85264, University of Bonn, February 2005.
8. F. Hohl. Time limited black box security: Protecting mobile agents from malicious hosts. In *Proc. Conf. on Mobile Agent Security*, Springer LNCS vol. 1419, pages 92–113, 1998.
9. F. Hohl. A framework to protect mobile agents by using reference states. In *Proc. 20th Int. Conf. on Distributed Computing Systems (ICDCS 2000)*, pages 410–417, 2000.
10. R. Klasing, E. Markou, T. Radzik, and F. Sarracco. Hardness and approximation results for black hole search in arbitrary graphs. In *Proc. 12th Int. Colloquium on Structural Information and Communication Complexity (SIROCCO 2005)*, Springer LNCS vol. 3499, pages 200–215, 2005.
11. S. Ng and K. Cheung. Protecting mobile agents against malicious hosts by intention of spreading. In H. Arabnia, editor, *Proc. Int. Conf. on Parallel and Distributed Processing and Applications (PDPTA'99) Vol. II*, pages 725–729, 1999.
12. T. Sander and C.F. Tschudin. Protecting mobile agents against malicious hosts. In *Proc. Conf. on Mobile Agent Security*, Springer LNCS vol. 1419, pages 44–60, 1998.
13. K. Schelderup and J. Olnes. Mobile agent security – issues and directions. In *Proc. 6th Int. Conf. on Intelligence and Services in Networks*, Springer LNCS vol. 1597, pages 155–167, 1999.

Revising UNITY Programs: Possibilities and Limitations[*]

Ali Ebnenasir, Sandeep S. Kulkarni, and Borzoo Bonakdarpour

Software Engineering and Network Systems Laboratory
Department of Computer Science and Engineering
Michigan State University
48824 East Lansing, Michigan, USA
{ebnenasi, sandeep, borzoo}@cse.msu.edu
http://www.cse.msu.edu/~{ebnenasi,sandeep,borzoo}

Abstract. We concentrate on automatic addition of UNITY properties unless, stable, invariant, and leads-to to programs. We formally define the problem of adding UNITY properties to programs while preserving their existing properties. For cases where one simultaneously adds a single leads-to property along with a conjunction of unless, stable, and invariant properties to an existing program, we present a sound and complete algorithm with polynomial time complexity (in program state space). However, for cases where one simultaneously adds two leads-to properties to a program, we present a somewhat unexpected result that such addition is NP-complete. Therefore, in general, adding one leads-to property is significantly easier than adding two (or more) leads-to properties.

Keywords: UNITY, Formal Methods, Program Synthesis.

1 Introduction

In this paper, we focus on automated addition of UNITY properties [1] to existing programs. To motivate the application of this work, consider two scenarios: In the first scenario, *a designer checks the model of a computing system to determine if it satisfies the given properties of interest using a model checker. The model checker provides a counterexample demonstrating that one of the properties is not met.* In this scenario, the designer needs to modify the given model so that it satisfies that property (while ensuring that the remaining properties continue to be satisfied). In another scenario, an existing program needs to be modified so that it satisfies an additional property of interest (while satisfying existing properties). Such a scenario occurs when the specification is incomplete and as designers gain more domain knowledge about the problem at hand, they may add new properties to the specification.

---

[*] This work was partially sponsored by NSF CAREER CCR-0092724, DARPA Grant OSURS01-C-1901, ONR Grant N00014-01-1-0744, NSF grant EIA-0130724, and a grant from Michigan State University.

J.H. Anderson, G. Prencipe, and R. Wattenhofer (Eds.): OPODIS 2005, LNCS 3974, pp. 275–290, 2006.

There exist two ways in which one can deal with the above scenarios: (1) *local redesign*, where the designer removes the program behaviors that violate the property of interest without adding any new behaviors, or (2) *comprehensive redesign*, where the designer introduces new behaviors in the program computations (e.g., by introducing new variables, or adding new computation paths). Clearly, the former approach is desirable, as it ensures that certain existing specifications (e.g., the UNITY specifications from [1]) are preserved. Moreover, in the second scenario, the designer may not have access to the complete specification of the existing system. Hence, in this case, local redesign, if successful, is highly desirable.

We expect that an algorithm for local redesign would be especially useful if it were sound and complete. A sound algorithm ensures that the redesigned program meets the new specification (in addition to preserving existing specification); i.e., the redesigned program is correct by construction. Moreover, a complete algorithm provides an insight for the designer to decide if a program can be redesigned locally or it should be redesigned from scratch to satisfy a new property while preserving its exiting properties. Such automated assistance for the designer is highly desirable since it significantly decreases the design time by warning the designers about spending time on fixing a program that is not *fixable*.

With this motivation, we present an incremental method for adding UNITY properties to programs. Our incremental approach has the potential to reuse the computations of an existing program while adding new properties to it. Also, we focus on UNITY since it provides (i) a simple and general computational model for a variety of computing systems, and (ii) a proof system for refining programs [1]. We expect to benefit from simplicity and generality of UNITY in automatic design of programs.

The basic UNITY properties from [1] are *unless, stable, invariant, ensures*, and *leads-to*. (We refer the reader to Section 2 for precise definitions.) Of these, *ensures* can be expressed in terms of *leads-to* and *unless*. Hence, we focus on adding *unless, stable, invariant*, and *leads-to* to programs. In particular, we present a sound and complete algorithm for simultaneous addition of a single *leads-to* property and a conjunction of *unless, stable*, and *invariant* properties. The time complexity of our algorithm is polynomial in program state space. However, we present an unexpected result that simultaneous addition of two *leads-to* properties to a program is NP-complete. Based on this result, we find that adding one *leads-to* property is significantly easier than simultaneous addition of two (or more) *leads-to* properties.

Contributions. The contributions of this paper are as follows: (1) We formally define the problem of adding UNITY properties to programs; (2) We present a sound and complete algorithm for automatic addition of a *leads-to* property and a conjunction of *unless, stable*, and *invariant* properties to programs, and (3) We show that simultaneous addition of two *leads-to* properties to a program is NP-complete.

Organization of the Paper. First, we present preliminary concepts in Section 2. In Section 3, we formally define the problem of adding UNITY properties to programs. Then, in Section 4, we present our sound and complete algorithm for adding a *leads-to* property to programs. In Section 5, we present our NP-completeness result. Subsequently, in Section 6, we demonstrate our addition algorithm using a mutual exclusion program. In Section 7, we compare the results of this paper with related work. We discuss the limitations and the applications of our results in Section 8. Finally, we make concluding remarks in Section 9.

2   Preliminaries

In this section, we give formal definitions of programs and properties in UNITY [1]. Programs are defined in terms of their state space and their transitions. UNITY properties are defined in terms of infinite sequences of transitions.

Program.   A program p is of the form $\langle S_p, I_p, \delta_p \rangle$, where S_p is a finite set of states, $I_p \subseteq S_p$ is the set of initial states of p, and $\delta_p \subseteq S_p \times S_p$ is the set of transitions of p.

A state predicate of p is any subset of S_p. A sequence of states, $\sigma = \langle s_0, s_1, \cdots \rangle$ is a computation of p iff (if and only if) the following three conditions are satisfied: (1) $s_0 \in I_p$; (2) if σ is infinite then $\forall j : j > 0 : (s_{j-1}, s_j) \in \delta_p$ holds, and (3) if σ is finite and terminates in state s_f then there does not exist state s such that $(s_f, s) \in \delta_p$, and $\forall j : 0 < j \leq f : (s_{j-1}, s_j) \in \delta_p$ holds. A sequence of states, $\langle s_0, s_1, ..., s_n \rangle$, is a computation prefix of p iff $\forall j : 0 < j \leq n : (s_{j-1}, s_j) \in \delta_p$.

Properties of UNITY Programs.   We reiterate the definition of the UNITY properties from [1]. In the following definitions, P and Q are state predicates.

- *Unless.* An infinite sequence of states $\sigma = \langle s_0, s_1, ... \rangle$ satisfies P *unless* Q iff $\forall i : 0 \leq i : (s_i \in (P \cap \neg Q)) \Rightarrow (s_{i+1} \in (P \cup Q))$. Intuitively, the sequence σ satisfies P *unless* Q iff if P holds in some state of σ then either (1) Q never holds in σ and P is continuously true, or (2) Q eventually becomes true and P holds at least until Q becomes true.
- *Stable.* An infinite sequence of states $\sigma = \langle s_0, s_1, ... \rangle$ satisfies $stable(P)$ iff σ satisfies $(P$ *unless* $false)$. Intuitively, P is stable iff once it becomes true it remains true forever.
- *Invariant.* An infinite sequence of states $\sigma = \langle s_0, s_1, ... \rangle$ satisfies $invariant(P)$ iff $s_0 \in P$ and σ satisfies $stable(P)$. An invariant property always holds.
- *Ensure.* An infinite sequence of states $\sigma = \langle s_0, s_1, ... \rangle$ satisfies P *ensures* Q iff (σ satisfies P *unless* Q) and ($\exists j : 0 \leq j : s_j \in Q$). In other words, there exists a state s_j , where (i) Q eventually becomes true in s_j , and (ii) P remains true everywhere between the first state s_i, $i \leq j$, where P becomes true and s_j.
- *Leads-to* (denoted $\mapsto$). An infinite sequence of states $\sigma = \langle s_0, s_1, ... \rangle$ satisfies $P \mapsto Q$ iff $(\forall i : 0 \leq i : (s_i \in P) \Rightarrow (\exists j : i \leq j : s_j \in Q))$. If P holds in some state $s_i \in \sigma$ then there exists a state $s_j \in \sigma$ where Q holds and $i \leq j$.

Since *ensures* can be expressed as a conjunction of an *unless* property and a *leads-to* property, we do not consider it explicitly in this paper. The properties *unless, stable,* and *invariant* are safety properties, as defined by Alpern and Schneider [2]. These properties can be modeled in terms of a set of *bad* transitions that should never occur in a program computation. For example, $stable(P)$, requires that transitions of the form (s_0, s_1), where $s_0 \in P$ and $s_1 \notin P$ should never occur in any program computation. Hence, for simplicity, in this paper, when dealing with these properties, we assume that they are represented as a set of transitions $\mathcal{B} \subseteq S_p \times S_p$ that must not occur in any computation.

Now, let *spec* be any conjunction of the above properties; i.e., $spec = \mathcal{L}_1 \wedge \cdots \wedge \mathcal{L}_n$, where $\mathcal{L}_i$ belongs to the set of properties *unless, stable, invariant,* and *leads-to* $(1 \le i \le n)$. A sequence of states $\sigma = \langle s_0, s_1, ... \rangle$ satisfies *spec* iff $\forall i : 1 \le i \le n : \sigma$ satisfies $\mathcal{L}_i$. We say that program p satisfies a given UNITY specification, *spec*, iff all computations of p are infinite and every computation of p satisfies *spec*.

Remark. We distinguish between a terminating computation and a deadlocked computation. To model a computation that terminates in state s_f, we include the transition (s_f, s_f) in program p. When a computation c of p reaches s_f, c can be extended to an infinite computation by stuttering at s_f. If there exists a state s_d such that there is no outgoing program transition from s_d then s_d is a deadlocked state and a computation of p that reaches s_d is a deadlocked computation. Such computations cannot be extended to an infinite computation. We want to ensure that such deadlocked computations do not occur while revising a program.

3   Problem Statement

In this section, we formally define the problem of adding UNITY specifications to programs. Given is a program p (with state space S_p, initial states I_p and transitions δ_p) that satisfies a UNITY specification $spec_e$. The goal is to generate a modified version of p, denoted p', in such a way that p' satisfies a UNITY specification $spec_n$, in addition to preserving its existing specification $spec_e$. Moreover, this addition should be done in such a way that one does not need to know the existing specification $spec_e$; during the addition, we only want to reuse the correctness of p with respect to $spec_e$ so that the correctness of p' with respect to $spec_e$ is derived from 'p satisfies $spec_e$'.

Now, we identify constraints on $S_{p'}$, $I_{p'}$ and $\delta_{p'}$. Clearly, in obtaining $S_{p'}$, no new states should be added to S_p; otherwise, there is no guarantee that the correctness of p can be reused to ensure that existing specification will continue to be preserved. Moreover, since S_p denotes the set of all states (not just reachable states) of p, removing states from S_p is not advantageous. Likewise, $I_{p'}$ should not have any states that were not there in I_p. Moreover, since I_p denotes the set of all initial states of p, we should preserve them during the transformation. Finally, likewise, $\delta_{p'}$ should be a subset of δ_p. Note that not all transitions of δ_p may be preserved in p'. However, we must ensure that p' does not deadlock in any reachable state. Based on the definition of the UNITY specification, if

(i) $\delta_{p'} \subseteq \delta_p$, (ii) p' does not deadlock in any reachable state, and (iii) p satisfies $spec_e$, then p' also satisfies $spec_e$. Thus, the problem statement is defined as follows:

The Problem of Adding UNITY Properties
Given a program p, its state space S_p, its set of initial states I_p, and a UNITY specification $spec_n$, identify
$\delta_{p'}$, $S_{p'}$, and $I_{p'}$ such that
    $(C1)$ $S_{p'} = S_p$
    $(C2)$ $I_{p'} = I_p$
    $(C3)$ $\delta_{p'} \subseteq \delta_p$
    $(C4)$ p' satisfies $spec_n$ □

Note that the requirement of deadlock freedom is not explicitly specified in the above problem statement, as it follows from 'p' satisfies $spec_n$'.

4   Adding Single Leads-to and Multiple Safety Properties

In this section, we present a simple solution for the addition problem (defined in Section 3) for the case where the new specification $spec_n$ is a conjunction of a single *leads-to* property and multiple safety properties. We note that the goal of our algorithm is simply to illustrate the feasibility of this solution. Hence, although our algorithm in this section can be modified to reduce complexity further, we have chosen to present a simple (and not so efficient) solution. In Section 8, we give an intuition as to how one can implement our algorithm using counterexamples provided by model checkers.

Given are a program $p = \langle S_p, I_p, \delta_p \rangle$ and a specification $spec_n = \mathcal{B} \wedge \mathcal{L}$, where $\mathcal{B}$ represents the conjunction of a set of safety properties and $\mathcal{L}$ is a $R \mapsto T$ property for state predicates R and T. Our goal is to generate a new program p' that satisfies $spec_n$ and preserves the existing specification. To guarantee that p' satisfies $\mathcal{B}$ (i.e., p' never executes a transition in the set of bad transitions $\mathcal{B}$), we exclude all transitions of p that belong to $\mathcal{B}$ (see Step 1 in Figure 1). To add the *leads-to* property $\mathcal{L} \equiv (R \mapsto T)$ to p, we need to guarantee that any computation of p' that reaches a state in R will eventually reach a state in T. Towards this end, we rank all states s based on the length of the shortest computation prefix of p from s to a state in T. In such ranking, if no state of T is reachable from s then the rank of s will be *infinity*. Also, the rank of states in T is zero.

There exist two obstacles in guaranteeing the reachability from R to T: (1) the deadlock states reachable from R, and (2) cycles reachable from R where the computations of p' may be trapped forever. We may create deadlock states by (i) removing safety-violating transitions (Step 1 in Figure 1), and (ii) making infinity-ranked states unreachable in Step 3.

To deal with the deadlock states, we make them unreachable by removing transitions that reach a deadlock state (Step 4 in Figure 1). Such removal of transitions may introduce new deadlock states that are removed in the *while* loop in Step 4. If the removal of deadlock states culminates in making an initial

Add_UNITY(I_p: state predicate, p: set of transitions, R, T: state predicate, $\mathcal{B}$: safety specification)
{ // S_p is the state space of p.

$$p_1 := p - \{(s_0, s_1) \mid (s_0, s_1) \in \mathcal{B}\}; \tag{1}$$
$$\forall s : s \in S_p : Rank(s) = \text{ the length of the shortest computation prefix of } p_1 \tag{2}$$
$$\text{that starts from } s \text{ and ends in a state in } T;$$
$$//Rank(s) = \infty \text{ means } T \text{ is not reachable from } s.$$
  repeat{
$$p_1 := p_1 - \{(s_0, s_1) \mid (s_1 \in R) \wedge Rank(s_1) = \infty\}; \tag{3}$$
$$\text{while } (\exists s_0 :: (\forall s_1 : s_1 \in S_p : (s_0, s_1) \not\in p_1)) \{ \tag{4}$$
$$\text{If } (s_0 \not\in I_p) \text{ then } p_1 := p_1 - \{(s, s_0) \mid (s, s_0) \in p_1\};$$
$$\text{else} \qquad\qquad \text{declare that the addition is not possible; exit();}$$
$$\}$$
$$\forall s : s \in S_p : Rank(s) = \text{ the length of the shortest computation prefix of } p_1 \tag{5}$$
$$\text{that starts from } s \text{ and ends in a state in } T;$$
$$\} \text{ until } (\forall s : (s \in R) \wedge (s \text{ is reachable in } p_1) : Rank(s) \neq \infty) \tag{6}$$
$$\text{return } p_1 - \{(s_0, s_1) \mid Rank(s_0) < Rank(s_1)\}; \tag{7}$$
}

Fig. 1. Adding one *leads-to* and multiple safety properties

state deadlocked then $(R \mapsto T)$ cannot be added to p. Otherwise, we again rank all states (in Step 5) since we might have removed some deadlock states in T, and as a result, we might have created new infinity-ranked states. We repeat the above steps until no reachable state in R has the rank infinity. At this point (end of repeat-until in Step 6), there is a path from each state in R to a T state. However, there may be cycles that are reachable from a state in R.

To deal with such cycles from R, we remove transitions from low-ranked states to high-ranked states (Step 7 in Figure 1). In particular, if $Rank(s_0) < Rank(s_1)$ then that means there exists a shorter computation prefix from s_0 to T with respect to the computation prefix from s_1 to T. Thus, removing (s_0, s_1) will not make s_0 deadlocked. (Note that in Step 7, transitions of the form (s_0, s_1), where $Rank(s_0) = \infty$ and $Rank(s_1) = \infty$, are not removed. Hence, computations in which neither predicates R and T are reached will not be affected.)

Theorem 4.1. The algorithm Add_UNITY is sound.

Proof. Since Add_UNITY does not add any new states to S_p, we have $S_{p'} = S_p$. Likewise, Add_UNITY does not remove (respectively, introduce) any initial states; we have $I_{p'} = I_p$. The Add_UNITY algorithm only updates δ_p by excluding some transitions from δ_p in Steps 1, 3, 4, and 7. It follows that $\delta_{p'} \subseteq \delta_p$. By construction, Add_UNITY removes all deadlock states in Step 4. Thus, if Add_UNITY generates a program p' in Step 7 then reachability from R to T is guaranteed in p'. Thus, p' meets all the requirements of the addition problem. □

Theorem 4.2. The algorithm Add_UNITY is complete.

Proof. Note that any transition removed in Add_UNITY (in Steps 1, 3, and 4) must be removed in any program that meets the requirements of the addition problem. Hence, when failure is declared (in Step 4), it follows that a solution to the addition problem does not exist. □

Theorem 4.3. The time complexity of Add_UNITY algorithm is polynomial in S_p.

Proof. The proof follows from the polynomial-time complexity of each step of Add_UNITY.   □

In Section 6, we demonstrate our algorithm in the local redesign of a token passing mutual exclusion program. We have also used our algorithm in the local redesign of a readers-writers program in [3].

5 Adding Two *Leads-to* Properties

In this section, we show that the addition of a UNITY specification, which is the conjunction of two *leads-to* properties, to a program is NP-complete. We show this by presenting a reduction from the 3-SAT problem to an instance of the decision problem defined below. The instance and the decision problem for adding two *leads-to* properties are as follows:

Instance. An instance of the addition problem for two *leads-to* properties consists of a program p, its state space S_p, set of initial states I_p, transitions δ_p, and $spec_n = \mathcal{L}_1 \wedge \mathcal{L}_2$, where $\mathcal{L}_1 \equiv P \mapsto Q$ and $\mathcal{L}_2 \equiv R \mapsto T$, and P, Q, R, and T are state predicates.

The Decision Problem
Given is an instance of the addition problem for two *leads-to* properties:
> Does there exist a program p', its state space $S_{p'}$, and its set of initial states $I_{p'}$ such that
> $S_p = S_{p'}$, $I_{p'} = I_p$, $\delta_{p'} \subseteq \delta_p$, and p' satisfies $spec_n = \mathcal{L}_1 \wedge \mathcal{L}_2$?

The 3-SAT problem is as follows: Let $x_1, x_2, ..., x_n$ be propositional variables. Given is a Boolean formula $y = y_1 \wedge y_2 \cdots \wedge y_M$, where each y_j $(1 \leq j \leq M)$ is a disjunction of exactly three literals. Does there exist an assignment of truth values to $x_1, x_2, ..., x_n$ such that y is satisfiable?
  Next, in Subsection 5.1, we present a polynomial-time mapping from 3-SAT to an instance of the decision problem. Then, in Subsection 5.2, we show that the 3-SAT problem is satisfiable iff the answer to the above decision problem is affirmative for the instance introduced in Subsection 5.1.

5.1 Mapping 3-SAT to the Addition of Two *Leads-to* Properties

We now present the mapping of an instance of the 3-SAT problem to an instance of the problem of adding two *leads-to* properties. First, we introduce the state space and the initial states of the instance of the addition problem corresponding to each variable x_i and each disjunction y_j. We also introduce the state predicates P, Q, R, and T that define $spec_n$. Then, we present the transitions of the instance corresponding to each variable x_i and each disjunction y_j.

The State Space, Initial States, and State Predicates $P, Q, R,$ **and** T.
Corresponding to each variable x_i of the given 3-SAT instance, we introduce
six states $P_i, a_i, Q_i, R_i, b_i,$ and T_i, where $1 \leq i \leq n$ (see Figure 2). For each
disjunction y_j, we introduce a state c_j, where $1 \leq j \leq M$, in the state space.
Thus,

- $S_p = \{P_i, a_i, Q_i, R_i, b_i, T_i \mid 1 \leq i \leq n\} \cup \{c_j \mid 1 \leq j \leq M\}$
- $I_p = \{c_j \mid 1 \leq j \leq M\}$
- $P = \{P_i \mid 1 \leq i \leq n\}$, $Q = \{Q_i \mid 1 \leq i \leq n\}$, $R = \{R_i \mid 1 \leq i \leq n\}$, and
  $T = \{T_i \mid 1 \leq i \leq n\}$

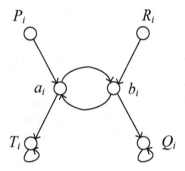

Fig. 2. Mapping of variables in the 3-SAT problem

The Program Transitions. Corresponding to each variable x_i, we include
transitions $(P_i, a_i), (a_i, b_i), (b_i, Q_i), (Q_i, Q_i), (R_i, b_i), (b_i, a_i), (a_i, T_i),$ and (T_i, T_i)
in the set of program transitions δ_p (see Figure 2). Moreover, corresponding to
each disjunction y_j, we include the following transitions:

- If x_i is a literal in y_j then we include the transition (c_j, P_i).
- If $\neg x_i$ is a literal in y_j then we include the transition (c_j, R_i).

5.2   Reduction from the 3-SAT Problem

In this subsection, we show that the given instance of 3-SAT is satisfiable iff
both *leads-to* properties $\mathcal{L}_1 \equiv (P \mapsto Q)$ and $\mathcal{L}_2 \equiv (R \mapsto T)$ can be added to the
problem instance defined in Subsection 5.1.

Part I.   First, we show that if the given instance of the 3-SAT formula is
satisfiable then there exists a solution that meets the requirements of the decision
problem. Since the 3-SAT formula is satisfiable, there exists an assignment of
truth values to variables $x_i, 1 \leq i \leq n$, so that each $y_j, 1 \leq j \leq M$, is *true*. Now,
we identify a program p' that is obtained by adding the *leads-to* properties $\mathcal{L}_1$
and $\mathcal{L}_2$ to program p as follows.

- The state space of p' consists of all the states of p, i.e., $S_{p'} = S_p$.
- The initial states of p' consists of all the initial states of p, i.e., $I_{p'} = I_p$.
- For each variable x_i, if x_i is *true* then we include the transitions (P_i, a_i), (a_i, b_i), (b_i, Q_i), and (Q_i, Q_i).
- For each variable x_i, if x_i is *false* then we include the transitions (R_i, b_i), (b_i, a_i), (a_i, T_i), and (T_i, T_i).
- For each disjunction y_j that contains x_i, we include the transition (c_j, P_i) if x_i is *true*.
- For each disjunction y_j that contains $\neg x_i$, we include the transition (c_j, R_i) if x_i is *false*.

As an illustration, we show the partial structure of p', for the formula $[(x_1 \vee \neg x_2 \vee x_3) \wedge (x_1 \vee x_2 \vee \neg x_4)]$, where $x_1 = true$, $x_2 = false$, $x_3 = false$, and $x_4 = false$ in Figure 3.

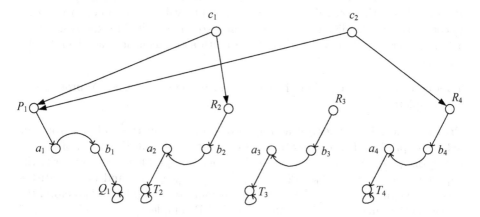

Fig. 3. The partial structure of the revised program

Now, we show that p' meets the requirements of the decision problem.

- The first three constraints of the decision problem are trivially satisfied.
- It is easy to observe that by construction, there are no deadlock states. Hence, for the UNITY specification $spec_e$ if p satisfies $spec_e$ then p' also satisfies $spec_e$. Moreover, if a computation of p' reaches P_i from some initial state (i.e., x_i is *true*) then that computation will eventually reach Q_i and will stay there, since p' does not include the transition (b_i, a_i). Likewise, if a computation of p' reaches R_i from some initial state (i.e., x_i is *false*) then that computation will eventually reach T_i and will stay there, since p' does not include the transition (a_i, b_i). Thus, p' satisfies both $\mathcal{L}_1$ and $\mathcal{L}_2$.

Part II. Next, we show that if there exists a solution to the instance identified in Subsection 5.1, then the given 3-SAT formula is satisfiable. Let p' be the program that is obtained by adding the two *leads-to* properties to program p.

Now, to obtain the solution for 3-SAT, we proceed as follows. If there exists a computation of p' where state P_i is reachable then we assign x_i the truth value *true*. Otherwise, we assign it the truth value *false*.

We now show that the above truth assignment satisfies all disjunctions. Let y_j be any disjunction and let c_j be the corresponding state in p'. Since c_j is an initial state and p' cannot deadlock, there must be some transition from c_j. This transition terminates in either P_i or R_i, for some i. If the transition from c_j terminates in P_i then y_j contains literal x_i and x_i is assigned the truth value *true*. Hence, y_j evaluates to true. If the transition from c_j terminates in R_i then P_i should not be reachable. Otherwise, (i) transitions $(R_i, b_i), (b_i, a_i)$, and (a_i, T_i) must be included to ensure that $R \mapsto T$ is satisfied, and (ii) transitions $(P_i, a_i), (a_i, b_i)$, and (b_i, Q_i) must also be included to guarantee that $P \mapsto Q$ is satisfied. Since the inclusion of all six transitions (P_i, a_i), (a_i, b_i), (b_i, Q_i), (R_i, b_i), (b_i, a_i), and (a_i, T_i) causes violation of $P \mapsto Q$ and $R \mapsto T$, it follows that P_i must not be reached in any computation of p' if R_i is reachable. Thus, if R_i is reachable then x_i will be assigned the truth value *false*. Since in this case y_j contains $\neg x_i$, the disjunction y_j evaluates to *true*. Therefore, the assignment of values considered above is a satisfying truth assignment for the given 3-SAT formula. $\square$

Theorem 5.1. The addition of two *leads-to* properties to UNITY programs is NP-complete.

Proof.   The NP-hardness of adding two *leads-to* properties follows from the reduction presented in this section. Also, given a solution (in terms of p' consisting of $S_{p'}, I_{p'}, \delta_{p'}$) to the instance of the decision problem, one can verify the requirements (1) $S_{p'} = S_p$, (2) $I_{p'} = I_p$, (3) $\delta_{p'} \subseteq \delta_p$, and (4) p' satisfies $spec_n$ in polynomial time. Thus, the membership to NP follows. Therefore, the problem of adding two *leads-to* properties is NP-complete. $\square$

6   Example: Mutual Exclusion

In this section, we illustrate the role of the algorithm Add_UNITY in deciding about local or comprehensive redesign of a token passing mutual exclusion (ME) program. We use Dijkstra's guarded commands (*actions*) [4] as the shorthand for representing the set of program transitions. A guarded command $g \rightarrow st$ captures the transitions $\{(s_0, s_1) :$ the state predicate g is true in s_0, and s_1 is obtained by *atomic* execution of statement st in state s_0 $\}$.

The initial ME program has two competing processes P_1 and P_2. Each process P_j $(j = 0, 1)$ has three Boolean variables n_j, c_j, and t_j, where (i) t_j represents whether or not P_j is trying to enter its critical section (i.e., trying section), (ii) c_j represents whether or not P_j is in its critical section, and (iii) n_j represents whether or not P_j intends to enter its trying section (i.e., non-trying section). The variables of P_j are mutually exclusive; i.e., the condition $(t_j \Rightarrow (\neg n_j \land \neg c_j)) \land (n_j \Rightarrow (\neg t_j \land \neg c_j)) \land (c_j \Rightarrow (\neg n_j \land \neg t_j))$ holds. We denote a state of ME by $\langle s_0, s_1 \rangle$, where s_0 represents the state of P_0 and s_1 represents the state of P_1. Also, we represent the actions of a process j ($j = 0, 1$) as follows:

$$ME1_j: \quad n_j \quad \longrightarrow \quad t_j := true; n_j := false;$$
$$ME2_j: \quad t_j \quad \longrightarrow \quad c_j := true; t_j := false;$$
$$ME3_j: \quad c_j \quad \longrightarrow \quad n_j := true; c_j := false;$$

For simplicity, we illustrate the reachability graph of the initial ME program in Figure 4 that shows all reachable states from the initial state s_{init} , where both processes are in their non-critical sections. We have annotated each transition with the index of the process that executes that transition.

In the initial state of ME, both processes are in their non-trying section (i.e., $n_0 = true$ and $n_1 = true$). The ME program satisfies its safety property that stipulates P_0 and P_1 must not enter the critical section simultaneously (i.e., $Invariant(\neg(c_0 \wedge c_1)))$. Also, the initial ME program only satisfies $c_j \mapsto n_j$. Next, we trace Add_UNITY to add the leads-to property $t_0 \mapsto c_0$ to ME while preserving $c_0 \mapsto n_0$. For reasons of space, we omit the addition of $t_1 \mapsto c_1$ as it is similar to the addition of $t_0 \mapsto c_0$.

Step 1. Since ME already satisfies its safety property, no transitions are removed at the first step of Add_UNITY.

Step 2. The Add_UNITY algorithm ranks all states based on their shortest computation prefix to states where c_0 is *true*. As a result, the rank of $\langle t_0, t_1 \rangle$ becomes 1 and the rank of $\langle t_0, c_1 \rangle$ becomes 2.

Step 3. Since there exist no states with rank ∞, Add_UNITY does not remove any transitions in Step 3.

Step 4. Since the execution of Steps 2 and 3 does not create any deadlock states, Add_UNITY does not modify the program structure in Step 4.

Step 5 and 6. The ranking of the states will not be changed in Step 5. Also, Add_UNITY exits the repeat-until loop since no state where t_0 holds has a rank of ∞.

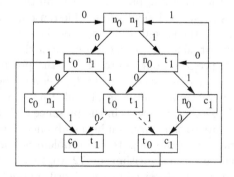

Fig. 4. The reachability graph of program ME

Step 7. Finally, in Step 7, Add_UNITY removes the transition $\langle t_0, t_1 \rangle \to$ $\langle t_0, c_1 \rangle$ since the rank of $\langle t_0, t_1 \rangle$ is 1 and the rank of $\langle t_0, c_1 \rangle$ is 2 (see Figure 4). Likewise, in the addition of $t_1 \mapsto c_1$, the transition $\langle t_0, t_1 \rangle \to \langle c_0, t_1 \rangle$ is removed (see Figure 4).

A similar execution of Add_UNITY for the addition of $t_1 \mapsto c_1$ results in the synthesis of the following ($\oplus$ denotes modulo 2 addition):

$$
\begin{aligned}
ME1'_j : \quad & n_j \wedge \neg t_{(j\oplus 1)} & \longrightarrow \quad & t_j := true; n_j := false; \\
ME2'_j : \quad & t_j \wedge n_{(j\oplus 1)} & \longrightarrow \quad & c_j := true; t_j := false; \\
ME3'_j : \quad & c_j & \longrightarrow \quad & n_j := true; c_j := false;
\end{aligned}
$$

Note that, the above program does not satisfy $n_j \mapsto t_j$. Now, if we use Add_UNITY for the addition of $n_j \mapsto t_j$, while preserving $t_j \mapsto c_j$ and $c_j \mapsto n_j$, then Add_UNITY will declare failure because the initial state will be deadlocked. In the context of this example, the addition of the above properties will fail regardless of the order of their addition. Thus, based on the completeness of Add_UNITY, it follows that the initial program cannot be revised to a program that simultaneously satisfies the above *leads-to* properties. This is an interesting result that enlightens designers to search for other solutions where one adds new variables and computations to the ME program (e.g., Peterson's solution) instead of spending time on modifying the initial ME program.

7   Related Work

In this section, we illustrate how the contributions of this paper differ from existing approaches for program synthesis and verification. Existing synthesis methods in the literature mostly focus on deriving the synchronization skeleton of a program from its specification (expressed in terms of temporal logic expressions or finite-state automata) [5–11], where the synchronization skeleton of a program is an *abstract structure* of the code of the program implementing inter-process synchronization. Although such synthesis methods may have differences with respect to the input specification language and the program model that they synthesize, the general approach is based on the satisfiability proof of the specification. This makes it difficult to provide reuse in the synthesis of programs; i.e., any change in the specification requires the synthesis to be restarted from scratch. By contrast, since the input to our algorithm (cf. Figure 1) is the set of transitions of a program, our approach has the potential to reuse those transitions in incremental synthesis of a revised version of the input program.

The algorithms for automatic addition of fault-tolerance [12–16] add fault-tolerance concerns to existing programs in the presence of faults, and guarantee not to add new behaviors to that program in the absence of faults. The problem of adding fault-tolerance is orthogonal to the problem of adding UNITY properties in that one could use the algorithms of [12–16] to add fault-tolerance concerns to a UNITY program synthesized by the algorithm presented in this paper.

On the other hand, we plan to investigate the addition of UNITY properties to fault-tolerant programs while preserving their fault-tolerance properties.

Run-Time Verification. Runtime verification techniques focus on monitoring the program behavior at runtime with respect to a given specification [17]. Also, such techniques provide a mechanism for ensuring the correctness of program execution after monitoring violations of desired properties [18]. Such approaches mostly focus on the verification of safety properties [19–22] and also provide mechanisms for exception handling and dealing with deadlocks at runtime. By contrast, our focus is on off-line addition of UNITY properties to programs where we ensure that the synthesized program satisfies its existing and newly added properties. Also, to the best of our knowledge, the runtime verification of *leads-to* properties is still an open question.

8   Discussion

In this section, we address some questions raised about the limitations and the applications of the results presented in this paper. We proceed as follows:

Stepwise Application of Add_UNITY. The Add_UNITY algorithm can be used in a stepwise fashion. While such a stepwise use of Add_UNITY to add multiple *leads-to* properties will be sound, it is not complete. This is due to the fact that during the addition of the first *leads-to* property, the transitions removed in the last step (Step 7 in Figure 1) may cause failure in adding the subsequent *leads-to* property. Therefore, this does not contradict the NP-completeness result in Section 5.

Addition of Other UNITY Properties. The Add_UNITY algorithm shows that it is possible to add several safety (*stable, invariant* and *unless*) properties and one *leads-to* property in polynomial time. Since *ensures* is a conjunction of *unless* and *leads-to* properties, this algorithm can be trivially extended to deal with the case where one adds several safety properties and an *ensures* property. Also, one can use Add_UNITY to add the *until* property in Linear Temporal Logic (LTL) [23] to programs as *ensures* is semantically the same as *until* in LTL.

However, in the context of adding multiple *leads-to* properties, there are several open questions. For example, is it possible to combine these *leads-to* properties with other (specific) properties to obtain efficient solutions? To illustrate this, it is straightforward to observe that adding '*invariant*$(\neg P) \wedge (P \mapsto Q) \wedge (R \mapsto T)$' can be added efficiently, as it corresponds to adding '*invariant*$(\neg P) \wedge (R \mapsto T)$'. Moreover, the complexity of adding two *ensures* properties is still an open question. (Note that the complexity of adding two *ensures* properties does not necessarily follow from the results in Section 5; as discussed earlier in this paragraph, combining *leads-to* properties with certain safety properties, does permit polynomial time solutions.)

Implementing Add_UNITY Using Model Checking. The algorithm Add_UNITY can also be implemented with the help of a model checker as follows: For this exposition, consider the case where a program, say p, is specified as a set of transitions, as defined in Section 2. When p is checked with a model checker with respect to a *leads-to* property $(R \mapsto T)$ and found to be incorrect, the counterexamples will be of one of the following two forms: (1) There exists a state s_d such that s_d is reachable in computations of p and s_d is a deadlocked state, or (2) There exists a state, say $s_r \in R$ that is reachable in a program computation and that program computation can be extended to reach a cycle, say $s_0, s_1, \cdots, s_n (= s_0)$ such that T is never satisfied. In the former case, transitions terminating in s_d need to be removed. In the latter case, we need to check if there exists a computation prefix of p that starts in one of the states in the cycle and reaches T. (This case could also be checked with a model checker.) If such a computation prefix does not exist then the state s_r and all its incident transitions should be removed. If such a computation prefix exists and s_j is the last state from the cycle to appear on that path then the transition (s_j, s_{j+1}) in the cycle should be removed. After removing the transitions in this fashion, we can repeat the process with the new program until a solution is found. (We leave it to the reader to verify that this approach is also sound and complete.)

The Choice of the Initial Program. The algorithm Add_UNITY takes the initial program p and adds a set of UNITY properties to p if possible. The choice of the initial program can affect the result of addition in that if we start with an initial program that is maximal, i.e., has the maximal non-determinism, then the chance of a successful addition is higher. This issue is particularly important for a step-wise application of the Add_UNITY algorithm.

9   Conclusion and Future Work

In this paper, we focused on the problem of revising UNITY [1] programs where one adds a conjunction of UNITY properties *unless, stable, invariant, ensures,* and *leads-to* to an existing program to provide new functionalities while preserving the existing functionalities. This is an important problem given the dynamic nature of the requirements of computing systems, where developers need to constantly revise existing programs due to newly-discovered user requirements. In particular, we formally defined the problem of adding UNITY properties to programs. Afterwards, we presented a sound and complete algorithm for such addition where one automatically (i) verifies if it is possible to add a conjunction of UNITY properties to a program and preserve the existing properties, and (ii) adds a conjunction of UNITY properties to a program if such addition is possible.

More importantly, we showed that if one adds a single *leads-to* property and a conjunction of *unless, stable,* and *invariant* properties to a program then the complexity of such addition will be polynomial in program state space. However, in general, we showed a surprising result that simultaneous addition of two *leads-to* properties to a program is NP-complete. Hence, revising UNITY programs would be significantly easier if one added a single *leads-to* property instead of adding more than one *leads-to* property. Since *ensures* can be expressed as the conjunction of an *unless* property and a *leads-to* property, the algorithm presented in this paper for adding a *leads-to* property and a conjunction of *unless, stable,* and *invariant* properties can be used for the addition of *ensures* property as well. Nonetheless, to the best of our knowledge, the complexity of adding two *ensures* properties to UNITY programs is still an open problem.

To extend the results of this paper, we plan to integrate the algorithm presented in this paper with model checking algorithms to provide automated assistance for developers. As a result, if the model checking of a model with respect to a UNITY property fails then our algorithm automatically (i) determines whether or not the model is *fixable*, and (ii) fixes the model if it is fixable.

References

1. K. M. Chandy and J. Misra. *Parallel Program Design: A Foundation.* Addison-Wesley, 1988.
2. B. Alpern and F. B. Schneider. Defining liveness. *Information Processing Letters,* 21:181–185, 1985.
3. Ali Ebnenasir and Sandeep Kulkarni. Automatic addition of liveness. Technical Report MSU-CSE-04-22, Department of Computer Science, Michigan State University, East Lansing, Michigan, June 2004.
4. E. W. Dijkstra. *A Discipline of Programming.* Prentice-Hall, 1990.
5. E.A. Emerson and E.M. Clarke. Using branching time temporal logic to synthesize synchronization skeletons. *Science of Computer Programming,* 2(3):241–266, 1982.
6. Z. Manna and P. Wolper. Synthesis of communicating processes from temporal logic specifications. *ACM Transactions on Programming Languages and Systems,* 6(1):68–93, 1984.
7. A. Pnueli and R. Rosner. On the synthesis of a reactive module. *In Proceedings of the 16th ACM Symposium on Principles of Programming Languages,* pages 179–190, 1989.
8. A. Pnueli and R. Rosner. On the synthesis of an asynchronous reactive module. *In Proceeding of 16th International Colloqium on Automata, Languages, and Programming,* Lec. Notes in Computer Science 372, Springer-Verlag:652–671, 1989.
9. A. Arora, P. C. Attie, and E. A. Emerson. Synthesis of fault-tolerant concurrent programs. *ACM Transactions on Programming Languages and Systems (TOPLAS),* 26(1):125–185, 2004. (A preliminary version of this paper appeared in Proceedings of the 17th ACM Symposium on Principles of Distributed Computing, 1998.).
10. P. Attie. Synthesis of large concurrent programs via pairwise composition. *CONCUR'99: 10th International Conference on Concurrency Theory, Lecture Notes In Computer Science,* 1664:130–145, 1999.
11. P. Attie and A. Emerson. Synthesis of concurrent programs for an atomic read/write model of computation. *ACM TOPLAS,* 23(2):187–242, March 2001. (A preliminary version of this paper appeared in PODC96.).
12. S. S. Kulkarni and A. Arora. Automating the addition of fault-tolerance. *Proceedings of the 6th International Symposium of Formal Techniques in Real-Time and Fault-Tolerant Systems,* pages 82–93, 2000.
13. S. S. Kulkarni, A. Arora, and A. Chippada. Polynomial time synthesis of Byzantine agreement. *Symposium on Reliable Distributed Systems,* pages 130–139, 2001.

14. S. S. Kulkarni and A. Ebnenasir. The complexity of adding failsafe fault-tolerance. *Proceedings of the 22nd International Conference on Distributed Computing Systems*, pages 337–344, 2002.

15. S. S. Kulkarni and A. Ebnenasir. Enhancing the fault-tolerance of nonmasking programs. *Proceedings of the 23rd International Conference on Distributed Computing Systems*, pages 441–449, 2003.

16. S. S. Kulkarni and A. Ebnenasir. Automated synthesis of multitolerance. *In Proceedings of the International Conference on Dependable Systems and Networks, Palazzo dei Congressi, Florence, Italy*, pages 209 – 218, June 28 - July 1 2004.

17. K. Havelund and G. Rosu. Runtime verification. *Formal Methods in System Design. Special issue dedicated to RV'01*, 24(2), 2004.

18. F. Chen, M. D'Amorim, and G. Rosu. A formal monitoring-based framework for software development and analysis. *Sixth International Conference on Formal Engineering Methods (ICFEM)*, pages 357–372, November 2004.

19. Bernd Fisher, Johann Schumann, and Mike Whalen. Synthesizing certified code. *Proceedings of the International Symposium of Formal Methods Europe (FME'02), Lecture Notes In Computer Science*, 2391:431–450, 2002.

20. Ewen Denney, Bernd Fischer, and Johann Schumann. Adding assurance to automatically generated code. *In Proceedings the 8th IEEE International Symposium on High Assurance Systems Engineering (HASE 2004)*, pages 297–299, March 2004.

21. Klaus Havelund and Grigore Rosu. Synthesizing monitors for safety properties. *In Tools and Algorithms for Construction and Analysis of Systems (TACAS'02), volume 2280 of Lecture Notes in Computer Science*, pages 342–356, October 2002.

22. K. Sen, G. Rosu, and G. Agha. Runtime safety analysis of multithreaded programs. *In ACM SIGSOFT Conference on the Foundations of Software Engineering /European Software Engineering Conference, Helsinki, Finland*, pages 337–346, 2003.

23. E.A. Emerson. *Handbook of Theoretical Computer Science: Chapter 16, Temporal and Modal Logic.* Elsevier Science Publishers B. V., 1990.

The Partitioned, Static-Priority Scheduling of Sporadic Real-Time Tasks with Constrained Deadlines on Multiprocessor Platforms*

Nathan Fisher and Sanjoy Baruah

Department of Computer Science, The University of North Carolina at Chapel Hill
{fishern, baruah}@cs.unc.edu

Abstract. We consider the partitioned scheduling of sporadic, hard-real-time tasks on a multiprocessor platform with static-priority scheduling policies. Most previous work on the static-priority scheduling of sporadic tasks upon multiprocessors has assumed implicit deadlines (i.e. a task's relative deadline is equal to its period). We relax the equality constraint on a task's deadline and consider task systems with constrained deadlines (i.e. relative deadlines are at most periods). In particular, we consider the *first-fit decreasing* partitioning algorithm. Since the partitioning problem is easily seen to be NP-hard in the strong sense, this algorithm is unlikely to be optimal. We quantitatively characterize the partitioning algorithm's worst-case performance in terms of *resource augmentation*.

1 Introduction

Over the years, the sporadic task model [23] has proven remarkably useful for the modelling of recurring processes in hard-real-time systems where the release times of jobs are not known *a priori*. In this model, a *sporadic task* $\tau_i = (e_i, d_i, p_i)$ is characterized by a *worst-case execution requirement* e_i, a *(relative) deadline* d_i, and a *minimum inter-arrival separation* p_i, which is, for historical reasons, also referred to as the *period* of the task. Such a sporadic task generates a potentially infinite sequence of jobs, with successive job-arrivals separated by at least p_i time units. Each job has a worst-case execution requirement equal to e_i and a deadline that occurs d_i time units after its arrival time. A *sporadic task system* is comprised of several such sporadic tasks. Let τ denote a system of sporadic tasks: $\tau = \{\tau_1, \tau_2, \ldots \tau_n\}$, with $\tau_i = (e_i, d_i, p_i)$ for all i, $1 \leq i \leq n$.

A sporadic task system is said to be *feasible* upon a specified platform if it is possible to schedule the system on the platform such that all jobs of all tasks will meet all deadlines, under all permissible (also called *legal*) combinations of job-arrival sequences by the different tasks comprising the system. The feasibility-analysis of sporadic task systems on preemptive *uni*processors has been extensively studied. It is known (see, e.g. [9]) that a sporadic task system is feasible on a preemptive uniprocessor if and only if all deadlines can be

---

* Supported in part by the National Science Foundation (Grant Nos. ITR-0082866, CCR-0204312, and CCR-0309825).

J.H. Anderson, G. Prencipe, and R. Wattenhofer (Eds.): OPODIS 2005, LNCS 3974, pp. 291–305, 2006.

met when each task in the system has a job arrive at the same time-instant, and subsequent jobs arrive as rapidly as legal (such a combination of job-arrival sequences is sometimes referred to as a *synchronous arrival sequence* for the sporadic task system).

Feasibility of a sporadic task system under static-priority scheduling has a more restrictive definition. In static-priority systems, each task is assigned a distinct priority, and all jobs of a task execute at the task's priority. A task system is said to be feasible *with respect to a static-priority scheduling algorithm* if the resulting priority assignment results in all deadlines being met under all legal combinations of job-arrival sequences. For *constrained-deadline systems* (i.e. each task has $d_i \leq p_i$), a sporadic system is feasible on a preemptive uniprocessor if and only if it can be scheduled according to the Deadline-Monotonic algorithm (DM) [19]; DM assigns priority to task according to on the inverse of its relative deadline. Several exact algorithms for feasibility-analysis of static-priority task systems (both unconstrained- and constrained-deadline) upon uniprocessor platforms have been developed [16,1,17].

On multiprocessor systems, two alternative paradigms for scheduling collections of sporadic tasks have been considered: *partitioned* and *global* scheduling. In the partitioned approach, the tasks are statically partitioned among the processors, i.e., each task is assigned to a processor and is always executed on it. Leung and Whitehead [19] showed that determining the feasibility of a task system under the partitioned paradigm is NP-hard. Under global scheduling, it is permitted that a job that has previously been preempted on one processor can resume execution at a later point in time upon a different processor, at no additional cost (however, each job may be executing on at most one processor at each instant in time).

Most prior theoretical research on multiprocessor scheduling of collections of sporadic tasks has assumed that *all tasks have their deadlines equal to their period parameters* (i.e., $d_i = p_i$ for all tasks τ_i) — such sporadic systems are sometimes referred to in the literature as **implicit-deadline** systems[1]. Oh [25] gives a performance bound on the *first-fit decreasing* heuristic using exact feasibility tests for deadline-monotonic scheduling. A significant portion of prior research has focused on deriving partitioning algorithms based on *utilization bounds*. A utilization bound represents the highest utilization in which any task system possessing a utilization at most the bound is guaranteed to be feasible on the multiprocessor system. Oh and Baker [24] derive a sufficient utilization test for feasibility of a task system that is partitioned scheduled using DM algorithm and assuming an implicit-deadline task system. Burchard, et al. [12] present utilization conditions for partitioned DM based on tightened uniprocessor utilization bounds derived from Liu and Layland [20].

The research described in this report is part of a larger project that is aimed at obtaining a better understanding of the multiprocessor scheduling of *arbi-*

---

[1] Notable and important exceptions are the recent work of Baker [4,5,6,7], Baruah and Fisher [8], and Bertogna et al. [10] which consider systems of sporadic tasks with $d_i \neq p_i$.

trary sporadic task systems – i.e., systems comprised of tasks that do not satisfy the "$d_i = p_i$" constraint. We are motivated to perform this research for two major reasons. First, sporadic task systems that do not necessarily satisfy the implicit-deadline constraint often arise in practice in the modelling of real-time application systems, and it therefore behooves us to have a better understanding of the behavior of such systems. Second, we observe that in the case of *uni*processor real-time scheduling, moving from implicit-deadline systems (the initial work of Liu and Layland [20]) to arbitrary systems (as represented in, e.g. [23, 18, 19, 17, 2] etc.[2], had a major impact in the maturity and development of the field of uniprocessor real-time systems; we are hopeful that progress in better understanding the multiprocessor scheduling of arbitrary sporadic task systems will result in a similar improvement in our ability to build and analyze multiprocessor real-time application systems.

Organization. In this paper, we report our findings concerning the preemptive multiprocessor scheduling of constrained-deadline sporadic real-time systems under the partitioned paradigm. The remainder of the paper is organized as follows. In Section 2, we formally specify the task model, and define the *request-bound function* and *demand-bound function* as characterizations of the maximum amount of execution time that has been requested by a task over a time interval of a given length. In Section 3, we position our finds within a larger context of multiprocessor real-time scheduling theory, and compare and contrast our results with related research. In Section 4, we describe an exact feasibility test for *uni*processor static-priority scheduling. In Section 5, we describe the *first-fit decreasing* algorithm for the partitioning of sporadic tasks upon a multiprocessor system. In Section 6, we theoretically evaluate the conditions under which first-fit decreasing is guaranteed to be able to successfully partition a task system on a multiprocessor platform. In Section 7, we state some future directions of our research.

2   Task/Machine Model and Definitions

In the sporadic task model, a *sporadic task* $\tau_i = (e_i, d_i, p_i)$ is characterized by a *worst-case execution requirement* e_i, a *(relative) deadline* d_i, and a *minimum inter-arrival separation* p_i (historically, referred to as the *period* of a task). The ratio $u_i \stackrel{\text{def}}{=} e_i/p_i$ of sporadic task τ_i is often referred to as the *utilization* of τ_i.

We will assume that we have a multiprocessor platform comprised of m identical processors $\pi_1, \pi_2, \ldots, \pi_m$, on which we are to schedule a system τ of n sporadic tasks: $\tau = \{\tau_1, \tau_2, \ldots \tau_n\}$, with $\tau_i = (e_i, d_i, p_i)$ for all i, $1 \leq i \leq n$. Depending upon what additional restrictions are placed on the relationship between the values of d_i and p_i for each sporadic task $\tau_i \in \tau$, we may define special subclasses of sporadic task systems:

---

[2] This is merely a small sample, and by no means an exhaustive list of citations of important and influential papers.

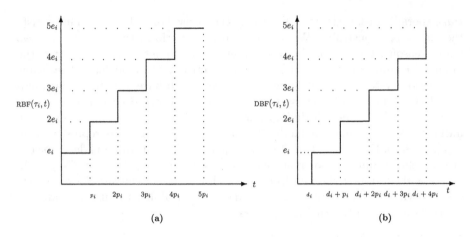

Fig. 1. (a) denotes a plot of RBF(τ_i, t) as a function of t. (b) denotes a plot of DBF(τ_i, t) as a function of t.

- Sporadic task systems in which each task satisfies the additional constraint that $d_i = p_i$ for each task τ_i are referred to as **implicit-deadline** sporadic tasks systems.
- Sporadic task systems in which each task satisfies the additional constraint that $d_i \leq p_i$ for each task τ_i are often referred to as **constrained** sporadic tasks systems.

Where necessary, the term **arbitrary** sporadic task system will be used to refer to task systems which do not satisfy the above constraints. The results we obtain in this work is for constrained task systems. Therefore, we will assume that a given task system, τ, is constrained, unless otherwise specified.

2.1   The Request-Bound Function

For any sporadic task τ_i and any real number $t \geq 0$, the *request-bound function* RBF(τ_i, t) is the largest cumulative execution requirement of all jobs that can be generated by τ_i to have their arrival times within a contiguous interval of length t. Every time a task τ_i releases a job, e_i additional units of processor time are requested. The following function provides an upper bound on the total execution time requested by task τ_i at time t (i.e. the scenario where a task releases jobs as soon as legally possible):

$$\text{RBF}(\tau_i, t) \stackrel{\text{def}}{=} \left\lceil \frac{t}{p_i} \right\rceil e_i. \tag{1}$$

Figure 1a shows an example of a RBF. Notice that the "step" function, RBF(τ_i, t) increases by e_i units every p_i time units.

To determine the response-time for the first job of task τ_i on a preemptive uniprocessor, we must consider execution requests of τ_i and all jobs of tasks which may preempt τ_i. We define the following *cumulative request-bound function* based on RBF. Let $\mathbf{T}_{H_i}$ be the set of tasks with priority greater than τ_i. Then, the cumulative request-bound function is defined as:

$$W_i(t) \overset{\text{def}}{=} e_i + \sum_{\tau_j \in \mathbf{T}_{H_i}} \text{RBF}(\tau_j, t). \tag{2}$$

The cumulative request-bound function $W_i(t)$ is simply the total execution requests of all tasks of higher priority than τ_i over the interval $[0, t)$, and the execution request of one job of τ_i.

2.2 The Demand-Bound Function

For any sporadic task τ_i and any real number $t \geq 0$, the *demand-bound function* $\text{DBF}(\tau_i, t)$ is the largest cumulative execution requirement of all jobs that can be generated by τ_i to have both their arrival times *and their deadlines* within a contiguous interval of length t (see Figure 1b for a visual example). It has been shown [9] that the cumulative execution requirement of jobs of τ_i over an interval $[t_o, t_o + t)$ is maximized if one job arrives at the start of the interval – i.e., at time-instant t_o – and subsequent jobs arrive as rapidly as permitted — i.e., at instants $t_o + p_i$, $t_o + 2p_i$, $t_o + 3p_i$, ... Equation (3) below follows directly [9]:

$$\text{DBF}(\tau_i, t) \overset{\text{def}}{=} \max \left(0, \left(\left\lfloor \frac{t - d_i}{p_i} \right\rfloor + 1 \right) \times e_i \right). \tag{3}$$

2.3 Relationship Between RBF and DBF

For all task systems, $\text{RBF}(\tau_i, t)$ exceeds or equals $\text{DBF}(\tau_i, t)$ for all $t > 0$. In a constrained task system τ, an important property regarding the ratio between RBF and DBF holds. For each task $\tau_i \in \tau$, the ratio between the RBF and DBF, for all $t \geq d_i$, is bounded by two. The following lemma formally states this observation:

Lemma 1. *If $d_i \leq p_i$, then for all $t \in [d_i, \infty)$, $\text{RBF}(\tau_i, t) \leq 2 \cdot \text{DBF}(\tau_i, t)$.*

Proof: Recall that $d_i \leq p_i$; thus, $\frac{d_i}{p_i} \leq 1$. So, for $t \geq d_i$:

$$\left\lceil \frac{t}{p_i} \right\rceil - \left\lfloor \frac{t - d_i}{p_i} \right\rfloor \leq \left\lceil \frac{t}{p_i} \right\rceil - \left\lfloor \frac{t}{p_i} \right\rfloor + 1 \leq 2. \tag{4}$$

Multiplying both sides of Equation 4 by e_i, we get:

$$\left\lceil \frac{t}{p_i} \right\rceil e_i - \left\lfloor \frac{t - d_i}{p_i} \right\rfloor e_i \leq 2 e_i$$

$$\Rightarrow \left\lceil \frac{t}{p_i} \right\rceil e_i \qquad \leq \left(\left\lfloor \frac{t - d_i}{p_i} \right\rfloor + 1 \right) e_i + e_i$$

$$\Rightarrow \text{RBF}(\tau_i, t) \qquad \leq \text{DBF}(\tau_i, t) + e_i \quad \text{(by definition of RBF and DBF)}$$

$$\Rightarrow \text{RBF}(\tau_i, t) \qquad \leq 2 \cdot \text{DBF}(\tau_i, t).$$

The last step follows because for $t \geq d_i$, $\text{DBF}(\tau_i, t) \geq e_i$. □

Lemma 1 will be useful in Section 6 for deriving quantitative results for the first-fit decreasing partitioning algorithm.

3   Context and Related Work

Given the specifications of a multiprocessor sporadic task system, **feasibility analysis** is the process of determining whether it is possible for the system to meet all timing constraints under all legal combinations of job arrivals. For **implicit-deadline** systems, partitioned feasibility-analysis can be transformed to a bin-packing problem [14] and shown to be NP-hard in the strong sense; sufficient feasibility tests for various bin-packing heuristics have recently been obtained [22, 21]. The **constrained** and **arbitrary** task models are generalizations of the implicit-deadline model; therefore, the intractability result (feasibility analysis being NP-hard in the strong sense) continues to hold. To our knowledge, there have been no prior non-trivial positive theoretical results (other than [8]) concerning partitioned feasibility analysis of constrained and arbitrary sporadic task systems — "trivial" results include the obvious ones that τ is feasible on m processors if **(i)** it is feasible on a single processor; or **(ii)** the system obtained by replacing each task τ_i by a task $\tau_i' = (e_i, \min(d_i, p_i), \min(d_i, p_i))$ is deemed feasible using the heuristics presented in [22, 21, 24].

While feasibility analysis is a very interesting and important question from a theoretical perspective, the following question is more relevant to the system designer: *Given the specifications of a multiprocessor sporadic task system and a scheduling algorithm that will be used to schedule the system during run-time, how do we determine whether the system will meet all its deadlines when scheduled using this scheduling algorithm?* More formally, for any scheduling algorithm A, a real-time system is said to be A-**schedulable** if the system meets all its deadlines during run-time when scheduled using algorithm A. (Note that, at least for the designer of <u>hard</u> real-time systems, schedulability analysis must be performed beforehand during the design of the system, and prior to run-time.)

The technique of **resource augmentation** [15, 26] is sometimes used to relate the concepts of feasibility and A-schedulability, for specific algorithms A. The technique is as follows: given that a system is known to be feasible upon a particular platform, can we guarantee that algorithm A will always successfully schedule the system if we *augment* the platform in some particular, quantifiable, way (e.g., by increasing the speed, or the number, of processors available to A as compared to the platform on which the system was shown to be feasible)?

In prior work [8], we developed a partitioning algorithm for constrained and arbitrary task systems using dynamic-priority scheduling policies, and analyzed its performance from the perspective of resource augmentation. Our results, in this paper, are with respect to *partitioned* static-priority scheduling of sporadic, *constrained* task systems. We will derive the following resource-augmentation bound from these results (see Corollary 2):

> <u>If</u> a system of sporadic tasks is feasible under the global paradigm (and consequently, under the partitioned paradigm as well) on m identical processors, <u>then</u> this system of sporadic tasks is partitioned by the first-fit decreasing algorithm on m identical processors in which the individual processors are $(3 - \frac{1}{m})$ times as fast as in the original system, such that each partition is uniprocessor DM-schedulable.

4   Uniprocessor Exact-Feasibility Test

In this section, we present uniprocessor exact-feasibility tests for a sporadic task set, τ, in a static-priority system. We will use these tests as the basis for the partitioning algorithm defined in Section 5 and the sufficient feasibility conditions developed in Section 6.

For static-priority task systems with relative deadlines bounded by periods, Liu and Layland [20] showed that the *worst-case* response time for a job of task τ_i occurs when all tasks of priority greater than τ_i release a job simultaneously with τ_i under the synchronous arrival sequence. In a sporadic task system with constrained deadlines, it is necessary and sufficient to only check the worst-case response time of the first job of each task. If the worst-case response time of the first job of task τ_i is at most its relative deadline, then τ_i is schedulable; else, it is not schedulable. A task system τ is feasible on a uniprocessor *if and only if* the first job of each task τ_i has a worst-case response time at most d_i.

Audsley *et al.* [3] presented an exact feasibility test for task τ_i using DM: a task always meets all deadlines on a preemptive uniprocessor if and only if there exists a fixed point, t, of $W_i(t)$ such that t occurs before τ_i's deadline . The following theorem restates their test:

Theorem 1 (from [3]). *In a constrained sporadic task system, task τ_i always meets all deadlines using* DM *on a preemptive uniprocessor if and only if* $\exists t \in (0, d_i]$ *such that* $W_i(t) \leq t$. □

5   A Partitioning Algorithm

Given sporadic task system τ comprised of n tasks $\tau_1, \tau_2, \ldots \tau_n$, and a platform comprised of m unit-capacity processors $\pi_1, \pi_2, \ldots, \pi_m$, we now describe an algorithm for partitioning the tasks in τ among the m processors. With no loss of generality, let us assume that *tasks are indexed according to non-decreasing order of their relative deadline parameter* (i.e., $d_i \leq d_{i+1}$ for all i, $1 \leq i < n$). The algorithm considers the tasks in the order $\tau_1, \tau_2, \ldots$. Suppose that tasks τ_1, $\tau_2, \ldots, \tau_{i-1}$ have all been successfully allocated among the m processors, and we are now attempting to allocate task τ_i to a processor. The algorithm for doing this is a variant of the *First-Fit Decreasing* [13, 25] algorithm for bin-packing, and is as follows (see Figure 2 for a pseudo-code representation of FFD-DM). For any processor π_ℓ, let $\tau(\pi_\ell)$ denote the tasks from among $\tau_1, \ldots, \tau_{i-1}$ that have already been allocated to processor π_ℓ. Considering the processors $\pi_1, \pi_2, \ldots, \pi_m$, in order, we will assign task τ_i to the first processor π_ℓ, $1 \leq \ell \leq m$, that satisfies the following condition:

$$\exists t \in (0, d_i] :: W_{i,\pi_\ell}(t) \leq t, \tag{5}$$

where

$$W_{i,\pi_\ell}(t) \stackrel{\text{def}}{=} e_i + \sum_{\tau_j \in \mathbf{T}_{H_i} \cap \tau(\pi_\ell)} \text{RBF}(\tau_j, t). \tag{6}$$

FFD-DM(τ, m)

> ▷ The collection of sporadic tasks $\tau = \{\tau_1, \ldots, \tau_n\}$ is to be partitioned on
> m identical, unit-capacity processors denoted $\pi_1, \pi_2, \ldots, \pi_m$. (Tasks are
> indexed according to non-decreasing value of relative deadline parame-
> ter: $d_i \leq d_{i+1}$ for all i.) $\tau(\pi_\ell)$ denotes the tasks assigned to processor π_ℓ;
> initially, $\tau(\pi_\ell) \leftarrow \varnothing$ for all ℓ.

```
1    for i ← 1 to n
     ▷ i ranges over the tasks, which are indexed by non-decreasing value of
     the deadline parameter
2         for ℓ ← 1 to m
          ▷ ℓ ranges over the processors, considered in order
3              if τᵢ satisfies Condition 5 on processor πℓ then
               ▷ assign τᵢ to πℓ; proceed to next task
4                   τ(πℓ) ← τ(πℓ) ⋃ {τᵢ}
5                   goto line 7
6         end (of inner for loop)
7         if (ℓ > m) return PARTITIONING FAILED
8    end (of outer for loop)
9    return PARTITIONING SUCCEEDED
```

Fig. 2. Pseudo-code for partitioning algorithm

If no such π_ℓ exists, then we declare failure: we are unable to conclude that sporadic task system τ is feasible upon the m-processor platform.

The following lemma asserts that, in assigning a task τ_i to a processor π_ℓ, the partitioning algorithm does not adversely affect the feasibility of the tasks assigned earlier to each processor.

Lemma 2. *If the tasks previously assigned to each processor were* DM-*feasible on that processor and the algorithm above assigns τ_i to processor π_ℓ (according to Condition 5), then the tasks assigned to each processor (including processor π_ℓ) remain feasible on that processor.*

Proof: Observe that the feasibility of processors other than processor π_ℓ is not affected by the assignment of task τ_i to processor π_ℓ. It remains to demonstrate that, if the tasks assigned to π_ℓ were feasible on π_ℓ prior to the assignment of τ_i and Condition 5 is satisfied, then the tasks on π_ℓ remain feasible after adding τ_i.

Observe that the following conditions held prior to adding τ_i to processor π_ℓ (due to Condition 5 of partitioning algorithm):

$$\forall \tau_j \in \mathbf{T}_{H_i} \cap \tau(\pi_\ell) : (\exists t \in (0, d_j] :: W_{j,\pi_\ell}(t) \leq t) . \tag{7}$$

In a static-priority, uniprocessor system adding a lower-priority task τ_i does not affect the $W_{j,\pi_\ell}(t)$ function for all $\tau_j \in \mathbf{T}_{H_i} \cap \tau(\pi_\ell)$. Therefore, Condition 7 continues to hold after the assignment of τ_i to processor π_ℓ. By Theorem 1, all tasks τ_j previously assigned to processor π_ℓ remain feasible.   □

The correctness of the partitioning algorithm follows, by repeated applications of Lemma 2:

Theorem 2. *If the* FFD-DM *partitioning algorithm returns* PARTITIONING SUC-CEEDED *on constrained task system* τ, *then the resulting partitioning is* DM-*feasible.*

Proof Sketch: Observe that the algorithm returns PARTITIONING SUCCEEDED if and only if it has successfully assigned each task in τ to some processor.

Prior to the assignment of task τ_i, each processor is trivially DM-feasible. It follows from Lemma 2 that all processors remain DM-feasible after each task assignment as well. Hence, all processors are DM-feasible once all tasks in τ have been assigned.   □

5.1   Run-Time Complexity

It may appear that a potentially infinite number of values of t must be checked in order to ensure that Equation 5 is satisfied. However, Lehoczky, et al [16] showed that it suffices to check only the values in the set,

$$S_{i,\pi_\ell} \stackrel{\text{def}}{=} \left\{ t = bp_j : \tau_j \in \tau(\pi_\ell) \cap \mathbf{T}_{H_i}, b = 1, \ldots, \left\lfloor \frac{d_i}{p_j} \right\rfloor \right\} \tag{8}$$

to determine whether τ_i fits on π_ℓ. We may have to check all m processors to determine whether τ_i "fits" on the multiprocessor platform. Thus, in the worst-case, we need to check all the points in

$$S_i \stackrel{\text{def}}{=} S_{i,\pi_1} \cup \ldots \cup S_{i,\pi_m} = \left\{ t = bp_j : j = 1, \ldots, i; b = 1, \ldots, \left\lfloor \frac{d_i}{p_j} \right\rfloor \right\}. \tag{9}$$

The number of elements in S_i is $\mathcal{O}(i \left\lfloor \frac{d_i}{p_1} \right\rfloor)$. Therefore, to check Equation 5 for a task τ_i requires $\mathcal{O}(i \left\lfloor \frac{d_i}{p_1} \right\rfloor + m)$. The time complexity for testing the feasibility of the entire task set τ is $\mathcal{O}(n^2 \left\lfloor \frac{d_n}{p_1} \right\rfloor)$ under the reasonable assumption that $m \leq n$. Since the time complexity of the (exact-test-based) partitioning algorithm depends upon the period and relative deadline parameters of τ, the algorithm runs in *pseudo-polynomial* time. The run-time of determining whether Equation 5 is satisfied can be further reduced by considering the tunable feasibility test of Bini and Buttazzo [11].

6   Evaluation

As stated in Section 1, the first-fit decreasing partitioning algorithm represents a sufficient, rather than exact, test for feasibility — it is possible that there are systems that are feasible under the partitioned paradigm but which will be incorrectly flagged as "infeasible" by FFD-DM. Indeed, this is to be expected since a simpler problem – partitioning collections of sporadic tasks that all have their deadline parameters equal to their period parameters – is known to be NP-hard in the strong sense while the FFD-DM algorithm runs in pseudo-polynomial time. In this section, we offer a quantitative evaluation of the efficacy the algorithm. Specifically, we derive some properties (Theorem 3 and Corollary 2) of the FFD-DM partitioning algorithm, which characterize its performance. We would like to stress that *these properties are not intended to be used as feasibility tests to determine whether* FFD-DM *would successfully schedule a given sporadic task system.* Rather, these properties are intended to provide a quantitative measure of how effective FFD-DM partitioning is *vis a vis* the performance of an optimal scheduler. For an empirical evaluation of the FFD-DM algorithm considered in this paper, we refer the reader to [7].

For given task system $\tau = \{\tau_1, \ldots, \tau_n\}$, let us define the following notation:

$$\delta_{\max}(\tau) \stackrel{\text{def}}{=} \max_{i=1}^{n} (e_i/d_i) , \tag{10}$$

$$\delta_{\text{sum}}(\tau) \stackrel{\text{def}}{=} \max_{t>0} \left(\frac{\sum_{j=1}^{n} \text{DBF}(\tau_j, t)}{t} \right) . \tag{11}$$

Lemma 3. *If task system τ is feasible (under either the partitioned or the global paradigm) on an identical multiprocessor platform comprised of m_o processors of computing capacity ξ each, it must be the case that*

$$\xi \geq \delta_{\max}(\tau) ,$$

and

$$m_o \cdot \xi \geq \delta_{\text{sum}}(\tau) .$$

Proof: Observe that each job of each task of τ can receive at most $\xi \cdot d_i$ units of execution by its deadline; hence, we must have $e_i \leq \xi \cdot d_i \equiv \lambda_i \leq \xi$. Taken over all tasks in τ, this observation yields the first condition.

The requirement that $m_o \xi \geq \delta_{\text{sum}}(\tau)$ is obtained by considering a sequence of job arrivals for τ that defines $\delta_{\text{sum}}(\tau)$; i.e., a sequence of job arrivals over an interval $[0, t_o)$ such that $\frac{\sum_{j=1}^{n} \text{DBF}(\tau_j, t_o)}{t_o} = \delta_{\text{sum}}(\tau)$. The total amount of execution that all these jobs may receive over $[0, t_o)$ is equal to $m_o \cdot \xi \cdot t_o$; hence, $\delta_{\text{sum}}(\tau) \leq m_o \cdot \xi$. □

Lemma 3 above specifies necessary conditions for the FFD-DM algorithm to successfully partition a sporadic task system; Theorem 3 below specifies a *sufficient* condition. But first, a technical lemma that will be used in the proof of Theorem 3.

Lemma 4. *Suppose that the* FFD-DM *partitioning algorithm is attempting to schedule a constrained sporadic task system τ on a platform comprised of unit-capacity processors.*

If $\delta_{\text{sum}}(\tau) \leq \frac{1}{2}$, then Equation 5 is always satisfied.

Proof: Observe that $\delta_{\text{sum}}(\tau) \leq \frac{1}{2}$ implies that $\sum_{\tau_j \in \tau} \text{DBF}(\tau_j, t_o) \leq \frac{t_o}{2}$ for all $t_o \geq 0$. For any task $\tau_i \in \tau$, $\sum_{j=1}^{i} \text{DBF}(\tau_j, t_o) \leq \frac{t_o}{2}$. By Lemma 1, this in turn implies that $\sum_{j=1}^{i} \text{RBF}(\tau_j, t_o) \leq t_o$ for all $t_o \geq d_i$; notice that $\text{RBF}(\tau_i, d_i) \geq e_i$.

Thus, for all $\tau_i \in \tau$, $\sum_{j=1}^{i-1} \text{RBF}(\tau_j, d_i) + e_i \leq d_i$. This implies for any processor π_ℓ:

$$\exists t_o \in (0, d_i] :: W_{i,\pi_\ell}(t_o) \leq t_o.$$

Therefore, Equation 5 is satisfied. $\qquad\square$

Corollary 1. *Any constrained sporadic task system τ satisfying ($\delta_{\text{sum}}(\tau) \leq \frac{1}{2}$) is successfully partitioned on any number of processors ≥ 1.*

Thus, any sporadic task system satisfying $\delta_{\text{sum}}(\tau) \leq \frac{1}{2}$ is successfully scheduled by the FFD-DM. We now describe, in Theorem 3, what happens when this condition is not satisfied.

Theorem 3. *Any <u>constrained</u> sporadic task system τ is successfully scheduled by FFD-DM on m unit-capacity processors, for any*

$$m \geq \frac{2\delta_{\text{sum}}(\tau) - \delta_{\text{max}}(\tau)}{1 - \delta_{\text{max}}(\tau)}. \tag{12}$$

Proof: The proof is by contradiction. Assume that m satisfies the antecedent of the theorem, but cannot schedule τ on m processors by FFD-DM. Then there exists a task τ_i which does not fit on any processor according Equation 5. It must be the case (by Theorem 1) that each such processor π_ℓ satisfies

$$\begin{aligned} W_{i,\pi_\ell}(d_i) &> d_i \\ \Rightarrow \sum_{\tau_j \in \tau(\pi_\ell)} \text{RBF}(\tau_j, d_i) + e_i &> d_i \\ \Rightarrow \sum_{\tau_j \in \tau(\pi_\ell)} 2 \cdot \text{DBF}(\tau_j, d_i) &> d_i - e_i \text{ (according to Lemma 1).} \end{aligned}$$

Observe that $\text{DBF}(\tau_i, d_i) = e_i$ and $\text{DBF}(\tau_j, d_i) = 0$ for all $j > i$. Summing over all m such processors and noting that the tasks on these processors is a subset of the tasks in τ, we obtain

$$2 \sum_{j=1}^{n} \text{DBF}(\tau_j, d_i) > m(d_i - e_i) + e_i$$

$$\Rightarrow \frac{\sum_{j=1}^{n} \text{DBF}(\tau_j, d_i)}{d_i} > \frac{m}{2}\left(1 - \frac{e_i}{d_i}\right) + \frac{e_i}{2d_i}. \tag{13}$$

By definition of $\delta_{\text{sum}}(\tau)$ (Equation 11)

$$\frac{\sum_{j=1}^{n} \text{DBF}(\tau_j, d_i)}{d_i} \leq \delta_{\text{sum}}(\tau). \tag{14}$$

Chaining Inequalities 13 and 14 above, we obtain

$$\frac{m}{2}\left(1 - \frac{e_i}{d_i}\right) + \frac{e_i}{2d_i} < \delta_{\text{sum}}(\tau)$$

$$\Rightarrow m < \frac{2\delta_{\text{sum}}(\tau) - \frac{e_i}{d_i}}{1 - \frac{e_i}{d_i}}.$$

By Corollary 1, it is necessary that $\delta_{\mathrm{sum}}(\tau) > \frac{1}{2}$ hold. Since $\delta_{\max}(\tau) \leq 1$ (if not, the system is trivially non-feasible), the right-hand side of the above inequality is maximized when $\frac{e_i}{d_i}$ is as large as possible, this implies that

$$m < \frac{2\delta_{\mathrm{sum}}(\tau) - \delta_{\max}(\tau)}{1 - \delta_{\max}(\tau)} \ ,$$

which contradicts Inequality 12 above.   □

The technique of **resource augmentation** may be used to quantify the "goodness" (or otherwise) of an algorithm for solving problems for which optimal algorithms are either impossible in practice (e.g., because optimal decisions require knowledge of future events), or computationally intractable. In this technique, the performance of the algorithm being discussed is compared with that of a hypothetical optimal one, under the assumption that the algorithm under discussion has access to *more resources* than the optimal algorithm. Using Theorem 3 above, we now present such a result concerning FFD-DM.

Theorem 4. FFD-DM *makes the following performance guarantees: if a constrained sporadic task system is feasible on m_o identical processors each of a particular computing capacity, then* FFD-DM *will successfully partition this system upon a platform comprised of m processors that are each $(2\frac{m_o}{m} + 1 - \frac{1}{m})$ times as fast as the original.*

Proof: Let us assume that $\tau = \{\tau_1, \tau_2, \dots, \tau_n\}$ is feasible on m_o processors each of computing capacity equal to ξ. Since τ is feasible on m_o ξ-speed processors, it follows from Lemma 3 that the tasks in τ satisfy the following properties:

$$\delta_{\max}(\tau) \leq \xi, \quad \text{and} \quad \delta_{\mathrm{sum}}(\tau) \leq m_o \cdot \xi$$

Suppose we attempt to schedule τ using FFD-DM on $m \geq \frac{2m_o \xi - \xi}{1 - \xi}$ unit-capacity processors. By substituting the inequalities above, we satisfy the condition of Theorem 3:

$$m \geq \frac{2\delta_{\mathrm{sum}}(\tau) - \delta_{\max}(\tau)}{1 - \delta_{\max}(\tau)}$$

$$\Leftarrow m \geq \frac{2m_o \xi - \xi}{1 - \xi}$$

$$\equiv \xi \leq \frac{m}{2m_o + m - 1}$$

$$\equiv \frac{1}{\xi} \geq 2\frac{m_o}{m} + 1 - \frac{1}{m}$$

which is as claimed in the statement of the theorem.   □

By setting $m_o \leftarrow m$ in the statement of Theorem 4 above, we immediately have the following corollary.

Corollary 2. FFD-DM *makes the following performance guarantees:*

> *If a constrained sporadic task system is feasible on m identical processors each of a particular computing capacity, then* FFD-DM *will successfully partition this system upon a platform comprised of m processors that are each $(3 - \frac{1}{m})$ times as fast as the original.* □

7   Conclusions and Future Work

Prior theoretical research [12, 24] on the static-priority scheduling of sporadic task systems upon partitioned multiprocessors has assumed that a task's deadline is equal to its period parameter. In this work, we have relaxed this constraint, and have allowed a task's period parameter to exceed its deadline parameter. We consider the scheduling of such sporadic task systems upon preemptive multiprocessor platforms, under the partitioned scheduling paradigm. To this end, we consider the first-fit decreasing partitioning algorithm using an exact-uniprocessor feasibility tests as a condition for a task "fitting" on a processor. We have proven the correctness of the partitioning algorithm, and have characterized the conditions under which the algorithm correctly partitions a task system. In particular, we have shown that the algorithm can partition a globally feasible task system by augmenting the speed of each processor by a multiplicative factor.

While we have assumed in this paper that our multiprocessor platform is comprised of identical processors, we observe that our results are easily extended to apply to *uniform multiprocessor* platforms — platforms in which different processors have different speeds or computing capacities — under the assumption that each processor has sufficient computing capacity to be able to accommodate each task in isolation. We are currently working on extending the results presented in this paper to uniform multiprocessor platforms in which this assumption may not hold.

We have not considered in this paper arbitrary sporadic task systems (i.e. task systems where there is no restriction between a task's relative deadline and its period parameter). Unfortunately, preliminary research indicates that the sufficient feasibility tests from this paper do not directly generalize for arbitrary sporadic tasks. Formally, the reason the results do not generalize is due to the fact that Lemma 1 does not hold for arbitrary task systems. We are currently working on devising sufficient feasibility tests for arbitrary sporadic task systems scheduled under the partitioned multiprocessor paradigm.

References

1. AUDSLEY, N., BURNS, A., RICHARDSON, M., TINDELL, K., AND WELLINGS, A. Applying new scheduling theory to static priority preemptive scheduling. *Software Engineering Journal 8*, 5 (1993), 285–292.
2. AUDSLEY, N., BURNS, A., AND WELLINGS, A. Deadline monotonic scheduling theory and application. *Control Engineering Practice 1*, 1 (1993), 71–78.

3. AUDSLEY, N. C., BURNS, A., RICHARDSON, M. F., AND WELLINGS, A. J. Hard Real-Time Scheduling: The Deadline Monotonic Approach. In *Proceedings 8th IEEE Workshop on Real-Time Operating Systems and Software* (Atlanta, May 1991), pp. 127–132.

4. BAKER, T. Multiprocessor EDF and deadline monotonic schedulability analysis. In *Proceedings of the IEEE Real-Time Systems Symposium* (December 2003), IEEE Computer Society Press, pp. 120–129.

5. BAKER, T. P. An analysis of deadline-monotonic schedulability on a multiprocessor. Tech. Rep. TR-030201, Department of Computer Science, Florida State University, 2003.

6. BAKER, T. P. An analysis of EDF schedulability on a multiprocessor. Tech. Rep. TR-030202, Department of Computer Science, Florida State University, 2003.

7. BAKER, T. P. Comparison of empirical success rates of global vs. partitioned fixed-priority and EDF scheduling for hard real time. Tech. Rep. TR-050601, Department of Computer Science, Florida State University, 2005.

8. BARUAH, S., AND FISHER, N. The partitioned multiprocessor scheduling of sporadic task systems. In *Proceedings of the 26th Real-Time Systems Symposium* (Miami, Florida, December 2005), IEEE Computer Society Press.

9. BARUAH, S., MOK, A., AND ROSIER, L. Preemptively scheduling hard-real-time sporadic tasks on one processor. In *Proceedings of the 11th Real-Time Systems Symposium* (Orlando, Florida, 1990), IEEE Computer Society Press, pp. 182–190.

10. BERTOGNA, M., CIRINEI, M., AND LIPARI, G. Improved schedulability analysis of EDF on multiprocessor platforms. In *Proceedings of the EuroMicro Conference on Real-Time Systems* (Palma de Mallorca, Balearic Islands, Spain, July 2005), IEEE Computer Society Press, pp. 209–218.

11. BINI, E., AND BUTTAZZO, G. The space of rate monotonic schedulability. In *Proceedings of the 23rd IEEE Real-Time Systems Symposium* (Austin, Texas, December 2002), IEEE Computer Society Press, pp. 169–178.

12. BURCHARD, A., LIEBEHERR, J., OH, Y., AND SON, S. H. Assigning real-time tasks to homogeneous multiprocessor systems. *IEEE Transactions on Computers 44*, 12 (December 1995), 1429–1442.

13. JOHNSON, D. Fast algorithms for bin packing. *Journal of Computer and Systems Science 8*, 3 (1974), 272–314.

14. JOHNSON, D. S. *Near-optimal Bin Packing Algorithms*. PhD thesis, Department of Mathematics, Massachusetts Institute of Technology, 1973.

15. KALYANASUNDARAM, B., AND PRUHS, K. Speed is as powerful as clairvoyance. In *36th Annual Symposium on Foundations of Computer Science (FOCS'95)* (Los Alamitos, Oct. 1995), IEEE Computer Society Press, pp. 214–223.

16. LEHOCZKY, J., SHA, L., AND DING, Y. The rate monotonic scheduling algorithm: Exact characterization and average case behavior. In *Proceedings of the Real-Time Systems Symposium - 1989* (Santa Monica, California, USA, Dec. 1989), IEEE Computer Society Press, pp. 166–171.

17. LEHOCZKY, J. P. Fixed priority scheduling of periodic tasks with arbitrary deadlines. In *IEEE Real-Time Systems Symposium* (Dec. 1990), pp. 201–209.

18. LEUNG, J., AND MERRILL, M. A note on the preemptive scheduling of periodic, real-time tasks. *Information Processing Letters 11* (1980), 115–118.

19. LEUNG, J., AND WHITEHEAD, J. On the complexity of fixed-priority scheduling of periodic, real-time tasks. *Performance Evaluation 2* (1982), 237–250.

20. LIU, C., AND LAYLAND, J. Scheduling algorithms for multiprogramming in a hard real-time environment. *Journal of the ACM 20*, 1 (1973), 46–61.

21. LOPEZ, J. M., DIAZ, J. L., AND GARCIA, D. F. Utilization bounds for EDF scheduling on real-time multiprocessor systems. *Real-Time Systems: The International Journal of Time-Critical Computing 28*, 1 (2004), 39–68.

22. LOPEZ, J. M., GARCIA, M., DIAZ, J. L., AND GARCIA, D. F. Worst-case utilization bound for EDF scheduling in real-time multiprocessor systems. In *Proceedings of the EuroMicro Conference on Real-Time Systems* (Stockholm, Sweden, June 2000), IEEE Computer Society Press, pp. 25–34.

23. MOK, A. K. *Fundamental Design Problems of Distributed Systems for The Hard-Real-Time Environment.* PhD thesis, Laboratory for Computer Science, Massachusetts Institute of Technology, 1983. Available as Technical Report No. MIT/LCS/TR-297.

24. OH, D.-I., AND BAKER, T. P. Utilization bounds for N-processor rate monotone scheduling with static processor assignment. *Real-Time Systems: The International Journal of Time-Critical Computing 15* (1998), 183–192.

25. OH, Y. *The Design and Analysis of Scheduling Algorithms for Real-Time and Fault-Tolerant Computer Systems.* PhD thesis, Department of Computer Science, The University of Virginia, 1994.

26. PHILLIPS, C. A., STEIN, C., TORNG, E., AND WEIN, J. Optimal time-critical scheduling via resource augmentation. In *Proceedings of the Twenty-Ninth Annual ACM Symposium on Theory of Computing* (El Paso, Texas, 4–6 May 1997), pp. 140–149.

New Schedulability Tests for Real-Time Task Sets Scheduled by Deadline Monotonic on Multiprocessors

Marko Bertogna, Michele Cirinei, and Giuseppe Lipari

Scuola Superiore Sant'Anna, Pisa, Italy
marko@sssup.it, cirinei@gandalf.sssup.it, lipari@sssup.it

Abstract. In this paper, we address the problem of schedulability analysis of a set of real-time periodic (or sporadic) tasks on multiprocessor hardware platforms, under fixed priority global scheduling. In a multiprocessor system with M processors, a global scheduler consists of a single queue of ready tasks for all processors, and the scheduler selects the first M tasks to execute on the M processors. We allow preemption and migration of tasks between processors.

This paper presents two different contributions. First, we derive a sufficient schedulability test for periodic and sporadic task system scheduled with fixed priority when priorities are assigned according to Deadline Monotonic. This test is efficient when dealing with heavy tasks (i.e. tasks with high utilization). Then, we develop an independent analysis for preperiod deadline systems. This leads to a new schedulability test with density and utilization bounds that are tighter than the existing ones.

1 Introduction

Recently, multicore hardware platforms (i.e. with more than one processor on a single chip) are gaining momentum both in the high-end processor market and in the embedded systems market. There are many reasons for this widespread popularity, the most important being the technological constraints that make it impossible to design and implement faster single-processor chips at reasonable costs.

However, the current state-of-practice programming methodologies have not yet shifted toward parallel computing. This is particularly unfortunate in real-time systems. As a matter of fact, the real-time scheduling theory for multiprocessor systems is not yet well studied as the corresponding single-processor scheduling theory. In particular, many negative results are known for real-time scheduling on multi-processors.

Recently, a number of research papers have addressed the problem of schedulability analysis of real-time task sets on a multi-processor platform when global scheduling is considered. In a multiprocessor system with m processors, global scheduling consists in having one single queue of ready tasks for all processors and a scheduler selects the first m tasks from the queue to be executed on the processors. Preemption and migration are allowed, i.e. a task may be interrupted by higher priority tasks at any time and it may resume execution on a different processor. A totally different approach is static partitioning of tasks to processors, where, before execution, tasks are statically allocated to processors and cannot migrate. On each processor, a single processor scheduler is run.

J.H. Anderson, G. Prencipe, and R. Wattenhofer (Eds.): OPODIS 2005, LNCS 3974, pp. 306–321, 2006.

In comparison to static partitioning, global scheduling suffers the cost of migration. This cost is mostly due to the cache: when moving a task from one processor to another, chances are that the task must reload the cache of the second processor. This cost, which might result excessive in traditional multiprocessor platforms, is greatly reduced in multicore chips, as the processors share part of the cache, and one processor can access the cache contents of another processor at little additional cost.

Moreover, global scheduling is particularly useful in case of open dynamic systems, where tasks may dynamically enter and leave the system. In fact, with static partitioning, every time a task enters the system, it must be allocated to a processor, and optimal allocation is an NP-Hard problem. Therefore, admission control and allocation become difficult and time consuming. Also, when a task leaves the system, there may be the need for re-allocation and load balancing, and this reintroduces migration overhead.

On the other hand, under global scheduling a task is not allocated to a processor. Therefore, when a task wants to enter the system, the only remaining problem is admission control, i.e. to understand if the task can be admitted into the system without jeopardizing the guarantee on the already admitted real-time tasks. This test is commonly referred to as *schedulability test*. In this paper we propose schedulability tests based on utilization and density bounds, which are polynomial in the number of tasks.

When considering global scheduling, schedulers can be roughly divided in three groups depending on the priority that a task has during its execution. If the priority of a task cannot change throughout the whole task lifetime, the scheduling algorithm has "fixed task priority". If the priority can change only at job boundaries, as with EDF, then the algorithm has "fixed job priority". The above classes are often referred to as "priority driven". Finally, if the priority can change also during the job execution, as for the P-fair class of algorithms described in [1], then the algorithm has "(fully) dynamic priority". Algorithms from the latter class can have a higher utilization bound, reaching the number of processors when deadlines are equal to periods. On the other side, they have a higher number of preemptions and migrations and a more difficult implementation. For these reasons, it may be more favorable to use a priority driven scheduler that has all the mentioned advantages related to the global scheduling.

This work will analyze the first group of algorithms, which assigns statically the priority to each task and that is often briefly called *fixed priority*. One of the most used priority assignment in this class is Rate Monotonic (RM), that assigns priorities proportional to the inverse of the periods. RM has been proved to be optimal in the uniprocessor case, in the sense that if a task set can be scheduled with fixed priority with a particular priority assignment, then it is also schedulable with RM. If a system can have deadlines less than periods, then the Deadline Monotonic priority assignment (DM) is optimal on a single processor. Efficient schedulability tests are known in the uniprocessor case for both DM and RM. When considering systems with more than one CPU, the above optimality is lost. This is mainly due to the "Dhall effect" [2], that takes place when scheduling on the same platform tasks with high utilization and tasks with low utilization. To overcome this effect reaching a higher utilization bound, there are proposed solutions that give maximum priority to the heaviest tasks and schedule the remaining ones with RM or DM.

1.1 Our Contribution

This paper presents various contributions. First, we discuss two recent solutions to the multiprocessor schedulability analysis using deadline-monotonic algorithm, one proposed by Andersson, Baruah and Jonsson [3], which will be denoted by ABJ, and the other one proposed by Baker [4], which will be denoted by BAK. We prove that neither test dominates the other.

Using a technique similar to the one used in [5] for the EDF case, we then propose a schedulability test that, bounding the interference imposed on a task, is able to succesfully guarantee a larger portion of schedulable task sets, especially in presence of *heavy tasks* (i.e. tasks whose utilization is greater than 0.5).

In order to derive a result that generalizes ABJ, as well as a utilization bound proposed by Baker, we develop a new scheduling analysis that leads to tighter density and utilization bounds. With these new results, we can evaluate the performances of DM-based hybrid scheduling algorithms, which are solutions that treat in a different way the tasks with high and with low utilization, overcoming Dhall's effect and reaching higher utilization bounds.

The paper is organized as follows. In Section 2 we introduce the terminology and notation. In Section 3, the two main existing results on the schedulability analysis with RM and DM are summarized and compared. In Section 4, we present our first test, which improves over the test proposed in [4] bounding the interference that can be imposed on a task. In Section 5, we propose a new scheduling analysis that leads to tighter density and utilization bounds. Using this result, we then characterize the performances of previously proposed hybrid algorithms based on RM and DM. Finally, in Section 6 we present our conclusions.

2 System Model

We consider a set τ of periodic or sporadic tasks to be scheduled on m identical processors. A task τ_k is a sequence of jobs J_k^j, each one with an arrival time r_k^j and a finishing time f_k^j. Each task $\tau_k = (C_k, D_k, T_k) \in \tau$ is characterized by a worst-case computation time C_k, a period or minimum interarrival time T_k, and a relative deadline D_k. Goal of the scheduling algorithm is to guarantee that each job will complete before its absolute deadline $d_k^j = r_k^j + D_k$.

For convenience, tasks are numbered in decreasing priority order. We denote with *constrained deadline* (resp. *implicit deadline*) the systems with $D_k \leq T_k$ (resp. $D_k = T_k$). We define the *utilization* of a task τ_k as $U_k = \frac{C_k}{T_k}$. We also define the *density* of a task τ_k as $\lambda_k = \frac{C_k}{D_k}$, which represents the "worst-case" request of a task in a generic time interval. Let $U_{\max}$ (resp. $\lambda_{\max}$) be the largest utilization (resp. the largest density) among all tasks.

The *workload* $W_k(a, b)$ of task τ_k is the sum of all intervals in which τ_k is executing in interval $[a, b]$. The *load* $L_k(a, b)$ of a task τ_k in $[a, b]$ is the workload divided by the length of the interval: $L_k(a, b) = \frac{W_k(a,b)}{b-a}$.

The *competing (work)load* of a task τ_k is the sum of the (work)loads of all tasks τ_i, with $i < k$.

The *interference* $I_k(a, b)$ on a task τ_k over an interval $[a, b]$ is the cumulative length of all intervals in which the task is ready to execute but it cannot execute due to higher priority jobs. We also define the *interference* $I_{i,k}(a, b)$ of a task τ_i on a task τ_k over an interval $[a, b]$ as the cumulative length of all intervals in which τ_k is ready to execute, τ_i is executing while τ_k is not. Notice that by definition: $I_{i,k}(a, b) \leq I_k(a, b), \forall i, k, a, b$.

We finally define the *interfering load* on a task τ_k over an interval $[a, b]$, as the interference $I_k(a, b)$ divided by the length of the interval, i.e.: $L_k^{int}(a, b) = \frac{I_k(a,b)}{b-a}$. Similarly, we define the *interfering load* of a task τ_i on a task τ_k in an interval $[a, b]$, as: $L_{i,k}^{int}(a, b) = \frac{I_{i,k}(a,b)}{b-a}$.

3   Summary of Existing Results

The schedulability problem for RM or DM has been widely studied in the uniprocessor case. Only recently the multiprocessor case has been analyzed in more detail. In particular, there are two previously proposed works that derive schedulability tests with polynomial time complexity, one proposed by Andersson, Baruah, Jonsson [3] and the other by Baker [4]. We will refer to both results with the first letters of the authors.

3.1   The ABJ Test

The following result has been presented in [3, 6] and is valid only for systems with deadlines equal to periods.

Theorem 1 (ABJ). *A task set with* $U_{tot} \leq \frac{m^2}{3m-2}$ *and* $U_{max} \leq \frac{m}{3m-2}$ *is schedulable with Rate Monotonic (RM) upon* m *processors.*

The test is very simple but is only applicable to task sets composed by tasks with limited utilization. In the same paper is proposed a slightly modified version of RM that allows to reach a utilization bound of $\frac{m^2}{3m-2}$ with no restriction on the utilization of a task. We will better describe this algorithm and the related bound in the last part of this paper.

3.2   The BAK Test

With a different approach, Baker derived in [4, 7] another test that is valid also for preperiod deadline systems with unrestricted task utilization. The idea is based on the consideration that if a job J_k^j of task τ_k misses its deadline d_k^j, it means that the competing load of task τ_k in interval $[r_k^j, d_k^j]$ is at least $m(1 - \lambda_k)$. The situation is depicted in Figure 1. Therefore, if it would be possible to show, for every job J_k^j, that the higher priority tasks cannot generate so much competing workload in interval $[r_k^j, d_k^j]$, then the schedulability would be guaranteed.

Unfortunately, checking the condition directly in $[r_k^j, d_k^j]$ is not simple without overestimating the contribution of each task. To find a better estimation, Baker proposes to *enlarge* the interval to the largest possible interval such that the competing load is still greater than $m(1 - \lambda_k)$. This new interval is called *busy window*. By deriving an upper bound on the combined load produced in the busy window, the final result is obtained.

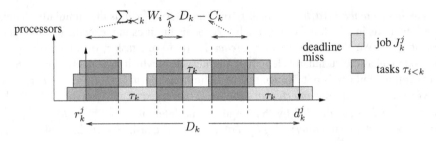

Fig. 1. Problem window

Theorem 2 (BAK). *A task set τ composed by n tasks is schedulable with DM on a SMP with m processors if*

$$\forall \tau_k : \sum_{i=1}^{k-1} \beta_i \leq m(1 - \lambda_k), \quad \text{where} \quad \beta_i = \begin{cases} U_i(1 + \frac{T_i - C_i}{D_k}) & \text{if } \lambda_k \geq U_i \\ U_i(1 + \frac{T_i - C_i}{D_k}) + \frac{C_i - \lambda_k T_i}{D_k} & \text{if } \lambda_k < U_i \end{cases}$$

It consists of $n - 1$ inequalities, one for each task, excluded the task with shortest deadline that doesn't have any interfering task.

Even if the BAK test is valid also for preperiod deadline systems with unrestricted task utilization, we show with a simple example that it doesn't dominate ABJ. Consider a platform with $m = 2$ processors and a task set $\tau = \{\tau_1 = (4, 9); \tau_2 = (4, 9); \tau_3 = (1, 10)\}$. Since the largest utilization is $\frac{4}{9} \leq \frac{m}{3m-2} = 0.5$, then ABJ is applicable. The total utilization is less than $\frac{m^2}{3m-2} = 1$ and ABJ is passed. On the other side, it is easy to verify that the BAK test fails for $k = 3$. Then, BAK is not more general than ABJ.

Note that this also proves that the utilization bound proposed in [4] for implicit deadline systems cannot follow from the general test. Anyway, we will prove along this paper that the bound is indeed correct, and our indipendent analysis will show that a similar result is valid also for preperiod deadline systems.

4 The BCL Test

A previous work [5] modified Baker's analysis for the EDF case, deriving a test that better behaves with tasks that have a high utilization. In this section, we briefly report some of the results derived in that work adapting them, when needed, to the fixed priority case. We will consider systems with constrained deadline. When a proof is not reported, it is identical to the EDF case and can be found in the cited paper.

4.1 Interference Time

The interference (resp. interfering load) that a task τ_i causes on another task τ_k in an interval $[a, b]$ is never greater than the workload (resp. load) of τ_i in the same interval:

$$\forall i, k, a, b : \quad I_{i,k}(a, b) \leq W_i(a, b) \leq b - a, \quad \text{and} \quad L_{i,k}^{int}(a, b) \leq L_i(a, b) \leq 1.$$

Moreover, note that the competing workload of a task τ_k in a generic interval cannot be less than the interference I_k in the same interval. Considering again Figure 1 and the definition of interference, we have that if a task τ_k misses a deadline in d_k^j, the interference on task τ_k in $[r_k^k, d_k^j]$ must be greater than $(D_k - C_k)$.

Since the fixed priority global scheduling algorithm is work-conserving, we have that in the time instants in which a job is ready but not executing, each processor must be occupied by a job of a higher priority task. Then, the followig results is valid.

Lemma 1. *The interference (resp.interfering load) that a task τ_k can suffer in interval $[a, b]$ is the sum of the interferences (resp. interfering loads) of all higher priority tasks in the same interval, divided by the number of processors:* $I_k(a, b) = \frac{\sum_{i<k} I_{i,k}(a,b)}{m}$ *(resp.:* $L_k^{int}(a, b) = \frac{\sum_{i<k} L_{i,k}^{int}(a,b)}{m}$ *).*

For constrained deadline systems scheduled with fixed priority, we then have that when a deadline d_k^j is missed: $\sum_{i<k} I_{i,k}(r_k^j, d_k^j) > m(D_k - C_k)$.

Therefore, for a job to meet its deadline, the competing interference on the task must be less than or equal to $m(D_k - C_k)$. For a task to be schedulable, the condition must hold for all its jobs.

We define the worst-case interference for task τ_k as: $\overline{I}_k = \max_j(I_k(r_k^j, d_k^j)) = I_k(r_k^{j*}, d_k^{j*})$, where $j*$ is the job instance in which the total interference is maximal. To simplify the notation, we define: $\overline{I}_{i,k} = I_{i,k}(r_k^{j*}, d_k^{j*})$. With the above notation we can easily extend a necessary and sufficient test derived in [5] for the EDF case.

Theorem 3. *A task set with constrained deadlines is schedulable with fixed priority iff, for each task τ_k, one of the following is true:*

1) $\sum_{i<k} \min\left(\overline{I}_{i,k}, D_k - C_k\right) < m(D_k - C_k)$
2) $\sum_{i<k} \min\left(\overline{I}_{i,k}, D_k - C_k\right) = m(D_k - C_k)$ *and* $\exists h < k : 0 < \overline{I}_{h,k} \leq D_k - C_k$

Proof. In [5], a corresponding theorem is proved for EDF. The difference is only in the tasks that have to be considered in the sum. In the EDF case, the sum is extended to all tasks (excluded τ_k). With fixed priority, the sum can be limited to the first $k - 1$ tasks, because the interference on task τ_k of each task $\tau_{i \geq k}$ is null.

To better understand the key idea behind Theorem 3, consider again the situation depicted in Figure 1. It is clear that, if the interference that a task τ_i can impose on task τ_k in window $[r_k^j, d_k^j]$ is greater than $D_k - C_k$, it is sufficient to consider only the portion $D_k - C_k$ in the sum to verify the schedulability of task τ_k.

4.2 Combined Workload

The schedulability test of Theorem 3 requires the interferences $\overline{I}_{i,k}$. Since we are not able to compute these values without a simulation of the system, we will use an upper bound, deriving only a sufficient condition. We know that an upper bound on the interference $I_{i,k}(r_k^j, d_k^j)$ is the workload $W_i(r_k^j, d_k^j)$. The workload of each interfering task $\tau_{i<k}$ is maximized when the last job is released at instant $(d_k^j - C_i)$, and the job has just the time to complete its execution requirements before the deadline of task τ_k. The situation is depicted in Figure 2 and detailed in [4]. In such a situation, let

$N_i = \left(\left\lfloor \frac{D_k - C_i}{T_i} \right\rfloor + 1 \right)$ be the number of requests r_i^h that τ_i makes in $[r_k^j, d_k^j]$. An upper bound on the workload of τ_i in a generic interval $[r_k^j, d_k^j]$ is then:

$$W_i(r_k^j, d_k^j) \le N_i C_i + \varepsilon_i(r_k^j, d_k^j)$$

where $\varepsilon_i(r_k^j, d_k^j)$ is the execution time that the first job of τ_i having execution in $[r_k^j, d_k^j]$ spends inside the considered interval. This is often called *carry-in* of task τ_i in interval $[r_k^j, d_k^j]$. Note that an upper bound on the carry-in is the following:

$$\varepsilon_i(r_k^j, d_k^j) \le \min \left(C_i, (D_k - N_i T_i + D_i - C_i)_0 \right),$$

where we used $(x)_0$ as a short notation for $\max(0, x)$. Obviously, the carry-in of a task cannot exceed the worst-case computation time C_i of the task. Moreover, since the first missed deadline is later at d_k^j, the finishing time of the first job of τ_i cannot be later than its deadline. From Figure 2, it follows that the carry-in cannot be greater than $(D_k - N_i T_i + D_i - C_i)$, when this term is positive, proving the bound.

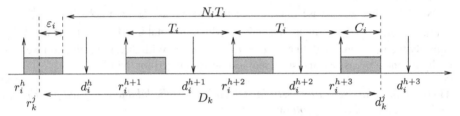

Fig. 2. Carry-in of a task $\tau_{i<k}$ in $[r_k^j, d_k^j]$

Denoting with β_i an upper bound on the load of task τ_i in interval $[r_k^j, d_k^j]$, we can then write:

$$\beta_i = \frac{N_i C_i + \min \left(C_i, (D_k - N_i T_i + D_i - C_i)_0 \right)}{D_k}. \tag{1}$$

Expressing Theorem 3 using the load instead of the workload and modifying it with the derived bound on the load of a task, we get the following sufficient condition.

Theorem 4 (BCL). *A task set with constrained deadlines is schedulable with fixed priority if, for each task τ_k, one of the followings is true:*

1) $\sum_{i<k} \min (\beta_i, 1 - \lambda_k) < m(1 - \lambda_k)$
2) $\sum_{i<k} \min (\beta_i, 1 - \lambda_k) = m(1 - \lambda_k)$ *and* $\exists i \ne k : 0 < \beta_i \le 1 - \lambda_k$.

where β_i is expressed by Equation (1).

One of the main differences between this test and the results presented in [4] lies in term $(1 - \lambda_k)$ in the minimum. This term directly derives from term $D_k - C_k$ in Theorem 3. The underlying idea is that when considering the interference of a heavy task τ_i over another task τ_k, we do not want to overestimate its contribution to the total interference. If we consider its entire load, when we sum it together with the load of the other tasks on all m processors, its contribution could be much higher than $\frac{D_k - C_k}{D_k}$ and we could end up overestimating the total interference. Therefore, we must consider only the fraction of its workload that can actually interfere with task τ_k. This fraction is bounded by $1 - \lambda_k$.

5   Density-Based Test

In this section we will develop an indipendent analysis of the multiprocessor schedulability problem when using a fixed priority scheduler with Deadline Monotonic priority assignment. This will allow to derive a new density based test that represents the corresponding version for DM of a utilization based test derived in [8] for implicit deadline systems scheduled with EDF, and extended for preperiod deadlines in [5].

We will then show that this test generalizes the ABJ test and allows to characterize hybrid algorithms based on DM that have better performances when scheduling heavy and light tasks on the same platform.

In [4], a similar bound for implicit deadline systems is presented but not correctly proved. The task set we introduced in Section 3 can be used to show that it cannot follow from the general BAK test. However, a corollary derived from our test when deadlines are equal to periods will show that the bound is indeed correct.

Lemma 2. *In a constrained deadline system scheduled with fixed priority, if a task τ_k misses a deadline d_k^j, then*

$$\sum_{i \leq k} L_i(r_k^j, d_k^j) > m(1 - \lambda_k) + \lambda_k$$

The proof is detailed in [4] and follows from Figure 1.

For the next results, we assume the constrained deadline model is used.

Lemma 3. *If the load $L_i(I)$ of a task τ_i in an interval $I = [a, b]$, with $|I| \geq D_i$, is greater than $2\lambda_i$, then τ_i has two and only two releases, r_i^1 and r_i^2, in I.*

Proof. First we prove that the interval should at least include two releases of task τ_i.

Suppose there exists a task τ_i with $L_i(I) > 2\lambda_i$ and less than two releases inside interval I. The load of τ_i inside that interval is due to at most two instances. Since $D_i \leq |I|$, such load is: $L_i(I) \leq \frac{2C_i}{|I|} \leq \frac{2C_i}{D_i} = 2\lambda_i$, contradicting the hypothesis.

We say that a job J_i^l is "entirely contained" inside an interval, if its arrival time, r_i^l, and the arrival time of the next released job of the same task, r_i^{l+1}, are both contained inside the considered interval. Let ξ be the number of jobs of τ_i entirely contained in I. We showed that $\xi \geq 1$. Now we prove that $\xi < 2$.

Note that task τ_i produces the maximal load in I when (see Figure 3):

(i) The first job of τ_i executing in I is released at instant $(a - D_i + C_i)$ and executes for C_i units at the beginning of the interval.
(ii) The last job of τ_i executing in I is released at instant $(b - C_i)$ and executes for C_i units at the end of the interval.

Suppose there exists a task τ_i for which $\xi \geq 2$ and $L_i(I) > 2\lambda_i$. The load of τ_i under conditions (i) and (ii) is:

$$L_i(I) = \frac{2C_i + \xi C_i}{\xi T_i + 2C_i + T_i - D_i} \leq \frac{2C_i + \xi C_i}{\xi T_i + 2C_i} = \frac{(2 + \xi)U_i}{\xi + 2U_i}$$

The above expression can be greater than $2U_i$ only when $\xi < 2$. So when $\xi \geq 2$ it will be $L_i(I) \leq 2U_i \leq 2\lambda_i$, contradicting the hypothesis. Therefore it should be $\xi = 1$, as the situation depicted in Figure 4.

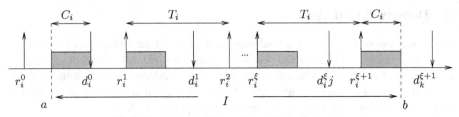

Fig. 3. Densest possible packing of jobs for task τ_i

From now on, we will call J_i^0 the first job of task τ_i that executes in interval I. The following jobs are numbered accordingly.

Lemma 4. *If the load $L_i(I)$ of a task τ_i in an interval $I = [a, b]$, with $|I| \geq D_i$, is greater than $2\lambda_i$, then:*

$$U_i < \frac{1}{4} \tag{2}$$

$$\sum_{h \leq i} L_h([r_i^0, a]) > m(1 - \lambda_i) + \lambda_i \tag{3}$$

$$D_i > \frac{2}{3}|I| \tag{4}$$

$$|[r_i^0, a]| > \frac{D_i}{2} + C_i \tag{5}$$

Proof. Lemma 3 guarantees that there is one and only one job of τ_i entirely contained in $[a, b]$, as in Figure 4. The load of τ_i in this situation is $L_i(I) < \frac{3C_i}{T_i + 2C_i} = \frac{3U_i}{1 + 2U_i}$. Since $L_i(I) > 2\lambda_i \geq 2U_i$, then $U_i < \frac{1}{4}$, proving Equation (2).

Let $x = [r_i^0, a]$, $y = [a, r_i^1]$ and $z = [r_i^1, b]$.
It is: $L_i(y + z) > 2\lambda_i$ and $L_i(x + y) \leq \lambda_i$. Moreover:

$$L_i(z) \leq \frac{2C_i}{T_i + C_i} = \frac{2U_i}{1 + U_i} < 2U_i \leq 2\lambda_i$$

$$L_i(y) = \frac{L_i(y + z)(|y| + |z|) - L_i(z)|z|}{|y|} > 2\lambda_i + \frac{|z|(2\lambda_i - L_i(z))}{|y|} \geq 2\lambda_i$$

$$L_i(x) = \frac{L_i(x + y)(|x| + |y|) - L_i(y)|y|}{|x|} \leq \lambda_i + \frac{|y|(\lambda_i - L_i(y))}{|y|} < \lambda_i \tag{6}$$

Since job J_i^0 didn't yet complete its execution at instant a, it means that when in interval x task τ_i is not executing, all m processors are executing higher priority tasks and $L_i(x) + L_i^{int}(x) = 1$. From Equation (6) we have: $L_i^{int}(x) > 1 - \lambda_i$.

Using Lemma 1, Equation (3) is proved by: $\sum_{h \leq i} L_h(x) \geq \sum_{h < i} L_{h,i}^{int}(x) + L_i(x) = mL_i^{int}(x) + L_i(x) = mL_i^{int}(x) + (1 - L_i^{int}(x)) > m(1 - \lambda_i) + \lambda_i$.

Now, let $w = [a, d_i^0]$. Note that an upper bound on $L_i(y + z)$ is $\frac{3C_i}{T_i + C_i + (T_i - D_i) + |w|}$. Since this quantity should be greater than $2\lambda_i$, we have: $|w| < \frac{5}{2}D_i - 2T_i - C_i$.

Then: $|I| = T_i + C_i + (T_i - D_i) + |w| < \frac{3}{2}D_i$, proving Equation (4).

And: $|[r_i^0, a]| = D_i - |w| > 2T_i - \frac{3}{2}D_i + C_i \geq \frac{D_i}{2} + C_i$, proving Equation (5).

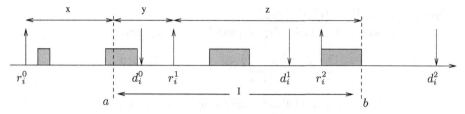

Fig. 4. A situation with $L_i(I) > 2\lambda_i$

Theorem 5. *A set of periodic or sporadic tasks with constrained deadlines is schedu-lable with Deadline Monotonic priority assignment on $m \geq 2$ processors if:*

$$\lambda_{tot} = \sum_{i=1}^{n} \frac{C_i}{D_i} \leq \frac{m}{2}(1 - \lambda_{max}) + \lambda_{max} \tag{7}$$

Proof. The proof is by contradiction. Using deadline monotonic priorities, suppose there exists a task set τ with $\lambda_{tot} \leq \frac{m}{2}(1-\lambda_{max})+\lambda_{max}$, which misses a deadline. Let d_k^j be the first missed deadline. Task τ_k is interfered by tasks in the set $T = \{\tau_1, \ldots, \tau_{k-1}\}$.

Case 1: $\forall \tau_i \in T : L_i(r_k^j, d_k^j) \leq 2\lambda_i$.
   Since $\sum_{i<k} L_{i,k}^{int}(r_k^j, d_k^j) > m(1 - \lambda_k)$, we get:

$$\lambda_{tot} \geq \sum_{i<k} \lambda_i + \lambda_k \geq \sum_{i<k} \frac{L_i(r_k^j, d_k^j)}{2} + \lambda_k \geq \sum_{i<k} \frac{L_{i,k}^{int}(r_k^j, d_k^j)}{2} + \lambda_k$$

$$> \frac{m}{2}(1 - \lambda_k) + \lambda_k \geq \frac{m}{2}(1 - \lambda_{max}) + \lambda_{max}.$$

Case 2: There is at least one task $\tau_i \in T : L_i(r_k^j, d_k^j) > 2\lambda_i$.
   Let $H = \{\tau_i \in T : L_i(r_k^j, d_k^j) > 2\lambda_i\}$. Since $D_i \leq D_k$, Lemma 3 guarantees that for every task $\tau_i \in H$ there is one and only one job entirely contained in $[r_k^j, d_k^j]$, as in Figure 4. Let τ_h be the task in H with the ear-liest released job that interferes τ_k in $[r_k^j, d_k^j]$. So it is: $r_h^0 \leq r_i^0, \forall \tau_i \in H$. Then no task in H can have only one job entirely contained in $[r_h^0, d_k^j]$. For Lemma 3 we then have:

$$\forall \tau_i \in H : L_i(r_h^0, d_k^j) \leq 2\lambda_i \tag{8}$$

Let $a = [r_h^0, r_k^j]$, $b = [r_k^j, d_k^j]$ and $(a + b) = [r_h^0, d_k^j]$.
   Since task τ_k can execute only when task τ_h is not interfered, and job J_h^0 has remaining execution time at instant r_k^j, then $L_k(a) \leq L_h(a)$. Equa-tion (6) (with $I = [r_k^j, d_k^j]$) gives $L_h(a) < \lambda_h$. So we have:

$$L_k(a) < \lambda_h \tag{9}$$

Case 2.1: $\forall \tau_i \in T : L_i(r_h^0, d_k^j) \le 2\lambda_i$.

Equation (3) with $I = [r_k^j, d_k^j]$ and $L_h(I) > 2\lambda_h$ gives:

$$\sum_{i \le k} L_i(a) \ge \sum_{i \le h} L_i(a) > m(1 - \lambda_h) + \lambda_h.$$

Using the above relation together with Lemma 2 we get:

$$\sum_{i \le k} L_i(a + b) = \sum_{i \le k} \frac{L_i(a)|a| + L_i(b)|b|}{|a + b|}$$
$$> \frac{(m(1 - \lambda_h) + \lambda_h)|a| + (m(1 - \lambda_k) + \lambda_k)|b|}{|a| + |b|} \qquad (10)$$

Consider separately the case $\lambda_h \le \lambda_k$ and $\lambda_h > \lambda_k$.

- Case $\lambda_h \le \lambda_k$:

Equation (10) gives: $\sum_{i \le k} L_i(a + b) > m(1 - \lambda_k) + \lambda_k$.

Equation (9) gives: $L_k(a) < \lambda_h \le \lambda_k$. Remember that $L_k(b) < \lambda_k$, because deadline d_k^j is missed. So, $L_k(a + b) = \frac{L_k(a)|a| + L_k(b)|b|}{|a+b|} < \frac{\lambda_k|a| + \lambda_k|b|}{|a+b|} < \lambda_k$.

Since $\forall \tau_i \in T : L_i(a + b) \le 2\lambda_i$, we get:

$$\lambda_{tot} \ge \sum_{i < k} \lambda_i + \lambda_k > \sum_{i \le k} \frac{L_i(a + b)}{2} + \frac{\lambda_k}{2} > \frac{m}{2}(1 - \lambda_k) + \lambda_k \ge \frac{m}{2}(1 - \lambda_{\max}) + \lambda_{\max}.$$

- Case $\lambda_h > \lambda_k$:

From Equation (10) with $(\lambda_h - \lambda_k) > 0$, $m \ge 2$ and $\frac{|b|}{|a|+|b|} > \frac{T_h + C_h}{2T_h + C_h} = \frac{1 + U_h}{2 + U_h} > \frac{1}{2}$:

$$\sum_{i \le k} L_i(a + b) > m(1 - \lambda_h) + \lambda_k + \frac{(\lambda_h - \lambda_k)|a| + m(\lambda_h - \lambda_k)|b|}{|a| + |b|}$$
$$> m(1 - \lambda_h) + \lambda_h + (\lambda_h - \lambda_k)\frac{|b|}{|a| + |b|}$$
$$> m(1 - \lambda_h) + \lambda_h + \frac{(\lambda_h - \lambda_k)}{2}$$

Since $|a| < D_h \le D_k$, then at most two jobs of τ_k can execute in interval $(a + b)$. So we have: $L_k(a + b) \le \frac{2C_k}{2T_h + C_h} < \frac{C_k}{T_h} \le \frac{C_k}{D_h} < \frac{C_k}{\frac{2}{3}D_k} = \frac{3}{2}\lambda_k$, where we used Equation (4) with $|I| = |b| = D_k$.

Moreover: $L_h(a + b) \le \frac{3C_h}{2T_h + C_h} = \frac{3U_h}{2 + U_h} < \frac{3}{2}U_h \le \frac{3}{2}\lambda_h$.

Since $\forall \tau_i \in T : L_i(a + b) \le 2\lambda_i$, it is:

$$\lambda_{tot} > \sum_{i < k, i \ne h} \frac{L_i(a + b)}{2} + \lambda_h + \lambda_k > \sum_{i \le k} \frac{L_i(a + b)}{2} + \frac{\lambda_h + \lambda_k}{4}$$
$$> \frac{m}{2}(1 - \lambda_h) + \lambda_h \ge \frac{m}{2}(1 - \lambda_{\max}) + \lambda_{\max}$$

contradicting the hypothesis.

Case 2.2: There is at least one task $\tau_g \in T : L_g(r_h^0, d_k^j) > 2\lambda_g$.

Lemma 3 guarantees that τ_g has one and only one job entirely contained in $(a + b)$.

Let $a' = [r_g^0, r_h^0]$. We will now prove that: $\forall \tau_i \in T : L_i(a'+a+b) \le 2\lambda_i$.

Suppose there is a task $\tau_f \in T$ for which $L_f(a'+a+b) > 2\lambda_f$. Applying repeatedly Equation (4) with $I = (a' + a + b)$, $I = (a + b)$ and $I = b$, we get:

$$D_f > \frac{2}{3}(2T_g + C_g) \ge \frac{4}{3}D_g > \frac{4}{3}\frac{2}{3}(2T_h + C_h) \ge \frac{16}{9}D_h > \frac{16}{9}\frac{2}{3}D_k > D_k.$$

Therefore, τ_f cannot be in T, proving the assertion.

Equation (4) with $I = (a + b)$ gives: $D_g > \frac{2}{3}(2T_h + C_h) > T_h \ge D_h$, showing that τ_g has lower priority than τ_h. This means that, since at instant r_k^j job J_h^0 still has to complete: $L_g(a) \le L_h(a)$. Equation (6) with $I = b$ gives $L_h(a) < \lambda_h$. Then:

$$L_g(a) < \lambda_h \tag{11}$$

Note that for Equation (8) $\tau_g \notin H$, so: $L_g(b) < 2\lambda_g$. Since $L_g(a + b) > 2\lambda_g$, then: $L_g(a) > 2\lambda_g$. Combining the latter relation with Equation (11), we get:

$$\lambda_g < \frac{\lambda_h}{2} \tag{12}$$

Equation (3) with $I = [r_h^0, d_k^j]$ gives: $\sum_{i \le k} L_i(a') \ge \sum_{i \le g} L_i(a') > m(1 - \lambda_g) + \lambda_g$. For what we said for Case 2.1, it is also: $\sum_{i \le k} L_i(a) > m(1 - \lambda_h) + \lambda_h$. Using the above relations together with Lemma 2 we get:

$$\sum_{i \le k} L_i(a'+a+b) > \frac{(m(1-\lambda_g)+\lambda_g)|a'|+(m(1-\lambda_h)+\lambda_h)|a|+(m(1-\lambda_k)+\lambda_k)|b|}{|a'|+|a|+|b|} \tag{13}$$

We consider separately the case $\lambda_h \le \lambda_k$ and $\lambda_h > \lambda_k$.
- Case $\lambda_h \le \lambda_k$:
Equations (12) and (13) give: $\sum_{i \le k} L_i(a' + a + b) > m(1 - \lambda_k) + \lambda_k$.
Being $D_g \le D_k$, task τ_k can execute only when task τ_g is not interfered. Considering that job J_g^0 has remaining execution at instant r_h^0, then: $L_k(a') \le L_g(a')$. Equation (6) for $I = [r_h^0, d_k^j]$ gives $L_g(a') < \lambda_g$. So we have: $L_k(a') < \lambda_g < \lambda_k$. Moreover, for Equation (9) it is: $L_k(a) < \lambda_h \le \lambda_k$. Using $L_k(b) < \lambda_k$, we get: $L_k(a'+a+b) = \frac{L_k(a')|a'|+L_k(a)|a|+L_k(b)|b|}{|a'+a+b|} < \frac{\lambda_k|a'|+\lambda_k|a|+\lambda_k|b|}{|a'|+|a|+|b||} = \lambda_k$.
Since $\forall \tau_i \in T : L_i(a' + a + b) \le 2\lambda_i$:

$$\lambda_{tot} \ge \sum_{i < k} \lambda_i + \lambda_k > \sum_{i \le k} \frac{L_i(a'+a+b)}{2} + \frac{\lambda_k}{2} > \frac{m}{2}(1-\lambda_k) + \lambda_k \ge \frac{m}{2}(1-\lambda_{max}) + \lambda_{max}.$$

- Case $\lambda_h > \lambda_k$:

Equation (4) with $I = (a + b)$ gives $D_g > \frac{2}{3}(2T_h + C_h)$. Since $D_k \geq D_g$, we get $T_h < \frac{3}{4}D_k - \frac{C_h}{2}$, and:

$$|a' + a + b| < D_g + (2T_h + C_h) < D_k + (2(\frac{3}{4}D_k - \frac{C_h}{2}) + C_h) = \frac{5}{2}D_k \quad (14)$$

This means that at most three jobs of task τ_k can execute in interval $(a' + a + b)$.

If $r_g^0 \geq r_k^{j-1}$, then $L_k(a' + a + b) \leq \frac{2C_k}{|a'+a+b|} < \frac{2C_k}{2T_h+C_h} < \frac{C_k}{T_h} < \frac{3}{2}U_k \leq \frac{3}{2}\lambda_k$, where we used $T_h > \frac{2}{3}D_k$. If $r_g^0 < r_k^{j-1}$, then $L_k(a' + a + b) < \frac{3C_k}{2T_k} < \frac{3}{2}U_k \leq \frac{3}{2}\lambda_k$.

In both cases: $L_k(a' + a + b) \leq \frac{3}{2}\lambda_k$.

Similarly: $L_g(a' + a + b) \leq \frac{3C_g}{2T_g+C_g} = \frac{3U_g}{2+U_g} < \frac{3}{2}U_g \leq \frac{3}{2}\lambda_g$.

Since $\forall \tau_i \in T : L_i(a' + a + b) \leq 2\lambda_i$:

$$\lambda_{tot} > \sum_{i<k, i \neq h, g} \frac{L_i(a' + a + b)}{2} + \lambda_h + \lambda_g + \lambda_k$$

$$> \sum_{i \leq k} \frac{L_i(a' + a + b)}{2} + \lambda_h + \frac{\lambda_g}{4} + \frac{\lambda_k}{4} - \frac{L_h(a' + a + b)}{2}$$

For Equation (12): $(\lambda_h - \lambda_g) > 0$. Using Equation (13), with $(\lambda_h - \lambda_k) > 0$ and $m \geq 2$:

$$\sum_{i \leq k} L_i(a'+a+b) > m(1-\lambda_h) + \frac{m(\lambda_h-\lambda_g)|a'|+m(\lambda_h-\lambda_k)|b|+\lambda_g|a'|+\lambda_h|a|+\lambda_k|b|}{|a'+a+b|}$$

$$> m(1-\lambda_h) + \lambda_h + \frac{(\lambda_h - \lambda_g)|a'| + (\lambda_h - \lambda_k)|b|}{|a'+a+b|}$$

Since for Equation (14) it is $\frac{|b|}{|a'+a+b|} > \frac{D_k}{\frac{5}{2}D_k} = \frac{2}{5}$, then:

$$\lambda_{tot} > \frac{m}{2}(1 - \lambda_h) + \lambda_h + \frac{(\lambda_h - \lambda_g)|a'|}{2|a'+a+b|} + \frac{7}{10}\lambda_h + \frac{\lambda_g}{4} - \frac{L_h(a' + a + b)}{2}$$

To derive an upper bound for $L_h(a' + a + b)$, note that, using Equation (4), it is:

$T_h \geq D_h > \frac{2}{3}D_k \geq \frac{2}{3}D_g > \frac{2}{3}|a'|$. Then at most two jobs of τ_h can execute in a'.

- If $|a'| \leq T_h$, at most one job of τ_h can execute in a'. Using twice Equation (4):

$$L_h(a'+a+b) \leq \frac{4C_h}{|a'+a+b|} < \frac{4C_h}{2T_g+C_g} < \frac{4C_h}{2D_g} < \frac{4C_h}{2\frac{2}{3}(2T_h+C_h)} < \frac{3}{2}U_h \leq \frac{3}{2}\lambda_h$$

Equation (4) and (5), with $I = [r_h^0, d_k^j]$, give:

$$\frac{|a'|}{|a'+a+b|} > \frac{\frac{D_g}{2}+C_g}{\frac{D_g}{2}+C_g+|a+b|} > \frac{\frac{1}{2}\frac{2}{3}|a+b|+C_g}{\frac{1}{2}\frac{2}{3}|a+b|+C_g+|a+b|} > \frac{1}{4}. \text{ Then:}$$

$$\lambda_{tot} > \frac{m}{2}(1-\lambda_h) + \lambda_h + \frac{(\lambda_h - \lambda_g)}{8} + \frac{7}{10}\lambda_h + \frac{\lambda_g}{4} - \frac{3}{4}\lambda_h$$
$$> \frac{m}{2}(1-\lambda_h) + \lambda_h \geq \frac{m}{2}(1-\lambda_{max}) + \lambda_{max}.$$

- If $|a'| > T_h$, then two jobs of τ_h can execute in a', and it is:

$$L_h(a'+a+b) \leq \frac{5C_h}{|a'|+|a+b|} < \frac{5C_h}{3T_h+C_h} < \frac{5}{3}U_h \leq \frac{5}{3}\lambda_h$$

Equation (2) for $I = [r_k^j, d_k^j]$ gives $C_h < \frac{T_h}{4}$.
So we have: $\frac{|a'|}{|a'+a+b|} > \frac{T_h}{T_h+2T_h+C_h} > \frac{T_h}{3T_h+\frac{T_h}{4}} = \frac{4}{13}$. And:

$$\lambda_{tot} > \frac{m}{2}(1-\lambda_h) + \lambda_h + \frac{2(\lambda_h-\lambda_g)}{13} + \frac{7}{10}\lambda_h + \frac{\lambda_g}{4} - \frac{5}{6}\lambda_h$$
$$> \frac{m}{2}(1-\lambda_h) + \lambda_h \geq \frac{m}{2}(1-\lambda_{max}) + \lambda_{max}.$$

When deadlines are equal to periods, a utilization based test immediately follows.

Corollary 1. *A set of periodic or sporadic tasks with deadline equal to period is schedulable with Rate Monotonic priority assignment on $m \geq 2$ processors if:*

$$U_{tot} \leq \frac{m}{2}(1 - U_{max}) + U_{max}$$

The above result is more general than **ABJ**. This is easy to see taking $U_{max} = \frac{m}{3m-2}$. Then a task set is schedulable when: $U_{tot} \leq \frac{m}{2}(1 - \frac{m}{3m-2}) + \frac{m}{3m-2} = \frac{m^2}{3m-2}$, as **ABJ**.

Theorem 5 is useful not only with RM and DM, but also with "hybrid" algorithms. Hybrid algorithms are modified versions of classic scheduling algorithms that can reach a higher utilization bound, dealing separately with heavy and light tasks (see [3, 4, 9, 10]). This is done in order to overcome Dhall's effect [2], an effect that limits the scheduling performances of the classic algorithms when tasks with high and low utilization have to be scheduled on the same platform. Consider Algorithm RM-US[U_{th}] (Rate Monotonic with Utilization Separation U_{th}) that assigns maximum priority up to the heaviest $m-1$ tasks having utilization greater than the threshold U_{th} and schedules the remaining tasks with priorities according to RM.

ALGORITHM RM-US[U_{th}](tasks ordered by decreasing utilization):

- For$(i=0, i<m, i=i+1)\{$If $(U_i > U_{th})$ {give τ_i maximum priority}; else break}
- Schedule the remaining tasks with priorities according to RM.

Andersson et al. showed that, when the threshold is $\frac{m}{3m-2}$, such algorithm can schedule any periodic task set with total utilization $U_{tot} \leq \frac{m^2}{3m-2}$.

Using Corollary 1, we can generalize the analysis to any utilization threshold. Being $H < m$ the number of tasks with $U_i > U_{th}$, the minimum total utilization needed for a task set to be schedulable is at least the minimum total utilization needed by an algorithm that schedules each one of the H "heavy" tasks on a dedicated processor and the others on the remaining $m - H$ processors with RM [3, 10]. Applying Corollary 1, the light tasks can be scheduled on $m - H$ processors if their total utilization is at most $\frac{m-H}{2}(1 - U_{th}) + U_{th}$. Therefore, the total utilization that still guarantees the schedulability with RM-US[U_{th}] is: $HU_{th} + \frac{m-H}{2}(1 - U_{th}) + U_{th}$. The maximum with respect to U_{th} of the minimum with respect to H of this expression is reached when $U_{th} = \frac{1}{3}$, which represents the utilization threshold that guarantees the highest utilization bound for the RM-US class of algorithms, relatively to our schedulability algorithm. Using this value inside the previous expression we have the following.

Corollary 2. *A periodic or sporadic task set with deadlines equal to periods is schedulable with RM-US[$\frac{1}{3}$] on m processors if $U_{tot} \leq \frac{m+1}{3}$.*

Note that the bound of Corollary 2 is better than the bound derived in [3] for RM-US[$\frac{m}{3m-2}$], when $m \geq 2$.

Since Theorem 5 is valid also for preperiod deadline systems, we can as well characterize a similar algorithm that uses as separation value the density of each task. We call this algorithm DM-DS[λ_{th}] (Deadline Monotonic with Density Separation λ_{th}), where λ_{th} is the density threshold that discriminate between maximum priority "heavy" task, and "light" task to be scheduled with DM.

ALGORITHM DM-DS[λ_{th}](tasks ordered by decreasing density):

- For$(i=0, i<m, i=i+1)\{$If $(\lambda_i > \lambda_{th})$ {give τ_i maximum priority}; else break;}
- Schedule the remaining tasks with priorities according to DM.

Proceding as before, but using Theorem 5 instead of Corollary 1, we can derive that the density threshold that guarantees the highest density bound using the test of Theorem 5 is $\lambda_{th} = \frac{1}{3}$, and state the following result.

Corollary 3. *A periodic or sporadic task set with preperiod deadlines is schedulable with DM-DS[$\frac{1}{3}$] on m processors if $\lambda_{tot} \leq \frac{m+1}{3}$.*

6   Conclusions

In this paper we presented two schedulability tests to be used with the fixed priority scheduling algorithm. The first test is very efficient in presence of heavy tasks and it is the correspondent version of a similar test appeared in [5] for the EDF case. The second test behaves well with a high number of light tasks, given that the total density of the task set doesn't exceed a derived bound. It represents the DM version of an EDF schedulability test presented in [8] and extended for constrained deadline systems in [5]. We showed that our result allows to generalize and improve the existing related bounds, as well as to characterize the performances of previously proposed hybrid algorithms. An advantage of our result is that it is valid also for sporadic task systems with unbounded task utilization and with preperiod deadlines. No density bounds for constrained deadline systems have been previously proposed.

References

1. Baruah, S., Cohen, N., Plaxton, C., Varvel, D.: Proportionate progress: A notion of fairness in resource allocation. Algorithmica **6** (1996)
2. Dhall, S.K., Liu, C.L.: On a real-time scheduling problem. Operations Research **26** (1978)
3. Andersson, B., Baruah, S., Jonsson, J.: Static-priority scheduling on multiprocessors. In IEEE, ed.: Proceedings of the IEEE Real-Time Systems Symposium. (2001)
4. Baker, T.: Multiprocessor EDF and deadline monotonic schedulability analysis. In: Proceedings of the 24th IEEE International Real-Time Systems Symposium, RTSS'03. (2003)
5. Bertogna, M., Cirinei, M., Lipari, G.: Improved schedulability analysis of EDF on multiprocessor platforms. In: Proceedings of the IEEE Euromicro Conference on Real Time Systems, Mallorca, Spain, IEEE (2005)
6. Andersson, B.: Static-priority scheduling on multiprocessors. PhD thesis, Department of Computer Engineering, Chalmer University of Technology, Goteborg, Sweden (2003)
7. Baker, T.: An analysis of deadline-monotonic schedulability on a multiprocessor. FSU computer science technical report, Department of Computer Science, Florida State University, Tallahassee, Florida (2003) available at http://www.cs.fsu.edu/research/reports.
8. Goossens, J., Funk, S., Baruah, S.: Priority-driven scheduling of periodic task systems on multiprocessors. Real-Time Systems **25**(2-3) (2003) 187–205
9. Baruah, S.K.: Optimal utilization bounds for the fixed-priority scheduling of periodic task systems on identical multiprocessors. IEEE Trans. Computers **53**(6) (2004) 781–784
10. Srinivasan, A., Baruah, S.K.: Deadline-based scheduling of periodic task systems on multiprocessors. Inf. Process. Lett. **84**(2) (2002) 93–98

Static-Priority Scheduling of Sporadic Messages on a Wireless Channel

Björn Andersson and Eduardo Tovar

Department of Computer Engineering, School of Engineering,
Polytechnic Institute of Porto (ISEP-IPP),
Rua Dr. António Bernardino de Almeida 431,
4200-072 Porto, Portugal
{bandersson, emt}@dei.isep.ipp.pt

Abstract. Consider the problem of scheduling sporadic messages with deadlines on a wireless channel. We propose a collision-free medium access control (MAC) protocol which implements static-priority scheduling and present a schedulability analysis technique for the protocol. The MAC protocol allows multiple masters and is fully distributed; it is an adaptation to a wireless channel of the dominance protocol used in the CAN bus. But unlike that protocol, our protocol does not require a node having the ability to receive an incoming bit from the channel while transmitting to the channel.

1 Introduction

The sporadic model [11] has proven to be very useful in the design of real-time systems. In this model, the exact time of a transmission request is unknown but a lower bound on the time between two consecutive transmission requests from the same message stream is known. This model is supported in processor scheduling [4] (where a message stream is called a task) and in wired communication channels [17]. Wireless communication is of increasing interest in the design of distributed real-time systems, and many scheduling algorithms and analysis techniques for wireless communication are available for periodic messages. But for sporadic messages such results are less well developed. Most of the current wireless protocols cannot be analyzed to offer pre-run-time guarantees that sporadic messages meet deadlines, and the protocols that do offer such guarantees rely on polling, which is inefficient when the deadline is short and the minimum time between two consecutive requests is long.

In this paper we solve the problem of sporadic scheduling on a wireless channel. We adapt the dominance protocols [12] (used in the CAN bus [5]) to a wireless channel and perform a schedulability analysis. The main idea of our dominance protocol is that a message stream is assigned a static priority and when message streams contend for the channel, they perform a tournament such that the highest-priority message is granted access to the channel. This tournament is performed bit-by-bit, starting with the most significant bit. A bit is assigned a time interval. If a node contends with a dominant bit then a carrier

J.H. Anderson, G. Prencipe, and R. Wattenhofer (Eds.): OPODIS 2005, LNCS 3974, pp. 322–333, 2006.

wave is transmitted in this time interval; if the node contends with a recessive bit, it transmits nothing but listens. This makes it possible for a node with a recessive bit to detect that another node has transmitted a dominant bit, and hence the node with the recessive bit withdraws. In order for this scheme to work, nodes must agree on which time interval to use. This requires a convention, something that is easy to state and which we do. It also requires that nodes have a common reference point in time. We provide this as well.

The remainder of this paper is structured as follows. Section 2 discusses related work and their ability to solve the problem of sporadic messages on a wireless channel. Section 3 presents the system model with our assumptions and terminology. Section 4 presents the protocol and discusses the rationale behind its design. Section 5 presents the schedulability analysis. Finally, Section 6 offers conclusions and future work.

2   Related Work

The introduction of the wireless LAN standard IEEE 802.11 [1] stimulated the development of many prioritized Carrier Sense Multiple Access (CSMA) protocols. Some of these protocols [2, 3, 7] changed parameters in the IEEE 802.11 standard to be a function of deadlines, either choosing (i) inter-frame spacing (the amount of time that a station waits before transmitting) or (ii) the back-off times after a collision has occurred. These techniques are useful to meet deadlines because they can implement algorithms such as deadline monotonic [9]. But they have two drawbacks (i) they only approximate priority scheduling; it may happen that a high-priority message has to wait for one or many lower-priority messages and (ii) collisions can occur hence causing deadline misses. Other prioritization protocols based on IEEE 802.11 use "black-bursts" [13, 15, 14]. They do not only change some parameters in the IEEE 802.11 but they also require other signals to be transmitted. If the channel is idle then a node transmits a message immediately. Otherwise the node waits until the channel becomes idle and transmits a "black-burst" (a jamming signal) for a time duration which is proportional to the priority. When a node finished transmitting its jamming signal, the node listens to find out whether other nodes transmit a jamming signal. If so, the node did not have the highest priority so it waits until the channel is idle again. The protocols based on "black-burst" were originally used to ensure that all real-time traffic is given a higher priority than non real-time traffic and dynamically change priorities of real-time traffic to achieve round-robin scheduling [15, 14]. These schemes treat all real-time messages in the same way and hence they are inappropriate for our purpose. The black-burst scheme in [13] implements static-priority scheduling though and is more interesting. However, all these black-burst schemes [13, 15, 14] have the drawback that (i) collisions can occur if the channel is idle and two nodes request to transmit simultaneously and (ii) the maximum length of the black-burst is proportionate to the number of priority levels, so only a small number of priority levels can be supported. Another technique [19], not based on IEEE 802.11, is to implement prioritization using two separate narrow band busy-tones to communicate that a node is backlogged with a high-priority message. This technique has the drawback of requiring specialized hardware (for listening to the narrow band signals), requires extra bandwidth (for the narrow band signals) and it supports only two priority levels.

The IEEE 802.11 standard also defined another MAC protocol where a base station polls a node, and gives it the right to transmit in a time interval. Naturally such an approach is inefficient to schedule sporadic messages. Recently, the IEEE 802.11e profile was introduced with the intention of offering better support for Quality-of-Service. The previous approach [2, 3, 7] of choosing back-off times as a function of priorities was adopted, and the polling scheme in IEEE 802.11 was refined with traffic classes.

MAC protocols have also been proposed from the real-time community with the goal of meeting deadlines. Some protocols use tables (sometimes called Time-Division Multiple-Access (TDMA) templates) with explicit start times of message transmission. These tables are created at run-time in a distributed fashion [16] or by a leader [10]. It is also conceivable to use a TDMA template designed before run-time [8] and use it to schedule wireless traffic. However, all these time-table approaches have the drawback of requiring that sporadic message streams are dealt with using polling, which, as previously stated, is inefficient. Another approach, Implicit EDF [6], is based on the assumption that all nodes know the traffic on the other nodes that compete for the medium, and all these nodes execute the EDF scheduling algorithm. If the message selected by the EDF scheduling algorithm is in the node's queue of outgoing messages, then the node transmits this message otherwise it does not transmit. Unfortunately, this algorithm is based on the assumption that a node knows the *arrival time* of messages on other nodes, and this implies that polling must be used to deal with sporadic message streams. MAC protocols based on token bus can be used in wireless channels and some of their analyses can be extended to sporadic messages [18]. Unfortunately, they only prioritize messages on a node; global prioritization is not achieved. As a result, deadlines can be missed although the utilization of the messages is low, and there exists a schedule of the messages that meets deadlines.

The dominance protocol [12] (used in for example the CAN bus [5]) uses global priorities and it can schedule sporadic message streams. Unfortunately, it requires that a node has the ability to receive an incoming bit from the channel while transmitting to the channel. Such a behavior is impossible on a wireless channel due to the large difference in transmitted energy and the received energy. The conclusion of this section is that several prioritization protocols and real-time scheduling algorithms exist, but they do not efficiently solve the problem of sporadic scheduling in wireless networks.

3   System Model

Consider n message streams $\tau_1, \tau_2, \tau_3, \ldots, \tau_n$ and m computer nodes $N_1, \ldots, N_m$. A message stream is assigned to exactly one node.

Workload. Message stream τ_i makes a sequence of requests to transmit a message. The exact time of a transmission request is unknown but a lower bound on the time between two consecutive transmission requests from the same message stream is known. This lower bound is denoted T_i. Every message from τ_i requires to transmit for C_i contiguous time units. The maximum time from a request of a message from τ_i to the completion of the transmission of that message is called the *response time* of τ_i, and it is denoted R_i.

Success and Failure. If there exists an overlap between a pair of transmission of data bits then both transmissions have failed. If a message finishes transmission later than D_i time units after it requested to be transmitted then the transmission has failed as well. The goal of our protocol is to schedule all messages in all message streams to finish their transmission before their deadlines. Then we say that the protocol has succeeded and we will (in Section 5) derive equations to compute whether a set of message streams succeeds using our protocol.

Priorities. Message streams are assigned unique priorities; these priorities are non-negative integers. Messages with low numbers have high priority. As a result, we will say that if a bit is "0" then it is dominant and if a bit is "1" then it is recessive. Let *npriobits* denote the number of bits required to represent the priorities. We use lower order first; that is, bit "0" is considered to be the most-significant bit in an integer. We do not assume any particular priority-assignment scheme.

Propagation. The time-of-flight between two arbitrary nodes i and j is unknown but it is non-negative and there is an upper bound α on the time-of-flights. We assume that when a node transmits and there is no collision, then all nodes receive exactly one copy of the message; that is, there is no noise, no hidden terminals and the transmitted signal takes only one path to the receiving node(s).

Nodes. We assume that nodes are equipped with real-time clocks. They are not synchronized; that is, their values may be different. For every unit of real-time, the clock increases by an amount. This amount is unknown but it is in the range $[1-\epsilon, 1+\epsilon]$, $0 < \epsilon < 1$. We let *CLK* denote the granularity of the clock. We assume that the clock does never "wrap-around". A message may have one intended node as a receiver (unicast) or all nodes (broadcast); our protocol can deal with both types of traffic. We assume, however, that when a node receives a message it does not send an acknowledgement. A node can sense other transmissions only if the node does not transmit. We do not assume any particular modulation technique or coding scheme for the data bits but we assume that when data bits are transmitted, there is no interval of continuous idle time that exceeds F time units. (F is a design parameter that will be discussed later). We assume that nodes can transmit a carrier wave and all nodes are able to detect that carrier wave if they do not transmit themselves. A node needs *TFCS* time units to detect that a carrier wave was transmitted. The transceiver of a node needs at most $turnaround_{RxTx}$ time units to switch from reception to transmission or vice-versa.

We will describe the protocol using a timed-automata like notation. States are represented as vertices and transitions are represented as edges. An edge is described by its guard (a condition which has to be true in order for the protocol to make the transition) and an update (an action that occurs when the transition is made). In figures, we let "/" separate the guards and the updates; the guards are before "/" and the update is after. We let "=" denote test for equality and let ":=" denote assignment to a variable.

We assume that when a time-out transition is enabled, it occurs immediately. The corresponding update of that transition and a continuing path of enabled transitions occur at most L time units later. Intuitively, L represents the delay due to executing on a finite-speed processor.

4   The Protocol

Figure 1 gives an informal overview of the protocol. Between the protocol and applications on the node, there is a queue storing messages that requested to be transmitted. In the starting state (marked as a circle with a circle inside), the protocol waits until the queue is non-empty. Then the protocol waits for a long idle time and then it transmits a pulse of the carrier wave. The beginning of the pulse represents a common reference point in time for all nodes. A node dequeues the highest priority message and then the nodes perform a tournament. If a node wins the tournament then it transmits the message. If a node loses the tournament then it continues to listen on the channel to figure out which priority

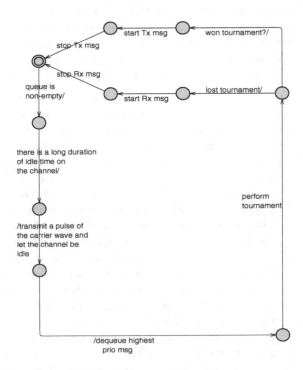

Fig. 1. Overview of the protocol

was the winner and then it receives the message. If the node which lost had an application that requested this message then it is delivered to that application, if not then the message is discarded.

The remainder of this section is structured as follows. Section 4.1 gives a detailed view of the protocol. Section 4.2 explains the rationale for the design of the protocol and why it is robust against imperfections in clocks.

4.1   Details of the Protocol

Figure 2 shows details of the protocol. The figure illustrates how the protocol is designed; the actual behavior is slightly different due to clock imperfection, time-of-flight of the carrier-signal and delays in the transitions.

States are numbered from 0 to 18. State 0 is the initial state. Each node has the following variables: a clock X, an integer i within the range $0..npriobits\text{-}1$, an integer prio occupying $npriobits$ bits, an integer winner_prio occupying $npriobits$ bits and a boolean variable winner. We let winner_prio[i] denote the bit i in the variable winner_prio. Analogously for prio[i]. We assume that when the protocol dequeues the highest-priority message then the variable prio is assigned the priority of that message. There are two functions carrierOn and carrierOff that can be called by a node. The function carrierOn requests to start the transmission of a carrier wave. It may take up to $turnaround_{RxTx}$ until the carrier actually starts to be transmitted but then it continues doing so. If carrierOff is called then it is requested that the carrier stops being transmitted but it may take up to $turnaround_{RxTx}$ until it stops. The symbol "carrier?" means: sense for a carrier and if there is a carrier then "carrier?" is true. E, F, G, H and SWX are constants used for time-outs, whose value we will choose later.

The states 1-5 in Figure 2 establish a common reference point in time between all nodes that requests to transmit. The transition $3\rightarrow4$ is designed to make the protocol robust to clock inaccuracies. The states 6-11 perform the tournament. During the tournament, nodes contend bit-by-bit, starting with the most significant bit.

If a node loses the contention of a bit then it loses the entire tournament but it continues to listen to find out which priority wins the tournament. If a node does not lose the contention during this bit, it continues with the contention for the next bit. Finally there is only one winner of the tournament because priorities are unique. This winning node makes the transition to state 14 and then transmits the message and then makes the transition to the initial state 0.

If the protocol contends with a dominant bit ("0") then it transmits a pulse of the carrier wave by taking the path $7 \rightarrow 8 \rightarrow 9 \rightarrow 11$. If the protocol contends with a recessive bit ("1") then it may take either the path $7 \rightarrow 10 \rightarrow 11$ or the path $7 \rightarrow 11$; it depends on whether the node heard a carrier wave (which signals that another node transmits a dominant bit). If a node contended with a recessive bit ("1") but heard a carrier wave then this node has lost.

Consider a node which has lost the tournament. It continues in the tournament and if such a node has a recessive bit then it acts in the same way as if it had not lost. The reason for this is that a recessive bit just listens; it does not transmit

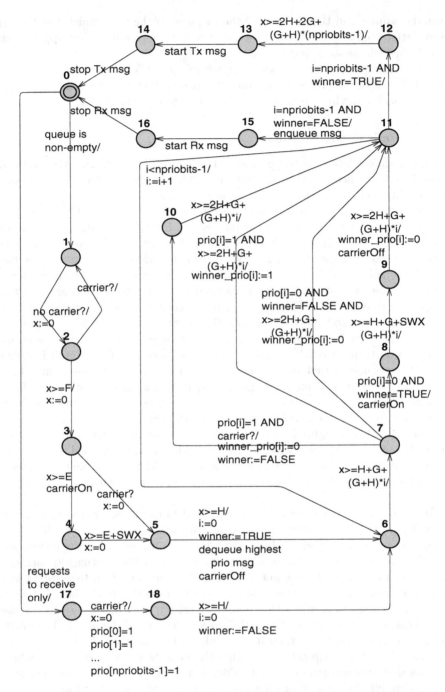

Fig. 2. Details about the protocol. This figure illustrates the design; the behavior is slightly different due to clock imperfection, time-of-flight of the carrier-signal and delays in the transitions.

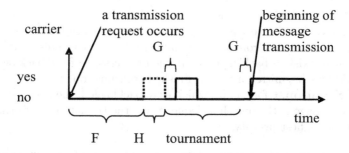

Fig. 3. An example of the carrier wave transmitted assuming *npriobits*=2 and the priority of the requested message is *1*. (The priority is encoded in a binary way as 01 which is signaled as: first a dominant bit and then a recessive bit). A solid box indicates that the node transmitted a carrier wave whereas a dotted box indicate that the node heard a carrier wave. The node that requested to transmit this message heard that another node transmitted a carrier wave so it did not need to transmit the carrier wave.

a carrier wave. However, if a node has a dominant bit and it has lost, then the protocol acts differently from the case when it had won; no carrier wave is transmitted. A node which only requests to receive, acts like a node losing the tournament from the start (see $0 \rightarrow 17 \rightarrow 18 \rightarrow 6$).

In order to understand the time-out parameters E, F, G, H and SWX, consider Figure 3. F denotes the initial idle time period. H represents the duration of a pulse of the carrier wave. G denotes a "guarding" time interval to separate pulses of carrier waves. This "guarding" time interval makes the protocol robust against clock inaccuracies, and takes into account that signals need a non-zero time to propagate from one node to another. E makes the protocol robust to inaccuracies of when the nodes measure F. SWX is used for the protocol to wait to be sure that a request to transmit a carrier really has resulted in a carrier being transmitted.

Consider the automata in Figure 2 again. Traverse the path of the transitions of the winning node and observe the last time-out (the transition $12 \rightarrow 13$). Based on this, we can compute the transmission time of a message taking the overhead of the protocol into account as:

$$C'_i = C_i + 2H + 2G + (G + H) \times (npriobits - 1) + 2L \tag{1}$$

By taking into account also the initial idle time (in state 2) we obtain:

$$C''_i = F + E + SWX + C'_i \tag{2}$$

4.2   Rationale of the Design and Correctness

We will now discuss the correctness of the protocol and discuss how assigning values to the constants E, F, G, H and SWX affects the correctness. The protocol must satisfy:

- **Mutual Exclusion.** At most one node is in state 14.
- **Progress.** There are two types of progress (i) state 0 is reached after at most C_i'' time units from any state and (ii) if a message finishes transmission and there exists a backlogged node then a message of the backlogged nodes should be transmitted after the finished transmission.
- **Prioritization.** Of all nodes which were backlogged, the one that will transmit a message is the one that dequeues (at the transition 5→6) the message with the highest priority.

In order to assure that these properties hold we need to assure that certain events do not occur at the wrong time. We need to assure that:

- **When a node transmits a dominant bit, it is received by all other nodes.** Consider an iteration of the tournament. It must have been sufficient overlap between the time interval where one node transmits the carrier to inform that it has a dominant bit and the time interval where a node with a recessive bit listens for nodes with a dominant bit. Due to clock drift, this overlap becomes smaller and smaller for each iteration of the tournament. Hence we consider the last iteration of the tournament. We require:

$$[2H + G + (H + G) \times (npriobits - 1)] \times [1 - \epsilon] -$$
$$[H + G + (H + G) \times (npriobits - 1)] \times [1 + \epsilon]$$
$$-2CLK - L - 2\alpha - (E + SWX) > TFCS + 2SWX \quad (3)$$

The motivation of Equation 3 is that the inaccuracy of the synchronization after the initial period of silence is $(E + SWX)$. Consequently, two different nodes can have different opinion on when a bit should be transmitted. If the time windows of the two nodes overlap by $TFCS + 2SWX$ then we can be sure that the node that attempts to detect the dominant bit will hear at least $TFCS$ time units of the carrier. The reason for requiring $2SWX$ extra time units is that it may take SWX for the sender to enter Tx mode and when it has transmitted the carrier for TFCS time units, when it switches the carrier off, this may take effect immediately.

- **If one node i has perceived a time of silence long enough (F time units) to make the transition from state 2 to state 3 but other nodes perceive that the duration of silence to be less than F time units so far due to different time-of-flight and clock-imperfections, then node i needs to wait until all nodes have perceived this long time of silence.** The protocol should stay in state 3 for E time units to ensure this. We require:

$$2CLK + L + 2\alpha + F \times 2\epsilon < E \quad (4)$$

- **A node which has lost the tournament must be in receiving mode in state 15 before it receives the data bits from the transmission of the winning node (which is in state 13).** This is taken care of by the delay between state 12 to state 13. We know that the node which lost was in receiving mode because in the last bit in the tournament, it was in receiving mode (if the losing node would have transmitted in the last bit in the tournament then it must have lost in the last bit and transmitted a dominant bit, something which is impossible). For this reason, it is only required that the delay between state 12 to state 13 is large enough to ensure that the losing node reaches state 15 before the winning node reaches state 13. To do so we require that the following inequality is satisfied:

$$[2H + 2G + (H + G) \times (npriobits - 1)] \times [1 - \epsilon] -$$
$$[2H + G + (H + G) \times (npriobits - 1)] \times [1 + \epsilon] -$$
$$-(E + SWX) > 0 \qquad (5)$$

- **During the tournament, the maximum time interval of idle time should be less than F, the initial idle period.** This assures that if one node makes the transition from state 2 to state 3 (the initial idle time period) then all nodes will do it at most $E+SWX$ time units later. We require:

$$[2H + 2G + (H + G) \times (npriobits - 1)] \times [1 + \epsilon] -$$
$$H \times [1 - \epsilon] -$$
$$+2CLK + L + 2\alpha + (E + SWX) < F \qquad (6)$$

- **The time interval between two successive dominant bits must be long enough to assure that no node interprets the first dominant bits to be transmitted in the time interval for the second dominant bit.** The worst case occurs when these two bits are the last ones in the tournament. We require:

$$[2H + 2G + (H + G) \times (npriobits - 2)] \times [1 - \epsilon] -$$
$$[2H + G + (H + G) \times (npriobits - 2)] \times [1 + \epsilon]$$
$$-2CLK - L - 2\alpha - (E + SWX) > 0 \qquad (7)$$

- **The time to wait from when a carrier is requested to be transmitted until it is known that a carrier is transmitted must be greater than the time required by the hardware.** Naturally, this requires:

$$SWX > turnaround_{RxTx} \qquad (8)$$

The values of E,F,G,H and SWX must be selected to satisfy the inequalities 3-8. In order to get an idea of the magnitude of these values, we will work out an example.

Consider a typical distributed real-time system (a car, a factory or a ship) with a diameter of at most *300m*. This gives:$\alpha=1\mu s$. Typical computers have $CLK=1\mu s$ and $\epsilon=10^{-5}$ (assuming a low resolution timer and a poor quality crystal). We assume that the protocol is implemented on dedicated hardware and use $L=2\mu s$. We choose $TFCS=5\mu s$ because busy tone detection of narrow-band signals have been estimated to need this time [19] and our application of carrier sensing is similar to busy tone detection. We choose $turnaround_{RxTx}=19\,\mu s$ based on the requirement in IEEE 802.11 standard (see page 180 in [1]). We choose $npriobits=20$. One choice that satisfies the constraints for this example is: $E=8\,\mu s$, $F=2349\,\mu s$, $G=35\,\mu s$, $H=79\,\mu s$ and $SWX=20\,\mu s$. Hence the overhead per message (calculated based on Equation 2) is $4775\mu s$.

5   Schedulability Analysis

Consider the mutual exclusion, the two progress properties and the prioritization property in Section 4.2. By combining them and a previous result on schedulability analysis of the CAN bus [17] we obtain that the response time can be calculated as a sum of the waiting time w_i and C_i''.

$$R_i = w_i + C_i'' \tag{9}$$

where C_i'' is defined as in Equation 2. The waiting time is obtained as:

$$w_i = B_i + \sum_{j \in hp(i)} \left\lceil \frac{w_i}{T_j} \right\rceil \times C_j'' \tag{10}$$

where $hp(i)$ is the set of all message streams with a higher priority than τ_i.
B_i can be computed as follows:

$$B_i = \max \left\{ C_j' : j \in lp(i) \right\} \tag{11}$$

where $lp(i)$ is the set of all message streams with a lower priority than τ_i. Note that the schedulability analysis considers the initial idle time between states 1-4 to be a part of the "message" when we compute interference. This initial idle period should not be included when computing the blocking in Equation 11.

6   Conclusions and Future Work

We have presented a MAC protocol for sporadic messages. The protocol is collision-free, does not require synchronized clocks and supports a large number of priority levels. We consider for future work (i) implementation of the protocol in Berkeley motes, (ii) automated formal verification of mutual exclusion, progress and prioritization, (iii) extending the protocol to deal with hidden nodes, (iv) analyzing the resilience of the protocol to noise in the carrier sensing and (v) techniques for achieving a low overhead and a large number of priorities on computer platforms with a large turnaround time from transmission to reception.

Acknowledgements

We are grateful to the reviewers for suggested improvements of the paper. This work was partially funded by Fundação para Ciência e Tecnologia (FCT).

References

1. IEEE 802.11, 1999 Edition (ISO/IEC 8802-11: 1999) IEEE Standards for Information Technology – Telecommunications and Information Exchange between Systems – Local and Metropolitan Area Network – Specific Requirements – Part 11: Wireless LAN Medium Access Control (MAC) and Physical Layer (PHY) Specifications.
2. Aad, I.,Castelluccia, C.: Differentiation mechanisms for IEEE 802.11. In *Infocom*, pages 209–218, 2001.
3. Barry, M., Campbell, A.T., Andras, V.: Distributed control algorithms for service differentiation in wireless packet networks. In *Infocom*, 2001.
4. Baruah, S. K. , Mok, A. K., Rosier, A. K.: Preemptively scheduling hard-real-time sporadic tasks on one processor. In *IEEE Real-Time Systems Symposium*, pages 182–190, 1990.
5. Bosch. CAN specification, ver. 2.0, Robert Bosch GmbH, Stuttgart. Technical report, 1991.
6. Caccamo, M.,Zhang, L. Y.: An implicit prioritized access protocol for wireless sensor networks. In *23rd IEEE Real-Time Systems Symposium (RTSS'02)*, pages 39–48, Austin, Texas, 2002.
7. Deng, D.-J.,Ruay-Shiung, C.: A priority scheme for IEEE 802.11 DCF access method. *IEICE Transactions on Communication*, E82-B:96–102, 1999.
8. Kopetz, H., Grunsteidl, G.: TTP - a protocol for fault-tolerant real-time systems. *IEEE Computer*, 27(1):14–24, 1994.
9. Leung, J.,Whitehead, J.: On the complexity of fixed-priority scheduling of periodic real-time tasks. *Performance Evaluation, Elsevier Science*, 22(4):237–250, 1982.
10. Li, H., Shenoy, P., Ramamrithan, K.: Scheduling communication in real-time sensor applications. In *IEEE Real-Time and Embedded Technology and Applications Symposium*, Toronto, Canada, 2004.
11. Mok, A.: *Fundamental Design Problems of Distributed Systems for the Hard Real-Time Environment.* PhD thesis, Massachusetts Institute of Technology, 1983.
12. Mok, A.K., and Ward, S.: Distributed broadcast channel access. *Computer Networks*, 3:327–335, 1979.
13. Sheu, J.-P., Liu, C.-H., Wu, S.-L., Tseng, Y.-C.: A priority MAC protocol to support real-time traffic in ad hoc networks. *Wireless networks*, 10(1):61–69, 2004.
14. Sobrinho, J. L., Krishnakumar, A. : Quality-of-service in ad hoc carrier sense multiple access networks. *IEEE J. Selec. Areas Commun.*, 17(8):1353–1368, 1999.
15. Sobrinho, J. L., Krishnakumar, A. S: Real-time traffic over the IEEE 802.11 medium access control layer. *Bell Labs Technical Journal*, 1(2):172–187, 1996.
16. Thomas, W. C., Moussa, A. B., Rajeev, B., David, B.S. Contention-free periodic message scheduler medium access control in wireless sensor / actuator networks. In *IEEE Real-Time Systems Symposium*, pages 298–307, Cancun, Mexico, 2003.
17. Tindell, K., Hansson, H., Wellings, A.: Analysing real-time communications: controller area network (CAN). In *15th Real-Time Systems Symposium (RTSS'94)*, pages 259–263, 1994.
18. Tovar, E., Vasques, V.: Non pre-emptive scheduling of messages on SMTV token-passing ne tworks. In *12th Euromicro Conference on Real Time Systems (ECRTS00)*, pages 209–218, 2000.
19. Yang, X., Vaidya, N.: Priority scheduling in wireless ad hoc networks. *Wireless networks*, to appear.

Implementing Reliable Distributed Real-Time Systems with the Θ-Model

Jean-François Hermant and Josef Widder*

1 INRIA Rocquencourt, Projet Novaltis, BP 105
F-78153 Le Chesnay Cedex (France)
jean-francois.hermant@inria.fr
2 Technische Universität Wien, Embedded Computing Systems Group E182/2
Treitlstraße 3, A-1040 Vienna (Austria)
widder@ecs.tuwien.ac.at

Abstract. A widely accepted viewpoint is that designs for distributed real-time systems should be based on synchronous computational models. Safety in such designs, however, requires that the target system behaves as the synchronous model postulates. We believe that this approach is rather risky, as it rests on solving distributed scheduling problems which are known to be NP-hard. We therefore advocate the use of more relaxed system models, namely asynchronous models equipped with unreliable failure detectors.

To this end, we introduce a novel implementation of the perfect failure detector, resting on an abstract model without upper bounds on end-to-end message delays. Then, we demonstrate how this algorithm can be transferred from the abstract model into a real network/system architecture. Finally, we prove that this solution exhibits real-time behavior.

1 Introduction

The research disciplines of distributed computing (DC) and real-time (RT), although often dealing with common problem domains — e.g. fault-tolerant systems/networks — seem not to reflect each others' results adequately. This might stem from apparently contrary research directions: Due to impossibility results, e.g. the impossibility of solving consensus in asynchronous systems [1], a major driver for DC research was to find weak timing models as close as possible to the asynchronous model (e.g. via unreliable failure detectors) that (1) match the highest possible number of real applications/systems and (2) allow fundamental non-trivial problems such as consensus or atomic broadcast to be solved [2, 3, 4]. Of course, with algorithms designed in some non synchronous model, liveness only can be proven to hold, not timeliness (known bounded finite delays).

In contrast, RT research traditionally focuses on queuing and scheduling disciplines in order to prove timeliness properties considering synchronous models.

---

* Partially supported by the BM:vit FIT-IT project *DCBA* (proj. no. 808198), and the Austrian FWF project *Theta* (proj. no. P17757-N04).

J.H. Anderson, G. Prencipe, and R. Wattenhofer (Eds.): OPODIS 2005, LNCS 3974, pp. 334–350, 2006.
© Springer-Verlag Berlin Heidelberg 2006

However, as is well known, proofs of timeliness properties involve solving combinatorial problems that are NP-hard, usually considering *simplified* models of reality (e.g. no failures, no cache-memory conflicts). We arrive at the mentioned gap: DC seeks solutions that are as far as possible independent of the system's timing behavior while RT considers underlying timing behaviors so as to ensure that, e.g. deadlines are met.

Is it the case that DC results regarding weak (partial) synchrony — assuming weak timing behavior — are of no use for designing RT systems, as the timeliness properties in RT should be predictable? (Exaggeratedly, one could rephrase this question to "Do DC results that guarantee safety and liveness in asynchronous *models* suddenly lose their properties when used in a synchronous *system?*")

Consider, e.g., the classic failure detector (FD) implementation by Chandra and Toueg [5]. The guarantee we get with such FDs is that crashes can eventually be detected *if eventually some unknown bound on message transmission and computing speeds holds*. At first sight, "eventually" and "some unknown bound" seem to be of little use when one wants to guarantee *hard real-time* behavior. This is mistaken. Just run Chandra and Toueg's FD implementation in a system where worst-case response times have been properly established via (distributed) schedulability analysis. In such systems one can derive worst-case response times for failure detection. Note again, that the *distributed algorithm* that implements the FD was designed for a generalized partially synchronous model (close to asynchrony), but now it provides real-time behavior!

But why should one take such a (not really straightforward) design approach? To this question there are several answers. Let us discuss two of them.

Safety. No timeliness failure — i.e., violation of the demonstrated timeliness properties — can ever lead to disagreement with asynchronous consensus algorithms based e.g. on eventually strong FD $\diamond\mathcal{S}$ [5].

This is of great interest as every solution to some RT scheduling problem inevitably rests on some schedulability analysis yielding "worst-cases under a given set of assumptions". As every assumption has a non-zero probability of being violated during operation (as we cannot tell the future) every derived bound on e.g. message delays could be violated. In such a case an algorithm that relies on these bounds will cease to work. That is, one loses safety (consistency) along with timeliness, although it need not be this way.

Performance. When trying to "implement" synchronous models, i.e., provide applications the illusion that they run in synchronous systems, timers (e.g. round durations, periods of scheduler activation) have to be set to worst-case values computed for worst-case load and failure conditions (e.g. re-transmissions of lost messages contributes to delay bounds). Thus, in many synchronous system designs, run-time behavior which is dictated by worst-case timeouts is bound to be worst-case behavior. Synchronous designs are inefficient by construction.

This deficiency increases even more as new applications for real-time systems demand highly dynamic computations. Dimensioning the systems according to rare (on demand) computations is expensive, and often not even required from a safety point of view. This can be avoided by favoring designs based on less restrictive assumptions. From these considerations emerged the concept of *design immersion* or *late binding*, which has been introduced and discussed formally by Le Lann [6, 7, 8].

Contribution. This paper provides an example of how weak synchrony assumptions can be immersed into systems to achieve real-time behavior. In Sect. 3, we present a novel algorithm for implementing the perfect FD $\mathcal{P}$ [5] in the Θ-Model, where one does not assume local clocks, or bounded computational step time or upper bounds on message transmission delay [9, 4, 10]. Rather, the Θ-Model assumes just eventual step/termination and a bounded ratio of end-to-end delays experienced by messages that are in transit simultaneously. We then show how to immerse our algorithm into a system where clocks may exist and bounded computational step times are used to implement and prove real-time behavior. To this end, we revisit the architecture that was employed in [11]. This allows us to compare timeout based FD implementations to our solutions that are message-driven and timer-free.

2   Model

For our presentation of the algorithm and our formal analysis[1] we consider a system of n distributed processes denoted as $p, q, \ldots$, which communicate through a reliable, error free and fully connected point-to-point network. We assume that a non-faulty receiver of a message knows the sender. The communication channels between processes need not provide FIFO transmission, and there is no authentication service.

At most f processes may stop by prematurely halting. A process is considered correct until it stops operation. Since we will immerse our solution into a broadcast network (Deterministic Ethernet [13]) later, we assume that any broadcast message is either received by all correct processes or by none (in the case the sender crashes before finishing its broadcast). This leads to simple fault semantics, i.e., clean crashes.

We now give two different models. The dynamic model of Sect. 2.1 will just be considered for coverage analysis. In this model, upper bounds on message end-to-end delays do not exist. There is just a relation of long and short transmission times of those messages which are simultaneously in transit. In order to keep the analysis simple we give the static model in Sect. 2.2 which is logically equivalent, i.e., any problem solvable in one of the models has a solution in the other model (see Theorem 1). However, both models assume that processes have no access to local clocks and can take a computational step only as a reaction to received messages, thus they are message-driven.

---

[1] Due to space restrictions we had to omit the full analysis of our algorithm. It can be found in the full version of the paper [12].

2.1 Dynamic Timing Model

In our dynamic model, processes communicate by message passing. The time interval a message m is in transit consists of three parts: Local message preparation and queuing at the sender, transmission over the link, and local receive computation and queuing at the receiver. We denote as t_s^m the instant the preparation of message m starts. The instant the receive computation is finished we denote as t_r^m. We assume that all communication is done by broadcasting.

In the dynamic model we say that message m is *in transit* during time interval $(t_s^m, t_r^m]$. We denote $\eta^m = t_r^m - t_s^m$ the finite end-to-end computational + queuing + transmission delay of message m sent from one correct process to another. Let $\mathcal{M}(t)$ be the set of all messages which are in transit at time t. Let $\delta(t)$ be a lower envelope function on transmission delays of all messages that are in transit at time t, such that for any time t it holds that $\delta(t) \leq min(\eta^m)$ for all $m \in \mathcal{M}(t)$ if $|\mathcal{M}(t)| > 0$ and $\delta(t) = 1$ otherwise. We define for a fixed $\Theta \in \mathbb{R}, \Theta \geq 1$ the upper envelope function $\Delta(t) = \Theta\delta(t)$. At any time t it must hold that $\Delta(t) \geq max(\eta^m)$ for all $m \in \mathcal{M}(t)$ if $|\mathcal{M}(t)| > 0$.

2.2 Static Timing Model

In contrast to the dynamic model, the static one stipulates an upper bound Δ on end-to-end delays as well as a lower bound δ such that $0 < \delta \leq \eta^m \leq \Delta < \infty$, where δ and Δ are not known in advance. Since $\Delta < \infty$, every message sent from a correct process to another one is eventually received. The *transmission delay ratio* is $\Theta = \Delta/\delta$. For our formal treatment we assume that processes have a priori knowledge of some integer Ξ (a function of Θ; cf. Theorem 5) but no knowledge on time bounds. Moreover, there is no access to an external time base, hardware clocks or similar devices that allow to get a notion of elapsed time; in other words, executions are message-driven. It follows that time passing information has to be obtained solely out of the message pattern.

In [10] we have shown the following theorem by proving that the runs of the dynamic and the static model cannot be distinguished by the processes. It follows that an algorithm that was proven correct in the static model is correct in the dynamic model as well.

Theorem 1 (Equivalence [10, Theorem 1]). *The dynamic model and the static model have the same expressive power.*

Uncertainty. Processes only communicate by broadcasting. In literature (in particular in work on clock synchronization [14]), usually, the delay uncertainty $E = \Delta - \delta$ is employed to discuss the effect of timing uncertainty (jitter). Our analysis reveals, however, that for our broadcast based algorithm we can employ a finer grained measure. Assume that a message m is broadcast at time t. It will be received by correct processes in the interval $[t + r_m, t + R_m]$ with $r_m \geq \delta$ and $R_m \leq \Delta$. We define the broadcast uncertainty $\varepsilon \geq R_m - r_m$ for all messages m. Obviously we have $\varepsilon \leq E < \Delta$. We will see in Sect. 5.2 that distinguishing between ε and E makes a big difference. It will turn out that in our targeted architecture the value of ε is close to 0 while E remains close to Δ.

Significant Timing Values. In this paper, we consider a round based algorithm that is executed in asynchronous rounds, i.e., every correct process sends a message in every round k. The transition to round $k + 1$ occurs when $n - f$ messages for the current round are received. It will turn out that the uncertainty we have to deal with does not stem from the ratio of message delays directly but rather from the ratio of the longest message delay and the shortest round switching intervals. The shortest round-switching interval δ^r, however, is not determined by only one single correct message. Rather it is determined by the sending time of the first message and the receive time of the $(n - f)^{\text{th}}$ message. This might seem irrelevant since any message is bounded by δ, and all could be sent simultaneously. From a practical point of view — as is confirmed by our analysis in Sect. 4 — this is very important, however. If one tries to establish an analytical expression for δ one would examine an idle system and the sending of a single message in this system — which could be a self reception as well. Obviously the receiver just has to deliver one message here. However, assuming that a receiver can process, say $n - f$ messages as fast as a single one is typically not valid in real systems — this would amount to assuming infinite computational power. Choosing $\delta^r = \delta$ hence would be overly conservative since round switching requires $n - f$ messages, i.e. is determined by the $(n - f)^{\text{th}}$ fastest message. Moreover, in broadcast bus networks one cannot transmit two messages simultaneously over the bus, i.e. the $n - f$ fastest messages must be transmitted one after the other. The time for $n - f$ messages to be transmitted in such networks is hence always larger than the best-case time of sending a single message in an idle system. Using δ in the analysis would lead to over-valuation of its significance.

In our analysis, we will hence set δ^r equal to the transmission time of the $(n - f)^{\text{th}}$ fastest message. That is, we will use δ^r as expression for the shortest time it may take to send $n - f$ messages from distinct processes to a single receiver (end-to-end). Let us formalize this:

Definition 1 (Incoming Messages). *For any correct process q, δ_q is the $n - f$ smallest η^m for all messages m sent by distinct correct processes that enable an event at q. δ^r is defined as the the smallest δ_q of all correct processes q.*

Lemma 1 (Sending Time). *If a correct process receives messages from at least $n - f$ distinct correct processes by time t, then at least one message was sent by time $t - \delta^r$.*

2.3 Event Generation

In previous work [15, 4] we considered purely message-driven algorithms. These algorithms are started by an external event, which triggers the first computational step. All steps after the first one are direct responses to received messages. As already shown in [4], such protocols can be employed efficiently in systems with large delay×bandwidth product; e.g. satellite broadcast communication link. In the architecture of Sect. 4, we show how to fine tune the overhead by introducing mute periods.[2] To this end we add local events to the model. Previous work that investigated the intersection of message-driven and time-driven semantics can be found in [16] where one has shown that message-driven semantics are weaker than time-driven ones by proving that the problem of self-stabilizing failure detection cannot have a message-driven solution [16] while time-driven solutions are known [17]. In fact, in [16] we proved even more. We showed that the impossibility result even holds if there are locally generated (deadlock prevention) events where no assumption is made on the occurrence of their arrival such that their semantics are too weak to employ them as clocks.

Following this result we add local events without assumptions on arrival laws to our model as well. We use local event generation in order to start instances of the basic round synchronization algorithm. In our theoretical analysis we show that the correctness of the algorithm does not depend on the actual intervals between these events. In our implementation example we then use these events in order to control the overhead such that we compare our performance with previous failure detector implementations [11].

3   General Implementation and Analysis of Perfect Failure Detector $\mathcal{P}$

The need for a definition of (unreliable) FDs emanated from the impossibility [1] of deterministic fault-tolerant consensus in asynchronous distributed systems. In their seminal paper, Chandra and Toueg [5] characterized FDs by the two properties completeness and accuracy. In an asynchronous distributed system equipped with FDs consensus is solvable. In this paper we will give an implementation of the perfect failure detector $\mathcal{P}$ that ensures the following two properties.

Strong Completeness. Eventually, every correct process permanently suspects every crashed process.
Strong Accuracy. No process is suspected before it crashes.

Our implementation of $\mathcal{P}$ follows an idea originally proposed in [9]; its pseudocode is given in Fig. 1. It is executed in consecutive instantiations which are numbered using variable i (see line 1). We will see that each instantiation can be regarded independently and that a process that crashes before instantiation j is started will be suspected at the end of j. The algorithm is started independently at each process by sending $(round, 0, 0)$ in line 4 — $round$ being just a message identifier. Note that round $k = 0$ is the only round where not all correct processes must send messages. The code inside the statement starting at line 6 is a simple round synchronization algorithm, i.e., the round number is a counter of the terminated rounds of computation. If a process has received $n - f$ messages from distinct processes for the current round k it increases k and sends its

---

[2] This is done in all FD implementations where e.g. heartbeats are sent every x (physical) time units while the FD remains mute in between.

0:   **VAR** k : integer := 0;   /* round number   */
1:   **VAR** i : integer := 0;   /* instantiation number   */
2:   **VAR** $SL[n]$: boolean := false;   /* list of suspected processes */
3:   **VAR** saw_max$[n][\infty]$: integer := 0;

4:   broadcast $(round, 0, 0)$ [once];   /* Initialization   */

5:   /* Round Synchronization */
6:   **if** received $(round, i, k)$ from at least $n - f$ distinct processes
7:        $\rightarrow$ $k := k + 1$;
8:            **if** $k > \Xi$
9:                $\rightarrow$ $\forall q$: **if** saw_max$[q][i] = 0 \rightarrow SL[q]:=$ true;
10:               $k := 0$;
11:               $i := i + 1$;
12:               $control\_overhead$;
13:           broadcast $(round, i, k)$ [once];   /* start next round   */

14: **if** received $(round, j, \ell)$ from q /* Store received messages   */
15:       $\rightarrow$ $saw\_max[q][j] := max(\ell, saw\_max[q][j])$;

Fig. 1. Perfect Failure Detector Implementation

message for the new round. Due to a priori knowledge of Ξ, a process can determine upon updating its counter whether messages from other processes for past rounds are missing. It does so in **line 8** where it checks whether all processes succeeded in sending at least $(round, i, 1)$. Processes which did not, must have crashed and are therefore suspected, i.e., added to the list of suspects SL which is the interface to upper layer applications (see Sect. 4). After that, k and i are updated and the next instantiation is started after the $control\_overhead$ command (see **line 12**), which will be used to create silent intervals between two instantiations, when the algorithm is immersed into our targeted architecture. It does so by, e.g., scheduling the transmission of the given message for some later point in time. Another way to implement timer-free local waiting are hardware instructions that exist in certain computers that allow to trigger some event when x instructions have been executed.

The chosen value of this timeout — we will introduce τ in Definition 3 as upper bound on it — neither has an influence on the correctness of the FD implementation (it could as well be set to 0) nor must be the same at every process. Moreover if there is no local timer, diverse local information may be used to get some rough estimate of elapsed time (counting interrupts or updates of the program counter etc.). In our example (Deterministic Ethernet in Sect. 5), we derive a timeout value which leads to a worst-case overhead of 5% for FD messages.

Contrary to most other FD implementations, we do not use hardware clocks to achieve FD properties, neither do we require upper bounds on message delays. Other FD implementations use local clocks or timers to timeout (1) τ and (2) the upper bound on end-to-end delays. Our solution neither relies on local information about τ nor on the existence of some upper bounds on end-to-end delays in order to detect a crashed process. It follows that our timeout mechanism remains message-driven.

To complete the description of our algorithm: The code of the statement in line 14 stores which processes have sent messages for which round. Only the message for the largest round number has to be stored here. (Note that the declaration of saw_max in line 3 includes an infinity of rows in the matrix just for conciseness of presentation. In real implementations, information from past instantiations need not be stored such that just bounded memory is needed in order to maintain the required information.)

In order to show that our algorithm does implement $\mathcal{P}$ we first analyze some properties of its included round synchronization algorithm (line 6) where k is the local round number. Since messages for different instantiations do not interfere logically with each other, we just examine the rounds for one instantiation here. For conciseness we therefore suppress i in the following. We follow the analysis of [15] where a logical clock synchronization algorithm in the presence of Byzantine faults was considered. We just focus on crashes and therefore have a simpler algorithm. After that we show the FD properties based upon these round synchronization properties. We start with some preliminary definitions.

Theorem 2 (Properties). *In the presence of $f < n$ faults, the algorithm given in Fig. 1 satisfies the following properties:*

(P) Uniform Progress. *If all correct processes set their round numbers to k by time t, then every process sets its round number at least to $k + 1$ by time $t + \Delta$.*

(U) Uniform Unforgeability. *If no process sets its round number to k by time t, then no process sets its round number to $k + 1$ by time $t + \delta^r$ or earlier.*

(S) Uniform Simultaneity. *If some process sets its round number to k at time t, then every process sets its round number at least to k by time $t + \varepsilon$.*

Lemma 2 (Fastest Progress). *Let the first correct process set its round number to k at time t. Then no correct process can reach a larger round number $k' > k$ before $t + \delta^r(k' - k)$.*

After discussing the fundamental round synchronization properties we now turn our attention to the problem of failure detection. We start with the behavior of instantiations.

Definition 2 (Instantiation). *The start of instantiation i is defined to be the earliest time b_i by which $n - f$ processes have sent $(round, i, 0)$. Further, the end of instantiation i is defined to be the time e_i the last process sets its round number to $k > \Xi$.*

The following corollary follows directly from (P) and Definition 2, which introduces D as the worst-case time between start and end of an instantiation.

Corollary 1 (Instantiation Termination Time). *For all instantiations i it holds that $e_i - b_i \leq D$, where $D = (\Xi + 1)\Delta$.*

As discussed above, we would like to fine tune the overhead of the FD algorithm to application requirements by inserting silent periods in our algorithm. In order to give a bound on detection latency we have to assume an upper bound on the duration of these periods. The value τ that we introduce in the following definition can in fact be arbitrary (depending on the required overhead) such that it cannot be used as a weak clock [3] that could be used to timeout processes.

Definition 3 (Intermission). $\tau \geq 0$ *is the upper bound on the timeout of the* control_overhead *call.*

Corollary 2 (Intermission Period). *For all instantiations i and $i+1$ it holds that $b_{i+1} - e_i \leq \tau$.*

With the results regarding timing we now turn our attention to FD semantics.

Theorem 3 (Strong Completeness). *Let $\varXi$ be some positive integer. In a system with $n > f$ processes, the algorithm given in Fig. 1 ensures that each process p that crashes by time b_i is suspected by all correct processes by time e_i.*

We now give two theorems for strong accuracy. Theorem 5 is typical for results in the $\varTheta$-Model as no time unit parameters show up but just the integer $\varXi \geq \varTheta$. From Theorem 4, however, one sees the parameters that have to be evaluated during immersion more explicitly, i.e., $\varDelta$, ε, and δ^r.

Theorem 4 (Strong Accuracy). *Let $\varXi \geq \left\lfloor \frac{\varDelta}{\delta^r} + \frac{\varepsilon}{\delta^r} \right\rfloor + 1$. In a system with $n > f$ processes, the algorithm given in Fig. 1 ensures that no process is suspected before it crashes.*

Theorem 5 (Strong Accuracy in the $\varTheta$-Model). *Let $\varXi \geq \lfloor 2\varTheta \rfloor$. In a system with $n > f$ processes, the algorithm given in Fig. 1 ensures that no process is suspected before it crashes.*

Assume that we have a system with $\varepsilon = 0$ and $\left\lfloor \frac{\varDelta}{\delta^r} \right\rfloor = 1$ which according to Theorem 4 requires $\varXi \geq 2$ for failure detection with our algorithm. Following Theorem 5, we say that the system *behaves as* a system obeying the $\varTheta$-Model with $\varTheta = 1$. Similarly we show in Sect. 5 that our architecture built upon Deterministic Ethernet requires just $\varXi \geq 2$ as well.

To achieve real-time behavior we require an upper bound on detection time. We give such a bound only for crashes that happen after time b_0, since obviously we cannot bound detection latencies for crashes that occurred before the algorithm was running. Such crashes, however, will be detected by all correct processes by time e_0 by Theorem 3.

Theorem 6 (Detection Latency). *Let $\varXi$ be according to Theorem 4 resp. Theorem 5. In a system with $n > f$ processes, the algorithm given in Fig. 1 ensures that a crash occurring at time $t \geq b_0$ is detected by time $t + L$, with detection latency $L = \tau + 2D$.*

Theorems 3 and 5 show that completeness and accuracy just depend on Θ while only *timeliness* depends on Θ and Δ (i.e., the assumed time bound). If Δ is violated but Θ still holds (which is possible in many real systems/networks [9]) we still guarantee completeness and accuracy while just timely detection is lost. This is the best one can hope for, given that Δ is violated here!

Despite Theorem 6 we have no solution to a real-time problem yet, since we did not show how to implement both the system model and the algorithm in a real network. To this end we have to show that the assumed timing behavior in the abstract model can be matched by demonstrated timeliness properties in real systems. We do so in the following section in order to give a complete solution to the RT FD problem for a network architecture based on Deterministic Ethernet and suitable scheduling algorithms.

4   Architectural Model

In this section, we sketch out a generic architectural model of the systems under consideration. See [11] for a detailed presentation of that model.

We consider a finite set Π of processors, interconnected by a network, referred to as Net. The nominal size of Π is $n > 1$. The model of a processor is given in Fig. 2. The software/hardware architecture is modeled after a number of levels, such as the application software level, the middleware level, the executive/operating system level, various communication protocol levels, the input/output (I/O) level. Processors act as sources of messages. There are two

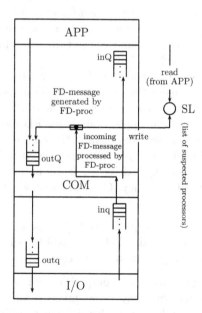

Fig. 2. Architectural model of a processor

types of messages. Messages handled by FDs are denoted FD-messages. Messages other than FD-messages are referred to as ordinary messages (e.g. application, middleware, system). Let COM denote the level of communication protocols where one finds FD modules. An FD module consists of a process, denoted FD-proc, which maintains a local list of suspects, denoted SL. At any time, $SL(p)$ contains the names of those processors that p's FD suspects (rightly or erroneously) of having failed. In addition, FD-proc receives and broadcasts FD-messages so as to "prove" that its processor has not failed. Let APP denote the application level.

Let us model those waiting queues visited by outgoing messages, from the APP level down to the COM level, as a single queue, denoted $outQ$, and those waiting queues visited by outgoing messages, from the COM level down to the I/O level, as a single queue, denoted $outq$. We define inq and inQ similarly. An FD-message is initially deposited by FD-proc in $outQ$, moved to $outq$ after being serviced in $outQ$, transmitted across Net after being serviced in $outq$, deposited in inq, then delivered to FD-proc after being serviced in inq. An ordinary message is initially deposited by an algorithm A in $outQ$, moved to $outq$ after being serviced in $outQ$, transmitted across Net after being serviced in $outq$, deposited in inq, then moved to inQ after being serviced in inq, and delivered to A after being serviced in inQ.

Correct modeling of reality leads to considering that a processor servicing a message pending in a waiting queue is not preempted. Consequently, we define variables w_{outQ}, w_{outq}, w_{inq}, and w_{inQ} as the service times corresponding to the four waiting queues, respectively, that is the worst-case times for servicing a message pending in each of these queues. We define d_m as the blocking factor with Net, i.e., d_m is the exact time needed for transmitting the longest ordinary message over the physical link between a processor and Net.

Let γ stand for an upper bound on end-to-end delays for an FD-message, measured at the COM level.

Under worst-case processor and Net "loads", waiting queues build up and Net contention arises for transmitting concurrent FD-messages and ordinary messages on the one hand, concurrent FD-messages on the other hand. Fast failure detection is achievable only if upper bounds for FD-messages' sojourn times in waiting queues and Net nodes are optimal, the case whenever FD-messages are serviced prior to ordinary messages. This can be enforced by resorting to classical priority-driven, or deadline-driven, scheduling policies that implement the well-known head-of-the-line policy. Consequently, we retain the following $\mathcal{SW}$ algorithm:

$\mathcal{SW}$. In every visited waiting queue, an FD-message is always deposited ahead of ordinary messages and behind possibly pending FD-messages. It is serviced prior to any ordinary message.

In order to resolve interprocessor competition for network and processor resources optimally, processors may be assigned priorities or messages may be assigned different relative deadlines. Priorities or deadlines being fixed, they define a total order over any set of FD-messages whenever contention develops.

Any such assignment is equivalent to assigning indices $1, \ldots, n$ over set Π, one index per processor. Moreover, whenever possible, preemption (of a broadcast medium, of a Net node) should be exercised, to the benefit of FD-messages, for it is known that preemption may be needed to achieve optimality. Therefore, we retain the following SN algorithm:

SN. Net resources are allocated to FD-messages, prior to ordinary messages; in case of interprocessor competition for transmitting FD-messages, FD-messages are serviced in increasing index order.

Let $\psi(x)$ stand for the worst-case time it takes for x processors to preempt Net locally and to fully resolve Net contention involving x FD-messages and $\psi'(x')$ stand for the worst-case time it takes for a processor to fully service a set of x incoming FD-messages, both measured at the COM level (x' is a function of x). Let ν be the smallest FD-message inter-arrival delay. Bound x' is the maximum number of FD-messages (out of x) that are not serviced at the time the last incoming FD-message is deposited into inq. Given SW, $x' = 1$ if $\nu \geq w_{inq}$, $x' = \lceil x\,(1 - \nu/w_{inq}) \rceil$ if $\nu < w_{inq}$, and $\psi'(x') = x'\,w_{inq}$.

Bound $\psi(x)$ is determined by policies SW and SN and bound $\psi'(x')$ is determined by algorithm SW. Hence, $\psi(x)$ and $\psi'(x')$ are tight. Let θ stand for the worst-case time needed for transmitting an FD-message across Net, measured at the I/O level, including the time needed for delivery into inq. A tight bound θ can be computed, considering that optimal schedulers (proper to Net) service FD-messages prior to ordinary messages. Consequently, for an FD-message generated by that processor assigned index x, tight bound $\gamma(x)$ is as follows:

$$\gamma(x) = w_{outQ} + w_{outq} + d_m + \psi(x) + \theta + x'\,w_{inq}.$$

Note the importance of differentiating between end-to-end delays proper to every process in a system. If no such differentiation is made, one faces a circular dependency. A distributed system consists of some architecture (processors, links) and all the system processes and application processes that run on the architecture. It makes no sense to talk about upper bounds on message delays in the "system" if one part of the system, i.e., the system processes and application processes are not known since they may produce unknown loads on the processors and/or links. Conversely, if one specifies the exact scheduling policy used for every class of processes, the circular dependency vanishes. For a given process p, only processes scheduled prior to p may influence upper bounds on response times. When choosing a head-of-the-line policy for a process (our case, for the FD process), then it is possible to conduct a worst-case schedulability analysis for that process ignoring all other processes (to the exception of simple blocking factors in case of non preemption). This is what we have shown how to do.

In Sect. 5, we consider Deterministic Ethernets and establish the analytical expression of γ for such networks. Then, we derive ρ, the worst-case overhead induced by FD-messages, and finally L, a tight upper bound on processor failure detection latencies. Before that we shortly discuss the network traffic which is induced by our FD implementation.

5   Illustration with Ethernets

We illustrate our generic results with Ethernet-like networks. Let COM be the ISO/OSI data link level. With Ethernets, $\theta = 0$ as $\psi(x)$ includes local physical transmission delays and there is no additional transmission delay. Hence, $\gamma(x) = w_{outQ} + w_{outq} + d_m + \psi(x) + x' w_{inq}$. Being concerned with real-time systems, we must consider a deterministic variant of the original Ethernet CSMA/CD protocol. This variant has been implemented in COTS products and is called CSMA/DCR (Carrier Sense Multi Access / Deterministic Collision Resolution), which is based on distributed deterministic balanced m-ary tree searches [13].

5.1   CSMA/DCR

Broadcast media are physically characterized by a channel slot time, denoted σ. Sources of messages are processors. Channel sharing between sources works like CSMA-CD whenever there is no unresolved collision pending. When a collision is detected (and there is no previous collision pending), sources initiate a deterministic balanced m-ary tree search collectively. To this end, every source is assigned some unique index. For this illustration, it suffices to consider exactly one index per source. A tree search proceeds from left to right, searching for subtrees that either are empty or contain exactly one active leaf. A leaf is active if its index is that of a source which has a message pending. Obviously, during a tree search, a message submitted by a source assigned index i is transmitted prior to messages submitted by sources assigned indexes greater than i. A tree search is time bounded, which permits computing $\psi(x)$.

Consider x sources, each attempting to transmit a pending message (rank 1 in $outq$). Let $\Sigma(x)$ be the time needed to physically transmit these x messages locally, in the absence of contention. Consider now that these x sources "collide." Let ξ_x^l be the maximum number of steps needed to search x leaves in a m-ary tree of l leaves. In [18] and [19], one shows for $x \in \{2, \ldots, l\}$:

$$\xi_x^l = \frac{m^{\lceil \log_m(m\lfloor \frac{x}{2}\rfloor)\rceil} - 1}{m - 1} + m\left\lfloor \frac{x}{2}\right\rfloor\left\lfloor \log_m\left(\frac{l}{m\lfloor \frac{x}{2}\rfloor}\right)\right\rfloor - \left(x - m\left\lfloor \frac{x}{2}\right\rfloor\right).$$

This formula applies for any assignment of x indexes over l sources. The worst-case delay involved with resolving a collision fully is $\Sigma(x) + \xi_x^l\,\sigma$.

CSMA/DCR has been designed to be fault-tolerant. This protocol may be defeated whenever sources get out of synchrony, which is revealed by detecting a collision on some tree leaf. Whenever this occurs, a channel jamming sequence $\mathcal{JS}$ of duration at least equal to $\log_m(l)\,\sigma$ is generated by the sources. Message transmissions are resumed when the channel returns to idle.

5.2   Behavior of the FD in Our Architecture

Evaluating ε. Our FD algorithm requires a priori knowledge of Ξ. Therefore, we examine the timing of our architecture in order to derive values for the timing parameters used in Theorem 4. Due to the physical properties of Net, all messages are received by all processes at I/O level within σ. Due to our queuing algorithm $\mathcal{SW}$, all FD-messages are taken out of inq by the FD-processes within σ as well. That is, $\varepsilon = \sigma$.

Bound on γ. We now derive a term for calculating the worst-case end-to-end delay of a message that participates in a collision on Net with x messages.

We use the $\mathcal{JS}$ mechanism to indicate that an on-going tree search performed for ordinary messages must be stopped, in order to transmit FD-messages. The channel is preempted without aborting any ordinary message, hence the blocking factor is d_m. After $\mathcal{JS}$ has been generated, only FD-messages are transmitted during the same tree search. Transmission of ordinary messages is resumed from its preemption state when the channel returns to idle. Given that the body of an FD-message requires only to contain 2 bits[3] (which can easily be stored within the smallest possible Ethernet message), its physical transmission delay is that of a message of minimum duration, i.e., slot time σ. Therefore, $\Sigma(x) = x\sigma$. Tight bound $\psi(x)$ is as follows:

$$\psi(x) = \left(log_m(l) + x + \xi_x^l\right)\sigma.$$

The smallest FD-message inter-arrival delay is σ. Hence, $x' = \lceil x\left(1 - \sigma/w_{inq}\right)\rceil$ if $\sigma < w_{inq}$, $x' = 1$ if $\sigma \geq w_{inq}$. Tight bound γ for the xth FD-message is:

$$\gamma(x) = w_{outQ} + w_{outq} + d_m + \psi(x) + x' w_{inq}.$$

Evaluating δ^r. We already partially discussed the expression of Theorem 4 (i.e., ε), which can be used to determine a numerical value for Ξ. What remains to do is to give an analytical expression of $\frac{\Delta}{\delta^r}$. In the worst-case, $\Delta = \gamma(n)$. It remains to derive an expression for δ^r. Recall that δ^r is defined as a *lower bound* on the time between when the first of $n - f$ messages is sent to some process p and when p receives the last of the $n - f$ messages. Let us assume pessimistically that on the bus the $n - f$ messages are sent back to back, i.e., on the bus they require $(n - f) \cdot \sigma$ time units. (Note that this lower bound is by no means tight as our solution always requires $\mathcal{JS}$ which leads to a distributed tree search.) At inq the $(n - f)$ messages, however, queue up such that from the time the last message arrives additional $(n - f)' \cdot w_{inq}$ time units are required. At the respective outgoing queues at the first sender we have to add w_{outQ} and w_{outq} while we assume that there is no congestion at Net. Summing up, we see that:

$$\delta^r = w_{outQ} + w_{outq} + (n - f) \cdot \sigma + (n - f)' \cdot w_{inq}.$$

5.3 Numerical Examples and Discussion

We use the same numerical values as in [11] to have a meaningful comparison. Let us consider 10 MBit/s Ethernets. According to the ISO/OSI standard, $n \leq 1,024$

---

[3] We will justify this in Sect. 5.3 by showing that $\Xi = 2$ suffices for failure detection.

Case 1: $n = l = 16$

results of [11]	our results
$D = 5.93\,ms$	$D = 17.78\,ms$
$\tau = 103.55\,ms$	$\tau = 292.87\,ms$
$L = 114.61\,ms$	$L = 328.44\,ms$

Case 2: $n = l = 1,024$

results of [11]	our results
$D = 275.39\,ms$	$D = 826.18\,ms$
$\tau = 6.52288\,s$	$\tau = 18.74246\,s$
$L = 7.07287\,s$	$L = 20.39482\,s$

Fig. 3. Comparison to [11]

and $\sigma = 51.2\ \mu s$ (microseconds). We assume that the size of the longest ordinary message (I/O level framing) is $10,000$ bits, i.e., $d_m = 1$ ms (millisecond). Let us pick up $250\ \mu s$ for each of the service times w_{outQ}, w_{outq}, and w_{inq}. Hence $\gamma(x) = 1.5 + \psi(x) + 0.25\,x'$ (in ms), with $x' = \lceil 0.7952\,x \rceil$. Results shown below are rounded up to a precision of $10\ \mu s$. We consider quaternary trees $(m = 4)$.

With Perfect FDs, $x = n$. As in [11] we pick up $f = 5$ as the upper bound on the number of processes that can crash during the execution of the algorithm (a very high number given practical fault probabilities). Thus, we get:

Case 1: $n = l = 16$, $f = 5$. $x' = 13$, $\psi(16) = \psi_1 = 1.18$ ms, hence $\gamma(16) = \gamma_1 = 5.93$ ms.

$(n - f)' = 9$, $\delta_1^\tau = 3.31$ ms, hence $\frac{\Delta}{\delta_1^\tau} = \frac{\gamma_1}{\delta_1^\tau} = \frac{5.93\ \text{ms}}{3.31\ \text{ms}} = 1.79$. Adding $\frac{\varepsilon}{\delta_1^\tau} = \frac{51.2\ \mu s}{3.31\ \text{ms}} = 0.02$ to this and applying the floor function (cf. Theorem 4) we get $\Xi = 2$. By Corollary 1 the termination time of an instantiation $D = (\Xi + 1)\Delta$ such that we get $D_1 = 3\gamma_1 = 17.78$ ms

Case 2: $n = l = 1024$, $f = 5$. $x' = 815$, $\psi(1,024) = \psi_2 = 70.14$ ms, hence $\gamma(1,024) = \gamma_2 = 275.39$ ms.

$(n - f)' = 811$, $\delta_2^\tau = 255.42$ ms, hence $\frac{\Delta}{\delta_2^\tau} = \frac{\gamma_2}{\delta_2^\tau} = \frac{275.39\ \text{ms}}{255.42\ \text{ms}} = 1.08$. Additionally, $\frac{\varepsilon}{\delta_2^\tau} = \frac{51.2\ \mu s}{255.42\ \text{ms}} = 0.0002$ such that again $\Xi = 2$. $D_2 = 3\gamma_2 = 826.18$ ms.

The worst-case FD-message overhead is $\rho = 3(\psi(x) + x\,w_{inq})/(D + \tau)$. Let us pick up $\rho = 5\%$. We get $\tau = 60\,(\psi(x) + 0.25\,x) - D$ (in ms). Thus we derive the following values for the mute periods τ and the tight upper bound on the failure detection latency L (cf. Theorem 6).

Case 1: $\tau_1 = 292.87$ ms, $L_1 = 328.44$ ms.

Case 2: $\tau_2 = 18.74246$ s, $L_2 = 20.39482$ s.

Let us compare our results with those presented in [11]. In Fig. 3, we see that the "worst-case price" for our message-driven implementation is a factor 3. This means that we have a worst-case detection latency that is 3 times larger with the same overhead or that one can achieve the same detection latency by tripling the overhead.

At first sight, these results seem to contradict one of the arguments (performance) at the core of the design immersion or late binding principle (cf. Sect. 1). This is not the case. Firstly, a complete comparison should take coverage into consideration. In other words, one should compare numerical results considering violations of the assumed timing behavior postulated in a synchronous model, i.e. timing bounds that are not tight, these bounds being such that the probability of having a bound violated or Θ violated is the same. Secondly, the run-time behavior induced by the synchronous design of [11] is always the actual worst-case behavior, even if actual delays are smaller than their postulated bounds most of the time (e.g. the blocking factor d_m). Conversely, the run-time behavior induced by the asynchronous design given in this paper simply matches the best-case or average-case message delay scenarios, yielding actual failure detection latencies (much) smaller than values computed for L.

Finally, experimental results [20] confirm the analytical ones, showing that broadcast bus based systems are particularly well suited for the Θ-Model. In our architecture we have seen that the value of Θ (derived from Ξ) is much smaller than the ratio of absolute bounds on worst-case and best-case message end-to-end delays.

6 Conclusions

In this paper, we have illustrated a number of concepts related to real-time computing and asynchronous models of computation. From a theoretical viewpoint, an interesting result is that we showed that local physical clocks are not required to detect crashed processes in bounded finite time. To this end, we have presented an implementation of the perfect FD $\mathcal{P}$ in the Θ-Model. One major merit of this implementation is its very high coverage, since the FD $\mathcal{P}$ semantics are not violated when postulated end-to-end upper bounds are violated, provided that Θ is not violated, which is not the case with implementations in partially synchronous models.

Acknowledgments. We are grateful to Gérard Le Lann and Ulrich Schmid for many valuable discussions on the Θ-Model.

References

1. Fischer, M.J., Lynch, N.A., Paterson, M.S.: Impossibility of distributed consensus with one faulty process. Journal of the ACM **32**(2) (1985) 374–382
2. Aguilera, M.K., Delporte-Gallet, C., Fauconnier, H., Toueg, S.: On implementing Omega with weak reliability and synchrony assumptions. In: Proceeding of the 22nd Annual ACM Symposium on Principles of Distributed Computing (PODC'03). (2003)
3. Fetzer, C., Schmid, U., Süßkraut, M.: On the possibility of consensus in asynchronous systems with finite average response times. In: Proceedings of the 25th International Conference on Distributed Computing Systems (ICDCS'05), Columbus, Ohio, USA (2005)
4. Widder, J., Le Lann, G., Schmid, U.: Failure detection with booting in partially synchronous systems. In: Proceedings of the 5th European Dependable Computing Conference (EDCC-5). Volume 3463 of LNCS., Budapest, Hungary, Springer Verlag (2005) 20–37
5. Chandra, T.D., Toueg, S.: Unreliable failure detectors for reliable distributed systems. Journal of the ACM **43**(2) (1996) 225–267

6. Le Lann, G.: On real-time and non real-time distributed computing. In: Proc. 9th Int'l Workshop on Distributed Algorithms. Volume 972 of LNCS., Springer-Verlag (1995) 51–70 invited paper.
7. Le Lann, G.: Proof-based system engineering and embedded systems. In: Proc. European School on Embedded Systems. Volume 1494 of LNCS., Springer Verlag (1996) 208–248 invited paper.
8. Le Lann, G.: Asynchrony and real-time dependable computing. In: 8th IEEE International Workshop on Object-Oriented Real-Time Dependable Systems (WORDS 2003), Guadalajara, Mexico. (2003) 18–25
9. Le Lann, G., Schmid, U.: How to implement a timer-free perfect failure detector in partially synchronous systems. Technical Report 183/1-127, Department of Automation, Technische Universität Wien (2003)
10. Widder, J.: Distributed Computing in the Presence of Bounded Asynchrony. PhD thesis, Vienna University of Technology, Fakultät für Informatik (2004)
11. Hermant, J.F., Le Lann, G.: Fast asynchronous uniform consensus in real-time distributed systems. IEEE Transactions on Computers **51**(8) (2002) 931–944
12. Hermant, J.F., Widder, J.: Implementing time free designs for distributed real-time systems (a case study). Research Report 23/2004, Technische Universität Wien, Institut für Technische Informatik (2004) Joint Research Report with INRIA Rocquencourt.
13. Le Lann, G., Rolin, P.: Process and device for the transmission of messages between different stations through a local distribution network. US Patent Number 4,847,835, July 1989, French Patent Number 84-16957, November 1984 (1984)
14. Lundelius-Welch, J., Lynch, N.A.: An upper and lower bound for clock synchronization. Information and Control **62** (1984) 190–204
15. Widder, J.: Booting clock synchronization in partially synchronous systems. In: Proceedings of the 17th International Symposium on Distributed Computing (DISC'03). Volume 2848 of LNCS., Sorrento, Italy, Springer Verlag (2003) 121–135
16. Hutle, M., Widder, J.: On the possibility and the impossibility of message-driven self-stabilizing failure detection. In: Proceedings of the 7th International Symposium on Self Stabilizing Systems (SSS 2005). Volume 3764 of LNCS., Barcelona, Spain, Springer Verlag (2005) 153–170 — Appeared also as brief announcement in *Proceedings of the 24th ACM Symposium on Principles of Distributed Computing (PODC'05)*.
17. Beauquier, J., Kekkonen-Moneta, S.: Fault-tolerance and self-stabilization: Impossibility results and solutions using self-stabilizing failure detectors. International Journal of Systems Science **28**(11) (1997) 1177–1187
18. Hermant, J.F., Le Lann, G.: A protocol and correctness proofs for real-time high-performance broadcast networks. Proc. IEEE Int'l Conf. Distributed Computing Systems (1998) 360–369
19. Hermant, J.F.: Quelques problèmes et solutions en ordonnancement temps réel pour systèmes répartis. PhD thesis, Paris-VI-Pierre-et-Marie-Curie Univ. (1999)
20. Albeseder, D.: Evaluation of message delay correlation in distributed systems. In: Proceedings of the Third Workshop on Intelligent Solutions for Embedded Systems, Hamburg, Germany (2005)

Reconfigurable Distributed Storage for Dynamic Networks*

Gregory Chockler[1,2], Seth Gilbert[1], Vincent Gramoli[3,4], Peter M. Musial[3], and Alex A. Shvartsman[1,3]

[1] CSAIL, Massachusetts Institute of Technology, Cambridge, MA 02139, USA.
grishac@csail.mit.edu, sethg@mit.edu, alex@theory.csail.mit.edu
[2] IBM Haifa Labs, Haifa University Campus, Mount Carmel, Haifa 31905, Israel.
[3] Dep. of Comp. Sci. and Eng., University of Connecticut, Storrs, CT 06269, USA.
piotr@cse.uconn.edu
[4] IRISA, Campus de Beaulieu, 35042 Rennes Cedex, France.
vgramoli@irisa.fr

Abstract. This paper presents a new algorithm, *RDS* (Reconfigurable Distributed Storage), for implementing a reconfigurable distributed shared memory in an asynchronous dynamic network. The algorithm guarantees atomic consistency (linearizability) in all executions in the presence of arbitrary crash failures of processors and message loss and delays. The algorithm incorporates a quorum-based read/write algorithm and an optimized consensus protocol, based on Paxos. RDS achieves the design goals of: (i) allowing read and write operations to complete rapidly, and (ii) providing long-term fault tolerance through reconfiguration, a process that evolves the quorum configurations used by the read and write operations. The new algorithm improves on previously developed alternatives by using a more efficient reconfiguration protocol, thus guaranteeing better fault tolerance and faster recovery from network instability. This paper presents RDS, a formal proof of correctness, conditional performance analysis, and experimental results.

Keywords: Distributed algorithms, reconfiguration, atomic objects, performance.

1 Introduction

Providing consistent and available data storage in a dynamic network is an important basic service for modern distributed applications. To be able to tolerate failures, such services must replicate data, which results in the challenging problem of maintaining consistency despite a continually changing computation and communication medium. The techniques that were previously developed to maintain consistent data in static network are largely inadequate for the dynamic settings of extant and emerging networks.

Recently a new direction was proposed that integrates dynamic reconfiguration within a distributed data storage service. The goal of this research was to enable the storage service to guarantee consistency (safety) in the presence of asynchrony, arbitrary changes in the collection of participating network nodes, and varying connectivity. The original service, called RAMBO (Reconfigurable Atomic Memory for Basic

---

* This work is supported in part by the NSF Grants 0311368 and 0121277.

J.H. Anderson, G. Prencipe, and R. Wattenhofer (Eds.): OPODIS 2005, LNCS 3974, pp. 351–365, 2006.
© Springer-Verlag Berlin Heidelberg 2006

Objects) [1, 2], supports multi-reader/multi-writer atomic objects in dynamic settings. The reconfiguration service is loosely coupled with the read/write service. This allows for the service to separate data access from reconfiguration, during which the previous set of participating nodes can be upgraded to an arbitrary new set of participants. Of note, read and write operations can continue to make progress while the reconfiguration is ongoing. Reconfiguration is a two step process. First, the next configuration is agreed upon by the members of the previous configuration; then obsolete configurations are removed using a separate configuration upgrade process. As a result, multiple configurations can co-exist in the system if the removal of obsolete configurations is slow. This approach leads to an interesting dilemma. (a) On the one hand, decoupling the choice of new configurations from the removal of old configurations allows for better concurrency and simplified operation. Thus each operation requires weaker fault-tolerance assumptions. (b) On the other hand, the delay between the installation of a new configuration and the removal of obsolete configurations is increased. Delaying the removal of obsolete configurations can slow down reconfiguration, lead to multiple extant configurations, and require stronger fault-tolerance assumptions.

Our broader current research direction is to study the trade-off between the simplicity of loosely coupled reconfiguration protocols, as in [1,2], and the fault tolerance properties that they require. This paper presents a new algorithm that more tightly integrates the two stages of reconfiguration. Our goal is to reduce the cost of reconfiguration, both in terms of latency and the fault-tolerance properties required of the configurations. We bound and reduce the time during which the old configurations need to remain active, without impacting the efficiency of data access operations. Reducing this time can substantially increase the fault-tolerance of the service, despite the more complicated integrated reconfiguration operation.

Contributions. In this paper we present a new distributed algorithm for implementing a read/write distributed shared memory in a dynamic asynchronous network. This algorithm, named *RDS* (Reconfigurable Distributed Storage), is fault-tolerant, using replication to ensure that data can survive node failures, and reconfigurable, tolerating continuous changes in the set of participating nodes. As in the original approach [1], we implement atomic (linearizable) object semantics, where in order to maintain consistency in the presence of small and transient changes, the algorithm uses *configurations* consisting of *quorums* of locations. Read and write operations consist of two phases, each phase accessing the needed read- or write-quorums. In order to tolerate significant changes in the computing medium we implement *reconfiguration* that evolves quorum configurations over time.

In RDS we take a radically different approach to reconfiguration. To speed up reconfiguration and reduce the time during which obsolete configurations must remain accessible, we present an integrated reconfiguration algorithm that overlays the protocol for choosing the next configuration with the protocol for removing obsolete configurations. The protocol for choosing and agreeing on the next configuration is based on an optimized version of Paxos [3,4,5,6]. The protocol for removing obsolete configurations is a two-phase protocol, involving quorums of the old and the new configurations.

In summary, RDS improves on the previous solutions [1, 2, 7] by using a more efficient reconfiguration protocol that relaxes some of the fault tolerance assumptions made in prior work and that provides faster recovery following network instability. In this paper we present the new algorithm, a formal proof of correctness, conditional performance results, and highly encouraging experimental results of additional operation latency due to reconfiguration. The highlights of our approach are as follows:

- *Read/write independence:* Read and write operations are independent of ongoing reconfigurations, and can make progress regardless of ongoing reconfiguration or the time it takes for reconfiguration to terminate (e.g., due to the instability of leaders selected by the reconfiguration algorithm). Even if the network is completely asynchronous, as long as reconfigurations are not too frequent (with respect to network latencies), then read and write operations are able to complete.
- *Fully flexible reconfiguration:* The algorithm imposes no dependencies between the quorum configurations selected for installation.
- *Fast reconfiguration:* The reconfiguration uses a leader-based protocol; when the leader is stable, reconfigurations are very fast: 3 network delays. Since halting consensus requires at least 3 network delays, this is seemingly optimal. Combining quorum reconfiguration with optimized 3-delay "Fast Paxos" requires new techniques since (i) prior attempts to use Paxos for reconfiguration depend on each reconfiguration using the existing quorum system to install the next, while (ii) "Fast Paxos" uses preparatory work from earlier configurations that may be obsolete.
- *Fast read operations:* Read operations require only two message delays when no write operations interfere with it.
- *Fast recovery:* Our solution eliminates the need for recovery following network instability and the associated clean-up of obsolete quorum configurations. Specifically, and unlike the prior RAMBO algorithms [1,2] that may generate a backlog of old configurations, there is never more than one old configuration at a time.

Our reconfiguration algorithm can be viewed as an example of protocol composition advocated by van der Meyden and Moses [8]. Instead of waiting for the establishment of a new configuration and then running the obsolete configuration removal protocol, we compose (or overlay) the two protocols so that the upgrade to the next configuration takes place as soon as possible.

Background. Several approaches have been used to implement consistent data in (static) distributed systems. Starting with the work of Gifford [9] and Thomas [10], many algorithms have used collections of intersecting sets of objects replicas (such as quorums) to solve the consistency problem. Upfal and Wigderson [11] use majority sets of readers and writers to emulate shared memory. Vitányi and Awerbuch [12] use matrices of registers where the rows and the columns are written and respectively read by specific processors. Attiya, Bar-Noy and Dolev [13] use majorities of processors to implement shared objects in static message passing systems. Extension for limited reconfiguration of quorum systems have also been explored [14, 15].

Virtually synchronous services [16], and group communication services (GCS) in general [17], can also be used to implement consistent data services, e.g., by implementing a global totally ordered broadcast. While the universe of processors in a GCS can evolve, in most implementations, forming a new view takes a substantial time, and client operations are interrupted during view formation. However the dynamic algorithms, such as the algorithm presented in this work and [1, 2, 7], allow reads and writes to make progress during reconfiguration.

Reconfigurable storage algorithms are finding their way into practical implementations [18, 19]. The new algorithm presented here has the potential of making further impact on system development.

Document Structure. Section 2 defines the model of computation. We present the algorithm in Section 3. In Section 4 we present the correctness proofs. In Section 5 we present conditional performance analysis of the algorithm. Section 6 contains experimental results about operation latency. The conclusions are in Section 7.

2   System Model and Definitions

We use a message-passing model with asynchronous processors that have unique identifiers (the set of processor identifiers need not be finite). Processors may crash. Processors communicate via point-to-point asynchronous unreliable channels. In normal operation any processor can send a message to any other processor. In safety (atomicity) proofs we do not make *any* assumptions about the length of time it takes for a message to be delivered.

To analyze the performance of the new algorithm, we make additional assumptions as to the performance of the underlying network. In particular, we assume that eventually (at some unknown point) the network stabilizes, becoming synchronous and delivering messages in bounded (but unknown) time. We also restrict the rate of reconfiguration after stabilization, and limit node failures such that some quorum remains available in an active configuration. (For example, in majority quorums, this means that only a minority of nodes in a configuration fail between reconfigurations.) We present a more detailed explanation in Section 5.

Our algorithm uses *quorum configurations*. A *configuration c* consists of three components: (i) *members*(c), a finite set of processor ids, (ii) *read-quorums*(c), a set of quorums, and (iii) *write-quorums*(c), a set of quorums, where each quorum is a subset of *members*(c). We require that the read quorums and write quorums of a common configuration intersect: formally, for every $R \in$ *read-quorums*(c) and $W \in$ *write-quorums*(c), the intersection $R \cap W \neq \emptyset$.

3   RDS Algorithm

In this section, we present a description of RDS. An overview of the algorithm appears in Figure 1 and Figure 2 (the algorithm is formally specified in the full paper). We present the algorithm for a single object; atomicity is preserved under composition and the complete shared memory is obtained by composing multiple objects. See [20] for an example of a more streamlined support of multiple objects.

In order to ensure fault tolerance, data is replicated at several nodes in the network. The key challenge, then, is to maintain the consistency among the replicas, even as the underlying set of replicas may be changing. The algorithm uses *quorum configurations* to maintain consistency, and *reconfiguration* to modify the set of replicas. During read() or write(v) operation at node i:

- **RW-Phase-1a:** Node i chooses a unique id, t, and sends a $\langle RW1a, t \rangle$ message to a read quorum of every active configuration. Node i stores the set of active configurations in *op-configs*.
- **RW-Phase-1b:** If node j receives a $\langle RW1a, t \rangle$ message from i, it sends a $\langle RW1b, t, tag, value \rangle$ message back to node i.
- **RW-Phase-2a:** If node i receives a $\langle RW1b, t, tag, value \rangle$ message from j, it updates its tag and value. If it receives $RW1b$ messages from a read quorum of *all* configurations in *op-configs*, then the first phase is complete. If the ongoing operation is a read operation and the tag has already been confirmed, node i returns the current value; otherwise it sends a $\langle RW2a, t, tag', value' \rangle$ message to a write quorum of every active configuration where tag' and $value'$ depend on whether it is a read or a write operation: in the case of a read, they are just equal to the local tag and $value$; in the case of a write, they are a newly unique chosen tag, and v, the value to write. Node i resets *op-configs* to the set of active configurations.
- **RW-Phase-2b:** If j receives a $\langle RW2a, t, tag, value \rangle$ message from i, it updates its tag and value and sends to i, $\langle RW2b, t, configs \rangle$, where *configs* is the set of active configurations.
- **RW-Done:** If node i receives message $\langle RW2b, t, c \rangle$, it adds any new configurations from c to its set of active configurations and to *op-configs*. If it receives a $RW2b$ message from a write quorum of *all* configurations in *op-configs*, then the read or write operation is complete and the tag is marked confirmed. If it is a read operation, node i returns its current value to client.

Fig. 1. The phases of the read and write protocols. Each protocol requires up to two phases.

normal operation, there is a single active configuration; during reconfiguration, when the set of replicas is changing, there may be two active configurations. Throughout the algorithm, each node maintains a set of *active configurations*. A new configuration is added to the set during a reconfiguration, and the old one is removed at the end of a reconfiguration.

Read and Write Operations. Read and write operations proceed by accessing the currently active configurations. Each replica maintains a *tag* and a *value* for the data being replicated. Tag is a counter-id pair used as a write operation version number where its node id serves as a tiebreaker. Each read or write operation potentially requires two phases: **RW-Phase-1** to *query* the replicas, learning the most up-to-date tag and value, and **RW-Phase-2** to *propagate* the tag and value to the replicas. In a *query* phase, the initiator contacts one read quorum from each active configuration, and remembers the largest tag and its associated value. In a *propagate* phase, read and write operations behave differently: a write operation chooses a new tag that is strictly larger than the one discovered in the query phase, and sends the new tag and new value to a write quorum; a read operation sends the tag and value discovered in the query phase to a write quorum.

Sometimes, a read operation can avoid performing the propagation phase, **RW-Phase-2**, if some prior read or write operation has already propagated that particular tag and value. Once a tag and value has been propagated, be it by a read or a write operation, it is marked confirmed. If a read operation discovers that a tag has been confirmed, it can skip the second phase.

One complication arises when during a phase, a new configuration becomes active. In this case, the read or write operation must access the new configuration as well as the

recon(c,c') at node i: If c is the only configuration in the set of active configurations, then reconfiguration can begin. The request is forwarded to the putative leader, ℓ. If it has already completed Phase 1 for some ballot b, then it can skip Phase 1, and use this ballot in Phase 2. Otherwise, it performs Phase 1.

- **Recon-Phase-1a:** Leader ℓ chooses a unique ballot number b larger than any previously used ballots and sends $\langle Recon1a, b \rangle$ messages to a read quorum of configuration c (the old configuration).
- **Recon-Phase-1b:** When node j receives $\langle Recon1a, b \rangle$ from ℓ, if it has not received any message with a ballot number greater than b, then it replies to ℓ with $\langle Recon1b, b, configs, \langle b'', c'' \rangle \rangle$ where $configs$ is the set of active configurations and b'' and c'' represent the largest ballot and configuration that j voted to replace configuration c.
- **Recon-Phase-2a:** If leader ℓ has received a $\langle Recon1b, b, configs, b'', c'' \rangle$ message, it updates its set of active configurations; if it receives "Recon1b" messages from a read quorum of configuration c, then it sends a $\langle Recon2a, b, c, v \rangle$ message to a write quorum of configuration c, where: if all the $\langle Recon1b, b, \ldots \rangle$ messages contained empty last two parameters, then v is c'; otherwise, v is the configuration with the largest ballot received in the prepare phase.
- **Recon-Phase-2b:** If a node j receives $\langle Recon2a, b, c, c' \rangle$ from ℓ, and if c is the only active configuration, and if it has not already received any message with a ballot number greater than b, it sends $\langle Recon2b, b, c, c', tag, value \rangle$ to a read quorum and a write quorum of c.
- **Recon-Phase-3a:** If a node j receives $\langle Recon2b, b, c, c', tag, value \rangle$ from a read quorum and a write quorum of c, and if c is the only active configuration, then it updates its tag and value, and adds c' to the set of active configurations *and* to *op-configs*. It then sends a $\langle Recon3a, c, c', tag, value \rangle$ message to a read quorum and a write quorum of configuration c.
- **Recon-Phase-3b:** If a node j receives $\langle Recon3a, c, c', tag, value \rangle$ from a read quorum and a write quorum of configuration c, then it updates its tag and value, and removes configuration c from its active set of configurations (but not from *op-configs*, if it is there).

Fig. 2. The phases of the recon protocol. The protocol requires up to three phases.

old one. In order to accomplish this, read or write operations save the set of currently active configurations, *op-configs*, when a phase begins; a reconfiguration can only add configurations to this set—none are removed during the phase. Even if a reconfiguration finishes with a configuration, the read or write phase must continue to use it.

Reconfiguration. When a client wants to change the set of replicas, it initiates a reconfiguration, specifying a new configuration. The nodes then initiate a consensus protocol, ensuring that everyone agrees on the active configuration, and that there is a total ordering on configurations. The resulting protocol is somewhat more complicated than typical consensus, however, since at the same time, the reconfiguration operation propagates information from the old configuration to the new configuration.

The reconfiguration protocol uses an optimized variant of Paxos [3]. The reconfiguration request is forwarded to a leader, which coordinates the reconfiguration, consisting of three phases: a *prepare* phase, **Recon-Phase-1**, in which a ballot is made ready, a *propose* phase, **Recon-Phase-2**, in which the new configuration is proposed, and a *propagate* phase, **Recon-Phase-3**, in which the results are distributed.

The prepare phase accesses a read quorum of the old configuration, thus learning about any earlier ballots. When the leader concludes the prepare phase, it chooses a configuration to propose: if no configurations have been proposed to replace the current old configuration, the leader can propose its own preferred configuration; otherwise, the leader must choose the previously proposed configuration with the largest ballot. The propose phase then begins, accessing both a read and a write quorum of the old configuration. This serves two purposes: it requires that the nodes in the old configuration vote on the new configuration, and it collects information on the tag and value from the old configuration. Finally, the propagate phase accesses a read and a write quorum from the old configuration; this ensures that enough nodes are aware of the new configuration to ensure that any concurrent reconfiguration requests obtain the desired result.

There are two optimizations included in the protocol. First, if a node has already prepared a ballot as part of a prior reconfiguration, it can continue to use the same ballot for the new reconfiguration, without redoing the prepare phase. This means that if the same node initiates multiple reconfigurations, only the first reconfiguration has to perform the prepare phase. Second, the propose phase can terminate when *any* node, even if it is not the leader, discovers that an appropriate set of quorums has voted for the new configuration. If all the nodes in a quorum send their responses to the propose phase to all the nodes in the old configuration, then all the replicas can terminate the propose phase at the same time, immediately sending out propagate messages. Again, when any node receives a propagate response from enough nodes, it can terminate the propagate phase. This saves the reconfiguration one message delay. Together, these optimizations mean that when the same node is performing repeated reconfigurations, it only requires three message delays: the leader sending the propose message to the old configuration, the nodes in the old configuration sending the responses to the nodes in the old configuration, and the nodes in the old configuration sending a propagate message to the initiator, which can then terminate the reconfiguration.

4   Proof of Correctness (Atomic Consistency)

We now outline the safety proof of RDS, i.e., we show that the read and write operations are atomic (linearizable). We depend on two lemmas commonly used to show linearizability: Lemmas 13.10 and 13.16 in [21]. We use the tags of the operations to induce a partial ordering on operations that allows us to prove the key property necessary to guarantee atomicity: if π_1 is an operation that completes before π_2 begins, then the tag of π_1 is no larger than the tag of π_2; if π_2 is a write operation, the inequality is strict.

Ordering Configurations. Before we can reason about the consistency of read and write operations, we must show that nodes agree on the active configurations. For a reconfiguration replacing configuration c, we say that reconfiguration $\langle c, c' \rangle$ is *well-defined* if no node replaces configuration c with any configuration except c'. This is, essentially, showing that the consensus protocol successfully achieves agreement. The proof is an extension of the proof in [3] which shows that Paxos guarantees agreement, modified to incorporate optimizations in our algorithm and reconfiguration (for lack of space we omit the proof).

Theorem 1. *For all executions, there exists a sequence of configurations, $c_1, c_2, \ldots$, such that reconfiguration $\langle c_i, c_{i+1} \rangle$ is well-defined for all i.*

Ordering Operations. We now proceed to show that tags induce a valid ordering on the operations. If both operations "use" the same configuration, then this property is easy to see: operation π_1 propagates its tag to a write quorum, and π_2 discovers the tag when reading from a read quorum. The difficult case occurs when π_1 and π_2 use differing configurations. In this case, the reconfigurations propagate the tag from one configuration to the next.

We refer to the smallest tag at a node that replaces configuration c_ℓ with configuration $c_{\ell+1}$ as the "tag for configuration $c_{\ell+1}$." We can then easily conclude from this definition, along with a simple induction argument, that:

Invariant 2. *If some node i has configuration $c_\ell + 1$ in its set of active configurations, then its tag is at least as large as the tag for configuration $c_{\ell+1}$.*

This invariant allows us to conclude two facts about how information is propagated by reconfiguration operations: the tag of each configuration is no larger than the tag of the following configuration, and the tag of a read/write operation is no larger than the tag of a configuration in its set of active configurations. The next lemma requires showing how read and write operations propagate information *to* a reconfiguration operation:

Lemma 1. *If c_ℓ is the largest configuration in i's op-config set of operational configurations when **RW-Phase-2** completes, then the tag of the operation is no larger than the tag of configuration $c_{\ell+1}$.*

Proof. During the **RW-Phase-2**, the tag of the read or write operation is sent to a write quorum of the configuration c_ℓ. This quorum must intersect the read quorum during the **Recon-Phase-2** propagation phase of the reconfiguration that installs $c_{\ell+1}$. Let i' be a node in the intersection of the two quorums. If i' received the reconfiguration message prior to the read/write message, then node i would learn about configuration $c_{\ell+1}$. However we assumed that c_ℓ was the largest configuration in *op-config* at i at the end of the phase. Therefore we can conclude that the read/write message to i preceded the reconfiguration message, ensuring that the tag was transfered as required.   □

Theorem 2. *For any execution, α, it is possible to determine a linearization of the operations.*

Proof. As discussed previously, we need to show that if operation π_1 precedes operation π_2, then the tag of π_1 is no larger than the tag of π_2, and if π_1 is a write operation, then the inequality is strict.

There are three cases to consider. First, assume π_1 and π_2 use the same configuration. Then the write quorum accessed during the propagate phase of π_1 intersects the read quorum accessed during the query phase of π_2, ensuring that the tag is propagated.

Second, assume that the *smallest* configuration accessed by π_1 in the propagate phase is larger than the *largest* configuration accessed by π_2 in the query phase. This case cannot occur. Let c_ℓ be the largest configuration accessed by π_2. Prior to π_1, some configuration installing configuration $c_{\ell+1}$ must occur. During the final phase **Recon-Phase-2** of the reconfiguration, a read quorum of configuration c_ℓ is notified of the new configuration. Therefore, during the query phase of π_2, the new configuration for $c_{\ell+1}$ would be discovered, contradicting our assumption.

Third, assume that the *largest* configuration c_ℓ accessed by π_1 in the propagate phase **RW-Phase-2** is smaller than the *smallest* configuration $c_{\ell'}$ accessed by π_2 in the query phase **RW-Phase-1**. Then, Lemma 1 shows that the tag of π_1 is no larger than the tag of c_ℓ; Invariant 2 shows that the tag of c_ℓ is no larger than the tag of $c_{\ell'}$ and that the tag of $c_{\ell'}$ is no larger than the tag of π_2. Together, these show the required relationship of the tags.

If π_1 skips the second phase, **RW-Phase-2**, then an earlier read or write must have performed a **RW-Phase-2** for the same tag, and the proof follows as before.   □

5   Conditional Performance Analysis

Here we examine the performance of RDS, focusing on the efficiency of reconfiguration and how the algorithm responds to instability in the network. To ensure that the algorithm makes progress in an otherwise asynchronous system, we make a series of assumptions about the network delays, the connectivity, and the failure patterns. In particular, we assume that, eventually, the network stabilizes and delivers messages with a delay of d. The main results in this section are as follows. (i) we show that the algorithm "stabilizes" within $e + 2d$ time after the network stabilizes, where e is the time required for new nodes to fully join the system and notify old nodes about their existence. (By contrast, the original RAMBO algorithm [1] might take arbitrarily long to stabilize under these conditions.) (ii) we show that after the algorithm stabilizes, reconfiguration completes in $5d$ time; if a single node performs repeated reconfigurations, then after the first, each subsequent reconfiguration completes in $3d$ time. (iii) we show that after the algorithm stabilizes, reads and writes complete in $8d$ time, reads complete in $4d$ time if there is no interference from ongoing writes, and in $2d$ if no reconfiguration is pending.

Assumptions.   Our goal is to model a system that becomes stable at some (unknown) point during the execution. Formally, let α be a (timed) execution and α' a finite prefix of α during which the network may be unreliable and unstable. After α' the network is reliable and delivers messages in a timely fashion.

We refer to $\ell time(\alpha')$ as the time of the last event of α'. In particular, we assume that following $\ell time(\alpha')$: (i) all local clocks progress at the same rate, (ii) messages are not lost and are received in at most d time, where d is a constant unknown to the algorithm, (iii) nodes respond to protocol messages as soon as they receive them and they broadcast messages every d time to all service participants, (iv) all enabled actions are processed with zero time passing on the local clock.

Generally, in quorum-based algorithms, the operations are guaranteed to terminate provided that at least one quorum does not fail. In constrast, for a reconfigurable quorum system we assume that at least one quorum does not fail prior to a successful reconfiguration replacing it. For example, in the case of majority quorums, this means that only a minority of nodes fail in between reconfigurations. Formally, we refer to this as *configuration-viability*: at least one read quorum and one write quorum from each installed configuration survive $4d$ after (i) the network stabilizes and (ii) a following successful reconfiguration operation.

We place some easily satisfied restrictions on reconfiguration. First, we assume that each node in a new configuration has completed the joining protocol at least time e prior to the configuration being proposed, for a fixed constant e. We call this *recon-readiness*. Second, we assume that after stabilization, reconfigurations are not too frequent: $5d$-*recon-spacing* implies that recons are at least $5d$ apart.

Also, after stabilization, we assume that nodes, once they have joined, learn about each other quickly, within time e. We refer to this as *join-connectivity*.

Finally, we assume that a leader election service chooses a single leader at time $\ell time(\alpha') + e$ and that it remains alive until the next leader is chosen and for a sufficiently long time for a reconfiguration to complete. For example, a leader may be chosen among the members of a configuration based on the value of an identifier.

Bounding Reconfiguration Delays. We now show that reconfiguration attempts complete within at most five message delays after the system stabilizes. Let ℓ be the node identified as the leader when the reconfiguration begins.

The following lemma describes a preliminary delay in reconfiguration when a non-leader node forwards the reconfiguration request to the leader.

Lemma 2. *Let the first* recon(c,c') *event at some active node i, where $i \neq \ell$, occur at time t and let t' be* max$(\ell time(\alpha'),t) + e$. *Then, the leader ℓ starts the reconfiguration process at the latest at time $t' + 2d$.*

Proof (sketch). When the recon(c,c') occurs at time t, one of two things happen: either the reconfiguration fails immediately, if c is not the current, unique, active configuration, or the recon request is forwarded to the leader. Observe that *join-connectivity* ensures that i knows the identity of the leader at time t', so no later than time $t' + d$, i sends a message to ℓ that includes reconfiguration request information. By time $t' + 2d$ the leader receives message from i and starts the reconfiguration process.   □

The next lemma implies that after some time following reconfiguration request, there is a communication round where all messages include the same ballot.

Lemma 3. *After time $\ell time(\alpha') + e + 2d$, ℓ knows about the largest ballot in the system.*

Proof (sketch). Let b be the largest ballot in the system at time $\ell time(\alpha') + e + 2d$, we show that ℓ knows it. We know that after $\ell time(\alpha')$, only ℓ can create a new ballot. Therefore ballot b must have been created before $\ell time(\alpha')$. Since ℓ is the leader at time $\ell time(\alpha') + e$, we know that ℓ has joined before time $\ell time(\alpha')$.

If ballot b still exists after $\ell time(\alpha')$ (the case we are interested in), then there are two possible scenarios. Either ballot b is conveyed by an in transit message or it exists an active node i aware of it at time $\ell time(\alpha') + e$. In the former case, gossip policy implies that the in transit message is received at time t, such that $\ell time(\alpha') + e < t < \ell time(\alpha') + e + d$. However, it might happen that ℓ does not receive it, if the sender ignored its identity at the time the send event occurred. Thus, at this time one of the receiver sends a message containing b to ℓ. Its receipt occurs before time $\ell time(\alpha') + e + 2d$ and ℓ learns about b. In the latter case, by join-connectivity assumption at time $\ell time(\alpha') + e$, i knows about ℓ. Gossip policy implies i sends a message to ℓ before $\ell time(\alpha') + e + d$ and this message is received by ℓ before $\ell time(\alpha') + e + 2d$, informing it of ballot b.   □

Next theorem says that any reconfiguration completes in at most $5d$ time, following the system stabilization. The proof is straightforward from the code and is omitted for lack of space. In Theorem 4 we show that when the leader node has successfully completed the previous reconfiguration request then it is possible for the subsequent reconfiguration to complete in at most $3d$.

Theorem 3. *Assume that ℓ starts the reconfiguration process initiated by* recon(c, c') *at time $t \geq \ell time(\alpha') + e + 2d$. Then the corresponding reconfiguration completes no later than $t + 5d$.*

Theorem 4. *Let ℓ be the leader node that successfully conducted the reconfiguration process from c to c'. Assume that ℓ starts a new reconfiguration process from c' to c'' at time $t \geq \ell time(\alpha') + e + 2d$. Then the corresponding reconfiguration from c' to c'' completes at the latest at time $t + 3d$.*

Proof (sketch). By *configuration-viability*, at least one read and one write quorums of c' are active. By Lemma 3, ℓ knows the largest ballot in the system at the beginning of the new reconfiguration. This means that ℓ may keep its ballot and start from **Recon-Phase-2a** (since it has previously executed **Recon-Phase-1b**). Hence only a single message exchange in **Recon-Phase-2a/Recon-Phase-2b** and a single broadcast following **Recon-Phase-3a** take place. Therefore, the last phase of Paxos occurs at time $t + 3d$.

Bounding Read-Write Delays. In this section we present bounds on the duration of read/write operations under assumptions stated in the previous section. Recall from Section 3 that both the read and the write operations are conducted in two phases, first the query phase and second the propagate phase. We begin by first showing that each phase requires at least $4d$ time. However, if the operation is a read operation and no reconfiguration and no write propagation phase is concurrent, then it is possible for this operation to terminate in only $2d$ – see proof of Lemma 4. The final result is a general bound of $8d$ on the duration of any read/write operation.

Lemma 4. *Consider a single phase of a read or a write operation initiated at node i at time t, where i is a node that joined the system at time $\max(t - e - 2d, \ell time(\alpha'))$. Then this phase completes at the latest at time $\max(t, \ell time(\alpha') + e + 2d) + 4d$.*

Proof. Let c_k be the largest configuration in any active node's *op-configs* set, at time $t - 2d$. By the *configuration-viability* assumption, at least one read and at least one write quorum of c_k are active for the interval of $4d$ after c_{k+1} is installed. By the *join-connectivity* and the fact that i has joined at time $\max(t - e - 2d, \ell time(\alpha'))$, i is aware of all active members of c_k by the time $\max(t - 2d, \ell time(\alpha') + e)$.

Next, by the timing of messages we know that within d time a message is sent from each active members of c_k to i. Hence, at time $\max(t, \ell time(\alpha') + e + 2d)$ node i becomes aware of c_k, i.e. $c_k \in$ *op-configs*.

At d time later, messages from phase **RW-Phase-1a** or **RW-Phase-2a** are received and **RW-Phase-1b** or **RW-Phase-2b** starts. Consequently, no later than $\max(t, \ell time(\alpha') + e + 2d) + 2d$, the second message of **RW-Phase-1** or **RW-Phase-2** is received.

Now observe that configuration might occur in parallel, therefore it is possible that a new configuration is added to the *op-configs* set during **RW-Phase-1** or **RW-Phase-2**.

Discovery of new configurations results in the phase being restarted, hence completing at time $\max(t, \ell time(\alpha') + e + 2d) + 4d$. By *recon-spacing* assumption no more than one configuration is discovered before the phase completes. □

Theorem 5. *Consider a read operation that starts at node i at time t:*

1. *If no write propagation is pending at any node and no reconfiguration is ongoing, then it completes at time* $\max(t, \ell time(\alpha') + e + 2d) + 2d$.
2. *If no write propagation is pending, then it completes at time* $\max(t, \ell time(\alpha') + e + 2d) + 8d$.

Consider a write operation that starts at node i at time t. Then it completes at time $\max(t, \ell time(\alpha') + e + 2d) + 8d$.

Proof. At the end of the **RW-Phase-1**, if the operation is a write, then a new non confirmed tag is set. If the operation is a read, the tag is the highest received one. This tag was maintained by a member of the read queried quorum, and it is confirmed only if the phase that propagated it to this member has completed. From this point, if the tag is not confirmed, then in any operation the fix-point of propagation phase **RW-Phase-2** has to be reached. But, if the tag is already confirmed then the read operation can terminate directly at the end of the first phase. By Lemma 4, this occurs at the latest at time $\max(t, \ell time(\alpha') + e + 2d) + 4d$; or at time $\max(t, \ell time(\alpha') + e + 2d) + 2d$ if no reconfiguration is concurrent. Likewise by Lemma 4, the **RW-Phase-2** fix-point is reached in at most $4d$ time. That is, any operation terminates by confirming its tag no later than $\max(t, \ell time(\alpha') + e + 2d) + 8d$. □

6   Experimental Results

We implemented the new algorithm based on the existing RAMBO codebase [7] on a network of workstations. The primary goal of our experiments was to gauge the cost introduced by reconfiguration. When reconfiguration is unnecessary, there are simpler and more efficient algorithms to implement a replicated DSM. Our goal is to achieve performance similar to the simpler algorithms while using reconfiguration to tolerate dynamic changes.

To this end, we designed three series of experiments where the performance of RDS is compared against the performance of an atomic memory service which has no reconfiguration capability — essentially the algorithm of Attiya, Bar Noy, and Dolev [13] (the "ABD protocol"). In this section we briefly describe these implementations and present our initial experimental results. The results primarily illustrate the impact of reconfiguration on the performance of read and write operations.

For the implementation we manually translated the IOA specification (from the appendix) into Java code. To mitigate the introduction of errors during translation, the implementers followed a set of precise rules to guide the derivation of Java code [22]. The target platform is a cluster of eleven machines running Linux. The machines are various Pentium processors up to 900 MHz interconnected via a 100 Mbps Ethernet switch.

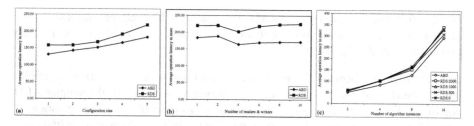

Fig. 3. Average operation latency: (a) as size of configurations changes, (b) as number of nodes performing read/write operations changes, and (c) as the reconfiguration and the number of participants changes

Each instance of the algorithm uses a single socket to receive messages over TCP/IP, and maintains a list of open, outgoing connections to the other participants of the service. The nondeterminism of the I/O Automata model is resolved by scheduling locally controlled actions in a round-robin fashion. The ABD and RDS algorithm share parts of the code unrelated to reconfiguration, in particular that related to joining the system and accessing quorums. As a result, performance differences directly indicate the costs of reconfiguration. While these experiments are effective at demonstrating comparative costs, actual latencies most likely have little reflection on the operation costs in a fully-optimized implementation.

Experiment (a). In the first experiment, we examine how the RDS algorithm responds to different size configurations (and hence different levels of fault-tolerance). We measure the average operation latency while varying the size of the configurations. Results are depicted in Figure 3(a). In all experiments, we use configurations with majority quorums. We designate a single machine to continuously perform read and write operations and compute average operation latency for different size configurations, ranging from 1 to 5. In the tests involving the RDS algorithm, we chose a separate machine to continuously perform reconfiguration of the system – when one reconfiguration request successfully terminates another is immediately submitted.

Experiment (b). In the second set of experiments, we test how the RDS algorithm responds to varying load. Figure 3(b) presents results of the second experiment, where we compute the average operation latency for a fixed-size configuration of five members, varying the number of nodes performing read/write operations changes from 1 to 10. Again, in the experiments involving RDS algorithm a single machine is designated to reconfigure the system. Since we only have eleven machines to our disposal, nodes that are members of configurations also perform read/write operations.

Experiment (c). In the last experiment we test the effects of reconfiguration frequency. Two nodes continuously perform read and write operations, and the experiments were run varying the number of instances of the algorithm. Results of this test are depicted in Figure 3(c). For each of the sample points on the x-axis, the size of configuration used is half of the algorithm instances. As in the previous experiments, a single node is dedicated to reconfigure the system. However, here we insert a delay between the successful termination of a reconfiguration request and the submission of another. The delays used are 0, 500, 1000, and 2000 milliseconds. Since we only have eleven machines to our disposal, in the experiment involving 16 algorithm instances, some of the machines run two instances of the algorithm.

Interpretation. We begin with the obvious. In all three series of experiments, the latency of read/write operations for RDS is competitive with that of the simpler ABD algorithm. Also, the frequency of reconfiguration has little effect on the operation latency. These observations lead us to conclude that the increased cost of reconfiguration is only modest.

This is consistent with the theoretical operation of the algorithm. It is only when a reconfiguration exactly intersects an operation in a particularly bad way that operations are delayed. This is unlikely to occur, and hence most read/write operations suffer only a modest delay.

Also, note that the messages that are generated during reconfiguration, and read and write operations, include replica information as well as the reconfiguration information. Since the actions are scheduled using a round-robin method, it is likely that in some instances a single communication phase might contribute to the termination of both the read/write and the reconfiguration operation. Hence, we suspect that the dual functionality of messages helps to keep the system latency low.

A final observation is that the latency does grow with the size of the configuration and the number of participating nodes. Both of these require increased communication, and result in larger delays in the underlying network when many nodes try simultaneously to broadcast data to all others. Some of this increase can be mitigated by using an improved multicast implementation; some can be mitigated by choosing quorums optimized specifically for read or write operations.

7   Conclusion

We have presented RDS, a new distributed algorithm for implementing a reconfigurable consistent shared memory in dynamic, asynchronous networks. Prior solutions (e.g., [1, 2]) used a separate new configuration selection service that did not incorporate the removal of obsolete configurations. This resulted in longer delays between the time of new-configuration installation and old configuration removal, hence requiring configurations to remain viable for longer periods of time and decreasing algorithm's resilience to failures. In this work we capitalized on the fact that RAMBO and Paxos solve two different problems using a similar mechanism, namely round-trip communication phases involving sets of quorums. This observation led to the development of RDS that allows rapid reconfiguration and removal of obsolete configurations, hence reducing the window of vulnerability. Finally, our experiments show that reconfiguration is inexpensive, since performance of our algorithm closely mimics that of an algorithm that has no reconfiguration functionality. However, our experiments are limited to a small number of machines and a controlled lab setting. Therefore, as future work we would like to extend the experimental study to a wide area network where many machines participate thereby allowing us to capture a more realistic behavior of this algorithm for arbitrary configuration sizes and network delays.

References

1. Lynch, N., Shvartsman, A.: RAMBO: A reconfigurable atomic memory service for dynamic networks. In: Proc. of 16th Int-l Symposium on Distributed Computing. (2002) 173–190
2. Gilbert, S., Lynch, N., Shvartsman, A.: RAMBO II: Rapidly reconfigurable atomic memory for dynamic networks. In: Proc. of International Conference on Dependable Systems and Networks. (2003) 259–268
3. Lamport, L.: The part-time parliament. ACM Transactions on Computer Systems **16(2)** (1998) 133–169
4. Lamport, L.: Paxos made simple. ACM SIGACT News (Distributed Computing Column) **32**(4) (2001) 18–25
5. Lampson, B.W.: How to build a highly available system using consensus. In: WDAG '96: Proceedings of the 10th International Workshop on Distributed Algorithms, London, UK, Springer-Verlag (1996) 1–17
6. Boichat, R., Dutta, P., Frolund, S., Guerraoui, R.: Reconstructing paxos. SIGACT News **34**(2) (2003) 42–57
7. Georgiou, C., Musial, P., Shvartsman, A.: Long-lived RAMBO: Trading knowledge for communication. In: Proc. of 11'th Colloquium on Structural Information and Communication Complexity, Springer (2004) 185–196
8. van der Meyden, R., Moses, Y.: Top-down considerations on distributed systems. In: 12th Int. Symp. on Distributed Computing, DISC'98. (1998) 16–19
9. Gifford, D.K.: Weighted voting for replicated data. In: Proceedings of the seventh ACM symposium on Operating systems principles, ACM Press (1979) 150–162
10. Thomas, R.H.: A majority consensus approach to concurrency control for multiple copy databases. ACM Trans. Database Syst. **4**(2) (1979) 180–209
11. Upfal, E., Wigderson, A.: How to share memory in a distributed system. Journal of the ACM **34(1)** (1987) 116–127
12. Awerbuch, B., Vitanyi, P.: Atomic shared register access by asynchronous hardware. In: Proc. of 27th IEEE Symposium on Foundations of Computer Science. (1986) 233–243
13. Attiya, H., Bar-Noy, A., Dolev, D.: Sharing memory robustly in message-passing systems. J. ACM **42**(1) (1995) 124–142
14. Englert, B., Shvartsman, A.: Graceful quorum reconfiguration in a robust emulation of shared memory. In: Proc. of Int-l Conference on Distributed Computer Systems. (2000) 454–463
15. Lynch, N., Shvartsman, A.: Robust emulation of shared memory using dynamic quorum-acknowledged broadcasts. In: Proc. of 27th Int-l Symp. on Fault-Tolerant Comp. (1997) 272–281
16. Birman, K., Joseph, T.: Exploiting virtual synchrony in distributed systems. In: Proc. of the 11th ACM Symposium on Operating systems principles, ACM Press (1987) 123–138
17. : Special issue on group communication services. Communications of the ACM **39**(4) (1996)
18. Albrecht, J., Yasushi, S.: RAMBO for dummies. Technical report, HP Labs (2005)
19. Saito, Y., Frolund, S., Veitch, A.C., Merchant, A., Spence, S.: Fab: building distributed enterprise disk arrays from commodity components. In: ASPLOS04. (2004) 48–58
20. Georgiou, C., Musial, P., Shvartsman, A.A.: Developing a consistent domain-oriented distributed object service. In: Proceedings of the 4th IEEE International Symposium on Network Computing and Applications, NCA 2005, Cambridge, MA, USA (2005)
21. Lynch, N.: Distributed Algorithms. Morgan Kaufmann Publishers (1996)
22. Musial, P., Shvartsman, A.: Implementing a reconfigurable atomic memory service for dynamic networks. In: Proc. of 18'th International Parallel and Distributed Symposium — FTPDS WS. (2004) 208b

Skip B-Trees

Ittai Abraham[1], James Aspnes[2,*], and Jian Yuan[3]

[1] The Institute of Computer Science, The Hebrew University of Jerusalem
ittaia@cs.huji.ac.il
[2] Department of Computer Science, Yale University
aspnes@cs.yale.edu
[3] Google
yuanjian@gmail.com

Abstract. We describe a new data structure, the **Skip B-Tree**, that combines the advantages of skip graphs with features of traditional B-trees. A skip B-Tree provides efficient search, insertion and deletion operations. The data structure is highly fault tolerant even to adversarial failures, and allows for particularly simple repair mechanisms. Related resource keys are kept in blocks near each other enabling efficient range queries.

Using this data structure, we describe a new distributed peer-to-peer network, the **Distributed Skip B-Tree**. Given m data items stored in a system with n nodes, the network allows to perform a *range search* operation for r consecutive keys that costs only $O(\log_b m + r/b)$ where $b = \Theta(m/n)$. In addition, our distributed Skip B-tree search network has provable polylogarithmic costs for all its other basic operations like insert, delete, and node join. To the best of our knowledge, all previous distributed search networks either provide a range search operation whose cost is worse than ours or may require a linear cost for some basic operation like insert, delete, and node join.

1   Introduction

Peer-to-peer systems provide a decentralized way to share resources among machines. An ideal peer-to-peer network should have such properties as decentralization, scalability, fault-tolerance, self-stabilization, load-balancing, dynamic addition and deletion of nodes, efficient query searching and exploiting spatial as well as temporal locality in searches.

Much of academic work on peer-to-peer systems has concentrated on building **distributed hash tables** or DHTs. In a DHT, the hash value of the key of resource is used to determine which node it will be stored at (typically the node whose own hashed identity is closest), and the use of random-looking hash values roughly balances out the load on the nodes in the system. An overlay graph is then constructed on top of the nodes in order to allow efficient searches for the nearest node to a target hash using some sort of routing algorithm. The major form of variation between these DHTs is the routing algorithm used to locate

* Supported in part by NSF grants CCR-0098078, CNS-0305258, and CNS-0435201.

J.H. Anderson, G. Prencipe, and R. Wattenhofer (Eds.): OPODIS 2005, LNCS 3974, pp. 366–380, 2006.

resources; however, in each case the underlying structure is built on pointers between nodes, so the resulting mechanism typically looks like some sort of tree search.

Even though traditional DHT systems effectively construct balanced search trees in order to find nodes, they generally do not support range queries since hashing destroys the ordering on keys. They also typically lack load balancing mechanisms other than the limited randomized balancing provided by hashing. For example, in Chord it is likely that some machine will own $\Omega(\log N/N \log \log N)$ fraction of the key space. There are some recent extensions of DHT systems which try to mitigate this problem. An extension of Chord called a p-tree [CLGS04] supports $O(\log_b N)$ search as well as providing efficient range query. However, there is no analysis on deletion and insertion, and the addition and removal of nodes are based on a complicated self-stabilization mechanism whose performance is based on empirical data only. Karger and Ruhl [KR04] propose algorithms to do address space balancing and item balancing in Chord, which ensures with high probability no node will be responsible for more than $O(1/N)$ of the key space. The item balancing algorithm is dependent on nodes being able to move freely in the key space and is incompatible with the address space balancing algorithm though. Ratnasamy etc. [RRHS04] proposes a new data structure called Prefix Hash Tree (PHT) that could be put on top of existing DHT. PHT is essentially a binary trie built over data sets being indexed. The system supports range queries and is load balanced, but it suffers from hot spots since the top-level trie nodes tend to be accessed more frequently than bottom-level trie nodes.

Though continued research on DHTs is likely to lead to further improvements, some of the difficulties with reconciling range queries and DHT structures is inherent in the use of hashing to perform load balancing. Another line of research has focused on providing searchable concurrent data structures by applying the tree structure in order to support efficient range queries using mechanisms similar to those in traditional balanced binary trees. For example, **Skipnet**, developed by Harvey etc. [HJS+03], is a trie of circular, singly-linked skip lists that link the machines in the system. It provides path locality and content locality, and its hashing provides some form of load balancing. However, transparent remapping of resources to other domains is not possible. Aspnes and Shah [AS02] concurrently devised a data structure called a **skip graph** which applies skip lists in a similar way to support $O(\log N)$ search, insertion and deletion operations, while maintaining the inherent tree structure in the network so that range queries are also supported. Skip graphs are also tolerant to node failures, including both adversarial failures and random failures.

The original skip graph construction in [AS02] was marred by the lack of any policy for assigning resources to nodes, excessive internode pointers, and a cumbersome self-repair mechanism. Recently Aspnes *et al.*[AKK04] have proposed a mechanism to do global load balancing by pairing heavily loaded machines with lightly loaded ones, while using sampling to reduce the number of pointers in the data structure from $O(\log N)$ per resource to $O(\log N)$ per machine. However, search times in such binned skip graphs still suffer from large constants, and exploiting the large memory capacity of typical machines may allow much faster searching.

1.1   Our Contribution

We describe a new data structure, the **Skip B-Tree**, which has the following features:

1. By combining skip graphs with features of traditional B-trees, the skip B-Tree avoids the drawbacks of traditional skip graphs while providing $O(\log_b N)$ search, insertion and deletion operations, where b is the block size. When $b = N^{1/k}$ for some constant k, then for any set of N items, all operations take constant time, $O(k)$.
2. The high connectivity of our data structure makes it highly fault tolerant even to adversarial failures, and allows for particularly simple repair mechanisms.
3. Related resource keys are kept in blocks near each other, which may enhance the performance of applications such as web page prefetching which utilize the locality of resources.

Using this data structure, we describe a new distributed network, the **Distributed Skip B-Tree**. We show that our distributed Skip B-tree is the first distributed search network with provable polylogarithmic costs for all its basic operations[1]. It employs balancing techniques from [AAA+03] to locally update system parameters and hence avoids costly global re-balancing. Moreover, given m data items stored in a system with n nodes, a range search for r consecutive keys costs only $O(\log_b m + r/b)$ where $b = \Theta(m/n)$. To the best of our knowledge, all previous distributed search networks may require a linear cost for some operation or do not provide cost efficient range queries. Aspnes *et al.*[AKK04] has a load balancing scheme that may cause an insert operation to trigger a global re-balancing that costs $\Omega(n)$. Awerbuch and Scheideler [AS03] have a scheme for which a range search for r consecutive keys costs $O(r \log n)$. Hence their solution obtains no locality of resources and incurs a high cost relative to our solution.

1.2   Distributed Search Trees vs Distributed Hash Tables

Skip B-trees are instances of the general concept of **Distributed Search Trees** (DSTs), which we now define. Essentially, DSTs are to search trees what DHTs are to hash tables. We begin by defining the interface to a **Distributed Hash Table** (DHT). A DHT is a distributed network on n nodes storing m (key,value) pairs with the following operations.

1. *Add:* Add a node to the system.
2. *Remove:* Gracefully remove a node from the system.

---

[1] See Section 1.2 for a formal definition of the operations and their cost measures.

3. *Insert:* add a (key,value) pair.
4. *Delete:* remove a (key, value) pair.
5. *Search:* Given a key, find the corresponding value(s).

The typical cost measures of a DHT are to achieve worst case guarantees for the following:

1. Network change cost: Message complexity of Add or Remove operations. For example $O(\log^2 n)$ in Chord [SMLN+03] and $O(\log n/\sqrt{\log \log n})$ in [KM05].
2. Data change cost: Message complexity of Insert, Delete, and Search operations. For example, $O(\log n)$ in [SMLN+03] and $O(\log n/\log \log n)$ in Koorde [KK03].
3. Data load: The maximal fraction of data items stored in one machine. For example $O(\log n/n)$ in [SMLN+03] and $O(1/n)$ in [KR04].
4. Network load: The maximal fraction of traffic a node receives given that random nodes search for random data. For example $O(\log n/n)$ in [SMLN+03].

The interface of a DST contains all the operations of a DHT and includes one new operation, the *Range search*. This search operation gets two parameters (k, r) and must return the r minimal keys whose value is larger than the search key k (one can also require a search for the r keys that are smaller than k). The cost metrics for DSTs are the same as for DHTs with the only difference being that the complexity of a range search operation is measured as a function of the required range r. Ideally, an efficient distributed search tree that stores m data items over a network with n nodes should store the index sorted with each node storing a consecutive block of size $b = \Theta(m/n)$ of the index. In such a case a range search operation for r keys should ideally require only $O(\log_b m + r/b)$ messages. Indeed we will show that our solution obtains this asymptotic bound while keeping all other operations at a polylogarithmic cost.

Finally we mention that handling faulty nodes (non-graceful node removals) is also an important issue both for DHTs and for DSTs. This usually requires data replication and techniques that are out of the scope of this short paper.

2   Skip B-Trees

The B-tree was originally introduced by Bayer [Bay72]. The B-tree algorithms utilized the locality of data and were designed to minimize the cost of sequential search/insert/delete operations. There has been a lot of research on building a distributed B-tree that supports concurrency and parallelism. Gilon and Peleg [GP91] proposed several structures for implementing a distributed dictionary, with the focus on reducing complexity of message passing as well as data balancing. Colbrook etc. [CBDW91] have proposed a pipelined distributed B-tree. Johnson etc. [JC94] describe a data structure called a dB-tree which permits concurrent updates on a replicated tree node, and rarely blocks operations.

A skip graph, introduced by Aspnes and Shah [AS02], is organized as a tower of increasing sparse linked lists, much like a skip list [Pug90]. Level 0 of a skip graph is just a doubly linked list of all nodes in increasing order by key. For each i greater than 0, each node appears randomly in one of the many link lists in level i (unlike a skip list where there is only one linked list per level), with two constraints. First, if node x is a singleton at level $i-1$, it doesn't appear in any of the linked list at levels higher than $i-1$. Second, for every linked list L at level i, there must be another linked list L' at level $i-1$ where the elements in L are a subset of the elements in L'.

Our skip B-tree can be viewed as a non-trivial extension of the skip graph, combined with the idea of a distributed B-tree. We specify a block size b, and for every linked list on any level we divide it into blocks where the expected size of each block is $O(b)$ (we will explain how to do this later). The division into blocks is independent of the skip graph structure.

As in a skip graph, each element x is assigned a membership vector $m(x)$, where the characters in $m(x)$ are taken from a finite alphabet set Σ. The cardinality of the alphabet, $|\Sigma|$, is typically taken to be the same as the block size b. Every doubly-linked list in the skip B-tree is labeled by some finite word w. An element x is in the list labeled by w if and only if w is a prefix of $m(x)$. Each element in the block keeps two pointers, one to the corresponding element in the upper level (called "parent") and one to the corresponding element in the lower level (called "child"). The block itself keeps two pointers to its two neighbors at the same level. It also keeps a count of how many elements there are in the block. According to Lemma 1, the expected height of the skip B-tree is $O(\log_b N)$. By making b large enough (say $b = 10^7$), in practice the height of a skip B-tree can be a very small constant (say, 2 or 3 for any data set).

We adopt much of the notation of [AS02]. In particular, for any element w, write $w \upharpoonright i$ for the prefix of w of length i. Write ϵ for the empty word. For each block b at level ℓ, write $m_\ell \ell(b)$ to denote the ℓ-th character of the membership

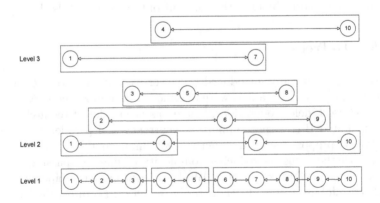

Fig. 1. A skip B-tree with $n = 10$ nodes and $\lceil \log_b n \rceil = 3$ levels. The block size $b = 3$.

vector of any element in b. In the implementation of the algorithm we actually store a number in each block indicating the ℓ-th element in the membership vector of all elements belonging to it instead of storing a membership vector in each element.

As in a skip graph, the bottom level of a skip B-tree is always a doubly-linked list S_ϵ consisting of all the nodes in order, divided into blocks with size of $O(b)$. In general, for each w in Σ^*, the doubly-linked list S_w contains all x for which w is a prefix of $m(x)$, in increasing order, divided into blocks with size of $O(b)$. We say that a particular list S_w is part of level i if $|w| = i$. This gives an infinite family of doubly-linked lists; in an actual implementation, only those S_w with at least two nodes are represented.

Lemma 1. *With high probability, the height of a skip B-tree is $O(\log_b N)$.*

3   Algorithms for a Skip B-Tree

Here we describe the search, insert and delete operation for a skip B-tree. We summarize the variables stored at each node in Table 1. For simplicity, our description assumes a supply of **blocks** that can hold many data items. The question of how these blocks are mapped to actual physical machines is deferred to Section 6.

Table 1. List of all the variables stored at each node

Variable	Meaning
MaxKey	the maximum resource key in a block
MinKey	the minimum resource key in a block
currentBlock	the block receiving the message
Right	the right neighbor of the current block
Left	the left neighbor of the current block
Level	the level of the block
m	Membership vector
[key]	the element in the block indexed by *key*
Parent	pointer to the block one level higher which contains the same resource key as the element
Child	pointer to the block one level lower which contains the same resource key as the element
Group	indicates the grouping of the block

In this section, we will give the algorithms and analyze their performance.

3.1   The Search Operation

The search operation (Algorithm 1) is basically the same as that of a skip list, except that our unit of search is now a block. The search is initiated by a top level block seeking a key and it proceeds down the same level without over-shooting, continuing at a lower level if required, until it reaches level 0. Either the block at level 0 which contains the key, if it exists, or the block at level 0 storing the key closest to the search key is returned. The algorithm is described below:

Algorithm 1. Search for the file indexed by $searchKey$

```
upon receiving ⟨searchOp, startBlock, searchKey, level⟩:
if (searchKey exists in unmarked elements of currentBlock) then
    if (level = 0) then
    |   send ⟨foundOp, currentBlock⟩ to startBlock
    else
    |   send ⟨searchOp, startBlock, searchKey, level − 1⟩ to currentBlock[searchKey].Child

if (searchKey > currentBlock.MaxKey) then
    while (level ≥ 0) do
        if (currentBlock.Right.MinKey < searchKey) then
        |   send ⟨searchOp, startBlock, searchKey, level⟩ to currentBlock.Right
        |   break
        else if (level > 0) then
        |   send ⟨searchOp, startBlock, searchKey, level − 1⟩ to currentBlock[currentBlock.MaxKey].Child

else
    while (level ≥ 0) do
        if (currentBlock.Left.MaxKey > searchKey) then
        |   send ⟨searchOp, startBlock, searchKey, level⟩ to currentBlock.Left
        |   break
        else if (level > 0) then
        |   send ⟨searchOp, startBlock, searchKey, level − 1⟩ to currentBlock[currentBlock.MinKey].Child

if (level = 0) then
|   send ⟨notFoundOp, currentBlock⟩ to startBlock
```

Lemma 2. *The search operation in a skip B-tree S with N nodes and block size b takes $O(\log_b N)$ time and $O(\log_b N)$ messages with high probability.*

Skip graphs can support range queries in which one is asked to find a key within a specified range. For most of these queries, the procedure is an obvious modification of Algorithm 1 and runs in $O(\log_b N)$ time with $O(\log_b N)$ messages. For finding all nodes in an interval, we can use a modified Algorithm 1 to find the closest element to the upper (or lower) bound. We then walk from this element in level 0 list until we hit the lower (or upper) bound, and return all the elements we have encountered. If there are r elements in the interval, the running time is $O(log_b N + r)$.

3.2   The Insert Operation

A new element n knows some introducing block *introducer* which helps it to join the network. n inserts itself in one list at each level until it finds itself a singleton list at top level. At level 0, n will be added to the block which contains a key closest to n.Key. At each level i, $i >= 1$, n will try to find the closest element x in level $i − 1$ with $x \lceil i = n \lceil i$ and add to the block x belongs to at level i. To ensure load balancing, we adopt the approach described in [AKK04]. Specifically, we call a block "closed" if it has more than $b/2$ elements, and we call it "open" if it has no more than $b/2$ elements. We group the blocks into groups of 2 or 3, with each group having the following property: it must either contain one closed block followed by one open block, or it may contain 2 closed blocks and 1 open block while the open block is in the middle. This is the invariant we try to keep for our insertion and deletion algorithm. When we insert a new element, if we insert it into a closed block we always move the largest element to the adjacent open block in the same group. If the open block is still open after insertion, nothing happens. If it is in a group of 2 and it becomes closed, we add a new empty block in the middle of these two blocks and mark it "open". We move the element to this new block instead. If the open block is in a group of 3, we create a new block, link it to the right of the rightmost closed block, and move the largest element in the open block in the middle to its neighbor to the right, which in turn causes the movement of the largest element in the rightmost closed block to the new block. We also split it into two groups of size 2 since we have 4 blocks now. Notice that in this way we guarantee that the average block size of any group is not smaller than $b/4$. To simplify analysis, we do not allow duplicates here, but it is quite easy to extend the algorithm so that duplicates are allowed. Also when we create a new block, we assume that there exists a routine which allocates the space for the block and distribute it to a random machine in the network.

Algorithm 2. Insert a new element n

```
if (introducer = ⊥) then
    create a new block and add n to the block
    block.Left ← ⊥
    block.Right ← ⊥
    block.Group ← 2
else
    send ⟨searchOp, currentBlock, n.Key, introducer.Level⟩ to introducer
    wait until foundOp or notFoundOp is received
    upon receiving ⟨foundOp, clone⟩:
        terminate insert
    upon receiving ⟨notFoundOp, block⟩:
    childblock ← ⊥
    while true do
        level ← block.Level
        send ⟨buddyOp, currentBlock, n, n⊳level, ⊥⟩ to block
        wait until receipt of ⟨setLinkOp, newblock⟩:
        send ⟨linkOp, n, childblock, newblock⟩ to block
        if (newblock ≠ ⊥) then
            childblock ← block
            block ← newblock
        else
            newBlock ← create a new block
            m(newBlock) ← uniformly chosen random element of Σ
            add n to newBlock
            n.Child ← block
            n.Parent ← ⊥
            break
```

3.3 The Delete Operation

Deletion works as follows: we recursively delete the element from each level it belongs to in a bottom-up fashion. When we delete an element, we check the block's size. If it remains closed/open after deletion, we simply remove the element from it. Notice that we allow an empty block to be in the group here. If it changes from closed to open and the open block in the group is not empty, we move the largest/smallest in the open block to the current block. If the open block in the group is empty, we then check the group size. If it is a group of size 3, we simply remove the empty block in the middle and form a group of size 2 since the block is open now. If it is a group of size 2, we check the size of the group to the left. If it is also a group of size 2, we move the largest key in the open block of the left neighbor to the current block, delete the empty open block and form a group of 3. If it is a group of size 3, we delete the empty block, and

Algorithm 3. Block's message handler for physically inserting new element n

```
upon receiving ⟨linkOp, n, childBlock, parentBlock⟩:
add n to currentBlock
n.Child ← childBlock
n.Parent ← parentBlock
currentBlock.Count++
//the block is open
if (currentBlock.Count <= b⊲2) then
 | return
//this is the first block on this level and it is closed
if (currentBlock.Left = currentBlock.Right = ⊥) then
 | block ← create a new block
 | block.Group ← 2
 | insert block to the right of currentBlock
 | m ← largest element in currentBlock
 | send ⟨linkOp, m, m.Child, m.Parent⟩ to block
 | remove m from currentBlock
 | return
//if the block was closed before, swap element with the open block in the group
if (currentBlock.Count > b⊲2 + 1) then
 | if (currentBlock.Left.Count <= b⊲2 and currentBlock.Group = 3) then
 |  | block ← create a new block
 |  | block.Group ← 2
 |  | insert block to the right of currentBlock
 |  | currentBlock.Left.Left.Group ← 2
 |  | currentBlock.Left.Group ← 2
 |  | currentBlock.Group ← 2
 |  | m ← largest element in currentBlock
 |  | send ⟨linkOp, m, m.Child, m.Parent⟩ to currentBlock.Right
 |  | remove m from currentBlock
 |  | return
 | else
 |  | m ← largest element in currentBlock
 |  | send ⟨linkOp, m, m.Child, m.Parent⟩ to currentBlock.Right
 |  | remove m from currentBlock
 | return
//currentBlock must have b⊲2 + 1 elements now
if (currentBlock.Group = 2) then
 | currentBlock.Left.Group ← 3
 | currentBlock.Group ← 3
 | block ← create a new block
 | block.Group ← 3
 | insert block to the left of currentBlock
 | m ← smallest element in currentBlock
 | send ⟨linkOp, m, m.Child, m.Parent⟩ to currentBlock.Right
 | remove m from currentBlock
 | return
else
 | m ← largest element in currentBlock
 | send ⟨linkOp, m, m.Child, m.Parent⟩ to currentBlock.Right
 | remove m from currentBlock
 | return
```

Algorithm 4. Block's message handler for finding the closest block one level higher to insert new element n, whose $b⊳Level$-th component of membership vector is val

```
upon receiving ⟨buddyOp, startBlock, n, val, side⟩:
foreach (element x in currentBlock)
if (m(x⊳Parent) = val) then
 | send ⟨setLinkOp, x.Parent⟩ to startBlock
 | return
if (side = ⊥) then
 | if (currentBlock.Left ≠ ⊥) then
 |  | send ⟨buddyOp, startBlock, n, val, Left⟩ to currentBlock.Left
 | if (currentBlock.Right ≠ ⊥) then
 |  | send ⟨buddyOp, startBlock, n, val, Right⟩ to currentBlock.Right
 | if (currentBlock.Left = ⊥ and currentBlock.Right = ⊥) then
 |  | send ⟨setLinkOp, ⊥⟩ to startBlock

else
 | if (currentBlock.side ≠ ⊥) then
 |  | send ⟨buddyOp, startBlock, val, side⟩
 |  |  to currentBlock.side
 | else
 |  | send ⟨setLinkOp, ⊥⟩ to startBlock
```

form 2 groups of size 2 with the left neighbor. Notice that the invariant of group structure is still preserved by our deletion algorithm.

The proof of the correctness of this mechanism is essentially the same as the proof of Theorem 4 in [AKK04].

Lemma 3. *The insertion and deletion operations in a skip B-tree S with N nodes and block size b take $O(\log_b N)$ messages and $O(\log_b N)$ time with high probability.*

3.4 Concurrency Issues

In order to ensure the correctness of the algorithm under concurrent updates, we need a lock-free doubly linked list in a distributed setting. Shasha and Goodman [SG88] provide a framework for proving the correctness of non-replicated concurrent data structures. For example, we could use the underlying doubly linked list of dB-tree [JC94] as our doubly linked list. Since our insertion and deletion operations all work in a bottom-up fashion, as long as each level is consistent the whole data structure must be intact, and a lock-free doubly-linked list ensures the consistency of each level. The only thing that could be missing during updates is the pointers between different levels, but this will only slow down the search operation and has no effect on the consistency of the data structure.

4 Fault Tolerance

In this section, we describe some of the fault tolerance properties of a skip B-tree. Fault tolerance of related data structures, such as augmented versions of linked lists and binary trees, has been well-studied and some results can be seen in [MP84, AB96]. Section 5 gives a repair mechanism that detects node failures and initiates actions to repair these failures. Before we explain the repair mechanism, we are interested in the number of blocks that can be separated from the primary component by the failure of other blocks, as this determines the size of the surviving skip B-tree after the repair mechanism finishes.

Notice that if multiple blocks are stored on a single machine, if that machine crashes all of its blocks are lost. Our results are stated in terms of the fraction of blocks that are lost; if the blocks are roughly balanced across machines, this will be proportional to the fraction of machine failures. Nonetheless, it would be useful to have a better understanding of fault tolerance when the mapping of resources to machines is taken into account; this may in fact dramatically improve fault tolerance, as blocks stored on surviving machines can always find other blocks stored on the same machine, and so need not be lost even if all of their neighbors in the skip B-tree are lost.

We give analysis of adversarial failures here, as this will be the worst case failure pattern. In this section we look at the expansion ratio of a skip B-tree, which gives the number of nodes that can be separated from the primary component even with adversarial failures.

Let G be a graph. Recall that the expansion ratio of a set of nodes A in G is $|\delta A|/|A|$, where $|\delta A|$ is the number of nodes that are not in A but are adjacent to some node in A. The expansion ratio of the graph G is the minimum expansion ratio for any set A, for which $1 \leq |A| \leq n/2$. The expansion ratio determines the resilience of a graph in the presence of adversarial failures, because separating a set A from the primary component requires all nodes in δA to fail. We will show that skip B-trees have $\Omega(\frac{1}{b})$ expansion ratio with high probability, implying that only $O(f \cdot b)$ nodes can be separated by f failures, even if the failures are carefully targeted.

Since all the real data is stored on level 0 blocks, we only need to consider the case when A consists entirely of level 0 blocks. The probability for a level 1 block to have no neighbor in A is $(\frac{m_0 - |A|}{m_0})^b$ since none of its pointers to level 0 blocks can point to any block in A, where m_0 is the total number of blocks on level 0. Thus the expected number of neighbors at level 1 is $m_1(1 - (1 - \frac{|A|}{m_0})^b)$, which is greater than $\frac{b|A|m_1}{m_0}$. Since $m_1 = \Theta(m_0)$, the expansion ratio is $\Omega(\frac{1}{b})$, which is pretty good since there are only $O(|A|b)$ links from A to level 1 blocks. It is comparable to the guarantee provided by data structures based on explicit use of expanders such as censor-resistant networks [FS02, SFG+02, Dat02].

5   Repair Mechanism

In this section we describe a self-stabilization mechanism that repairs our skip B-tree in case of block failure. We assume that a block either works or fails in its entirety. The repair mechanism is quite simple: each block sends message to its neighbors periodically to see if they are alive. If one of the neighbors is dead, we try to fix the link to the next live neighbor. Without loss of generality, we assume that the right neighbor fails, and the block resides on level 0.

Lemma 4. *For any two adjacent blocks b_1 and b_2 on level 0, the probability that there is an element x_1 from b_1 and an element x_2 from b_2 such that $x_1 \uparrow 1 = x_2 \uparrow 1$ is at least $1 - e^{-b/4}$.*

Thus we can see that the repair mechanism would finish in expected $O(1)$ time if we assume the node can process $O(b)$ messages simultaneously, and sends expected $O(b)$ messages with high probability.

Algorithm 5. Algorithm for repairing right neighbor for block *block* at level 0

```
send ⟨repairOp, block.maxKey, block⟩ to block
upon receiving ⟨repairOp, key, block⟩:
  minKey ← ∞
  foreach element x in block
  send message to x.Parent and x.Parent.Right asking for the smallest key greater than key
  if (the reply is not ⊥ and the key returned is < minKey) then
    | minKey ← the key returned
    | newBlock ← the block containing the key
    //make sure that newBlock's left neighbor is indeed missing if (newBlock.Left = ⊥) then
    | newBlock.Left ← block
    | block.Right ← newBlock
  else
    | send ⟨repairOp, key, block⟩ to the left neighbor of current block
```

---

6   Distributed Skip B-Trees

In this section, we detail how to map skip B-trees to machines and build an efficient DST. Consider a network with n machines that stores m data items, we would like to have a skip B-tree with block size $b \approx m/n$. We use the load balancing strategy of [AAA+03] in order to label nodes with $\Theta(\log n)$ identifiers. This can be done so that all nodes have unique binary identifiers that form a prefix code whose size is between $\log n - C$ and $\log n + C$ for a predetermined constant C. The add node and remove node operations maintain this invariant with cost $O(\log^2 n)$ [AAA+03].

In order to map a skip B-Tree to nodes we must map nodes to blocks in a manner that balances load between nodes and maintains low degree (an edge is formed between any two nodes that store two consecutive blocks of any of the linked lists of the skip B-Tree structure). The idea is that each node estimates b to be about m/n, the estimation of b will always be always a power of two.

We now explain how to maintain the base linked list S_ϵ that is maintained by all the network nodes. However, the same techniques are used to store all the linked lists. Specifically, for any binary word w, the nodes whose identifiers are a prefix of w maintain the linked list S_w in the same fashion.

Insertion of a block into a linked list is performed in the following manner. A sample of $\Theta(\log n)$ random nodes are queried, and the least loaded node gets to store the block. The nodes that store the previous and next blocks now store a network link to this new location and the chosen node adds links to them. If the adversary is oblivious to the random choices then with high probability [MRS01, ABKU00] all machines will have the same load (number of blocks) up to a constant factor. If $b = \Theta(m/n)$ and n nodes maintain the list then the number of blocks per node is $O(1)$ and hence the number of links of each node is also $O(1)$.

We now analyze the number of network links each node needs to maintain for all the lists it belongs to. Fix a node u with id $id(u)$, it participates in maintaining all the linked lists S_w such that w is a prefix of $id(u)$ or $id(u)$ is a prefix of w. Hence there are $O(\log m)$ such lists. Each such list S_w with $|w| = i$ contains $\Theta(2^{-i}m)$ elements and since node identifiers are balanced there are $O(2^{-i}n)$ nodes whose prefix is a prefix of w. Since $b = \Theta(m/n)$ then each such list requires $O(1)$ links for each node maintaining it. Therefore, for maintaining all lists of the skip B-Tree the degree of each node is $O(\log m)$. So the cost of adding a node and setting up its connections is $O(\log n \log m)$.

Finally, we need a mechanism to update b as the size of n and m dynamically change over time. We want to avoid global pitfalls that would require the whole system to do a global update as such operations are not scalable. Each node maintains b at a power of two, for a node v let $b = 2^{B(v)}$ be its local estimate. Several events described below may cause $B(v)$ to change. Whenever $B(v)$ changes this effects the open or closed status of the nodes blocks. We use the bucket compression technique of [AKK04] (section 3.3) and a similar bucket expansion algorithm to locally adjust the nodes blocks to the new value of $b = 2^{B(v)}$. The details will appear in the full paper.

When a node joins the system, we use the node split mechanism of [AAA⁺03]. When node v splits, it decreases its $B(v)$ by one and the new node also takes the updated value of $B(v)$. Similarly, when a node leaves, we use the merge mechanism of [AAA⁺03]. The two merged nodes increase their $B(\cdot)$ value by one. Changes in $B(v)$ also occur due to change in the number of blocks stored. Once a node stores more that a given constant number of blocks, it locally increase its value of $B(v)$ by one. Similarly, when a node has less than a given constant number of blocks, it locally decreases $B(v)$ by one. The estimation of b is adequate since the load balancing algorithms give each node an estimate of n and m up to constant factors with high probability. In the full paper, we prove that using this strategy the nodes' estimates of b are all within a constant factor of each other. Moreover, locally updating b has low cost as only $O(\log n \log m)$ messages are sent.

One remaining obstacle is that the skip B-tree now has different members having slightly different estimates of b. As long as estimates are bounded by a constant factor it is easy to see that insert, delete, and search operations can still be carried out using $O(\log_b m)$ messages. The resulting distributed data structure is a DST with the following costs.

Lemma 5. *Given an n node network storing m items, both the network change cost and the data change cost is $O(\log n \log_b m)$. A range search for r consecutive keys costs only $O(\log_b m + r/b)$. Both the data load and network load are $O(\log n/n)$.*

7   Conclusion

In this paper we defined a new data structure called skip B-tree which has several desirable properties. Insertion, deletion and search in skip B-tree all take $O(\log_b N)$ time for any set of elements that be arbitrarily unbalanced. In practice just as in B-trees, our cost is a very small constant (2-3) for reasonably large b (say, 10^7). Also under the condition of no additional node failures, the skip B-tree can repair itself in a very efficient way. Finally, skip B-tree also supports range queries, and it exploits the geographical proximity in location of resources. We use skip B-trees to build a distributed peer-to-peer network that provides the first polylogarithmic cost DST that allows to perform efficient range search operations.

References

[AAA⁺03]   Ittai Abraham, Baruch Awerbuch, Yossi Azar, Dahlia Malkhi, and Elan Pavlov. A generic scheme for building overlay networks in adversarial scenarios. In *Proceedings of the International Parallel and Distributed Processing Symposium (IPDPS 2003)*, April 2003.

[AB96]   Yonatan Aumann and Michael A. Bender. Fault Tolerant Data Structures. In *Proceedings of the Thirty-Seventh Annual Symposium on Foundations of Computer Science (FOCS)*, pages 580–589, Burlington, VT, USA, October 1996.

[ABKU00]   Yossi Azar, Andrei Z. Broder, Anna R. Karlin, and Eli Upfal. Balanced allocations. *SIAM J. Comput.*, 29(1):180–200, February 2000.

[AKK04]   James Aspnes, Jonathan Kirsch, and Arvind Krishnamurthy. Load balancing and locality in range-queriable data structures. In *Twenty-Third ACM Symposium on Principles of Distributed Computing*, pages 115–124, July 2004.

[AS02]   James Aspnes and Gauri Shah. Skip Graphs. In *Fourteenth Annual ACM-SIAM Symposium on Discrete Algorithms(SODA)*, pages 384–393, January 2002. Submitted to *Journal of Algorithms*.

[AS03]   Baruch Awerbuch and Christian Scheideler. Peer-to-peer Systems for Prefix Search. In *Proceedings of the Twenty-Second ACM Symposium on Principles of Distributed Com puting (PODC)*, Boston, MA, USA, July 2003.

[Bay72]   Rudolf Bayer. Symmetric Binary B-trees: Data Structure and Maintainance Algorithms. *Acta Informatica*, pages 290–306, 1972.

[CBDW91]   Adrian Colbrook, Eric A. Brewer, Chrysanthos Dellarocas, and William E. Weihl. An Algorithm for concurrent search trees. In *Proceedings of the 20th International Conference on Parallel Processing*, pages III138–III141, 1991.

[CLGS04]   Adina Crainiceanu, Prakash Linga, Johannes Gehrke, and Jayavel Shanmugasundaram. P-Tree: A P2P Index for Resource Discovery Applications. *The 13th International World Wide Web Conference*, pages 390–392, May 2004.

[Dat02]   Mayur Datar. Butterflies and Peer-to-Peer Networks. In Rolf Möhring and Rajeev Raman, editors, *Proceedings of the Tenth European Symposium on Algorithms (ESA)*, volume 2461 of *Lecture Notes in Computer Science*, pages 310–322, Rome, Italy, September 2002.

[FS02]   Amos Fiat and Jared Saia. Censorship Resistant Peer-to-Peer Content Addressable Networks. In *Proceedings of the Thirteenth Annual ACM-SIAM Symposium on Discrete Algorithms (SODA)*, pages 94–103, San Francisco, CA, USA, January 2002. Submitted to a special issue of *Journal of Algorithms* dedicated to select papers of SODA 2002.

[GP91]   Karni Gilon and David Peleg. Compact Deterministic Distributed Dictionaries. In *Proceedings of the Tenth Annual ACM Symposium on Principles of Distributed Computing*, pages 81–94, 1991.

[HJS+03]   Nicholas J. A. Harvey, Michael B. Jones, Stefan Saroiu, Marvin Theimer, and Alec Wolman. SkipNet: A Scalable Overlay Network with Practical Locality Properties. In *Proceedings of the Fourth USENIX Symposium on Internet Technologies and Systems (USITS)*, pages 113–126, Seattle, WA, USA, March 2003.

[JC94]   Theodore Johnson and Adrian Colbrook. A Distributed, Replicated, Data-Balanced Search Structure. In *International Journal of High Speed Computing*, volume 6, pages 475–500, 1994.

[KK03]   Frans Kaashoek and David R. Karger. Koorde: A simple degree-optimal hash table. In *Proceedings of the 2nd International Workshop on Peer-to-Peer Systems (IPTPS03)*, Berkeley, CA, 2003.

[KM05]   Krishnaram Kenthapadi and Gurmeet Singh Manku. Decentralized algorithms using both local and random probes for p2p load balancing. In *SPAA'05: Proceedings of the 17th annual ACM symposium on Parallelism in algorithms and architectures*, pages 135–144, New York, NY, USA, 2005. ACM Press.

[KR04]   David R. Karger and Matthias Ruhl. Simple Efficient Load Balancing
             Algorithms for Peer-to-Peer Systems. In *ACM SPAA*, 2004.
[MP84]   J. Ian Munro and Patricio V. Poblete. Fault Tolerance And Storage
             Reduction In Binary Search Trees. *Information and Control*, 62(2/3):
             210–218, August 1984.
[MRS01]   Michael Mitzenmacher, Andréa W. Richa, and Ramesh Sitaraman. The
             power of two random choices: A survey of techniques and results, 2001.
[Pug90]   William Pugh. Skip Lists: A Probabilistic Alternative to Balanced Trees.
             Communications of the ACM, 33(6):668–676, June 1990.
[RRHS04]   Sriram Ramabhadran, Sylvia Ratnasamy, Joseph M. Hellerstein, and
             Scott Shenker. Brief Announcement: Prefix Hash Tree. In *Proceedings of
             ACM PODC*, St. Johns, Canada, July 2004.
[SFG⁺02]   Jared Saia, Amos Fiat, Steven Gribble, Anna Karlin, and Stefan Saroiu.
             Dynamically Fault-Tolerant Content Addressable Networks. In Peter Dr-
             uschel, Frans Kaashoek, and Antony Rowstron, editors, *Proceedings of the
             First International Workshop on Peer-to-Peer Systems (IPTPS)*, volume
             2429 of *Lecture Notes in Computer Science*, pages 270–279, Cambridge,
             MA, USA, March 2002.
[SG88]   Dennis Shasha and Nathan Goodman. Concurrent search structure
             algorithms. *ACM Transactions on Database Systems*, pages 53–90, 1988.
[SMLN⁺03]   Ion Stoica, Robert Morris, David Liben-Nowell, David R. Karger,
             M. Frans Kaashoek, Frank Dabek, and Hari Balakrishnan. Chord: A Scal-
             able Peer-to-peer Lookup Service for Internet Applications. *IEEE/ACM
             Transactions on Networking*, 11:17–32, February 2003.

Bounding Communication Cost in Dynamic Load Balancing of Distributed Hash Tables*

Marcin Bienkowski[1] and Miroslaw Korzeniowski[2],**

[1] Institute of Computer Science,
University of Wroclaw, Poland
mbi@ii.uni.wroc.pl
[2] International Graduate School of Dynamic Intelligent Systems,
University of Paderborn, Germany
rudy@upb.de

Abstract. In Peer-to-Peer networks based on consistent hashing and ring topology each peer is responsible for an interval chosen (pseudo-) randomly on a circle. The topology of the network, the communication load and the amount of data a peer stores depends heavily on the length of its interval.

Additionally, peers are allowed to join the network or to leave it at any time. Such operations can destroy the balance of the network even if all the intervals had equal lengths in the beginning.

This paper deals with the task to keep such a system balanced, so that the lengths of intervals assigned to the peers differ at most by a constant factor. We propose a simple scheme which achieves this and its communication cost can be amortized against the cost of keeping the system connected. Our procedure requires $O(\log n)$ times more messages than any procedure maintaining the connectivity, even if the an oblivious adversary decides about the dynamics of the system.

The scheme is a continuous process which does not have to be informed about the current size or possible imbalance in the network to start working. As a byproduct, we show how to compute a constant approximation of the current number of nodes n in the system, provided that we know an upper bound on $\log n$.

1 Introduction

Peer-to-Peer networks are an efficient tool for storage and location of data, since there is no central server which could become a bottleneck, and the data is evenly distributed among the participants.

* Partially supported by DFG-Sonderforschungsbereich 376 "Massive Parallelität: Algorithmen, Entwurfsmethoden, Anwendungen" and by the Future and Emerging Technologies programme of EU under EU Contract 001907 DELIS "Dynamically Evolving, Large Scale Information Systems".

** This work was done while the author was in the International Graduate School of Dynamic Intelligent Systems, University of Paderborn, Germany.

J.H. Anderson, G. Prencipe, and R. Wattenhofer (Eds.): OPODIS 2005, LNCS 3974, pp. 381–395, 2006.
© Springer-Verlag Berlin Heidelberg 2006

The Peer-to-Peer networks which we are considering are based on consistent hashing [1] with ring topology like Chord [2], Tapestry [3], Pastry [4], and a topology inspired by de Bruijn graph [5, 6]. In short, Distributed Hash Tables work as follows. Each peer chooses a number between 0 and 1 and takes responsibility for the interval from the chosen place to the next node. When a peer wants to insert or find an item x in the network, it computes a global hash function on the item's name which is a value $h(x)$ between 0 and 1. It can then contact the node responsible for $h(x)$ using the network structure that has been built among the participating nodes.

There are several approaches to build an efficient topology, however the exact structure of the network is not relevant for us. It is only important that each node has direct links to its successor and predecessor on the ring and that there is a routine that lets any node contact the node responsible for any given point in the network in time $\mathcal{D}$.

A crucial parameter of a network defined in this way is its *smoothness* which is the ratio of the length of the longest interval to the length of the shortest interval. The smoothness is a parameter, which informs about three aspects of the load balance.

- Storage load of a peer: The longer its interval is, the more data has to be stored in the peer. On the other hand, if there are n nodes and $\Omega(n \cdot \log n)$ items distributed (pseudo-)randomly on the ring, then, with high probability, the items are distributed evenly among the peers provided that the smoothness is constant.
- Degree of a node: A longer interval has a higher probability of being contacted by many short intervals which increases its in-degree.
- Congestion and dilation: Having constant smoothness is necessary to keep these routing parameters small, for example in [5, 6].

Even if we choose the points for the nodes fully randomly, the smoothness is as high as $\Omega(n \cdot \log n)$ with constant probability,[1] whereas we would like it to be constant (n denotes the current number of nodes).

1.1   Related Work

Load balancing has been a crucial issue in the field of Peer-to-Peer networks since the design of the first network topologies like Chord [2]. In [7] the concept of virtual servers was introduced and it was proposed that each real peer works as $\log n$ virtual servers, thus greatly decreasing the probability that some peer will get a large part of the ring. Some extensions of this method were proposed in [8] and [9], where more schemes based on virtual servers were introduced and experimentally evaluated. Unfortunately, such an approach increases the degree of each peer by a factor of $\log n$, because each peer has to keep all the links of all its virtual servers.

---

[1] With constant probability (w.c.p.) means with probability at least $1 - \epsilon$ for an arbitrary constant $\epsilon > 0$.

The paradigm of many random choices [10] was used by Byers et al. [11] and by Naor and Wieder [5, 6]. When a peer joins, it contacts $\log n$ random places in the network and chooses to cut the longest of all the found intervals. This yields constant smoothness with high probability.[2]

A similar approach was proposed in [12]. It extensively uses the structure of the hypercube to decrease the number of random choices to one and the communication to only one node and its neighbors. It also achieves constant smoothness with high probability.

The two approaches above have a certain drawback. They both assume that peers join the network sequentially. What is more important, they do not provide analysis for the problem of balancing the intervals afresh when peers leave the network.

Karger and Ruhl [13, 14] propose a scheme, in which each node chooses $\Theta(\log n)$ places in the network and takes responsibility for only one of them. This can change, if some nodes leave or join, but each node migrates only among the $\Theta(\log n)$ places it chose, and after each operation $\Theta(\log \log n)$ nodes have to migrate on expectation. The advantage of our algorithm is that it performs a migration only if there really is a too long interval in the network. Both their and our algorithms use only tiny messages for checking the network state, and in both approaches the number of messages in half-life[3] can be bounded by $\Theta(\log n)$ per peer. Their scheme is claimed to be resistant to attacks thanks to the fact that each node can only join in logarithmically bounded number of places on the ring. However, in [15] it is stated that such a scheme cannot be secure and that more sophisticated algorithms are needed to provide provable security. The reasoning for this is that with IPv6 protocol the adversary has access to thousands of IP numbers, and she can join the system with the ones falling into an interval that she has chosen. She does not have to join the system with each possible IP to check if this IP is useful, because the hash functions are public and she can compute them offline.

Manku [16] presented a scheme based on a virtual binary tree that achieves constant smoothness with low communication cost for peers joining or leaving the network. It is also shown that the smoothness can be diminished to as low as $(1 + \epsilon)$ with communication cost per operation increased to $O(1/\epsilon)$. All the nodes form a binary tree, where some of them (called *active*) are responsible for perfect balancing of subtrees rooted at them. Our scheme treats all peers evenly and is substantially simpler.

In [17] the authors present a scheme that extends [16] and generalizes [12]. Nodes are grouped into clusters of size h. Each node checks k clusters when it joins the network (In [12], $h = \log n$ and $k = 1$). The authors prove that it is sufficient that $h \cdot k = \Omega(\log n)$ to guarantee that the resulting smoothness is constant, with high probability. Similarly to the other two approaches, this algorithm does not consider nodes leaving the network.

---

[2] With high probability (w.h.p.) means with probability at least $1 - O\left(\frac{1}{n^l}\right)$ for an arbitrary constant l.

[3] For now, we define half-life of the network to be the time it takes for half of the peers in the system to arrive or depart.

1.2 Our Results

In [18] we showed a self-stabilizing distributed algorithm that rebalances the system in the static case, that is when no nodes join or leave it. Such strong assumption was needed in the analysis, but the algorithm itself was designed to work in a dynamic environment.

In this paper we extend and modify the scheme so, that it can be analyzed as an ever-running process. We show formally that the communication in a half-life is bounded to $\log n$ messages per node. Unbounded communication was the main drawback of our previous scheme. Consider a scenario in which the sequence of join and leave requests is generated by an oblivious adversary and the algorithm responsible for keeping the system connected is optimal with respect to communication cost. We show that our algorithm keeps the system smooth with only slight delay with additional communication cost by a logarithmic factor larger than the cost of keeping the system connected.

Consider any phase of length equal to half-life, in which the sequence of join and leave requests is generated by an oblivious adversary. We show that our algorithm smooths the imbalance present in the beginning of the phase.

As a byproduct we present a scheme, which gives a constant approximation of the number of nodes in the network n. The scheme needs the knowledge of an upper bound of $\log n$.

Finally, we present the results of the experimental evaluation that we performed. It shows that the constants used in the theoretical analysis can be notably reduced in practice.

2   The Algorithm

We assume that each node knows an upper bound Δ on $\log n$, the logarithm of the current number n of nodes in the system. In order to avoid complex terms in the analysis, we assume that Δ is a sharp bound (up to constant factors), that is $\Delta = \Theta(\log n)$. This bound should be global for the whole network. Most of the existing systems already assume such knowledge. It will be used to estimate the value of n, in order to enable each node to decide whether its current load is below or above the average.

An assumption already mentioned in the introduction is that each node can communicate directly with its successor and predecessor on the ring.

Let $\mathcal{D}$ denote the dilation of the network, i.e. the maximum number of hops needed to route from any node to any other node. $\mathcal{D}$ is $O(\log n)$ in Chord [2] and $O(\log n / \log \log n)$ in de Bruijn graph [5, 6].

In Subsection 2.1 we introduce a notion of weight of an interval. It is a measure supplementary to the interval's length. We show the relationships between these two measures and how to use them to efficiently approximate the number of participants of the network. In Subsection 2.2 we state the algorithm and in Subsection 2.3 we show that it achieves constant smoothness and its communication is bounded. In Section 3 we present the experimental evaluation of our algorithm.

2.1   Estimating the Current Number of Nodes

The goal of this subsection is to provide a scheme, which, for an arbitrary node i responsible for an interval I_i of sufficient length, returns an estimate n_i of the total number of nodes, so that each n_i is within a constant factor of n, with high probability.

Let Δ be the upper bound on $\log n$ mentioned above. Each node keeps connections to $\delta = \alpha \cdot \Delta$ random positions on the ring, for sufficiently large global constant α. We assume each of these connections is visible for the node responsible for the interval containing the chosen position. These connections are called markers and define weights of intervals and nodes in the following way.

Definition 1. *For a node i and its interval I_i, the weight of the interval I_i, denoted $w(I_i)$, is the number of markers which fall into I_i. The weight of a node is the weight of the interval it is responsible for.*

It is clear that $\mathrm{E}[w(I_i)] = \delta \cdot l(I_i) \cdot n$, so $n_i = \frac{w(I_i)}{\delta \cdot l(I_i)}$ is a good estimate for n. In the following lemma we state precisely the relation between the length and the weight of an interval and prove, using Chernoff bounds, that the quality of the estimate is sufficient.

Lemma 1. *There exist constants $w_{\min} < \frac{1}{2}$, $l_{\min}$ and $l_{\max}$, such that for arbitrary interval I_i and timestep t, if α is large enough, the following holds with high probability. If $w(I_i) \geq w_{\min} \cdot \delta$, then $l_{\min} \cdot \frac{w(I_i)}{\delta \cdot n} \leq l(I_i) \leq l_{\max} \cdot \frac{w(I_i)}{\delta \cdot n}$.*

Proof. Consider an interval I of length $l(I) \leq \frac{l_{\min}}{n}$ and let I' be any interval containing I such that $l(I') = \frac{l_{\min}}{n}$. Let $X = w(I')$ be the random variable denoting how many of the $\delta \cdot n$ markers hit I'; we have $\mathrm{E}[X] = l_{\min} \cdot \delta = \Theta(\delta) = \Omega(\log n)$. Using Chernoff bound, we obtain $X = \Theta(\delta)$, with high probability. Since I is contained in I', its weight is always smaller than the weight of I', so $w(I) = O(\delta)$, with high probability. Thus, if an interval I has weight $w(I) \geq w_{\min} \cdot \delta = \Omega(\delta)$ then, with high probability, $l(I) \geq \frac{l_{\min}}{n} = \Omega\left(\frac{w(I)}{\delta \cdot n}\right)$, which proves the first inequality.

For the proof of the second inequality, we assume that $l(I) \geq \frac{l_{\min}}{n}$. The random variable $X = w(I)$ has expectation $\mathrm{E}[X] = l(I) \cdot \delta \cdot n = \Omega(\log n)$, so with high probability, $w(I) = \Omega(l(I) \cdot \delta \cdot n)$. This finishes the proof.

It is hard for nodes to compare their length to the average length (which is $1/n$) due to the lack of knowledge about the exact number of participants n. On the other hand it is easy for them to compare their weight to the average weight, since the latter is a global constant equal to δ.

2.2   The Balancing Algorithm

Our algorithm reorganizes the positions of the nodes on the ring, so that the resulting intervals I_i' have weights between $w_{\min} \cdot \delta$ and $32 \cdot \delta$, where $w_{\min}$ is the constant defined in Lemma 1. By Lemma 1, this implies that in the end the smoothness is constant, with high probability.

We call the intervals of weight at most $16 \cdot \delta$ *light* and intervals of weight at least $32 \cdot \delta$ *heavy*. Intervals of intermediate weight are called *medium*.

The algorithm minimizes the weight of the heaviest interval, but we also have to take care that no interval is too light. This is needed, since smoothness demands not only the longest interval to be sufficiently short but also the shortest interval to be sufficiently long. Therefore, before we begin the routine we force all the nodes responsible for intervals with weight smaller than $w_{min} \cdot \delta$ to leave the network; we call such nodes *very light*. Doing this, we assure that the weight of the lightest interval in the network is bounded from below. We have to explain why this does not destroy the structure of the network. That is, that the algorithm does not worsen the balance of the system instead of improving it and that the removed nodes can still communicate with others.

First of all, it is possible that we remove a huge fraction of the nodes. It is even possible that a very long interval appears even though the network was very near to a balanced state before. This is not a problem, since the algorithm rebalances the system. Besides, if this algorithm is used also for new nodes at the moment of joining, this initialization is not necessary. We do not completely remove the nodes with too light intervals from the network. The number of nodes n, and thus also the weight δ of a perfect interval is unaffected, and the removed nodes act as though they were simple light nodes. Each of the very light nodes knows its virtual position on the ring and contacts the network through the node responsible for that position. We assume that the node is not heavy since it could immediately split using the light node.

The routine works differently for different nodes, depending on the node's interval weight. The heavy nodes only wait for help proposals in order to split their intervals. The medium nodes do nothing as they are too light to split their intervals and too heavy to help. In order to be able to bound the communication cost we distinguish two types of light nodes. A light node can be *passive* and do nothing until it is *stimulated*, i.e. until it loses or receives a marker, which is noticed by a loss or gain of a connection. Then the node becomes *active* and stays active until it successfully sends a constant ($\mathcal{A}$) number of help proposals. An active node sends help proposals to random places until it finds a heavy node or it becomes passive. In order not to create any heavy nodes, an active node sends a proposal only if its predecessor is light and has been locked. Locking means that the predecessor will not send any proposals, and thus guarantees that the predecessor will not migrate.

The routines for two types of light nodes are depicted in Figure 1. The parameters $\mathcal{A}$ and $\mathcal{F}$, responsible for the maximum activity time and the forwarding distance, are sufficiently large constants, which will be defined later.

The very light nodes act in the following way. The light node responsible for such nodes informs them of its markers and they are stimulated at the same time as it is. They behave in the same way as the light nodes except that they do not have to lock anything.

---

passive light (permanently in staying state)
   if (any change in markers)
   {
      change activity level to $\mathcal{A}$
      become active
   }

active light
   if (locked)
      wait until unlocked by successor
   if (predecessor is light)
   {
      do
         perform one of the following choosing equiprobably at random
            let the successor lock me and wait until unlocked
            try to lock the predecessor
      until (predecessor locked)
      p := random(0..1)
      P := the node responsible for p
      if (P is heavy and migrating to p does not produce a very light interval)
         migrate to p
      else
         contact consecutively the node P and its $\mathcal{F} \cdot \Delta$ successors on the ring
         if (a contacted node R is heavy)
            migrate to the middle of the interval of R
      unlock the predecessor
   }
   if (any change in markers)
      change activity level to $\mathcal{A}$
   decrease activity level
   if (activity level = 0)
      become passive

Fig. 1. The algorithm for two types of light nodes

2.3   Performance and Communication Cost

In [18] we showed an algorithm that can be treated as the algorithm we are currently analyzing with parameter $\mathcal{A} = \infty$, and we proved that it is self-stabilizing, that is after a constant number of rounds the smoothness becomes constant, provided that no new nodes join the system and no nodes leave it during this time. Alas, such approach causes a lot of communication even if the system is already balanced and there are no changes. Therefore we adapted the algorithm and we analyze it in the situation with $\mathcal{A}$ set to a sufficiently large constant.

The environment, in which the algorithm has to work, is not a process that starts and ends but rather a system that runs forever. In order to measure the communication not as the total bandwidth used, but rather as rate at which each node has to communicate we introduce the following definition from [19].

Definition 2 ([19]). *If there are n live nodes at time t, then:*

1. *the doubling time from time t is the time that elapses before n additional nodes arrive*
2. *the halving time from time t is the time required for half of the nodes alive at time t to depart*
3. *the half-life τ_t from time t is the smaller of the doubling and halving times from time t*
4. *the half-life τ of the entire system is the minimum half-life over all times t*

In order to show that our algorithm is competitive with respect to communication cost we also cite the following theorem from [19].

Theorem 1 ([19]). *Any n-node P2P network that remains connected with high probability for any sequence of joins and leaves with half-life τ must notify every node with an average of $\Omega(\log n)$ messages per τ time.*

We model an oblivious adversary, against which the cost of the algorithm is measured in the following way.

1. The adversary generates a pattern of insertions and removals of nodes in any way she wants as long as she does not measure the performance of our algorithm. Thus, she can generate the worst possible starting situation in an adaptive way.
2. The adversary chooses a moment in time t_0, at which she wants to start the measurement. The number of nodes at time t_i for $i \geq 0$ is denoted n_i. As mentioned above, the distribution of the nodes on the ring at t_0 can be arbitrary. However, it has to be an output of our algorithm, so there are no very light nodes in the system.
3. The adversary chooses the patterns of insertions and removals for the current phase. She can decide about insertions online in an adaptive way, that is the number of nodes inserted at time i may depend on the behavior of the algorithm up to time $i - 1$. The removals are generated in an oblivious way, i.e. the adversary decides about TTL (Time To Live) of each node at the moment of its insertion; for the nodes present in the network at time t_0, TTLs can be generated at t_0. The algorithm does not know the TTLs.
4. At every timestep nodes are inserted and removed according to the pattern chosen by the adversary. The algorithm responds with communication and possible migrations of nodes.
5. After a half-life the phase ends, and the adversary is switched off. The algorithm is allowed to communicate and migrate in an extension of $\Theta(\log n)$ timesteps.

In order to precisely express the performance of the algorithm, we consider the following virtual process after the half-life has ended. For each node which left during the considered half-life, we re-insert it into the network provided that such an insertion does not create a very light interval. We perform the re-insertions sequentially in any order, so that there are no ambiguities with parallel checks. If we prove that after performing such process the system is balanced, we prove that our algorithm copes with the imbalance present in the network at the beginning of the half-life. The imbalance created by the adversarial deletions of nodes will be repaired in the next half-life.

In the rest of this subsection we prove the following theorem characterizing the communication cost of the algorithm in a half-life and stating how well the algorithm rebalances the system.

Theorem 2. *In the game described above, the following properties hold with high probability:*

1. *The communication cost of the algorithm in half-life is at most $O(\log n)$ times larger than the communication cost of maintaining the system.*
2. *If we re-insert the nodes removed in the current half-life as described above, the smoothness is constant at the end of the half-life.*

For further analysis we need the following claims about the behavior of the network in a half-life.

Lemma 2. *Denote the number of nodes in the network in the beginning of a half-life by n_0, the number of nodes present at time t by n_t, and the number of markers at time t as m_t, for $t \geq 0$. Then during a half-life*

1. *the number of nodes in the network at time t is bounded by $\frac{n_0}{2} \leq n_t \leq 2 \cdot n_0$,*
2. *the number of markers in the network at time t is bounded by $\frac{n_0 \cdot \delta}{2} \leq m_t \leq 2 \cdot n_0 \cdot \delta$.*
3. *the number of insert / delete operations in a half-life ranges from $\frac{n_0}{2}$ to $\frac{5 \cdot n_0}{2}$,*

Proof. Let the nodes present at time t_0 be called *old* and the nodes inserted during half-life *new*. Before the half-life ends the adversary can remove at most $\frac{n_0}{2}$ old nodes and insert at most $2 \cdot n_0$ new nodes. Thus, the total number of nodes ranges from $\frac{n_0}{2}$ to $\leq 2 \cdot n_0$ and the number of markers ranges from $\frac{n_0 \cdot \delta}{2}$ to $2 \cdot n_0 \cdot \delta$.

It is straightforward that removing $n_0/2$ nodes is the fastest way to end the half-life, whereas inserting $n_0 - 1$ new nodes and removing them and $n_0/2$ old ones is the best way for the half-life to last long. Thus, the last statement follows.

We are now ready to prove the communication-competitiveness of the algorithm.

Proof (of Property 1 of Theorem 2). For the exact analysis we modify our algorithm slightly. Instead of δ markers, each node inserts $\delta/2$ insertion-markers and $\delta/2$ deletion-markers into the system. If a node u stores a marker of a node v then u is activated in two cases: if v joins the network and the marker is an insertion-marker or if v leaves the network and the marker is a deletion-marker. Since the adversary is oblivious, we may think that the deletion-markers are generated at the moment when a node leaves the network. Thus, when a node joins or leaves the network, it contacts $\Theta(\delta)$ places chosen uniformly at random at the moment in which the operation happens. Since the total number of joins and leaves in a half-life is $\Theta(n)$, the total number of contacted places in a half-life is $\Theta(n \cdot \delta)$, all of which are independent.

Since each light node has length $\Theta(1/n)$ during the whole half-life we can use Chernoff bounds to show that each light node is activated $\Theta(\delta)$ times, with high probability. Each activation is responsible for a constant number of messages, so the total number of messages sent by a light node is $O(\delta) = O(\log n)$ in a half-life, with high probability. Each of these messages is sent to a distance of $O(\mathcal{D} + \log n) = O(\log n)$ and the total communication cost is $O(\log^2 n)$ messages per node. By Theorem 1, this proves the first property of Theorem 2.

It remains to prove that such communication is still sufficient to keep the system balanced. First, we show that the number of proposals in a half-life is sufficiently high.

Lemma 3. *There exist $\frac{n_0}{16}$ light nodes alive during the whole half-life which send the maximum number $\mathcal{A}$ of proposals and still are not accepted anywhere. With high probability, a fraction $\frac{1}{3}$ of the messages they want to send is sent in the half-life or in the extension.*

Proof. There are at least $n_0/2$ nodes which are alive during the whole half-life - we call them immortals. Since an interval is light when its weight is below $16 \cdot \delta$ and, by Lemma 2, the total weight in the network is at most $2 \cdot n_0 \cdot \delta$, at most $n_0/8$ nodes are not light, and thus at every timestep at least $\frac{3}{8} \cdot n_0$ immortals are light.

Consider the distribution of the immortals in the beginning of the half-life and ignore other nodes for a while. We couple the immortals in the following way. Any immortal is chosen as the first element of the first pair and its successor is the second element of the first pair. Consecutive immortals (according to the order on the ring) build consecutive pairs. We want to bound the number of pairs with two light nodes. There are $n_0/4$ pairs, at most $n_0/8$ of which can have at least one middle or heavy node, thus in at least $n_0/8$ pairs, an immortal will be willing to migrate when it is activated. Notice that presence of other nodes can only decrease the weight and cannot discourage any immortals from sending proposals.

As a node only wishes to share its load with another node, if its current weight exceeds $32 \cdot \delta$, $n_0/16$ immortals suffice to store all load. Thus, only $n_0/16$ immortals have a chance to migrate and at least $n_0/16$ send the maximum number $\mathcal{A}$ of messages.

Assume that in order to send a message, a node does not have to lock its predecessor. Then all $\mathcal{A}$ messages sent by a node will be sent in time $O(\log n)$. Suppose that the part of the algorithm responsible for trying to lock a neighbor is performed immediately. Then at every timestep if a node is not sending a message, it means that either it cannot lock its predecessor or that it has been locked by its successor. In either case it implies that one of its neighbors is sending a message. This means that at least $\frac{1}{3}$ of the messages will be delivered in the time, in which all messages would be delivered if locking was immediate.

We assign additional $\Theta(\log n)$ timesteps to each active node. Each time a node fails to lock a predecessor or fails to let the successor lock itself, because the other node tries to synchronize with its other neighbor, we pay for such waste of time from these additional timesteps. If within these $\Theta(\log n)$ timesteps a node succeeds $\mathcal{A}$ times, it manages to send all its messages. At each such trial the node succeeds with probability at least $\frac{1}{4}$, as at least one of its neighbors tries to contact it at the same time and the probability that at a timestep they try to contact each other is exactly $\frac{1}{4}$. With high probability, there is at least one success in $\Theta(\log n)$ timesteps, and thus also $\mathcal{A}$ successes in $\Theta(\log n)$ trials. Also, all nodes use $\Theta(\log n)$ additional timesteps to succeed $\mathcal{A}$ times, w.h.p.

Below we prove the second part of Theorem 2. As writing all constants exactly significantly decreases the readability of the proof, we simplify it by assuming that nodes operate on lengths instead of weights and that an interval is considered very short, if its length is below $\frac{1}{n}$. This assumption is justified by Lemma 1.

Proof (of Property 2 of Theorem 2). We know that in the half-life (or in the extension guaranteed by the definition of the model) $\Theta(n)$ proposals from immortals are generated in the system, and that we can make the constant in the Θ notation arbitrarily large just by increasing the $\mathcal{A}$ constant in the algorithm.

Let $y \in [0, 1)$ be an arbitrary real number on the ring. Consider the interval I_y of length $\frac{\log n}{n}$ starting in y. Let x and z be equal to $y - \frac{\log n}{n}$ and $y + \frac{\log n}{n}$ respectively. I_x and I_z are intervals of the same length as the length of I_y and are the predecessor and successor of I_y on the ring.

Using Chernoff bound we can show that with high probability the number of proposals from immortals that fall into I_x is $\Theta(\log n)$. We say that a proposal reaches z, if it contacts the node responsible for z. The parameter $\mathcal{F}$ is chosen so, that even if all intervals between x and z have the lowest possible length, a proposal travelling from x and forwarded through all the nodes can reach z.

At this point of the analysis we allow the adversary to be adaptive. She can choose, which of the mortal nodes die and when. When she removes a node from the network, a heavy interval can appear, which should be split by an immortal. Our analysis is based on the fact that when an immortal splits a heavy interval, it does it at least until the end of the half-life. The adversary may remove some nodes from I_y after all immortals have been forwarded through I_y and the algorithm repairs such imbalance in the next half-life.

Below we show that the following event happens at least $2 \cdot \log n$ times: a proposal that hit I_x reaches z at the moment when there is a node in I_z. If such an event happens, then either there are no heavy nodes in I_y, or the immortal is inserted somewhere between y and the node in I_z. At most $2 \cdot \log n$ immortals can be inserted in the interval $I_y \uplus I_z$, so after $2 \cdot \log n$ such events there are no heavy nodes in I_y.

First, we show that $\Theta(\log n)$ of the proposals reach z in the process of forwarding (not necessarily when there exists a node in I_z). This is true, since in I_x and I_y there is place for at most $2 \cdot \log n$ of them. Notice that we cannot be sure which proposals (in order of coming) reach z: it may happen that the first one gets through, right after that many nodes die in the network, and the next immortals split the heavy intervals that appear in I_x and I_y.

We introduce a notion of a *steady barrier* as the first node behind z on the ring which will survive until the end of the half-life. At the beginning of the process we can bound the distance between y and the barrier by 1. When during our process an immortal reaches z and there is no node in I_z then the immortal is inserted between y and the current steady barrier and becomes the new steady barrier. In the worst case, the distance between y and the steady barrier halves each time when it happens, so after fewer than $\log n$ such events there is a steady barrier in I_z. Thus, $\log n$ immortals can be used to assure that there is a steady barrier in z and further $2 \cdot \log n$ to assure that I_y is balanced.

If we divide the ring into $\frac{n}{\log n}$ disjoint intervals each of length $\frac{\log n}{n}$, then the probability that the algorithm fails for at least one of them is at most n times larger than the probability of failure for a single interval. Thus, our algorithm succeeds on the whole ring with high probability.

3   Experimental Evaluation

In this paper we focused on theoretical proofs of correctness and efficiency of our algorithm. Additionally, we performed a series of experiments on a single machine, in order to show that constants emerging from our analysis are reasonable. We did not experimentally compare our approach with others, as such comparisons should probably be done in a large distributed environment. We did not model the dynamics of the system, either, as our approach copes with adversarial dynamics and in this matter we consider proofs of correctness to be much better than any experiments. In all tests the underlying space was the ring of natural numbers $\{0, \ldots, 2^{64} - 1\}$ with arithmetic modulo 2^{64}.

There were two groups of experiments. The first group was to find the best parameters for the algorithm in the static case. In the tests in this group n nodes were inserted in the very beginning and all lived until the end of the test. The number of nodes n was $2^5, 2^{11}, 2^{14}$ or 2^{17}; they were chosen to be powers of two only for easier implementation. We present the results for the highest number of nodes.

The first parameter we tested was the number of markers that each node should insert into the network. The number of markers δ ranged from 8 to 128 and the other parameters were set as follows. Each packet was forwarded through 128 nodes to assure quick convergence. An interval could send a proposal, if the sum of the weight of itself and its successor was at most δ. An interval was considered very light if its weight was below $\delta/2$. We measured the final smoothness in the system and noticed that choosing a value of 40 already yields smoothness below 20 and values larger than 64 do not improve the system much. The final smoothness for different δ parameters is depicted in Figure 2.

With the number of markers fixed to 64 we performed tests which had to estimate the best definition of a very light interval. The forward parameter $\mathcal{F} \cdot \Delta$

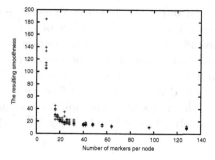

Fig. 2. Smoothness according to approximation of $\log n$

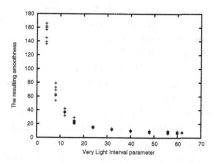

Fig. 3. Smoothness according to the weight of the very light interval

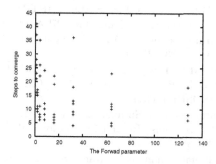

Fig. 4. Convergence according to the forward parameter

was 128 again. The final smoothness for different weights of a very light interval is depicted in Figure 3. We consider the constant 56 to be the best.

The last set of tests for the static scenario was developed to optimize the distance to which a packet should be forwarded. This time the output of the analysis was not smoothness but the time it takes for the scheme to stabilize. From Figure 4 it can be seen that already very short forwarding gives good results. We chose the forward parameter to be 16.

To test the behavior of our algorithm in a dynamic scenario, we took the model from [20]. For each time step the number of nodes joining at this time step was chosen according to the Poisson distribution with mean λ, and for each node its time to stay in the system was chosen according to the exponential distribution with mean μ. For parameters (λ, μ) equal to $(10, 100)$ and $(100, 100)$ the smoothness never exceeded 14 and was in 97% time steps at most 9. For comparison, if we insert the nodes uniformly and independently at random the smoothness is approximately 23 for 2^{14} and 127 for 2^{17} nodes.

References

1. Karger, D.R., Lehman, E., Leighton, F.T., Levine, M.S., Lewin, D., Panigrahy, R.: Consistent Hashing and Random Trees: Distributed Caching Protocols for Relieving Hot Spots on the World Wide Web. In: Proc. of the 29th ACM Symp. on Theory of Computing (STOC). (1997) 654–663

2. Stoica, I., Morris, R., Karger, D.R., Kaashoek, M.F., Balakrishnan, H.: Chord: A Scalable Peer-to-Peer Lookup Service for Internet Applications. In: Proc. of the ACM SIGCOMM. (2001) 149–160

3. Hildrum, K., Kubiatowicz, J.D., Rao, S., Zhao, B.Y.: Distributed Object Location in a Dynamic Network. In: Proc. of the 14th ACM Symp. on Parallel Algorithms and Architectures (SPAA). (2002) 41–52

4. Rowstron, A., Druschel, P.: Pastry: Scalable, Decentralized Object Location, and Routing for Large-Scale Peer-to-Peer Systems. Lecture Notes in Computer Science (2001) 329–350

5. Naor, M., Wieder, U.: A Simple Fault Tolerant Distributed Hash Table. In: 2nd International Workshop on Peer-to-Peer Systems (IPTPS). (2003)

6. Naor, M., Wieder, U.: Novel Architectures for P2P Applications: the Continuous-Discrete Approach. In: Proc. of the 15th ACM Symp. on Parallel Algorithms and Architectures (SPAA). (2003) 50–59

7. Dabek, F., Kaashoek, M.F., Karger, D., Morris, R., Stoica, I.: Wide-Area Cooperative Storage with CFS. In: Proceedings of the 18th ACM Symposium on Operating Systems Principles (SOSP). (2001)

8. Rao, A., Lakshminarayanan, K., Surana, S., Karp, R.M., Stoica, I.: Load Balancing in Structured P2P Systems. In: 2nd International Workshop on Peer-to-Peer Systems (IPTPS). (2003)

9. Godfrey, B., Lakshminarayanan, K., Surana, S., Karp, R.M., Stoica, I.: Load Balancing in Dynamic Structured P2P Systems. In: 23rd Conference of the IEEE Communications Society (INFOCOM). (2004)

10. Michael Mitzenmacher, Andra W. Richa, R.K.S.: The Power of Two Random Choices: A Survey of Techniques and Results. In: Handbook of Randomized Computing. P. Pardalos, S.Rajasekaran, J.Rolim, and Eds. Kluwer, editors. (2000)

11. Byers, J.W., Considine, J., Mitzenmacher, M.: Simple Load Balancing for Distributed Hash Tables. In: 2nd International Workshop on Peer-to-Peer Systems (IPTPS). (2003)

12. Adler, M., Halperin, E., Karp, R.M., Vazirani, V.: A stochastic process on the hypercube with applications to peer-to-peer networks. In: Proc. of the 35th ACM Symp. on Theory of Computing (STOC). (2003) 575–584

13. Karger, D.R., Ruhl, M.: Simple Efficient Load Balancing Algorithms for Peer-to-Peer Systems. In: 3rd International Workshop on Peer-to-Peer Systems (IPTPS). (2004)

14. Karger, D.R., Ruhl, M.: Simple Efficient Load Balancing Algorithms for Peer-to-Peer Systems. In: Proc. of the 16th ACM Symp. on Parallelism in Algorithms and Architectures (SPAA). (2004) 36–43

15. Awerbuch, B., Scheideler, C.: Group Spreading: A protocol for provably secure distributed name service. In: Proc. of the 31st Int. Colloquium on Automata, Languages, and Programming (ICALP). (2004) 183–195

16. Manku, G.S.: Balanced Binary Trees for ID Management And Load Balance in Distributed Hash Tables. In: Proc. of the 23rd annual ACM symposium on Principles of Distributed Computing (PODC). (2004) 197–205

17. Kenthapadi, K., Manku, G.S.: Decentralized Algorithms Using Both Local and Random Probes for P2P Load Balancing. In: Proc. of the 17th ACM Symp. on Parallel Algorithms and Architectures (SPAA). (2005)

18. Bienkowski, M., Korzeniowski, M., Meyer auf der Heide, F.: Dynamic Load Balancing in Distributed Hash Tables. In: 4th International Workshop on Peer-to-Peer Systems (IPTPS). (2005)

19. Liben-Nowell, D., Balakrishnan, H., Karger, D.R.: Analysis of the Evolution of Peer-to-Peer Systems. In: Proc. of the 21st annual ACM symposium on Principles of Distributed Computing(PODC). (2002) 233–242

20. Pandurangan, G., Raghavan, P., Upfal, E.: Building Low-Diameter Peer-to-Peer Networks. In: Proc. of the 42nd IEEE symposium on Foundations of Computer Science (FOCS). (2001) 492–499

On the Power of Anonymous One-Way Communication

Dana Angluin[1], James Aspnes[1,*], David Eisenstat[2], and Eric Ruppert[3,**]

[1] Yale University, Department of Computer Science
[2] University of Rochester, Department of Computer Science
[3] York University, Department of Computer Science and Engineering

Abstract. We consider a population of anonymous processes communicating via anonymous message-passing, where the recipient of each message is chosen by an adversary and the sender is not identified to the recipient. Even with unbounded message sizes and process states, such a system can compute only limited predicates on inputs held by the processes. In the finite-state case, we show how the exact strength of the model depends critically on design choices that are irrelevant in the unbounded-state case, such as whether messages are delivered immediately or after a delay, whether a sender can record that it has sent a message, and whether a recipient can queue incoming messages, refusing to accept new messages until it has had a chance to send out messages of its own. These results may have implications for the design of distributed systems where processor power is severely limited, as in sensor networks.

1 Introduction

We introduce and study certain variants of the population protocol model [2, 3] modified to use forms of one-way communication progressively more similar to those of traditional asynchronous message-passing. In the population protocol model, finite-state agents interact in pairs, updating their states according to a joint transition function whose value depends upon the previous states of both agents. Because the new state of both agents may depend on the prior state of the other, we call such an interaction a **bidirectional interaction**. Protocols in this model must work correctly regardless of the order in which these bidirectional interactions occur. Motivating scenarios include models of the propagation of trust in populations of agents [10] and interactions of passively mobile sensors [3]. Similar models of pairwise interaction have been used to study the propagation of rumors in a population of agents [9] and to justify the Chemical Master Equation [13], suggesting that the model of population protocols may be fundamental in several fields.

Because the agents in a population protocol have only a constant number of states, it is impossible for them to adopt distinct identities, making them

---

* Supported in part by NSF grants CNS-0305258 and CNS-0435201.
** Supported in part by the Natural Sciences and Engineering Research Council of Canada.

J.H. Anderson, G. Prencipe, and R. Wattenhofer (Eds.): OPODIS 2005, LNCS 3974, pp. 396–411, 2006.

effectively anonymous. An agent encountering another agent cannot tell in general whether it has interacted with that agent before. Despite these limitations, populations of such agents can compute surprisingly powerful predicates on their initial states under a reasonable global fairness condition. When each agent may interact with every other agent, any predicate over the counts of initial states definable in Presburger arithmetic is computable [3]. When each agent has only a bounded set of neighbors with which it can interact, linear space computable predicates are computable [2].

The assumption of bidirectional interaction, however, may be unrealistic in the context of sensor networks, where radio communication, even between nearby sensors, may not be bidirectional. Moreover, one-way message-passing primitives may be easier to implement in practice. In this paper, we study how the power of the population protocol model changes when the assumption of bidirectional interaction is replaced by certain forms of one-way communication. The pairwise interactions are split into separate send and receive events that each may affect only a single agent.

We consider the effect of two primary attributes of the models: (1) send and receive events may occur simultaneously (**immediate** delivery) or may involve delayed messages subject to various constraints (**delayed** delivery and **queued** delivery), and (2) a sender may be allowed to change its state as a result of sending a message (**transmission**), or not (**observation**). The transmission model is more typical in distributed computing. A web page that increments its counter in response to a visit is an example of such an interaction. Examples of interactions that fit the observation model, where the receiver observes an unknowing sender, include a person reading a post to a discussion forum or a device reading a passive RFID (radio frequency identification) tag. (Of course to preserve the anonymity of our model, the device would not get a unique identity from the tag.) For models with delayed messages, we also consider whether the number of messages in transit is linearly bounded in the population size. Precise definitions are given in Sect. 2.

1.1 Comparing the Models

Comparing the computational power of the resulting models highlights the differences between the forms of one-way communication we consider. As in [3], we assume that every pair of agents eventually come into contact with each other, and seek to characterize the class of predicates on multisets of inputs that are stably computable by protocols in each model. Let $\#(a)$ denote the number of agents assigned input a in the initial configuration. We consider three kinds of predicates: (1) Threshold: $\#(a) \geq t$, (2) Modulo: $\#(a) \equiv j \pmod{k}$, and (3) Comparison: $\#(a) \geq \#(b)$. These three kinds of predicates turn out to be well-suited for characterizing the power of the various versions of our model but they arise in some interesting distributed tasks. The threshold function is applicable to a motivating example of [3]: a network of sensors monitoring individual birds could detect when at least five birds in the flock have an elevated temperature in order to raise an alarm of a possible epidemic. The modulo-k

predicate is useful if the system must determine whether processes can be evenly partitioned into groups of size k. A majority voting scheme could use a comparison predicate.

More complicated predicates can be built up from the basic predicates using Boolean operators. We define classes of predicates on finite multisets of symbols from a finite input alphabet Σ as follows. $\mathbf{TH}_k$ is the Boolean closure of all threshold predicates $\#(a) \geq t$ where $a \in \Sigma$ and $t \leq k$. Predicates in $\mathbf{TH}_k$ are determined by the multiplicities of input symbols up to a maximum of k; in particular, predicates in $\mathbf{TH}_1$ are determined by the presence or absence of each input symbol. $\mathbf{TH}_*$ is the union of $\mathbf{TH}_k$ over all positive integers k. $\mathbf{REG}$ is the Boolean closure of all threshold predicates $\#(a) \geq t$ and modulo predicates $\#(a) \equiv j \pmod{k}$ where $a \in \Sigma$, $t \geq 1$, $j \geq 0$, and $k \geq 2$. Predicates in $\mathbf{REG}$ are those recognizable by finite-state acceptors when fed the input symbols in any order. $\mathbf{SLIN}$ is the class of semilinear predicates over multisets of symbols from Σ, that is, the class definable by Presburger predicates [21] over the counts of symbols from Σ. It is the Boolean closure of threshold predicates, modulo predicates and comparisons of linear combinations of input multiplicities. We have the following relationships between these classes:

$$\mathbf{TH}_1 \subset \mathbf{TH}_2 \subset \ldots \subset \mathbf{TH}_* \subset \mathbf{REG} \subset \mathbf{SLIN},$$

where the containments are strict. The predicate $(\#(a) = 1) \wedge (\#(b) \geq 3)$ is in $\mathbf{TH}_3$ but not $\mathbf{TH}_2$. The predicate $(\#(a) \geq 13) \vee (\#(b) \equiv 3 \pmod{5})$ is in $\mathbf{REG}$, but not $\mathbf{TH}_*$, which does not contain the modulo predicates. The predicate $((3 * \#(a) + 1) < (5 * \#(b))) \vee (\#(b) = 2)$ is in $\mathbf{SLIN}$ but not $\mathbf{REG}$, which does not contain the comparison predicate. Every predicate in $\mathbf{SLIN}$ is stably computable by a population protocol in the standard two-way model [3]; whether other predicates are stably computable in this model is open.

We define the class of core-$\mathbf{REG}$ predicates over an alphabet Σ as follows. A finite multiset of elements of Σ is k-rich if it contains each element of Σ with multiplicity at least k. Given a predicate P and a nonnegative integer k, define the k-core of P to be $P \wedge Q$ where Q is the property of being k-rich. Then a predicate P is in core-$\mathbf{REG}$ if some k-core of P is in $\mathbf{REG}$.

Our results for the finite-state models appear in Sect. 3. A summary is provided in Fig. 1. For each variant of the model, the corresponding box in the figure describes known facts about the class of predicates that can be stably computed.

The power of the delayed observation model is exactly $\mathbf{TH}_1$; protocols can only detect the presence or absence of each input symbol. The power of the immediate observation model is exactly $\mathbf{TH}_*$. A protocol in this model may determine the multiplicity of each input symbol up to some fixed limit k. Thus, this model is strictly stronger than the delayed observation model. The power of the immediate and delayed transmission models properly includes $\mathbf{REG}$, but does not include the comparison predicate. Thus, these two models are strictly more powerful than the immediate observation model. The immediate transmission model is strictly weaker than the standard two-way model and the delayed transmission model is strictly weaker than the queued transmission model.

	observation	transmission	transmission with linear message bound
immediate	= **TH**$_*$ (Thm 5)	$\supset$ **REG** (Thm 9) $\not\supseteq$ comparison (Cor 12) = two-way $\cap$ core-**REG** (Thm 13)	*not applicable*
delayed	= **TH**$_1$ (Thm 1)	$\supseteq$ immediate transmission $\not\supseteq$ comparison (Cor 12) $\subseteq$ queued $\cap$ core-**REG** (Thm 11)	= immediate transmission (full paper)
queued	*not applicable*	$\supseteq$ two-way $\supseteq$ **SLIN** (Thm 14 & [3])	= two-way $\supseteq$ **SLIN** (Thm 14 & [3])

Fig. 1. Summary of our results for finite-state models

The queued transmission model, which is essentially an anonymous finite-state version of the usual asynchronous message-passing model, is at least as powerful as the standard two-way model, and equal to it in power with a linear bound on messages in transit. Without such a bound, the queued transmission model admits protocols that spawn an unbounded number of new simulated agents; the exact characterization of the power of the model in this case is an open question.

1.2 Anonymous Communication and Fairness

The question of what computations can be performed in anonymous systems, where processes start with the same state and the same programming, has a long history in theoretical distributed computing. Many early impossibility results such as [1] assume both anonymity and symmetry in the communication model, which limits what can be done without some mechanism for symmetry-breaking. See [12] for a survey of many such impossibility results. More recent work targeted specifically at anonymity has studied what problems are solvable in message-passing systems under various assumptions about the initial knowledge of the processes [6, 7, 22], or in anonymous shared-memory systems where the properties of the supplied shared objects can often (but not always, depending on the details of the model) be used to break symmetry and assign identities [4, 5, 8, 11, 15, 17, 18, 19, 20, 23]. This work has typically assumed few limits on the power of the processes in the system other than the symmetry imposed by the model.

Agents in the population protocol model are assumed to be finite-state. Together with a transition rule that depends only on the states of the two interacting agents, the finite-state assumption naturally yields a model in which agents are effectively anonymous. This makes the model much weaker than a typical message-passing model, where processes have identities. On the other hand, in one respect the population protocol model is much stronger than a typical message-passing model: communication between two interacting agents is instantaneous and bidirectional.

Implicit in the structure of a population protocol is that message-passing is rather strongly anonymous: not only does a receiver not learn the identity of the sender, but a sender cannot direct its message to a particular receiver. This is unusual even in anonymous message-passing models, which typically assume that a process can use some sort of local addressing to direct messages to specific neighbors. It also leads to a very weak message-passing model if we adopt the traditional fairness assumption of eventual delivery to all destinations of any message that is sent often enough. We show in Sect. 4 that even with unbounded states and message lengths, this fairness condition provides only enough power to detect the presence or absence of each possible input, giving additional support for the global fairness condition used in the rest of the paper.

2   Model

We give a model that unifies both the standard asynchronous message-passing model, adapted so that processes are anonymous and no longer control the destinations of their messages; and the population protocol model of [3], restricted so that interactions between two agents are one-way. We first describe these two models separately, and then define our combined model and its variations.

2.1   Asynchronous Message-Passing

In an **asynchronous message-passing model**, processes communicate by sending messages. A process may spontaneously send a message at any time, which is delivered to a recipient at some later time. The recipient may respond to the message by updating its state and possibly sending one or more messages. In the standard model, senders can choose the recipients of their messages, and recipients are aware of the identities of the senders of messages they receive; in our model, we drop these assumptions.

Message-passing systems may be vulnerable to a variety of failures, including failures at processes such as crashes or Byzantine faults, and failures in the message delivery system such as dropped or duplicated messages. We assume fault-free executions. Since message delivery is asynchronous, making any sort of progress requires adopting a fairness condition to exclude executions in which indefinitely-postponed delivery becomes equivalent to no delivery.

A minimal fairness condition might be that if some process sends a particular message m infinitely often, then each other process receives the same message m infinitely often. In Sect. 4, we show that this minimal fairness condition is not enough to solve more than a small class of problems, even in a message-passing model with unbounded states and message sizes. So instead we adopt a stronger global fairness condition derived from that used in [3]. We define this condition formally below.

2.2   Population Protocols

We call this model the **standard two-way model** of population protocols to distinguish it from the one-way models we define in Sect. 2.3. A **population**

protocol [3] consists of a finite population V of agents with states drawn from a finite state set Q. The identities of agents $v \in V$ are used in describing the model, but are not accessible to the agents themselves. Agents interact in pairs; each interaction updates the state of both agents according to a joint transition rule $\delta : Q \times Q \to Q \times Q$ that maps pairs of states $(p, q) \mapsto (p', q')$. Interactions are asymmetric: the left-hand agent is called the **initiator** and the right-hand agent the **responder**. We think of the initiator as the **sender** of a message and the responder as the **receiver** of a message, but in the original model information may flow in both directions.

A **configuration** C of a population protocol describes the states of all agents; the state of agent v in C is denoted $C(v)$. An interaction takes a configuration C to a new configuration C' by updating the states of exactly two agents. If there is a transition from C to C', we write $C \to C'$. We write $C \xrightarrow{*} C'$ if there is a sequence of zero or more transitions that transform C to C'. In this case, C' is said to be **reachable** from C.

A **computation** is a sequence of configurations $C_0, C_1, C_2, \ldots$ with $C_i \to C_{i+1}$ for each i. Computations may be finite or infinite. Achieving positive results in this model depends on excluding computations in which subpopulations are isolated from each other or are only permitted to communicate at inopportune times. In [3], a computation was defined to be **fair** if for every configuration C that occurs infinitely often in the computation, if $C \to C'$, then C' also occurs infinitely often in the computation. This condition is intended to capture the effect of a probability 1 property without directly incorporating probabilities; for example, if pairs of agents are selected at random to interact, the resulting computation is fair with probability 1. In Sect. 2.4 we generalize this fairness condition to deal with messages in transit.

To allow agent states to contain information other than the output value, states in Q are mapped to outputs from a finite output alphabet Y by an **output function**. Similarly, inputs from a finite input alphabet Σ are mapped to states in Q by an **input function** $I : \Sigma \to Q$. An input X assigns a symbol from Σ to each agent in the population; the corresponding input configuration is denoted $I(X)$. Because the agents are anonymous and every pair may interact and because we consider predicates, it is immaterial which agent is assigned each symbol [3], and we may consider inputs and configurations as finite multisets. Multisets are denoted by upper-case letters, and individual elements are denoted by lower-case letters. We use the notation $A + B$ for the union of multisets A and B, and $A + a$ for the union of multisets A and $\{a\}$. The notation kA, where k is a non-negative integer and A is a multiset, is used for the multiset in which every element occurs with k times its multiplicity in A.

A configuration C is **output-stable** if, for any C' reachable from C by a sequence of zero or more transitions, the vector of output values in C' is equal to the vector of output values in C. A predicate P on finite multisets X of elements from Σ is **stably computed** by a given protocol if every fair computation of the protocol from an input configuration $I(X)$ eventually reaches an output-stable state in which all agents output the correct value for $P(X)$. As an example, a protocol with inputs $\{0, 1\}$ and identity input and output functions in which $(1, q) \mapsto (1, 1)$ and $(0, q) \mapsto (0, q)$ stably computes the OR of all the initial inputs. Output-stability does not require that the states of individual agents do not change; it is enough that any changes are not visible in the outputs of agents. This fact is exploited by protocols that include "leader bits" or similar tokens that move freely among agents without affecting the output after convergence.

2.3 One-Way Communication in Population Protocols

To model one-way communication in a population protocol, we restrict the transition function so that the new state of the sender does not depend on the state of the receiver. There are two natural ways to do this. We may stipulate that an interaction does not change the state of the sender at all. This is an **observation** model, in which the sender is passively observed by the receiver. Formally, if $(p, q) \mapsto (p', q')$, then $p' = p$.

Alternatively, in a **transmission** model, the sender of a message can detect that it has sent the message, but learns nothing about the state of the recipient. This corresponds to requiring that for any two transitions $(p_1, q_1) \mapsto (p'_1, q'_1)$ and $(p_2, q_2) \mapsto (p'_2, q'_2)$, that if $p_1 = p_2$ then $p'_1 = p'_2$. Since each transmission model formally includes the corresponding observation model, it is at least as powerful.

In both cases, the result is that communication is **one-way**: only the receiver obtains any information about its partner's state. We will refer to any protocol with such one-way communication as a **one-way population protocol**. In an **immediate delivery** model, these are the only changes to the basic population protocol model. Immediate delivery models can be thought of as models of interaction.

However, the standard asynchronous message-passing model assumes that (1) processes cannot be compelled to send messages if they do not want to and (2) messages may not be delivered immediately. Including the first feature requires classifying states based on whether or not they are enabled to send messages. For the non-immediate models we assume that send events only occur for states q in some subset Q_S of Q; states in Q_S are called **send-enabled**.

To address (2), we split a joint transition into two separate sending and receiving events. Configurations are extended to include two components: the **population configuration**, giving the states of all the agents, and the multiset of **messages in transit**, which for simplicity we take to be pairs consisting of sender ids and elements of the state space Q. (The sender ids are used only in the model discussed in Sect. 4.) Each transition $(p, q) \mapsto (p', q')$ is split into a **send event** which changes the state of an agent from p to p' and adds p to the multiset of messages in transit, and a **receive event** in which p is removed from the multiset of messages in transit and the state of some agent is updated from q to q'. As with immediate delivery, we can consider both a **delayed transmission** model in which a sender can record that it sent a message and a **delayed observation** model in which a sender cannot.

Both the delayed transmission and delayed observation models require that any agent be prepared to receive any message in any state. This may not give an agent enough time to respond to a message before the next incoming message arrives. With **queued** delivery, an agent can enter into a state in which it refuses to receive messages. Formally, we assume that only states in some subset Q_R of Q can receive messages; states in Q_R are called **receive-enabled**. In the delayed or queued models, the transition rule becomes a partial function whose domain is $Q_S \times Q_R$, where $Q_R = Q$ for delayed transmission or delayed observation and $Q_R \subseteq Q$ for queued transmission.[1]

Separating message transmission and receipt creates the possibility that an agent may receive its own message. This can be thought of as including self-loops in the **interaction graph** controlling which agents can communicate, which we otherwise take to be complete. In general, we assume that this does not occur in the immediate delivery models (which are interaction models) but may occur in the delayed and queued delivery models (once a message is sent it may be delivered to anyone.) In the full paper it will be shown that this has at most a minor effect on the power of the models we consider.

2.4 Fairness Revisited

We generalize the fairness condition from [3], given in Sect. 2.2, to deal with messages in transit. Because we permit partial transition rules, we also extend the definition of a computation to be any sequence of configurations $C_0, C_1, \ldots$ such that for each i, $C_i \to C_{i+1}$ or $C_{i+1} = C_i$. This does not change the reachability relation on computations, but it does permit a simpler definition of fairness that applies to computations that terminate (when no further transitions are enabled) as well as non-terminating ones.

Let $C_0, C_1, \ldots$ be an infinite computation. A population configuration C **occurs infinitely often** in this computation if there are infinitely many j such that C is the population component of C_j. A population configuration C is **infinitely often enabled** in this computation if there exist infinitely many j such that C is the population component of some configuration reachable from C_j. We say that this computation is **fair** if for every population configuration C that is infinitely often enabled in the computation, C occurs infinitely often in the computation.[2]

3 The Power of One-Way Population Protocols

We investigate what predicates on the multiset of input symbols are stably computable in the models defined in Sect. 2.3 Note that for each of these models, a direct product construction permits parallel execution of a finite collection of different protocols, and therefore the set of stably computable predicates is closed under Boolean combinations in each model.

---

[1] In an observation model an agent cannot leave a non receive-enabled state; thus we do not consider a queued observation model.

[2] The antecedent of the condition may never be satisfied if the state space is unbounded, as is often implicit in the standard asynchronous message-passing model.

3.1   Delayed Observation

The delayed observation model is very weak: an agent is unaware that it has sent a message, and may receive messages that were sent in the distant past. This effectively means that an agent may at any time receive messages containing any state that has ever appeared in the computation. As a result, the most that a protocol can do is detect the presence or absence of particular symbols in the input.

Theorem 1. TH$_1$ *is the class of predicates stably computable in the delayed observation model.*

Lemma 2. *Let P be a predicate in* **TH$_1$**. *Then P is stably computable by a delayed observation protocol.*

Proof. Each state is a subset of the finite input alphabet. Input a is mapped to $\{a\}$. Whenever an agent in state q receives a message q', it updates its state to $q \cup q'$. The output function maps q to the value of P on this set of inputs. By the fairness condition, the value of every state must converge to the set of inputs present in the initial configuration, and the outputs will then be the correct value of P. □

The following cloning technique applies to both the observation models.

Lemma 3. *Suppose a protocol in the delayed or immediate observation model stably computes the predicate P. Suppose $C \xrightarrow{*} D$ and v is an agent such that $C(v) = p$ and $D(v) = q$. Let v' be a new agent, and let C' be C with v' in state p and let D' be D with v' in state q. Then $C' \xrightarrow{*} D'$.*

Proof sketch. We use the computation from C to D to construct a computation from C' to D' by duplicating every message eventually delivered to v in the computation from C to D, and delivering one copy to v and one copy to v'. The agents sending the duplicate messages are unaffected by the change because these are observation models. □

Lemma 4. *Suppose P is stably computed by a delayed observation protocol. Then P is in* **TH$_1$**.

Proof. We show that for any multiset X of inputs, if $a \in X$ then $P(X + a) = P(X)$, which implies that P is determined solely by the presence or absence of each input symbol and hence is in **TH$_1$**.

Consider the finite graph whose nodes are configurations reachable from $I(X)$ that contain no messages in transit, with a directed edge from C to C' if $C \xrightarrow{*} C'$. A **final** strongly connected component of this graph is one from which no other strongly connected component of the graph is reachable. From $I(X)$ we can reach a configuration in a final strongly connected component $\mathcal{F}$ of this graph. Let $\hat{\mathcal{F}}$ denote all the configurations D, including those with undelivered messages, such that $C \xrightarrow{*} D$ for some $C \in \mathcal{F}$. For any configurations D and D' in $\hat{\mathcal{F}}$, $D \xrightarrow{*} D'$

by first delivering all messages in D. This implies that all configurations in $\hat{\mathcal{F}}$ are output-stable.

The set T of states that occur in configurations in $\hat{\mathcal{F}}$ is closed, that is, if $p, q \in T$ and $(p, q) \mapsto (p, q')$, then $q' \in T$. To see this, assume not. Then, take a configuration D in $\hat{\mathcal{F}}$ that contains p and let an agent in state p send a message, putting p into messages in transit. Now mimic a computation from D to a configuration D' in $\hat{\mathcal{F}}$ containing q, leaving the message p undelivered. Then deliver p to an agent in state q, arriving at a configuration in $\hat{\mathcal{F}}$ containing q', a contradiction.

Now consider any a in X. Let C be an output-stable configuration in $\mathcal{F}$ that is reachable from $I(X)$. Let q be the state in configuration C of an agent that began with input a. Then by Lemma 3, a configuration C' equal to C with a new agent in state q is reachable from $I(X + a)$. Because T is closed and the states of C' are all in T, C' is output-stable and therefore $P(X + a) = P(X)$. □

3.2 Immediate Observation

In the immediate observation model, transitions are of the form $(p, q) \mapsto (p, q')$ and there is no multiset of undelivered messages. For any constant k, an immediate observation protocol can count the number of copies of each input symbol up to k, making this model more powerful than the delayed observation model. However, this is also the extent of its power.

Theorem 5. $\mathbf{TH}_*$ *is the class of predicates stably computable in the immediate observation model.*

Lemma 6. *Every predicate in* $\mathbf{TH}_*$ *is stably computable by an immediate observation protocol.*

Proof. By Boolean closure, it suffices to give an immediate observation protocol that stably computes an arbitrary threshold predicate: $\#(a) \geq k$. The states are $0, 1, 2, \ldots, k$. The input map takes a to 1 and every other symbol to 0; the protocol must determine whether there are at least k 1's in the initial configuration. The transitions are $(i, i) \mapsto (i, i + 1)$ for all $i = 1, 2, \ldots, k - 1$ and $(k, i) \mapsto (k, k)$ for all $i = 0, 1, 2, \ldots, k - 1$, where all other transitions leave the argument pair unchanged. The output map takes k to 1 and every other state to 0.

If there are no 1's in the initial configuration, then it never changes. If there are j 1's in the initial configuration for some $0 < j < k$, then any fair computation eventually reaches a configuration in which the only nonzero states are $1, 2, \ldots, j$, and this configuration never changes. In both cases, every output is 0 throughout the computation.

If there are $j \geq k$ 1's in the initial configuration, then any fair computation must reach the configuration in which all states are k, and this configuration never subsequently changes. In this configuration, every output is 1. (The full paper will contain a proof that the number of states used in this protocol is optimal.) □

Consider an immediate observation protocol that stably computes a predicate P. The following property of output-stable configurations of P is very useful. A set $\mathcal{L}$ of finite multisets of elements from some set S is called **linear** if there exist a base element $B \in \mathcal{L}$ and a finite set of periods $P_1, \ldots, P_d$ such that the elements of $\mathcal{L}$ are precisely those of the form $B + m_1 P_1 + \ldots + m_d P_d$, where the m_i are nonnegative integers and the P_i are multisets of elements of S.

Lemma 7. *The set of output-stable accepting (resp., rejecting) configurations is a union of a finite collection of linear sets in which every period consists of a singleton state.*

Proof. A set is **semilinear** if it is a finite union of linear sets. The set $\mathcal{A}$ of output-stable accepting configurations is downward closed, so its complement is upward closed and therefore semilinear by Higman's Lemma [16]. Because the semilinear sets are closed under complement [14], $\mathcal{A}$ is semilinear.

Thus, $\mathcal{A}$ is a finite union of linear sets. Consider one of the linear sets, say $\mathcal{L}$. It has a base element B and a finite collection of periods, $P_1, \ldots, P_d$. Consider the linear set $\mathcal{L}'$ with base B and periods $\{q\}$ for any state q that occurs in some P_i. Clearly, $\mathcal{L} \subseteq \mathcal{L}'$, and we claim $\mathcal{L}' \subseteq \mathcal{A}$, so that replacing each $\mathcal{L}$ by its corresponding $\mathcal{L}'$ gives the decomposition of $\mathcal{A}$ required by the lemma. To see that the claim is true, consider any element C of $\mathcal{L}'$. C consists of B plus multiples of states q in the periods P_i. By taking B plus sufficiently large multiples of the P_i's we get a configuration $C' \in \mathcal{L}$ such that $C \subseteq C'$. Because $\mathcal{A}$ is downward closed, $C \in \mathcal{A}$. The same proof works for the output-stable rejecting configurations. $\qquad\square$

Lemma 8. *Let P be a predicate that is stably computed by a protocol in the immediate observation model. Then P is in $\mathbf{TH}_*$.*

Proof. By Lemma 7, the output-stable accepting configurations of the protocol are the union of a finite collection of linear sets $\mathcal{L}_i$ with singleton periods, and similarly for the output-stable rejecting configurations, where the linear sets are $\mathcal{M}_j$. Let k be one more than the maximum cardinality of any of the bases of the $\mathcal{L}_i$'s or $\mathcal{M}_j$'s.

Consider any finite multiset X of inputs for which $\#(a) \geq k$ for some a. Suppose X is accepted; a similar proof applies if X is rejected. If $I(a) = q$ then q occurs with multiplicity at least k in $I(X)$. Consider any output-stable configuration D reachable from C. D is in one of the linear sets $\mathcal{L}_i$. Because the multiplicity of q exceeds the cardinality of the base of $\mathcal{L}_i$, some agent v in state q in $I(X)$ must have state q' in D, where q' is the singleton state of one of the periods of $\mathcal{L}_i$. Thus, $D + q'$ is also in $\mathcal{L}_i$, so $D + q'$ is output-stable and accepting. However, by Lemma 3, $I(X) + q \xrightarrow{*} D + q'$, and $I(X) + q = I(X + a)$, so $X + a$ must also be accepted by the protocol. Thus, for any input symbol a, if $\#(a) \geq k$ in input X, $P(X + a) = P(X)$, which implies that P is in $\mathbf{TH}_k$, and therefore in $\mathbf{TH}_*$. $\qquad\square$

3.3   Immediate and Delayed Transmission

The immediate and delayed transmission models can stably compute all threshold and modulo predicates, and therefore all predicates in **REG**. Thus they are more powerful than the immediate observation model.

Theorem 9. *Predicates in* **REG** *are stably computable in the immediate and delayed transmission models.*

Proof. By Boolean closure, it suffices to prove that all the threshold and modulo predicates are stably computable in both models. We assume data values in the set $S = \{0, 1, \ldots, k\}$ and a commutative monoid operation $g(d_1, d_2)$ on this set with identity 0. We describe a protocol to compute the g-sum of all the data values in the input states. The states are (b, d), where $b \in \{0, 1\}$ is a leader bit, and $d \in S$. A transition with sender state (b, d) and receiver state (b', d') updates the sender state to $(0, d)$ and the receiver state to $(1, g(d, d'))$ if $b = b' = 1$, to $(1, d)$ if $b = 1$ and $b' = 0$, and leaves it unchanged otherwise.

The following invariant is preserved by each transition: the g-sum of the data values of those agents and messages in transit with leader bit equal to 1 is the g-sum of all the input data values. By fairness, eventually there will be just one agent (or message in transit) with leader bit equal to 1, and its data value will be the correct g-sum of all the input data values. Again by fairness, that data value will be copied to every agent as the leader bit is passed among them.

For the threshold predicate $\#(a) \geq k$, a is mapped to $(1, 1)$ and all other input symbols are mapped to $(0, 0)$. State (b, d) is mapped to output 1 if and only if $d = k$. The monoid sum $g(d_1, d_2)$ is $\min(k, d_1 + d_2)$. For the modulo predicate $\#(a) \equiv j \pmod{(k + 1)}$ we take the same input function, map (b, d) to output 1 if and only if $d = j$, and take the monoid sum $g(d_1, d_2)$ to be $(d_1 + d_2) \bmod (k + 1)$.   □

The following theorem shows that **REG** does not exhaust the class of predicates stably computable in the immediate and delayed transmission models. Let $ be a symbol not in Σ and P a predicate over alphabet Σ. Define $P_\$$ be the predicate over $\Sigma \cup \{\$\}$ that is true if there are at least two agents in the population, there is exactly one $ in the input, and P is true on the multiset of other input symbols. For example, if P is the comparison predicate, $\#(a) > \#(b)$, then $P_\$$ is the predicate that is true when the input contains exactly one $ and more a's than b's, which is not in **REG**.

Theorem 10. *Let P be a predicate over Σ that is stably computable in the standard two-way model. Then $P_\$$ is stably computable in the immediate and delayed transmission models.*

Proof sketch. We run three protocols in parallel, one to verify that there are at least two agents in the population, one to verify that there is just one $ in the input, and one that performs a simulation of the two-way protocol computing P on the rest of the input symbols, assuming that the first two conditions are satisfied. The first two conditions are in $\textbf{TH}_2$ and $\textbf{TH}_1$, respectively, and are therefore computable, by Theorem 9.

The idea of the simulation is to use the unique input \$ to generate a leader token that passes from one simulated agent to another in the population. The leader token nondeterministically chooses a simulated agent to be the initiator and picks up its state (leaving behind a place marker), chooses another simulated agent to be the responder, updates the responder's state and waits until it returns to the place marker to update the simulated initiator's state, and then repeats the whole sequence. The state of the extra agent (that had the input \$) is updated to reflect the outputs of the simulated agents.   □

The following theorem is an important restriction on the power of both transmission models; its proof will appear in the full paper. Recall the definitions of k-rich, k-core, and core-$\textbf{REG}$ from Sect. 1.1.

Theorem 11. *Let P be a predicate that is stably computable by an immediate or delayed transmission protocol. Then for some k, the k-core of P is in $\textbf{REG}$.*

Let P be the comparison predicate, $\#(a) > \#(b)$. The 2-core of $P_\$$ is empty, and therefore in $\textbf{REG}$, but no k-core of P is in $\textbf{REG}$, yielding the following corollary.

Corollary 12. *The comparison predicate is not stably computable in the immediate or delayed transmission models.*

By generalizing Theorem 10 and combining it with Theorem 11, we get the following characterization of the power of immediate transmission protocols; its proof will appear in the full paper.

Theorem 13. *A predicate P is stably computable in the immediate transmission model if and only if P is stably computable in the standard two-way model and some k-core of P is in $\textbf{REG}$.*

3.4   Queued Transmission

The queued transmission model is the most powerful of the models we consider; it is capable of simulating the standard model of two-way population protocols, and (if no bounds are placed on the size of the multiset of messages in transit) can generate an unbounded number of additional simulated agents. The intuition is that a simulation can use messages in transit to represent agents of the standard population protocol, and collect pairs of simulated agents at real nodes to simulate transitions. To avoid deadlocks, we also include a floating population of "release messages" that trigger nodes to release the simulated agents collected so far.

Theorem 14. *A predicate P is stably computable by a standard two-way population protocol if and only if P is stably computable in the queued transmission model using at most a linear number of messages in transit.*

A detailed proof is given in the full paper. The full paper will also include a proof that the delayed transmission model with a linear bound on messages in transit is equivalent in power to the immediate transmission model, based on Theorems 11 and 14.

4   Local Fairness Is Weak Even with Unbounded States

In this section, we consider an anonymous message-passing model with the following local fairness condition: if some process sends a particular message m infinitely often, then each process receives message m infinitely often. This model turns out to be surprisingly weak. Even if the states of processes and the lengths of messages may grow without bound, protocols in this model cannot distinguish two multisets of inputs if the same set of values appears in each. Since this model subsumes the finite-state models of the preceding sections, it demonstrates why the stronger global fairness condition assumed there is necessary. The definition of $\mathbf{TH}_k$ generalizes straightforwardly to an infinite alphabet Σ.

Theorem 15. *Let Σ denote the (finite or infinite) set of possible input values. A predicate P on finite multisets of elements from Σ is stably computable in the asynchronous message-passing model with the weak fairness condition if and only if P is in $\mathbf{TH}_1$.*

Proof. Consider the delayed observation protocol from the proof of Lemma 2 to determine the set of all inputs that occur in the initial configuration, modified so that each agent sends its state every time it runs. Clearly every message is a subset of the initial set of input values, so there are only finitely many possible messages in each computation. Every message sent by a process with input value x contains the element x, and it sends infinitely many messages, so eventually every process receives a message containing x. Thus, the state of every process eventually consists of the initial set of input values.

For the converse, assume that we have an algorithm to stably compute a predicate P, and let A and B be two multisets of values from Σ such that the same set of values appears in each. Let $n = |A|$ and $n' = |B|$. Let C_0 and C_0' be initial configurations where processes have inputs from A and B, respectively. We construct two executions α and α' starting from C_0 and C_0'. Let $m_1, m_2, \ldots$ be an arbitrary sequence of messages where every possible message appears infinitely often. We construct the executions α and α' in phases, where phase i will ensure that message m_i gets delivered to everyone if that message has been sent enough times. Let C_i and C_i' be the configurations of α and α' at the end of phase i.

Our goal is to prove the following claim: for all $i \geq 0$ and for all $x \in \Sigma$, the state of each process with input x in C_i is the same as the state of each process with input x in C_i'. Assume that we have constructed the first $i - 1$ phases of the two executions so that the claim is satisfied. Suppose we run all processes in lock step from C_{i-1} and C_{i-1}' without delivering any messages. There are two cases.

Case (i): Eventually, after r_i rounds, the run from C_{i-1} will have at least n copies of m_i in transit and, after r_i' rounds, the run from C_{i-1}' will have at least n' copies of m_i in transit. Then, the ith phase of α and α' is constructed by running each process for $\max(r_i, r_i')$ rounds without delivering any messages, and then delivering one copy of m_i to every process. This ensures the claim will be true for C_i and C_i'.

Case (ii): Otherwise, we allow every process to take one step without delivering any messages. (This clearly satisfies the claim for C_i and C_i'.)

It remains to show that both α and α' satisfy the weak fairness condition, and then it will follow from the claim that $P(A) = P(B)$. First, notice that every process takes infinitely many steps in α and α'. If some process v sends a message m infinitely many times in α or α', it will also be sent infinitely many times by a process with the same input value in the other execution (since a process with a particular input experiences the same sequence of events in both executions). Suppose m is never delivered after phase i to some process w in one of the two executions. Eventually, there will be n copies of m in transit in C_j for some $j > i$ and n' copies of m in transit in $C'_{j'}$ for some $j' > i$. Consider the first occurrence of m in the sequence $m_1, m_2, \ldots$ that comes after m_j and m'_j. During the corresponding phase, m will be delivered to every process, including w, a contradiction. Thus, α and α' satisfy the weak fairness condition. $\square$

5   Conclusion

We defined several models incorporating one-way communication and message-passing into population protocols and compared their ability to compute predicates on multisets of inputs. We have fully characterized the power of the delayed and immediate observation models, the immediate transmission model, and the delayed and queued transmission models with a linear bound on messages in transit. The queued transmission model with a linear bound on messages in transit is equivalent in power to the original model of two-way population protocols. In contrast to traditional message-passing systems, the strongest model is the most asynchronous: in the queued transmission model, messages in transit can effectively act as extra storage. An important feature of the queued transmission model is that receivers can exercise flow control over incoming messages; the delayed transmission model, lacking such flow control, is strictly weaker. The problems of characterizing the power of the delayed and queued transmission models with no bound on messages in transit remains open, as does the related problem from [3] of whether the power of standard two-way model is more than **SLIN**.

References

1. Dana Angluin. Local and global properties in networks of processors. In *Proceedings of the 12th ACM Symposium on Theory of Computing*, pages 82–93, 1980.
2. Dana Angluin, James Aspnes, Melody Chan, Michael J. Fischer, Hong Jiang, and René Peralta. Stably computable properties of network graphs. *IEEE/ACM International Conference on Distributed Computing in Sensor Systems*, June 2005.
3. Dana Angluin, James Aspnes, Zoë Diamadi, Michael J. Fischer, and René Peralta. Computation in networks of passively mobile finite-state sensors. In *Proc. 23rd Annual ACM Symposium on Principles of Distributed Computing*, pages 290–299, 2004.
4. James Aspnes, Gauri Shah, and Jatin Shah. Wait-free consensus with infinite arrivals. In *Proceedings of the 34th ACM Symposium on Theory of Computing*, pages 524–533, 2002.

5. Hagit Attiya, Alla Gorbach, and Shlomo Moran. Computing in totally anonymous asynchronous shared memory systems. *Information and Computation*, 173(2): 162–183, March 2002.

6. Paolo Boldi and Sebastiano Vigna. Computing anonymously with arbitrary knowledge. In *Proceedings of the 18th ACM Symposium on Principles of Distributed Computing*, pages 173–179, 1999.

7. Paolo Boldi and Sebastiano Vigna. An effective characterization of computability in anonymous networks. In *Distributed Computing, 15th International Conference*, pages 33–47, 2001.

8. Harry Buhrman, Alessandro Panconesi, Riccardo Silvestri, and Paul Vitanyi. On the importance of having an identity or, is consensus really universal? *Distributed Computing*, 18(3):167–176, 2006.

9. D. J. Daley and D. G. Kendall. Stochastic rumours. *Journal of the Institute of Mathematics and its Applications*, 1:42–55, 1965.

10. Zoë Diamadi and Michael J. Fischer. A simple game for the study of trust in distributed systems. *Wuhan University Journal of Natural Sciences*, 6(1–2):72–82, March 2001. Also appears as Yale Technical Report TR–1207, January 2001.

11. Ömer Eğecioğlu and Ambuj K. Singh. Naming symmetric processes using shared variables. *Distributed Computing*, 8(1):19–38, 1994.

12. Faith Fich and Eric Ruppert. Hundreds of impossibility results for distributed computing. *Distributed Computing*, 16(2-3):121–163, September 2003.

13. Daniel T. Gillespie. A rigorous derivation of the chemical master equation. *Physica A*, 188:404–425, 1992.

14. Seymour Ginsburg. *The Mathematical Theory of Context Free Languages*. McGraw-Hill, New York, 1966.

15. Rachid Guerraoui and Eric Ruppert. What can be implemented anonymously? In *19th International Symposium on Distributed Computing*, pages 244–259, 2005.

16. G. Higman. Ordering by divisibility in abstract algebras. *Proceedings of the London Mathematical Society*, 3(2):326–336, 1952.

17. Prasad Jayanti and Sam Toueg. Wakeup under read/write atomicity. In *Distributed Algorithms, 4th International Workshop*, volume 486 of *LNCS*, pages 277–288, 1990.

18. Shay Kutten, Rafail Ostrovsky, and Boaz Patt-Shamir. The Las-Vegas processor identity problem (How and when to be unique). *Journal of Algorithms*, 37(2): 468–494, November 2000.

19. Richard J. Lipton and Arvin Park. The processor identity problem. *Information Processing Letters*, 36(2):91–94, October 1990.

20. Alessandro Panconesi, Marina Papatriantafilou, Philippas Tsigas, and Paul Vitányi. Randomized naming using wait-free shared variables. *Distributed Computing*, 11(3):113–124, August 1998.

21. Mojzesz Presburger. Über die Vollständigkeit eines gewissen Systems der Arithmetik ganzer Zahlen, in welchem die Addition als einzige Operation hervortritt. In *Comptes-Rendus du I Congrès de Mathématiciens des Pays Slaves*, pages 92–101, Warszawa, 1929.

22. Naoshi Sakamoto. Comparison of initial conditions for distributed algorithms on anonymous networks. In *Proc. 18th ACM Symposium on Principles of Distributed Computing*, pages 173–179, 1999.

23. Shang-Hua Teng. Space efficient processor identity protocol. *Information Processing Letters*, 34(3):147–154, April 1990.

Quality-Aware Resource Management for Wireless Sensor Networks*

Roland Gémesi, Nirvana Meratnia, and Paul Havinga

University of Twente, Department of Computer Science,
P.O. Box 217, 7500 AE, Enschede, The Netherlands
{r.gemesi, n.meratnia, p.j.m.havinga}@ewi.utwente.nl

Abstract. Due to the distributed and resource constrained nature of
wireless sensor networks, their design proves to be difficult. We present a
resource management framework, which integrates a data-centric lightweight operating system with a publish/subscribe middleware. In this
framework, the main system abstraction is data for both local and networked processing. The resultant system software is extended with a
quality-aware adaptation mechanism, which configures system timeliness
according to the actual application requirements. A feedback-based control mechanism is used to iteratively tune the resultant data granularity
in order to fit user requirements. Our design is evaluated by simulations
and the concepts were also implemented in our sensor network testbed.

1 Introduction

Wireless Sensor Networks represent the first step towards ubiquitous computing
[1]. They are massively distributed systems built of small embedded devices with
computing and wireless communication capabilities and provide data-collection
or possibly real-time control functionality by means of collaboration. Typically,
a number of sensor nodes are scattered over the target area to monitor and
provide information about requested phenomena.

The considered distributed platform differs from traditional computing systems in numerous aspects. Sensor nodes are usually small, battery powered,
and possess extremely limited hardware resources, such as CPU and storage capacity. Due to the finite battery supply, the utilised mechanisms have to be as
energy-efficient as possible to maximize the lifetime of the system. Despite these
constraints, complex tasks can be performed by means of collaboration. These
embedded devices use self-organised wireless networking to interact with each
other; however, their communication is very limited as well. Since nodes may
arbitrarily arrive or leave the network, the available resources can dynamically
change during the operation. Moreover, both nodes and their communication
are characterised by uncertainty.

Designing distributed applications in a harsh environment having the above-
mentioned characteristics proves to be difficult. The management of distributed,

---

* This work was funded by STW under the Featherlight Project number TES-6388.

J.H. Anderson, G. Prencipe, and R. Wattenhofer (Eds.): OPODIS 2005, LNCS 3974, pp. 412–426, 2006.

scarce and dynamic system resources is too complicated to be performed by each application, consequently mechanisms are needed to automate common distributed system functionalities. Moreover, the possibly immense number of nodes might produce a vast amount of information, usually much more than required. The quality and granularity of the acquired output should be managed according to the actual user/application requirements. Thus, resource management should also be capable of adapting service qualities, consequently managing what resources are spent for.

We introduce a system software framework that integrates a data-centric real-time operating system with a publish/subscribe middleware. This results in a resource management framework, which presents similar system abstractions for local and networked application development. We extend the resultant resource management framework with quality-awareness, which supports dynamic quality-aware reconfiguration of distributed mechanisms based on the application requirements. The provided framework is evaluated through simulations and the mechanisms are also implemented in our sensor network testbed.

The rest of this paper is organized as follows. Section 2 introduces the problems that motivate our work in more details. The middleware that extends the local abstractions of our local operating system is proposed in Section 3. Section 4 describes our feedback-based quality-management mechanism, followed by evaluation of the proposed framework in Section 5. Section 6 overviews related work and finally Section 7 concludes the paper.

2   Motivation

Collaborative applications involve several entities and utilise several resources concurrently in order to fulfil a common goal. The management and coordination of such distributed entities make the development very complex. Moreover, dealing with the dynamic and uncertain nature of the underlying system poses additional burden on the application developer.

The issue of handling system complexity is already present in traditional distributed systems, in which the objective of *System Software* is to support managing the system, consequently easing application development [12]. System software presents programming interfaces to perform standard operations, thus prevents designers to handle all the underlying issues of the actual system. This results not only in a simpler and generic development framework, but also helps avoiding reimplementing common features in each of the applications. Traditionally, the system software of distributed systems was divided into three parts: (i) *Operating System* (OS), which hides low-level hardware concepts by providing APIs for standard concerns, such as starting or stopping processes or allocating memory (ii) *Communication Protocol Stack*, which decomposes network communication tasks into a set of standardized layers (iii) *Middleware* that aims at hiding the networked nature of the underlying system and providing high-level, often application-dependent, programming primitives for distributed applications.

Providing generic system primitives calls for abstractions that shield developers from the underlying complexities of the distributed system. These high-level concepts should be useful for development purposes, however should not contain any details regarding the specific low-level system implementation. Selecting suitable abstractions for sensor networks is especially challenging. The complex distributed nature of the system makes it difficult to provide simple interfaces that can be maintained with a wide range of resources. For instance, the offered programming primitives should be independent of the number of available nodes or the topology they are actually organised in.

On top of that, the resources to manage can change dynamically. As new nodes enter the network, their offered services should get involved in the collaboration, although, when nodes leave or fail during operation, the system should tolerate the lack of their effort. The dynamic changes occurring in the actual network should not be realised by the applications that rely on high-level system primitives. System support should resolve such changes by reacting and adapting to changing resources.

As severe resource changes occur, some system services might not be maintained without degradation. However, in sensory environments *quality-resource tradeoffs* are usual between the accuracy of their acquired readings and the resource consumption. The system might operate at several quality levels, however the availability of resources and the minimal quality requirement specified by the application decide on suitable choices.

Resource management of sensor networks should consider such tradeoffs as tunable *knobs* of the system. Adaptively influencing quality metrics and consequently regulating resource demands has considerable benefits. It increases the resource-tolerance, because in case of insufficient resources the system might keep on operating with decreased quality levels. On the other hand, even if resources allow high granularity, avoiding acquiring unnecessary details saves energy. Thus, resource management should not only satisfy mechanisms with dynamic resource availabilities, but also manage quality-resource tradeoffs to regulate resource demands.

In this article, we introduce the design and evaluation of a resource management framework that provides system primitives suiting dynamic systems. The aim of our design is to set up a framework, in which both local and distributed applications rely on similar system primitives. Moreover, the proposed system software is capable of adapting qualities according to the available resources and user requirements, thus actively influencing the timeliness of system mechanisms.

3   Data-Centric System Software for Sensor Networks

A major issue in designing system software is to find the suitable system abstractions that are practical for common application needs and are not related to the actual resources. Since sensor networks are built of processing elements that might arrive and leave the network arbitrarily, processing models that explicitly describe the actual processing flow are not practical.

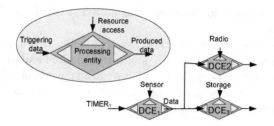

Fig. 1. Data-Centric Entities in AmbientRT

Our framework follows the data-centric concept [5]. In a *data-centric* system, actions are triggered by the data that is available in the network. Thus it focuses on the data being produced and consumed, but does not explicitly define the actions to be taken with produced data. That is the role of the system to pass the data to a suitable processing entity and activate it.

In the following, we show both the operating system and middleware levels of our data-centric system software.

3.1 AmbientRT

AmbientRT [8] is an embedded operating system developed and successfully applied by our research group. It was designed to fit the extremely limited memory and computing capacity of sensor nodes, while being able to provide real-time guarantees and facilitating energy-efficient operation.

AmbientRT is a data-centric operating system, in which the main system abstraction, called an *event*, can range from a system event to data measured from an environmental phenomena. The system is built of software components called *Data Centric Entities (DCE)*, which perform the processing tasks. As illustrated in Figure 1, the execution of DCEs are triggered by the availability of a data. During their execution, they usually require system resources and produce output data that can trigger other entities.

In the example illustrated in Figure 1, entity DCE_1 is activated by the periodic event *timer*, and perform a sensor *measurement*, presenting output data as a result. This periodically produced data activates two other entities: DCE_2 and DCE_3 representing storage and radio transmission functionality.

The central element of AmbientRT is the *Data Centric Scheduler*, which keeps track of all entities and has two main functionalities: to control which entities should be activated and to manage the data flow between the entities. The kernel uses a scheduling method called *Earliest Deadline First with Inheritance* [10] that enforces mutual exclusion of shared resources without the need of semaphores. This scheduling mechanism enables entities to meet real-time requirements.

The data-centric architecture of AmbientRT enables dynamic runtime reconfiguration, which makes it especially suitable for dynamic environments. As new entities appear and others are removed, the execution flow reconfigures automatically. AmbientRT makes the development of data-centric applications simple, enabling the developer to focus on evolving data instead of tracking dynamically available entities.

AmbientRT is a lightweight operating system facilitating a data-driven model for application development. It suits systems with limited and dynamic resources, but focuses only on the local aspects of system management. Since we consider distributed systems, it is still difficult to implement networked applications by using only local system support.

3.2 Publish/Subscribe Middleware for AmbientRT

To facilitate the development of networked applications, a network-wide resource management framework is required. We propose a middleware that extends the concepts of AmbientRT and provides efficient support for developing distributed applications.

To suit the data-centric philosophy, we apply a *publish/subscribe middleware*. In a publish/subscribe middleware, some nodes publish data that others are subscribed for. These abstractions are independent of the actual network topology and of available resources; it is focused on the data, therefore it is suitable to extend our operating system. The role of the middleware is to offer simple application interfaces and to manage disseminating data to the subscribed nodes.

The communication of the proposed middleware relies on the services offered by LMAC, our energy-efficient medium access control (MAC) protocol [14]. LMAC uses *Time Division Multiple Access* (TDMA) to share the communication channel among the participants. It divides time into slots and sets up schedules that determine when the nodes are allowed to transmit. LMAC uses a distributed algorithm that relies only on local information to create the schedules. LMAC is especially efficient in resource constrained environments, because nodes that do not communicate in a time slot might turn off their radios, consequently saving significant amount of energy.

LMAC also includes a basic routing functionality, which enables nodes to send data to the sink node, consequently supporting data collection in sensor networks. Each node chooses one of its neighbours that is closer to the sink node, and maintains it as a parent in the data collection tree. Our middleware relies on this data collection tree, thus no energy is wasted to set up an additional routing hierarchy.

With this basic routing support, we aimed at building a multicast routing scheme to disseminate data to the subscribed places. Our routing scheme is similar to the Protocol Independent Multicast (PIM) [4] protocol. Similarly to PIM, subscribers send requests to a rendezvous point setting routing states along the path. A published message is first sent to the rendezvous point, which subsequently routes it to all subscribers. However, PIM was proposed for wide area networks, and our mechanism contains additional optimizations to save as much energy as possible.

The nodes of the proposed publish/subscribe middleware perform as follows. When a node subscribes for a data type, it sends a *subscription message* to the root node. This message registers the interest both at the root as well as

ST_i : subscription table of node i

PST_i^j : proxied subscripiton table of node i for neighbour node j

$uplink_i$: uplink of node i

$downlink_i^j$: downlink of node i to neighbour j

$inlink$: the link on which event e arrived from

$Procedure_1$: node i subscribes for event e:
    if $((e \notin ST_i) \wedge (\neg\exists j : e \in PST_i^j))$ send e on $uplink_i$;
    add e to ST_i;
End;

$Procedure_2$: node i publishes event e:
    if $(e \in ST_i)$ dispatch to local operating system;
    send e on $uplink_i$;
    $\forall j$: if $(e \in PST_i^j)$ send e on $downlink_i^j$;
End;

$Procedure_3$: Subscribing network packet arrives:
    if $((e \notin ST_i) \wedge (\neg\exists j : e \in PST_i^j))$ send e on $uplink_i$
    add e to PST_i^{inlink};
End;

$Procedure_4$: Publishing network packet arrives:
    if $(e \in ST_i)$ dispatch to local operating system.
    $\forall j$: if $((e \in PST_i^j) \wedge (j \neq inlink))$ send e on $downlink_i^j$;
    if $(inlink \neq uplink_i)$ send e on $uplink_i$
End;

Fig. 2. Pseudocode of Event Dissemination

at each intermediate hops, so the delivery paths from the root node towards each interested parties are formed. When an arbitrary node wants to publish a data, it sends the data to the root node first, which disseminates it along all the interested links of the tree. The pseudocode of the message dispatching algorithm run by the nodes is shown in Figure 2. The actions of the root node differ slightly, because it cannot send messages further in the uplink direction.

Each node i in the network is a participant of the data delivery tree, consequently each node maintains links both to its parent ($uplink_i$) and to all its descendants ($downlink_i^j$). Since the tree is set up by LMAC, the middleware assumes that this information is available. The middleware registers subscriptions in order to maintain the dissemination tree. Each node i stores a *subscription table* for maintaining its own interest (ST_i), and also *proxied subscription tables* (PST_i^j) for the interests of all the descendants.

When a node subscribes to a new data type, an entry is added to its local subscription table. Then, if the data is neither present among the local nor the proxied subscriptions, the subscription message is sent to the parent. If the data is already present in any of the subscription tables, an interest has already been registered at the parent, thus it is not necessary to do it again. Similarly, as a subscription message arrives, the packet is sent to the parent only if it has

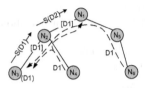

Fig. 3. Example Data Dissemination in the Proposed Middleware

not been sent before. The incoming interest is stored in the proxied subscription table of the particular incoming link.

When data is published, the middleware disseminates it to all the subscribed parties. If the actual node itself is subscribed, the message has to be dispatched to the local operating system first. Afterwards, the publishing message is disseminated to the parent node, and to each of the interested descendants. When a publishing network packet arrives, it is not necessary to disseminate the message on the incoming link. Thus, if the publishing message arrived from a descendant, it is sent to the parent and also to each interested downlinks, except the one it arrived from. When a publication arrives from the parent, it is disseminated only to the interested descendants.

An example is illustrated in Figure 3. Nodes $(N_1 \ldots N_7)$ form a tree rooted at N_1. When N_3 subscribes for data type D_1, its subscription message (S_{D_1}) is sent to N_2 first. N_2 registers that the link towards N_3 is interested in D_1, then it forwards S_{D_1} to the root (N_1), which registers the interest of N_2. When N_6 publishes D_1, it is first delivered to the root through N_5, then it is sent through the previously registered route to N_3. However, when N_4 publishes the data, N_3 gets the message directly from N_2 even before N_1 receives it, thus making a shortcut in the network.

Although not shown in the pseudocode, the routing mechanism can recover from errors, because the subscription tables hold enough redundancy to avoid loosing routing information. When a branch of the tree is broken, the root of the subtree knows all subscription information of the nodes below it. Thus, as it is reattached to an arbitrary parent, it can send its subscription tables in one step, and the system is just ready to operate again.

Since LMAC is a schedule-based protocol, nodes that are willing to transmit have to wait first until their time slot arrives. However, the delay of transmissions is quite deterministic. It was shown previously, that when time slots are randomly chosen amongst the available slots, the average transmission delay is a half time frame. Because our routing uses the shortest possible path to connect the sink to the receivers, the resultant dissemination delay is the smallest possible, dependent on the depth of the tree.

The introduced mechanism runs at each node of the network, forming a collaborative middleware service. Towards the operating system, it provides interfaces to publish or subscribe data. Consequently, the data-centric entities of the local operating system can be easily extended to publish their output events network-wide. Other nodes, that are subscribed, automatically get the data delivered.

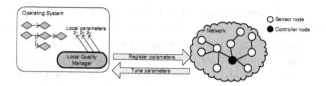

Fig. 4. Quality Management in a Data-Centric System

The dissemination of data and the management of the network are not a burden on the application developer any more.

The mentioned middleware extends the data-centric concepts of AmbientRT for networked applications. The events of AmbientRT can be easily exported to the network, thus making local and networked processing almost identical from the development point of view. The proposed middleware relies on the communication services offered by LMAC, thus efficiently utilising already existing communication infrastructure. However the solution is centralized at the root node, such topology is reasonable in systems that perform data collection.

4   Quality-Aware Adaptation

The resource management of sensor networks should be capable of managing the hosted mechanisms by controlling their resultant quality levels, consequently regulating their resource demands. With the support of the introduced data-centric architecture, we propose a quality management scheme, which adapts network services according to application/network/user requirements. In this section, the applied architecture and our feedback-based quality management mechanism are introduced.

4.1   Quality Management Architecture

The mechanisms capable of operating with several quality levels usually possess parameters that influence the granularity of their output. Unfortunately, these parameters are often kept as fixed internal values, not supplying any interfaces to change them. To facilitate the system managed tuning of quality levels, we made the introduced system software capable of accessing and adjusting these *control knobs* accordingly.

The idea is depicted in Figure 4. We let the processing entities of AmbientRT define their parameters, which manipulate the quality of their resultant data. The quality tuning changes only the accuracy of the provided information but not the data type itself. Entities offer these knobs to the local operating system, where a *local quality manager* is in charge for setting them to suit the actual requirements.

We utilised the proposed publish/subscribe middleware to facilitate network-wide quality management. The network of local quality managers utilise data-centric middleware services to enable remote quality changing. Thus, they subscribe for control messages and rely on the middleware to get control messages relevant to local knobs delivered. When such control occurs, the middleware is in charge for delivering the control messages to each tunable party. As a result, all members of the given distributed service are configured accordingly.

For instance, the distributed service providing periodic temperature measurements might offer knobs to influence the sampling frequency or the resolution of the measurements. The processing entities thus offer their knobs for the operating system, which subscribes for them at the middleware. During the operation of the system, such control messages can speed up or slow down measurements.

The resultant quality management scheme is thus capable of reconfiguring collaborative services, since it delivers data to all its members. By relying on the dissemination service offered by the middleware, the required implementation effort remains quite small.

4.2 Feedback-Based Quality Control

Even though the knobs can be controlled network-wide, choosing an adequate configuration is challenging.

Control messages might be sent by any of the network participants, but we assume that a particular entity exists for quality management. This entity might be the base station, the network maintainer or the user of the application. The manager has to evaluate the actual conditions and make decision about the suitable control parameters accordingly. The choice is determined by the amount of available resources and the application requirements.

Using a centralised quality manager is a limiting factor, because in many cases local control needs to be executed. For instance, nodes around areas of interest need to perform more accurate measurements than nodes that do not observe any interesting data. Such local control can be performed by forming multiple smaller groups, and executing the control mechanism within the group.

Applications express their interest by *Quality of Interest* (QoI) specifications. If the terms of QoI specify high-level properties, such as the confidence of pattern detection algorithm, determining the required parameters requires additional models. Thus, the terms in which the QoI is expressed might require application-dependent knowledge to facilitate finding the parameters resulting in the required quality.

Such models are usually not available, but the QoI requirements can also be expressed in more generic terms. We focus on the case, when QoI is given as statistical requirements over the provided data. For instance, QoI might specify the number of required samples or the standard deviation of the result. Such metrics can be evaluated independently of the actual application, therefore the parameter adjustment results in a more general framework.

Since such statistical properties can be evaluated based on purely resultant data, we apply a feedback-based approach to continuously adapt the system to meet the requirements. As shown in Figure 5, the quality of the result is continuously evaluated and compared to the expectations. If the difference makes it reasonable, parameters of the mechanism are changed.

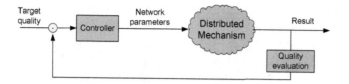

Fig. 5. Closed Loop Quality Control

The design of such a closed loop control is well supported by the design framework of digital control engineering. The basic task is to find the suitable controller for the given real world system to achieve an expected output. However, when choosing the controller the behaviour of the controllable system has to be considered. Whether the actual statistical QoI involves delays or transient events, the controller has to fit the proportional, integral or derivative nature of the controlled system.

Thus, our proposed quality-management scheme is based on the continuous analysis of results and applies closed-loop feedback control to satisfy requirements. Since application-dependent models might support abstract QoI adjustment, in case of purely statistical requirements such models are not required.

5 Evaluation

We have investigated the efficiency of the proposed schemes by simulations as well as by real experiments. This section introduces the evaluation of the middleware and the quality adjustment scheme.

5.1 Overhead of Data Dissemination

First we evaluate the efficiency of the proposed publish/subscribe middleware. Since the routing topology of LMAC was used, our focus is to investigate how efficiently it is used and not to examine the tree itself.

We implemented the proposed publish/subscribed scheme in the OMNeT++ discrete event simulator [11]. For simulations, we applied a random topology of 40 nodes scattered uniformly in a 600x600m area. The communication range was given 125m.

First, we investigated the overhead of the dissemination tree. We define *overhead* as the number of nodes participating in the data dissemination without being among the subscribers. We have changed the number of subscribers from 1 to 40 and recorded the number of such nodes. We evaluated both cases when the subscribers were randomly selected and geographically nearby. The results are shown in Figure 6.

When the subscribers were randomly selected, the overhead grows for a while and then decreases to zero. It grows as long as new branches became involved in the delivery tree, possibly involving nodes to forward the message without actually being interested in it. As the tree becomes more and more saturated

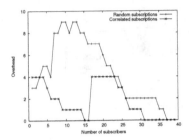
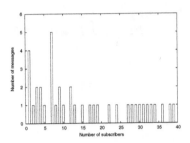

Fig. 6. Overhead of the Data Delivery Tree

Fig. 7. Messages Needed to Register New Subscriptions

with subscribers, the chance that such a purely forwarding node becomes a subscriber grows. Consequently, the overhead decreases and when all the nodes are subscribed for the data, the overhead reaches zero.

The overhead has a different trend when the subscribers are geographically nearby. Nearby nodes often have the same node as their parent, thus the overhead does not grow as new nodes subscribe. Moreover, if the chosen node is the parent of a previous subscriber, the overhead just decreases. Consequently, the overhead gradually decreases, except for the case when a completely new branch of the tree becomes involved in the dissemination. It can be seen from Figure 6 that the overhead reaches zero when 15 subscribers are present. In this case, all members of a tree branch are subscribed, however after this point a completely new branch has to be involved again.

Another interesting metric is the number of messages needed for a new node to join the data delivery tree. The subscription is sent upwards in the tree until it reaches either the root or a node that is already subscribed. Figure 7 shows how many times the subscription messages has to be transmitted. As expected, it is always less than the depth of the tree, which is actually 6. It can be seen, that except the two peaks at second 1 and 7, the number of required messages is quite small. The reason that peaks occur is that as nodes in a new branch subscribe, the subscription message should travel several hops upwards in the tree to meet an already registered node.

Our evaluation focused on how efficient our data delivery service is over a given routing tree. We have evaluated the overhead, and have seen that it depends on the spatial distribution of subscribers. The dissemination is usually more efficient if the subscribers are nearby. We have also seen that the number of messages required for subscriptions usually remains quite small, because it has to reach only the closest actually subscribed node.

5.2   Quality-Aware Adaptive Control

We evaluate the feedback-based quality control mechanism through a sample. Assume a typical sensor network to collect measurements periodically over a target area. The QoI specification describes how many of the nodes need to provide measurements. It specifies minimum and maximum thresholds for the number of samples received by the sink node. Since the number of available sensors might be very large, it is sufficient to sample only a subset of nodes and turn the rest off or to power-saving mode. The sink evaluates the received samples in specified time intervals and controls the system accordingly.

To influence the number of nodes participating in the sampling process, we use probabilistic sampling with a p probability value as a parameter. Each node receiving p decides to participate the measurements with probability p and is turned off otherwise.

The sink node is in charge of determining p according to the received number of samples. Since the controller entity is also a resource constrained unit, we decided to keep the controller mechanism as simple as possible. Changing the applied p probability results in immediate changing of the number of collected samples and does not contain dynamic effects. Consequently, the applied controller adjusts p proportionally to the ratio of required and desired number of samples.

First, we evaluated the control mechanism by simulation, in which the previously described setup of 40 nodes was used. The root node collects the measured data, and performs the control in every second if it is necessary. The QoI requirement was chosen to require 8 to 12 samples per interval. The simulation starts with a stationary environment, then after second 25 nodes die uniformly.

The number of actually received samples and the number of available nodes can be seen in Figure 8. First, it can be seen that despite the large number of nodes, only the required number of samples was produced. Second, notice that as the number of available nodes decreases, the number of received samples mostly remains within the specified interval. When the specification is not met (for instance at second 50), the network is immediately re-adjusted so that the target QoI is met again. Finally, after second 88 the requirements cannot be met any more.

Besides, we have also implemented this quality-aware control mechanism in our sensor network testbed and evaluated it through real experiments. The target number of samples was set to be either 2 or 3 in each 4 seconds time intervals. We used 10 sensors that are gradually deployed in the first half of the time, then started to turn them off. The number of samples received by the sink node are shown in Figure 9. It can be seen that the number of received samples has never

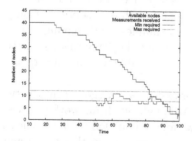

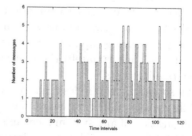

Fig. 8. Number of Received Samples in a Time Interval

Fig. 9. Experimental Results of Received Samples

reached 10, thus the system did not activate some of the sensors in order to save their battery capacity. After deploying all the nodes, we started turning off those nodes that were actually sampling. No degradation can be seen in the second half of the time, thus the system reacted to changes and reconfigured well in order to maintain the specifications.

Although the number of acquired samples did not grow more than 5, unattractive fluctuations can be observed. The reason is that as some samples were missing due to transmission errors, the system thought nodes became unavailable and proportionately increased the probability. Since the actual node was available at the following sampling, the resultant amount of acquired information was increased unnecessarily. Thus, the system overreacted communication errors and resulted in transients. However these transients might be suppressed by filtering techniques, which would result in increased responsiveness and longer convergence time.

As we have shown, adjusting sampling parameters based on the QoI requirements is efficient to avoid unnecessary actions. Resource management controls system qualities to meet and maintain the target quality level even during resource changes. With the support of the proposed publish/subscribe middleware; controlling of distributed control knobs is simple. However, the experimental results show that even if the controllable quantity does not produce dynamic behaviour, communication uncertainties might call for more complex controllers.

6   Related Work

The massively distributed, dynamic and uncertain environment poses several new concerns to system software [12]. To respond to these concerns, several operating system platforms have been proposed for extremely resource constrained systems. TinyOS [7] is one of the first and best known among them. Its component-based development model is easy to use, however it is not capable of providing real-time execution guarantees and the dynamic reconfiguration of system components is not easy. In contrast, AmbientRT [8] is a data-centric operating system, enabling real-time execution guarantees and supporting simple runtime reconfiguration.

In addition to operating systems, numerous sensor network middleware platforms have been evolved to provide high level distributed services. Cougar[2] and SINA [13] are two middleware platform examples, both having database-like query processing support, which is usually required by typical sensor network applications. Unfortunately, these platforms are not able to guarantee quality of service requirements.

QoS support for Wireless Sensor Networks can be categories into network, reliability and application guarantees [3]. Although our framework enables the reconfiguration of any system mechanism, we focused on QoS on the application-level. MiLAN [6] is a middleware platform, also supporting quality requirements. It is proactive, meaning that it is capable of influencing its mechanisms according to higher level requirements. It aims at utilising only the most suitable set of resources to meet the actual requirements, although its scheme of expressing quality requirements is quite limited. Similarly, MASTAQ [9] is a middleware, supporting quality of service requirements, which uses a dynamic quality management mechanism, similar to our solution.

Existing QoS-aware middleware platforms do not involve the operating system in the reconfiguration process. To the best of our knowledge, there is no resource management framework for sensor networks integrating the same concepts ranging from operating system to middleware, and also enabling quality-aware dynamic reconfiguration.

7   Conclusion and Future Work

The contribution of this paper is twofold. First, we proposed a system software that integrates a real-time lightweight operating system and a publish/subscribe middleware. The resulted framework provides similar data-centric abstractions for the development of both local and networked applications. It results in easier application development, because shields developers from the possibly distributed nature of the system.

By extending this system support we built a resource management framework that supports quality-aware adaptation. It allows the system to tune quality levels according to application requirements and actual resource availabilities. Its feedback-based control loop mechanism continuously evaluates the resultant quality metrics and satisfies application QoI requirements by tuning knobs of possibly distributed applications.

Future research will look into combining the publish/subscribe middleware with the MAC protocol, because it might result in additional energy savings. Influencing the routing hierarchy based on the distribution of subscribers might result in a more efficient routing tree. The time slot allocation could also be changed based on the amount of information to be disseminated, consequently influencing throughput and delay of the data dissemination.

As the experiments pointed out, designing a closed loop controller is not straightforward even in case of a simplistic controllable quantity. The quality should converge into the desired range rapidly, however transient events should be suppressed. We aim at developing models to facilitate quality management based on higher level quality concerns. Moreover, we aim at making the quality-management scheme more distributed, applying local control mechanisms.

References

1. I.F. Akyildiz, W. Su, Y. Sankarasubramaniam, and E. Cayirci. Wireless sensor networks: A survey. *Computer Networks*, 38:393–422, 2002.
2. Philippe Bonnet, Johannes Gehrke, and Praveen Seshadri. Querying the physical world. *IEEE Personal Communications*, October 2000.
3. Dazhi Chen and Pramod K. Varshney. Qos support in wireless sensor networks: A survey. In *Proc. of the 2004 Int. Conf. on Wireless Networks (ICWN 2004)*, June 2004.

4. Stephen Deering, Deborah L. Estrin, Dino Farinacci, Van Jacobson, Ching-Gung Liu, and Liming Wei. The PIM architecture for wide-area multicast routing. *IEEE/ACM Trans. Netw.*, 4(2):153–162, 1996.

5. Stefan Dulman. *Data-centric architecture for wireless sensor networks*. PhD thesis, Centre for Telematics and Information Technology, Univ. of Twente, The Netherlands, October 2005.

6. Wendi B. Heinzelman, Amy L. Murphy, Hervaldo S. Carvalho, and Mark A. Perillo. Middleware to support sensor network applications. *IEEE Network Magazine*, 18(1):6–14, 2004.

7. Jason Hill, Robert Szewczyk, Alec Woo, Seth Hollar, David Culler, and Kristofer Pister. System architecture directions for networked sensors. In *Proc. of the 9th international conference on Architectural support for programming languages and operating systems*, pages 93–104, Cambridge, Massachusetts, United States, 2000.

8. T. Hofmeijer, S. Dulman, P. G. Jansen, and P. J. M. Havinga. AmbientRT - real time system software support for data centric sensor networks. In *2nd Int. Conf. on Intelligent Sensors, Sensor Networks and Information Processing*, pages 61–66, Melbourne, Australia, Dec 2004. IEEE Computer Society Press.

9. Inseok Hwang, Qi Han, and Archan Misra. MASTAQ: A Middleware Architecture for Sensor Applications with Statistical Quality Constraints. In *The First Int. Workshop on Sensor Networks and Systems for Pervasive Computing (PerSeNS 2005)*, Kauai Island, Hawaii, USA, March 2005.

10. P. G. Jansen, S. J. Mullender, P. J. M. Havinga, and J. Scholten. Lightweight EDF scheduling with deadline inheritance. Technical report TR-CTIT-03-23, Centre for Telematics and Information Technology, Univ. of Twente, The Netherlands, May 2003.

11. Omnet++ discrete event simulator. `http://www.omnetpp.org`.

12. Anu Purhonen and Esa Tuulari. *Ambient intelligence and the development of embedded system software*, pages 51–67. Kluwer Academic Publishers, Norwell, MA, USA, 2003.

13. Chien-Chung Shen, Chavalit Srisathapornphat, and Chaiporn Jaikaeo. Sensor information networking architecture and applications. *IEEE Personal Communications Magazine*, 8(4):52–59, August 2001.

14. L. van Hoesel and P.Havinga. A lightweight medium access protocol (LMAC) for wireless sensor networks: Reducing preamble transmissions and transceiver state switches. In *Proc. of 1st Int. Workshop on Networked Sensing Systems*, 2004.

Topology Control with Limited Geometric Information

Kevin Lillis and Sriram V. Pemmaraju

Department of Computer Science
The University of Iowa, Iowa City, IA 52242-1419, USA
{lillis, sriram}@cs.uiowa.edu

Abstract. Topology control is the problem of selecting neighbors for each node in a wireless network, so that the resulting network has a number of useful properties. More precisely, a topology control protocol P takes as input a network G and aims to construct a spanning subgraph G_P, that is sparse, "energy minimizing" and has sufficient connectivity so as to guarantee multiple short paths between pairs of nodes in G. Currently, topology control protocols assume that nodes in G reside in some Euclidean (usually, 2-dimensional) space and rely on geometric information such as node locations and pairwise distances between nodes to produce G_P with appropriate properties. However, these protocols are extremely sensitive to errors in location information and this feature makes them impractical because errors in location and distance information are pervasive in practical systems. This paper presents and analyzes two randomized topology control protocols that are tolerant to errors in pairwise distance estimates. The first protocol, called RTC (short for randomized topology control) uses *no* geometric information, relying only on connectivity information and is therefore completely immune to errors in location or distance information. The second protocol, called ε-RTC, generalizes the first protocol. Allowing for errors in distance estimates, but assuming that relative errors are bounded above by ε, the second protocol produces an output network that is symmetric, connected, sparse, and has good spanner properties. As $\varepsilon \to 0$, ε-RTC behaves like the XTC protocol (R. Wattenhofer and A. Zollinger, "XTC: A practical topology control algorithm for ad-hoc networks", WMAN 2004) and for large values of ε, it behaves like RTC. Our results hold whenever the input network is a unit disk graph or even a quasi unit disk graph.

1 Introduction

An ad-hoc wireless network consists of a set of nodes, each equipped with a wireless radio. Each node u can send messages to all nodes within its radio range and all such nodes are potential neighbors of u. However, for reasons explained below, it is preferable for u to communicate with an appropriately chosen subset of these reachable nodes. Informally speaking, the *topology control* problem is one of selecting neighbors for each node so that the resulting network has a number of useful properties. More precisely, let V be a set of nodes that can communicate via wireless radios and for each $v \in V$, let $N(v)$ denote the

J.H. Anderson, G. Prencipe, and R. Wattenhofer (Eds.): OPODIS 2005, LNCS 3974, pp. 427–442, 2006.
© Springer-Verlag Berlin Heidelberg 2006

set of all nodes that v can reach when transmitting at maximum power. The induced digraph $G = (V, E)$, where $E = \{(u, v) \mid v \in N(u)\}$, represents the network in which every node has chosen to transmit at maximum power and has designated every node it can reach, as its neighbor. The topology control problem is the problem of devising a protocol P for selecting a set of neighbors $N_P(v) \subseteq N(v)$ for each node $v \in V$. The induced digraph $G_P = (V, E_P)$, where $E_P = \{(u, v) \mid v \in N_P(u)\}$ is typically required the satisfy properties such as symmetry (if $v \in N_P(u)$ then $u \in N_P(v)$), sparseness ($|E_P| = O(|V|)$) or bounded degree ($|N_P(v)| \leq c$ for all nodes v and some constant c), connectivity, and the spanner property.

Current Research on Topology Control. In the last few years, a generation of topology control protocols have been proposed that achieve many of the properties mentioned above by assuming that the nodes in V lie in some Euclidean (typically, 2-dimensional) space and each node knows its spatial location with respect to some global coordinate system [6, 7, 8, 9, 14]. In our view, the main problem with these protocols is the reliance on node location information and the lack of robustness with respect to errors in this information. Node location information is typically available only if nodes are GPS enabled or if an expensive protocol called *localization* [2] is run. For sensor networks, which typically consist of a large scale deployment of small devices, assuming that nodes are GPS enabled is unrealistic because of cost and size requirements [2, 3, 11]. No matter which approach is used to find node locations, errors in location information are quite likely. Unfortunately, none of the topology control protocols mentioned above make allowances for any errors in location information and are extremely sensitive to these errors. In other words, critical properties of the output network such as connectivity or bounded maximum degree are not guaranteed to hold even if there is a small amount of error in location information.

More recently, Wattenhofer and Zollinger [15] have proposed a topology control protocol called XTC that does not rely on specific location information for each node, but rather requires each node to only know the distance to each of its neighbors. Although this is an improvement over location-based topology control algorithms, XTC still suffers from lack of robustness to errors in distance information. As we show in Sect. 2, there are networks modeled as unit disk graphs (UDGs) such that when XTC is run on these, its output network is disconnected and contains vertices with unbounded degree, even in the presence of arbitrarily small errors in pairwise distance estimates. This is a significant problem because in general it seems hard to accurately estimate pairwise node distances. For example, [15] mentions the use of the strength of the received signal (RSSI) as a way to estimate distances. While this technique is relatively cheap and does not need additional hardware, it is known to have low accuracy. Alternate techniques such as the use of ultrasound hardware have been proposed [13]. These have better accuracy than RSSI, but are significantly costlier, both in terms of additional hardware and in terms of energy consumption.

Our Results. We present two randomized topology control protocols. The first protocol, called RTC (short for "randomized topology control") uses *no* geometric information, relying only on connectivity information. As a result RTC is completely immune to errors in distance or location information. Our second protocol, called ε-RTC is parameterized by $\varepsilon > 0$, which stands for the maximum relative error on pairwise distance estimates. This error represents the uncertainty of the measured distance between pairs of nodes. A precise uncertainty model would include errors due to noise, response time, energy consumption, device deterioration, ambient influences, as well as calibration equipment [5]. Such an uncertainty model is beyond the scope of this paper. Allowing for errors in distance estimates, but assuming that relative errors are bounded above by ε, ε-RTC produces an output graph that is symmetric, connected, sparse, and has spanner properties. As $\varepsilon \to 0$, ε-RTC behaves like XTC and for large values of ε, ε-RTC behaves like RTC. In general, ε-RTC combines the advantages of XTC and RTC. Unlike XTC, ε-RTC is tolerant to errors bounded by ε and unlike RTC, ε-RTC uses distance information to the extent they are reliable and attempts to drop long links in favor of short links, thereby saving on energy consumption. Both RTC and ε-RTC are randomized variants of XTC and are therefore extremely light weight, needing only two rounds of communication. We prove properties of the output network of RTC and ε-RTC assuming that the input network G is a UDG. However, our results hold even when G is a quasi UDG [1].

2   The XTC Protocol

We start this section by reproducing the XTC protocol from [15], followed by a description of properties of XTC.

1. Establish order $\prec_u$ over u's neighbors in G
2. Broadcast $\prec_u$ to each neighbor in G; receive orders from all neighbors
3. Select topology control neighbors:
4. $N_u := \{\ \}; \tilde{N}_u := \{\ \}$
5.   **while** ($\prec_u$ contains unprocessed neighbors)$\{$
6. $v :=$ least unprocessed neighbor in $\prec_u$
7.   **if**($\exists w \in N_u \cup \tilde{N}_u : w \prec_v u$)
8. $\tilde{N}_u := \tilde{N}_u \cup \{v\}$
9.   **else**
10. $N_u := N_u \cup \{v\}$
11. $\}$

As mentioned in [15], the XTC protocol (shown above) consists of three main steps: (i) neighbor ordering (Line 1), (ii) neighbor order exchange (Line 2), and (iii) edge selection (Lines 3-11). In the edge selection step a vertex u decides to drop v from its set of neighbors if there is a vertex w that u and v both agree is mutually better. More precisely, u drops v from its neighborhood if there exists w such that $w \prec_u v$ and $w \prec_v u$. In the protocol, the variable N_u

is the set of neighbors that u has chosen to retain and the variable $\widetilde{N}_u$ is the set of neighbors that u has chosen to drop. Let $E_{XTC} = \{(u,v) \mid v \in N_u\}$ and $G_{XTC} = (V, E_{XTC})$. Also, let $\prec = \{\prec_u \mid u \in V(G)\}$ denote the collection of neighborhood orderings. Note that the protocol leaves $\prec$ unspecified. Thus G_{XTC} is a function, not only of the input network G, but also of the neighborhood orderings $\prec$. An appropriate choice of $\prec$ is critical to the success of XTC.

It is shown in [15] that G_{XTC} is symmetric provided G is and this is independent of $\prec$. It is also shown that if G is a Euclidean graph and $\prec_u$ is defined as

$$v \prec_u w \Leftrightarrow (|uv|, \min\{id_u, id_v\}, \max\{id_u, id_v\}) < (|uw|, \min\{id_u, id_w\}, \max\{id_u, id_w\}),$$
(1)

then G_{XTC} is connected. We will call the above neighborhood ordering, a *distance-based* ordering. Note that in the distance-based ordering, ids are only used to break ties. Finally, it is shown that if $\prec$ is a distance-based ordering and G is a UDG, then the maximum degree in G_{XTC} is at most 6 and G_{XTC} is planar.

Even though XTC is fast and simple and its output graph has many desired properties, it is extremely sensitive to small perturbations in the neighborhood orderings. In the following subsections we show XTC's lack of robustness to small errors.

2.1 G_{XTC} May Be Disconnected

We now present a simple example of a 4-vertex unit disk graph that illustrates the lack of robustness of XTC. As shown in [15], if neighborhood orderings are distance-based (as in (1)), then G_{XTC} is connected. Note that according to this definition, each node u orders its neighbors in increasing order of distance, breaking ties using ids. We show that if the distance estimates are erroneous, even slightly, then the resulting neighborhood orderings are such that G_{XTC} becomes disconnected.

Consider the unit disk graph shown in Fig. 1. Pick an ε, $0 < \varepsilon < 1 - \frac{1}{\sqrt{2}}$. Let the lengths of the edges be $|ab| = |dc| = (1 - \varepsilon)/2$ and $|ac| = |bd| = 1/2$. Then the neighborhood orderings $\prec$ according to (1) are:

$$d \prec_a b \prec_a c \qquad c \prec_b a \prec_b d \qquad b \prec_c d \prec_c a \qquad a \prec_d c \prec_d b.$$

Now suppose that node b incorrectly estimates distance $|ba|$ as $(1+\varepsilon)/2$ and node c incorrectly estimates distance $|cd|$ as $(1 + \varepsilon)/2$. The resulting neighborhood orderings $\widetilde{\prec} = \{\widetilde{\prec}_a, \widetilde{\prec}_b, \widetilde{\prec}_c, \widetilde{\prec}_d\}$ are shown below.

$$d \widetilde{\prec}_a b \widetilde{\prec}_a c \qquad c \widetilde{\prec}_b d \widetilde{\prec}_b a \qquad b \widetilde{\prec}_c a \widetilde{\prec}_c d \qquad a \widetilde{\prec}_d c \widetilde{\prec}_d b.$$

If XTC is run with input $\widetilde{\prec}$ then G_{XTC} contains just the two edges $\{a, d\}$ and $\{b, c\}$ and is therefore disconnected. Thus two incorrect estimates by an arbitrarily small amount ε is sufficient to break connectivity.

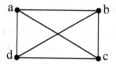

Fig. 1. A unit disk graph for showing the sensitivity of XTC to small perturbations. The lengths of the edges are $|ab| = |dc| = (1 - \varepsilon)/2$ and $|ac| = |bd| = 1/2$.

2.2 G_{XTC} May Have High Degree

To start with, suppose that we have three nodes u, v_1, and v_2 (refer to Fig. 2). Fix an $\varepsilon, 0 < \varepsilon < 1/2$ and let $|uv_1| = d$ and $|v_1v_2| = \frac{d}{1+\varepsilon}$. If the length of the third edge $|uv_2|$ is $\frac{\varepsilon d}{1+\varepsilon}$, then the three points u, v_2, and v_1 would be collinear. To make $\triangle uv_1v_2$ a non-trivial triangle, pick $|uv_2| = \frac{2\varepsilon d}{1+\varepsilon}$. If XTC were run, just on $\triangle uv_1v_2$, then vertex u would drop v_1 from its set of neighbors in favor of vertex v_2. Likewise vertex v_1 would drop u from its set of neighbors in favor of vertex v_2. This would eliminate the edge $\{u, v_1\}^1$ from the output graph. Now suppose that there are errors in distance estimates such that lengths $|uv_1|$ and $|uv_2|$ are unchanged, but the length $|v_1v_2|$ is overestimated by a factor of $(1 + \varepsilon)$, thus making $|v_1v_2| = |uv_1|$. Now, because ties are broken by node ids, we can assume that $id_u < id_{v_2}$, thus forcing XTC to drop edge $\{v_1, v_2\}$, but retain $\{u, v_1\}$. This phenomenon can be forced to repeat arbitrarily. Specifically, u could have a third neighbor v_3 that plays the role relative to v_2 that v_2 played relative to v_1. Let the actual distances to the new vertex v_3 satisfy

$$|v_2v_3| = \frac{2\varepsilon d}{(1 + \varepsilon)^2}, \qquad |uv_3| = \left(\frac{2\varepsilon}{1 + \varepsilon}\right)^2 d, \qquad |v_1v_3| > \frac{d}{(1 + \varepsilon)},$$

and perturb $|v_1v_3|$ and $|v_2v_3|$ by a factor of $(1 + \varepsilon)$ such that it would appear that $|v_2v_3| = |uv_2|$ and $|v_1v_3| > d$. In addition, if we assume that $id_u < id_{v_3}$, then $\{v_1, v_3\}$ and $\{v_2, v_3\}$ would be dropped and $\{u, v_2\}$ would be retained. By continuing this construction, we can force u to have arbitrarily high degree. Note that in this example, some distances are unchanged while some are increased by a factor of $(1 + \varepsilon)$.

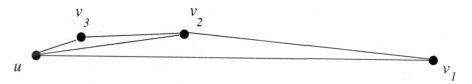

Fig. 2. A unit disk graph to illustrate how XTC may produce an output graph with unbounded node degree

---

[1] XTC outputs a symmetric network independent of the neighborhood orderings $\prec$. This allows us to think of the edges of G_{XTC} as undirected edges.

2.3   Experimental Evidence

We have experimentally studied XTC's sensitivity to errors in distance information. We implemented XTC, RTC, and ε-RTC on a Pentium 4 PC running Mathematica 5.0, release 1, with the Combinatorica add-on package. All algorithms were run on UDGs and quasi UDGs that were generated by distributing nodes in the plane in a variety of ways. One series of input graphs was constructed by distributing nodes uniformly at random, at a density of 10 nodes per unit square, and increasing the area of the square linearly from 1 to 77 square units. Another series of input graphs was constructed by fixing the dimensions of the graph at 5×5 and increasing the density of nodes, placed uniformly at random, linearly form 3 to 30 nodes per unit square. A final series of input graphs was constructed by distributing nodes uniformly at random on a 5×5 square, at a density of 3 nodes per unit square, and then adding small regions ($\frac{1}{2} \times \frac{1}{2}$) with node density of 30 nodes per unit square.

To introduce errors in distance information, we fixed a value for $\varepsilon > 0$ and for each edge $\{u, v\}$ in each generated graph G, we picked two distance estimates for $|uv|$, one to be assigned to u and the other to v. Both distance estimates are picked uniformly at random from the interval $[|uv| \cdot (1 - \varepsilon), |uv| \cdot (1 + \varepsilon)]$. Our experiments show that even for randomly generated instances of UDGs, XTC produces disconnected output networks a substantial fraction of the time. For example, for UDGs generated with node density of 3 nodes per unit square, for $\varepsilon = 0.4$, XTC produces a disconnected network 60% of the time. Even for UDGs of higher density, say 12 nodes per unit square, XTC produces a disconnected network 40% of the time at $\varepsilon = 0.4$. See [10] for more details.

The plots below shows the increase in the maximum degree of G_{XTC}, as $\varepsilon \to 1$. The plot on the left is for input UDGs with a density of 15 nodes per unit square and the plot on the right is for input UDGs with a density of 30 nodes per unit square. In each case, at a certain value of ε, the maximum degree of G_{XTC} exceeds beyond 5, which is the upper bound on $\Delta(G_{XTC})$ assuming completely accurate distances. Notice that in the case of the higher density graphs, $\Delta(G_{XTC})$ exceeds 5 at around $\varepsilon = 0.25$.

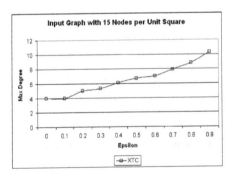 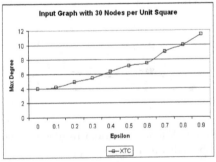

Fig. 3. These are plots showing the increase in the maximum degree of G_{XTC} as the error bound ε increases

3   Randomized Topology Control

Here we describe two randomized topology control protocols, RTC and ε-RTC. Both are variants of XTC in that they first construct specific neighborhood orderings and then run XTC with these orderings as input. RTC ignores geometric information completely, relying on randomization alone to obtain good expected performance. ε-RTC does use the distance estimates, even though they may be erroneous. However, in an attempt to foil the adversary, ε-RTC first does a random perturbation of the distance estimates. The amount of perturbation is a function of ε.

3.1   The RTC Protocol

RTC consists of two phases. In phase 1, a randomized edge labeling is constructed and this is used by each node u to define a neighborhood ordering $\prec_u$ on $N(u)$. In Phase 2, XTC is executed with these neighborhood orderings as input. Phase 1 of RTC, which we call `NeighborhoodOrdering`, is shown below. It simply consists of picking for each edge, a real number, uniformly at random from the range $[0, 1]$. The choices for different edges are independent. Each node u maintains an array $d_u[v]$, $v \in N(u)$, of local variables and for each edge $\{u, v\} \in E(G)$, one of the two endpoints u or v whichever has higher id, picks a real number $d \in [0, 1]$ to serve as the edge label for $\{u, v\}$ and this is assigned to both $d_u[v]$ and to $d_v[u]$. Finally, each node u constructs $\prec_u$ by ordering its neighbors in increasing order of the values $d_u[v]$, $v \in N(u)$. We call the output of RTC, G_{RTC}.

Algorithm `NeighborhoodOrdering`(u)

1. Node u sends to each neighbor $v \in N(u)$, the value id_u. It receives from each neighbor $v \in N(u)$, the value id_v.
2. For each neighbor v with $id_v < id_u$, node u picks $d \in [0, 1]$ uniformly at random and assigns $d_u[v] := d$ and sends $d_u[v]$ to v.
3. For each neighbor v with $id_v > id_u$, node u receives $d_v[u]$ from v and assigns $d_u[v] := d_v[u]$.
4. Node u computes an ordering $\prec_u$ of its neighborhood $N(u)$ such that for any pair of vertices $v_1, v_2 \in N(u)$:

$$v_1 \prec_u v_2 \Leftrightarrow (d_u[v_1], id_{v_1}) < (d_u[v_2], id_{v_2}).$$

3.2   The ε-RTC Protocol

Let $\alpha(u, v)$ denote the distance between u and v, *as estimated by u*. It is possible that $\alpha(u, v) \neq \alpha(v, u)$. We assume that the errors in distance estimates are bounded. That is, there is an $\varepsilon > 0$, such that

$$(1 - \varepsilon) \cdot |uv| \leq \alpha(u, v) \leq (1 + \varepsilon) \cdot |uv|.$$

When the distance estimates satisfy this property, we say that they are ε-*error bounded*.

Like RTC, the ε-RTC protocol also consists of two phases, the first involves constructing neighborhood orderings and the second involves calling XTC. The first phase, called ε-NeighborhoodOrdering, is shown below. We assume that all nodes know the value of ε and each node u can compute distance estimates $\alpha(u, v)$ to all neighbors $v \in N(u)$. Unlike in RTC, ε-NeighborhoodOrdering does make explicit use of the estimated pairwise distances $\alpha(\cdot, \cdot)$. For each edge $\{u, v\}$, first the average of $\alpha(u, v)$ and $\alpha(v, u)$ is computed. Then, an interval around this average is constructed and a value is picked, uniformly at random from this interval. This value is assigned to both $d_u[v]$ and $d_v[u]$ as the final label of the edge $\{u, v\}$. We call the output of ε-RTC, $G_{\varepsilon\text{-}RTC}$.

Algorithm ε-NeighborhoodOrdering(u)

1. Node u sends to each neighbor $v \in N(u)$, the value id_u. It receives from each neighbor $v \in N(u)$, the value id_v.
2. Node u estimates the distance $\alpha(u, v)$ to each neighbor $v \in N(u)$. Then node u sends to each neighbor $v \in N(u)$ the estimate $\alpha(u, v)$ and receives from each neighbor $v \in N(u)$ the estimate $\alpha(v, u)$.
3. For each neighbor v with $id_v < id_u$, node u computes $a := (\alpha(u, v) + \alpha(v, u))/2$ and then picks $d \in [a(1 - \delta_L), a(1 + \delta_R)]$ uniformly at random and assigns $d_u[v] := d$ and sends $d_u[v]$ to v. Here, $\delta_L = 2\varepsilon/(1 + \varepsilon)$ and $\delta_R = 2\varepsilon/(1 - \varepsilon)$.
4. For each neighbor v with $id_v > id_u$, node u receives $d_v[u]$ from v and assigns $d_u[v] := d_v[u]$.
5. Node u computes an ordering $\prec_u$ of its neighborhood $N(u)$ such that for any pair of vertices $v_1, v_2 \in N(u)$:

$$v_1 \prec_u v_2 \Leftrightarrow (d_u[v_1], id_{v_1}) < (d_u[v_2], id_{v_2}).$$

---

4   Analysis of RTC and ε-RTC

In this section we show that the output networks produced by RTC and ε-RTC are sparse. Specifically, we show that for any node u, its expected degree in G_{RTC} is bounded above by $O(\log deg_G(u))$ and its expected degree in $G_{\varepsilon\text{-}RTC}$ is bounded above by $O(1)$. We use the notation $deg_G(u)$ to denote degree of node u in the graph G. Before we prove our sparsity results, we quickly show that both G_{RTC} and $G_{\varepsilon\text{-}RTC}$ are symmetric and connected.

It is observed in [15] that if G is symmetric, then so is G_{XTC} no matter what $\prec$ is. As a corollary we obtain that both G_{RTC} and $G_{\varepsilon\text{-}RTC}$ are symmetric since the algorithms RTC and ε-RTC are just implementations of XTC with specific choices of $\prec$. Connectivity of G_{RTC} and $G_{\varepsilon\text{-}RTC}$ follows from the following result due to [4, 15]. Before we state the result we need a definition.

Definition. Let S be an arbitrary set on which a total order $<_S$ is defined. The collection of neighborhood orderings $\prec = \{\prec_u | u \in V(G)\}$ is said to be *consistent* if there is a labeling of the edges $\ell : E \to S$ such that for any two neighbors $v_1, v_2 \in N(u)$,

$$v_1 \prec_u v_2 \Leftrightarrow (\ell\{u, v_1\}, id_{v_1}) < (\ell\{u, v_2\}, id_{v_2}).$$

In the above, $<$ denotes the lexicographic ordering on $S \times ID$, where ID is the space of all node ids. It is worth emphasizing that E is the set of *undirected* edges and therefore every edge $\{u, v\}$ gets a single label, that is, $\ell\{u, v\} = \ell\{v, u\}$.

Theorem 1. *[4, 15] Let $\prec$ be a collection of consistent neighborhood orderings of G. If XTC is executed with input $\prec$ and G is connected then G_{XTC} is connected.*

The above theorem essentially says that as long as some edge labels are agreed upon and used to construct the neighborhood orderings, connectivity is guaranteed. These edge labels need have nothing to do with actual pairwise distances. From the fact that RTC and ε-RTC both execute XTC with a consistent collections of neighborhood orderings, we obtain that both G_{RTC} and $G_{\varepsilon\text{-}RTC}$ are connected.

Theorem 2. *G_{RTC} and $G_{\varepsilon\text{-}RTC}$ are both symmetric and connected.*

4.1   Bound on Vertex Degrees

Here is a simple and useful fact about the probability that the neighbors of a node u are ordered in $\prec_u$ in a certain way. This follows from the fact that in RTC, for any node u, each ordering of its neighbors is equally likely to be $\prec_u$.

Lemma 1. *Let $v_1, v_2, \ldots, v_t$ be neighbors of u. Then, $Prob[\bigwedge_{i=2}^{t} v_1 \prec_u v_i] = \frac{1}{t}$.*

Theorem 3. *Let G be a UDG and let $H = G_{RTC}$. For any vertex u of G*

$$E[deg_H(u)] = O(\log deg_G(u)).$$

Proof. Since G is a UDG, the neighborhood $N(u)$ of u can be partitioned into at most 5 cliques. For some integer t, $1 \leq t \leq 5$, let $\{N^i(u) \mid i = 1, 2, \ldots, t\}$ be a partition of $N(u)$ into t cliques. Let $deg_G^i(u) = |N^i(u)|$, for each $i = 1, 2, \ldots, t$ and let $deg_H^i(u)$ be the number of nodes in $N^i(u)$ that continue to be neighbors of u in H. Then $deg_H(u) = \sum_{i=1}^{t} deg_H^i(u)$ and by linearity of expectation $E[deg_H(u)] = \sum_{i=1}^{t} E[deg_H^i(u)]$. We will now show that

$$E[deg_H^i(u)] = \Theta(\log deg_G^i(u)) = O(\log deg_G(u)).$$

Since $t \leq 5$, we have that $E[deg_H(u)] = O(\log deg_G(u))$.

Fix i, $1 \leq i \leq t$, and let $d = deg_G^i(u)$ and $N^i(u) = \{v_1, v_2, \ldots, v_d\}$ such that $v_1 \prec_u v_2 \prec_u \cdots \prec_u v_d$. For each $j = 1, 2, \ldots, d$, let X_j denote the indicator random variable that equals 1 if $\{u, v_j\} \in E(H)$ and 0 otherwise. Then, by linearity of expectation, $E[deg_H^i(u)] = \sum_{j=1}^{d} E[X_j] = \sum_{j=1}^{d} Prob[X_j = 1]$. Given that $v_\ell \prec_u v_j$ for each $\ell = 1, 2, \ldots, j - 1$, for the edge $\{u, v_j\}$ to be present in H, it must be the case that $u \prec_{v_j} v_\ell$, for each $\ell = 1, 2, \ldots, j - 1$. Therefore,

$$Prob[X_j = 1] \leq Prob[\wedge_{\ell=1}^{j-1} u \prec_{v_j} v_\ell].$$

By Lemma 1, $\text{Prob}[\wedge_{\ell=1}^{j-1} u \prec_{v_j} v_\ell] = 1/j$. Therefore,

$$E[deg_H^i(u)] = \sum_{j=1}^{d} \text{Prob}[X_j = 1] \le \sum_{j=1}^{d} \frac{1}{j} = \Theta(\log d) = \Theta(\log deg_G^i(u)).$$

This completes the proof.   □

The above proof can be modified to obtain a corresponding "high probability" result.

Theorem 4. *Let G be an n-vertex UDG and $H = G_{RTC}$. Then, $\Delta(H) = O(\log n)$ with high probability.*

Proof. Assuming that $n \ge 3$, we extend the last line of the above proof.

$$E[deg_H^i(u)] = \sum_{j=1}^{d} \text{Prob}[X_j = 1] \le \sum_{j=1}^{d} \frac{1}{j} \le \ln d + 1 < 2 \ln n.$$

Since $deg_H^i(u) = \sum_{j=1}^{d} X_j$ and the X_j's are negatively correlated binary random variables, we can use the standard Chernoff bound [12] to show that $deg_H^i(u)$ exceeds $6 \ln n$ with very small probability. Specifically,

$$\text{Prob}[deg_H^i(u) > 6 \ln n] < \left(\frac{e^2}{3^3}\right)^{2 \ln n} < \frac{1}{n^2}.$$

Using the union bound we observe that the probability that there exists a vertex u and index i, $1 \le i \le 5$ such that $deg_H^i(u) > 6 \ln n$ is less than $5/n$. This implies that the probability that $\Delta(H)$ exceeds $30 \ln n$ is less than $5/n$. Thus, $\Delta(H)$ is at most $30 \ln n$ with probability at least $1 - 5/n$.   □

Now we prove the sparseness of $G_{\varepsilon\text{-}RTC}$. Specifically, we show that the expected degree of each vertex u in $G_{\varepsilon\text{-}RTC}$ is bounded above by a constant. Before we embark on this proof, we state a simple inequality that expresses a connection between the actual distance $|uv|$ between a pair of neighbors u and v and the eventual edge label $d_u[v]$ assigned by ε-RTC.

Lemma 2.
$$|uv| \cdot \frac{(1-\varepsilon)^2}{(1+\varepsilon)} \le d_u[v] \le |uv| \cdot \frac{(1+\varepsilon)^2}{(1-\varepsilon)}.$$

Theorem 5. *Let G be a UDG and suppose that the pairwise distance estimates $\alpha : V \times V \to \Re^+$ are ε-error bounded. Let $H = G_{\varepsilon\text{-}RTC}$. Then there is a constant C such that for any vertex $u \in V$, $E[deg_H(u)] \le C$.*

Proof. Set $\eta = (1+\varepsilon)^3/(1-\varepsilon)^3$. For this proof to go through, we require that $\eta < 2$. This happens whenever

$$\varepsilon < \frac{(2^{1/3} - 1)}{(2^{1/3} + 1)} = 0.115013....$$

For notational ease we denote the constant 0.115013... above by Ω. In other words, our proof goes through when ε is around $1/9$ or smaller. A more complicated analysis can be used for larger values of ε between Ω and 1; we skip that for conciseness.

Set $\theta = \pi/2 - \sin^{-1}(\eta/2)$ and $t = \lceil \frac{2\pi}{\theta} \rceil$. Partition the unit disk centered at u into cones, $C_1, C_2, \ldots, C_t$ such that each cone C_i, $1 \le i < t$, makes an angle θ at u, C_t makes an angle of at most θ at u. It is worth noting that as $\varepsilon \to 0$, we see that $\eta \to 1$ and therefore $\theta \to \pi/3$. Also, when $\varepsilon \to \Omega$ from below, we see that $\eta \to 2$ from below and $\theta \to 0$. In short, as ε increases, our cone partition becomes more fine.

Let $\{N^i(u) \mid i = 1, 2, \ldots, t\}$ be a partition of $N(u)$ into t subsets such that all nodes in $N^i(u)$ lie in cone C_i. Note that each $N^i(u)$ induces a clique in G because $\theta \le \pi/3$ for all values of $\varepsilon < \Omega$. Let $deg_G^i(u) = |N^i(u)|$, for each $i = 1, 2, \ldots, t$ and let $deg_H^i(u)$ be the number of nodes in $N^i(u)$ that continue to be neighbors of u in H. Then $deg_H(u) = \sum_{i=1}^t deg_H^i(u)$ and by linearity of expectation $E[deg_H(u)] = \sum_{i=1}^t E[deg_H^i(u)]$. We will now show that $E[deg_H^i(u)] \le c$, where c is a constant in the sense that it is independent of the size of the network, but does depend on ε. From this, it immediately follows that $E[deg_H(u)] \le t \cdot c$. Note that t is also independent of the size of network and depends only on ε. Hence, we have that $E[deg_H(u)] \le C$, for some constant C.

Fix i, $1 \le i \le t$, and let $d = deg_G^i(u)$ and $N^i(u) = \{v_1, v_2, \ldots, v_d\}$ such that $v_1 \prec_u v_2 \prec_u \cdots \prec_u v_d$. For each $j = 1, 2, \ldots, d$, let X_j denote the indicator random variable that equals 1 if $\{u, v_j\} \in E(H)$ and 0 otherwise. Then, by linearity of expectation, $E[deg_H^i(u)] = \sum_{j=1}^d E[X_j] = \sum_{j=1}^d \text{Prob}[X_j = 1]$. We now calculate $\text{Prob}[X_j = 1]$.

Given that $v_\ell \prec_u v_j$ for each $\ell = 1, 2, \ldots, j-1$, for the edge $\{u, v_j\}$ to be present in H, it must be the case that $u \prec_{v_j} v_\ell$, for each $\ell = 1, 2, \ldots, j-1$. Therefore,

$$\text{Prob}[X_j = 1] \le \text{Prob}[\wedge_{\ell=1}^{j-1} u \prec_{v_j} v_\ell],$$
$$= \text{Prob}[\wedge_{\ell=1}^{j-1} d_{v_j}[u] < d_{v_j}[v_\ell]],$$
$$= \prod_{\ell=1}^{j-1} \text{Prob}[d_{v_j}[u] < d_{v_j}[v_\ell]]. \tag{2}$$

The last equality follows from the mutual independence of the events $\{d_{v_j}[u] < d_{v_j}[v_\ell] \mid \ell = 1, 2, \ldots, j-1\}$. These events are mutually independent because in ε-RTC each edge label $d_u[v]$ is obtained by a random perturbation and these are done *independently*. We will now compute an upper bound on $\text{Prob}[d_{v_j}[u] < d_{v_j}[v_\ell]]$, where $1 \le \ell \le j-1$. Fix ℓ and for notational ease let $v \equiv v_\ell$. We now prove a geometric property that follows from the fact that $d_{v_j}[v] < d_{v_j}[u]$ and from our choice of θ.

Claim: Given that $\theta = \pi/2 - \sin^{-1}(\eta/2)$ and that $d_{v_j}[v] < d_{v_j}[u]$, it follows that $|v_j v| \le |v_j u|$.

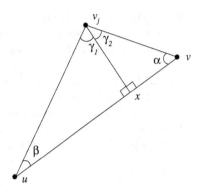

Fig. 4. This shows the triangle uv_jv

Proof. Refer to Fig. 4. To show that $|v_jv| \leq |v_ju|$, we will show that $\beta \leq \alpha$. This is equivalent to showing that $\gamma_1 \geq \gamma_2$. To obtain a contradiction suppose that $\gamma_1 < \gamma_2$. This implies that $|ux| < |xv|$.

Since $v \prec_u v_j$, we have that $d_u[v] < d_u[v_j]$. Combining this with Lemma 2 we obtain

$$|uv| \cdot \frac{(1-\varepsilon)^2}{(1+\varepsilon)} \leq d_u[v] < d_u[v_j] \leq |uv_j| \cdot \frac{(1+\varepsilon)^2}{(1-\varepsilon)}.$$

This yields

$$|uv| < \frac{(1+\varepsilon)^3}{(1-\varepsilon)^3} \cdot |uv_j| = \eta \cdot |uv_j|.$$

Combining the inequalities $|ux| < |xv|$, $|uv| < \eta \cdot |uv_j|$ with the fact that $|ux| + |xv| = |uv|$, we get that $|ux| < \eta/2 \cdot |uv_j|$. Now notice that $\sin\gamma_1 = |ux|/|uv_j| < \eta/2$, implying that $\gamma_1 < \sin^{-1}(\eta/2)$. Using the fact that $\beta \leq \theta$ and that θ was chosen to satisfy $\theta = \pi/2 - \sin^{-1}(\eta/2)$, we get that $\beta < \pi/2 - \gamma_1$. In other words, $\beta + \gamma_1 < \pi/2$, which is a contradiction. $\square$

Let $b = |v_jv|$. Then, both $\alpha(v_j, v)$ and $\alpha(v, v_j)$ are bounded above by $b \cdot (1+\varepsilon)$ and therefore their mean, which we will denote by $\overline{\alpha}\{v_j, v\}$, is also bounded above by $b \cdot (1+\varepsilon)$. Since $b = |v_jv| \leq |v_ju|$, we obtain in a similar manner that $\overline{\alpha}\{v_j, u\}$, the mean of $\alpha(v_j, u)$ and $\alpha(u, v_j)$ is bounded below by $b \cdot (1-\varepsilon)$.

Now recall that $d_{v_j}[u]$ is chosen uniformly at random from the interval $[L_u, R_u]$, where $L_u = \overline{\alpha}\{v_j, u\} \cdot (1 - \delta_L)$ and $R_u = \overline{\alpha}\{v_j, u\} \cdot (1 + \delta_R)$. Note that R_u satisfies

$$R_u = \overline{\alpha}\{v_j, u\} \cdot (1 + \delta_R) \geq b \cdot (1-\varepsilon) \cdot (1 + \delta_R) = b \cdot (1+\varepsilon).$$

Thus, as shown in Fig. 5, the right endpoint R_u lies to the right of $\overline{\alpha}\{v_j, v\}$. Similarly, recall that $d_{v_j}[v]$ is chosen uniformly at random from the interval $[L_v, R_v]$, where $L_v = \overline{\alpha}\{v_j, v\} \cdot (1 - \delta_L)$ and $R_v = \overline{\alpha}\{v_j, v\} \cdot (1 + \delta_R)$. Now note that L_v satisfies:

$$L_v = \overline{\alpha}\{v_j, v\} \cdot (1 - \delta_L) \leq b \cdot (1+\varepsilon) \cdot (1 - \delta_L) \leq b \cdot (1-\varepsilon).$$

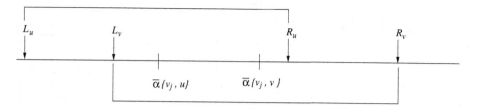

Fig. 5. This is the configuration of the point $\overline{\alpha}\{v_j, u\}$, the interval $[L_u, R_u]$ around it, the point $\overline{\alpha}\{v_j, v\}$, and the interval $[L_v, R_v]$ around it. Note that L_v is to the left of $\overline{\alpha}\{v_j, u\}$ and R_u is to the right of $\overline{\alpha}\{v_j, v\}$.

Thus, as shown in Fig. 5, the left endpoint L_v lies to the left of $\overline{\alpha}\{v_j, u\}$.

We now show that the interval $[L_v, R_u]$ is fairly large, compared to both $[L_u, R_u]$ and $[L_v, R_v]$. Recalling that $R_u \geq b \cdot (1 + \varepsilon)$ and $L_v \leq b \cdot (1 - \varepsilon)$, we see that $R_u - L_v \geq b \cdot (2\varepsilon)$. Furthermore, we have that

$$R_v - L_v = \overline{\alpha}\{v_j, v\} \cdot (1 + \delta_R) - \overline{\alpha}\{v_j, v\} \cdot (1 - \delta_L) \leq b \cdot (1 + \varepsilon) \cdot (\delta_R + \delta_L) = b \cdot (2\varepsilon) \cdot \frac{2}{(1 - \varepsilon)}.$$

Therefore,

$$\frac{R_u - L_v}{R_v - L_v} \geq \frac{1 - \varepsilon}{2} \quad \text{and} \quad \frac{R_u - L_v}{R_u - L_u} \geq \frac{1 - \varepsilon}{2}.$$

The latter follows from the fact that $R_u - L_u \leq R_v - L_v$. From these bounds, it follows that

$$\text{Prob}\Big[d_{v_j}[u] \in [L_v, R_u] \text{ and } d_{v_j}[v_\ell] \in [L_v, R_u]\Big] \geq \frac{1 - \varepsilon}{4}.$$

Given that both $d_{v_j}[u]$ and $d_{v_j}[v]$ are in $[L_v, R_u]$, either the event $d_{v_j}[u] < d_{v_j}[v]$ or the event $d_{v_j}[u] > d_{v_j}[v]$ occurs. Because of symmetry, the likelihood of these two possibilities is the same and therefore,

$$\text{Prob}\Big[d_{v_j}[u] > d_{v_j}[v]\Big] \geq \frac{1 - \varepsilon}{8},$$

implying that

$$\text{Prob}\Big[d_{v_j}[u] < d_{v_j}[v]\Big] \leq \frac{7 + \varepsilon}{8}.$$

Plugging this upper bound in (2), we get that $\text{Prob}[X_j = 1] \leq (\frac{7 + \varepsilon}{8})^{j-1}$. Therefore,

$$E[deg_H^i(u)] \leq \sum_{j=1}^{d} \Big(\frac{7 + \varepsilon}{8}\Big)^{j-1} \leq \frac{8}{1 - \varepsilon}. \qquad \square$$

4.2 Experimental Evidence for Sparseness

In this subsection we report on experiment results related to the maximum degree of G_{RTC} and $G_{\varepsilon\text{-}RTC}$. Figure 6 shows the ratio $\Delta(G_{RTC})/\log \Delta(G)$ as

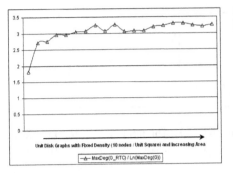 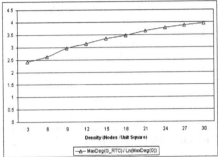

Fig. 6. Although maximum degree of G_{RTC} is not bounded, it is comparable to $log(\Delta)$

the size of G increases. In the plot on the left, the increase in the size of G is due to an increase in the area in which the nodes of G are distributed. In this case, the density of G remains fixed. In the plot on the right, the size of G is increased by increasing the density of the graph, while keeping the area of the graph fixed.

Theorem 3 claims that for any vertex u, the expected value of $\deg_{G_{RTC}}(u)$ is bounded above by $O(\log deg_G(u))$. This does not imply that $E[\Delta(G_{RTC})] = O(log\Delta(G))$. To see this consider a graph G in which there are many nodes whose degrees are equal to $\Delta(G)$. While it is true that for each of these high degree nodes u, we would *expect* the degree of u in G_{RTC} to be equal to $O(\log deg_G(u))$, it is also true that with significant probability at least one of these nodes will have a degree in the output graph that is much larger than $\log deg_G(u)$. As a result, $\Delta(G_{RTC})$ may drift above $O(\log \Delta(G))$ and this drift is more pronounced as the number of high degree nodes increases. This phenomenon is illustrated by the two plots. In the plot on the left the ratio $\Delta(G_{RTC})/\log \Delta(G)$ tends to a constant because even though the size of G is increasing, the density is not. The plot on the right shows a steady increase because as the density of G increases, there are more and more high degree vertices.

Below (Fig. 7) we show a 3-dimensional plot of the behavior of $\Delta(G_{\varepsilon\text{-}RTC})$ with respect to varying values of ε and the density of the input UDG. For $\varepsilon = 0$ the plot shows that $\Delta(G_{\varepsilon\text{-}RTC})$ is bounded above by a constant. This is to be expected because ε-RTC is the same as XTC for $\varepsilon = 0$. For large values of ε (say, 0.8 or more) the behavior of $\Delta(G_{\varepsilon\text{-}RTC})$ is similar to the behavior of $\Delta(G_{RTC})$. This is also to be expected. What is more interesting is the behavior of $\Delta(G_{RTC})$ for small, positive values of ε. Our plot shows that for small, positive ε, the value of $\Delta(G_{\varepsilon\text{-}RTC})$ remains, more or less, a constant even though the density of G increases. Theorem 5 claims that for any node u, the degree of u in $G_{\varepsilon\text{-}RTC}$ is bounded above by a constant C (whose value depends on ε). While this implies that the average degree of $G_{\varepsilon\text{-}RTC}$ is bounded above by $C/2$, it does not imply that $\Delta(G_{\varepsilon\text{-}RTC})$ is bounded above by a constant. Hence, it is a pleasant surprise to see $\Delta(G_{\varepsilon\text{-}RTC})$ so well behaved for small values of ε.

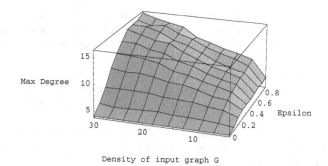

Fig. 7. The behavior of $\Delta(G_{\varepsilon\text{-}RTC})$, as ε increases and as the density of G increases

4.3   Spanner Properties

Due to lack of space we do not present a detailed analysis of the spanner properties of G_{RTC} and $G_{\varepsilon\text{-}RTC}$ here. We simply state our results without proof and postpone the proofs and a discussion of the implications of these results to the full version of the paper. Note that our results hold for arbitrary graphs and not just UDGs.

Definition. Let H be a spanning subgraph of the graph G. H is said to be a *t-hop spanner* of G if for any u and v in G, $c_H(u,v)/c_G(u,v) \leq t$, where $c_G(u,v)$ (respectively, $c_H(u,v)$) is the number of hops in a shortest u,v-path in G (respectively, H).

Theorem 6. *Let G be an arbitrary graph. G_{RTC} is a t-spanner of G for $t = O(1)$ and $G_{\varepsilon\text{-}RTC}$ is a t-spanner of G for $t = \log(1/\delta)$, where δ is the smallest distance $|uv|$ between any pair of nodes in G.*

References

1. L. Barriére, P. Fraigniaud, and L. Narayanan. Robust position-based routing in wireless ad hoc networks with unstable transmission ranges. In *Proceedings of the 5th international workshop on Discrete algorithms and methods for mobile computing and communications (DIALM)*, pages 19–27, 2001.
2. N. Bulusu, J. Heidemann, and D. Estrin. GPS-less low cost outdoor localization for very small devices. *IEEE Wireless Communications*, 7(5):27–34, 2000.
3. S. Capkun, M. Hamdi, and J. Hubaux. Gps-free positioning in mobile ad-hoc networks. In *Proceedings of the 34th Annual Hawaii International Conference on System Sciences (HICSS)*, volume 9, page 9008, Washington, DC, USA, 2001. IEEE Computer Society.
4. S. Ghosh, K. Lillis, S. Pandit, and S. Pemmaraju. Robust topology control algorithms. In *Proceedings of the 8th International Conference on Principles of Distributed Systems (OPODIS)*, 2004.
5. F. K. Harris, N. B. Belecki, and Jr. R. J. Soulen. Measurements and instruments. In D. G. Fink and H. W. Beaty, editors, *Standard Handbook for Electrical Engineers*, pages 3–1–3–98. McGraw Hill, 1987.

6. L. Li, J. Halpern, V. Bahl, Y.-M. Wang, and R. Wattenhofer. Analysis of a cone-based distributed topology control algorithm for wireless multihop networks. In *Twentieth ACM Symposium on Principles of Distributed Computing (PODC)*, 2001.
7. X.-Y. Li, G. Calinescu, and P. Wan. Distributed construction of planar spanner and routing for ad hoc wireless networks. In *Proceedings of the 21st Annual Joint Conference of the IEEE Computer and Communications Societies (INFOCOM)*, 2002.
8. X.-Y. Li, G. Calinescu, P.-J. Wan, and Y. Wang. Localized delaunay triangulation with application in ad hoc wireless networks. *IEEE Trans. Parallel Distrib. Syst.*, 14(10):1035–1047, 2003.
9. Xiang-Yang Li and Yu Wang. Efficient construction of low weight bounded degree planar spanner. In *Proceedings of the 9th International Computing and Combinatorics Conference (COCOON)*, 2003.
10. K. Lillis and S. Pemmaraju. Topology control with limited geometric information. Full paper: `www.cs.uiowa.edu/~sriram/randomTopControl.pdf`, 2005.
11. D. Moore, J. Leonard, D. Rus, and S. Teller. Robust distributed network localization with noisy range measurements. In *Proceedings of the Second ACM Conference on Embedded Networked Sensor Systems (SenSys)*, 2004.
12. Rajeev Motwani and Prabhakar Raghavan. *Randomized algorithms*. Cambridge University Press, New York, NY, USA, 1995.
13. N. B. Priyantha, A. Chakraborty, and H. Balakrishnan. The cricket location-support system. In *Mobile Computing and Networking*, pages 32–43, 2000.
14. W.-Z. Song, Y. Wang, X.-Y. Li, and O. Frieder. Localized algorithms for energy efficient topology in wireless ad hoc networks. In *Proceedings of the 5th ACM International Symposium on Mobile Ad Hoc Networking and Computing (MobiHoc)*, pages 98–108. ACM Press, 2004.
15. R. Wattenhofer and A. Zollinger. XTC: A practical topology control algorithm for ad-hoc networks. In *4th International Workshop on Algorithms for Wireless, Mobile, Ad Hoc and Sensor Networks (WMAN)*, 2004.

Author Index

Lecture Notes in Computer Science

For information about Vols. 1–4263

please contact your bookseller or Springer